**Eleventh Edition**

# Entrepreneurship and Effective Small Business Management

**Norman M. Scarborough**

Presbyterian College

**Jeffrey R. Cornwall**

Belmont University

**PEARSON**

Boston   Columbus   Indianapolis   New York   San Francisco   Upper Saddle River
Amsterdam   Cape Town   Dubai   London   Madrid   Milan   Munich   Paris   Montreal   Toronto
Delhi   Mexico City   São Paulo   Sydney   Hong Kong   Seoul   Singapore   Taipei   Tokyo

**Editor in Chief:** Stephanie Wall
**Acquisitions Editor:** Daniel Tylman
**Program Management Lead:** Ashley Santora
**Program Manager:** Claudia Fernandes
**Editorial Assistant:** Linda Albelli
**Director of Marketing:** Maggie Moylan
**Senior Marketing Manager:** Erin Gardner
**Project Management Lead:** Judy Leale
**Project Manager:** Ann Pulido
**Art Director:** Kenny Beck
**Text Designer:** S4Carlisle Publishing Services
**Art Cover Director:** Bruce Kenselaar
**Cover Designer:** Suzanne Behnke
**VP, Director of Digital Strategy & Assessment:** Paul Gentile
**Digital Editor:** Brian Surette
**Digital Development Manager:** Robin Lazrus
**Digital Project Manager:** Alana Coles
**MyLab Product Manager:** Joan Waxman
**Digital Production Project Manager:** Lisa Rinaldi
**Full-Service Project Management:** Christian Holdener/S4Carlisle Publishing Services
**Composition:** S4Carlisle Publishing Services
**Printer:** LSC Communications
**Cover Printer:** LSC Communications
**Text Font:** 10/12, Times LT Std

Photo credits front cover (from top to bottom): © PhotoSG/Fotolia, © monjiro/Fotolia, © JJAVA/Fototlia, © ducdao/Fotolia, © Jacques PALUT/Fotolia, © Gina Sanders/Fotolia. Credits and acknowledgments borrowed from other sources and reproduced, with permission, in this textbook appear on the appropriate page within text with the exception of the chapter opening photo which appears throughout the text and is credited to © Tyler Olson/Fotolia.

Microsoft® and Windows® are registered trademarks of the Microsoft Corporation in the U.S.A. and other countries. Screen shots and icons reprinted with permission from the Microsoft Corporation. This book is not sponsored or endorsed by or affiliated with the Microsoft Corporation.

Many of the designations by manufacturers and sellers to distinguish their products are claimed as trademarks. Where those designations appear in this book, and the publisher was aware of a trademark claim, the designations have been printed in initial caps or all caps.

**Library of Congress Cataloging-in-Publication Data**

Scarborough, Norman M.
  Entrepreneurship and effective small business management/Norman Scarborough, Jeff Cornwall.—Eleventh Edition.
    pages cm
  Includes bibliographical references and index.
  ISBN-13: 978-0-13-350632-7
  ISBN-10: 0-13-350632-0
  1. Small business—Management. 2. New business enterprises—Management. 3. Small business—United States—Management. 4. New business enterprises—United States—Management. I. Cornwall, Jeffrey. II. Title.
HD62.7.S27 2013
657'.9042—dc23
                                                                                    2013039406

ISBN-10:    0-13-350632-0
ISBN-13: 978-0-13-350632-7

# Brief Contents

# Contents

In memory of Lannie H. Thornley and Mildred T. Myers

To Louise Scarborough and John Scarborough. Your love, support, and encouragement have made all the difference.

—NMS

To my grandchildren Lucy Kuyper, Ellie Cornwall, and Isaac Cornwall.

—JRC

# Preface

The field of entrepreneurship is experiencing incredible rates of growth, not only in the United States but around the world as well. People of all ages, backgrounds, and nationalities are launching businesses of their own and, in the process, are reshaping the global economy. Entrepreneurs are discovering the natural advantages that result from their companies' size—speed, agility, flexibility, sensitivity to customers' needs, creativity, a spirit of innovation, and many others—give them the ability to compete successfully with companies many times their size and that have budgets to match. As large companies struggle to survive wrenching changes in competitive forces by downsizing, merging, and restructuring, the unseen army of small businesses continues to flourish and to carry the nation's economy on its back. Entrepreneurs who are willing to assume the risks of the market to gain its rewards are the heart of capitalism. These men and women, with their bold entrepreneurial spirits, have led our nation into prosperity throughout its history. Entrepreneurship also plays a significant role in countries throughout the world. Across the globe, entrepreneurs are creating small companies that lead nations to higher standards of living and hope for the future.

In the United States, we can be thankful for a strong small business sector. Small companies deliver the goods and services we use every day, provide jobs and training for millions of workers, and lead the way in creating the products and services that make our lives easier and more enjoyable. Small businesses were responsible for introducing to the world the elevator, the airplane, FM radio, the zipper, the personal computer, and a host of other marvelous inventions. The imaginations of the next generation of entrepreneurs of which you may be a part will determine other fantastic products and services that lie in our future! Whatever those ideas may be, we can be sure of one thing: Entrepreneurs will be there to make them happen.

The purpose of this book is to open your mind to the possibilities, the challenges, and the rewards of owning your own business and to provide the tools you will need to be successful if you choose the path of the entrepreneur. It is not an easy road to follow, but the rewards—both tangible and intangible—are well worth the risks. Not only may you be rewarded financially for your business ideas, but also, like entrepreneurs the world over, you will be able to work at something you love! If you do not pursue a career as an entrepreneur, you still need to understand entrepreneurship because you most likely will be working in, doing business with, or competing against small businesses throughout your career.

Now in its eleventh edition, *Entrepreneurship and Effective Small Business Management* has stood the test of time by bringing to generations of students the material they need to launch and manage a small business successfully in a hotly competitive environment. In writing this edition, we have worked hard to provide you with plenty of practical, "hands-on" tools and techniques to make your business ventures successful. Many people launch businesses every year, but only some of them succeed. This book provides the tools to help you learn the *right* way to launch and manage a small business with the staying power to succeed and grow.

## What's New to This Edition?

The first change you will notice is in the title of the book. We believe that the new title, *Entrepreneurship and Effective Small Business Management,* reflects this edition's emphasis on the entrepreneurial process. When we started writing this book nearly 35 years ago, small business management was the topic of choice on college campuses; today, the emphasis of college courses is on entrepreneurship. This edition reflects that change by including enhanced coverage of the entrepreneurial process, including the creative process and developing a business model, while retaining thorough coverage of traditional topics that are required for entrepreneurial success, such as e-commerce, managing cash flow, selecting the right location and designing the proper layout, and supply chain management.

Another important change is the addition of Jeff Cornwall as coauthor. Jeff, who holds the Jack C. Massey Chair of Entrepreneurship at Belmont University, is an experienced and successful entrepreneur, a dedicated teacher, a respected author, and an acknowledged expert in the field of entrepreneurship. The United States Association for Small Business and Entrepreneurship has honored Jeff on numerous occasions for his contributions to the field of entrepreneurship, naming him a Longnecker/USASBE Fellow in 2006 and awarding the Center for Entrepreneurship that he headed at Belmont University the USASBE National Model Undergraduate Program of the Year Award in 2008. USASBE also recognized Jeff in 2013 with the prestigious Outstanding Educator of the Year award. He served as USASBE's president in 2010. Jeff's blog, *The Entrepreneurial Mind*, is one of the most popular small business blogs on the Internet, named by *Forbes* as a "Best of the Web" selection.

This edition of *Entrepreneurship and Effective Small Business Management* also includes many new pedagogical features that reflect the dynamic and exciting field of entrepreneurship.

- The addition of a chapter on the creative process that explores how the entrepreneurial mind works. This innovative chapter also explains how entrepreneurs can stimulate their own creativity and the creativity of the people in their organizations.

- Because your generation is keenly interested in ethics and social responsibility, we placed the updated chapter on ethics and social responsibility right up front (Chapter 2). This thought-provoking chapter gives you the opportunity to wrestle with some of the ethical dilemmas that entrepreneurs face every day in business. Encouraging you to think about and discuss these issues now prepares you for making the right business decisions later. We also have included more extensive coverage of social entrepreneurship in this edition, including new forms of ownership designed specifically for social entrepreneurs.

- This edition includes enhanced coverage of social media, such as Facebook, Twitter, Pinterest, YouTube, and others, throughout the entire book, including ways to use social media as a powerful bootstrap marketing technique; a fund-raising tool; a quick, inexpensive way to test business models; and many others.

- We have included more material on bootstrapping throughout the book because today's young entrepreneurs must be prepared to launch their ventures with limited resources and little access to outside funding.

- We have updated the chapters on financing small businesses to reflect the current state of financial markets. Included in these updates is discussion of the newest form of financing known as crowdfunding.

- We have revised the chapter on creating a business plan to reflect the modern view of the business planning process. In addition to retaining extensive coverage of how to write a business plan, we have expanded the section on conducting a feasibility analysis and added a section on using the business model canvas to develop a viable business model. This chapter also shows how to take the ideas that pass the feasibility analysis, build a business model around them, and create a business plan that serves as a guide to a successful launch.

- Almost all of the real-world examples in this edition are new and are easy to spot because they are highlighted by in-margin markers. These examples allow you to see how entrepreneurs are putting into practice the concepts that you are learning in the book and in class. The examples are designed to help you to remember the key concepts in the course. The business founders in these examples also reflect the diversity that makes entrepreneurship a vital part of the global economy.

- To emphasize the practical nature of this book, every chapter includes a new or updated "Lessons from the Street-Smart Entrepreneur" feature that focuses on a key concept and offers practical advice about how you can put it to practice in your own business. These features include topics such as "Questions to Spur the Imagination," "Thriving on Change," "How to Make Your Business Ready for Global E-Commerce," "E-Mail Ads That Produce Results," "How to Set Up an ESOP," and many others.

- We have updated all of the "Entrepreneurship in Action" features that have proved to be so popular with both students and professors. Every chapter contains at least one of these short cases that describes a decision that an entrepreneur faces and asks you to assume the role of consultant and advise the entrepreneur on the best course of action.

This feature includes the fascinating stories of entrepreneurs who see space as the next entrepreneurial frontier (including Elon Musk's SpaceX and Richard Branson's Virgin Galactic), professional athletes who have become successful franchisees (including Jamal Mashburn, Drew Brees, and Angelo Crowell), and using bootstrap marketing techniques to build a name in the music industry (Erin Anderson, founder of Olivia Management). Each one poses a problem or an opportunity, includes questions that focus your attention on key issues, and helps you hone your analytical and critical thinking skills.

- This edition includes 10 new brief cases that cover a variety of topics (see the Case Matrix that appears on the inside cover). All of the cases are about small companies, and most are real companies that you can research online. These cases challenge you to think critically about a variety of topics that are covered in the book—from managing cash flow in a seasonal business and choosing a location for a restaurant's second branch to deciding how to deal with the Affordable Care Act and setting prices for a social entrepreneur's eco-friendly apparel.

- Almost all of the "In the Entrepreneurial Spotlight" features are new to this edition as well. These inspirational true stories invite you to explore the inner workings of entrepreneurship by advising entrepreneurs who face a variety of real-world business issues. Topics addressed in these "Spotlights" include college students applying the entrepreneurial skills they are learning in their classes by starting businesses while they are still in school, entrepreneurs who discover that for them franchising is the ideal path to entrepreneurship, a television makeup artist who launched her own line of makeup and faces decisions about promoting it, entrepreneurs who are enhancing their companies' e-commerce efforts with social media, and many others.

- The content of every chapter reflects the most recent statistics, studies, surveys, and research about entrepreneurship and small business management. Theory, of course, is important, but this book explains how entrepreneurs are *applying* the theory of entrepreneurship every day. You will learn how to launch and manage a business the *right* way by studying the most current concepts in entrepreneurship and small business management.

- A sample business plan for The Picturebooth Company serves as a model for you as you create plans for your own business ideas. Ross Hill wrote this plan for a business that sells and rents portable photo booths while he was a student and used it to launch his business. Not only has Ross used this plan to guide his successful company, but he also has used it to raise more than $70,000 in start-up capital. Hill's plan won three business plan competitions, including the national competition sponsored by Collegiate DECA.

- This edition features an updated, attractive, full-color design and layout that is designed to be user-friendly. Each chapter begins with learning objectives, which are repeated as in-margin markers within the chapter to guide you as you study.

Policymakers across the world are discovering that economic growth and prosperity lie in the hands of entrepreneurs—those dynamic, driven men and women who are committed to achieving success by creating and marketing innovative, customer-focused new products and services. Not only are these entrepreneurs creating economic prosperity, but many of them are also striving to make the world a better place in which to live by using their businesses to solve social problems. Those who possess this spirit of entrepreneurial leadership continue to lead the economic revolution that has proved repeatedly its ability to raise the standard of living for people everywhere. We hope that by using this book in your small business management or entrepreneurship class, you will join this economic revolution to bring about lasting, positive changes in your community and around the world. If your goal is to launch a successful business of your own, *Entrepreneurship and Effective Small Business Management* is the ideal book for you!

This eleventh edition of *Entrepreneurship and Effective Small Business Management* provides you with the knowledge you need to launch a business that has the greatest chance for success. One of the hallmarks of every edition of this book has been a very practical, "hands-on" approach to entrepreneurship. Our goal is to equip you with the tools you need for entrepreneurial success. By combining this textbook with your professor's expertise and enthusiasm, we believe that you will be equipped to follow your dreams of becoming a successful entrepreneur.

## CourseSmart eTextbook

CourseSmart eTextbooks were developed for students looking to save on required or recommended textbooks. Students simply select their eText by title or author and purchase immediate access to the content for the duration of the course using any major credit card. With a CourseSmart eText, students can search for specific keywords or page numbers, take notes online, print out reading assignments that incorporate lecture notes, and bookmark important passages for later review. For more information or to purchase a CourseSmart eTextbook, visit *www.coursesmart.com*.

## Acknowledgments

Supporting every author is a staff of professionals who work extremely hard to bring a book to life. They handle the thousands of details involved in transforming a rough manuscript into the finished product you see before you. Their contributions are immeasurable, and I appreciate all they do to make this book successful. We have been blessed to work with the following outstanding publishing professionals:

- Claudia Fernandes, our exceptionally capable program manager, who was always just an e-mail away when we needed her help with a seemingly endless number of details. She always does a masterful job of coordinating the many aspects of this project. Her ability to juggle the demands of multiple projects at once is amazing!

- Ann Pulido, project manager who skillfully guided the book through the long and sometimes difficult production process with wonderful "can-do" attitude. Ann is capable, experienced, and reliable, and we appreciate her hard work.

- Cordes Hoffman, photo researcher, who took our ideas for photos and transformed them into the meaningful images you see on these pages. Her job demands many hours of research and hard work.

- Erin Gardner, marketing manager, whose input helped focus this edition on an evolving market.

We also extend a big "Thank You" to the corps of Pearson Education sales representatives, who work so hard to get our books into customers' hands and who represent the front line in our effort to serve our customers' needs. They are the unsung heroes of the publishing industry.

Special thanks go to the following academic reviewers, whose ideas, suggestions, and thought-provoking input have helped to shape this edition and previous editions of *Entrepreneurship and Effective Small Business Management*. We always welcome feedback from our customers!

Joseph Adamo, *Cazenovia College*

H. Lon Addams, *Weber State University*

Mainuddin Afza, *Bloomsburg University of Pennsylvania*

Corinne Asher, *Henry Ford Community College*

Calvin Bacon, *University of South Alabama*

Judy Beebe, *Western Oregon University*

Tony Bledsoe, *Meredith College*

Jim Bloodgood, *Kansas State University*

Steven Bradley, *Austin Community College*

Kimberly Brown-King, *Southeast Arkansas College*

James H. Browne, *University of Southern Colorado*

Judy Dietert, *Southwest Texas State University*

Brian Dyk, *Heritage College*

Todd Finkle, *University of Akron*

Olene Fuller, *San Jacinto College North*

Pat Galitz, *Southeast Community College–Lincoln*

Joyce Gallagher, *Maysville Community and Technical College*

Bill Godair, *Landmark College*

Mark Hagenbuch, *University of North Carolina–Greensboro*

Ronald Hagler, *California Lutheran University*

Jeff Hornsby, *Ball State University*

Chris Howell, *New Mexico Junior College*

Eddie Hufft, *Alcorn State University*

Ralph Jagodka, *Mt. San Antonio College*

Richard Judd, *University of Illinois at Springfield*

Kyoung-Nan Kwon, *Michigan State University*

Stephen Lovejoy, *University of Maine at Augusta*

John F. McMahon, *Mississippi County Community College*

John Moonen, *Daytona Beach Community College*

Joseph Neptune, *St. Leo University*

Linda M. Newell, *Saddleback College*

Randy Nichols, *Sullivan University*

Marcella Norwood, *University of Houston*

David Orozco, *Michigan Technological University*

Ben Powell, *University of Alabama*

Khaled Sartawi, *Fort Valley State University*

Jack Sheeks, *Broward Community College*

Herbert Sherman, *Southampton College–LIU*

Lindsay Sholdar, *Art Institute of California, San Diego*

Howard Stroud, *LeTourneau University*

Ram Subramanian, *Montclair State University*

Charles N. Toftoy, *George Washington University*

Steve Varga-Sinka, *Saint Leo University*

Tony Warren, *Pennsylvania State University*

Tanisha Washington, *Wade College*

Willie Williams, *Tidewater Community College*

Bill Wise, *Metropolitan State College of Denver*

We also are grateful to our colleagues who support us in the often grueling process of writing a book: Foard Tarbert, Sam Howell, Jerry Slice, Suzanne Smith, Jody Lipford, Tobin Turner, Cindy Lucking, and Talisa Koon of Presbyterian College and Mark Schenkel, Mark Phillips, and Jose Gonzalez of Belmont University.

Finally, we thank Cindy Scarborough and Ann Cornwall for their love, support, and understanding while we worked many long hours to complete this book. For them, this project represents a labor of love.

**Norman M. Scarborough**
William H. Scott III Associate Professor of Entreprenuership
Presbyterian College
Clinton, South Carolina
nmscarb@presby.edu

**Jeffrey R. Cornwall**
Jack C. Massey Chair in Entrepreneurship
Belmont University
Nashville, Tennessee
jeff.cornwall@belmont.edu

CHAPTER 1

# Entrepreneurs: The Driving Force Behind Small Business

*All our dreams can come true, if we have the courage to pursue them.*

—Walt Disney

*Success is the prize given to those who try and fail willingly.*

—Jeffrey Bryant

## Learning Objectives

**Upon completion of this chapter, you will be able to:**

1. Define the role of the entrepreneur in the U.S. economy.
2. Describe the entrepreneurial profile.
3. Explain how entrepreneurs spot business opportunities.
4. Describe the benefits of owning a small business.
5. Describe the potential drawbacks of owning a small business.
6. Explain the forces that are driving the growth of entrepreneurship.
7. Discuss the role of diversity in small business and entrepreneurship.
8. Describe the contributions small businesses make to the U.S. economy.
9. Put business failure into the proper perspective.
10. Explain how small business owners can avoid the major pitfalls of running a business.

## The Role of the Entrepreneur

**1.**

Define the role of the entrepreneur in the U.S. economy.

Welcome to the world of the entrepreneur! Every year, entrepreneurs in the United States alone launch more than 6.5 million businesses.[1] These people, who come from diverse backgrounds, are striving to realize that Great American Dream of owning and operating their own businesses. Some of them have chosen to leave the security of the corporate hierarchy in search of independence, others have been forced out of large corporations as a result of downsizing, and still others have from the start chosen the autonomy that owning a business offers. The impact of these entrepreneurs on the nation's economy goes far beyond their numbers, however. The resurgence of the entrepreneurial spirit they are spearheading is the most significant economic development in recent business history. These heroes of the business world are introducing innovative products and services, pushing back technological frontiers, creating new jobs, opening foreign markets, and, in the process, sparking the U.S. economy.

Entrepreneurs, once shunned as people who could not handle a "real" job in the corporate world, now are the celebrities of the global economy. They create companies, jobs, wealth, and innovative solutions to some of the world's most vexing problems, from relief for sore feet to renewable energy sources. "The story of entrepreneurship entails a never ending search for new and imaginative ways to combine the factors of production into new methods, processes, technologies, products, or services," says one government economist who has conducted extensive research on entrepreneurship's impact.[2] In short, small business is "cool," and entrepreneurs are the rock stars of the business world.

The last several decades have seen record numbers of entrepreneurs launching businesses. One important indicator of the popularity of entrepreneurship is the keen interest expressed by students in creating their own businesses. According to a recent Gallup survey, 77 percent of students in grades 5 through 12 say that they "want to be their own bosses."[3] Growing numbers of young people are choosing entrepreneurship as a career (some of them while they are still in school) rather than joining the ranks of the pin-striped masses in major corporations. A recent poll by the Young Entrepreneur Council reports that 21 percent of recent college graduates started businesses out of necessity because they could not find jobs elsewhere.[4] Many others choose to start their own companies because they prefer the autonomy of entrepreneurship to the hierarchy of corporate America. In fact, when many young people hear the phrase "corporate America," they do not think of career opportunities; instead, images of the film *Office Space* come to mind. In short, the probability that you will become an entrepreneur at some point in your life has never been higher!

Research suggests that entrepreneurial activity remains vibrant not only in the United States but around the world as well. According to the Global Entrepreneurship Monitor, a study of entrepreneurial activity across the globe, 13 percent of the U.S. population aged 18 to 64, more than one in eight adults, is engaged in entrepreneurial activity. The level of entrepreneurial activity in the United States is the same as the global average of 13.0 percent and above the average (7.1 percent) for innovation-driven economies (see Figure 1.1).[5]

Entrepreneurship has been part of the fabric of the United States since its earliest days. Many of the nation's founding fathers were entrepreneurs. Thomas Jefferson started a nailery (a business that transformed iron into nails) in 1794 and purchased high-tech (at the time) nail-making machinery in 1796 to increase his company's production. Benjamin Franklin was an inventor and in 1729 at the age of 21, convinced several friends to finance his purchase of a newspaper that he renamed *The Pennsylvania Gazette*, a business that made him quite wealthy.[6] That same entrepreneurial spirit remains strong today as it does in other countries. Entrepreneurs in every corner of the world are launching businesses thanks to technology that provides easy access to both local and global markets at start-up. Even countries that traditionally are not known as hotbeds of entrepreneurial activity are home to promising start-up companies. Despite decades of economic problems, Zimbabwe's economy is growing once again, and small businesses are driving much of its growth.

**ENTREPRENEURIAL PROFILE: Divine Ndhlukula: Securio** One of Zimbabwe's most successful entrepreneurs is Divine Ndhlukula, who in 1998 started a small security company, Securico, in her home with a modest investment and just four employees. Ndhlukula says that she dreamed of an entrepreneurial career while she was a student studying accounting. After brief stints in farming, broadcasting, and insurance, she saw an opportunity in the security services business and

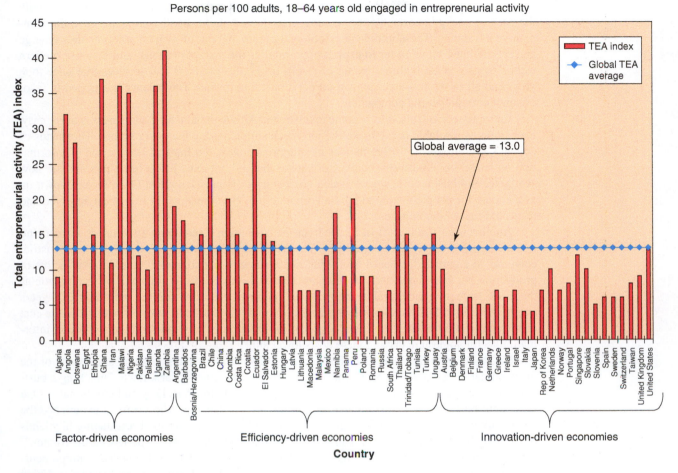

Persons per 100 adults, 18–64 years old engaged in entrepreneurial activity

**FIGURE 1.1**

**Entrepreneurial Activity Across the Globe**

*Source:* Based on Siri Roland Xavier, Donna Kelley, Jacqui Kew, Mike Herrington, and Arne Vorderwülbecke, *Global Entrepreneurship Monitor 2012 Global Report,* Babson College, Universidad del Desarrollo, Universiti Tun Abdul Razak, and Global Entrepreneurship Research Consortium, 2012, pp. 58–59.

started Securico, which targets multinational companies operating in Zimbabwe. "People who aspire to be in business think that you have to have lots of money to start," Ndhlukula says. "It's not that. It's really the passion." Today Securico, which now provides a full range of security services, employs more than 3,500 people, generates sales of more than $16 million, and was recently was recognized by Africa Awards for Entrepreneurship.[7]

In recent years, large companies in the United States and around the world have engaged in massive downsizing campaigns, dramatically cutting the number of managers and workers on their payrolls. This flurry of "pink slips" has spawned a new population of entrepreneurs—"castoffs" from large corporations (many of whom thought they would be lifetime ladder climbers in their companies) with solid management experience and many productive years left before retirement.

One casualty of this downsizing has been the long-standing notion of job security in large corporations, which all but destroyed the notion of loyalty and has made workers much more mobile. In the 1960s, the typical employee had worked for an average of four employers by the time he or she reached age 65; today, the average employee has had eight employers by the time he or she is 30.[8] Members of Generation X (those born between 1965 and 1980) and Generation Y (those born between 1981 and 1995), in particular, no longer see launching a business as being a risky career path. Having witnessed large companies lay off their parents after many years of service, these young people see entrepreneurship as the ideal way to create their own job security and career success! They are eager to control their own destinies.

This downsizing trend among large companies also has created a more significant philosophical change. It has ushered in an age in which "small is beautiful." Thirty years ago, competitive conditions favored large companies with their hierarchies and layers of management; today, with the pace of change constantly accelerating, fleet-footed, agile, small companies have the competitive advantage. These nimble competitors dart into and out of niche markets as they emerge and recede, they move faster to exploit opportunities the market presents, and they use modern technology to create within a matter of weeks or months products and services that once took years and all of the resources a giant corporation could muster. The balance has tipped in favor of small entrepreneurial companies.

Entrepreneurship also has become mainstream. Although launching a business is never easy, the resources available today make the job much simpler today than ever before. Thousands of colleges and universities offer courses in entrepreneurship, the Internet hosts a sea of information on launching a business, sources of capital that did not exist just a few years ago are now available, and business incubators hatch companies at impressive rates. Once looked down on as a choice for people unable to hold a corporate job, entrepreneurship is now an accepted and respected part of our culture.

Another significant shift in the bedrock of our nation's economic structure is influencing this swing in favor of small companies. The nation is rapidly moving away from an industrial economy to a knowledge-based one. What matters now is not so much the traditional factors of production but *knowledge* and *information*. The final impact of this shift will be as dramatic as the move from an agricultural economy to an industrial one that occurred more than 200 years ago in the United States. A knowledge-based economy favors small businesses because the cost of managing and transmitting knowledge and information is very low, and computer and information technologies are driving these costs lower still.

No matter why they start their businesses, entrepreneurs continue to embark on one of the most exhilarating—and one of the most frightening—adventures ever known: launching a business. It's never easy, but it can be incredibly rewarding, both financially and emotionally. One successful business owner claims that an entrepreneur is "anyone who wants to experience the deep, dark canyons of uncertainty and ambiguity and wants to walk the breathtaking highlands of success. But I caution: Do not plan to walk the latter until you have experienced the former."[9] True entrepreneurs see owning a business as the real measure of success. Indeed, entrepreneurship often provides the only avenue for success to those who otherwise might have been denied the opportunity.

Who are these entrepreneurs, and what drives them to work so hard with no guarantee of success? What forces lead them to risk so much and to make so many sacrifices in an attempt to achieve an ideal? Why are they willing to give up the security of a steady paycheck working for someone else to become the last person to be paid in their own companies? This chapter will examine the entrepreneur, the driving force behind the American economy.

*Source:* CartoonStock.

# What Is an Entrepreneur?

Adapted from the French verb *entreprendre*, which means "to undertake" or "to attempt," the word "entrepreneur" was introduced in 1755 in economist Richard Cantillon's book *Essay on the Nature of Trade in General*. Cantillon defined an entrepreneur as a producer with nonfixed income and uncertain returns.[10] At any given time, an estimated 9 million adults in the United States are engaged in launching a business, traveling down the path of entrepreneurship that Cantillon first wrote about more than 250 years ago.[11] An **entrepreneur** is one who creates a new business in the face of risk and uncertainty for the purpose of achieving profit and growth by identifying opportunities and assembling the necessary resources to capitalize on those opportunities. Entrepreneurs usually start with nothing more than an idea—often a simple one—and then find and organize the resources necessary to transform that idea into a sustainable business. Harvard Business School professor Howard Stevenson says that entrepreneurs "see an opportunity and don't feel constrained from pursuing it because they lack resources. They're *used* to making do without resources."[12] In essence, entrepreneurs are *disrupters*, upsetting the traditional way of doing things by creating new ways to do them.

What entrepreneurs have in common is the ability to spot opportunities and the willingness to capitalize on them.

**ENTREPRENEURIAL PROFILE: Ted Southern and Nikolay Moiseev: Final Frontier Design** Ted Southern, an artist and designer, and Nikolay Moiseev, a mechanical engineer, launched Final Frontier Design, when they saw the opportunity to create functional, affordable space suits for the burgeoning commercial space flight industry (see the accompanying "Entrepreneurship in Action" feature on page 9). "We recognized a new market in the suborbital space flight industry," says Southern. Their Brooklyn, New York–based start-up makes space suits that are more flexible than the traditional space suits designed by NASA and include ergonomic designs, clever reinforcements, and innovative joints that allow space travelers (the suits are designed for use inside spacecraft, not for space walks) to move more easily and fluidly. Existing space suits are "expensive, heavy, and not very functional," says Southern. "We think we can offer real improvements in both performance and cost." Moiseev designed space suits for the Russian Space Agency for nearly 20 years before moving to the United States, where he and Southern, who was best known for designing wings for the models in Victoria's Secret runway shows, teamed up to design gloves for astronauts in a competition sponsored by NASA. (They won a $100,000 prize that they used to launch Final Frontier Design.) After raising more than $27,000 on crowdfunding site Kickstarter, the entrepreneurs have enough capital to create a prototype of their "3G" spacesuit that they say will sell for as little as $50,000, far below the $12 million cost for a traditional space suit.[13]

Nikolay Moiseev (left) and Ted Southern (right), cofounders of Final Frontier Design.

*Source:* Final Frontier Design, LLC.

Although many people dream of owning a business, most of them never actually launch a company. Those who do take the entrepreneurial plunge, however, will experience the thrill of creating something grand from nothing; they will also discover the challenges and the difficulties of building a business "from scratch." Whatever their reasons for choosing entrepreneurship, many recognize that true satisfaction comes only from running their own businesses the way they choose.

Researchers have invested a great deal of time and effort over the last decade studying these entrepreneurs and trying to paint a clear picture of the entrepreneurial personality. Not surprisingly, the desire for autonomy is the single most important factor motivating entrepreneurs to start businesses (see Table 1.1). Although these studies have produced several characteristics that entrepreneurs tend to exhibit, none of them has isolated a set of traits required for success. We now turn to a brief summary of the entrepreneurial profile.[14]

**1. *Desire and willingness to take initiative.*** Entrepreneurs feel a personal responsibility for the outcome of ventures they start. They prefer to be in control of their resources and to use those resources to achieve self-determined goals. They are willing to step forward and build businesses based on their creative ideas.

**2. *Preference for moderate risk.*** Entrepreneurs are not wild risk takers but are instead *calculating* risk takers. Unlike "high-rolling, riverboat gamblers," they rarely gamble. Entrepreneurs often have a different perception of the risk involve in a business situation. The goal may appear to be high—even impossible—from others' perspective, but entrepreneurs typically have thought through the situation and believe that their goals are reasonable and attainable. Entrepreneurs

**2.** _____

Describe the entrepreneurial profile.

**TABLE 1.1 Why Entrepreneurs Start Businesses**

Noam Wasserman and Timothy Butler of the Harvard Business School surveyed nearly 2,000 entrepreneurs about their motivations for starting their businesses, analyzed the results by gender and age, and compared them to thousands of nonentrepreneurs. The primary motivator for entrepreneurs is autonomy, but security and a congenial work environment top the list for nonentrepreneurs. Entrepreneurs' source of motivation shifts slightly as they age, more so for women than for men. The following tables summarize the researchers' findings:

| Men by Age | | |
| --- | --- | --- |
| **20s** | **30s** | **40s+** |
| Autonomy | Autonomy | Autonomy |
| Power and Influence | Power and Influence | Power and Influence |
| Managing People | Managing People | Altruism |
| Financial Gain | Financial Gain | Variety |

| Women by Age | | |
| --- | --- | --- |
| **20s** | **30s** | **40s+** |
| Autonomy | Autonomy | Autonomy |
| Power and Influence | Power and Influence | Intellectual Challenge |
| Managing People | Variety | Variety |
| Altruism | Altruism | Altruism |

*Source:* Adapted from Leigh Buchanan, "The Motivation Matrix," *Inc.*, March 2012, pp. 60–62.

launched many now famous businesses, including Burger King, Microsoft, FedEx, Disney, CNN, MTV, Hewlett Packard, and others, during economic recessions when many people believed their ideas and their timing to be foolhardy.

**ENTREPRENEURIAL PROFILE: Nicholas Pelis: Denizen Rum** While working for SKYY Vodka, Nicholas Pelis spotted an opportunity to create a new blend of rum, a product that had been "sanitized" by the mass-production mind-set of large modern distilleries. Pelis and his wife sold their house in San Francisco to return to his native New York and used the proceeds of the sale and $300,000 raised from family and friends to launch Denizen Rum, a company whose distilled spirits blend the mixability of white rum with the bold, smooth flavors of traditional dark rum from Amsterdam, where rum blending has been a tradition since the 1700s. Introduced in 2011, Denizen Rum quickly won critical acclaim, which allowed the Pelis's young company to sign a national distribution contract with one of the largest wine and spirits distributors in the United States. Although some people criticized Pelis for the risk that he took, his industry experience and market research convinced him that his idea was sound and that his company would be successful.[15]

This attitude explains why so many successful entrepreneurs failed many times before finally achieving their dreams. For instance, Milton Hershey, founder of one of the world's largest and most successful chocolate makers, started four candy businesses, all of which failed, before he launched the chocolate business that would make him famous. The director of an entrepreneurship center says that entrepreneurs "are not crazy, wild-eyed risk takers. Successful entrepreneurs understand the risks [of starting a business] and figure out how to manage them."[16] Good entrepreneurs become risk *reducers*, and one of the best ways to minimize the risk in any entrepreneurial venture is to conduct a feasibility study and create a sound business plan, which is the topic of Chapter 8.

**3. *Confidence in their ability to succeed.*** Entrepreneurs typically have an abundance of confidence in their ability to succeed, and they tend to be optimistic about their chances for business success. Entrepreneurs face many barriers when starting and running their companies, and a healthy dose of optimism can be an important component in their ultimate success. "Entrepreneurs believe they can do anything," says one researcher.[17]

**4. *Self-reliance.*** Entrepreneurs do not shy away from the responsibility for making their businesses succeed. Perhaps that is why many entrepreneurs persist in building businesses even when others ridicule their ideas as follies. Against the advice of his father, a fifth-generation brewmaster, entrepreneur Jim Koch left his high-paying job as a management consultant to start

Boston Beer Company from his kitchen using his family's beer recipe. Koch recalls thinking, "I'm on this path, and it doesn't lead anywhere I want to go." He made the decision to launch his business to "own my life and make decisions that are not the result of other people's plans or expectations." Today, Boston Beer Company sells 32 types of beer, has 800 employees, and generates sales of $371 million.[18]

**5. *Perseverance.*** Even when things don't work out as they planned, entrepreneurs don't give up. They simply keep trying. Real entrepreneurs follow the advice contained in the Japanese proverb, "Fall seven times; stand up eight."

**ENTREPRENEURIAL PROFILE: Gail Borden: Borden Inc.** Entrepreneur Gail Borden (1801–1874) was a prolific inventor, but most of his inventions, including the terraqueous wagon (a type of prairie schooner that could travel on land or water) and a meat biscuit (a mixture of dehydrated meat and flour that would last for months), never achieved commercial success. After witnessing a small child die from contaminated milk, Borden set out to devise a method for condensing milk to make it safer for human consumption in the days before refrigeration. For two years he tried a variety of methods, but every one of them failed. Finally, Borden developed a successful vacuum condensation process, won a patent for it, and built a company around the product. It failed, but Borden persevered. He launched another condensed milk business, this time with a stronger capital base, and it succeeded, eventually becoming Borden Inc., a multi-billion-dollar conglomerate that still makes condensed milk using the process Borden developed 150 years ago. When he died, Borden was buried beneath a tombstone that reads, "I tried and failed. I tried again and succeeded."[19]

**6. *Desire for immediate feedback.*** Entrepreneurs like to know how they are doing and are constantly looking for reinforcement. Tricia Fox, founder of Fox Day Schools, Inc., claims, "I like being independent and successful. Nothing gives you feedback like your own business."[20]

**7. *High level of energy.*** Entrepreneurs are more energetic than the average person. That energy may be a critical factor given the incredible effort required to launch a start-up company. Long hours—often 60 to 80 hours a week—and hard work are the rule rather than the exception. Building a successful business requires a great deal of stamina and dedication. "Entrepreneurs have zero sense of balance," says serial entrepreneur Jeff Stibel, CEO of Dun & Bradstreet Credibility Corporation. "We're all in all the time. It doesn't matter if it's day or night, weekday or weekend. Each of us focuses on our vision with a single-minded passion. We'd probably work in our sleep if we could."[21]

**8. *Competitiveness.*** Entrepreneurs tend to exhibit competitive behavior, often early in life. They enjoy competitive games and sports and always want to keep score.

**9. *Future orientation.*** Entrepreneurs tend to dream big and then formulate plans to transform those dreams into reality. They have a well-defined sense of searching for opportunities. They look ahead and are less concerned with what they accomplished yesterday than what they can do tomorrow. Ever vigilant for new business opportunities, entrepreneurs *observe* the same events other people do, but they *see* something different. "Entrepreneurial brains are full-time pattern recognizers," says Steve Blank, professor of entrepreneurship at Stanford University.[22]

Taking this trait to the extreme are **serial entrepreneurs**, those who create multiple companies, often running more than one business simultaneously. These entrepreneurs take multitasking to the extreme. Serial entrepreneurs get a charge from taking an idea, transforming it into a business, and repeating the process.

**ENTREPRENEURIAL PROFILE: Paul Hurley: ideeli** At age 12, Paul Hurley purchased the equipment to start a lawn care business with the profits he earned investing in small oil company stocks. (He came up with the investment strategy after reading his father's copies of *Forbes*.) Hurley's first hire was a kid who had a driver's license because he was too young to drive the company truck. While attending Yale University, Hurley started a series of companies, learning the fundamentals of developing a workable business model, importing, mastering direct mail, and other business skills. After college, he and his brother started Aveo, a communications software company that attracted investments from venture capital firms before folding. "I was completely wiped out," he recalls. From 2001 to 2006, the serial entrepreneur launched seven businesses in quick succession before devoting his full energy to ideeli, a shopping Web site that runs weekly flash sales that feature thousands of clothing, household, and accessory items from brand-name companies at discounts of up to 80 percent. "We put up a new store every day," says Hurley. The site, with more than 4.5 million members, has more than 1,000 suppliers and has raised $70 million in capital from top venture capital companies. Just three years after its launch, ideeli's annual sales reached nearly $78 million, but Hurley's vision is much grander. "We're going to build something big and have a meaningful impact," he says.[23]

**10.** *Skill at organizing.* Building a company "from scratch" is much like piecing together a giant jigsaw puzzle. Entrepreneurs know how to put the right people and resources together to accomplish a task. Effectively combining talent and resources enables entrepreneurs to bring their visions to reality.

**11.** *Value of achievement over money.* One of the most common misconceptions about entrepreneurs is that they are driven wholly by the desire to make money. To the contrary, *achievement* seems to be one of the primary motivating forces behind entrepreneurs; money is simply a way of "keeping score" of accomplishments—a *symbol* of achievement. "Money is not the driving motive of most entrepreneurs," says Nick Grouf, founder of a high-tech company. "It's just a very nice by-product of the process."[24]

Other characteristics entrepreneurs exhibit include the following:

• *High degree of commitment.* Launching a company successfully requires total commitment from the entrepreneur. Business founders often immerse themselves completely in their businesses. "The commitment you have to make is tremendous; entrepreneurs usually put everything on the line," says one expert.[25] That commitment helps overcome business-threatening mistakes, obstacles, and pessimism from naysayers, however. Entrepreneurs' commitment to their ideas and the businesses those ideas spawn determine how successful their companies ultimately become.

• *Tolerance for ambiguity.* Entrepreneurs tend to have a high tolerance for ambiguous, ever-changing situations—the environment in which they most often operate. This ability to handle uncertainty is critical because these business builders constantly make decisions using new, sometimes conflicting information gleaned from a variety of unfamiliar sources.

• *Flexibility.* One hallmark of true entrepreneurs is their ability to adapt to the changing demands of their customers and their businesses. In this rapidly changing world economy, rigidity often leads to failure. As society, its people, and their tastes change, entrepreneurs also must be willing to adapt their businesses to meet those changes. Successful entrepreneurs are willing to allow their business models to evolve as market conditions warrant.

• *Tenacity.* Obstacles, obstructions, and defeat typically do not dissuade entrepreneurs from doggedly pursuing their visions. Successful entrepreneurs have the willpower to conquer the barriers that stand in the way of their success. "[Entrepreneurship] is about staying focused on the summit," explains Jim Koch, founder of Boston Beer. "No one climbs a mountain to get to the middle. You don't focus on the difficulties. You take it one step at a time, knowing that you're going to get to the top."[26]

What conclusion can we draw from the volumes of research conducted on the entrepreneurial personality? Entrepreneurs are not of one mold; no one set of characteristics can predict who will become entrepreneurs and whether they will succeed. Indeed, *diversity* seems to be a central characteristic of entrepreneurs. As you can see from the examples in this chapter, *anyone*—regardless of age, race, gender, color, national origin, or any other characteristic—can become an entrepreneur. There are no limitations on this form of economic expression, and Fabian Ruiz is living proof.

Catherine Rohr, founder of Defy Ventures.

*Source:* Christian Science Monitor/ Getty Images.

**ENTREPRENEURIAL PROFILE: Fabian Ruiz: Infor-Nation** After serving a 21-year prison term for killing the man who shot his brother, Ruiz, 37, enrolled in Defy Ventures, a nonprofit organization founded by former Wall Street executive Catherine Rohr that teaches the tools of entrepreneurship to former inmates. "The purpose of Defy is to change the way these men think about themselves and their lives," says Rohr. Participants take a yearlong course of instruction in both business and life skills and work with mentors from colleges, churches, and the business community. They compete in a business plan competition in which the winners share $100,000 in seed funding and earn a spot in Defy Venture's business incubator. Ruiz is in Defy Venture's first class, and when he graduates, he will start Infor-Nation, a company that will sell printouts of Web pages to inmates in the New York prison system, who are blocked from using the Internet. "This company is helping me fulfill a lot of expectations," says Ruiz. "Things I expected for myself and things my family expected from me."[27]

Entrepreneurship is not a genetic trait; it is a skill that is learned. The editors of *Inc.* magazine claim, "Entrepreneurship is more mundane than it's sometimes portrayed. . . . You don't need to be a person of mythical proportions to be very, very successful in building a company."[28] As you read this book, we hope that you will pay attention to the numerous small business examples and will notice not only the creativity and dedication of the entrepreneurs behind them but also the diversity of those entrepreneurs.

 **Entrepreneurship in Action**

## Space: The Next Entrepreneurial Frontier?

Entrepreneur-turned-venture-capitalist Guy Kawasaki says that entrepreneurs are willing to ask the fundamental question, "Wouldn't it be neat if . . .?" Steve Jobs wondered, "Wouldn't it be neat if people could take their favorite music with them wherever they go?" and the result was the best-selling iPod. Recently, several serial entrepreneurs asked, "Wouldn't it be neat if people could ride into space?" and have launched commercial "spaceline" businesses to take customers into the final frontier.

In 2011, the National Aeronautic and Space Administration (NASA) completed its final manned space flight when the space shuttle *Atlantis* touched down, ending the 135th space shuttle flight and marking the end of a program that began in 1981, when the launch of the shuttle *Columbia* began a new era in space travel. The end of NASA's program has created an opportunity for entrepreneurs who are interested in exploring the business potential of space much like the entrepreneurs who capitalized on the new field of aviation in the 1920s. Although NASA is planning no space flights in the immediate future, the agency is helping private companies develop spacecraft and space flight capability through its Commercial Crew Development program, which so far has invested $320 million in four companies, three of which are entrepreneurial ventures. "We're at the dawn of a new era of space exploration, one where there's a much bigger role for commercial companies," says Elon Musk, founder of SpaceX. Musk, a serial entrepreneur and cofounder of PayPal, which he sold to eBay for $1.5 billion in 2002. Musk used $100 million of the proceeds from the sale to start SpaceX that same year and later invested $50 million to launch Tesla Motors, a company that makes head-turning, high-performance electric cars. After SpaceX's first three launches of its Falcon 9 booster rocket ended in failure, the company was on the verge of going out of business. The company's fourth attempt was successful, however, and its *Dragon* space capsule became the first from a private company to rendezvous 240 miles above the earth with the International Space Station carrying a modest cargo of 162 meal packets, a laptop computer, clothing, and 15 student experiments. The successful flight resulted in a $1.6 billion contract for SpaceX, which is based in Hawthorne, California, from NASA, under which it will fly 12 cargo missions to the space station. Musk also intends for SpaceX to be one of the companies that NASA selects to take astronauts back to the space station. SpaceX currently launches its flights from NASA's Cape Canaveral center but plans to build its own launch pad somewhere along the Gulf Coast.

Another serial entrepreneur, Richard Branson, founder of Virgin Galactic, which is part of Branson's Virgin Group, a collection of companies in industries that range from health care and air travel to book publishing and wine, has developed a vehicle, *SpaceShipTwo*, that will carry passengers into suborbital space 70 miles above the earth, where they will experience weightlessness and breathtaking views. After being launched from a mother ship called *LauncherOne*, the two-pilot rocket plane will take six passengers into space but will not orbit the earth. Purchasing a seat on a *SpaceShipTwo* flight costs $200,000, and already more than 500 space tourists from 40 countries have paid deposits of more than $60 million to reserve seats on upcoming flights. "We want to enable people all over the world to experience what only about 500 people have seen: Earth from space and the surrounding universe," says Virgin Galactic CEO George Whitesides.

Another start-up company with several high-profile investors has its eyes on space but with a different twist than SpaceX and Virgin Galactic. The founders of Planetary Resources Inc. are developing a series of low-cost unmanned spacecraft that are designed to prospect and mine valuable minerals on near-Earth asteroids (NEAs). Eric Anderson and Peter Diamandis, the entrepreneurs behind Planetary Resources, say that of the 10,000 known NEAs, more than 1,500 are as easy to reach as the moon. Diamandis says that a typical asteroid that is 265 feet in diameter could contain $100 billion worth of metals and provide enough energy-generating material to power every space shuttle that has ever traveled into space. The solar system is "full of resources that we could bring back to humanity," he says. In addition, studying the composition of asteroids could help humans develop methods for preventing them from colliding with earth, an event that could threaten the survival of the human race. Anderson estimates that sending six spacecraft into space to identify the asteroids that offer the greatest potential for mining will cost $25 million to $30 million. Hitching a ride on other company's rockets could lower that cost significantly, which is the reason that the company has entered into a deal with Virgin Galactic to use *LauncherOne* to send Planetary Resources' *Arkyrd* spacecraft into space to explore and eventually mine asteroids.

Investors in Planetary Resources, which currently has more than 30 employees with plans to expand to 100 people who will "devote their lives" to the project, include Google cofounder Larry Page; Ross Perot Jr., chairman of the Perot Group; movie director James Cameron; Chris Lewicki, former Mars mission manager at NASA; and others. "We're trying to do something so audacious, and we might fail," acknowledges Anderson. "But we believe that attempting this and moving the needle in space

*(continued)*

# Entrepreneurship in Action *(continued)*

is worth it." The company says its ultimate goal is to "Planetary Resources' plan to mine Near-Earth Asteroids for raw materials, ranging from water to precious metals, which will deliver multiple benefits to humanity and grow to be valued at tens of billions of dollars annually."

1. Assume that you are one of the wealthy potential investors whom the founders of the companies profiled here approached for start-up capital. How would you have responded? What questions would you have asked them?

2. What do you predict for the future of the businesses described here?

3. "If no one is calling you crazy, you're probably not thinking big enough," says entrepreneur Linda Rottenberg. What does she mean? Do you agree?

*Sources:* Based on Emma Haak, "Space, the Private Frontier," *Fast Company*, February 2012, p. 15; Andrew Shafer, "Up, Up, and Away," *Inc.*, July/August 2011, pp. 34–35; Andy Pasztor, "Private Space Run Makes History," *Wall Street Journal*, May 26–27, 2012, pp. A1–A2; George Abbey, "A New Generation of Space Entrepreneurs," Chron.com, June 2012, *http://blog.chron.com/bakerblog/2012/06/a-new-generation-of-space-entrepreneurs*; Christian Cotroneo, "Virgin Galactic Taking Reservations, Calgary Teen Poised to Be Youngest in Space," *Huffington Post*, August 26, 2011, *www.huffingtonpost.ca/2011/06/26/virgin-galactic-reservations-calgary-teen_n_884735.html*; Kenneth Chang, "Big Day for a Space Entrepreneur Promising More," *New York Times*, May 22, 2012, *www.nytimes.com/2012/05/23/science/space/spacexs-private-cargo-rocket-heads-to-space-station.html*; Amir Efrati, "Asteroid Venture Is About Politics, Not Just Mining," *Wall Street Journal*, April 24, 2012, pp. B1–B2; Amir Efrati, "Asteroid Mining Strategy Is Outlined by a Start-Up," *Wall Street Journal*, April 25, 2012, p. B3; "Planetary Resources Inc. Announces Agreement with Virgin Galactic for Payload Services," Planetary Resources, July 11, 2012, *www.planetaryresources.com/2012/07/planetary-resources-inc-announces-contract-with-virgin-galactic-for-payload-services*.

## How to Spot Entrepreneurial Opportunities

**3.**

Explain how entrepreneurs spot business opportunities.

One of the tenets of entrepreneurship is the ability to create new and useful ideas that solve the problems and challenges people face every day. "Entrepreneurs innovate," said management legend Peter Drucker. "Innovation is the special instrument of entrepreneurship."[29] Entrepreneurs achieve success by creating value in the marketplace when they combine resources in new and different ways to gain a competitive edge over rivals. Entrepreneurs can create value in a number of ways. Indeed, finding new ways of satisfying customers' needs, inventing new products and services, putting together existing ideas in new and different ways, and creating new twists on existing products and services are hallmarks of the entrepreneur. At first glance, some entrepreneurs' ideas seem outlandish, but "illogical ideas are how society achieves progress," observes Steve Blank, professor of entrepreneurship at Stanford.[30]

What is the entrepreneurial "secret" for creating value in the marketplace? In reality, the "secret" is no secret at all: it is applying creativity and innovation to solve problems and to exploit opportunities that people face every day. **Creativity** is the ability to develop new ideas and to discover new ways of looking at problems and opportunities. **Innovation** is the ability to *apply* creative solutions to those problems and opportunities to enhance or to enrich people's lives. Harvard's Ted Levitt says that creativity is *thinking* new things and that innovation is *doing* new things. In short, entrepreneurs succeed by *thinking and doing* new things or old things in new ways. Simply having a great new idea is not enough; turning the idea into a tangible product, service, or business venture is the essential next step.

Entrepreneurs' ability to build viable businesses around their ideas has transformed the world. From King Gillette's invention of the safety razor (Gillette) and Mary Kay Ash's use of a motivated team of consultants to sell her cosmetics (Mary Kay Cosmetics) to Steve Jobs and Steve Wozniak building the first personal computer in a California garage (Apple) and Fred Smith's concept for delivering packages overnight (FedEx), entrepreneurs have made the world a better place to live. How do entrepreneurs spot opportunities? Although there is no single process, the following techniques will help you discover business opportunities in the same way these successful entrepreneurs did.

### Monitor Trends and Exploit Them Early On

Astute entrepreneurs watch both national and local trends that are emerging and then build businesses that align with those trends. Detecting a trend early on and launching a business to capitalize on it enables an entrepreneur to gain a competitive advantage over rivals.

**ENTREPRENEURIAL PROFILE: Kian Saneii: Independa** Kian Saneii watched his parents, both in their 70s, care for his grandmother, who was in her 90s. Frequent telephone calls to check on her and to remind her to take her medications were part of their daily routine. Saneii realized that his family was facing an issue that was becoming more prevalent in the United States. His research confirmed that the number of U.S. citizens who are 65 or older will more than double from 40 million to 89 million by 2050. Saneii decided to tap into this trend and invested a year of research before launching Independa, a telecommunications platform that uses telephones, computers, and tablets to deliver reminders to elderly people about taking medications and going to medical appointments. Independa's "aging in place" service also allows people who know nothing about technology to use a television or touch-screen device to video chat or use Facebook, reducing feelings of isolation and depression. It offers games and puzzles for entertainment and mental engagement and a calendar with reminders of family celebrations. Independa also offers a service that uses wireless sensors to monitor a person's vital signs and transmit them via the Internet at regular intervals. Saneii recently acquired $2.35 million in financing from venture capital firms.[31]

## Travel—and Be Inspired

One of the benefits of traveling is the exposure to new ideas. When entrepreneurs travel, they take the time to observe and to be inspired by what they see, always on the lookout for new ideas they can turn into businesses.

**ENTREPRENEURIAL PROFILE: Eileen Fisher: Eileen Fisher** Legendary fashion designer Eileen Fisher never really thought about becoming a fashion designer even though she learned to sew as a young girl and made her own prom dress. After graduating from college, Fisher worked for a New York City graphic designer, giving her the opportunity to travel to Japan, where she was captivated by the beautiful fabrics and simple styles, such as cropped pants and kimonos. At the time, Fisher recalls, "I hated shopping for clothes because I couldn't find what I wanted." She believed that women's clothes were too complicated and decided to "make simple clothes that would last and that would transcend fashions." In 1984, recalling the simple styles she had seen on her travels in Japan, Fisher designed four garments, found a seamstress to make them, and took them to a boutique fashion show in New York City, where she sold small orders to eight stores. The next year, Fisher expanded her line and took $40,000 in orders at the same show. Six years later, she opened the first Eileen Fisher store on Madison Avenue in New York City. Today, the entrepreneur, who is still known for her simple mix-and-match collections, has 57 stores in the United States, Canada, and Great Britain and a company that generates more than $300 million in annual sales.[32]

## Take a Different Approach to an Existing Market

Another way to spot opportunities is to ask whether there is another way to reach an existing market with a unique product, service, or marketing strategy. Entrepreneurs are famous for finding new, creative approaches to existing markets and turning them into business opportunities.

**ENTREPRENEURIAL PROFILE: Joshua Opperman: I Do Now I Don't** After Joshua Opperman and his fiancé broke up in 2006, he attempted to get a refund on the diamond ring he had purchased, but the jewelry store would issue only a store credit, and other jewelers and pawn shops offered him just 28 percent of the original $10,000 purchase price. The painful experience prompted him to start an e-commerce business, cleverly named I Do Now I Don't, that provides a secure Web site on which people can sell slightly used engagement rings. A seller who lists a ring on the site negotiates a price with a buyer, who sends payment to I Do Now I Don't to hold in escrow. The seller sends the ring to I Do Now I Don't, where it is appraised before the company completes the transaction by sending it to the buyer. Opperman's company collects a 15 percent commission for its services. In response to customers' requests, I Do Now I Don't also buys some rings outright from customers and resells them to dealers. Already the company's annual sales are $3 million and are growing fast.[33]

## Put a New Twist on an Old Idea

Sometimes entrepreneurs find opportunities by taking an old idea and giving it a unique twist. The result can lead to a profitable business venture.

**ENTREPRENEURIAL PROFILE: Jason Brown and David Waxman: Vitaband** While jogging one day, Jason Brown was nearly hit by a car, and the near miss gave him the idea for a rubber identification wristband containing a chip that would allow emergency responders to access the wearer's medical history in case of an accident. Brown told his best friend, David Waxman, about his idea, and the two launched Vitaband to bring the product to market. As they built their business, Brown and Waxman added a prepaid debit chip to Vitaband so that runners could make purchases simply by waving the band near a wireless payment reader without having to carry a wallet, a credit card, or cash. Brown and Waxman invested $50,000 of their own money and raised an additional $750,000 from family members, friends, and, most recently, angel investors to develop prototypes and market the Vitaband. The next challenge is marketing the Vitaband to other customers, including parents who want a safety device for their children and children who want another layer of security for their aging parents.[34]

## Look for Creative Ways to Use Existing Resources

Another way entrepreneurs uncover business opportunities is to find creative ways to use existing resources. This requires them to cast aside logic and traditional thinking.

**ENTREPRENEURIAL PROFILE: Ed Munn: Dig This** While using heavy equipment to clear land, build a pond, and dig the foundation for the house he was building for him and his wife in Steamboat Springs, Colorado, contractor Ed Munn thought about how much fun he had operating the equipment and how other people would enjoy the experience as well. Munn used his inventory of equipment to launch Dig This, a business that transforms almost anyone into a heavy equipment operator for a day. Three years later, Munn moved his business to Las Vegas, Nevada, where a real estate collapse had freed up many pieces of heavy equipment and customers would have plenty of room to dig in the dirt like kids but with adult-size toys. For as little as $250, customers can experience the thrill of moving dirt, digging trenches, and playing "excavator basketball" under the watchful eye of experienced instructors.[35]

## Realize That Others Have the Same Problem You Do

Another way entrepreneurs spot business opportunities is by recognizing the "pain points" they encounter from flaws in existing products or services and asking whether other people face the same problems. Providing a product or service that solves those problems offers the potential for a promising business.

**ENTREPRENEURIAL PROFILE: Sanjay Kothari and Vinay Pulim: MileWise** Like most frequent fliers, Sanjay Kothari experienced difficulty trying to redeem the miles he accumulated on various airlines. Doing so usually required many hours of searching for available flights, poring over rules and restrictions, and making numerous telephone calls. Kothari discovered that many of the 90 million frequent fliers in the United States never use the airline miles they accumulate because the process of redeeming them is so onerous. Spotting an opportunity, Kothari worked with fellow entrepreneur Vinay Pulim to launch MileWise, a specialized search engine that allows travelers to find flights that they can purchase with airline miles, hotel or credit card points, or cash. The Web site also recommends the best way to pay for a trip based on a user's reward program and travel preferences. "It usually takes people several hours to figure out whether to pay for travel with cash or rewards," says Kothari. "We're trying to help them do that in under 30 seconds." Kothari and Pulim raised $1.5 million in start-up financing for MileWise from angel investors and venture capital firms and within one month of the site's launch had attracted 12,000 users.[36]

## Take Time to Play

Children are so creative because they play and have not yet been subjected to all of the "rules" about how things should work that adults have. When it comes to creativity, entrepreneurs can take a lesson from playful children. Play can be a source of business ideas.

**ENTREPRENEURIAL PROFILE: Doug Stienstra: Flash Pals** While he was a student at the University of Iowa, Doug Stienstra's girlfriend wanted a "cute" flash drive. After scouring the Internet and retail stores, Stienstra could not find one, so he decided to make one for her. He bought an animal-shaped finger puppet from a toy store and glued it to a standard flash drive. His girlfriend loved the gift, and "her friends starting asking me to make one for them," says Stienstra. "I knew I was on to something. I tested the market, and there was clearly a demand, so I kept at it." Stienstra worked with the Bedell Entrepreneurship Learning Laboratory at the university and launched a business, Flash Pals, that sells the playful flash drives for $25 to $30 and donates a portion of each sale to wildlife charities.[37]

## Notice What Is Missing

Sometimes entrepreneurs spot viable business opportunities by noticing what is *missing*—the "white space" in a market. "Realize that when people say, 'You're starting *what?*' that you're on to something," says one writer.[38] The first step is to determine whether a market for the missing product or service actually exists (perhaps the reason it does not exist is that there is no market potential), which is one of the objectives of a feasibility analysis.

**ENTREPRENEURIAL PROFILE: Fred Carl: Viking Range Corporation** In 1980, while designing the kitchen for their new house, Fred Carl's wife, Margaret, said that she wanted a heavy-duty gas range like the one her mother had. Carl searched but soon discovered that no company made commercial-grade ovens for home use, so he decided to build one himself. Eventually, he says, "Because no one was doing it, I thought, 'This is a business.'" Carl contacted every oven manufacturer in the country, and it took two years for him to convince one company to build the oven he had designed. In 1984, he formed a company, Viking Range Corporation, in Greenwood, Mississippi, using his own money, credit cards, and a $325,000 bank loan, and today the company generates annual sales of more than $300 million from a full line of quality kitchen appliances.[39]

No matter which methods they use to detect business opportunities, true entrepreneurs follow up their ideas with action, building companies to capitalize on their ideas.

## The Benefits of Owning a Small Business

Surveys show that owners of small businesses believe they work harder, earn more money, and are happier than if they worked for a large company. Entrepreneurs enjoy many benefits of owning a small business, including the following.

**4.**

Describe the benefits of owning a small business.

### Opportunity to Gain Control over Your Own Destiny

Entrepreneurs cite controlling their own destinies as one of the benefits of owning their own businesses. Owning a business provides entrepreneurs the independence and the opportunity to achieve what is important to them. Entrepreneurs want to "call the shots" in their lives, and they use their businesses to bring this desire to life. Numerous studies of entrepreneurs in several countries report that the primary incentive for starting their businesses is "being my own boss." Entrepreneurs reap the intrinsic rewards of knowing they are the driving forces behind their businesses. "When you're in the driver's seat, you are making decisions on how to steer your company into the future," explains Kasey Gahler, who left his corporate job to start his own financial services company, Gahler Financial.[40]

### Opportunity to Make a Difference

Increasingly, entrepreneurs are starting businesses because they see an opportunity to make a difference in a cause that is important to them. Known as **social entrepreneurs**, these business builders seek to find innovative solutions to some of society's most pressing and most challenging problems. Their businesses often have a triple bottom line that encompasses economic, social, and environmental objectives. These entrepreneurs see their businesses as mechanisms for achieving social goals that are important to them. Whether it is providing sturdy low-cost housing for families in developing countries, promoting the arts in small communities, or creating a company that educates young people about preserving the earth's limited resources, entrepreneurs are finding ways to combine their concerns for social issues and their desire to earn good livings. Although they see the importance of building viable, sustainable businesses, social entrepreneurs' primary goal is to use their companies to make a positive impact on the world. Women are slightly more likely than men to start companies for social rather than economic reasons.[41]

**ENTREPRENEURIAL PROFILE: Gabrielle Palermo, Bill Walters, Susanna Young and Clay Tyler: G3Box** When two professors at Arizona State University challenged their engineering students to develop creative ideas for using the hundreds of used shipping containers that are abandoned at ports around the world, Gabrielle Palermo, Bill Walters, Susanna Young, and Clay Tyler came up with the idea of converting the containers into medical clinics that can be deployed anywhere in the world. They created a company, G3Box (the G3 stands for "generating global good"), that transforms the shipping containers into mobile medical clinics and sells them to nonprofit and nongovernmental organizations. The mobile clinics are outfitted with insulation, ventilation, power (some units are equipped with solar panels), potable water, and other necessities and can be set up as permanent housing for medical care or transported into disaster areas as temporary clinics. Outfitting a container costs between $12,000 and $18,000, depending on the particular setup, but Palermo says that G3Box can modify containers for practically any use, such as classrooms, food distribution units, dental offices, and more. "When I started college, I didn't really think I was going to be growing a business," says Palermo, "but doing G3Box as a career or starting other companies that focus on social good is my passion now."[42]

## Opportunity to Reach Your Full Potential

Too many people find their work boring, unchallenging, and unexciting. But to most entrepreneurs, there is little difference between work and play; the two are synonymous. Roger Levin, founder of Levin Group, the largest dental practice management consulting firm in the world, says, "When I come to work every day, it's not a job for me. I'm having fun!"[43]

Entrepreneurs' businesses become the instrument for self-expression and self-actualization. Owning a business challenges all of an entrepreneur's skills, abilities, creativity, and determination. The only barriers to success are self-imposed. "It's more exciting to get a company from zero to $100 million than to get a billion-dollar company to its next $100 million," says Dick Harrington, former CEO of Thomson Reuters and now a principal at Cue Ball, a venture capital firm that invests in promising small companies.[44] Entrepreneurs' creativity, determination, and enthusiasm—not limits artificially created by an organization (e.g., the "glass ceiling")—determine how high they can rise.

## Opportunity to Reap Impressive Profits

Although money is *not* the primary force driving most entrepreneurs, the profits their businesses can earn are an important motivating factor in their decisions to launch companies. If accumulating wealth is high on your list of priorities, owning a business is usually the best way to achieve it. Most entrepreneurs never become superrich, but many of them do become quite wealthy. Indeed, nearly 75 percent of those on the *Forbes* list of the 400 richest Americans are first-generation entrepreneurs (and most of the others are part of successful family businesses)![45] Self-employed people are four times more likely to become millionaires than those who work for someone else. According to Russ Alan Prince and Lewis Schiff, authors of *The Middle Class Millionaire*, more than 80 percent of middle-class millionaires, those people with a net worth between $1 million and $10 million, own their own businesses or are part of professional partnerships. (They also work an average of 70 hours a week.)[46]

**ENTREPRENEURIAL PROFILE: Kevin Plank: Under Armour** As a special teams captain on the University of Maryland football team, Kevin Plank grew weary of wearing a heavy, sweat-soaked cotton T-shirt under his football pads. He began to research the properties of various fabrics and produced sample shirts made with a polyester-blend base layer that fit as snugly as Spiderman's suit and were extremely lightweight, durable, and capable of wicking away perspiration so that they stayed dry. He tested early prototypes himself, and, at first, his teammates laughed at him because the fabric resembled lingerie. Before long, however, his teammates were asking for shirts of their own. After graduating, Plank launched a company, Under Armour, from the basement of his grandmother's townhouse in Washington, D.C., which served as the company's first office, warehouse, distribution center—and his bedroom. He started Under Armour with $20,000 of his own money and $40,000 in credit card debt before landing a $250,000 loan guaranteed by the U.S. Small Business Administration. Fifteen years later, Plank's company, which sells a full line of athletic apparel and shoes, generates annual sales of $1.83 billion. With a personal net worth of $1.7 billion, Kevin Plank has reaped the financial rewards of entrepreneurship.[47]

## Opportunity to Contribute to Society and Be Recognized for Your Efforts

Often, small business owners are among the most respected—and most trusted—members of their communities. A recent survey by the Public Affairs Council reports that 90 percent of Americans have a favorable view of small businesses, far more than those who view large corporations, news media, and the government.[48] Entrepreneurs enjoy the trust and the recognition they receive from the customers they have served faithfully over the years. A recent Pew Research Center survey reports that small businesses make up the most trusted institution in the United States, ranking ahead of churches and colleges.[49] Playing a vital role in their local business systems and knowing that the work they do has a significant impact on how smoothly our nation's economy functions is yet another reward for entrepreneurs.

### Opportunity to Do What You Enjoy Doing

A common sentiment among small business owners is that their work *really* isn't work. In fact, a recent survey by Wells Fargo/Gallup Small Business Index reports that 47 percent of business owners say they do not plan to retire from their businesses unless they are forced to because of health reasons![50] Most successful entrepreneurs choose to enter their particular business fields because they have an interest in them and enjoy those lines of work. Many of them have made their avocations (hobbies) their vocations (work) and are glad they did! These entrepreneurs are living the advice Harvey McKay offers: "Find a job doing what you love, and you'll never have to work a day in your life."

**ENTREPRENEURIAL PROFILE: Jeff Archer and Tom Losee: YOLO Board** Jeff Archer was hooked on the sport of stand-up paddling on his first outing when he followed a pod of dolphins and watched them teach a young dolphin how to catch fish. Two weeks later, Archer and business partner Tom Losee, both lifelong aficionados of water sports and fitness, had launched YOLO ("You Only Live Once") Board, a company in Santa Rosa Beach, Florida, that makes a modern version of the stand-up paddle boards invented by the Polynesians centuries ago. YOLO Board manufactures 18 different boards that range in price from $700 to $2,000 to accommodate various types of water and paddler preferences. Similar to a surfboard only wider, longer, and more stable, stand-up paddle boards allow users to get exercise, enjoy the beauty of a variety of bodies of water, and experience a sense of calmness. Gliding on the surface of the water, one newcomer to the sport says, "It feels as if we're walking on water." Through YOLO Board, Archer and Losee, whose work wardrobes include board shirts, T-shirts, and flip-flops rather than suits, ties, and wingtips, are able to do what they enjoy and share their passion for the sport with others.[51]

## The Potential Drawbacks of Entrepreneurship

Although owning a business has many benefits and provides many opportunities, anyone planning to enter the world of entrepreneurship should be aware of its potential drawbacks. "Building a start-up is incredibly hard, stressful, chaotic, and—more often than not—results in failure," says entrepreneur Eric Ries. "So why become an entrepreneur? Three reasons: change the world, make customers' lives better, and create an organization of lasting value. If you want to do only one of these things, there are better options. Only start-ups combine all three."[52] Let's explore the "dark side" of entrepreneurship.

**5.** _____

Describe the potential drawbacks of owning a small business.

### Uncertainty of Income

Opening and running a business provides no guarantees that an entrepreneur will earn enough money to survive. Even though business owners tend to earn more than wage-and-salary workers, some small businesses barely generate enough revenue to provide the owner-manager with an adequate income. The median income of small business owners ($72,806) is 82 percent higher than the median income of full-time wage and salary workers ($40,092), but business owners' income tends to be much more variable.[53] In the early days of a start-up, a business often cannot provide an attractive salary for its founder and meet all of its financial obligations, which means that the entrepreneur may have to live on savings for a time. The regularity of income that comes with working for someone else is absent because the owner is always the last one to be paid. A recent survey by Citibank reports that 54 percent of small business owners have gone without a paycheck to help their businesses survive.[54] The founder of a flavor and fragrances manufacturing operation recalls the time his bank unexpectedly called the company's loans just before Thanksgiving, squeezing both the company's and the family's cash flow. "We had planned a huge Christmas party, but we canceled that," recalls his wife. "And Christmas. And our usual New Year's trip."[55]

### Risk of Losing Your Entire Invested Capital

The small business failure rate is relatively high. According to a research by the Bureau of Labor Statistics, 31 percent of new businesses fail within two years, and 51 percent shut down within five years. Within 10 years, 66 percent of new businesses will have folded.[56] "In the wake of a company failure, the founder knows that he has kicked his family's fortune back to Square One, or past that, to Square Zero, or Minus Three," says Meg Hirshberg, wife of Gary Hirshberg, founder of yogurt maker Stonyfield Farm. "The [failure] of Stonyfield Farm would have meant the loss of our home, our lifestyle, our children's college funds."[57]

A failed business can be financially and emotionally devastating. Before launching their businesses, entrepreneurs should ask themselves whether they can cope financially and psychologically with the consequences of failure. They should consider the risk-reward tradeoff before putting their financial and mental well-being at risk:

- What is the worst that could happen if I open my business and it fails?
- How likely is the worst to happen?
- What can I do to lower the risk of my business failing?
- If my business were to fail, what is my contingency plan for coping?

### Long Hours and Hard Work

The average small business owner works 54 hours per week, compared to the 35 hours per week the typical U.S. employee works.[58] In many start-ups, 10- to 12-hour days and six- or seven-day workweeks with no paid vacations are the *norm*. A recent survey by Manta Media found that 48 percent of small business owners say that they had no time to take a summer vacation.[59] "I just took the first vacation in years," says Greg Selkoe, founder of Karmaloop, a Web site that sells clothing and shoes. "I've never taken a vacation in which I don't work. In one sense, my life is stressful. In another, it's a vacation because I love what I'm doing. Work is my fun."[60]

Sleep researcher James Maas of Cornell University estimates that entrepreneurs lose 700 hours of sleep the year in which they launch their companies, which is equivalent to the amount of sleep that a parent loses in the first year of a baby's life.[61] Dan Croft left a top management job at a large mobile communications company to start Mission Critical Wireless, a small business that helps other businesses select and implement wireless communication systems. Croft's 25 years of experience in the industry allowed him to make a smooth transition to entrepreneurship, but there were a few surprises. "The highs are much higher, the lows are much lower, and the lack of sleep is much greater," jokes Croft, referring to the long hours his new role requires.[62]

Because they often must do everything themselves, owners experience intense, draining workdays. "I'm the owner, manager, secretary, and janitor," says Cynthia Malcolm, who owns a salon called the Hand Candy Mind and Body Escape in Cheviot, Ohio.[63] Many business owners start down the path of entrepreneurship thinking that they will own a business only to discover later that the business owns them!

### Lower Quality of Life Until the Business Gets Established

The long hours and hard work needed to launch a company can take their toll on the remainder of an entrepreneur's life. Business owners often find their roles as husbands and wives or fathers and mothers take a backseat to their roles as company founders. Marriages and friendships are too often casualties of small business ownership. Part of the problem is that entrepreneurs are most likely to launch their businesses between the ages of 25 and 34, just when they start their families.

**ENTREPRENEURIAL PROFILE: Peyton Anderson and Affinergy, Inc.** Peyton Anderson, owner of Affinergy Inc., a 12-person biotech firm located in Research Triangle Park, North Carolina, struggles to balance the demands of his young company and his family, which includes three children under the age of four. "I do a lot of work from 9 p.m. to midnight," says Anderson, "and I try to keep Saturday open to do things with the kids." He also uses flextime during the week to spend more time with his family, but maintaining balance is an ongoing battle, especially when managing a young company. "Even while I'm singing to them in the bathtub, in the back of my mind, I'm grinding on stuff at work," admits Anderson.[64]

### High Levels of Stress

Launching and running a business can be an extremely rewarding experience, but it also can be a highly stressful one. Most entrepreneurs have made significant investments in their companies, left behind the safety and security of a steady paycheck, and mortgaged everything they own to get into business. Failure often means total financial ruin as well as a serious psychological blow, and that creates high levels of stress and anxiety. "Being an entrepreneur takes sheer guts and demands far more than an 'employee' mentality," says Jamie Kreitman, founder of Kreitman Knitworks Ltd., a company specializing in whimsical apparel and footwear.[65]

## Complete Responsibility

Owning a business is highly rewarding, but many entrepreneurs find that they must make decisions on issues about which they are not really knowledgeable. When there is no one to ask, pressure can build quickly. The realization that the decisions they make are the cause of success or failure of the business has a devastating effect on some people. Small business owners realize quickly that *they* are the business.

## Discouragement

Launching a business requires much dedication, discipline, and tenacity. Along the way to building a successful business, entrepreneurs will run headlong into many obstacles, some of which may appear to be insurmountable. Discouragement and disillusionment can set in, but successful entrepreneurs know that every business encounters rough spots and that perseverance is required to get through them.

Entrepreneurs are not easily dissuaded by the disadvantages of owning a business. In a recent survey by Citibank, 76 percent of small business owners say they would start their businesses again if they knew then what they know now about the challenges they would face.[66]

# Why the Boom: The Fuel Feeding the Entrepreneurial Fire

What forces are driving this entrepreneurial trend in our economy? Which factors have led to this age of entrepreneurship? Some of the most significant ones follow.

**6.**

Explain the forces that are driving the growth of entrepreneurship.

## Entrepreneurs as Heroes

An intangible but very important factor is the attitude that Americans have toward entrepreneurs. Around the world, the most successful entrepreneurs have hero status and serve as role models for aspiring entrepreneurs. Business founders such as Michael Dell (Dell Computers), Oprah Winfrey (Harpo Studios and Oxygen Media), Richard Branson (Virgin), Robert Johnson (Black Entertainment Television), and Mark Zuckerburg (Facebook) are to entrepreneurship what LeBron James and Peyton Manning are to sports. The media reinforce entrepreneurs' hero status with television shows such as *The Apprentice* with Donald Trump and *Shark Tank and Dragons' Den*, both of which features entrepreneurs who pitch their ideas to a panel of tough business experts who have the capital and the connections to make a budding business successful. Nearly 7.5 million people in 123 countries on six continents participate in nearly 34,000 activities during Global Entrepreneurship Week, a celebration of entrepreneurship that is sponsored by the Kauffman Foundation.[67]

## Entrepreneurial Education

People with more education are more likely to start businesses than those with less education, and entrepreneurship, in particular, is an extremely popular course of study among students at all levels. A rapidly growing number of college students see owning a business as an attractive career option, and in addition to signing up for entrepreneurship courses, many of them are launching companies while in school. Today, more than two-thirds of the colleges and universities in the United States (more than 2,300) offer courses in entrepreneurship or small business, up from just 16 in 1970. More than 200,000 students are enrolled in entrepreneurship courses, and many colleges and universities have difficulty meeting the demand for courses in entrepreneurship and small business.[68]

## Shift to a Service Economy

The service sector accounts for 86 percent of the jobs (up from 70 percent in the 1950s) and 48 percent of the GDP in the United States.[69] Because of their relatively low start-up costs, service businesses have been very popular with entrepreneurs. The booming service sector has provided entrepreneurs with many business opportunities, from hotels and health care to computer maintenance and Web-based services.

## Technology Advancements

With the help of modern business tools—the Internet, cloud computing, personal computers, tablet computers, smart phones, apps, copiers, color printers, instant messaging, and voice mail—even one person working at home can look like a big business. At one time, the high cost of such technological wizardry made it impossible for small businesses to compete with larger companies that could afford the hardware. Now the cost of sophisticated technology is low enough that even the smallest companies can use a multitude of devices creatively to gain a competitive edge. One recent survey by AT&T reports that 96 percent of small businesses use wireless technology and that 64 percent of owners say that their companies could not survive without it.[70] With the help of modern technology, entrepreneurs can run their businesses from almost anywhere very effectively and look like any *Fortune* 500 company to their customers and clients.

**ENTREPRENEURIAL PROFILE: Drew Houston and Arash Ferdowsi: Dropbox** Drew Houston, just 24 years old and a student at the Massachusetts Institute of Technology, met fellow MIT student, 21-year-old Arash Ferdowsi, and the two began working on a problem that plagued many people: how to store all of your files in one place so that they are accessible from anywhere. Their solution was to create a virtual storage cabinet in the cloud that enables users to save and access documents, spreadsheets, photographs, music, videos, and anything else from any computer, tablet, or smart phone. (Houston actually began writing the code for the software in a Boston train station.) In 2007, Houston and Ferdowsi launched Dropbox Inc. and moved to San Francisco, where they raised $7.2 million in equity financing from top-tier venture capital firms. In 2011, the duo attracted another $250 million in capital to fuel Dropbox's growth. Today, 100 million users save about one billion files on Dropbox each day, generating more than $500 million in annual revenue for the company.[71]

## Outsourcing

Entrepreneurs have discovered that they do not have to do everything themselves. Because of advances in technology, entrepreneurs can outsource many of the operations of their companies and retain only those in which they have a competitive advantage. Doing so enhances their flexibility and adaptability to ever-changing market and competitive conditions.

**ENTREPRENEURIAL PROFILE: Evan Solida: Cerevellum** Evan Solida left his job as a designer for a kayak manufacturer in Easley, South Carolina, to launch Cerevellum, a company that makes a unique digital rearview mirror for bicyclists. An avid cyclist, Solida came up with the idea a decade earlier as part of a college class project but didn't bring the product to life until he was struck by a car while bicycling. After receiving funding from the Upstate Carolina Angel Network and Michelin Development Corporation, Solida was able to bring to market the Hindsight 35, which attaches a small camera at the rear of the bicycle to a handlebar-mounted screen that also serves as a cyclometer and a "black box" in case of an accident. Solida outsources production of the device to a specialty manufacturer in China, and a company in Texas handles distribution for Cerevellum. Solida's outsourcing strategy allowed him to minimize his start-up costs and enables him to focus on the tasks that he performs best.

## Independent Lifestyle

Entrepreneurship fits the way Americans want to live—independent and self-sustaining. Increasingly, entrepreneurs are starting businesses for lifestyle reasons. They want the freedom to choose where they live, the hours they work, and what they do. Although financial security remains an important goal for most entrepreneurs, lifestyle issues such as more time with family and friends, more leisure time, and more control over work-related stress also are important. To these "lifestyle entrepreneurs," launching businesses that give them the flexibility to work the hours they prefer and live where they want to are far more important than money.

## E-Commerce, the Internet, and Mobile Computing

The proliferation of the Internet and mobile computing has spawned thousands of entrepreneurial ventures since the beginning in 1993. Currently, more than 167 million customers in the United States alone shop online.[72] As online shopping becomes easier, more engaging, and more secure for shoppers, e-commerce will continue to grow. eMarketer predicts that online retail sales in the United States will increase from $224.2 billion in 2012 to $361.9 billion in 2016.[73] Many entrepreneurs see the power of the Internet and mobile computing and are putting them to use, but some small businesses have been slow to adopt the technology. A recent study by Web.com reports that only 60 percent of small businesses have Web sites, and only 26 percent of those Web sites are mobile friendly. (Just 14 percent of small businesses have a stand-alone Web site designed specifically for mobile devices.)[74]

**ENTREPRENEURIAL PROFILE: Boris Saragaglia: Spartoo** In Europe, e-commerce sales are growing nearly as fast as in the United States. In 2006, 23-year-old French entrepreneur Boris Saragaglia decided to capitalize on that opportunity and launched Spartoo.com, an e-commerce site that sells shoes. Inspired by the success of online retailer Zappos, Saragaglia made customer service the focal point of Spartoo's strategy, offering customers free delivery and returns on 25,000 shoe styles from 500 brands. His strategy has been successful. With more than a dozen local language versions of its Web site, Spartoo sells more than 1.5 million pairs of shoes annually and generates revenue of $195 million, mostly from customers across Europe.[75]

## International Opportunities

No longer are small businesses limited to pursuing customers within their own borders. The dramatic shift to a global economy has opened the door to tremendous business opportunities for those entrepreneurs willing to reach across the globe. Although the United States is an attractive market for entrepreneurs, approximately 95 percent of the world's population lives outside its borders. With so many opportunities in international markets, even the smallest businesses can sell globally, particularly with the help of the Internet. Jonathan Forgacs, cofounder of Pillow Décor, a Vancouver, Canada–based company that sells more than 1,000 types of decorative pillows online, says that more than 98 percent of sales originate outside of Canada.[76]

Although only 280,000 companies in the United States—less than 1 percent of U.S. small businesses—export, companies with fewer than 20 employees account for 72 percent of all exporters.[77] Small and medium-size companies generate 33 percent of the nation's export sales.[78] The barriers to international trade that small business owners encounter most frequently are high shipping costs, language and cultural differences, and difficulty finding potential customers.[79] Although "going global" can be fraught with many dangers and problems, many entrepreneurs are discovering that selling their products and services in foreign markets is not really as difficult as they originally thought. Patience, diligence, and a management commitment to exporting are essential elements. As business becomes increasingly global in nature, international opportunities for small businesses will continue to grow rapidly.

# In the Entrepreneurial Spotlight

# Collegiate Entrepreneurs

For growing numbers of students, college is not just a time of learning, partying, and growing into young adulthood; it is fast becoming a place for building a business. Today, more than 2,300 colleges and universities offer courses in entrepreneurship and small business management, and many of them have trouble meeting the demand for these classes. "There's been a change in higher education," says William Green, dean of the entrepreneurship program at the University of Miami. "Entrepreneurship has become a mainstream activity." Greater numbers of students are pursuing careers in entrepreneurship and see their college experience as an opportunity to get an early start not only by studying entrepreneurship but also by putting what they learn into practice. In addition to regular classroom courses, colleges increasingly are building an extra dimension in their entrepreneurship programs, including internships with local businesses, mentoring relationships with other entrepreneurs, networking opportunities with potential investors, and participation in business plan competitions. "Entrepreneurial education is a contact sport," says Allan R. Cohen, dean of the graduate program at Babson College.

As the following examples prove, many college students expect to apply the entrepreneurial skills they are learning in their classes by starting businesses while they are still in college.

**ThinkLite**

When Dinesh Wadhwani and Enrico Palmerino were students at Babson College in Wellesley, Massachusetts, they saw an ad for a new technology that produces customized energy-efficient lightbulbs but realized that the $24-per-bulb price tag would dissuade many potential buyers despite the fact that the bulbs produce energy and maintenance savings of up to 90 percent. They approached several large companies that make the bulbs, negotiated discounts for bulk purchases, and started ThinkLite, a Boston-based company that installs the energy efficient bulbs at no up-front cost in exchange for a fixed percentage of the energy savings their customers' realize. The young entrepreneurs have signed on many retail clients, a high-rise apartment building in New York City, and a factory. "College is the best time to have a business venture because all of the money that we make we put back into the business to grow it, and it gives us the liquidity to finance more projects," says Wadhwani.

After graduating, Wadhwani and Palmerino made their college start-up a full-time venture and have expanded ThinkLite into other cities across the United States and in other countries. Looking back, Wadhwani says that his collegiate entrepreneurial education and experience were "priceless" and credits Babson College with encouraging his entrepreneurial spirit. "Babson has educated me

*(continued)*

# In the Entrepreneurial Spotlight *(continued)*

on the two different ways one could make a living: conforming to a standard, or being a pioneer of innovation," he says.

## Skida

While Corinne Prevot was in high school in East Burke, Vermont, the avid skier found some soft, brightly colored Lycra and fleece fabrics and made ski caps and headbands for herself and the teammates on her cross-country ski team. Soon, other people were asking how they could buy some of the unique hats, and before she knew it, Prevot had started a business making them. To expand her market, she drove to a local sporting goods store in a borrowed car and approached the owner with a boxful of brightly colored caps and headbands. "I have these hats and headbands, and a lot of my friends have been interested in them," she told the owner. "I think your cold weather cyclists would like them, too." The owner purchased the box of caps and headbands, giving Prevot her first big sale.

Now attending Middlebury College, Prevot continues to operate her company, Skida, which currently sells its line of hats, headbands, and scarves—all sporting neon polka dots, bright plaids, and happy geisha flowers—in 47 retail stores across the United States and through the Skida Web site. Prevot, who has a double major in anthropology and geography, says that Skida is profitable and generates annual sales of more than $100,000.

## Bump technologies

In an accounting class in the University of Chicago's MBA program, David Lieb began thinking about an easy way for smart phone users to share contact information with one another. During the first week of classes, "I found myself entering in phone number after phone number and name after name," he recalls. Lieb, a former employee at Texas Instruments, believed that he could create an easy, automated way for smart phone users to share information. He explained his idea to fellow students Andy Huibers and Jake Mintz, and the trio of entrepreneurs began developing a prototype based on Lieb's idea. Two weeks later, they had a rudimentary prototype operating on a laptop, and within five months the entrepreneurs launched Bump Technologies, featuring their mobile app that allows smart phone users to share photos and contact information simply by bumping their phones together. "The first day we got 222 downloads, and soon we were getting thousands," says Lieb. Today, more than 100 million people have downloaded the Bump app. Lieb, Mintz, and Huibers have

raised $19.9 million in financing, primarily from venture capital firms, and their company now has 26 full-time employees and 11 interns. Looking back, the entrepreneurs say that much of their success originates in two principles that they have relied on since they started their business: (1) creating a strong team of founders whose skill sets complement one another and that is capable of handling the unpredictable tasks of starting a company and (2) regularly testing not only products but also the assumptions on which their business is built.

College can be one of the best places to start a business, but doing so requires discipline, good time management, and a willingness to make mistakes and learn from them. "An entrepreneur's career may include 30 or 40 ventures," says Andrew Bachman, who started Tatto Media, a digital advertising company, from his dorm room and sold it a few years later for $60 million. "Each one should be a stepping stone and a learning experience."

1. "Entrepreneurship can't be taught in a regular classroom any more than surfboarding can," says one venture capitalist. "To learn it, you have to get your feet wet in the real world." What do you think?

2. In addition to the normal obstacles of starting a business, what other barriers do collegiate entrepreneurs face?

3. What advantages do collegiate entrepreneurs have when launching a business?

4. What advice would you offer a fellow college student about to start a business?

5. Work with a team of your classmates to develop ideas about what your college or university could do to create a culture that supports entrepreneurship on your campus or in your community.

*Sources:* Based on LeeAnn Maton, "College Entrepreneurs Part 2: Looking for A's in Money Making," *Daily Finance*, June 15, 2012, *www.dailyfinance.com/2010/06/15/college-entrepreneurs-part-2-looking-for-as-in-making-money*; Lauren Monsen, "Lighting the Way: College Students Help Businesses Go Green," *IIP Digital*, January 26, 2012, *http://iipdigital.usembassy.gov/st/english/article/2012/01/20120126142229nerual0.3576471.html#axzz1pAhYRzqZ*; David Port, "Get Smarter," *Entrepreneur*, April 2009, pp. 51–56; Nichole L. Torres, "Launch Pad to Success," *Entrepreneur*, October 2008, pp. 61–81; Joel Holland, "Breaking Business Models," *Entrepreneur*, March 2009, p. 102; Patricia B. Gray, "Can Entrepreneurship Be Taught?," *FSB*, March 2006, pp. 34–51; Susan Adams, Helen Coster, and Elizabeth Woyke, "All-Star Student Entrepreneurs," *Forbes*, August 22, 2011, pp. 74–79; "About Us," Skida, *www.skidasport.com/pages/about-us*; Joel Holland, "It's a Hit," *Entrepreneur*, September 2011, p. 98; Andrew Bachman, "3 Golden Rules for College Entrepreneurs," *Young Entrepreneur Council*, April 30, 2012, *http://theyec.org/3-golden-rules-for-college-entrepreneurs*; Victor W. Hwang, "Can Entrepreneurship Be Taught?," *Wall Street Journal*, March 19, 2012, p. R4.

# The Cultural Diversity of Entrepreneurship

**7.**

Discuss the role of diversity in small business and entrepreneurship.

As you have seen, virtually anyone has the potential to become an entrepreneur. The entrepreneurial sector of the United States consists of a rich blend of people of all races, ages, backgrounds, and cultures. It is this cultural diversity that is one of entrepreneurship's greatest strengths. We turn our attention to those who make up this diverse fabric we call entrepreneurship.

## Young Entrepreneurs

Young people are setting the pace in entrepreneurship. Disenchanted with their prospects in corporate America and willing to take a chance to control their own destinies, scores of young

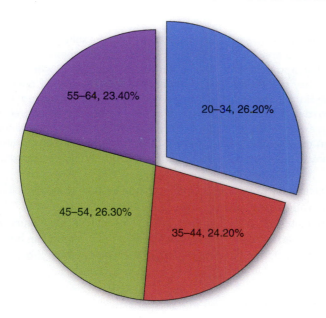

**FIGURE 1.2**

**New Entrepreneurs by Age Group**

*Source:* Based on Robert W. Fairlie, *Kauffman Index of Entrepreneurial Activity*, 1996–2012, April 2013, Kauffman Foundation, p. 12.

people are choosing entrepreneurship as their primary career path. Although people 55 and older have demonstrated the greatest increase in entrepreneurial activity over the last 25 years, Generation Y, made up of people born between 1980 and 2000, is one of the most entrepreneurial generations in history (see Figure 1.2).[80] Research shows that children whose parents are entrepreneurs are two to three times more likely to pursue entrepreneurship as a career than those whose parents are wage earners.[81]

There is no age requirement to be a successful entrepreneur.

**ENTREPRENEURIAL PROFILE: Mallory Kievman: Hiccupops** When 11-year-old Mallory Kievman developed a stubborn case of the hiccups one summer, she tried a variety of home remedies, including swallowing salt water, eating a spoonful of sugar, and sipping pickle juice, but her hiccups persisted. The experience prompted Kievman to develop a cure for hiccups. After two years and testing 100 remedies in her family's kitchen, Kievman developed the Hiccupop, a product that blends the most successful hiccup-fighting remedies she discovered—lollipops, sugar, and apple cider vinegar. She entered her product in the Connecticut Invention Convention, an annual new product competition for kids, and won prizes for innovation and patentability. "Hiccupops solves a very simple, basic need," observes Sanny Briere, a serial entrepreneur who is serving as an adviser to Hiccupops. Explaining the science behind the Hiccupop, Kievman says, "It triggers a set of nerves in your throat and mouth that are responsible for the hiccup reflex arc. It overstimulates those nerves and cancels out the message to hiccup." Kievman currently is working with a team of MBA students from the University of Connecticut to bring her patented hiccup-fighting lollipops to market.[82]

## Women Entrepreneurs

Despite years of legislative effort, women still face discrimination in the workforce. However, small business has been a leader in offering women opportunities for economic expression through employment and entrepreneurship. Many women are discovering that the best way to break the "glass ceiling" that prevents them from rising to the top of many organizations is to start their own companies (see Figure 1.3). The freedom that owning their own companies gives them is one reason that entrepreneurship is a popular career choice for women. In fact, women now own almost 30 percent of all businesses in the United States, and many of them are in fields that traditionally have been male dominated.[83]

**ENTREPRENEURIAL PROFILE: Jessica Alba: The Honest Company** After film star Jessica Alba became a mother, she "was horrified to find out how many toxic chemicals are in baby products." Inspired by a book about creating a clean home without relying on potentially harmful chemicals that she had read during her first pregnancy, Alba contacted Christopher Gavigan, the book's author, and proposed that they create a business that would provide mothers with the products to implement the strategies featured in the book. "You've given me a handbook, but you

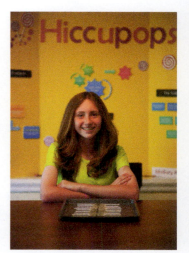

Mallory Kievman, founder of Hiccupops.
*Source:* Andrew Douglas Sullivan.

Jessica Alba, cofounder of Honest Company.
*Source:* © A. Ariani/Corbis.

haven't given me a solution," Alba told Gavigan. "Let's make the solution." Working with serial entrepreneur Brian Lee, Alba and Gavigan launched The Honest Company, a business that sells safe, eco-friendly, affordable products for babies and the home. They started with an eco-friendly disposable diaper because they saw disposable diapers as "the greatest area of opportunity for innovation," says Alba. The Honest Company's diapers, which are 85 percent biodegradable, use a mix of wheat, corn, and wood fluff to achieve 35 percent more absorbency than conventional diapers. The Honest Company has expanded its product line to include detergents, soaps, shampoos, and cleaners; more products are in the planning stage. Sales are growing, but according to Alba, "We're still this scrappy little company where everybody is working long hours and doing everything at once."[84]

Although the businesses women start tend to be smaller than those men start, their impact is anything but small. Women-owned companies in the United States employ 7.7 million workers and generate approximately $1.3 trillion in revenue.[85] Women entrepreneurs have even broken through the comic strip barrier. Blondie Bumstead, long a typical suburban housewife married to Dagwood, owns her own catering business with her best friend and neighbor, Tootsie Woodly!

## Minority Enterprises

Like women, minorities also are choosing entrepreneurship more often than ever before. Hispanics, African Americans, and Asians are most likely to become entrepreneurs. Hispanics represent the fastest-growing segment of the U.S. population, and Hispanic entrepreneurs represent the largest segment of minority-owned businesses in the United States (see Figure 1.4). More than 2.3 million Hispanic-owned companies employ more than 1.9 million people and generate more than $345 billion in annual sales.[86]

Minority entrepreneurs see owning their own businesses as an ideal way to battle discrimination, and minority-owned companies have come a long way in the last decade. The most recent Index of Entrepreneurial Activity by the Ewing Marion Kauffman Foundation shows that Hispanics are 38 percent more likely to start a business than whites, and Asians are 7 percent more likely.[87] Minority entrepreneurs own 22 percent of all businesses in the United States, generate $1 trillion in annual revenues, and start their businesses for the same reason that most entrepreneurs do: to control their own destinies.[88] The future is promising for this new generation of minority entrepreneurs who are better educated, have more business experience, have more entrepreneurial role models, and are better prepared for business ownership than their predecessors.

## FIGURE 1.3

**Entrepreneurial Activity Index by Gender**

*Source:* Based on Robert W. Fairlie, *Kauffman Index of Entrepreneurial Activity,* 1996–2012, Kauffman Foundation, April 2013, p. 5.

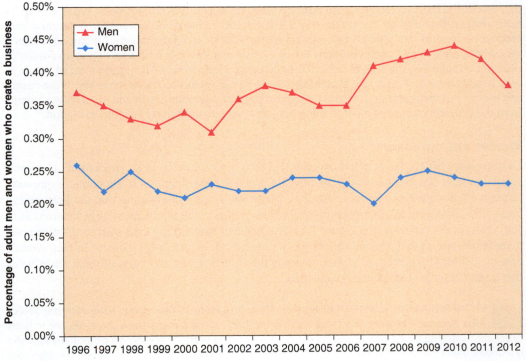

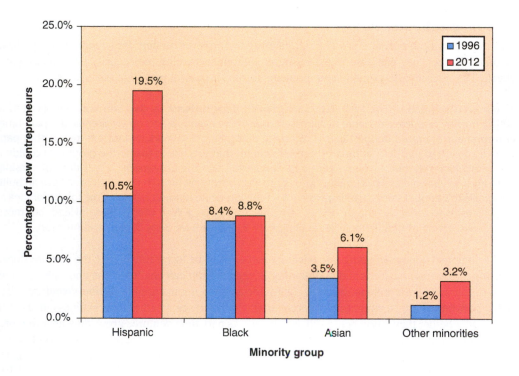

**FIGURE 1.4**

**Percentage of New Entrepreneurs by Minority Group 1996 and 2012**

*Source:* Based on Robert W. Fairlie, *Kauffman Index of Entrepreneurial Activity*, 1996–2012, p. 9.

**ENTREPRENEURIAL PROFILE: Venus Williams: V\*Star Interiors and Jamba Juice** Not only has Venus Williams been a dominant force in the world of professional tennis since she turned pro in 1994, but she also has exercised her entrepreneurial muscles, starting an interior design company, V\*Star Interiors, in 2002 and two Jamba Juice franchises in the Washington, D.C., area in 2011 and 2012. V\*Star, located in Jupiter, Florida, has done design work for high-profile professional athletes, upscale residential communities, university athletic facilities, and sets for television shows. Williams's affiliation with Jamba Juice, which offers a wide selection of healthy, vegetarian, and vegan menu items, is "a perfect fit" given her interest in inspiring young people to stay active and make good dietary choices.[89]

## Immigrant Entrepreneurs

The United States has always been a "melting pot" of diverse cultures, and many immigrants have been lured to this nation by its economic freedom. Unlike the unskilled "huddled masses" of the past, today's immigrants arrive with far more education and experience and a strong desire to succeed. They play an especially important role in technology industries. A study by the Kauffman Foundation reports that immigrant entrepreneurs are responsible for 52 percent of Silicon Valley technology start-ups, including Google, PayPal, and YouTube.[90]

Although immigrants make up 13 percent of the U.S. population, immigrant entrepreneurs own 18 percent of businesses in the United States; in 1992, immigrants owned just 9 percent of businesses in the United States. Their companies generate $776 billion in annual revenues and employ 4.7 million workers.[91] Although many immigrants come to the United States with few assets, their dedication and desire to succeed enable them to achieve their entrepreneurial dreams. "Most immigrants have the risk gene already built in," explains Al Guerra, who emigrated to the United States from Cuba and now owns Kelvin International, a business that makes cryogenic (ultralow temperature) equipment.[92]

**ENTREPRENEURIAL PROFILE: Delfino Bello: El Faro** When Delfino Bello emigrated to the United States from Mexico, he spoke no English but learned quickly working various jobs in the restaurant industry. "I had nothing, nothing when I arrived in this country," he recalls. Bello worked hard, saved his money, and in 1995 opened a restaurant, El Faro, that specialized in authentic Mexican food in a modest shopping center in Bartlett, Illinois. El Faro flourished, and over the next several years, Bello opened two other locations in Bartlett and Elgin and now has plans to open a fourth location.[93]

Venus Williams, entrepreneur and tennis star.

*Source:* Ezio Petersen/UPI/Newscom.

## Part-Time Entrepreneurs

Starting a part-time business is a popular gateway to entrepreneurship. Part-timers have the best of both worlds. They can ease into a business without sacrificing the security of a steady paycheck. The Internet allows many entrepreneurs to run successful part-time businesses.

**ENTREPRENEURIAL PROFILE: Sari Crevin: BooginHead** By day, Sari Crevin worked as a human resources manager at Microsoft, but in the evenings and on weekends, the part-time entrepreneur operated BooginHead, a company that makes and markets fabric fasteners that parents can attach to pacifiers, sippy cups, and other items that tots like to toss to the ground. "I couldn't find a product that met my own needs and standards," says the busy mom. "I was tired of chasing after my one-year-old's sippy cup that he loved to throw from his high chair and stroller." Crevin built BooginHead's annual sales to an impressive $1.1 million while holding her full-time job before leaving Microsoft to focus her energy on her company. Crevin has a Web site for BooginHead, but most of her sales are at wholesale to large retailers, such as Babies R Us, Baby Depot, and Amazon.[94]

A major advantage of going into business part-time is the lower risk in case the venture flops. Starting a part-time business and maintaining a "regular" job can challenge the endurance of the most determined entrepreneur, but it does provide a safety net in case the business venture fails. Many part-timers are "testing the entrepreneurial waters" to see whether their business ideas will work and whether they enjoy being self-employed. As part-time ventures grow, they absorb more of the entrepreneur's time until they become full-time businesses. "There comes a point when you cannot get up and go to work because the only thing you want to do is your company," says Divya Gugnani, who left her job with a venture capital firm to start BehindtheBurner.com, a Web site that features cooking tips and techniques. "The passion is so infectious."[95]

## Home-Based Business Owners

Entrepreneurs in the United States operate 18.3 million home-based businesses, generating $427 billion a year in sales. Fifty-three percent of all small businesses are home based, but most of them are very small with no employees.[96] In the past, home-based businesses tended to be rather unexciting cottage industries, such as making crafts or sewing. Today's home-based businesses are more diverse; modern home-based entrepreneurs are more likely to be running high-tech or service companies with six-figure sales. Eight percent of home-based businesses generate more than $500,000 in annual revenues.[97] Their success rate also is higher than companies that have locations outside the home; nearly 70 percent succeed for at least three years.[98] Less costly and more powerful technology and the Internet, which are transforming ordinary homes into "electronic cottages," are driving the growth of home-based businesses.

On average, someone starts a home-based business every 11 seconds.[99] The biggest advantage home-based businesses offer entrepreneurs is the cost savings of not having to lease or buy an external location, something that allows them to generate higher profit margins. Home-based entrepreneurs also enjoy the benefits of flexible work and lifestyles.

**ENTREPRENEURIAL PROFILE: Natalie Cox: Natty by Design** Natalie Cox, a 28-year-old mother of four children, used her do-it-yourself furniture refurbishing skills to start Natty by Design, a home-based business that gives old pieces of furniture new life by refinishing or repainting them and adding new hardware. She launched the company in the basement of her family's home in Phoenix, Arizona, to supplement her husband's salary while he returned to college to earn an MBA degree. Cox describes the style of furniture she sells from a front room of her house that serves as both her office and showroom as "shabby chic." Most of her company's sales come from repeat business and referrals from existing customers and from her listings on Craigslist. "[My company] allows me to stay at home with my kids," says Cox, "and business is thriving."[100]

Table 1.2 offers 20 guidelines home-based entrepreneurs should follow to be successful.

## Family Business Owners

A **family-owned business** is one that includes two or more members of a family with financial control of the company. They are an integral part of the global economy. More than 80 percent of all companies in the world are family owned, and their contributions to the global economy are significant. In the United States alone, family businesses create 57 percent of the nation's GDP,

**TABLE 1.2  Rules for a Successful Home-Based Business**

*Rule 1. Do your homework.* Much of a home-based business's potential for success depends on how much preparation an entrepreneur makes *before* ever opening for business. Your local library and the Web are excellent sources of information on customers, industries, competitors, and other important topics.

*Rule 2. Find out what your zoning restrictions are.* In some areas, local zoning laws make running a business from home illegal. Avoid headaches by checking these laws first. You can always request a variance.

*Rule 3. Create distinct zones for your family and business dealings.* Your home-based business should have its own dedicated space. About half of all home-based entrepreneurs operate out of spare bedrooms. The best way to determine the ideal office location is to examine the nature of your business and your clients. Avoid locating your business in your bedroom or your family room.

*Rule 4. Focus your home-based business idea.* Avoid the tendency to be "all things to all people." Most successful home-based businesses focus on a niche, whether it is a particular customer group, a specific product line, or in some other specialty.

*Rule 5. Discuss your business rules with your family.* Running a business from your home means that you can spend more time with your family—and that your family can spend more time with you. Establish the rules for interruptions up front.

*Rule 6. Select an appropriate business name.* Your first marketing decision is your company's name, so make it a good one! Using your own name is convenient, but it's not likely to help you sell your product or service.

*Rule 7. Buy the right equipment.* Modern technology allows a home-based entrepreneur to give the appearance of any *Fortune 500* company, but only if you buy the right equipment. A well-equipped home office should have a separate telephone line, a fast computer, a sturdy printer, a high-speed Internet connection, a copier/scanner, and an answering machine (or voice mail).

*Rule 8. Dress appropriately.* Being an "open-collar worker" is one of the joys of working at home. However, when you need to dress up (to meet a client, make a sale, meet your banker, or close a deal), do it! Avoid the tendency to lounge around in your bathrobe all day.

*Rule 9. Learn to deal with distractions.* The best way to fend off the distractions of working at home is to create a business that truly interests you. Budget your time wisely. Remember: Your productivity determines your company's success.

*Rule 10. Realize that your phone can be your best friend—or your worst enemy.* As a home-based entrepreneur, you'll spend lots of time on the phone. Be sure you use it productively.

*Rule 11. Be firm with friends and neighbors.* Sometimes friends and neighbors get the mistaken impression that because you're at home, you're not working. If someone drops by to chat while you're working, tactfully ask him or her to come back "after work."

*Rule 12. Maximize your productivity.* One advantage of working from home is flexibility. Learn the times during which you tend to work at peak productivity, whether that occurs at 2 P.M. or 2 A.M., and build your schedule around them.

*Rule 13. Create no-work time zones.* Because their businesses are always nearby, the tendency for some home-based entrepreneurs is to work all the time, which is not healthy. Set boundaries that separate work and no work times and stick to them.

*Rule 14. Take advantage of tax breaks.* Although a 1993 Supreme Court decision tightened considerably the standards for business deductions for an office at home, many home-based entrepreneurs still qualify for special tax deductions on everything from computers to cars. Check with your accountant.

*Rule 15. Make sure you have adequate insurance coverage.* Some home-owner's policies provide adequate coverage for business-related equipment, but many home-based entrepreneurs have inadequate coverage on their business assets. Ask your agent about a business owner's policy, which may cost as little as $300 to $500 per year.

*Rule 16. Understand the special circumstances under which you can hire outside employees.* Sometimes zoning laws allow in-home businesses, but they prohibit hiring employees. Check local zoning laws carefully.

*Rule 17. Be prepared if your business requires clients to come to your home.* Dress appropriately. (No pajamas!) Make sure your office presents a professional image.

*Rule 18. Get a post office box.* With burglaries and robberies on the rise, you are better off using a P.O. Box address rather than your specific home address. Otherwise, you may be inviting crime.

*Rule 19. Network.* Isolation can be a problem for home-based entrepreneurs, and one of the best ways to combat it is to network. It's also an effective way to market your business.

*Rule 20. Be proud of your home-based business.* Merely a decade ago, there was a stigma attached to working from home. Today, home-based entrepreneurs and their businesses command respect. Be proud of your company!

*Sources:* Based on Pamela Slim, "5 Keys to Making Your Home Office Work," *Open Forum*, June 24, 2009, *www.openforum.com/idea-hub/topics/the-world/article/5-keys-to-making-your-home-office-work-pamela-slim*; Lynn Beresford, Janean Chun, Cynthia E. Griffin, Heather Page, and Debra Phillips, "Homeward Bound," *Entrepreneur*, September 1995, pp. 116–118; Jenean Huber, "House Rules," *Entrepreneur*, March 1993, pp. 89–95; Hal Morris, "Home-Based Businesses Need Extra Insurance," *AARP Bulletin*, November 1994, p. 16; Stephanie N. Mehta, "What You Need," *Wall Street Journal*, October 14, 1994, p. R10; Jeffery Zbar, "Home Free," *Business Start-Ups*, June 1999, pp. 31–37.

employ 60 percent of the private sector workforce, and account for 65 percent of all wages paid. Not all family-owned businesses are small, however; 35 percent of *Fortune 500* companies are family businesses.[101] Family firms also create 78 percent of the U.S. economy's net new jobs and are responsible for many famous products, including Heinz ketchup, Levi's jeans, and classic toys such as the Slinky and the Wiffle Ball.[102]

"When it works right," says one writer, "nothing succeeds like a family firm. The roots run deep, embedded in family values. The flash of the fast buck is replaced with long-term plans. Tradition counts."[103]

**ENTREPRENEURIAL PROFILE: Domino, Julio, and Rene Diaz: Diaz Foods** When Fidel Castro's regime seized Domingo Diaz's cattle ranches in Cuba in 1966, he fled to the United States and settled in Atlanta, Georgia, where he found work as a janitor. He eventually saved enough money to purchase a small grocery store that he and his son, Julio, managed. As Diaz Foods grew to four locations, more family members, including Julio's son Rene, began to work there. Today, Rene is head of the family business, which sells Hispanic food products to restaurants and grocery stores in 25 states from a new 250,000-square-foot warehouse on the outskirts of Atlanta. Diaz Foods employs 370 workers and generates annual sales of $200 million. "I can't count how many family members work here," says Rene. "I always want it to be a privately-held business with family values."[104]

Despite their magnitude, family businesses face a major threat—a threat from within: management succession. Only 33 percent of family businesses survive to the second generation, just 12 percent make it to the third generation, and only 3 percent survive to the fourth generation and beyond.[105] Business periodicals are full of stories describing bitter disputes among family members who have crippled or destroyed once-thriving businesses, usually because the founder failed to create a succession plan. To avoid the senseless destruction of valuable assets, founders of family businesses should develop plans for management succession long before retirement looms before them. We will discuss family businesses and management succession in more detail in Chapter 22.

## Copreneurs

**Copreneurs** are entrepreneurial couples who work together as co-owners of their businesses. More than 1.2 million husband-and-wife teams operate businesses in the United States.[106] Unlike the traditional "Mom & Pop" (Pop as "boss" and Mom as "subordinate"), copreneurs divide their business responsibilities on the basis of their skills, experience, and abilities rather than on gender.

Managing a small business with a spouse may appear to be a recipe for divorce, but most copreneurs say not. "There are days when you want to kill each other," says Mary Duty, who has operated Poppa Rollo's Pizza with her husband for 20 years. "But there's nothing better than working side-by-side with the [person] you love."[107] Successful copreneurs learn to build the foundation for a successful working relationship *before* they ever launch their companies. Some of the characteristics they rely on include the following:

- An assessment of how well their personalities will mesh in a business setting.
- Mutual respect for each other and one another's talents.
- Compatible business and life goals—a common "vision."
- A view that they are full and equal partners, not a superior and a subordinate.
- Complementary business skills that each acknowledges in the other and that lead to a unique business identity for each spouse.
- A clear division of roles and authority—ideally based on each partner's skills and abilities—to minimize conflict and power struggles.
- The ability to keep lines of communication open, talking and listening to each other about personal as well as business issues.
- The ability to encourage each other and to lift up a disillusioned partner.
- Separate work spaces that allow them to escape when the need arises.
- Boundaries between their business life and their personal life so that one doesn't consume the other.
- A sense of humor.
- An understanding that not every couple can work together.

Although copreneuring isn't for every couple, it works extremely well for many couples and often leads to successful businesses.

**ENTREPRENEURIAL PROFILE: Karine and Aaron Hirschhorn: DogVacay** When Karine and Aaron Hirschhorn traveled, they dreaded boarding their beloved dogs, Rocky and Rambo, in a kennel but had little choice. Poor kennel experiences prompted the Hirschhorns to launch DogVacay, an online marketplace that allows dog owners to browse hundreds of online profiles of people nearby who are willing to provide temporary homes for dogs for fees that range between $15 and $70 per night. DogVacay subjects all host families to a vetting process using background checks and interviews. The average price for dog-sitting is $25 per night (host families set their own rates), and DogVacay, which is based in Santa Monica, California, collects 3 to 10 percent of each transaction. DogVacay has more than 4,000 host families in major cities across the United States, and the 12-employee company is growing fast. The potential market for DogVacay is huge; pet owners in the United States spend $10 billion annually on pet boarding, and the Hirschhorns are making plans to expand DogVacay across the nation. The copreneurs have landed a total of $22 million in financing from several venture capital firms to fuel their company's growth.[108]

## Corporate Castoffs

Concentrating on trying to operate more efficiently, corporations have been downsizing, shedding their excess bulk, and slashing employment at all levels in the organization. These downsizing victims or "corporate castoffs" have become an important source of entrepreneurial activity. Skittish about downsizing at other large companies they might join, many of these castoffs are choosing instead to create their own job security by launching their own businesses or buying franchises. They have decided that the best defense against future job insecurity is an entrepreneurial offense. Armed with years of experience, tidy severance packages, a working knowledge of their industries, and a network of connections, these former managers are starting companies of their own.

**ENTREPRENEURIAL PROFILE: Forrest Graves: JumpinGoat** Forrest Graves spent many years selling equipment to the printing industry for one of the largest corporations in the United States only to become a victim of the Great Recession. After he was laid off, Graves considered finding another corporate job but knew "that I would be better off to do my own thing," he recalls. He created a business plan for a coffee roasting company, JumpinGoat, that purchases green coffee that comes from the 10 major coffee regions around the world, roasts it, and sells packages of premium coffee through a retail outlet in tiny Helen, Georgia, to other retail coffee shops and online through its Web site. JumpinGoat has been successful, and within six months of launching the company, Graves was earning more than he did in his corporate job. However, the income is not what matters most to Graves. "My passion and income are now fueled with the truth that I'm actually building something sustainable," he says. "I am now the benefactor of a better 'work life balance,' freedom to make my own mistakes and failures, and the notion that there is no cap on my financial well-being."[109]

## Corporate "Dropouts"

The dramatic downsizing in corporate America has created another effect among the employees left after restructuring: a trust gap. The result of this trust gap is a growing number of "dropouts" from the corporate structure who then become entrepreneurs. Although their workdays may grow longer and their incomes may shrink, those who strike out on their own often find their work more rewarding and more satisfying because they are doing what they enjoy and they are in control.

Because they often have college degrees, a working knowledge of business, and years of management experience, both corporate castoffs and dropouts will likely increase the small business survival rate. Better-trained, more experienced entrepreneurs are less likely to fail in business. Many corporate castoffs and dropouts choose franchising as the vehicle to business ownership because it offers the structure and support with which these former corporate executives are most comfortable. *Entrepreneur* magazine surveyed the companies on its *Franchise 500* list recently and discovered that 77 percent of franchisors report that "second-career executives" (i.e., corporate dropouts and castoffs) were among the primary purchasers of their franchises.[110]

**FIGURE 1.5**

**Entrepreneurial Activity by Age Group 1996–2012**

*Source:* Based on Robert W. Fairlie, *Kauffman Index of Entrepreneurial Activity*, 1996–2012, Kauffman Foundation, April 2013, p. 12.

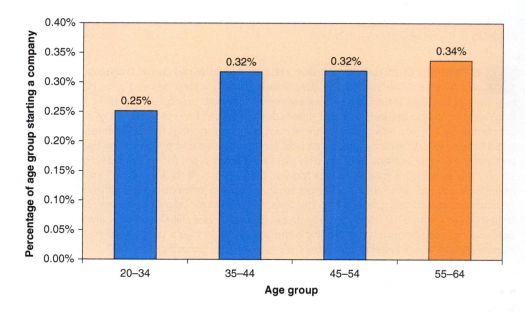

### Retired Baby Boomers

Members of the Baby Boom Generation (1946–1964) are retiring, but many of them are not idle; instead, they are launching businesses of their own. A survey by Robert Half reports that 54 percent of Baby Boomers plan to work beyond the traditional retirement age, and many of those who do will choose entrepreneurship as their second career.[111] A study by the Kauffman Foundation shows that the average level of entrepreneurial activity over the last 15 years among people age 55 to 64 actually is higher than that among people of any other age-group (see Figure 1.5). One advantage that older entrepreneurs have is wisdom that has been forged by experience. Because people are living longer and healthier than ever before, many entrepreneurs start their entrepreneurial ventures late in life. At age 65, Colonel Harland Sanders, for example, began franchising the fried chicken business that he had started three years earlier, a company that became Kentucky Fried Chicken (now known as KFC).

To finance their businesses, retirees often use some of their invested "nest eggs," or they can rely on the same sources of funds as younger entrepreneurs, such as banks, private investors, and others.

**ENTREPRENEURIAL PROFILE: Michael Brown: MJB Organics** At age 66, Michael Brown, a retired human resources manager at a large security firm, launched MJB Organics, a company in New Addington, England, that sells a line of organic shaving soaps manufactured by another local small business, John Perry Soaps. A longtime user of the soaps, Brown says, "As I was shaving one morning, I came up with the idea of setting up my own business selling the line of soaps. I may have retired, but I didn't want to put my feet up." The retired grandfather started selling the soaps at indoor markets near his home, but sales have grown so rapidly that Brown now sells to other retailers and has plans to move into upscale shops in Brighton and London. "I think organic products are the future," says the eager entrepreneur.[112]

## The Contributions of Small Businesses

**8.**

Describe the contributions small businesses make to the U.S. economy.

Since 1997, the number of small businesses in the United States has grown more than 30 percent.[113] Of the 27.2 million businesses in the United States today, approximately 27.1 million, or 99.7 percent, can be considered "small." Although there is no universal definition of a small business, a common delineation of a **small business** is one that employs fewer than 100 people. They thrive in virtually every industry, although the majority of small companies are concentrated in the service industry (see Figure 1.6). Their contributions to the economy are as numerous as the businesses themselves. For example, small companies employ 49.2 percent of the nation's private sector workforce and pay 43 percent of the total private payroll in the United States. Although 79 percent of small companies have no employees other than the founder, the 21 percent that do have employees actually create more

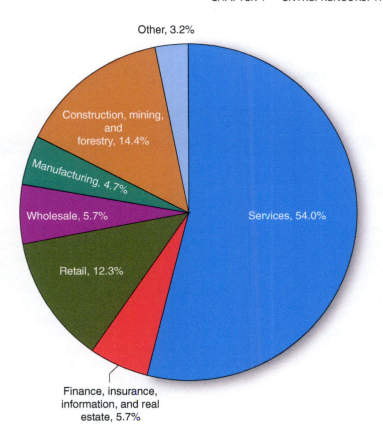

**FIGURE 1.6**

**Small Businesses by Industry**

*Source:* Based on Small Business Administration, 2012.

jobs than do big businesses. Small businesses have created 65 percent of the net new jobs in the United States between 1993 and 2009.[114]

David Birch, president of the research firm Arc Analytics, says that the ability to create jobs is not distributed evenly across the small business sector, however. His research shows that just 6 percent of these small companies create 70 percent of the net new jobs, and they do so across all industry sectors—not just in "hot" industries. Birch calls these job-creating small companies "gazelles," those growing at 20 percent or more per year with at least $100,000 in annual sales. His research also identified "mice," small companies that never grow much and don't create many jobs. The majority of small companies are "mice." Birch tabbed the country's largest businesses "elephants," which have continued to shed jobs for several years.[115] In an updated study, researchers found that small companies with fewer than 20 employees accounted for 93.8 percent of all "high-impact firms," those that have both fast revenue and employment growth. These high-impact companies make up less than 3 percent of all businesses but account for almost all of the employment and revenue growth in the U.S. economy.[116]

Not only do small companies lead the way in creating jobs, but they also bear the brunt of training workers for them. Small businesses provide 67 percent of workers with their first jobs and basic job training. Small companies offer more general skills instruction and training than large ones, and their employees receive more benefits from the training than do those in larger firms. Although their training programs tend to be informal, in-house, and on-the-job, small companies teach employees valuable skills—from written communication to computer literacy.[117]

Small businesses also produce 46 percent of the country's private GDP and account for 47 percent of business sales.[118] In fact, the U.S small business sector is the world's third-largest "economy," trailing only the economies of the United States and China. Small businesses also play an integral role in creating new products, services, and processes. Small companies produce 16.5 times more patents per employee than do large firms, and many of those patents are among the most significant inventions in their fields. A study by the SBA reports that the smallest businesses, those with fewer than 25 employees, produce the greatest number of patents per employee.[119] Many important inventions trace their roots to an entrepreneur; for example, the zipper, the personal computer, FM radio, air conditioning, the escalator, the lightbulb, the helicopter, and the automatic transmission all originated in small businesses. Entrepreneurs continue to create innovations designed to improve people's lives in areas that range from energy and communications to clothing and toys.

 **Lessons from the Street-Smart Entrepreneur**

## Bulletproofing Your Start-Up

It happens thousands of times every day: Someone comes up with a great idea for a new business, certain that the idea is going to be "the next big thing." Technology advances, the Internet, increased global interconnectivity, and computer-aided-design tools that allow inventors to go from the idea stage to creating a prototype faster than ever have made transforming a great idea into reality much easier than at any point in the past. In addition, entrepreneurial training, improved access to information, and greater awareness of entrepreneurship as a career choice have made it easier than ever to launch a business. However, *succeeding* in business today is as challenging as it ever was.

What steps can a potential entrepreneur with a great idea take to build a "bulletproof" start-up? Take these tips from the Street-Smart Entrepreneur:

### Step 1. Test to see whether your idea really is a good one

The reality is that transforming an idea into a successful business concept is much like the television show *American Idol*. For every person who really is a great singer, there are 99 people who can't stay on key but who *think* they are great singers. This step involves getting a reality check from other people—and not just friends and relatives who may not tell you what they really think about your idea because they don't want to hurt your feelings. The goal is to determine whether your business idea really has market potential. One key is to get your product or service into potential customers' hands and see how they respond. In 2009, Terry Danielson started Simmer Down Teas in Eagan, Minnesota, as a part-time business after spending time with the owner of a teahouse on a business trip to Taiwan and learning the intricacies of blending teas. Danielson began by testing his business idea at Eagan's Market Fest, a weekly farmer's market that runs from June to September and draws more than 34,000 visitors annually, a practice that he continues to use. "It's fertile ground, and it's very inexpensive to test products," he says. Customer feedback has helped Danielson identify the most popular tea blends and has helped him to validate his business idea. He is planning to make Simmer Down Teas a full-time venture. "I put my big toe in the water, and now I'm ready to dive in," he says.

Entrepreneur Hugh Crean suggests another technique that involves strangers called the "$20 Starbucks Test" and is designed to judge the validity of new product, service, or start-up ideas: Take $20 to a nearby Starbucks and offer to buy someone a cup of coffee in exchange for his or her opinion about a business idea that your "brother" has. Explain that your "brother" is about to get a second mortgage on his house, raid his retirement plan, and quit his job to pursue his start-up idea. (Making the idea your

"brother's" means that people are more likely to tell you the truth about your idea than if you tell them it's your idea.) His wife and your parents are afraid that he will lose everything and have come to you for help to try to talk him out of starting the business. Then give the person your best two- to three-minute elevator pitch, ask him or her for reasons why the idea won't work, and listen to his or her comments. Resist the temptation to argue with his or her reasoning. Finally, thank the person and repeat the experiment with someone else until your $20 runs out.

"The most likely outcome is that you will hear the same obvious rejections of your idea that you already have and believe are surmountable," says Crean. "Your $20 didn't generate any great new insight but was an inexpensive check that you aren't blind to an obvious shortcoming. A good outcome is that you hear sound new objections that you never thought of before. This should give you real pause about your idea. A not-so-likely outcome is that your strangers will find themselves agreeing with you and your 'brother' that it is a great idea. If this happens, you probably have a real hit on your hands. Run with it!"

Sometimes entrepreneurs discover that step 1 is as far as they should go; otherwise, they would be wasting time, talent, and resources. Other entrepreneurs receive confirmation that they really are on to something at this step and move forward.

### Step 2. Conduct a feasibility analysis

The purpose of a feasibility analysis is to subject a business idea to what one entrepreneur calls a "quick scrub," judging its merits in four areas: the attractiveness of the industry and market segment, the ability to provide the proposed product or service at a reasonable cost, the ability of the entrepreneurial team to implement the idea successfully, and the capacity to generate a reasonable profit and return on investment. If an idea passes the feasibility test, entrepreneurs can begin building their new venture team and creating a business plan.

### Step 3. Start building your entrepreneurial team

Nearly half of all new business ventures are started by teams of people. As one business writer observes, "Launching a company isn't just a full-time job; in many cases, it's three full-time jobs." Perhaps that is why a study of 2,000 businesses by researchers at Marquette University found that companies started by teams of entrepreneurs are nearly 16 times more likely to become high-growth ventures than those started by solo entrepreneurs. Indeed, launching a company is a demanding task that requires a diverse blend of skills, abilities, and experience that not every individual possesses. If that is the case, the best alternative is to launch your company with others whose skills, abilities, and experience *complement* rather than *mirror* yours. Picking the right entrepreneurial players is as essential to business success as picking the best kids to be on your kickball team was in grammar school! However many people it may require, ideally a start-up team includes a "big-picture" strategic thinker, a top-notch networker with marketing and sales know-how, and a hands-on technical person who understands the business opportunity at the "nuts-and-bolts" level.

### Step 4. Do your research and create a business plan

Smart entrepreneurs know that creating a business plan is an important step in building a successful company even if they are not seeking capital from external sources. Starting a company without a business plan is like trying to build a house without a set of blueprints. Even though a business plan is a valuable document that entrepreneurs use in many ways, the real value in creating a plan lies in the *process*. Developing a plan requires entrepreneurs to address an array of important issues, ranging from which form of ownership is best and how much capital is required to researching their target customers and preparing financial and cash flow forecasts.

David Langer and Andy Young met at an entrepreneurial club while they were students at Oxford University. Both young men were officers in campus organizations and began talking about how the processes for contacting members, keeping track of dues payments, and maintaining membership records were scattered, inefficient, and time consuming and required the use of multiple tools. To solve their problem, they decided to create a platform that would handle all of the administrative activities for clubs and organizations conveniently and in one place. They soon realized that other people would be interested in their solution and created a company, GroupSpaces, to market it. "The key is in bringing everything together in one place," says Langer. The duo created a business plan and within three months used it to secure $244,000 in seed capital from an Oxford, England–based angel capital network. GroupSpace provides its basic service for free to small groups but charges a subscription for large groups and groups that want additional functionality. It also collects a small percentage of each payment it processes. GroupSpaces's software now helps manage more than 1 million groups in more than 30 countries and has raised a total of $2.1 million in capital from angel capital networks.

*Sources:* Based on David Henke, "Eagan's Market Fest a Hotbed of Entrepreneurial Spirit," *EaganPatch*, June 21, 2012, *http://eagan.patch.com/articles/eagan-s-market-fest-a-hotbed-of-entrepreneurial-spirit*; Jennifer Hill, "Start-Up Execs Schooled from Oxbridge," *Venture Capital Journal*, April 6, 2011, pp. 47–50; Peter Day, "Top Tips for Starting Your Own Business," *BBC News*, January 18, 2012, *www.bbc.co.uk/news/business-16595152*; Sara Wilson, "Laid Off in 2008? Start a Business in 2009," *Entrepreneur*, February 2009, pp. 73–77; Michael V. Copeland and Om Malik, "How to Build a Bulletproof Start-up," *Business 2.0*, June 2006, pp. 76–92; Michael V. Copeland and Andrew Tilin, "The New Instant Companies," *Business 2.0*, June 2005, pp. 82–94; Daniel Roth, "The Amazing Rise of the Do-It-Yourself Economy," *Fortune*, May 30, 2005, pp. 45–46; Sean Johnson, "The $20 Start-Up Test," *Monkey Opus*, December 2010, *http://blog.snootymonkey.com/post/2432103782/the-20-starbucks-test*.

## Putting Failure into Perspective

Because of their limited resources, inexperienced management, and lack of financial stability, small businesses suffer relatively high mortality rates (see Figure 1.7). Research shows that 52 percent of new businesses will have failed within five years. Why are entrepreneurs willing to endure these odds? Because they are building businesses in an environment filled with uncertainty and shaped by rapid change, entrepreneurs recognize that failure is likely to be a part of their lives, yet they are not paralyzed by that fear. "The excitement of building a new business from scratch is far greater than the fear of failure," says one entrepreneur who failed in business several times before finally succeeding.[120] Instead, they use their failures as a rallying point and as a means of defining their companies' reason for being more clearly. They see failure for what it really is: an opportunity to learn what doesn't work! Successful entrepreneurs are what one author calls "rebounders," people who suffer great setbacks, often repeatedly, but who demonstrate the persistence and tenacity necessary to rise above the challenges and succeed.[121] They understand that failures are simply stepping-stones along the path to success. Author J. K. Rowling was a penniless, unemployed, single parent when she penned a book about a boy wizard and his adventures. She submitted her manuscript to 12 publishers, all of whom rejected it. Rowling persisted, however, and a small London publisher, Bloomsbury, finally decided to take a chance on *Harry Potter and the Philosopher's Stone* after a glowing review from the CEO's young daughter. The seven-book Harry Potter series went on to sell more than 450 million copies worldwide, making Rowling the first billionaire author.[122]

Failure is a natural part of the creative process. The only people who never fail are those who never do anything or never attempt anything new. Baseball fans know that Babe Ruth held the record for career home runs (714) for many years, but how many know that he also held the record for strikeouts (1,330)? Successful entrepreneurs realize that hitting an entrepreneurial home run requires a few strikeouts along the way, and they are willing to accept that. In an address at Harvard University's graduation, author J. K. Rowling told students, "You might never

**9.**
Put business failure into the proper perspective.

J. K. Rowling.
*Source:* © jeremy sutton-hibbert/Alamy.

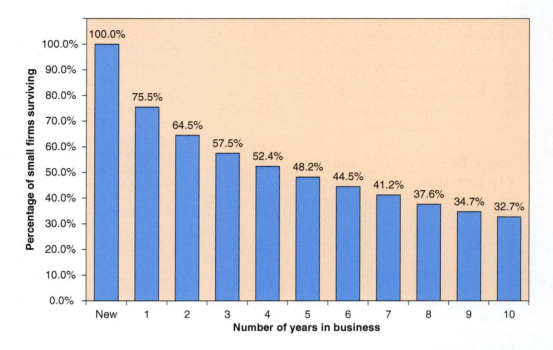

fail on the scale I did, but some failure in life is inevitable. It is impossible to live without failing at something, unless you live so cautiously that you might as well not have lived at all—in which case, you fail by default."[123] Although entrepreneurs don't always succeed, they are not willing to fail by default.

One hallmark of successful entrepreneurs is the ability to fail *intelligently*, learning why they failed so that they can avoid making the same mistake again. They know that business success does not depend on their ability to avoid making mistakes but to be open to the lessons each mistake brings. They *learn* from their failures and use them as fuel to push themselves closer to their ultimate target. Many entrepreneurs became successful by becoming adept at failing quickly and cheaply, learning from their failures, and moving on to the next business idea. Entrepreneurs are less worried about what they might lose if they try something and fail than about what they miss if they fail to try.

Entrepreneurial success requires both persistence and resilience, the ability to bounce back from failures. Inventor James Dyson, founder of the company that sells vacuum cleaners, fans, heaters, and hand dryers and that bears his name, discovered 5,127 ways not to build a bagless vacuum cleaner before he developed a design that worked—and revolutionized the world of vacuum cleaners.[124] R. H. Macy failed in business seven times before his department store in New York City became a success. Entrepreneur Bryn Kaufman explains this "don't-quit" attitude: "If you are truly an entrepreneur, giving up is not an option."[125]

## How to Avoid the Pitfalls

**10.**

Explain how small business owners can avoid the major pitfalls of running a business.

As valuable as failure can be to the entrepreneurial process, no one sets out to fail. We now examine the ways to avoid becoming another failure statistic and gain insight into what makes a start-up successful. Entrepreneurial success requires much more than just a good idea for a product or service. It also takes a solid plan of execution, adequate resources (including capital and the right people), the ability to assemble and manage those resources, and perseverance. The following suggestions for success follow naturally from the causes of business failures.

### Know Your Business in Depth

We have already emphasized the need for the right type of experience in the business. Get the best education in your business area you possibly can *before* you set out on your own. Read everything you can—trade journals, business periodicals, books, and Web pages—relating to your industry. Personal contact with suppliers, customers, trade associations, and others in the same industry is another excellent way to get important knowledge.

**ENTREPRENEURIAL PROFILE: Jessica Gold Newman and Catherine Doyle: Dobbin Clothing** Jessica Gold Newman and Catherine Doyle grew up working as sales associates in retail stores near Boston and met while working at Liz Lange Maternity, where Gold Newman led the company's marketing department, and Doyle was responsible for fashion design. Gold Newman left to work as a retail consultant, and Doyle began developing store concepts for another major retail chain. In 2011, building on their knowledge of and experience in the retail clothing industry, the business partners launched Dobbin (from the British nickname for a workhorse), a clothing line aimed at working women over the age of 35. Dobbin offers customers a mix of classic and vintage-inspired designs made of washable European fabrics in flattering fits made for "real women" that sell at reasonable prices.[126]

Like Jessica Gold Newman and Catherine Doyle, successful entrepreneurs are like sponges, soaking up as much knowledge as they can from many sources, and they continue to learn about their businesses, markets, and customers as long as they are in business.

## Prepare a Business Plan

To wise entrepreneurs, a well-written business plan that defines the company's business model and defines the market opportunity is a crucial ingredient in business success. Without a sound business plan, a company merely drifts along without any real direction and often stalls out when it faces its first challenge. Yet entrepreneurs, who tend to be people of action, often jump right into a business venture without taking time to prepare a written plan outlining the essence of the business. "Most entrepreneurs don't have a solid business plan," says one business owner. "But a thorough business plan and timely financial information are critical. They help you make the important decisions about your business; you constantly have to monitor what you're doing against your plan."[127] We will discuss the process of developing a business plan in Chapter 8.

## Manage Financial Resources

The best defense against financial problems is developing a practical financial information system and then using this information to make business decisions. No entrepreneur can maintain control over a business unless he or she is able to judge its financial health.

The first step in managing financial resources effectively is to have adequate start-up capital. Too many entrepreneurs begin their businesses with too little capital. One experienced business owner advises, "Estimate how much capital you need to get the business going and then double that figure." In other words, launching a business almost always costs more than *any* entrepreneur expects. Establishing a relationship early on with at least one reliable lender or investor who understands your business is a good way to gain access to financing when a company needs capital for growth or expansion.

The most valuable financial resource to any small business is *cash*; successful entrepreneurs learn early on to manage it carefully. Although earning a profit is essential to its long-term survival, a business must have an adequate supply of cash to pay its bills. Some entrepreneurs count on growing sales to supply their company's cash needs, but it almost never happens. Growing companies usually consume more cash than they generate; and the faster they grow, the more cash they gobble up! We will discuss cash management techniques in Chapter 15.

## Understand Financial Statements

Every business owner must depend on records and financial statements to know the condition of his or her business. All too often, these records are used only for tax purposes rather than as vital control devices. To truly understand what is going on in the business, an owner must have at least a basic understanding of accounting and finance.

When analyzed and interpreted properly, financial statements are reliable indicators of a small company's health. They can be quite helpful in signaling potential problems. For example, declining sales or profits, rising debt, and deteriorating working capital are all symptoms of potentially lethal problems that require immediate attention. We will discuss financial statement analysis in Chapter 14.

### Learn to Manage People Effectively

No matter what kind of business you launch, you must learn to manage people. Every business depends on a foundation of well-trained, motivated employees. No entrepreneur can do everything alone. The people an entrepreneur hires ultimately determine the heights to which the company can climb—or the depths to which it can plunge. Attracting and retaining a corps of quality employees is no easy task, however; it remains a challenge for every small business owner. One entrepreneur alienated employees with a memo chastising them for skipping lines on interoffice envelopes (the cost of a skipped line was two-thirds of a penny) while he continued to use a chauffeur-driven luxury car and to stay at exclusive luxury hotels while traveling on business.[128] Entrepreneurs quickly learn that treating their employees with respect and compassion usually translates into their employees treating customers in the same fashion. Successful entrepreneurs value their employees and constantly find ways to show it. We will discuss the techniques of managing and motivating people effectively in Chapter 21.

### Set Your Business Apart from the Competition

The formula for almost certain business failure involves becoming a "me-too business"—merely copying whatever the competition is doing. Successful entrepreneurs find a way to convince their customers that their companies are superior to their competitors even if they sell similar products or services. We will discuss the strategies for creating a unique footprint in the marketplace in Chapter 4 and Chapter 9.

### Maintain a Positive Attitude

Achieving business success requires an entrepreneur to maintain a positive mental attitude toward business and the discipline to stick with it. Successful entrepreneurs recognize that their most valuable resource is their time, and they learn to manage it effectively to make themselves and their companies more productive. None of this, of course, is possible without passion—passion for their businesses, their products or services, their customers, and their communities. Passion is what enables a failed business owner to get back up, try again, and make it to the top! One business writer says that growing a successful business requires entrepreneurs to have great faith in themselves and their ideas, great doubt concerning the challenges and inevitable obstacles they will face as they build their businesses, and great effort—lots of hard work—to make their dreams become reality.[129]

## Conclusion—and a Look Ahead

As you can see, entrepreneurship lies at the heart of this nation's free enterprise system; small companies truly are the backbone of our economy. Their contributions are as many and as diverse as the businesses themselves. Indeed, diversity is one of the strengths of the U.S. small business sector. Although there are no secrets to becoming a successful entrepreneur, there are steps that entrepreneurs can take to enhance the probability of their success. The remainder of this book will explore those steps and how to apply them to the process of launching a successful business with an emphasis on building a sound business plan.

- Section 2, Launching a Venture: Entry Strategies (Chapters 5–8), discusses the classic start-up questions every entrepreneur faces, particularly developing a strategy, choosing a form of ownership, alternative methods for becoming a business owner (franchising and buying an existing business), and building a business plan.

- Section 3, Building a Marketing Plan: (Chapters 9–13), focuses on creating an effective marketing plan for a small company. These chapters address developing advertising and promotional campaigns, establishing pricing and credit strategies, penetrating global markets, and creating an effective e-commerce strategy.

- Section 4, Building a Business Plan: Financial Issues (Chapters 14–17), explains how to develop the financial component of a business plan, including creating projected financial statements and forecasting cash flow. These chapters also offer existing business owners practical financial management tools and explain how entrepreneurs can find the financing, both debt (borrowed capital) and equity (invested capital) they need to launch their businesses.

- Section 5, Building an Operating Plan (Chapters 18–21), describes how entrepreneurs should select a location for their businesses and how to create a layout that enhances sales and employee productivity. This section also explains the practical aspects of supply chain management and inventory control. It concludes with a chapter on assembling a strong new venture team and leading its members to success.

- Section 6, Legal Aspects of Business Ownership: Succession and Government Regulation (Chapters 22 and 23), discusses the important topics of management succession and risk management and avoiding legal and regulatory pitfalls.

As you can see, the journey down the road of entrepreneurship will be an interesting and exciting one. Let's get started!

# Chapter Review

1. Define the role of the entrepreneur in business.
   - Record numbers of people have launched companies over the past decade. The boom in entrepreneurship is not limited solely to the United States; many nations across the globe are seeing similar growth in the small business sector. A variety of competitive, economic, and demographic shifts have created a world in which "small is beautiful."
   - Society depends on entrepreneurs to provide the drive and risk taking necessary for the business system to supply people with the goods and services they need.

2. Describe the entrepreneurial profile.
   - Entrepreneurs have some common characteristics, including a desire for responsibility, a preference for moderate risk, confidence in their ability to succeed, desire for immediate feedback, a high energy level, a future orientation, skill at organizing, and a value of achievement over money. In a phrase, they are high achievers.

3. Describe the benefits of owning a small business.
   - Driven by these personal characteristics, entrepreneurs establish and manage small businesses to gain control over their lives, become self-fulfilled, reap unlimited profits, contribute to society, and do what they enjoy doing.

4. Describe the potential drawbacks of owning a small business.
   - Small business ownership has some potential drawbacks. There are no guarantees that the business will make a profit or even survive. The time and energy required to manage a new business may have dire effects on the owner and family members.

5. Explain the forces that are driving the growth in entrepreneurship.
   - Several factors are driving the boom in entrepreneurship, including entrepreneurs portrayed as heroes, better entrepreneurial education, economic and demographic factors, a shift to a service economy, technological advancements, more independent lifestyles, and increased international opportunities.

6. Discuss the role of diversity in small business and entrepreneurship.
   - Several groups are leading the nation's drive toward entrepreneurship—women, minorities, immigrants, "part-timers," home-based business owners, family business owners, copreneurs, corporate castoffs, corporate dropouts, and retired Baby Boomers.

7. Describe the contributions small businesses make to the U.S. economy.
   - The small business sector's contributions are many. They make up 99.7 percent of all businesses, employ 49.2 percent of the private sector workforce, create 65 percent of the new jobs in the economy, produce 46 percent of the country's private GDP, and account for 47 percent of business sales. Small companies also create 16.5 times more innovations per employee than large companies.

8. Explain the reasons small businesses fail.
   - The failure rate for small businesses is higher than for big businesses, and profits fluctuate with general economic conditions. SBA statistics show that 52 percent of new businesses will have failed within five years.

9. Put business failure into the proper perspective.
   - Because they are building businesses in an environment filled with uncertainty and shaped by rapid change, entrepreneurs recognize that failure is likely to be a part of their lives, yet they are not paralyzed by that fear. Successful entrepreneurs have the attitude that failures are simply stepping stones along the path to success.

10. Explain how small business owners can avoid the major pitfalls of running a business.
    - There are several general tactics the small business owner can employ to avoid failure. The entrepreneur should know the business in depth, develop a solid business plan, manage financial resources effectively, understand financial statements, learn to manage people effectively, set the business apart from the competition, and maintain a positive attitude.

## Discussion Questions

**1-1.** What forces have led to the boom in entrepreneurship in the United States?

**1-2.** What is an entrepreneur? Give a brief description of the entrepreneurial profile.

**1-3.** *Inc.* magazine claims, "Entrepreneurship is more mundane than it's sometimes portrayed . . . you don't need to be a person of mythical proportions to be very, very successful in building a company." Do you agree? Explain.

**1-4.** What are the major benefits of business ownership?

**1-5.** Which of the potential drawbacks to business ownership are most critical?

**1-6.** Briefly describe the role of the following groups in entrepreneurship: women, minorities, immigrants, "part-timers," home-based business owners, family business owners, copreneurs, corporate castoffs, and corporate dropouts.

**1-7.** What contributions do small businesses make to our economy?

**1-8.** Describe the small business failure rate.

**1-9.** How can the small business owner avoid the common pitfalls that often lead to business failures?

**1-10.** Why is it important to study the small business failure rate?

**1-11.** Explain the typical entrepreneur's attitude toward failure.

**1-12.** One entrepreneur says that too many people "don't see that by spending their lives afraid of failure, they *become* failures. But when you go out there and risk as I have, you'll have failures along the way, but eventually the result is great success if you are willing to keep risking. . . . For every big 'yes' in life, there will be 199 'nos.'" Do you agree? Explain.

**1-13.** What advice would you offer an entrepreneurial friend who has just suffered a business failure?

**1-14.** Noting the growing trend among collegiate entrepreneurs launching businesses while still in school, one educator says, "A student whose main activity on campus is running a business is missing the basic reason for being here, which is to get an education." Do you agree? Explain.

# CHAPTER 2

# Ethics and Social Responsibility: Doing the Right Thing

*A man does what he must . . . in spite of personal consequences, in spite of obstacles and dangers, and pressures . . . and that is the basis of all human morality.*

—John F. Kennedy

*If ethics are poor at the top, that behavior is copied down through the organization*

—Robert Noyce,
Inventor of the Silicon Chip

## Learning Objectives

**On completion of this chapter, you will be able to:**

1. Define business ethics and describe three levels of ethical standards.
2. Determine who is responsible for ethical behavior and why ethical lapses occur.
3. Explain how to establish and maintain high ethical standards.
4. Explain the difference between social entrepreneurs and traditional entrepreneurs.
5. Define social responsibility.
6. Understand the nature of business's responsibility to the environment.
7. Describe business's responsibility to employees.
8. Explain business's responsibility to customers.
9. Discuss business's responsibility to investors.
10. Discuss business's responsibility to the community.

Business ethics involves the moral values and behavioral standards that businesspeople draw on as they make decisions and solve problems. It originates in a commitment to do what is right. Ethical behavior—doing what is "right" as opposed to what is "wrong"—starts with the entrepreneur. The entrepreneur's personal values shape the business from day one. Entrepreneurs' personal values and beliefs influence the way they lead their companies and are apparent in every decision they make, every policy they write, and every action they take. The entrepreneurs' values set the tone for the culture that will guide the ethical actions of every employee they bring into their businesses. Entrepreneurs who succeed in the long term have a solid base of personal values and beliefs that they articulate to their employees, put into practice in ways that others can observe, and are carried out through the culture of the organization. Values-based leaders do more than merely follow rules and regulations; their consciences dictate that they do what is right.

For many entrepreneurs, the ability to determine the values and ethics that shape how business will be conducted is a major motivation to launching a venture. For example, when Bob Wahlstedt and his partners left successful corporate careers to found Reell Precision Manufacturing (RPM), a major driving force in their decision was to be able to found a company that values workers and customers over short-term profits and allows employees to put their families ahead of their jobs. "If there's a conflict between the job and the family, *we expect the employee to resolve the matter in favor of the family*, says Wahlstedt."[1] To bring these values to life, RPM does not require employees to travel on weekends to ensure that they can be home with their families and has implemented a generous sick leave policy that allows the use of sick time for any purpose, even attending a child's ball game!

The values and morals that entrepreneurs draw on to guide their ethical behaviors can come from a variety of sources, including their family upbringing, their faith traditions, mentors who have shaped their lives, and the communities they grew up in. Bringing their personal values into their decision making and actions in their businesses ensures that entrepreneurs will act with integrity. Acting with integrity means that entrepreneurs do what is right no matter what the circumstances.

In some cases, ethical dilemmas are apparent. Entrepreneurs must be keenly aware of the ethical entrapments awaiting them and know that society will hold them accountable for their actions. More often, however, ethical issues are less obvious, cloaked in the garb of mundane decisions and everyday routine. Because they can easily catch entrepreneurs off guard and unprepared, these ethical "sleepers" are most likely to ensnare business owners, soiling their reputations and those of their companies. To make proper ethical choices, entrepreneurs must first be aware that a situation with ethical implications exists.

Complicating the issue even more is that, in some ethical dilemmas, no clear-cut, right or wrong answers exist. There is no direct conflict between good and evil, right and wrong, or truth and falsehood. Instead, there is only the issue of conflicting interests among a company's **stakeholders**, the various groups and individuals who affect and are affected by a business. These conflicts force entrepreneurs to identify their stakeholders and to consider the ways in which entrepreneurs will deal with them (see Figure 2.1). For instance, when the founders of a local

**FIGURE 2.1**

**Key Stakeholders**

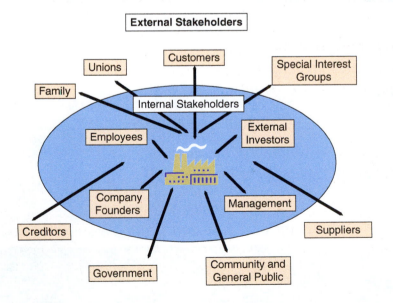

coffee shop make business decisions, they must consider the impact of those decisions on many stakeholders, including the team of employees who work there, the farmers and companies that supply the business with raw materials, the union that represents employees in collective bargaining, the government agencies that regulate a multitude of activities, the banks that provide the business with financing, the founding partners and other external investors who helped fund the start-up, the general public the business serves, the community in which the company operates, the customers who buy the company's products, and their families. When making decisions, entrepreneurs often must balance the needs and demands of a company's stakeholders, knowing that whatever the final decision is, not all groups will be satisfied.

Ethical leaders approach their organizational responsibilities with added dimensions of thought and action. They link ethical behaviors to organizational outcomes and incorporate social responsibility into daily decisions. They establish ethical behavior and concern for the environment as an integral part of organizational training and eventually as part of company culture. What does this mean from a practical standpoint? How does a commitment to "doing the right thing" apply to employees, customers, and other stakeholders, and how does it affect an entrepreneur's daily decision making? For example, Facebook has been facing an ethical dilemma as it has attempted to find a way to gain access to the Chinese market. Facebook and other social networking services such as Twitter have been banned by China's Ministry of Industry and Information Technology. Facebook has been pursuing a partnership with Baidu, which is the leading Chinese-language search engine. To enter the Chinese market, Facebook would have to comply with the restrictive Internet censorship protocol strictly enforced by the Chinese government. The Chinese government also uses the Internet as a surveillance tool to monitor its citizens for political dissent. If Facebook enters into this partnership, it faces the high cost associated with complying with the Chinese Internet restrictions and controls, and it faces an even greater risk of damaging its reputation with its current users and the general public by agreeing to comply with restrictions that allow for censorship and violations of the privacy of its users. On the other hand, from a shareholder perspective, entering the Chinese market is an attractive business opportunity that would potentially add hundreds of millions of new users to Facebook.[2] Balancing the demands of various stakeholders to make ethical decisions is no easy task.

Business operates as an institution in our often complex and ever-evolving society. As such, every entrepreneur is expected to behave in ways that are compatible with the values system of society. It is society that imposes the rules of conduct for all business owners in the form of ethical standards of behavior and responsibilities to act in ways that benefit the long-term interest of all. Society expects business owners to strive to earn a profit on their investment. Ethics and social responsibility simply set behavioral boundaries for decision makers. **Ethics** is a branch of philosophy that studies and creates theories about the basic nature of right and wrong, duty, obligation, and virtue. **Social responsibility** involves how an organization responds to the needs of the many elements in society, including shareholders, lenders, employees, consumers, governmental agencies, and the environment. Because business is allowed to operate in society, it has an obligation to behave in ways that benefit all of society.

## An Ethical Perspective

**Business ethics** consist of the fundamental moral values and behavioral standards that form the foundation for the people of an organization as they make decisions and interact with stakeholders. Business ethics is a sensitive and highly complex issue, but it is not a new one. In 560 BC, the Greek philosopher Chilon claimed that a merchant does better to take a loss than to make a dishonest profit.[3] Maintaining an ethical perspective is essential to creating and protecting a company's reputation, but it is no easy task. Ethical dilemmas lurk in the decisions—even the most mundane ones—that entrepreneurs make every day. Succumbing to unethical temptations ultimately can destroy a company's reputation, one of the most precious and most fragile possessions of any business.

Building a reputation for ethical behavior typically takes a long time; unfortunately, destroying that reputation requires practically no time at all, and the effects linger for some time. One top manager compares a bad reputation to a hangover. "It takes a while to get rid of, and it makes everything else hurt," he says.[4] Many businesses flounder or even fail after their owners or managers are caught acting unethically.

**1.**

Define business ethics and describe three levels of ethical standards.

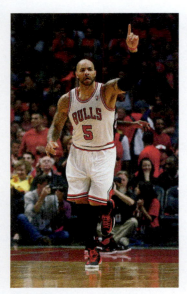

Carlos Boozer.

*Source:* © epa european pressphoto agency b.v./Alamy.

**ENTREPRENEURIAL PROFILE: Claudio Osorio: InnoVida Holdings** Claudio Osorio had been a well-respected entrepreneur, once being designated as "Entrepreneur of the Year" by the tax and consulting firm Ernst & Young. Osorio was the president and owner of the Miami-based company InnoVida Holdings, which manufactured fiber composite panels that could be used to build homes and other buildings without cement, steel, or wood. The company had many prominent people on its board, including former Florida governor Jeb Bush and General Wesley Clark. One of his investors was Chicago Bulls basketball star Carlos Boozer. In an indictment by the U.S. Attorney's Office, prosecutors said that Osorio defrauded investors from 2007 to 2010, exaggerating the company's finances and pocketing millions of dollars to fund a lavish lifestyle that included a Miami Beach mansion, a Maserati car, and a Colorado mountain retreat home.[5]

### Three Levels of Ethical Standards

As displayed in Figure 2.2, there are three levels of ethical standards:

1. *The law*, which defines for society as a whole those actions that are permissible and those that are not. The law is the narrowest level of ethical standards. The law merely establishes the minimum standard of behavior. Actions that are legal, however, may not be ethical. Simply obeying the law is insufficient as a guide for ethical behavior; ethical behavior requires more. Few ethical issues are so simple and one dimensional that the law can serve as the acid test for making a decision.

2. *Organizational policies and procedures*, which serve as specific guidelines for people as they make daily decisions. Policies and procedures include a broader definition of ethical standards that go beyond what is defined by the law. Many colleges and universities have created honor codes, and companies rely on policies covering everything from sexual harassment and gift giving to hiring and whistle-blowing.

3. The *moral stance* that employees take when they encounter a situation that is not governed by levels 1 and 2. It is the broadest and most fundamental definition of ethical standards. The values people learn early in life at home, from their religious upbringing, in the communities they were raised in, in school, and at work are key ingredients at this level. Morality is what shapes a person's character. A strong determinant of moral behavior is *training*. As Aristotle said thousands of years ago, you get a good adult by teaching a child to do the right thing. A company's culture can serve either to support or undermine its employees' concept of what constitutes ethical behavior.

Ethics is something that every business person faces daily; most decisions involve some degree of ethical judgment. Over the course of a career, entrepreneurs can be confident that they will face some tough ethical choices. But that is not necessarily bad! Situations such as these give

**FIGURE 2.2**

**Levels of Ethical Standards**

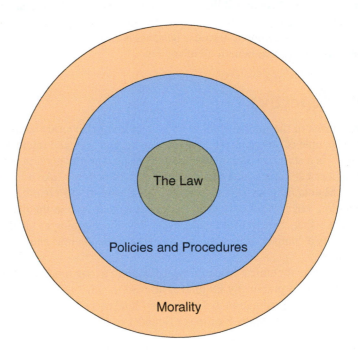

entrepreneurs the opportunity to flex their ethical muscles and do what is right. Entrepreneurs set the ethical tone for their companies. The ethical stance employees take when faced with difficult decisions often reflects the values that entrepreneurs have used to intentionally shape the culture within their businesses.

## Immoral, Amoral, and Moral Management

Although companies may set ethical standards and offer guidelines for employees, the ultimate decision on whether to abide by ethical principles rests with the *individual*. In other words, companies really are not ethical or unethical; individuals are. Managers, however, can greatly influence individual behavior within the company. That influence must start at the *top* of the organization. The entrepreneur who practices ethical behavior establishes the moral tone for the entire organization. Table 2.1 summarizes the characteristics of the three ethical styles of management: immoral, amoral, and moral management.

**IMMORAL MANAGEMENT** Immoral managers are motivated by selfish reasons such as their own gains or those of the company. The driving force behind immoral management is *greed*: achieving personal or organizational success at any cost. Immoral management is the polar opposite of ethical management; immoral managers do what they can to circumvent laws and moral standards and are not concerned about the impact that their actions have on others.

**AMORAL MANAGEMENT** The principal goal of amoral managers is to earn a profit, but their actions differ from those of immoral managers in one key way: They do not purposely violate laws or ethical standards. Instead, amoral managers neglect to consider the impact their decisions have on others; they use free-rein decision making without reference to ethical standards. Amoral management is not an option for socially responsible businesses.

**MORAL MANAGEMENT** Moral managers also strive for success but only within the boundaries of legal and ethical standards. Moral managers are not willing to sacrifice their values and violate ethical standards just to make a profit. Managers who operate with this philosophy see the law as a minimum standard for ethical behavior.

## TABLE 2.1 Approaches to Business Ethics

| Organizational Characteristics | Immoral Management | Amoral Management | Moral Management |
|---|---|---|---|
| Ethical norms | Management decisions, actions, and behavior imply a positive and active opposition to what is moral (ethical). Decisions are discordant with accepted ethical principles. An active negation of what is moral is implicit. | Management is neither moral nor immoral; decisions are not based on moral judgments. Management activity is not related to any moral code. A lack of ethical perception and moral awareness may be implicit. | Management activity conforms to a standard of ethical, or right, behavior. Management activity conforms to accepted professional standards of conduct. Ethical leadership is commonplace. |
| Motives | Selfish. Management cares only about its or its company's gains. | Well-intentioned but selfish in the sense that impact on others is not considered. | Good. Management wants to succeed but only within the confines of sound ethical precepts such as fairness, justice, and due process. |
| Goals | Profitability and organizational success at any price. | Profitability. Other goals are not considered. | Profitability within the confines of legal obedience and ethical standards. |
| Orientation toward law | Legal standards are barriers that management must overcome to accomplish what it wants. | Law is the ethical guide, preferably the letter of the law. The central question is, what can we do legally? | Obedience toward letter and spirit of the law. Law is a minimal ethical behavior. Prefer to operate well above what law mandates. |
| Strategy | Exploit opportunities for corporate gain. Cut corners when it appears useful. | Give managers free rein. Personal ethics may apply but only if managers choose. Respond to legal mandates if caught and required to do so. | Live by sound ethical standards. Assume leadership position when ethical dilemmas arise. Enlightened self-interest. |

*Source:* Adapted from Archie B. Carroll, "In Search of the Moral Manager," reprinted from *Business Horizons*, March/April, Copyright 1987 by the Foundation for the School of Business at Indiana University. Used with permission.

## The Benefits of Moral Management

One of the most common misconceptions about business is that there is a contradiction between earning a profit and maintaining high ethical standards. In reality, companies have learned that these two goals are consistent with one another. Tom Chappell, founder of Tom's of Maine and Rambler's Way Farm, companies known almost as well for their ethical and socially responsible behavior as for their natural personal care products and environmentally friendly clothing, says, "You can make money and do good at the same time. They are not separate acts."[6] Many entrepreneurs launch businesses with the idea of making a difference in society. They quickly learn that to "do good," their companies must first "do well." Bridget Hilton, founder of Jack's Soap, a for-profit company that addresses the problem of child mortality due to hygiene by donating one bar of soap to a child in need for every bar of soap sold, says, "Cynics believe there's no way to do good while reaping financial rewards. We beg to differ."[7]

According to a survey by the public relations firm Edelman, 83 percent of U.S. consumers say that transparent and honest practices and operating as a business that one can trust are the most important factors in a company's reputation.[8] The Edelman survey also reports that people in the United States (and globally) trust small businesses more than big businesses.[9]

 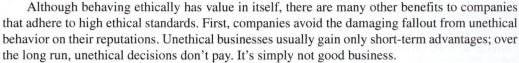

**ENTREPRENEURIAL PROFILE: Tal Dehtiar: Oliberté** Tal Dehtiar, founder of the for-profit company Oliberté, is helping to develop a middle class in Africa by creating fair-wage, sustainable jobs in Ethiopia, Liberia, and Kenya. The company hires women to manufacture shoes made of eco-friendly materials using ethical business practices to help build the local economy and strengthen the skills of its workforce. Due to the success of his business model, Dehtiar has plans to expand Oliberté manufacturing to Cameroon, Congo, Uganda, and Zambia. "At the end of the day, when you strip everything away, we're a shoe company," says Dehtiar. "We make shoes, and we want people to buy them. The more they buy, the more money we make. That being said, though, we do it fairly and properly. . . . In my opinion, that shouldn't be a social business. It should be every business."[10]

Tal Dehtiar, founder of Oliberté.
*Source:* Keith Beaty/Newscom.

Although behaving ethically has value in itself, there are many other benefits to companies that adhere to high ethical standards. First, companies avoid the damaging fallout from unethical behavior on their reputations. Unethical businesses usually gain only short-term advantages; over the long run, unethical decisions don't pay. It's simply not good business.

Second, a solid ethical framework guides managers as they cope with an increasingly complex network of influence from external stakeholders. Dealing with stakeholders is much easier if a company has a solid ethical foundation on which to build.

Third, businesses with solid reputations as ethical companies find it easier to attract and retain quality workers. Explaining why she came to work for shoemaker Timberland, Helen Kellogg, a senior manager, says, "I was looking for a company that had a conscience." Timberland gives every employee 40 hours of paid leave every year to work on volunteer projects. Bonnie Monahan, a Timberland vice president who organized a bike-a-thon that raised $50,000 for a local charity, says that she has turned down "several lucrative job offers" from larger companies to stay with Timberland, where "you don't have to leave your values at the door." Every year, Timberland sponsors Serv-a-palooza, a one-day blitz of community service that involves 170 projects in 27 countries.[11]

Fourth, ethical behavior has a positive impact on a company's bottom line. Research by Dov Seidman, a management consultant, shows that companies that outperform their competitors ethically also outperform them financially.[12] However, financial rewards should never become the motivating force behind acting ethically. Entrepreneurs must strive to do the right thing simply because it is the right thing to do!

Finally, a company's ethical philosophy has an impact on its ability to provide value for its customers. The "ethics factor" is difficult to quantify, yet it is something that customers consider when deciding where to shop and which company's products to buy. "Do I want people buying Timberland boots as a result of the firm's volunteer efforts?" asks CEO Jeffrey Swartz. "You bet."[13] Timberland's commitment to "doing good" in addition to "doing well" is expressed in its slogan, "Boots, Brand, Belief." Like other social entrepreneurs, Swartz's goal is to manage the company successfully so that he can use its resources to combat social problems.

Entrepreneurs must recognize that ethical behavior is an investment in the company's future rather than merely a cost of doing business. Table 2.2 shows the results of a comprehensive study

**TABLE 2.2  Reasons to Run a Business Ethically and the Factors that Drive Business Ethics**

**Top Five Reasons to Run a Business Ethically**

1. Protect brand and company reputation
2. It is the right thing to do
3. Maintain customers' trust and loyalty
4. Maintain investors' confidence
5. Earn public acceptance and recognition

**Top Five Factors that Drive Business Ethics**

1. Corporate scandals
2. Marketplace competition
3. Demands by investors
4. Pressure from customers
5. Globalization

*Source:* Adapted from *The Ethical Enterprise: A Global Study of Business Ethics 2005–2015* (American Management Association/Human Resource Institute, New York City: 2006), p. 2.

that was conducted by the American Management Association of global human resources directors who were asked about the reasons for their companies' engaging in ethical behavior and the factors that drive business ethics today.

## Establishing an Ethical Framework

To cope successfully with the many ethical decisions they face, entrepreneurs must develop a workable ethical framework to guide themselves and the organization. Although many frameworks exist, the following five-step process works quite well:

**Step 1.** *Identify the personal moral and ethical principles that shape all business decisions.* Entrepreneurs build the foundation for making ethical decisions by understanding how their personal values come to life in business situations. This starts with an inventory of the important principles that define one's personal values. The entrepreneur then determines how each of these principles affects each of the major stakeholders of the business. Many entrepreneurs integrate this proactive approach to ethical decision making into their business plans to ensure the integrity of their business actions as they launch and grow their business ventures.

**Step 2.** *Recognize the ethical dimensions involved in the dilemma or decision.* Before entrepreneurs can make informed ethical decisions, they must recognize that an ethical situation exists. Only then is it possible to define the specific ethical issues involved. Too often, business owners fail to take into account the ethical impact of a particular course of action until it is too late. To avoid ethical quagmires, entrepreneurs must consider the ethical forces at work in a situation—honesty, fairness, respect for the community, concern for the environment, trust, and others—to have a complete view of the decision.

**Step 3.** *Identify the key stakeholders involved and determine how the decision will affect them.* Every business influences and is influenced by a multitude of stakeholders. Frequently, the demands of these stakeholders conflict with one another, putting a business in the position of having to choose which groups to satisfy and which to alienate. Before making a decision, managers must sort out the conflicting interests of the various stakeholders by determining which ones have important stakes in the situation. Although this analysis may not resolve the conflict, it will prevent the company from inadvertently causing harm to people it may have failed to consider. More companies are measuring their performance using a **triple bottom line (or 3BL)** that, in addition to the traditional measure of profitability, includes the commitment to ethics and social responsibility and the impact on the environment ("profit, people, and planet").

**ENTREPRENEURIAL PROFILE: Corbin Clay: Azure Furniture** Corbin Clay founded Azure Furniture in Denver, Colorado, in 2009 to address two problems. The first problem was a dramatic decline in American-manufactured furniture over the past decades. The second problem was the loss of 4 million acres of pine trees in the Rocky Mountains to bark beetle infestation. Although the bark beetles kill the trees they infest, they do not harm the wood logs from these trees. Azure Furniture works with local sawmills, the Department of Forestry at Colorado State University, and the U.S. Department of Forestry to harvest this wood and use it to make hand-crafted, solid wood furniture. The process is both an efficient use of materials and an environmentally sound way to address the problem created by the bark beetle.[14]

**Step 4. *Generate alternative choices and distinguish between ethical and unethical responses.*** When entrepreneurs are generating alternative courses of action and evaluating the consequences of each one, they must consider the stakeholders who will be affected and what society considers to be "right" to ensure that everyone involved is aware of the ethical dimensions of the issue.

**Step 5. *Choose the "best" ethical response and implement it.*** At this point, there likely will be several ethical choices from which managers can pick. Comparing these choices with the "ideal" ethical outcome may help managers make the final decision. The final choice must be consistent with the company's goals, culture, and value system as well as those of the individual decision makers.

## Why Ethical Lapses Occur

**2.**
_____
Determine who is responsible for ethical behavior and why ethical lapses occur.

Although most small business owners run their companies ethically, business scandals involving Enron, WorldCom, Tyco, and other high-profile companies have sullied the reputations of businesses of all sizes. The best way for business owners to combat these negative public perceptions is to run their business ethically. When faced with an ethical dilemma, however, not every entrepreneur or employee will make the right decision. According to KPMG's Integrity Survey, 73 percent of workers say that they have observed ethical lapses in their companies within the last year. (Fifty-six percent of employees say that misconduct they observed would cause "a significant loss of public trust if discovered."[15]) Many unethical acts are committed by normally decent people who believe in moral values. Figure 2.3 shows the results of an integrity survey that identifies the primary causes of misconduct in businesses.

Let's explore some of these causes of ethical lapses in more detail.

**FIGURE 2.3**

**Causes of Ethical Lapses**

*Source:* Based on 2013 KPMG Integrity Survey, KPMG LLC, p. 12.

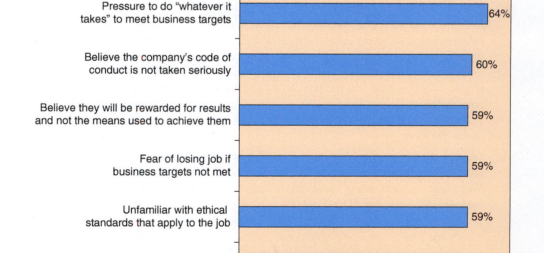

**Causes of Ethical Lapses**

| Cause | Percentage |
|---|---|
| Pressure to do "whatever it takes" to meet business targets | 64% |
| Believe the company's code of conduct is not taken seriously | 60% |
| Believe they will be rewarded for results and not the means used to achieve them | 59% |
| Fear of losing job if business targets not met | 59% |
| Unfamiliar with ethical standards that apply to the job | 59% |
| Lack resources to get the job done without taking shortcuts | 57% |

**Percentage of Employees Reporting**

### An Unethical Employee

Ethical decisions are individual decisions, and some people are corrupt. Try as they might to avoid them, small businesses occasionally find that they have hired a "bad apple." Eliminating unethical behavior requires eliminating these bad apples.

### An Unethical Organizational Culture

In some cases, a company's culture has been poisoned with an unethical overtone; in other words, the problem is not the "bad apple" but the "bad barrel." Pressure to prosper produces an environment that creates conditions that reward unethical behavior, and employees act accordingly. Studies show that companies with strong ethical cultures experience fewer ethical violations than those with weak ethical cultures.[16] In fact, an ethical culture positively influences the behaviors of employees *independently* of the degree to which there is a match between employee and organizational values.[17]

### Moral Blindness

Sometimes, fundamentally ethical people commit unethical blunders because they are blind to the implications of their conduct. Moral blindness may be the result of failing to realize that an ethical dilemma exists, or it may arise from a variety of mental defense mechanisms. One of the most common mechanisms is rationalization:

> "Everybody does it."
>
> "If they were in my place, they'd do it too."
>
> "Being ethical is a luxury I cannot afford right now."
>
> "The impact of my decision/action on (whomever or whatever) is not my concern."
>
> "I don't get paid to be ethical; I get paid to produce results."

Conducting ethics training and creating a culture that encourages employees to consider the ethical impact of their decisions reduces the likelihood of moral blindness. Instilling a sense of individual responsibility and encouraging people at all levels of an organization to speak up when they see questionable actions create a company-wide ethical conscience. However, employees are not the only ones who need guidance when facing ethical decisions. Entrepreneurs themselves should also seek advice and counsel when it comes to ethics. One reason entrepreneurs should establish advisory boards is to serve as a sounding board to help ensure that they understand the moral and ethical dimensions of major decisions.

### Competitive Pressures

If competition is so intense that a company's survival is threatened, managers may begin to view what were once unacceptable options as acceptable. Managers and employees are under such pressure to produce that they may sacrifice their ethical standards to reduce the fear of failure or the fear of losing their jobs. Without a positive organizational culture that stresses ethical behavior regardless of the consequences, employees respond to feelings of pressure and compromise their personal ethical standards to ensure that the job gets done.

### Opportunity Pressures

When the opportunity to "get ahead" by taking some unethical action presents itself, some people cannot resist the temptation. The greater the reward or the smaller the penalty for unethical acts, the greater is the probability that such behavior will occur. If managers, for example, condone or even encourage unethical behavior, they can be sure it will occur. Those who succumb to opportunity pressures often make one of two mistakes: They overestimate the cost of doing the right thing, or they underestimate the cost of doing the wrong thing. Either error can lead to disaster.

### Globalization of Business

The globalization of business has intertwined what once were distinct cultures. This cultural cross-pollination has brought about many positive aspects, but it has created problems as well. Companies have discovered that there is no single standard of ethical behavior applying to all business decisions in the international arena. Practices that are illegal in one country may be

**TABLE 2.3** Ethics Research Reveals Features of Ethical Cultures

1. Leaders support and model ethical behavior.
2. Consistent communications come from all company leaders.
3. Ethics is integrated into the organization's goals, business processes, and strategies.
4. Ethics is part of the performance management system.
5. Ethics is part of the company's selection criteria and its selection process.

*Source:* Adapted from *The Ethical Enterprise: A Global Study of Business Ethics 2005–2015* (American Management Association/Human Resource Institute, New York City: 2006), pp. 5, 6, 10.

perfectly acceptable, even expected, in another. Actions that would send a businessperson to jail in Western nations are common ways of working around the system in others.

Table 2.3 provides a summary of important ethics research concerning the characteristics that are most important to establishing an ethical culture.

## Establishing and Maintaining Ethical Standards

### Establishing Ethical Standards

**3.**

Explain how to establish and maintain high ethical standards.

A study by the Southern Institute for Business and Professional Ethics found that small companies are less likely than large ones to have ethics programs.[18] Although they may not have formal ethics programs, entrepreneurs can encourage employees to become familiar with the following ethical tests for judging behavior:

- The utilitarian principle. Choose the option that offers the greatest good for the greatest number of people.
- Kant's categorical imperative. Act in such a way that the action taken under the circumstances could be a universal law or rule of behavior.
- The professional ethic. Take only those actions that a disinterested panel of professional colleagues would view as proper.
- The Golden Rule. Treat other people the way you would like them to treat you.
- The television test. Would you and your colleagues feel comfortable explaining your actions to a national television audience?
- The family test. Would you be comfortable explaining to your children, your spouse, and your parents why you took this action?[19]

Although these tests do not offer universal solutions to ethical dilemmas, they do help employees identify the moral implications of the decisions they face. People must be able to understand the ethical impact of their actions before they can make responsible decisions. Table 2.4 describes ten ethical principles that differentiate between right and wrong, thereby offering a guideline for ethical behavior.

### Maintaining Ethical Standards

Establishing ethical standards is only the first step in an ethics-enhancing program; implementing and maintaining those standards is the real challenge facing management. What can entrepreneurs do to integrate ethical principles into their companies? To create an environment that encourages ethical behavior, entrepreneurs must make building an intentional culture that is based on a strong ethical foundation a core responsibility as leaders of their businesses.

**SET THE TONE** "The character of the leader casts a long shadow over the organization and can determine the character of the organization itself," says one business executive.[20] Entrepreneurs must remember that ethics starts at the top and set an impeccable ethical example at all times. If entrepreneurs and their managers talk about the importance of ethics and then act in an unethical manner, they send mixed signals to employees. Workers believe the *actions* of those in charge more than their words. What you do, how you do it, and what you say set the tone for your employees. The values you profess must be aligned with the behaviors you demonstrate.

## TABLE 2.4 Ten Ethical Principles to Guide Behavior

The study of history, philosophy, and religion reveals a strong consensus about certain universal and timeless values that are central to leading an ethical life.

1. *Honesty.* Be truthful, sincere, forthright, straightforward, frank, and candid; do not cheat, lie, steal, deceive, or act deviously.

2. *Integrity.* Be principled, honorable, upright, and courageous and act on convictions; do not be two-faced or unscrupulous or adopt an ends-justifies-the-means philosophy that ignores principle.

3. *Promise-keeping.* Be worthy of trust, keep promises, fulfill commitments, and abide by the spirit as well as the letter of an agreement; do not interpret agreements in a technical or legalistic manner to rationalize noncompliance or to create excuses for breaking commitments.

4. *Fidelity.* Be faithful and loyal to family, friends, employers, and country; do not use or disclose information earned in confidence; in a professional context, safeguard the ability to make independent professional judgments by scrupulously avoiding undue influences and conflicts of interest.

5. *Fairness.* Be fair and open-minded, be willing to admit error, and, when appropriate, change positions and beliefs and demonstrate a commitment to justice, the equal treatment of individuals, and tolerance for diversity; do not overreach or take undue advantage of another's mistakes or adversities.

6. *Caring for others.* Be caring, kind, and compassionate; share, be giving, and serve others; help those in need and avoid harming others.

7. *Respect for others.* Demonstrate respect for human dignity, privacy, and the right to self-determination for all people; be courteous, prompt, and decent; provide others with the information they need to make informed decisions about their own lives; do not patronize, embarrass, or demean.

8. *Responsible citizenship.* Obey just laws [if a law is unjust, openly protest it]; exercise all democratic rights and privileges responsibly by participation [voting and expressing informed views], social consciousness, and public service; when in a position of leadership or authority, openly respect and honor democratic processes of decision making, avoid secrecy or concealment of information, and ensure others have the information needed to make intelligent choices and exercise their rights.

9. *Pursuit of excellence.* Pursue excellence in all matters; in meeting personal and professional responsibilities, be diligent, reliable, industrious, and committed; perform all tasks to the best of your ability, develop and maintain a high degree of competence, and be well informed and well prepared; do not be content with mediocrity, but do not seek to win "at any cost."

10. *Accountability.* Be accountable; accept responsibility for decisions, for the foreseeable consequences of actions and inactions, and for setting an example for others. Parents, teachers, employers, many professionals, and public officials have a special obligation to lead by example and to safeguard and advance the integrity and reputation of their families, companies, professions, and the government; avoid even the appearance of impropriety and take whatever actions are necessary to correct or prevent inappropriate conduct by others.

*Source:* Michael Josephson, "Teaching Ethical Decision Making and Principled Reasoning," *Ethics: Easier Said Than Done,* Winter 1988, pp. 28–29, *www.JosephsonInstitute.org.*

**CREATE A COMPANY CREDO**  A **company credo** defines the values underlying the entire company and its ethical responsibilities to its stakeholders. It offers general guidance in ethical issues. The most effective credos capture the elusive essence of a company—what it stands for and why it's important—and they can be a key ingredient in a company's competitive edge. A company credo is especially important for a small company, where the entrepreneur's values become the values driving the business. A credo is an excellent way to transform those values into guidelines for employees' ethical behavior.

**ESTABLISH HIGH STANDARDS OF BEHAVIOR**  It is essential to emphasize to *everyone* in the organization the importance of ethics. All employees must understand that ethics is *not* negotiable. The role that an entrepreneur plays in establishing high ethical standards is critical; no one has more influence over the ethical character of a company than its founder. One experienced entrepreneur offers this advice to business owners: "Stick to your principles. Hire people who want to live by them, teach them thoroughly, and insist on total commitment."[21]

**INVOLVE EMPLOYEES IN ESTABLISHING ETHICAL STANDARDS**  Encourage employees to offer feedback on how to establish standards. Involving employees improves the quality of a company's ethical standards and increases the likelihood of employee compliance.

**CREATE A CULTURE THAT EMPHASIZES TWO-WAY COMMUNICATION** A thriving ethical environment requires two-way communication. Employees must have the opportunity to report any ethical violations they observe. A reliable, confidential reporting system is essential to a whistle-blowing program, in which employees anonymously report breaches of ethical behavior through proper channels. Eliminate "undiscussables." One of the most important things entrepreneurs can do to promote ethical behavior is to instill the belief that it is acceptable for employees to question what happens above them. Doing away with undiscussables makes issues transparent and promotes trust both inside and outside the company.[22]

**DEVELOP A CODE OF ETHICS** A **code of ethics** is a written statement of the standards of behavior and ethical principles a company expects from its employees. A code of ethics spells out what kind of behavior is expected (and what kind will not be tolerated) and offers everyone in the company concrete guidelines for dealing with ethics every day on the job. Although creating a code of ethics does not guarantee 100 percent compliance with ethical standards, it does tend to foster an ethical atmosphere in a company. Workers who will be directly affected by the code should have a hand in developing it.

**ENFORCE THE CODE OF ETHICS THROUGH POLICIES** Set appropriate policies for your organization. Communicate them on a regular basis and adhere to them yourself so that others can see. Show zero tolerance for ethical violations and realize that the adage "Don't do as I do; do as I say" does *not* work. Without a demonstration of real consequences and personal accountability from the CEO, organizational policies are meaningless. Managers must take action whenever they discover ethical violations. If employees learn that ethical breaches go unpunished, the code of ethics becomes meaningless. Enforcement of the code of ethics demonstrates to everyone that you believe that ethical behavior is mandatory.

**RECRUIT AND PROMOTE ETHICAL EMPLOYEES** Ultimately, the decision in any ethical situation belongs to the individual. Hiring people with strong moral principles and values is the best insurance against ethical violations. To make ethical decisions, people must have (1) *ethical commitment*— the personal resolve to act ethically and do the right thing; (2) *ethical consciousness*—the ability to perceive the ethical implications of a situation; and (3) *ethical competency*—the ability to engage in sound moral reasoning and develop practical problem-solving strategies.[23] Find colleges and universities that incorporate business ethics into courses and make them prime recruiting sources. Tina Byles Williams, owner of FIS Group, an investment advising and management firm, understands how important it is to hire honest employees with a strong sense of ethics. Although Williams knows that there is no foolproof hiring method, she has redesigned her company's selection process with an emphasis on screening for integrity.[24]

**CONDUCT ETHICS TRAINING** Instilling ethics in an organization's culture requires more than creating a code of ethics and enforcing it. Managers must show employees that the organization truly is committed to practicing ethical behavior. One of the most effective ways to display that commitment is through ethical training designed to raise employees' consciousness of potential ethical dilemmas. Ethics training programs not only raise employees' awareness of ethical issues but also communicate to employees the core of the company's value system. Rob Kaplan, professor of management practice at Harvard University, recommends that employees be trained to follow a simple yet powerful three-step process when facing an ethical situation:

1. Slow down.
2. Seek advice and elevate the issue.
3. Don't get bullied into making a quick decision that you might later regret.[25]

**REWARD ETHICAL CONDUCT** The reward system is a large window into the values of an organization. If you reward a behavior, people have a tendency to repeat the behavior.

**SEPARATE RELATED JOB DUTIES** This is a basic organizational concept. Not allowing the employee who writes checks to reconcile the company bank statement is one example.

**PERFORM PERIODIC ETHICAL AUDITS** One of the best ways to evaluate the effectiveness of an ethics system is to perform periodic audits. These reviews send a signal to employees that ethics is not just a passing fad.

**Entrepreneurship in Action**

# But Is It Safe?

Oxitec, a British biotech company, developed a new approach to tackling the mosquito-borne disease dengue fever. There are 50 million to 100 million cases of dengue fever every year, and the death rate from the disease is about 2.5 percent. There is no treatment or vaccine for dengue fever; patients are treated for their symptoms, and the disease must run its course. Many pests are becoming resistant to insecticides, and there are growing concerns over the long-term environmental and health impact of consistent use of insecticides. Using advanced genetics, Oxitec breeds and releases "sterile" male mosquitoes of the disease-carrying species. Oxitec claims that their new approach is a highly targeted form of biological control that is safe to other species, causes no lasting impact on the environment, and is cost-effective. In 2010, Oxitec released 3 million genetically altered mosquitoes into the Cayman Islands. The result: Dengue fever was cut by 80 percent within the first year.

In 2009, the Florida Keys suffered an outbreak of dengue fever. Although no one died from this outbreak, 93 people became ill with dengue fever in Key West that year. To avoid future outbreaks, the Florida Keys Mosquito Control District decided to contract with Oxitec to release their genetically altered mosquitoes in the Florida Keys. Key West would be only the fourth location worldwide to use Oxitec's mosquitoes to control the local mosquito population.

Some critics raise concerns about releasing genetically altered mosquitoes into the environment. "If we remove an insect like the mosquito from the ecosystem, we don't know what the impact will be," says Pete Riley, campaign director of a British nonprofit group that opposes genetic modification. He points out that we do not know the impact on animals that feed on these mosquitoes and cannot know what other organisms may move in to fill the ecological void once the mosquitoes are gone. The Florida Keys Environmental Coalition wrote to Florida Governor Rick Scott, asking him to stop Oxitec, pointing out that "biting female mosquitoes could inject an engineered protein into humans along with other proteins from the mosquitoes'

salivary gland. Oxitec has yet to conduct or publish any study showing that this protein is not expressed in the salivary gland and therefore cannot be passed on to humans."

A local real estate agent collected more than 117,000 signatures on a petition she posted on *Change.org* against the release of the altered mosquitoes in the Florida Keys.

Advocates of the plan point to the research conducted by Oxitec that has been published in peer-reviewed scientific journals and the problems associated with traditional spraying with insecticides. However, the use of the altered mosquitoes cannot move ahead until the Food and Drug Administration gives its formal approval.

One local resident offers this caution: "Why the rush here? We already have test cases in the world where we can watch what is happening and make the best studies, because wouldn't it be wonderful if we could find out how it can be fail-safe—which it is not right now. It's an open Pandora's box."

1. Is it ethical for a company to expose people to products that have not been definitively proven to be safe? Explain.

2. How should companies test the safety of products before they are introduced? Explain.

3. Create a detailed diagram of all of the stakeholders of Oxitec. How is each of the stakeholders affected by Oxitec's actions? Explain. What conclusions can you draw from this analysis? Explain.

*Sources:* www.oxitec.com; World Health Organization, "Dengue and Severe Dengue: Fact Sheet," November 2012, *www.who.int/mediacentre/factsheets/fs117/en*; Maria Cheng, "GM Mutant Mosquitoes Fight Dengue Fever in Cayman Islands," *Huffington Post*, November 11, 2010, *www.huffingtonpost.com/2010/11/11/gm-mosquitoes-fight-dengu_n_782068.html*; Chris Sweeney, "Genetically Modified Bugs Glow Red and Self-Destruct, But Can They Keep Away Disease?," *Broward Palm Beach New Times News*, Thursday, May 31, 2012, *www.browardpalmbeach.com/2012-05-31/news/genetically-modified-bugs-glow-red-and-self-destruct-but-can-they-keep-away-disease*; "Oxitec Wants to Release Genetically Modified Mosquitoes into Florida Keys," *Huffington Post*, July 16, 2012, *www.huffingtonpost.com/2012/07/16/oxitec-mutant-mosquitoes_n_1676344.html*.

## Social Entrepreneurship

Whereas traditional entrepreneurs seek opportunities to create market value, there is a growing trend to use entrepreneurship to pursue opportunities to create social value. These **social entrepreneurs,** people who start businesses so that they can create innovative solutions to society's most vexing problems, see themselves as change agents for society. Social entrepreneurs are finding the resources to tackle challenging problems confronting the global economy, including pollution, habitat destruction, human rights, AIDS, hunger, poverty, and others. Social entrepreneurship can be characterized by the following:

**4.** _____

Explain the difference between social entrepreneurs and traditional entrepreneurs.

1. Social entrepreneurs seek solutions for social problems that neither the market nor government provides.

2. Social entrepreneurs are motivated primarily by creating social benefit rather than commercial success.

3. Social entrepreneurs tackle social problems by taking full advantage of natural market forces.[26]

Social entrepreneurs use their creativity to develop solutions to social problems that range from cleaning up the environment to improving working conditions for workers around the world; their goal is to use their businesses to make money *and* to make the world a better place to live.

A recent Global Entrepreneurship Monitor survey of entrepreneurial activity in 54 countries reports that 36 percent of entrepreneurs launch for-profit companies that also include a social responsibility focus.[27] Bill Drayton, founder of Ashoka, an organization that promotes social entrepreneurship, says, "Social entrepreneurs are not content just to give a fish or teach [someone] how to fish. They will not rest until they have revolutionized the fishing industry."[28]

Ugandan woman/Krochet Kids.
*Source:* Krochet Kids International.

 **ENTREPRENEURIAL PROFILE: Kohl Crecelius: Krochet Kids International** Kohl Crecelius, CEO and cofounder of Krochet Kids International, learned how to crochet hats from his older brother. He passed on this skill to two of his friends who shared his passion for snow sports. The novelty of their hats caught on, and they soon began to sell their headwear to classmates as a means of supporting their wintertime recreation. A few years later, the three friends, who had all gone their separate ways in college, were trying to find a way to help those suffering the effects of two decades of civil war in Uganda. They decided to teach the Ugandan women who were refugees living in government camps how to crochet as a way for them to create a living wage and rise up out of poverty. Soon they had trained more than 150 people in Uganda who were then able to earn their own living, receive an education, and have hope for a brighter future all thanks to their hats. They also have expanded their operations into Peru. "This may sound weird," said Kohl, "but there was never really a doubt that this would help or that we would be able to accomplish our mission."[29]

## In the Entrepreneurial Spotlight

# Making a Profit and Making a Difference

There is a significant growth in young entrepreneurs pursuing social ventures. The business models these social entrepreneurs are developing are often based on the notion of a **triple bottom line**—profits, people and planet. "I believe capitalism is in the midst of an evolution," said Jim Schorr, a professor at Vanderbilt University's Owen School of Management. He goes on to state that social enterprise "represents a 21st-century version of capitalism that's more conscious of social and environmental responsibilities."

In his short career as a social entrepreneur, Kyle McCollum has already launched two social enterprises—the first that addresses the problem of inmate recidivism at a local level and the second that seeks to address the global issue of dehydration.

## Triple Thread

As an undergraduate student at Vanderbilt University, Kyle McCollum served as a volunteer at Dismas House, which is a halfway house for former offenders who recently had been released from jail. Kyle did not just drop in as a volunteer—he actually moved into the halfway house. The idea for Triple Thread came from dinner conversations at Dismas House where Kyle and other students heard the residents talk about their desire to start a business, rather than continue to face constant rejection in their efforts to find jobs due to their felony records. However, these ex-felons lacked the financial resources and business knowledge to launch businesses on their own.

William Williams is one of these residents. The convicted felon just got out of jail after serving years for a robbery charge. Williams had tried for a long time to find a job, but his criminal record kept him from finding work.

Then one day Kyle found inspiration for a business opportunity to help Williams and the other residents. He noticed how many students wore custom shirts on campus. He also recognized the demand for employment for former offenders. Like many entrepreneurs, Kyle made the connection between these two observations and came up with a business idea.

They convinced the administrators at Dismas House and some university professors to help create this business for residents to launch and operate. In 2010 they were able to use a $30,000 grant to help the ex-felons of Dismas House realize their dream of starting a business. During its first year of operation, Triple Thread provided more than 20 former offenders with job training and work and brought in revenue of more than $120,000.

Triple Thread is beginning to see returns on its triple bottom line. Many of the former offenders are now leading productive lives.

### Everly

By the time Kyle had graduated from Vanderbilt in spring of 2011, Triple Thread had become self-sufficient. The residents and former residents of Dismas House were able to run the operations of the tee shirt business with only occasional business advising from Kyle.

In the fall of 2011 Kyle McCollum launched a second social venture, this time with Vanderbilt classmate Chris Cole as his partner. The idea for this venture came from separate experiences each of the partners had while in school.

Kyle got the idea for a new drink mix to add to water while on a week-long canoe trek in the Boundary Waters of Minnesota. He had been sipping on drink mixes in his water bottle, but tired of their artificial taste and ingredients. He saw an opportunity to make a natural drink mix that could meet the needs of active, adventurous consumers.

Chris had spent a summer working in Bangladesh, where he learned of the horrors of waterborne disease. Chris learned about the needs for life-saving medicines called Oral Rehydration Salts (ORS) to save children sick with waterborne disease from death by dehydration.

The two friends realized that these two experiences could be linked together to create a venture with a triple bottom line. They could earn **profits** through the development and sale of the all-natural drink mix. They could help **people** by committing to send ORS packets to those in impoverished countries for each packet of drink mix they sold. They could help the **planet** by reducing the number of plastic bottles being thrown away by encouraging people to mix their own drinks in reusable water bottles.

Kyle McCollum was named a #Inspire 100 as a "World Changer" by Dell for his work in launching Everly.

"I'd like to spend my life being a social entrepreneur," Kyle says, "starting businesses like this that have an impact in addition to having a profit so that we can continue to give back."

1. Do you agree with the path Kyle McCollum is taking to use for-profit business to help support social causes? Explain.

2. What benefits does Everly realize by committing to donate Oral Rehydration Salts for every sale they make of their drink packets?

3. Select a local social issue and work with a team of your classmates to brainstorm ideas for a social venture that could help create a sustainable cash flow to help address this social cause. What advice can you offer social entrepreneurs on how to build ventures with a Triple Bottom Line?

*Sources:* Nevin Batiwalla, "Nashville's social entrepreneurs mix business, charity," *Nashville Business Journal,* September 14, 2012, *http://www.bizjournals.com/nashville/print-edition/2012/09/14/nashvilles-social-entrepreneurs-mix.html*; "Vanderbilt students create company to hire ex-offenders," *News 2 WKRN-TV,* September 10, 2010, *http://www.wkrn.com/story/13135456/vanderbilt-students-create-company-to-hire-ex-offenders?redirected=true*; Linda Bryant, "Money with a Mission," *Nashville Post,* July 5, 2011, *http://nashvillepost.com/news/2011/7/5/money_with_a_mission*; Amanda Hara, "Vanderbilt Student Finds Success for Felons," *NewsChannel5.com,* January 19, 2011, *http://www.newschannel5.com/story/13872304/vanderbilt-student-finds-success-for-felons*; "Vanderbilt students design Triple Thread Apparel to train ex-offenders," *jailstojobs.org,* March 1, 2012, *http://jailstojobs.org/wordpress/successstories/vanderbilt-students-design-triple-thread-apparel-to-train-ex-offenders/*; *http://triplethreadapparel.com/about/story/*; *http://www.goeverly.com/about/*; Kicking off Inspired Gifting This Holiday Season, Dell Announces the #Inspire 100, *DailyFinance,* November 20, 2012, *http://www.dailyfinance.com/2012/11/20/kicking-off-inspired-gifting-this-holiday-season-d/*.

## Social Responsibility

The concept of social responsibility has evolved from that of a nebulous "do-gooder" to one of "social steward" with the expectation that businesses will produce benefits not only for themselves but also for society as a whole. Society is constantly redefining its expectations of business and now holds companies of all sizes to high standards of ethics and social responsibility. Companies must go beyond "doing well"—simply earning a profit—to "doing good"—living up to their social responsibility. They also must recognize the interdependence of business and society. Each influences the other, and both must remain healthy to sustain each other over time. A growing recognition of social responsibility is true not only for large public corporations but also for small businesses. Two surveys by SurePayroll shed light onto the scope of small business owner's engagement in social responsibility. One survey reports that 55 percent of small business's mission statements include a reference to achieving some type of social goal, and a second report finds that 90 percent of small business owners give to charity and that 70 percent donate both money *and time* to local causes.[30]

Companies that are most successful in meeting their social responsibility select causes that are consistent with their core values and their employees' interests and skill sets. In fact, some entrepreneurs allow employees to provide input into the decision concerning which causes to support. A common strategy is to allow employees to provide pro bono work for the charitable organizations they support.

**5.** _____

Define social responsibility.

**ENTREPRENEURIAL PROFILE: Emma, Inc.** Emma, Inc., an e-mail marketing company with about 100 employees that is based out of Nashville, Tennessee, is an example of a small company that has an active giving program. Emma has five programs tied to giving back. First, for every new customer the company wins, Emma donates $5 to a program that supports the needs of teachers and their students. So far, Emma has helped 16,000 students in 37 states. The second program is also tied to new accounts. The employees of Emma plant five trees for every new customer. So far, they have planted more than 53,000 trees! Third, Emma gives away 25 free

*Source:* Scott Adams/Universal Uclick.

lifetime accounts to nonprofits each year. Fourth, a team of Emma employees manages the company's microloan program through Kiva, which gives microloans to entrepreneurs around the globe to help alleviate poverty. Finally, Emma has a program that allows employees to request funding and volunteer support for charities that they personally care about.[31]

In a free enterprise system, companies that fail to respond to their customers' needs and demands soon go out of business. Today, customers are increasingly demanding the companies they buy goods and services from to be socially responsible. When customers shop for "value," they no longer consider only the price–performance relationship of the product or service; they also consider the company's stance on social responsibility. Whether a company supports a social or an environmental cause has a significant effect on shoppers' behavior. A study by Penn Schoen Berland, in conjunction with Burson-Marsteller and Landor, reports that more than 75 percent of consumers say that social responsibility is important in their purchasing decisions. The survey finds that 55 percent are more likely to choose a product that supports a certain cause when choosing between otherwise similar products and that 38 percent of consumers are willing to pay more for products with added social benefits.[32] Other studies conclude that when price, service, and quality are equal among competitors, customers buy from the company that has the best reputation for social responsibility.

Other studies show a connection between social responsibility and profitability. One team of researchers evaluated 52 studies on corporate social responsibility that were conducted over 30 years and concluded that a positive correlation existed between a company's profitability and its reputation for ethical, socially responsible behavior. The relationship also was self-reinforcing. "It's a virtuous cycle," says Sara Rynes, one of the researchers. "As a company becomes more socially responsible, its reputation and financial performance go up, which causes them to become even more socially responsible."[33] The message is clear: Companies that incorporate social responsibility into their competitive strategies outperform those that fail to do so. Today's socially wired, transparent economy makes ethical and socially responsible behavior highly visible and, conversely, improper behavior more difficult to hide.

One problem businesses face is defining just what socially responsible behavior is. Is it manufacturing environmentally friendly products? Is it donating a portion of profits to charitable organizations? Is it creating jobs in inner cities plagued by high unemployment levels? The nature of a company's social responsibility efforts depends on how its owners, employees, and other stakeholders define what it means to be socially responsible. Typically, businesses have responsibilities to several key stakeholders, including the environment, employees, customers, investors, and the community.

## Business's Responsibility to the Environment

**6.**

Understand the nature of business's responsibility to the environment.

Due to a strong personal belief in environmental protection, many entrepreneurs seek to start ventures that have a positive impact on the environment or take steps to operate their businesses in ways that help protect the environment. Also driven by a commitment of their customers' interest in protecting the environment, small businesses have become more sensitive to the impact their products, processes, and packaging have on the planet. Environmentalism has become—and will continue to be—one of the dominant issues for companies worldwide because consumers have added another item to their list of buying criteria: environmental friendliness and safety. Companies have discovered that sound environmental practices make for good business. In addition to lowering their operating costs, environmentally safe products attract environmentally conscious customers and can give a company a competitive edge in the marketplace. Socially responsible business owners focus on the three Rs: reduce, reuse, and recycle:

- *Reduce* the amount of energy and materials used in your company, from the factory floor to the copier room.
- *Reuse* whatever you can.
- *Recycle* the materials that you must dispose of.

**ENTREPRENEURIAL PROFILE: Kyle Parsons: Indosole** On a trip to Indonesia, Kyle Parsons heard about landfills spontaneously combusting due to the number of tires thrown in every year. To address this environmental problem, Parsons founded Indosole, which creates sandals and shoes made from repurposed Indonesian motorcycle tires. Indosole creates two pairs of shoes from every tire it salvages from the landfill. The production process involves no melting down, off-gassing, or re-forming of materials salvaged. In addition, all the shoes are made by hand rather than by machine. Indosole strives to create sustainable local jobs with a clean, fair, and healthy working environment. The profits from Indosole are used to help send the workers' kids to school.[34]

Indonesian worker for Indosole.
*Source:* Indosole LLC.

Many progressive small companies are taking their environmental policies a step further, creating redesigned, "clean" manufacturing systems that focus on *avoiding* waste and pollution and using resources efficiently. That requires a different manufacturing philosophy. These companies design their products, packaging, and processes from the start with the environment in mind, working to eliminate hazardous materials and by-products and looking for ways to turn what had been scrap into salable products. This approach requires an ecological evaluation of every part of the process, from the raw materials that go into a product to the disposal or reuse of the packaging that contains it.

**ENTREPRENEURIAL PROFILE: Joshua Onysko: Pangea Organics** Joshua Onysko, founder of Pangea Organics, incorporates these principles into his business, which uses organic, all-natural ingredients, such as beeswax, almond oil, and sweet basil, to produce its line of soaps and body lotions. Pangea's packaging is made from 100 percent recycled paper using a "zero waste" process. The packages even include the seeds of herbs such as basil and amaranth. Once customers remove the product, they simply soak the package in water for one minute, plant it, and wait for the seeds to sprout! Pangea's 10,000-square-foot factory in Denver, Colorado, is powered completely by wind, and a 2,500-square-foot garden provides lunch for the company's 22 employees seven months out of the year. Onysko says that Pangea is gearing up for an audit of its environmental impact so that the company can be even more environmentally sensitive.[35]

## Business's Responsibility to Employees

Few other stakeholders are as important to a business as its employees. It is common for managers to *say* that their employees are their most valuable resource, but the truly excellent ones actually *treat* them that way. Employees are at the heart of increases in productivity, and they add the personal touch that puts passion in customer service. In short, employees produce the winning competitive advantage for an entrepreneur. Entrepreneurs who understand the value of their employees follow a few simple procedures by doing the following:

- Listening to employees and respecting their opinions.
- Asking for their input; involving them in the decision-making process.
- Providing regular feedback—positive and negative—to employees.
- Telling them the truth—always.
- Letting them know exactly what's expected of them.
- Rewarding employees for performing their jobs well.
- Trusting them; creating an environment of respect and teamwork.

**7.**

Describe business's responsibility to employees.

**ENTREPRENEURIAL PROFILE: Lee Company** Leon Lee started Lee Company in Franklin, Tennessee, in 1944 to provide service for refrigeration and heating equipment. His goal from the beginning was to focus on people—hiring the best people and treating them well. Now in its third generation of family ownership, Lee Company continues this focus as it has grown to hundreds of employees doing work with customers nationwide. Lee Company was recently named one of the top 10 companies to work for in the state of Tennessee. The mission statement of Lee Company begins with the following: "To create a workplace where our employees can thrive." Lee Company established an employee emergency assistance fund that allows employees to contribute both money and days off to a pool used to help coworkers facing an emergency or crisis. Because so many of their workers are young blue-collar workers, these employees can be particularly vulnerable to a financial crisis. "If they have a health insurance claim that's not covered or they have an unexpected death and they have funeral expenses, it is a real crisis for them," explains Bill Lee, current CEO of Lee Company. "So we set something up that would keep our folks from being financially devastated and also something to let the employees be involved in helping one another. Employees put the money into our Lee Employee Assistance Fund for their co-workers. It is not just the company doing something for them, but it is the workers doing something for one another." Lee Company also established a single benefit plan that applies to every employee in the company, no matter what level. "In our company we have had a long standing tradition of not having a different set of benefits for our field employees than we do for our office employees," said Bill Lee. "A lot of companies have dual benefits. Office workers get this, field workers get that. And there are certainly things inherent in their jobs that are different for field and office workers. One of the things that we have tried to do is keep the barriers broken down so that people feel like the $9 an hour entry-level, low-skilled worker is just as valuable to this company as the CFO. The entry level employee's benefit package is the same as the CFO's. He is treated as fairly and justly as anyone else in the company." Lee Company has experienced very low turnover among employees due in large part to the quality of the work environment and culture.[36]

Several important issues face entrepreneurs who are trying to meet their social responsibility to employees, including cultural diversity, drug testing, AIDs, sexual harassment and privacy.

## Cultural Diversity in the Workplace

The United States has always been a nation of astonishing cultural diversity (see Figure 2.4), a trait that has imbued it with an incredible richness of ideas and creativity. Indeed, this diversity is one of the driving forces behind the greatest entrepreneurial effort in the world, and it continues to grow. The United States, in short, is moving toward a "minority majority," and significant demographic shifts will affect virtually every aspect of business. Nowhere will this be more visible than in the makeup of the nation's workforce (see Figure 2.5). In 2020, members of five different generations will be working side by side in the United States.[37] By 2039, the *majority* of the workforce in the United States will be members of a minority.[38] The Hispanic population is

**FIGURE 2.4**

**Diversity Index by County**

The diversity Index measures the probability that two people chosen at random from the same area belong to two different race or ethnic groups. The Diversity Index ranges from 0 (no diversity) to 100 complete diversity). The diversity index for the entire United States is 62.1, an increase from 54 in 2000.

*Source:* Diversity Index Statement 2012, Ersi, p. 3.

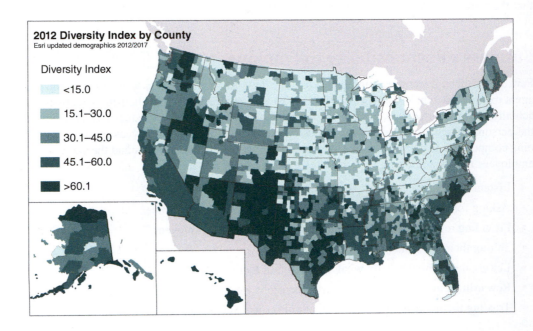

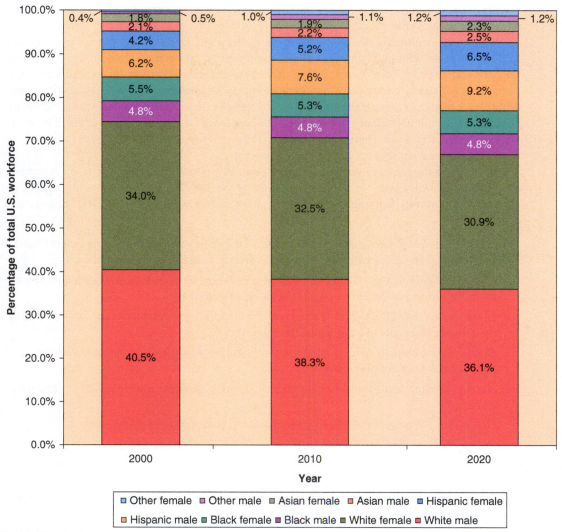

**FIGURE 2.5**

## Composition of U.S. Workforce by Race and Gender 2000, 2010, and 2020

*Source:* Based on Mitra Toossi, "Labor Force Projections to 2020: A More Slowly Growing Workforce," *Monthly Labor Review*, January 2012, pp. 43–64.

the fastest-growing sector in the United States, and Hispanics now make up the largest minority population in the nation.

This rich mix of generations, cultures, and backgrounds within the workforce presents both opportunities and challenges to employers. One of the chief benefits of a diverse workforce is the rich blend of perspectives, skills, talents, and ideas that employees have to offer. In addition, the changing composition of the nation's population will change business's customer base. What better way is there for an entrepreneur to deal with culturally diverse customers than to have a culturally diverse workforce? "No matter who you are, you're going to have to work with people who are different from you," says Ted Childs, vice president of global workforce diversity for IBM. "You're going to have to sell to people who are different from you, buy from people who are different from you, and manage people who are different from you."[39] Diversity is more than just checking boxes to ensure that a broad spectrum of people work in a business, however. Shirley Engelmeier, CEO of InclusionINC, recommends that entrepreneurs view diversity "through the lens of what are the diverse competencies you need to build your business, and those diverse competencies are going to show up in different people. Don't just do it to get numbers. Don't just do it to make your team look different. That's part of corporate diversity fatigue. For a couple of decades we've been counting women and people of color without linking it to what the bottom line business rationale is for that, and the bottom line business rationale is about skills."[40]

Managing a culturally diverse workforce presents a real challenge for employers, however. Molding workers with highly varied beliefs, backgrounds, and biases into a unified team takes time and commitment. Stereotypes, biases, and prejudices present barriers that workers and managers must constantly overcome. Communication may require more effort because of language differences. In many cases, dealing with diversity causes a degree of discomfort for entrepreneurs because of the natural tendency to associate with people who are similar to ourselves. These reasons and others cause some entrepreneurs to resist the move to a more diverse workforce, a move that threatens their ability to create a competitive edge.

How can entrepreneurs achieve unity through diversity? The only way is by *managing* diversity in the workforce. In its *Best Practices of Private Sector Employers*, an Equal Employment Opportunity Commission task force suggests following a "SPLENDID" approach to diversity:

- *Study*. Business owners cannot solve problems they don't know exist. Entrepreneurs must familiarize themselves with issues related to diversity, including relevant laws.
- *Plan*. Recognizing the makeup of the local population, entrepreneurs must set targets for diversity hiring and develop a plan for achieving them.
- *Lead*. A diversity effort starts at the top of the organization with managers communicating their vision and goals to everyone in the company.
- *Encourage*. Company leaders must encourage employees at levels of an organization to embrace the diversity plan.
- *Notice*. Entrepreneurs must monitor their companies' progress toward achieving diversity goals.
- *Discussion*. Managers must keep diversity on the company's radar screen by communicating the message that diversity is vital to business success.
- *Inclusion*. Involving employees in the push to achieve diversity helps break down barriers that arise.
- *Dedication*. Achieving diversity in a business does not happen overnight, but entrepreneurs must be persistent in implementing their plans.[41]

The goal of diversity efforts is to create an environment in which all types of workers— men, women, Hispanic, African American, white, disabled, homosexual, elderly, and others—can flourish and can give top performances to their companies. In fact, researchers at Harvard University report that companies that embrace diversity are more productive than those that shun diversity. A distinguishing factor the companies supporting diversity share is the willingness of people to learn from their coworkers' different backgrounds and life experiences.[42]

Managing a culturally diverse workforce requires a different way of thinking, and that requires training. In essence, diversity training helps make everyone aware of the dangers of bias, prejudice, and discrimination, however subtle or unintentional they may be. Managing a culturally diverse workforce successfully requires a business owner to do the following:

*Assess your company's diversity needs.* The starting point for an effective diversity management program is assessing a company's needs. Surveys, interviews, and informal conversations with employees can be valuable tools. Several organizations offer more formal assessment tools—cultural audits, questionnaires, and diagnostic forms—that also are useful.

*Learn to recognize and correct your own biases and stereotypes.* One of the best ways to identify your own cultural biases is to get exposure to people who are not like you. By spending time with those who are different from you, you will learn quickly that stereotypes simply don't hold up. Giving employees the opportunity to spend time with one another is an excellent way to eliminate stereotypes. The owner of one small company with a culturally diverse staff provides lunch for his workers every month with a seating arrangement that encourages employees to mix with one another.

*Avoid making invalid assumptions.* Decisions that are based on faulty assumptions are bound to be flawed. False assumptions built on inaccurate perceptions or personal bias have kept many qualified minority workers from getting jobs and promotions. Make sure that it does not happen in your company.

*Push for diversity in your management team.* To get maximum benefit from a culturally diverse workforce, a company must promote nontraditional workers into top management. A culturally diverse top management team that can serve as mentors and role models provides visible evidence that nontraditional workers can succeed.

*Concentrate on communication.* Any organization, especially a culturally diverse one, will stumble if lines of communication break down. Frequent training sessions and regular opportunities for employees to talk with one another in a nonthreatening environment can be extremely helpful.

*Make diversity a core value in the organization.* For a cultural diversity program to work, top managers must "champion" the program and take active steps to integrate diversity throughout the entire organization.

*Continue to adjust your company to your workers.* Rather than pressure workers to conform to the company, entrepreneurs with the most successful cultural diversity programs are constantly looking for ways to adjust their businesses to their workers. Flexibility is the key.

As business leaders look to the future, an increasingly diverse workforce stares back. People with varying cultural, racial, gender and lifestyle perspectives seek opportunity and acceptance from coworkers, managers, and business owners. Currently, women make up 46 percent of the U.S. workforce, and minority workers make up more than 33 percent of the labor force.[43] Businesses that value the diversity of their workers and the perspectives they bring to work enjoy the benefits of higher employee satisfaction, commitment, retention, creativity, and productivity more than those companies that ignore the cultural diversity of their workers. In addition, they deepen the loyalty of their existing customers and expand their market share by attracting new customers. In short, diversity is a winning proposition from every angle!

## Drug Testing

One of the realities of our society is substance abuse. Another reality, which entrepreneurs now must face head on, is that substance abuse has infiltrated the workplace. In addition to the lives it ruins, substance abuse takes a heavy toll on business and society. Drug and alcohol abuse by employees results in reduced productivity (an estimated $262.8 billion per year), increased medical costs, higher accident rates, and higher levels of absenteeism. Alarmingly, 66 percent of all drug abusers and 77 percent of alcohol abusers are employed.[44] Small companies bear a disproportionate share of the burden because they are less likely to have drug-testing programs than large companies and are more likely to hire people with substance abuse problems. Abusers who know that they cannot pass a drug test simply apply for work at companies that do not use drug tests. In addition, because the practice of drug testing remains a controversial issue, its random use can lead to a variety of legal woes for employers, including invasion of privacy, discrimination, slander, or defamation of character.

An effective, proactive drug program should include the following five elements:

1. *A written substance abuse policy.* The first step is to create a written policy that spells out the company's position on drugs. The policy should state its purpose, prohibit the use of drugs on the job (or off the job if it affects job performance), specify the consequences of violating the policy, explain the drug-testing procedures the company will use, and describe the resources available to help troubled employees.

2. *Training for supervisors to detect substance-abusing workers.* Supervisors are in the best position to identify employees with alcohol or drug problems and to encourage them to get help. The supervisor's job, however, is not to play "cop" or "therapist." The supervisor should identify problem employees early and encourage them to seek help. The focal point of the supervisor's role is to track employees' performances against their objectives

to identify the employees with performance problems. Vigilant managers look for the following signs:

- Frequent tardiness or absences accompanied by questionable excuses
- Long lunch, coffee, or bathroom breaks
- Frequently missed deadlines
- Withdrawal from or frequent arguments with fellow employees
- Overly sensitive to criticism
- Declining or inconsistent productivity
- Inability to concentrate on work
- Disregard for personal safety or the safety of others
- Deterioration of personal appearance

3. *An employee education program.* Business owners should take time to explain the company's substance abuse policy, the reasons behind it, and the help that is available to employees who have substance abuse problems. Every employee should participate in training sessions, and managers should remind employees periodically of the policy, the magnitude of the problem, and the help that is available. Some companies have used inserts in pay envelopes, home mailings, lunch speakers, and short seminars as part of their ongoing educational efforts.

4. *A drug-testing program, when necessary.* Experts recommend that business owners seek the advice of an experienced attorney before establishing a drug-testing program. Preemployment testing of job applicants generally is a safe strategy to follow as long as it is followed consistently. Testing current employees is a more complex issue, but, again, consistency is the key.

5. *An employee assistance program.* No drug-battling program is complete without a way to help addicted employees. An **employee assistance program** (EAP) is a company-provided benefit designed to help reduce workplace problems such as alcoholism, drug addiction, a gambling habit, and other conflicts and to deal with them when they arise. Although some troubled employees may balk at enrolling in an EAP, the company controls the most powerful weapon in motivating them to seek and accept help: *their jobs.* The greatest fear that substance-abusing employees have is losing their jobs, and the company can use that fear to help workers recover. EAPs, which cost between $18 and $30 per employee each year to operate, are an effective weapon in the battle against workplace substance abuse. Research shows that EAPs can pay for themselves quickly by reducing absenteeism and tardiness by 25 percent and increasing productivity by 25 percent.[45] Unfortunately, only 21 percent of small companies (compared to 76 percent of large companies) offer EAPs.[46]

**ENTREPRENEURIAL PROFILE: Eastern Industries** Eastern Industries, a Pennsylvania-based company that produces building supplies, concrete, asphalt, and stone, operates in an industry that traditionally has been plagued by substance abuse problems. (A recent study shows that 15.1 percent of workers in the construction industry had substance abuse problems, second only to the food service industry.) Initially, Eastern's substance abuse policy was simple: We test for drugs, and if you fail the test, you are fired. The all-or-nothing policy affected the company's ability to keep and retain skilled workers, and company managers decided to change it to a policy that includes prevention, testing, and rehabilitation. Eastern includes educational sessions on substance abuse in its employee orientation program and ongoing programs for all workers. If an employee fails a drug test, he or she can enroll in an employee assistance program that includes rehabilitation that, once successfully completed, allows the worker to return to his or her job. Managers at Eastern say the program has been a tremendous success, allowing them to keep good workers they would have lost under the old policy and giving employees the opportunity to correct bad decisions and keep their jobs.[47]

## HIV/AIDS

One of the most serious health problems to strike the world is HIV/AIDS (acquired immune deficiency syndrome). Health care experts estimate that more than 1.15 million people in the

United States have HIV/AIDS, and 50,000 new cases are diagnosed each year. HIV/AIDS claims the lives of about 15,500 people annually.[48] This deadly disease, for which no cure yet exists, poses an array of ethical dilemmas for business, ranging from privacy to discrimination. AIDS has had an impact on our economy in the form of billions of dollars in lost productivity and increased health care costs. For most business owners, the issue is not one of *whether* one of their employees will contract AIDS but *when*.

Coping with AIDS in the workplace is not like managing normal health care issues because of the fear and misunderstanding the disease creates among coworkers. When confronted by the disease, many employers and employees operate on the basis of misconceptions and fear, resulting in "knee-jerk" reactions that are illegal, including firing the worker and telling other employees. Too many entrepreneurs know very little about their legal obligation to employees with AIDS. In fact, AIDS is considered a disability and is covered by the Americans with Disabilities Act. This legislation prohibits discrimination against any person with a disability, including AIDS, in hiring, promoting, discharging, or compensation. In addition, employers are required to make "reasonable accommodations" that will allow an AIDS-stricken employee to continue working. Some examples of these accommodations include job sharing, flexible work schedules, job reassignment, sick leave, and part-time work.

Coping with AIDS in a socially responsible manner requires a written policy and an educational program, ideally implemented *before* the need arises. When dealing with AIDS, entrepreneurs must base their decisions on facts rather than on emotions, so they must be well informed. As with drug testing, it is important to ensure that a company's AIDS policies are legal. In general, a company's AIDS policy should include the following:

*Employment.*  Companies must allow employees with AIDS to continue working as long as they can perform the job.

*Discrimination.*  Because AIDS is a disability, employers cannot discriminate against qualified people with the disease who can meet job requirements.

*Employee benefits.*  Employees with AIDS have the right to the same benefits as those with any other life-threatening illness.

*Confidentiality.*  Employers must keep employees' medical records strictly confidential.

*Education.*  An AIDS education program should be a part of every company's AIDS policy. The time to create and implement one is before the problem arises. As part of its AIDS program, one small company conducted informational seminars, distributed brochures and booklets, established a print and video library, and even set up individual counseling for employees.

*Reasonable accommodations.*  Under the Americans with Disabilities Act, employers must make "reasonable accommodations" for employees with AIDS. These may include extended leaves of absence, flexible work schedules, restructuring a job to require less strenuous duties, purchasing special equipment to assist affected workers, and other modifications.

## Sexual Harassment

Sexual harassment is a problem in the workplace, and thousands of workers file sexual harassment charges with the Equal Employment Opportunity Commission against their employers every year (see Figure 2.6). A survey by Reuters-Ipsos reports that 10 percent of workers in 24 countries say that they have been physically or sexually harassed. Employees in India were most likely to report sexual harassment (26 percent), and those in France and Sweden were least likely (3 percent). The incidence of sexual harassment in the United States is slightly below the global average at 9 percent.[49] Sexual harassment is a violation of Title VII of the Civil Rights Act of 1964 and is considered to be a form of sex discrimination. Studies show that sexual harassment occurs in businesses of all sizes, but small businesses are especially vulnerable because they typically lack the policies, procedures, and training to prevent it.

**Sexual harassment** is any unwelcome sexual advance, request for sexual favors, and other verbal or physical sexual conduct made explicitly or implicitly as a condition of employment. Women bring about 84 percent of all sexual harassment charges.[50] Jury verdicts reaching into the millions of dollars are not uncommon. In 2011, there were 11,364 sexual harassment claims that yielded a total of $52.3 million in settlements to the victims.[51] Retaliation, such as demotions and

**FIGURE 2.6**

**Sexual Harassment Charges Filed**

*Source:* Based on "Sexual Harassment Charges EEOC & FEPAs Combined: FY 1997–GY 2011," US Equal Employment Opportunity Commission.

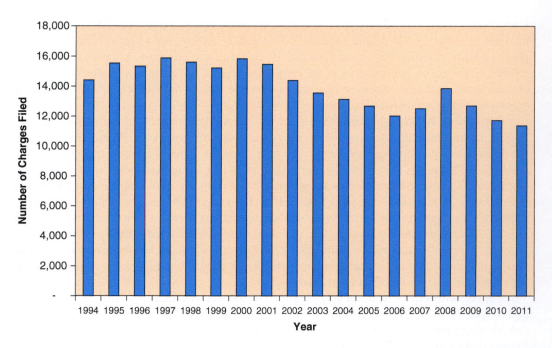

assignments to less attractive work against employees who file complaints of sexual harassment, occurs too often, but the most common form of employer retaliation is termination. Types of behavior that may result in sexual harassment charges include the following.

**QUID PRO QUO HARASSMENT** The most blatant and most potentially damaging form of sexual harassment is *quid pro quo* ("this for that"), in which a superior conditions the granting of a benefit (promotion, raise, and so on) on the receipt of sexual favors from a subordinate. Only managers and supervisors, not coworkers, can engage in quid pro quo harassment.

**HOSTILE ENVIRONMENT** Behavior that creates an abusive, intimidating, offensive, or hostile work environment also constitutes sexual harassment. A hostile environment usually requires a *pattern* of offensive sexual behavior rather than a single, isolated remark or display. When judging whether a hostile environment exists, courts base their decisions on how a "reasonable woman" would perceive the situation. (The previous standard was that of a "reasonable person.") Examples of what creates a hostile work environment might include the following:

- Displaying sexually suggestive pictures or posters.
- Engaging in sexually related humor within hearing of someone who takes offense.
- Talking about sexual matters where others can hear (as in colorfully relating one's "conquests").
- Making sexual comments to other employees.
- Dispensing assignments based on sexual orientation.
- Repeatedly asking a coworker for a date after having been refused multiple times.[52]

Although not easily defined, a hostile work environment is one in which continuing unwelcome sexual conduct in the workplace interferes with an employee's work performance. Most sexual harassment charges arise from claims of a hostile environment.

**HARASSMENT BY NONEMPLOYEES** An employer can be held liable for third parties (customers, sales representatives, and others) who engage in sexual harassment if the employer has the ability to stop the improper behavior. For example, one company required a female employee to wear an extremely skimpy, revealing uniform. She complained to her boss that the uniform encouraged members of the public to direct offensive comments and physical contact toward her. The manager ignored her complaints, and later she refused to wear the uniform, which resulted in her dismissal. When she filed a sexual harassment claim, the court held the company accountable for the employee's sexual harassment by nonemployees because it required her to wear the uniform after she complained of the harassment.[53]

No business wants to incur the cost of defending itself against charges of sexual harassment, but those costs can be devastating for a small business. Multi-million-dollar jury awards in harassment cases are becoming increasingly common because the Civil Rights Act of 1991 allows victims to collect punitive damages and emotional distress awards. A jury awarded Shannen De La Cruz $2.16 million in damages after she won a lawsuit in which she claimed that her supervisor at the casino where she worked as a card dealer made inappropriate comments and sexual innuendo toward her. After De La Cruz reported the behavior to the company's human resources manager, a woman who also had filed (and settled) a sexual harassment suit against the company, the supervisor began disciplining her for minor and fabricated violations. Managers at the company did nothing to stop the actions of the supervisor, who fired De La Cruz after he discovered that she was exploring legal action against the company over the harassment. On appeal, a judge affirmed the lower court's ruling but reduced the award to $1.26 million.[54]

The U.S. Supreme Court has expanded the nature of an employer's liability for sexual harassment, rejecting the previous standard that the employer had to be negligent to be liable for a supervisor's improper behavior toward employees. In *Burlington Industries v. Ellerth*, the court ruled that an employer can be held liable *automatically* if a supervisor takes a "tangible employment action," such as failing to promote or firing an employee whom he has been sexually harassing. The employer is liable even if he was not aware of the supervisor's conduct. If a supervisor takes no tangible employment action against an employee but engages in sexually harassing behavior, such as offensive remarks, inappropriate touching, or sexual advances, the employer is not *automatically* liable for the supervisor's conduct. However, an employer would be liable for such conduct if, for example, he knew (or should have known) about the supervisor's behavior and failed to stop it.[55]

A company's best weapons against sexual harassment are education, policy, and procedures.

**EDUCATION** Preventing sexual harassment is the best solution, and the key to prevention is educating employees about what constitutes sexual harassment. Training programs are designed to raise employees' awareness of what might be offensive to other workers and how to avoid sexual harassment altogether.

**POLICY** Another essential ingredient is a meaningful policy against sexual harassment that management can enforce. The policy should do the following:

- Clearly define what behaviors constitute sexual harassment.
- State in clear language that harassment will not be tolerated in the workplace.
- Identify the responsibilities of supervisors and employees in preventing harassment.
- Define the sanctions and penalties for engaging in harassment.
- Spell out the steps to take in reporting an incident of sexual harassment.

In another case, the Supreme Court ruled that an employer was liable for a supervisor's sexually harassing behavior even though the employee never reported it. The company's liability stemmed from its failure to communicate its sexual harassment policy throughout the organization. This ruling makes employers' policies and procedures on sexual harassment the focal point of their defense.

**PROCEDURES** Socially responsible companies provide a channel for all employees to express their complaints. Choosing a person inside the company (perhaps someone in the human resources area) and one outside the company (a close adviser or attorney) is a good strategy because it gives employees a choice about how to file a complaint. At least one of these people should be a woman. When a complaint arises, managers should do the following:

- Listen to the complaint carefully without judging. Taking notes is a good idea. Tell the complainant what the process involves. Never treat the complaint as a joke.
- Investigate the complaint *promptly*, preferably within 24 hours. Failure to act quickly is irresponsible and illegal. Table 2.5 offers suggestions for conducting a sexual harassment investigation.
- Interview the accused party and any witnesses who may be aware of a pattern of harassing behavior *privately* and separately.

**TABLE 2.5 What to Do When an Employee Files a Sexual Harassment Complaint**

When an employee files a sexual harassment complaint, the Equal Employment Opportunity Commission (EEOC) recommends that employers (1) question both parties in detail and (2) probe for corroborative evidence. Here is a checklist to help when following these EEOC recommendations:

- Analyze the victim's story for sufficient detail, internal consistency, and believability.
- Do not attach much significance to a general denial by the accused harasser.
- Search completely and thoroughly for evidence that corroborates either person's story.
- You can do this by:
  - interviewing coworkers, supervisors, and managers;
  - obtaining testimony from individuals who observed the accuser's demeanor immediately after the alleged incident of harassment; and
  - talking to people with whom the alleged victim discussed the incident (e.g., coworkers, a doctor, or a counselor).
- Ask other employees whether they noticed changes in the accusing individual's behavior at work or in the alleged harasser's treatment of him or her.
- Look for evidence of other complaints, either by the victim or other employees.
- Follow up on evidence that other employees were sexually harassed by the same person.

To make a fair and legal decision on a sexual harassment complaint, you must find out as much information as you can, not only on the incident itself but also on the victim's and accuser's personalities, surroundings, and relationships. To accomplish this task, you should ask many questions not only of the victim and the accuser but also of any witnesses to the incident.

*Source:* Adapted from "Questions for Investigations," Women's Studies Database at the University of Maryland, *www.mith2.umd.edu/WomensStudies/GenderIssues/SexualHarassment/questions-for-investigations*.

- Keep findings confidential.
- Decide what action to take, relying on company policy as a guideline.
- Inform both the complaining person and the alleged harasser of the action taken.
- Document the entire investigation.[56]

The accompanying "Lessons from the Street-Smart Entrepreneur" feature includes a quiz on sexual harassment for both employees and managers.

 **Lessons from the Street-Smart Entrepreneur**

## How to Avoid Sexual Harassment Charges

The Equal Employment Opportunity Commission handles about 12,000 charges of sexual harassment each year from both women and men. Not surprisingly, women file 84 percent of the charges. Experts say that many other employees are sexually harassed but never file charges because of the stigma associated with doing so. What can you do to ensure you provide your employees a safe work environment that is free of sexual harassment? Consider the following case and then take the quizzes below on sexual harassment.

Theresa Waldo was the only woman working in the Transmission Lines Department, a traditionally male-dominated job in which workers maintain and repair high-voltage power lines, sometimes at heights up to 250 feet, for Consumers Energy (CE).

Her supervisor told her that the company did not "have women in this department" and had never had them there and that "they are not strong enough" to do the job. Despite resistance from her supervisor and her coworkers, Waldo, who started her career with CE as a meter reader, was participating in a four-year Line Apprentice Training Program that would entitle her to a higher-paying job. On several occasions, Waldo's supervisor told her that he would "wash her out" of the apprenticeship program.

During her time in the apprenticeship program, Waldo alleges that she faced an "abusive and dysfunctional environment" in which she was constantly "bombarded with sexually abusive and derogatory language and conduct." Male coworkers subjected her to magazines, calendars, playing cards, and other items that contained photographs of nude women. They also referred to Waldo using derogatory, sexually offensive names and on one 90-degree day intentionally locked her in a port-a-potty for 20 minutes. On another occasion, her supervisor ordered her to clean up the tobacco spit of the male workers; when she refused, her coworkers locked her in a trailer. Waldo complained to the company's management about the sexual harassment on several occasions, but managers failed to take any meaningful action to stop the behavior.

After Waldo had successfully completed three years of the apprenticeship program, CE removed her from it and transferred her to the Sub Metro Department, where her pay was $4 less per hour. She filed a sexual harassment charge, alleging that the company had created a hostile work environment, committed sexual harassment, and engaged in gender discrimination and retaliation.

Does Waldo have a legitimate sexual harassment complaint? Explain.

[Yes. Although the jury ruled in the trial in favor of the employer on all claims, the judge granted Waldo's motion for a new trial, acknowledging that the jury's verdict on the hostile work environment and sexual harassment should be set aside because of the "clear evidence presented" in the case. The court ruled that the evidence "demonstrated egregious actions and sexually offensive and demeaning language" directed at Waldo. The court concluded that the harassment created "an intimidating, hostile, and offensive work environment" and that EC "knew of the harassment and failed to implement proper and appropriate corrective action." At the second trial, a jury ruled in Waldo's favor and granted her $400,000 in compensatory damages and $7.5 million in punitive damages.]

One of the primary causes of sexual harassment in the workplace is the lack of education concerning what constitutes harassment. The following quizzes ask you to assume the roles of an employee and of a manager when answering the questions. Learning from these quizzes can help your company avoid problems with sexual harassment.

## A test for employees

Answer the following true/false questions:

1. If I just ignore unwanted sexual attention, it will usually stop.

2. If I don't mean to sexually harass another employee, he or she cannot perceive my behavior as sexually harassing.

3. Some employees don't complain about unwanted sexual attention from another worker because they don't want to get that person in trouble.

4. If I make sexual comments to someone and that person doesn't ask me to stop, I can assume that my behavior is welcome.

5. To avoid sexually harassing a woman who comes to work in a traditionally male workplace, men simply should not haze her.

6. A sexual harasser may be told by a court to pay part of a judgment to the employee he or she harassed.

7. A sexually harassed man does not have the same legal rights as a woman who is sexually harassed.

8. About 84 percent of all sexual harassment in today's workplace is done by males to females.

9. Sexually suggestive pictures or objects in a workplace don't create a liability unless someone complains.

10. Displaying nude pictures can constitute a hostile work environment even though most employees in the workplace think they are harmless.

11. Telling someone to stop his or her unwanted sexual behavior usually doesn't do any good.

Answers (1) False, (2) False, (3) True, (4) False, (5) False, (6) True, (7) False, (8) True, (9) False, (10) True, (11) False.

## A test for managers

Answer the following true/false questions:

1. Men in male-dominated workplaces usually have to change their behavior when a woman begins working there.

2. Employers are not liable for the sexual harassment of one of their employees unless that employee loses specific job benefits or is fired.

3. Supervisors can be liable for sexual harassment committed by one of their employees against another.

4. Employers can be liable for the sexually harassing behavior of management personnel even if they are unaware of that behavior and have a policy forbidding it.

5. It is appropriate for a supervisor, when initially receiving a sexual harassment complaint, to determine whether the alleged recipient overreacted or misunderstood the alleged harasser.

6. When a supervisor is to tell an employee that an allegation of sexual harassment has been made against the employee, it is best to ease into the allegation instead of being direct.

7. Sexually suggestive visuals or objects in a workplace don't create a liability unless an employee complains about them and management allows them to remain.

8. The lack of sexual harassment complaints is a good indication that sexual harassment is not occurring.

9. It is appropriate for supervisors to tell an employee to handle unwelcome sexual behavior if they think that the employee is misunderstanding the behavior.

10. The *intent* behind employee A's sexual behavior is more important than the *impact* of that behavior on employee B when determining if sexual harassment has occurred.

11. If a sexual harassment problem is common knowledge in a workplace, courts assume that the employer has knowledge of it.

Answers (1) True, (2) False, (3) True, (4) True, (5) False, (6) False, (7) False, (8) False, (9) False, (10) False, (11) True.

*Sources:* Reprinted with permission from *Industry Week*, November 18, 1991, p. 40. Copyright Penton Publishing, Cleveland, Ohio; Sexual Harassment Manual for Managers and Supervisors (Chicago: Commerce Clearing House), 1992, p. 22; Andrea P. Brandon and David R. Eyler, *Working Together* (New York: McGraw-Hill), 1994; *Theresa Waldo v. Consumers Energy Company*, 2010 U.S. District Lexus 55068; 109 Fair Employment Practices Case (BNA) 11348, June 4, 2010; John Agar, "Consumers Energy Ordered to Pay $8 Million in Sexual Harassment Lawsuit Verdict," *Mlive*, October 8, 2010, *www.mlive.com/news/grand-rapids/index.ssf/2010/10/consumers_energy_ordered_to_pa.html*.

### Privacy

Modern technology has given business owners the ability to monitor workers' performances as they never could before, but where is the line between monitoring productivity and invasion of privacy? With a few mouse clicks, it is possible for managers to view e-mail messages employees send to one another, listen to voice-mail or telephone conversations, and actually see what is on their monitors while they are sitting at their computer terminals. Some employers have begun to demand Facebook usernames and passwords from job applicants. Employers have established policies that prohibit employees from stating negative information—or in some cases *any* information—about the company in any social media (including Facebook, Twitter, blogs, and so forth). Employers can monitor all activities, including Web usage and text messages that employees send on their employer-issued smart phones. Managers use electronic monitoring to track customer service representatives, word-processing clerks, data entry technicians, and other workers for speed, accuracy, and productivity. Even truck drivers, the lone rangers of the road, are not immune to electronic tracking. Most major trucking companies outfit their trucks with GPS devices that they use to monitor drivers' exact locations at all times, regulate their speed, make sure they stop only at approved fueling points, and ensure that they take the legally required hours of rest. Although many drivers support the use of these devices, others worry about their tendency to create George Orwell's "Big Brother" syndrome.

E-mail also poses an ethical problem for employers. Internet users have more than 4.1 billion e-mail accounts worldwide (974 million of which are business e-mail accounts), and people send more than 100 billion business e-mails per day.[57] Although most e-mails are unwanted spam, e-mail messages are a common way for employees to communicate with one another. Most workers do not realize that, in most states, employers legally can monitor their e-mail and voice-mail messages without notification. Only two states (Connecticut and Delaware) require companies to notify employees that they are monitoring e-mail. According to the Electronic Monitoring and Surveillance Survey, 43 percent of businesses monitor employees' e-mail, and 26 percent have fired employees for misusing e-mail.[58] To avoid ethical (and legal) problems, business owners should follow these guidelines:

- ***Establish a clear policy for monitoring employees' communications.*** Employees should know that the company is monitoring their e-mails and other forms of communication, and the best way to make sure they do is to create an unambiguous policy. Once you create a policy, be sure to follow it. Some managers ask employees to sign a consent form acknowledging that they have read and understand the company's monitoring policy.

- ***Create guidelines for the proper use of the company's communication technology and communicate them to everyone.*** A company's policies and guidelines should be reasonable and should reflect employees' reasonable expectations of privacy.

- ***Monitor in moderation.*** Employees resent monitoring that is unnecessarily invasive. In addition, excessively draconian monitoring may land a company in a legal battle.

 **Entrepreneurship in Action**

## Think Before You Hit "Post" on Facebook

There has been increasing attention given to employee posts on social media sites such as Facebook and Twitter. The National Labor Relations Board (NLRB) and several judges have begun to define what is protected, private speech when it is posted on a personal Facebook or Twitter account. Several cases have helped bring this issue into focus.

**Employee rant**

Dawnmarie Souza was a paramedic working for American Medical Response of Connecticut Inc. Souza was fired after calling her supervisor a "scumbag" on Facebook from her home computer. She was angry about her supervisor's actions after a customer complaint. She also posted a comment, "love how the company allows a 17 to become a supervisor." "17" is the company's terminology for a psychiatric patient. Her comments led to several supportive responses from her coworkers and more negative comments about the supervisor.

The NLRB filed a complaint on behalf of Souza, which was the first case they had ever filed involving social media. "You're allowed to talk about your supervisor with your coworkers," said Jonathan Kreisberg of the NLRB. "You're allowed to communicate the concerns and criticisms you have. The only difference in this case is she did it on Facebook and did it on her own time and her own computer."

The case was settled before it was ruled on by the judge.

### Employee threat?

A warehouse employee, Roy Rhone Jr., made comments on Facebook that indicated a threat of violence toward his employer. Frito-Lay fired Rhone after he posted on Facebook that he was "a hair away from setting it off in that b—." He had been told he would lose attendance points if he left work early because he felt ill. A human resources manager later told Rhone that the Facebook post sounded like a threat to shoot everyone in the warehouse.

Rhone told the manager that "setting it off" meant swearing at someone or walking out on the job. The NLRB said the comments weren't protected.

### When sarcasm goes too far

Robert Becker, a car salesperson, was fired by a Chicago-area car dealership Knauz BMW. Becker posted comments and pictures on Facebook of a sales event in which the dealership served hot dogs and bottled water to customers with the comment, "I was happy to see that Knauz went 'All Out' for the most important launch of a new BMW in years." That same day, he also posted on Facebook pictures of a Land Rover at a nearby dealership also owned by the Knauz group that the 13-year-old son of a customer who was allowed to sit in the driver's seat of the vehicle

had driven into a pond. Becker's comments on this post were, "This is your car: This is your car on drugs." Becker deleted the posts after his supervisor asked him to. He was still fired later that same day.

The NLRB said that Becker's Facebook posts were protected speech and that the dealership could not fire him. The posts about the food were just an extension of conversations that Becker and the other sales staff had about concerns that the food served might hurt their ability to sell cars and earn commission. The NRLB argued that the dealership could not fire Becker for making these comments on Facebook.

Although the judge ruled that Becker's online posts about the sales event were protected by federal law, he did not rule in favor of Becker regarding his comments and pictures about the Land Rover accident. They were not considered protected speech for an employee because they had nothing to do with his conditions of employment.

1. If you were the judge in the Becker case, how would you rule? Explain your reasoning.

2. If you were the judge and the Souza case had not been settled, how would you rule? Explain your reasoning.

3. What policies would you put in place as a business owner about employee comments on social media sites like Facebook and Twitter? Explain your policies based on the cases discussed above.

*Sources:* Ameet Sachdevhttp, "Judge Backs Car Dealer That Fired Employee over Facebook Post," *Chicago Tribune*, October 1, 2011, *http://articles.chicagotribune.com/2011-10-01/business/ct-biz-1001-nlrb-20111001_1_facebook-post-karl-knauz-bmw-dealership*; Julianne Pepitone, "Facebook Firing Test Case Settled Out of Court," *CNN Money*, February 1, 2011, *http://money.cnn.com/2011/02/08/technology/facebook_firing_settlement/index.htm*; Steven Greenhouse, "Company Accused of Firing over Facebook Post," *New York Times*, November 8, 2010, *www.nytimes.com/2010/11/09/business/09facebook.html?_r=0*; Melanie Trottman, "For Angry Employees, Legal Cover for Rants," *Wall Street Journal*, December 2, 2011, *http://online.wsj.com/article/SB10001424052970203710704577049822809710332.html*.

# Business's Responsibility to Customers

One of the most important groups of stakeholders that a business must satisfy is its *customers*. Building and maintaining a base of loyal customers is no easy task because it requires more than just selling a product or a service. The key is to build relationships with customers. Socially responsible companies recognize their duty to abide by the Consumer Bill of Rights, first put forth by President John Kennedy. This document gives consumers the following rights.

**8.** _____
Explain business's responsibility to customers.

## Right to Safety

The right to safety is the most basic consumer right. Companies have the responsibility to provide their customers with safe, quality products and services. The greatest breach of trust occurs when businesses produce products that, when properly used, injure customers.

 **ENTREPRENEURIAL PROFILE: New England Compounding Center** In 2012, a deadly outbreak of fungal meningitis affected more than 500 people, killing more than 30. Patients contracted the deadly fungal meningitis after being injected with a contaminated preservative-free steroid used to treat pain and inflammation that was manufactured at the New England Compounding Center, a small compounding pharmacy in Framingham, Massachusetts. Preliminary investigations indicated that there were unsanitary, dangerous conditions at the company. Federal authorities launched a criminal investigation into the practices at New England Compounding Center, and the state Board of Registration in Pharmacy has voted to revoke permanently the company's license to operate in Massachusetts.

*Source:* CJ GUNTHER/Newscom.

Product liability cases can be controversial, such as the McDonald's coffee lawsuit, in which a jury found that the fast-food giant's coffee was too hot when served and caused a serious injury when a customer at a drive-through window spilled coffee in her lap. In other situations, the evidence is clear that a product suffers from fundamental flaws in either design or construction and caused an injury to its user when used properly.

Many companies have responded by placing detailed warning labels on their products that sometimes insult customers' intelligence. Consider the following actual examples from product warning labels:

- "Do not eat toner" on a toner cartridge for a laser printer.
- "Never operate your speakerphone while driving," a warning attached to a "Drive 'N' Talk" speakerphone for use with cell phones.
- "Do not use orally" on a toilet bowl cleaning brush.
- "Do not try to dry your phone in a microwave oven" in the instructions for a cellular phone.
- "Caution: Remove infant before folding for storage" on a baby stroller.[59]

### Right to Know

Consumers have the right to honest communication about the products and services they buy and the companies that sell them. In a free market economy, information is one of the most valuable commodities available. Customers often depend on companies for the information they need to make decisions about price, quality, features, and other factors. As a result, companies have a responsibility to customers to be truthful in their advertising.

Unfortunately, not every business recognizes its social responsibility to be truthful in advertising. The Federal Trade Commission reached a settlement requiring Oreck Corporation to stop making allegedly false and unproven claims that two of its vacuum cleaners can reduce the risk of flu and other illnesses and eliminate virtually all common germs and allergens. The company also has agreed to pay $750,000 in fines.[60] Businesses that rely on unscrupulous tactics may profit in the short term, but they will not last in the long run.

### Right to Be Heard

The right to be heard suggests that the channels of communication between companies and their customers run in both directions. Socially responsible businesses provide customers with a mechanism for resolving complaints about products and services. Some companies have established a consumer ombudsman to address customer questions and complaints. Others have created customer hot lines, toll-free numbers designed to serve customers more effectively. Today, many businesses actively monitor social media, watching for customer complaints or negative comments that customers make about the company or its products and services and then addressing them promptly.

Another effective technique for encouraging two-way communication between customers and companies is the customer report card. The Granite Rock Company, a business that supplies a variety of building materials to construction companies, relies on an annual report card from its customers to learn how to serve them better. Although the knowledge an entrepreneur gets from customer feedback is immeasurable for making improvements, only 1 in 12 small companies regularly schedules customer satisfaction surveys such as Granite Rock's. It is a tool that can boost a company's profitability significantly.

### Right to Education

Socially responsible companies give customers access to educational material about their products and services and how to use them properly. The goal is to give customers enough information to make informed purchase decisions. A product that is the wrong solution to the customer's needs results in a disappointed customer who is likely to blame the manufacturer or retailer for the mistake. Consumer education is an inexpensive investment in customer satisfaction (especially when done online) and the increased probability that a satisfied customer is a repeat buyer.

## Right to Choice

Inherent in the free enterprise system is the consumer's right to choose among competing products and services. Socially responsible companies do not restrict competition, and they abide by U.S. antitrust policy, which promotes free trade and competition in the market. The foundation of this policy is the Sherman Antitrust Act of 1890, which forbids agreements among sellers that restrain trade or commerce and outlaws any attempts to monopolize markets (see Chapter 23).

## Business's Responsibility to Investors

Companies have the responsibility to provide investors with an attractive return on their investments. Although earning a profit may be a company's *first* responsibility, it is not its *only* responsibility; meeting its ethical and social responsibility goals is also a key to success. Investors today want to know that entrepreneurs are making ethical decisions and acting in a socially responsible manner. Those who invest in entrepreneurial ventures are a small community (see Chapter 16). Reputation can mean everything for an entrepreneur because most investors invest more on the basis of the entrepreneur's track record than on the entrepreneur's idea. Maintaining high standards of ethics and social responsibility translates into a business culture that sets the stage for future equity investments and in more profitable business operations.

Companies also have the responsibility to report their financial performances in an accurate and timely fashion to their investors. Businesses that misrepresent or falsify their financial and operating records are guilty of violating the fiduciary relationship with their investors.

**9.**
Discuss business's responsibility to investors.

**ENTREPRENEURIAL PROFILE: Richard Priddy and Charles Sample: TVI Corporation**
Richard Priddy, CEO of TVI Corporation, and Charles Sample, the company's CFO, were sentenced to prison time and ordered to pay $595,000 in restitution for defrauding the company of more than $1.4 million. Priddy and Sample learned that they could purchase from a company in Seattle at significantly lower prices the same parts that TVI had been buying. Rather than allow TVI to switch to the lower-cost supplier, they formed a separate company, Containment & Transfer Systems, LLC (CATS), to purchase the parts from the Seattle company and resell them to TVI. Over the next five years, Priddy and Sample hid the fact that they owned CATS from the TVI board and investors and defrauded TVI of more than $1.4 million before board members discovered the executives' illicit actions.[61]

## Business's Responsibility to the Community

As corporate citizens, businesses have a responsibility to the communities in which they operate. In addition to providing jobs and creating wealth, companies contribute to the local community in many different ways. Socially responsible businesses are aware of their duty to put back into the community some of what they take out as they generate profits; their goal is to become a neighbor of choice.

**10.**
Discuss business's responsibility to the community.

Experts estimate that 80 percent of companies worldwide engage in some type of socially responsible activity.[62] The following are just a few examples of ways small businesses have found to give back to their communities:

- Act as volunteers for community groups such as the American Red Cross, United Way, literacy programs, and a community food bank.
- Participate in projects that aid the elderly or economically disadvantaged.
- Adopt a highway near the business to promote a clean community.
- Volunteer in school programs, such as Junior Achievement.

In a recent survey, 75 percent of consumers say that companies living up to their social responsibility is important even during economic recessions.[63] Even small companies that may be short on funding can support causes by choosing them strategically and discovering creative ways to help them. The key to choosing the "right" cause is finding one that makes an impact and whose purpose resonates with customers, employees, and owners. Small companies can commit their employees' talent and know-how, not just dollars, to carefully chosen social causes and then tell the world about their cause and their dedication to serving it. By forging meaningful partnerships, both the businesses and the causes benefit in unique ways. Over the years, companies have helped social causes enjoy financial rewards and unprecedented support. In addition to doing good, companies have been able to enhance their reputations, deepen employee loyalty, strengthen ties with business partners, and sell more products or services.

**ENTREPRENEURIAL PROFILE: Ray Booska: Glacier Tek** Ray Booska, founder of Glacier Tek, a West Melbourne, Florida–based company that makes body-cooling vests for a variety of applications, learned about the challenges that the intense heat in the Middle East creates for bomb-sniffing dogs stationed there on military duty and decided that his company could help. Booska and his team of designers tested several prototypes on Booska's retired police dog, Fritz, before finding one that worked to their satisfaction. The vest is made of a nontoxic coolant that works like gel ice packs and can be recharged in just 15 minutes. Glacier Tek added the canine vest to its product line but has donated more than 500 of them to dogs in military zones in the Middle East. "These dogs save the lives of our sons and daughters," says Booska, "and we're going to do everything we can to help them."[64]

Entrepreneurs such as Booska who demonstrate their sense of social responsibility not only make their communities better places to live and work but also stand out from their competitors. Their efforts to operate ethical, socially responsible businesses create a strong sense of loyalty among their customers and their employees.

## Conclusion

Businesses must do more than merely earn profits; they must act ethically and in a socially responsible manner. Establishing and maintaining high ethical and socially responsible standards must be a top concern of every business owner. Managing in an ethical and socially responsible manner presents a tremendous challenge, however. There is no universal definition of ethical behavior, and what is considered ethical may change over time and may be different in other cultures.

Finally, business owners and managers must recognize the key role they play in influencing their employees' ethical and socially responsible behavior. What owners and managers *say* is important, but what they *do* is even more important! Employees in a small company look to the owner and managers as models; therefore, owners and managers must commit themselves to following the highest ethical standards if they expect their employees to do so.

## Chapter Review

1. Define business ethics and describe the three levels of ethical standards.
   - Business ethics involves the fundamental moral values and behavioral standards that form the foundation for the people of an organization as they make decisions and interact with organizational stakeholders. Small business managers must consider the ethical and social as well as the economic implications of their decisions.
   - The three levels of ethical standards are (1) the law, (2) the policies and procedures of the company, and (3) the moral stance of the individual.

2. Determine who is responsible for ethical behavior and why ethical lapses occur.
   - Managers set the moral tone of the organization. There are three ethical styles of management: immoral, amoral, and moral. Although moral management has value in itself, companies that operate with this philosophy discover other benefits, including a positive reputation among customers and employees.
   - Ethical lapses occur for a variety of reasons:
     Some people are corrupt ("the bad apple").
     The company culture has been poisoned ("the bad barrel").

Competitive pressures push managers to compromise.

Managers are tempted by an opportunity to "get ahead."

Managers in different cultures have different views of what is ethical.

3. Explain how to establish and maintain high ethical standards.
   - Philosophers throughout history have developed various tests of ethical behavior: the utilitarian principle, Kant's categorical imperative, the professional ethic, the Golden Rule, the television test, and the family test.
   - A small business manager can maintain high ethical standards in the following ways:

     Create a company credo.

     Develop a code of ethics.

     Enforce the code fairly and consistently.

     Hire the right people.

     Conduct ethical training.

     Perform periodic ethical audits.

     Establish high standards of behavior, not just rules.

     Set an impeccable ethical example at all times.

     Create a culture emphasizing two-way communication.

     Involve employees in establishing ethical standards.

4. Explain the difference between social entrepreneurs and traditional entrepreneurs.
   - Traditional entrepreneurs seek opportunities to create market value and profit.
   - Social entrepreneurs use entrepreneurship to pursue opportunities to create social value by creating innovative solutions to society's most vexing problems.

5. Define social responsibility.
   - Social responsibility is the awareness of a company's managers of the social, environmental,

political, human, and financial consequences of their actions.

6. Understand the nature of business's responsibility to the environment.
   - Environmentally responsible business owners focus on the three Rs: reduce, reuse, recycle: *reduce* the amount of materials used in the company from the factory floor to the copier room, *reuse* whatever you can, and *recycle* the materials that you must dispose of.

7. Describe business's responsibility to employees.
   - Companies have a duty to act responsibly toward one of their most important stakeholders: their employees. Businesses must recognize and manage the cultural diversity that exists in the workplace, establish a responsible strategy for combating substance abuse in the workplace (including drug testing) and dealing with AIDS, prevent sexual harassment, and respect employees' right to privacy.

8. Explain business's responsibility to customers.
   - Every company's customers have a right to safe products and services; to honest, accurate information; to be heard; to education about products and services; and to choices in the marketplace.

9. Discuss business's responsibility to investors.
   - Companies have the responsibility to provide investors with an attractive return on their investments and to report their financial performances in an accurate and timely fashion to their investors.

10. Describe business's responsibility to the community.
    - Increasingly, companies are seeing a need to go beyond "doing well" to "doing good"—being socially responsible community citizens. In addition to providing jobs and creating wealth, companies contribute to the local community in many different ways.

## Discussion Questions

2-1. What is ethics? Discuss the three levels of ethical standards.

2-2. List the core personal values that you intend to bring to your business (e.g., treating people fairly, giving something back to the community, and so on). Where does each of these core values come from (religious faith, family, and so on)? Why is each of these important to you?

2-3. In any organization, who determines ethical behavior? Briefly describe the three ethical styles of management. What are the benefits of moral management?

2-4. Why do ethical lapses occur in businesses?

2-5. Describe the various methods for establishing ethical standards. Which is most meaningful to you? Why?

2-6. What can business owners do to maintain high ethical standards in their companies?

2-7. What is a social entrepreneur? How do they differ from traditional entrepreneurs?

2-8. What are some social problems that you think could be tackled by social entrepreneurs?

2-9. What is social responsibility?

2-10. Describe business's social responsibility to each of the following areas:
   - The environment
   - Employees
   - Customers
   - Investors
   - The community

**2-11.** What can businesses do to improve the quality of our environment?

**2-12.** Should companies be allowed to test employees for drugs? Explain. How should a socially responsible drug-testing program operate?

**2-13.** Many owners of trucking companies use electronic communications equipment to monitor their drivers on the road. They say that the devices allow them to remain competitive and to serve their customers better by delivering shipments of vital materials exactly when their customers need them. They also point out

that the equipment can improve road safety by ensuring that drivers get the hours of rest the law requires. Opponents argue that the surveillance devices work against safety. "The drivers know they're being watched," says one trucker. "There's an obvious temptation to push?" What do you think? What ethical issues does the use of such equipment create? How should a small trucking company considering the use of such equipment handle these issues?

**2-14.** What rights do customers have under the Consumer Bill of Rights? How can businesses ensure those rights?

# CHAPTER 3
# Creativity and Innovation: Keys to Entrepreneurial Success

## Learning Objectives

**On completion of this chapter, you will be able to:**

1. Explain the differences among creativity, innovation, and entrepreneurship.

2. Describe why creativity and innovation are such integral parts of entrepreneurship.

3. Understand how the two hemispheres of the human brain function and what role they play in creativity.

4. Explain the 10 "mental locks" that limit individual creativity.

5. Understand how entrepreneurs can enhance the creativity of their employees as well as their own creativity.

6. Describe the steps in the creative process.

*The chief enemy of creativity is "good" sense.*

                    —Pablo Picasso

*Genius is born from a thousand failures.*

                    —Greg Linden

One of the tenets of entrepreneurship is the ability to create new and useful ideas that solve the problems and challenges people face every day. Entrepreneurs achieve success by creating value in the marketplace when they combine resources in new and different ways to gain a competitive edge over rivals. From Alexander Fleming's pioneering work that resulted in a cure for infections (penicillin) and the founders of the Rocket Chemical Company's fortieth try to create an industrial lubricant (WD-40) to Jeff Bezos's innovative use of the Internet in retailing (*Amazon .com*) and Ted Turner's around-the-clock approach to the availability of television news (CNN), entrepreneurs' ideas have transformed the world.

As you learned in Chapter 1, entrepreneurs can create value in a number of ways—inventing new products and services, developing new technology, creating new business models, discovering new knowledge, improving existing products or services, finding different ways of providing more goods and services with fewer resources, and many others. Indeed, finding new ways of satisfying customers' needs, inventing new products and services, putting together existing ideas in new and different ways, and creating new twists on existing products and services are hallmarks of the entrepreneur! "At the heart of any successful business is a great idea," says one business writer. "Some seem so simple we wonder why nobody thought of them before. Others are so revolutionary that we wonder how anybody could have thought of them at all."[1]

John Friedman and Brad McNamara, cofounders of Freight Farms.
*Source:* Freight Farms.

**ENTREPRENEURIAL PROFILE: Jon Friedman and Brad McNamara: Freight Farms** Jon Friedman and Brad McNamara came up with the idea of transforming used shipping containers, thousands of which sit abandoned in ports across the United States, into highly productive gardens that produce year-round and can be located almost anywhere, even in metropolitan areas. The entrepreneurs launched Freight Farms in 2010 to market their Leafy Green Machines, converted 320-square-foot modular, stackable shipping containers that can produce up to 900 heads of leafy green vegetables each week, the equivalent yield of a one-acre farm. The containers cost $60,000 and come fully "outfitted with advanced climate technology that creates the optimal growing conditions needed to maximize any harvest," seeds, and nutrients. LED lights simulate night and day, and a climate-control system ensures optimal growing conditions no matter what the weather is like outside. Every Leafy Green Machine comes with a tablet PC that allows a customer to monitor and control growing conditions remotely. Friedman and McNamara are targeting restaurants, food wholesalers, cooperatives, and nonprofit organizations that help with disaster relief and claim that their Leafy Green Machines deliver high-quality produce at low cost and use a fraction of the energy compared to traditional and greenhouse production. Currently, they are developing containers designed to grow vine crops and mushrooms.[2]

Like many innovators, Friedman and McNamara created a successful business by taking common items—shipping containers—that have existed for many years, looked at them in a different way, and put them to use in a creative fashion.

## Creativity, Innovation, and Entrepreneurship

**1.**

Explain the differences among creativity, innovation, and entrepreneurship.

According to the Battelle and *R&D Magazine*, U.S. companies, government agencies, and universities invest $501 billion annually in research and development (R&D), about one-third of $1.5 billion global expenditure on R&D.[3] Small companies are an important part of the total R&D picture. One study by the Small Business Administration reports that small companies that receive patents produce 16 times more patents per employee than their larger rivals that receive patents.[4] "Small businesses have an inherent innovative advantage over large businesses," says one writer. "They are less likely to have an interest in maintaining the status quo, and they are more responsive and quicker to change. As a result, they have a disproportionate impact on 'disruptive' innovation—change that creates an entirely new market—as opposed to large firms, which tend to engage in incremental innovation."[5]

What is the entrepreneurial "secret" for creating value in the marketplace? In reality, the "secret" is no secret at all: It is applying creativity and innovation to solve problems and to exploit opportunities that people face every day. **Creativity** is the ability to develop new ideas and to discover new ways of looking at problems and opportunities. **Innovation** is the ability to *apply* creative solutions to those problems and opportunities to enhance or to enrich people's lives. Harvard's Ted Levitt says that creativity is *thinking* new things and that innovation is *doing* new things. In short, entrepreneurs succeed by *thinking and doing* new things or old things in new ways. Simply having a great new idea is not enough; transforming the idea into a tangible product, service, or business venture is the essential next step. As management legend Peter Drucker said, "Innovation is the specific instrument of entrepreneurs, the act that endows resources with a new capacity to create wealth."[6]

Software maker Intuit published a study about how small businesses would compete in 2020 and identified six "enablers" of small business innovation:[7]

1. *Passion.* Entrepreneurs typically start businesses using ideas about which they are passionate. Their passion and enthusiasm makes them willing to test new business models and invent new products and services.

2. *Customer connection.* Because entrepreneurs are close to their customers, they listen to their customers, understand their needs and problems, and develop creative solutions for meeting and solving them.

3. *Agility and adaptation.* One hallmark of successful entrepreneurs is their ability to adapt and adjust, making the necessary "pivots" when their business models do not work the way they anticipated.

4. *Experimentation and improvisation.* Successful entrepreneurs understand that creativity and innovation produce big payoffs but also carry a high probability of failure. They accept that failure is merely a stepping-stone on the pathway to success.

5. *Resource limitations.* Because small companies usually operate with limited resources, they are accustomed to doing more with less. Entrepreneurs' resource limitations often require them to be highly innovative.

6. *Information sharing and collaboration.* Entrepreneurs rely on a strong network of people—customers, friends, family members, and social networks—from whom they get useful feedback on their ideas, giving them the ability to discard quickly ideas that do not work and improve those that do.

Successful entrepreneurs introduce new ideas, products, services, and business models that solve a problem or fill a need. In a world that is changing faster than most of us ever could have imagined, creativity and innovation are vital to a company's success—and ultimate survival. That's true for businesses in every industry—from automakers to tea growers—and for companies of all sizes. GE's Global Innovation Barometer reports that 84 percent of 3,100 global business executives believe that innovation can originate from companies of any size. The executives in the survey also say that incremental improvements of existing products and services has been and continues to be the most important factor in their companies' innovation engines but that creating new business models will play a much more important role in innovation in the future.[8] In an earlier version of the survey, executives say that their companies will have to innovate in ways that are "totally different than ever before." As Doreen Lorenzo, president of global innovation consulting firm, says, "Doing business as usual means that you could be out of business sooner than you think."[9] In other words, to be successful, business leaders must develop innovations in their business models as well as in their product and service lines. Table 3.1 summarizes the results of a study by Hal Gregersen, professor of innovation and leadership at Insead, that explains the components of discovery-driven leadership.

Although big businesses develop many new ideas, creativity and innovation are the signatures of small, entrepreneurial businesses. Creative thinking has become a core business skill, and entrepreneurs lead the way in developing and applying that skill. In fact, creativity and innovation often lie at the heart of small companies' ability to compete successfully with their larger rivals. Even though they cannot outspend their larger rivals, small companies can create powerful, effective competitive advantages over big companies by "out-creating" and "out-innovating" them! If they fail to do so, entrepreneurs don't stay in business very long. Leadership expert Warren Bennis says, "Today's successful companies live and die according to the quality of their ideas."[10]

Some small businesses create innovations *reactively* in response to customer feedback or changing market conditions, and others create innovations *proactively*, spotting opportunities on which to capitalize. Sometimes innovation is *revolutionary*, creating market-changing, disruptive breakthroughs that are the result of generating something from nothing. More often, innovation is *evolutionary*, developing market-sustaining ideas that elaborate on existing products, processes, and services that result from putting old things together in new ways or from taking something away to create something simpler or better. Apple did not invent the digital music

## TABLE 3.1 The Five Dimensions of Discovery-Driven Leadership

Hal Gregersen's research suggests the leaders engage in two types of leadership: delivery driven and discovery driven. Delivery-driven leadership includes the traditional management roles of analyzing, controlling, planning, and directing that often leads to only incremental innovations. Recognizing that many consumers misused Nyquil cold medicine to induce sleep even when they did not have colds, consumer products giant Procter & Gamble introduced an incremental "innovation" with Zzzquil, which is nothing more than its NyQuil cold relief medicine without the cold medication. "The reality is when you look at companies that produce long-term, organic profit growth, a huge amount of what they do is incremental innovation," says one innovation expert. Incremental innovations may produce profitable products, but can companies that become content with incremental innovation succeed in the long run, or will they be eclipsed by companies that create disruptive innovations?

Discovery-driven leadership, which innovative entrepreneurs exhibit, produces disruptive innovations and includes the following five dimensions:

1. *Associating* involves drawing connections among ideas, questions, processes, or problems from diverse and unrelated fields.

2. *Questioning* poses questions that challenge conventional thinking and common wisdom. Entrepreneurs recognize that well-established processes may not be the best way to accomplish a task.

3. *Networking* involves entrepreneurs engaging people from different backgrounds who have different ideas and perspectives from their own. Their goal is to learn from people who are different from themselves.

4. *Observing* the behavior of customers, suppliers, and competitors gives entrepreneurs insight into how they can develop new products, services, processes, and business models.

5. *Experimenting* involves constructing interactive experiences (often with customers or potential customers) to see whether their ideas are successful, to gauge customers' reactions, and to gather meaningful insights.

The following table shows the percentile rankings on the five dimensions of discovery-driven leadership for different types of leaders:

Percentile Rankings for Various Types of Leaders on the Five Dimensions

| Type of Leader | Dimension | | | | |
| --- | --- | --- | --- | --- | --- |
| | Associating | Questioning | Observing | Networking | Experimenting |
| Non-innovators | 48% | 49% | 48% | 47% | 39% |
| Process innovators | 70% | 65% | 68% | 61% | 68% |
| Product innovators | 78% | 77% | 79% | 72% | 74% |
| Corporate entrepreneurs | 76% | 67% | 75% | 77% | 69% |
| Start-up entrepreneurs | 78% | 72% | 75% | 74% | 73% |

Doron Shafrir and Sayre Swarztrauber, who cofounded Quadlogic Controls Corporation in New York City in 1984, demonstrated discovery-driven leadership in their company, which provides products that track energy usage for tenants living in the same building. Their business had just posted its best year ever with $15 million in annual sales when the housing market collapsed and Quadlogic's sales plummeted. A few years before, a conversation with a business associate about how energy theft was a major problem in many developing countries had led Shafrir and Swarztrauber to begin tinkering with a new product designed to prevent utility metering systems from being breached by energy thieves. However, the product was incomplete, and the entrepreneurs had not yet identified any potential customers.

They decided that the best strategy for their company was to introduce the new antitheft product and launch it with a big marketing blast. "We saw our survival threatened and that gave us the incentive to make it happen," says Swarztrauber. Their risk-taking strategy paid off; within five months, Quadlogic had signed a multi-million-dollar deal with a utility company in Jamaica. Since then, hundreds of customers in Mexico, Ecuador, Costa Rica, and other countries have purchased the antitheft device, and Quadlogic recently achieved a new sales record, generating $20 million in annual sales. Shafrir and Swarztrauber's discovery-driven leadership style, their ability to spot new business opportunities, and their willingness to take risks probably saved their company. "You have to place your bets," says Swarztrauber philosophically.

*Sources:* Based on Hal Gregersen, "The Entrepreneur's DNA," *Wall Street Journal*, February 26, 2013, p. B13; John Bussey, "The Innovator's Enigma," *Wall Street Journal*, October 4, 2012, *http://online.wsj.com/article/SB10000872396390443493304578036753351798378.html*; Sarah Needleman, Vanessa O'Connell, Emily Maltby, and Angus Loten, "And the Most Innovative Entrepreneur Is ..." *Wall Street Journal*, November 14, 2011, pp. R1, R4.

player, but Steve Jobs's company created a player that was easier to use and offered a "cool" factor that existing MP3 players did not have. One experimenter's research to improve the adhesive on tape resulted in a glue that hardly stuck at all. Although most researchers might have considered the experiment a total failure and scrapped it, this researcher asked a simple, creative question: What can you do with a glue when you take away most of its stickiness? The answer led to the invention of one of the most popular office products of all time: the Post-It Note, a product that now includes more than 4,000 variations. Although both types of innovation produce useful results, revolutionary innovation that produces disruptive changes is momentous—and often highly profitable.

Some entrepreneurs stumble onto their ideas by accident but are clever enough to spot the business opportunities they offer.

**ENTREPRENEURIAL PROFILE: Michael Maness and Bill Silva: CamCaddy Pro** Michael Maness, a professional golfer and PGA caddy, was hitting golf balls on a driving range one day and wanted to capture a video of his swing to share with his instructor. "I had my phone propped up on my golf bag," he recalls, which did not work very well. Maness mentioned the event to his friend Bill Silva, who also was at the range that day. Over lunch, the two friends began brainstorming ideas and making sketches of a simple device to which golfers could attach their phones and record their swings from the same perspective. That led them to create the CamCaddy Pro, an adjustable smart phone holder that snaps onto a standard alignment stick, a common tool that golfers use. "People have been using their phones to do this, but they haven't had a consistent way to get the same perspective," says Silva. In just six months, Maness and Silva sold 10,000 CamCaddy Pros and have since signed distribution agreements with Dick's Sporting Goods and several other major sporting goods retailers. They expect sales of the CamCaddy Pro, which won the award for best new product at a recent PGA Merchandise Show, to reach $1.2 million in the company's first full year of operation. Maness and Silva already are at work on a version of CamCaddy Pro that holds tablets and on variations that people can use anywhere they want to shoot hands-free videos, such as baseball fields, tennis courts, or the beach.[11]

More often, creative ideas arise when entrepreneurs look at something old and think something new or different. Legendary Notre Dame football coach Knute Rockne, whose teams dominated college football in the 1920s, got the idea for his constantly shifting backfields while watching a burlesque chorus routine! Rockne's innovations in the backfield (which included the legendary "Four Horsemen") and his emphasis on the forward pass (a legal but largely unused tactic in this era) so befuddled opposing defenses that his teams compiled an impressive 105–12–5 record.[12]

**ENTREPRENEURIAL PROFILE: SportsArt Fitness** Employees at SportsArt Fitness, a manufacturer of exercise machines based in Woodinville, Washington, developed a way to capture the energy that health club members generate while exercising on elliptical trainers and treadmills and use it to produce electricity. The company's Green System line of exercise equipment captures up to 72 percent of the power that exercisers create during a workout and directs it back into the local electrical system. Anita Miller, the company's senior product manager, says that 10 people using 10 elliptical trainers for an average of eight hours a day can cut a gym's electrical bill by $60 per month.[13]

Entrepreneurship is the result of a disciplined, systematic process of applying creativity and innovation to needs and opportunities in the marketplace. It involves applying focused strategies to new ideas and new insights to create a product or a service that satisfies customers' needs or solves their problems. It is much more than random, disjointed tinkering with a new gadget. Millions of people come up with creative ideas for new or different products and services; most of them, however, never do anything with them. Entrepreneurs are people who connect their creative ideas with the purposeful action and structure of a business. "Great ideas are abundant," says Samer Kurdi, head of Entrepreneurs' Organization, "but it is what we decide to do with them that counts."[14] Successful entrepreneurship is a constant process that relies on creativity, innovation, and application in the marketplace.

Innovation must be a constant process because most ideas don't work and most innovations fail. One writer explains, "Trial—and lots of error—is embedded in entrepreneurship."[15] For every 5,000 to 10,000 new drug discoveries, only about 250 get to preclinical trials, and only five of those make it to clinical trials. Just one or two drugs emerge from clinical trials for review by the U.S. Food and Drug Administration, and only one typically gets to the market in a process that typically takes 10 to 15 years.[16] New products are crucial to companies' success, however. According to Robert Cooper, a researcher who has analyzed thousands of new product launches, new products (those launched within the previous three years) account for an impressive 38 percent of sales at top-performing companies.[17] Still, successful entrepreneurs recognize that many failures will accompany innovations, and they are willing to accept their share of failures because they know that failure is merely part of the creative process. Rather than quit when they fail, entrepreneurs simply keep trying. While working as a textbook editor, James Michener had an idea for a book based on his experiences in the Solomon Islands during World War II. He sent the manuscript to a publisher and received the following note: "You are a good editor. Don't throw it all away trying to be a writer. I read your book. Frankly, it's not really that good." Michener persisted and went on to publish *South Pacific*, for which he won a Pulitzer Prize and which became the basis for one of Broadway's most successful musicals of all time.[18]

Entrepreneurship requires business owners to be bold enough to try their new ideas, flexible enough to throw aside those that do not work, and wise enough to learn about what will work based on their observations of what did not. We now turn our attention to creativity, the creative process, and methods for enhancing creativity.

## Creativity—Essential to Survival

**2.**

Describe why creativity and innovation are such integral parts of entrepreneurship.

In this fiercely competitive, fast-faced, global economy, creativity is not only an important source for building a competitive advantage but also a necessity for survival. When developing creative solutions to modern problems, entrepreneurs must go beyond merely relying on what has worked in the past. "A company that's doing all the things that used to guarantee success—providing quality products backed by great service, marketing with flair, holding down costs, and managing cash flow—is at risk of being flattened if it fails to become an engine of innovation," says one business writer.[19] Transforming their organizations into engines of innovation requires entrepreneurs to cast off limiting assumptions, beliefs, and behaviors and develop new insights into the relationship among resources, needs, and value. In other words, they must change their perspectives, looking at the world in new and different ways.

Entrepreneurs must always be on guard against traditional assumptions and perspectives about how things out to be because they are certain killers of creativity. These self-imposed mental constraints that people tend to build over time push creativity right out the door. These ideas become so deeply rooted in our minds that they become immovable blocks to creative thinking—even though they may be outdated, obsolete, and no longer relevant. In short, they act as logjams to creativity. That's why children are so creative and curious about new possibilities; society has not yet brainwashed them into an attitude of conformity, nor have they learned to accept *traditional* solutions as the *only* solutions. By retaining their creative "inner child," entrepreneurs are able to throw off the shackles on creativity and see opportunities for creating viable businesses where most people see what they've always seen (or, worse yet, see nothing). Creative exercises such as the one in Figure 3.1 can help adults reconnect with the creativity they exhibited so readily as children.

Many years ago, during an international chess competition, Frank Marshall made what has become known as one of the most beautiful—and one of the most creative—moves ever made on a chess board. In a crucial game in which he was evenly matched with a Russian master player, Marshall found his queen under serious attack. Marshall had several avenues of escape for his queen available. Knowing that the queen is one of the most important offensive players on the chessboard, spectators assumed that Marshall would make a conventional move and push his queen to safety.

Using all of the time available to him to consider his options, Marshall picked up his queen—and paused—and put it down on the most *illogical* square of all—a square from which the queen could easily be captured by any one of three hostile pieces. Marshall had done the unthinkable! He had sacrificed his queen, a move typically made only under the most desperate of circumstances. All of the spectators—even Marshall's opponent—groaned in dismay. Then the Russian—and finally the crowd—realized that Marshall's move was, in reality, a brilliant one. No matter how the Russian opponent took the queen, he would eventually be in a losing position. Seeing the inevitable outcome, the Russian conceded the game. Marshall had won the match in a rare and daring fashion: He had won by sacrificing his queen![20]

What lesson does this story hold for entrepreneurs? By suspending conventional thinking long enough to even consider the possibility of such a move, Marshall was able to throw off the usual assumptions constraining most chess players. He had looked beyond the traditional and orthodox strategies of the game and was willing to take the risk of trying an unusual tactic to win. The result: He won. Although not every creative business opportunity that entrepreneurs take will be successful, many who, like Frank Marshall, are willing to go beyond conventional wisdom will be rewarded for their efforts. Successful entrepreneurs, those who are constantly pushing technological and economic boundaries forward, constantly ask, "Is it time to sacrifice the queen?"

Merely generating one successful creative solution to address a problem or a need usually is not good enough to keep an entrepreneurial enterprise successful in the long run, however. Success—even survival—in the modern world of business requires entrepreneurs to tap their

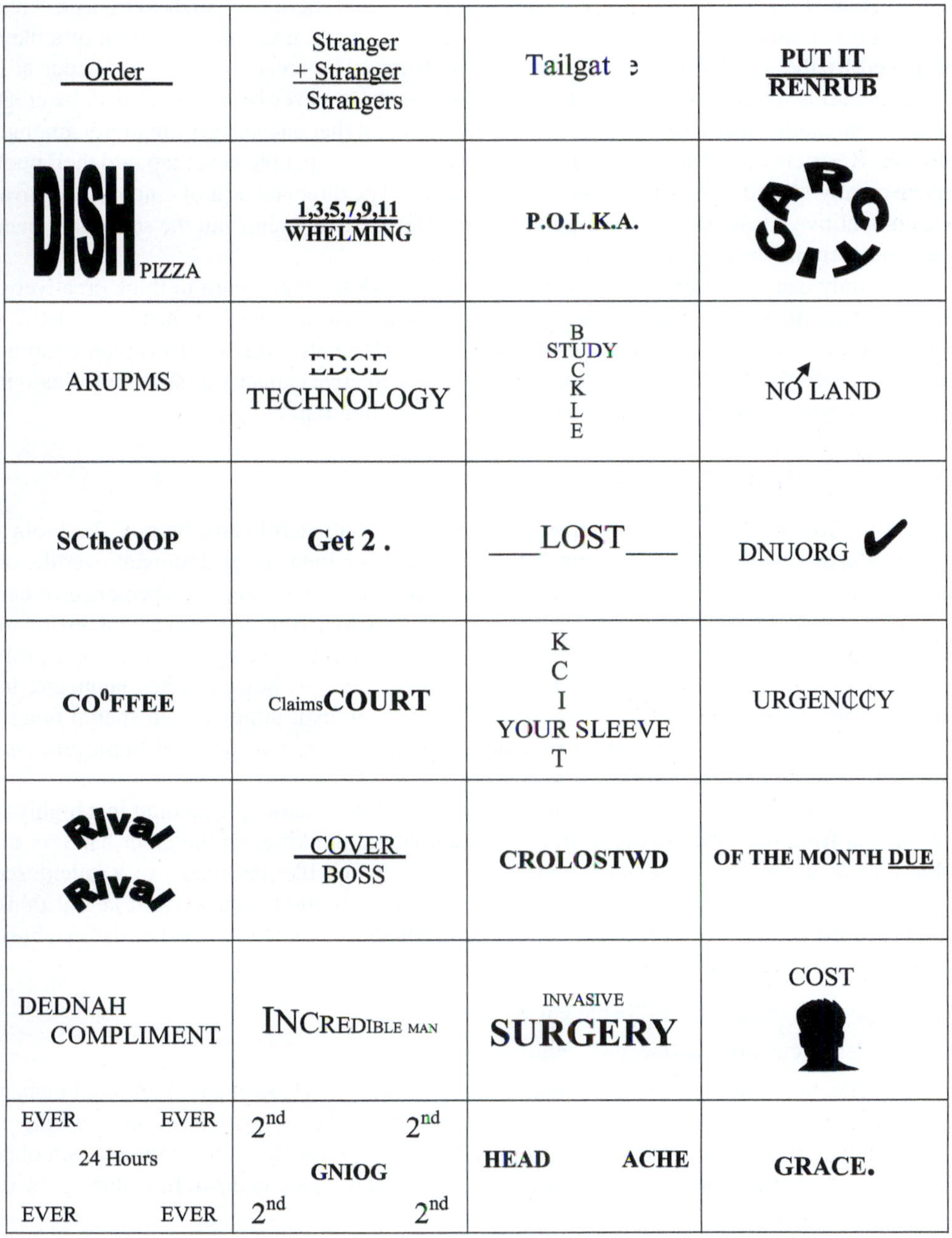

**FIGURE 3.1**

**"How Creative Are You?"**

| Order | Stranger + Stranger Strangers | Tailgat e | PUT IT / RENRUB |
|---|---|---|---|
| **DISH** PIZZA | 1,3,5,7,9,11 / WHELMING | P.O.L.K.A. | GARCITY |
| ARUPMS | EDGE TECHNOLOGY | B STUDY C K L E | NO LAND |
| SCtheOOP | Get 2 . | ___LOST___ | DNUORG ✔ |
| CO⁰FFEE | Claims**COURT** | K C I T YOUR SLEEVE | URGEN℃℃Y |
| Rival Rival | COVER / BOSS | CROLOSTWD | OF THE MONTH DUE |
| DEDNAH COMPLIMENT | INCREDIBLE MAN | INVASIVE **SURGERY** | COST |
| EVER    EVER / 24 Hours / EVER    EVER | 2ⁿᵈ      2ⁿᵈ / GNIOG / 2ⁿᵈ      2ⁿᵈ | HEAD      ACHE | GRACE. |

creativity (and that of their employees) constantly. Entrepreneurs can be sure that if they have developed a unique, creative solution to solve a problem or to fill a need, a competitor (perhaps one six times zones away) is hard at work developing an even more creative solution to render theirs obsolete. This rapid and accelerating rate of change has created an environment in which staying in a leadership position requires constant creativity, innovation, and entrepreneurship. A company that has achieved a leadership position in an industry but then stands still creatively is soon toppled from its number one perch. The entrepreneur's job is to keep the company focused on the future. Jay Walker, founder of *Priceline.com*, suggests that entrepreneurs constantly ask, "What might my customers want tomorrow? What might my customers want in six months, a year, two years, that they don't want today?"[21] As valuable as customer feedback is, merely soliciting it is not likely to produce disruptive innovation; that usually requires a company whose culture and employees are focused on developing new products, services, and business models.

### Can Creativity Be Taught?

Because creativity appears to be almost magical, conventional wisdom held that a person was either creative—imaginative, free-spirited, entrepreneurial—or not—logical, narrow-minded, rigid. Today, we know better. "Creativity is not magic, and there's no such thing as a 'creative type,'" says creativity expert Jonah Lehrer. "Creativity is not a trait that we inherit or a blessing bestowed by the angels. It is a skill. Anyone can learn to be creative and to get better at it."[22] The problem is that in most organizations, employees have never been expected to be creative. In addition, many businesses fail to foster an environment that encourages creativity among employees. Restricted by their traditional thinking patterns, most people never tap into their pools of innate creativity, and the company becomes stagnant. "The direct benefit of employee innovation is a competitive advantage," says creativity expert David Silverstein, "but the secondary benefits are greater employee empowerment and satisfaction."

Not only can entrepreneurs and the people who work for them learn to think creatively, but they must for their companies' sake! "Innovation and creativity are not just for artists," says Joyce Wycoff, author of several books on creativity. "These are skills with a direct, bottom-line payoff."[23] Before entrepreneurs can draw on their own creative capacity or stimulate creativity in their own organizations, they must understand creative thinking.

### Creative Thinking

**3.**

Understand how the two hemispheres of the human brain function and what role they play in creativity.

Research into the operation of the human brain shows that each hemisphere of the brain processes information differently and that one side of the brain tends to be dominant over the other. The human brain develops asymmetrically, and each hemisphere tends to specialize in certain functions. The left brain is guided by linear, vertical thinking (from one logical conclusion to the next), whereas the right brain relies on kaleidoscopic, lateral thinking (considering a problem from all sides and jumping into it at different points). The left brain handles language, logic, and symbols; the right brain takes care of the body's emotional, intuitive, and spatial functions. The left brain processes information in a step-by-step fashion, but the right brain processes it intuitively—all at once, relying heavily on images.

Left-brain vertical thinking is narrowly focused and systematic, proceeding in a highly logical fashion from one point to the next. Right-brain lateral thinking, on the other hand, is somewhat unconventional, unsystematic, and unstructured, much like the image of a kaleidoscope, whirling around to form one pattern after another. It is this right-brain-driven, lateral thinking that lies at the heart of the creative process. Those who have learned to develop their right-brain thinking skills tend to do the following:

- Always ask the question, "Is there a better way?"
- Challenge custom, routine, and tradition.
- Be reflective, often staring out windows, deep in thought. (How many traditional managers would stifle creativity by snapping these people out of their "daydreams," chastise them for "loafing," and admonish them to "get back to work?") Great ideas need time to percolate, and smart entrepreneurs give employees (and themselves) some down time during the day to think and reflect.
- Be prolific thinkers. They know that generating lots of ideas increases the likelihood of coming up with a few highly creative ideas. Nobel laureate Paul Berg, recalling his friend

Francis Crick, who also won a Nobel Prize as codiscoverer of the structure of DNA, says, "He had 10 ideas for every one that was truly brilliant."[24]

- Play mental games, trying to see an issue from different perspectives.
- Realize that there may be more than one "right answer."
- See mistakes as mere "pit stops" on the way to success.
- See problems as springboards for new ideas. While Cristy Clarke was on her way to a holiday party, she began to think of questions to serve as starters for meaningful, interesting conversations because she did not want to endure yet another dull evening of meaningless small talk. Her experiment was a success, and the next morning Clarke began developing the questions that would become part of the successful party game TableTopics, which Clarke markets along with 29 other products through her company, Ruby Mine Inc.[25]
- Understand that failure is a natural part of the creative process. James Dyson spent 15 years and nearly his entire savings before he succeeded in developing the bagless vacuum cleaner that made him rich and famous. "If you want to discover something that other people haven't," he says, "you need to do things the wrong way. You don't learn from success."[26]
- Have "helicopter skills," the ability to rise above the daily routine to see an issue from a broader perspective and then swoop back down to focus on an area in need of change.
- Relate seemingly unrelated ideas to a problem to generate innovative solutions.

**ENTREPRENEURIAL PROFILE Charles Kaman: Kaman Aircraft Company and Ovation Instruments** After graduating from college, Charles Kaman worked in the helicopter division of United Aircraft Corporation, where he helped to design helicopters for the military. Using a homemade calculator he called the Aeronalyzer, Kaman developed several innovations in rotor and wing designs, in none of which his employer showed any interest. In 1945, with $2,000 and his idea for a new dual rotor system that made helicopters more stable and safer to fly, 26-year-old Kaman, also an accomplished guitarist, turned down an offer to join Tommy Dorsey's famous swing band and decided to pursue his innovative designs for helicopters and start the Kaman Aircraft Company in his mother's garage. Over the next 50 years, Kaman built his company into a billion-dollar aviation business, creating many important innovations along the way, including turbine engines; blades made of lightweight, sturdy composite materials; and remote-controlled helicopters. Kaman also maintained an avid interest in guitars and in 1964 began working with a small team of aerospace engineers to build a better acoustic guitar. Drawing on their experience of removing vibrations from helicopters, the team reverse-engineered a guitar with a bowl-shaped body made of composite materials that incorporated more vibration into the instrument, giving it a bolder, richer sound. "In helicopters, engineers spend all of their time trying to figure out how to remove vibration," Kaman said. "To build a guitar, you spend your time trying to figure out how to put vibration in." Kaman founded Ovation Instruments in 1966 and began selling the Balladeer, an acoustical guitar that immediately attracted attention for its superior tone and volume among musicians, including famous artists such as John Lennon, Glen Campbell, Bob Marley, Carly Simon, Jimmy Page, and Melissa Etheridge.[27]

## In the Entrepreneurial Spotlight

# The Ingredients of Creativity

According to creativity expert Tina Seelig, a person must have three factors to be creative:

1. Imagination, the ability to allow your mind to come up with innovative ideas.
2. A knowledge base that allows you to understand a problem or situation and that serves as a base from which you can generate unique solutions. Seelig calls knowledge the "toolbox for your imagination."
3. The motivation and drive to solve the problem "because getting beyond the obvious answers requires a tremendous amount of energy."

Sometimes creative solutions arise as a result of solving a simple problem. Christoph Rochna's girlfriend wanted to shop a local flea market for mismatched chairs to go with the new dining room table and decorations that she had purchased from Ikea. Knowing that finding just the right chairs could take months,

*(continued)*

# In the Entrepreneurial Spotlight *(continued)*

Rochna took the corrugated cardboard packaging from their purchases and fashioned temporary chairs, which his girlfriend loved. "The chairs lasted for six months," says Rochna, "which got me thinking, 'If this crudely constructed furniture could last this long, it's something we should pursue.'" Rochna invited two friends, Mario Bauer and Benjamin Kwitek, to form a business to produce biodegradable furniture made from a patented composite of paper, viscose fabric, and biopolymer. With $200,000 in seed capital, the three entrepreneurs launched Papernomad and achieved immediate success selling their biodegradable furniture to companies for use at outdoor festivals and to consumers who wanted inexpensive outdoor furniture.

A year later, Rochna came up with a new product idea: protective sleeves and covers for electronic devices, such as tablet computers and smart phones. He realized that existing sleeves and covers were made of plastic and neoprene, materials that will outlast the devices they protect and will most likely end up in a landfill for several thousands of years. "It seemed sensible to create sleeves that lasted just as long as the device that lives in them," says Rochna. Papernomad's protective sleeves were a hit with consumers and won the prestigious red dot award for product design. Their success led Rochna and his team to drop their line of biodegradable furniture and focus solely on manufacturing protective sleeves and covers for electronic devices. Customers appreciate the environmentally friendly products, which sell for between €26 and €58, and the fact that they can customize their sleeves and covers simply by drawing any design they want on them.

Serendipity, stumbling onto a creative solution by chance, also plays a role in creativity. Steve Cox was the owner of Green Foam Blanks, a company that manufactured surfboard blanks, the core of every surfboard that is made from recycled polyurethane foam. Cutting the blanks and shaping surfboards from them creates mountains of "shaper dust," which many surfboard makers reluctantly dumped in landfills. "We'd been trying to figure out ways to get rid of this stuff without putting it in the landfill," says Jerry O'Keefe, owner of Soul Stix Surfboards, in San Clemente, California.

One day, after a machine in Cox's factory leaked two quarts of hydraulic fluid, Cox grabbed a handful of shaper dust and threw it on the spill. To his amazement, the dust soaked up the spill in seconds. Cox realized that he was on to something and decided to conduct another test. "I got some old oil from a mechanic's shop and went to a stagnant pond I knew and put in a quart," he recalls. "I threw the [shaper dust] on it, and it bonded immediately. I was able to scoop it out, and it left the water perfectly clear." The material's secret, Cox learned, lies in its cell structure, which resembles a honeycomb. The cells attract liquids but do not allow them to penetrate, characteristics that allow the dust to soak up spills, including those on water but without sinking as other absorbent materials do.

Cox abandoned his surfboard blank-making business and teamed up with Tom and T. J. Rossi and Daniel Fitzgerald to start a company, Monarch Green, to refine the shaper dust into a commercial product, Spillinex, a process that took the better part of a year. Monarch Green changed Spillinex's name to Incredisorb, which it sells for $1.99 per pound to companies for cleaning up oil and chemical spills, a $1-billion-per-year industry (compared to just $160 million in surfboard manufacturing). Studies show that Incredisorb can absorb 638 percent of its own weight in motor oil. Cox and his team also have developed Oilinator, mats covered with an absorbent shell and filled with Incredisorb. With 10 million to 25 million gallons of oil spilled in the United States annually, Monarch Green has a bright future.

Entrepreneurs can encourage creativity in their organizations by providing certain external factors, such as a culture that supports creativity, a work space that encourages creativity, the resources necessary for creativity, an attitude that expects and tolerates failure, and many others. To send a clear signal that creative ideas sometimes fail, every quarter Tor Myhren, a top manager at Grey New York, an advertising agency, gives one employee the "Heroic Failure" award, a garish two-foot-tall trophy that recognizes bold, brilliant ideas that do not always pan out. "How companies deal with failure is a very big part of innovation," observes Judy Estrin, a serial entrepreneur and innovation expert. The Heroic Failure award lets employees know that Grey New York values creativity and that they will not be punished for trying creative solutions that fail. "The most successful people tend to be those with the most failures," says Keith Simonton, an expert on creativity.

1. The three factors that Tina Seelig identifies as essential to creativity are internal factors that an individual must possess. List and describe five external factors that businesses can provide to encourage their employees' creativity.

2. Use a search engine to find an example of an entrepreneur who, like Christoph Rochna and Steve Cox, used their creative ability to develop a business idea. Write a brief summary of the entrepreneur's process.

*Sources:* Based on Suzanne Todd Woody, "Wipe Up," *Forbes*, October 24, 2011, pp. 70–72; Jodi Helmer, "Looks Good on Paper," *Entrepreneur*, October 2012, p. 96; Sue Shellenbarger, "Better Ideas Through Failure," *Wall Street Journal*, September 27, 2011, pp. D1, D4; Drake Baer, "A Crash Course in Creative Breakthroughs," *Fast Company*, April 18, 2012, www.fastcompany.com/1834454/crash-course-creative-breakthroughs.

Although each hemisphere of the brain tends to dominate in its particular functions, the two halves normally cooperate, with each part contributing its special abilities to accomplish those tasks best suited to its mode of information processing. Sometimes, however, the two hemispheres may even compete with each other, or one half may choose not to participate. Some researchers have suggested that each half of the brain has the capacity to keep information from the other! The result, literally, is that "the left hand doesn't know what the right hand is doing." Perhaps the most important characteristic of this split-brain phenomenon is that an individual can learn to control which side of the brain is dominant in a given situation. In other words, a person can learn to "turn down" the dominant left hemisphere (focusing on logic and linear thinking) and "turn up" the right hemisphere (focusing on intuition and unstructured thinking) when a situation requiring creativity arises.[28] With practice, a person can learn to control this mental shift, tapping the pool of creativity that lies hidden within the right side of the brain. This ability has tremendous power to unleash the creative capacity of entrepreneurs. The need to develop this creative ability means that exploring inner space (the space within our brains)—not outer space—becomes the challenge of the century.

Successful entrepreneurship requires both left- and right-brain thinking. Right-brain thinking draws on the power of divergent reasoning, which is the ability to create a multitude of original, diverse ideas. Left-brain thinking counts on convergent reasoning, the ability to evaluate multiple ideas and choose the best solution to a given problem. Entrepreneurs need to rely on right-brain thinking to generate innovative product, service, or business ideas. Then they must use left-brain thinking to judge the market potential of the ideas they generate. Successful entrepreneurs have learned to coordinate the complementary functions of each hemisphere of the brain, using their brains' full creative power to produce pragmatic innovation. Otherwise, entrepreneurs, who rarely can be accused of being "halfhearted" about their business ideas, run the risk of becoming "half-headed."

How can entrepreneurs learn to tap their innate creativity more readily? The first step is to break down the barriers to creativity that most of us have erected over the years. We now turn our attention to these barriers and some suggested techniques for tearing them down.

## Barriers to Creativity

The number of potential barriers to creativity is virtually limitless—time pressures, unsupportive management, pessimistic coworkers, overly rigid company policies, and countless others. Perhaps the most difficult hurdles to overcome, however, are those that individuals impose on themselves. In his book *A Whack on the Side of the Head*, Roger von Oech identifies 10 "mental locks" that limit individual creativity:[29]

**4.** _____
Explain the 10 "mental locks" that limit individual creativity.

**1.** *Searching for the one "right" answer.* Recent research by Kyung Hee Kim, a professor at the College of William and Mary, shows that creativity (as measured by the Torrance Test of Creative Thinking) among both children and adults in the United States has declined markedly since 1990. The decline, which Kim says is "very significant," is particularly acute among the youngest segment of the population, children from kindergarten to sixth grade.[30] "Children have become less emotionally expressive, less energetic, less talkative and verbally expressive, less humorous, less imaginative, less unconventional, less lively and passionate, less perceptive, less apt to connect seemingly irrelevant things, less synthesizing, and less likely to see things from a different angle," she says.[31] Part of the problem is that deeply ingrained in most educational systems is the assumption that there is one "right" answer to a problem. In reality, however, most problems are ambiguous. The average student who has completed four years of college has taken more than 2,600 tests; therefore, it is not unusual for this one-correct-answer syndrome to become an inherent part of our thinking. "Schools are educating creativity and innovation out of children," says Matt Goldman, a cofounder of the Blue Man Group, which recently started Blue School, a pre-K and elementary school that focuses on developing creativity in its students. Depending on the questions one asks, there may be (and usually are) several "right" answers.

**ENTREPRENEURIAL PROFILE: Ben Vigoda and David Reynolds: Lyric Semiconductor** From their earliest days, computers have processed information using the binary code, a system that uses only zeroes and ones. However, Ben Vigoda and David Reynolds, the cofounders of Lyric Semiconductor, a small company based in Cambridge, Massachusetts, realized that there might be other ways for computers to process information. They have developed a semiconductor chip (the "brain" of any computer) that also uses values between zero and one, an advancement that has the potential to revolutionize computing. Lyric's probability processing technology not only dramatically increases the speed with which a computer works, ranging from faster Google searches to speedier analysis of the human genome, but also reduces the size of computers because fewer chips are needed to process a given amount of data. "We are changing something that's been true for 50 or 60 years," says Vigoda. Lyric's creative technology holds so much potential that venture capital firms and the U.S. Department of Defense have invested $20 million in the company, which recently was named one of the world's most innovative companies by *Technology Review* magazine.[32]

**2.** *Focusing on "being logical."* Logic is a valuable part of the creative process, especially when evaluating ideas and implementing them. However, in the early imaginative phases of the process, logical thinking can restrict creativity. Focusing too much effort on being logical also discourages the use of one of the mind's most powerful creations: intuition. Von Oech advises us to "think something different" and to use nonlogical thinking freely, especially in the imaginative phase of the creative process. Intuition, which is based on the accumulated knowledge and experiences a person encounters over the course of a lifetime and resides in the subconscious, can be unlocked. It is a crucial part of the creative process because using it often requires one to tear down long-standing assumptions that limit creativity and innovation.

**ENTREPRENEURIAL PROFILE: Jae Lee: Georgia Chopsticks** When Jae Lee learned that China cannot harvest enough domestic wood to produce the billions of pairs of disposable chopsticks used there each year, the Americus, Georgia, resident launched Georgia Chopsticks, the only chopsticks manufacturer in the United States. His company uses the ample supply of local poplar to produce and export to China 80 million pairs of chopsticks annually—at a price that is 20 percent lower than Chinese-manufactured chopsticks. Lee recently expanded Georgia Chopsticks's product line to include toothpicks and tongue depressors, both of which he makes from the wood scraps that are left over from chopstick production.[33]

**3.** *Blindly following the rules.* We learn at a very early age not to "color outside the lines," and we spend the rest of our lives blindly obeying such rules. Sometimes, creativity depends on our ability to break the existing rules so that we can see new ways of doing things. Consider, for example, the top row of letters on a standard keyboard:

QWERTYUIOP

In the 1870s, Sholes & Company, a leading manufacturer of typewriters, began receiving numerous customer complaints about its typewriter keys sticking together when typists' fingers were practiced enough to go really fast. Company engineers came up with an incredibly creative solution to eliminate the problem of sticking keys. They designed a *less* efficient keyboard configuration, placing the letters O and I (the fourth and fifth most commonly used letters of the alphabet) so that the weaker middle and ring fingers would strike them. By slowing down typists with this inefficient keyboard, the engineers solved the sticking keys problem. Today, despite the fact that computer technology has eliminated all danger of sticking keys, this same inefficient keyboard configuration remains the industry standard!

**4.** *Constantly being practical.* Imagining impractical answers to "what if" questions can be powerful stepping-stones to creative ideas. Suspending practicality for a while frees the mind to consider creative solutions that otherwise might never arise. Whenever Thomas Edison hired an assistant to work in his creative laboratory, he would tell the new employee, "Walk through town and list 20 things that interest you." When the worker returned, Edison would ask him to split the list into two columns. Then he would say, "Randomly combine objects from column A and column B and come up with as many inventions as you can." Edison's methods for stimulating creativity in his lab proved to be successful; he holds the distinction of being the only person to have earned a patent every year for 65 consecutive years![34]

Periodically setting aside practicality allows entrepreneurs to consider taking a product or a concept from one area and placing it in a totally different application.

**ENTREPRENEURIAL PROFILE: Michelle Marciniak and Susan Walvius: Sheex** Former collegiate basketball coaches Michelle Marciniak and Susan Walvius enjoyed the moisture-wicking properties of the high-performance athletic clothing that they and their athletes wore. After a workout one day, Walvius said, "I'd love to have bed sheets made out of this stuff," and a business idea was born. That year, the entrepreneurs worked with students at the University of South Carolina's Moore School of Business to conduct a feasibility study and to create a business plan. "We learned that the big issue most people have that disrupts their sleep is being too warm," says Walvius. Within a year, the budding entrepreneurs gave up their coaching jobs to focus on launching Sheex. Sheex, which are made from microfiber polyester and spandex, are designed to transfer body heat twice as effectively as traditional sheets, breathe 50 percent better than cotton, and wick away moisture to keep sleepers dry. Marciniak and Walvius sell Sheex through several national retail chains, including

Bed, Bath, & Beyond, Brookstone, and Sleep Number, and their company now generates $240 million in annual sales.[35]

**5.** *Viewing laughter and play as frivolous.* A playful attitude is fundamental to creative thinking. There is a close relationship between the "haha" of humor and the "aha" of discovery. Laughter tends to help people relax, which in turn allows them to be more creative. Researchers have discovered that exposing people to short video clips of stand-up comedy or humorous comedy scenes increases their creativity.[36]

Play gives us the opportunity to reinvent reality and to rethink established ways of doing things. Play also stimulates the left side of the brain, which is responsible for creativity. Play at work causes people to remove idea filters that can be barriers to creativity and sends a signal to employees that they "work in a permissive and playful environment," says Tim Brown, CEO of global design company IDEO. "We need to be able to trust to play and be creative."[37] Children learn when they play, and so can entrepreneurs. Watch children playing, and you will see them invent new games, create new ways of looking at old things, and learn what works (and what doesn't) in their games. Entrepreneurs can benefit from playing in the same way that children do. They, too, can learn to try new approaches and discover what works and what doesn't. Creativity results when entrepreneurs take what they have learned at play, evaluate it, corroborate it with other knowledge, and put it into practice. Encourage employees to have fun when solving problems; they are more likely to push the boundaries and come up with a genuinely creative solution if they do. What kind of invention would Wile E. Coyote, who seems to have an inexhaustible supply of ideas for catching Roadrunner in those cartoons, create in this situation? How might the Three Stooges approach this problem? What would Seinfeld's Kramer suggest? What would a six-year-old do? The idea is to look at a problem or situation from different perspectives.

**ENTREPRENEURIAL PROFILE: Kim Vandenbroucke: Brainy Chick** For Kim Vandenbroucke, owner of Brainy Chick and a game inventor with a track record of hits such as Cranium Party Playoff, Barbie Mini Kingdom, and Scattergories Categories (part of which she came up with on her honeymoon), playing is an important part of the creative process. Vandenbroucke, who says she grew up in a household of game players, says she still plays at least one game a day, often drawing on the experience for inspiration. Although she keeps many sources of creative inspiration near her desk, one of her favorites is a copy of *Meet Mr. Product,* a book that features classic characters from the world of advertising. It's "a great place to get ideas," she says. "I love old advertising characters—the styles, the names, the nostalgia." Vandenbroucke also carries a small notebook in which she writes down game ideas, "seeds," she calls them, as they come to her.[38]

**6.** *Becoming overly specialized.* A common killer of creativity is **myopic thinking,** which is narrowly focused and limited by the status quo. Because experts are so immersed in what they know, they often are victims of myopic thinking. That's why creative companies include *nonexperts* in creative problem solving or idea generation sessions; they are free to ask questions and offer ideas that challenge the status quo and traditional solutions that experts "know" cannot work but often do. "The real disruptors will be those individuals who are not steeped in one industry of choice but individuals who approach challenges with a clean lens, bringing together diverse experiences, knowledge, and opportunities," says serial entrepreneur and philanthropist Naveen Jain.[39]

Creative thinkers tend to be "explorers," searching for ideas outside of their areas of specialty. The idea for the roll-on deodorant stick came from the ballpoint pen. The famous Mr. Potato Head toy was invented by a father sitting with his family at the dinner table who noted how much fun his children had playing with their food. Velcro was invented by a man who, while hiking one day to take a break from work, had to stop to peel sticky cockleburs from his clothing. As he picked them off, he noticed how their hooked spines caught on and held tightly to the cloth. When he resumed his hike, he began to think about the possibilities of using a similar design to fasten objects together. Thus was born Velcro!

**ENTREPRENEURIAL PROFILE: Jessica Smith: Casttoo** When Jessica Smith tried to jump a curb on her bicycle, she ended up with a broken wrist. The 21-year-old art student painted a beautiful floral design on her cast, and when she returned to the doctor to have it removed, "he said that if someone would produce art like that for casts, he'd buy them," she recalls. The comment inspired Smith, who transformed her artwork into the first generation of Casttoos, a special adhesive

## Lessons from the Street-Smart Entrepreneur *(continued)*

9. Can you combine ideas?

10. Are customers using your product or service in ways you never expected or intended?

11. Which customers are you not serving? What changes to your product or service are necessary to reach them?

12. Can you put it to other uses?

13. What else could we make from this?

14. Are there other markets for it?

15. Can you reverse it?

16. Can you rearrange it?

17. Can you put it to another use?

18. What idea seems impossible but, if executed would revolutionize your business?

When Chester Carlson was a boy, he was fascinated by chemistry and graphic arts, two distinct disciplines that he would later combine to create a popular invention. After graduating from the California Institute of Technology with a degree in physics, Carlson earned a law degree from New York Law School and became the head of the patent department for P.R. Mallory and Company, an electronics company in New York City. While studying law and working at Mallory, Carlson was frustrated by having to make handwritten copies of the information he needed from law books and patent applications and decided to create a machine that could make copies of documents. Rather than utilize the well-researched field of traditional photography as the foundation for his work, Carlson decided to use an emerging technology

called photoconductivity as the basis for his device. His research led him to conduct rudimentary experiments in the kitchen of his apartment in Jackson Heights, Queens, and in September 1938, Carlson filed his first patent for xerography, a process that used electrophotography and chemistry, to create images of documents. From 1939 to 1944, Carlson pitched his invention to more than 20 companies, but every one of them rejected it. Finally, the Battelle Memorial Institute signed a royalty-sharing agreement with Carlson and by 1947 had entered into a contract with a small company called Haloid (which would later change its name to Xerox) to develop the machine. It wasn't until 1959 that Xerox unveiled the first convenient office copier that could produce copies on plain paper with the touch of a single button. Carlson's invention, the photocopier, became the foundation of a huge global industry—all because he asked, "Can you combine ideas?"

*Sources:* Based on "How to Come Up with a Great Idea," *Wall Street Journal,* April 29, 2013, p. R1; "Chester F. Carlson," *The Great Idea Finder,* www.ideafinder.com/history/inventors/carlson.htm; "Timeline: The ATM's History," International Merchant Services, www.atm24.com/newssection/industry%20news/timeline%20-%20the%20atm%20history.aspx; Mary Bellis, "The ATM Machine of Don Wetzel," *About,* http://inventors.about.com/od/astartinventions/a/atm_3.htm; Chuck Frey, "How to Develop a Powerful Arsenal of Creative Questions," *Innovation Tools,* March 1, 2011, www.innovationtools.com/weblog/innovationblog-detail.asp?ArticleID=1570; David Lidsky, "Brain Calisthenics," *Fast Company,* December 2004, p. 95; Thea Singer, Christopher Caggiano, Ilan Mochari, and Tahl Raz, "If You Come, They Will Build It," *Inc.,* August 2002, p. 70; Creativity Web, "Question Summary," www.ozemail.com/au/~caveman/Creative/Techniques/osb_quest.html; *Bits & Pieces,* February 1990, p. 20; *Bits & Pieces,* April 29, 1993, "Creativity Quiz," *In Business,* November/December 1991, p. 18; Doug Hall, *Jump Start Your Brain,* (New York: Warner Books, 1995), pp. 86–87; Christine Canabou, "Imagine That," *Fast Company,* January 2001, p. 56; Steve Gillman, "Step Out of Business Mode to Solve Problems," *Regan's Manager's eBulletin,* May 22, 2008, p. 1; Tim McKeough, " The Shape-Shifting Car," *Fast Company,* November 2008, p. 84.

## How to Enhance Creativity

### Enhancing Organizational Creativity

**5.**
_____

Understand how entrepreneurs can enhance the creativity of their employees as well as their own creativity.

Creativity doesn't just happen in organizations; entrepreneurs must establish an environment in which creativity can flourish—for themselves and for their workers. "Everyone has a creative spark, but many factors can inhibit its ignition," says one writer. "Part of an [entrepreneur's] role is to see the spark in his or her people, encourage its ignition, and champion its success."[46] New ideas are fragile creations, but the right company culture can encourage people to develop and cultivate them. Ensuring that workers have the freedom and the incentive to be creative is one of the best ways to achieve innovation. Entrepreneurs can stimulate their own creativity and encourage it among workers by following the suggestions outlined in the following section; these suggestions are designed to create a culture of innovation.

**INCLUDE CREATIVITY AS A CORE COMPANY VALUE AND MAKE IT AN INTEGRAL PART OF THE COMPANY'S CULTURE** Innovative companies do not take a passive approach to creativity; they are proactive in their search for new ideas. One of the best ways to set a creative tone throughout an organization begins with the company's mission statement. Entrepreneurs should incorporate creativity and innovation into their companies' mission statements and affirm their commitment to them in internal communications. Innovation allows a company to shape, transform, and direct its future, and the natural place to define that future is in the mission statement. If creativity and innovation are vital to a company's success (and they are!), they also should be a natural part of its culture. "Innovation occurs only if it's an attitude that runs through a company's culture," says one expert on innovation.[47] Integrating an attitude of innovation into a company's culture is much easier in small companies than in large ones.

Innovation can be a particularly powerful competitive weapon in industries that are resistant to change and are populated by companies that cling to the same old ways of doing business.

Even small companies that are willing to innovate can have a significant impact on entire industries by shaking up the status quo with their creative approaches. The result often is growing market share and impressive profits for the innovator.

**HIRE FOR CREATIVITY** Research published in the *Sloan Management Review* concludes that the most effective way for companies to achieve continuous innovation over the long term is by hiring and cultivating talented people.[48] Often the most creative people also tend to be somewhat different, even eccentric. Two researchers call these employees "the odd clever people every organization needs" because they use their creativity to create disproportionate amounts of value for their companies.[49]

**EMBRACE DIVERSITY** One of the best ways to cultivate a culture of creativity is to hire a diverse workforce. When people solve problems or come up with ideas, they do so within the framework of their own experience. Hiring people from different backgrounds with different cultural experiences, hobbies, and interests provides a company with a crucial raw material needed for creativity. Smart entrepreneurs hire capable people of diverse backgrounds, different personalities, and varied work experience, confident that this eclectic mix of people will produce creative results for their businesses.

Focusing the talent and creativity of a diverse group of employees on a problem or challenge is one of the best ways to generate creative solutions. Research by Harvard Business School professor Karim Lakhani concludes that the experiences, viewpoints, and thought processes of diverse groups of people are powerful tools for solving problems creatively. "It's very counterintuitive," says Lakhani, "but not only did the odds of a [problem] solver's success actually increase in fields outside his expertise, but also the further a challenge was from his specialty, the greater was the likelihood of success."[50] The lesson for entrepreneurs: To increase the odds of a successful creative solution to a problem, involve in the process people whose background and experience lies *outside* of the particular problem area. One manager says, "They create a little grit to stimulate the oyster to produce a pearl."[51]

**ESTABLISH AN ORGANIZATIONAL STRUCTURE THAT NOURISHES CREATIVITY** John Kao, an economist whose nickname is "Mr. Creativity," says that innovative companies are structured like spaghetti rather than a traditional pyramid. In a spaghetti-style organization, employees are encouraged to mix and mingle constantly so that creative ideas flow freely throughout the company.[52] At innovative companies, managers create organizational structures and cultures that emphasize the importance of creativity. Managers at Dunkin' Donuts, with 9,235 coffee and donut outlets worldwide, recognize that innovation is the key to the 60-year-old company's success. A few years ago, they created the Dunkin' Brands Innovation Team, a group of 18 bakery specialists, and assigned them the task of developing new products for the company's menu. Although many product ideas never make it out of the test kitchen, the Innovation Team launches about 20 new product ideas each year. One of its most successful additions was the bagel twist, which took the team 10 months to perfect and comes in a variety of flavors.[53]

**EXPECT CREATIVITY** Employees tend to rise—or fall—to the level of expectations entrepreneurs have of them. One of the best ways to communicate the expectation of creativity is to encourage them to be creative.

**ENTREPRENEURIAL PROFILE: West Paw Design** West Paw Design, a company based in Bozeman, Montana, that produces eco-friendly pet toys, sponsors a creativity contest in which its 36 employees, from president to seamstresses, form small teams to develop prototypes of new product ideas. The winning team receives the coveted Golden Hairball Award, a statue reminiscent of the Oscar but with one of the company's cat toys perched atop its head. Employees develop ideas and sketches, scrounge through bins of discarded materials, and assemble prototypes in less than two hours. The entire staff votes on a winner by secret ballot, and in addition to the Golden Hairball Award, the winning team members receive $100 gift cards. The winning team in a recent contest was comprised of a sales representative, a seamstress, and a shipping department worker. Their idea: the Eco Bed, a stuffed dog bed made completely from recycled materials. West Paw included the bed in its product line, and it became an instant hit among customers.[54]

**EXPECT FAILURE AND LEARN FROM IT** Creative ideas produce failures as well as successes. People who never fail are not being creative. Creativity requires taking chances, and managers must remove employees' fear of failure. The surest way to quash creativity throughout an organization is to punish employees who try something new and fail. Failure is a natural part of the creative process; therefore, entrepreneurs must give employees the freedom to fail early and often by encouraging them to test their new ideas against the lens of reality. The key is not to attempt to avoid failures (which are inevitable) but to learn from them. Inspired by Google's well-known 20 percent policy in which employees spend 20 percent of their time working on "pet projects" that they find interesting and believe have potential, National Public Radio (NPR) gives employees two or three days off once a quarter during the company's "Serendipity Days" to team up with people from other departments with whom they normally do not work to come up with creative ideas and projects. One purpose of the sessions is to "work with groups you wouldn't ordinarily work with through the course of your week," says Lars Schmidt, NPR's director of talent acquisition and innovation, whose team recently developed a new social media training program for the NPR staff. The goal is to "tap the creative ideas of the team and create a vehicle for getting small, cool projects and research explored," says one NPR employee. "There are some failures," he admits, which led managers to introduce a special award for these pioneers: the Penguin Award, named to honor the first bird in the flock bold enough to jump off the ice floe, knowing that he risks being eaten by a leopard seal. NPR employees have incorporated several of the ideas spawned at Serendipity Days into the company.[55]

**INCORPORATE FUN INTO THE WORK ENVIRONMENT** Smart entrepreneurs know that work should be fun, and although they expect employees to work hard, they create a company culture that allows employees to have fun. "If you want creative workers, give them enough time to play," says actor John Cleese. At Radio Flyer, the Chicago-based company that makes the classic little red wagon for children, employees routinely participate in fun activities at work that include karaoke, tricycle races, pumpkin-carving contests, a Hollywood Squares game, and others. CEO Robert Pasin intentionally has made fun events a part of the company's culture. "There's method to the madness," says the company's "chief wagon officer," pointing out that the company's success depends on creative employees who are motivated and engaged in their work.[56]

**ENCOURAGE CURIOSITY** Entrepreneurs and their employees constantly should ask "what if" questions and to take a "maybe we could" attitude. Challenging standing assumptions about how something should be done ("We've always done it that way.") is an excellent springboard for creativity. Doing so allows people to break out of assumptions that limit creativity. Supporting employees' extracurricular activities also can spur creativity on the job. For instance, Clay Carley, owner of a real estate development company in Boise, Idaho, recently hired a local dance troupe, Trey McIntyre Project, to help him and his employees brainstorm ideas for creating a new mixed-use project in Old Boise, a historic downtown district. "They've helped us to imagine the space in non-traditional ways," says Carley. Watching the dancers perform and learning about their creative process "pulls our staff out of the same way we do things so that we can design better solutions and solve problems."[57]

Encouraging employees to "think big" also helps. "Incremental innovation is not a winner's game," says creativity expert John Kao. "The opportunity these days is to become a disruptive inventor," striving for major changes that can revolutionize an entire industry and give the company creating it a significant competitive advantage.[58]

**ENTREPRENEURIAL PROFILE: Joshua Silver** In the 1980s, Joshua Silver, an atomic physicist at Oxford University and a lifelong tinkerer, began working to develop adjustable eyeglasses whose focusing power users could change themselves. Over time, Silver created a system of two flexible, transparent membranes with a clear silicone fluid between them. Changing the volume of fluid changes the curvature and the power of the lenses. "I did it because I was curious," says Silver of his invention. The adjustable glasses are ideal for people in developed nations, where only 5 percent of people wear eyeglasses, primarily because they live in rural areas and have no access to eye care professionals or lack the money to afford glasses. Silver's glasses come with plastic syringes filled with silicone fluid; users add or remove fluid by turning a dial that controls a small pump until the focus is right. Then they remove the syringes, and the adjustable glasses are ready to use. "All users have to do is look at a reading chart and adjust the glasses until they can see the letters clearly," says Silver, who hopes to eventually distribute a billion pairs of the glasses. "It's as simple as that."[59]

**DESIGN A WORKSPACE THAT ENCOURAGES CREATIVITY** The physical environment in which people work has an impact on their level of creativity. The cubicles made so famous in the "Dilbert" cartoon strip can suck the creativity right out of a workspace. Transforming a typical office space—even one with cubicles—into a haven of creativity does not have to be difficult or expensive. Covering bland walls with funny posters, photographs, murals, or other artwork; adding splashes of color; and incorporating live plants enliven a work space and enhance creativity. Designs that foster employee interaction, especially informal interaction, enhance an organization's creative power. A study by the Massachusetts Institute of Technology reports that 80 percent of breakthrough innovations in products and services at companies came as a result of informal (sometimes chance) encounters among people. Many leading companies, including Google, Salesforce, and Zappos, have intentionally designed office layouts that encourage interaction among employees—informal employee "collisions." At Google, these informal encounters led to collaborations among employees that resulted in both Gmail and Street View. "We want Googlers to bump into each other and collaborate," says a company spokesperson. At Pixar, Steve Jobs insisted on placing bathrooms in the center of the building so that people working in different parts of the company would encounter one another. Salesforce has installed "lunch button" kiosks that employees can use to find other employees in the company with similar interests with whom to have lunch. Employees also can converse over meals with colleagues in other locations around the world using a "conversation portal," a videoconferencing system set up in the dining area.[60]

**ENTREPRENEURIAL PROFILE: Mark Pincus: Zynga** Mark Pincus, founder of Zynga, a maker of social media games, used Willie Wonka's chocolate factory as the inspiration for the design of the company's headquarters. Zynga offers employees a full-service gym and a health spa that provides free massages and acupuncture, and arcade games are scattered about the building. The office design is light and open, encouraging employees to interact with one another. Meeting rooms are filled with mismatched, retro furniture that lets employees know how important "being different" is to the company's culture. Employees also are free to bring their dogs to work. (After all, Pincus named the company after his beloved American bulldog.)[61]

Zynga's headquarters.
*Source:* Karsten Lemm/Newscom.

Although setting up arcade games may not be not practical for every business, entrepreneurs can still stimulate creativity by starting meetings with some type of short, fun exercise designed to encourage participants to think creatively.

**VIEW PROBLEMS AS OPPORTUNITIES** Every problem offers the opportunity for innovation. One of the best ways to channel a company's innovative energy productively is to address questions that focus employees' attention on customers' problems and how to solve them.

**ENTREPRENEURIAL PROFILE: Lihang Nong: PicoSpray** Lihang Nong, a student at the University of Michigan, participated in a competition that challenged participants make a small engine more fuel efficient and less polluting. Nong learned that small engines, those that power lawn mowers, mopeds, motorcycles, generators, and other products, outnumber automotive engines and that they produce more greenhouse gases than automotive engines, mainly because they rely on older, cheaper carburetors rather than the more efficient electronic fuel injection systems that modern cars and trucks use. Unfortunately, traditional fuel-injected engines cost five times more than engines equipped with carburetors. As a student pursuing a master's degree in mechanical engineering, Nong developed a simple, super-efficient fuel injection system designed that costs one-half to one-third as much as a standard fuel injection system because it eliminates the need for two of the three components traditionally used in fuel-injected engines. Nong's fuel injection system not only produces the same gains in fuel efficiency as traditional systems but also generates far lower levels of greenhouse gases. Nong has filed a patent application for his novel small engine fuel injection system and launched a company, PicoSpray, to produce and market it.[62]

**PROVIDE CREATIVITY TRAINING** Almost everyone has the capacity to be creative, but developing that capacity requires training. One writer claims, "What separates the average person from Edison, Picasso, or even Shakespeare isn't creative capacity—it's the ability to tap that capacity by encouraging creative impulses and then acting upon them."[63] Training accomplished through books, seminars, workshops, and professional meetings can help everyone learn to tap their creative capacity. Research shows that even a single creativity training session can enhance employees' creative ability.[64]

**PROVIDE SUPPORT** Entrepreneurs must give employees the tools and the resources they need to be creative. Entrepreneurs should remember that creativity often requires nonwork phases, and giving employees time to "daydream" is an important part of the creative process. The creativity that employees display when they know that managers value innovation can be amazing— and profitable. These **intrapreneurs**, entrepreneurs who operate within the framework of an existing business, sometimes can transform a company's future or advance its competitive edge. Jim Lynch, an electrical engineer at iRobot, a leading maker of robotic devices including the Roomba vacuum cleaner, was cleaning the gutters on his house one day and thought, "This is the perfect job for a robot because it fits our company's three criteria: dumb, dirty, and dangerous." Lynch began tinkering and built a gutter-cleaning robot using a spaghetti ladle and an electric screwdriver. At the company's "Idea Bake-Off," an event at which employees have 10 minutes to pitch a new product idea, Lynch's idea received solid support and became an official project. Fellow employees volunteered to work on Lynch's team, and within one year, iRobot introduced the Looj, the world's first gutter-cleaning robot![65]

**DEVELOP A PROCEDURE FOR CAPTURING IDEAS**  Small companies that are outstanding innovators do not earn that mantle by accident; they have a process in place to solicit and then collect new ideas. When workers come up with creative ideas, however, not every organization is prepared to capture them. The unfortunate result is that ideas that might have vaulted a company ahead of its competition or made people's lives better simply evaporate. Without a structured approach for collecting employees' creative concepts, a business leaves its future to chance. Clever entrepreneurs establish processes within their companies that are designed to harvest the results of employees' creativity. At Lark Technologies, a Mountain View, California–based consumer electronics company that makes wearable wellness monitors and a vibrating silent alarm clock, most of the walls are made of whiteboards on which employees write out and draw sketches of new product ideas and post problems that they have not been able to solve. Company founder and CEO Julia Hu says that employees constantly add to each other's ideas on the walls, creating an ongoing brainstorming session that has helped the young company expand its product line beyond its original vibrating silent alarm clock that links to an iPhone or iPod and that awakens only the person wearing it to include a diet, exercise, and sleep monitoring and feedback system. *Fast Company* magazine recently named Lark Technologies one of the 10 most innovative consumer electronics companies in the United States.[66]

**TALK WITH CUSTOMERS—OR, BETTER YET, INTERACT WITH THEM**  Innovative companies take the time to get feedback about how customers use the companies' products or services, listening for new ideas. The voice of the customer can be an important source of creative ideas, and the Internet allows entrepreneurs to hear their customers' voices quickly and inexpensively. Some companies engage their customers in social media conversations (or at least read what customers are writing about their products in social media); others observe their customers actually using their products or services to glean ideas that may lead to improvements and new features. Some companies go farther, forging alliances with customers to come up with creative ideas and develop new products based on them.

**ENTREPRENEURIAL PROFILE: Jack Groetzinger and Russ D'Souza: SeatGeek Inc.**  Jack Groetzinger and Russ D'Souza launched SeatGeek Inc. in 2009 in New York City as a service that predicted concert ticket prices, which can fluctuate wildly between the time promoters put them on sale and when the concert actually takes place. As customers signed up for the service, Groetzinger and D'Souza asked users permission to send them periodic e-mail surveys so that the company could get fresh ideas for improved or additional services. In its first questionnaire, which SeatGeek sent to 5,000 customers, the cofounders learned that customers wanted to see prices of available tickets listed in real time. "It really changed the way we thought about what we should do," says Groetzinger. Today, SeatGeek has morphed into the largest event ticket search engine in the world and helps customers find the best deals on tickets for thousands of concerts and sporting events across the United States.[67]

**MONITOR EMERGING TRENDS AND IDENTIFY WAYS YOUR COMPANY CAN CAPITALIZE ON THEM**  Taco Bell, the quick-service chain of Mexican restaurants, invests resources in monitoring demographic and social trends that influence customers' dining habits. Two trends that the company recently identified are the demand for healthier menus and customers' focus on value-priced meals. To capitalize on these trends, Taco Bell introduced a fresher, lighter, and healthier Fresco product line and is developing a "home replacement menu" that offers food in large containers that customers take home to share with their families. The company normally creates about 200 new product ideas each year before winnowing them down to about 20 products to introduce into test markets. Those that succeed in the test markets are rolled out nationwide. "Fail to innovate at your own risk," says Taco Bell's chief marketing officer, David Ovens.[68]

**LOOK FOR USES FOR YOUR COMPANY'S PRODUCTS OR SERVICES IN OTHER MARKETS** Focusing on the "traditional" uses of a product or service limits creativity—and a company's sales. Entrepreneurs can boost sales by finding new applications, often in unexpected places, for their products and services.

**ENTREPRENEURIAL PROFILE: Neil Wadhawan and Raj Raheja: Heartwood Studios** In 2002, Neil Wadhawan and Raj Raheja launched Heartwood Studios, a company that produced 3-D renderings and animations of buildings and products for architects and designers. Their business was successful, but a brainstorming session helped the entrepreneurs to realize that their company's 3-D renderings had applications in other industries as well. Today, Heartwood Studios has clients in the defense and aerospace industries as well as in the fields of entertainment and sports. In fact, the company creates animations for use on the giant screens in sports arenas for the Dallas Cowboys and the New Jersey Nets.[69]

**REWARD CREATIVITY** Entrepreneurs can encourage creativity by rewarding it when it occurs. Financial rewards can be effective motivators of creative behavior, but nonmonetary rewards, such as praise, recognition, and celebration, usually offer more powerful incentives for creativity.

**ENTREPRENEURIAL PROFILE: Mike Tattersfield: Caribou Coffee** At Caribou Coffee, a chain of coffee shops with nearly 500 locations in the United States and abroad, CEO Mike Tattersfield, whose desk doubles as a foosball table, celebrates employees' creative contributions to the company at an awards banquet, where winners receive watermelons as prizes. "You get it for using your melon," explains Tattersfield. The company also awards winners with a pair of custom Converse Chuck Taylor tennis shoes that they themselves design and that Tattersfield inscribes with a personal note of thanks. "All I ask is that they send me a photo of them wearing the sneakers," he says.[70]

**MODEL CREATIVE BEHAVIOR** Creativity is "caught" as much as it is "taught." Companies that excel at innovation find that the passion for creativity starts at the top. Entrepreneurs who set examples of creative behavior, taking chances, and challenging the status quo will soon find their employees doing the same. "Innovative companies are led by innovative chief executives," says creativity expert Hal Gregersen. "They spend their time asking provocative questions, observing the world, and networking with people who don't think, act, or talk like them. They are willing to experiment and try new things. It's the CEO who sets the stage for innovation."

**ENTREPRENEURIAL PROFILE: Jason Fried: 37signals** Jason Fried, cofounder of 37signals, a software company based in Chicago, understands the importance of innovation in the fast-moving software business. Fried worked with his staff recently to create an "end of the road" list of products that they will retire. One of the products marked for elimination, Sortfolio, generates more than $200,000 in annual revenue and significant profits. "What entrepreneur voluntarily parts with a profitable service? Are we crazy?" he asks. Fried decided to retire Sortfolio to free up his staff to work on improving the company's other software products and to give them the time and energy to come up with ideas for new products. Fried also used the same reasoning when he decided that the best way to improve Basecamp, the company's eight-year-old best-selling product, was to rebuild it from scratch. "We have ideas that are more revolutionary than incremental that will dramatically enhance Basecamp's speed, power, and flexibility," he says.[71]

## Enhancing Individual Creativity

Just as entrepreneurs can cultivate an environment of creativity in their organizations by using the techniques described above, they can enhance their own creativity by using the techniques discussed in the following section.

**ALLOW YOURSELF TO BE CREATIVE** As we have seen, one of the biggest obstacles to creativity occurs when a person believes that he or she is not creative. Giving yourself the permission to be creative is the first step toward establishing a pattern of creative thinking. Refuse to give in to the temptation to ignore ideas simply because you fear that someone else may consider them "stupid." When it comes to creativity, there are no stupid ideas!

**FORGET THE "RULES"** Creative individuals take a cue from Captain Jack Sparrow in the *Pirates of the Caribbean* series of movies. When faced with a difficult (sometimes impossible) situation, Sparrow (played by Johnny Depp) usually operates outside the rules and, as a result, comes up with innovative solutions. "[Sparrow] creates new degrees of freedom that enable him to act in ways that someone encumbered by the rules cannot," says one writer. "In that space outside the rules are some pretty interesting solutions."[72]

**GIVE YOUR MIND FRESH INPUT EVERY DAY** To be creative, your mind needs stimulation. Imagination is the fuel that drives creativity. Do something different each day—listen to a new radio station, take a walk through a park or a shopping center, or pick up a magazine you never read—to stimulate your imagination. "You're not going to get innovation if you don't have imagination," says Jay Walker, founder of *Priceline.com*.[73]

**ENTREPRENEURIAL PROFILE: Doris Raymond: The Way We Wore** The Way We Wore, a huge vintage clothing store in Los Angeles started by Doris Raymond in 2004 that stocks garments from the Victorian era to the 1980s, has become a destination for designers from many fashion houses and retailers, ranging from Marc Jacobs to Forever 21, who are looking for inspiration for their clothing collections. Recognizing that meeting customers' demand for fresh designs gives their clothing lines a competitive advantage, many designers are looking to the past for creative ideas, taking note not only of fabrics and patterns but also of the smallest details, such as buttons and the type of stitching used on pockets. These fashion experts have discovered that exposing their minds to "new" designs is a great way to stimulate their own creativity.[74]

**TRAVEL—AND OBSERVE** Visiting other countries (even other states) is a creativity stimulant. Travelers see new concepts and engage in new experiences that can spark creative ideas.

**ENTREPRENEURIAL PROFILE: Johanna Uurasjarvi: Leifsdottir** Johanna Uurasjarvi, creator and designer of the fashion brand Leifsdottir, draws the inspiration for her clothing from her Scandinavian heritage and from her passion for travel. Celebrities including Taylor Swift, Sarah Jessica Parker, and Melissa George often sport Uurasjarvi's fashions, which feature impeccable craftsmanship and unique patterns and sumptuous textures inspired by Uurasjarvi's travels to places as far-flung as Turkey and Brazil. "I wanted to combine the Scandinavian element with my global experience of traveling," she says. "You collect [ideas] until you have so much, you have to do something with it."[75]

**COLLABORATE WITH OTHER PEOPLE** Working with other people, particularly people from different backgrounds, is an excellent way to stimulate creativity. When he invented the lightbulb, Thomas Edison's team included chemists, mathematicians, and glassblowers.[76] "You need a group composed of individuals who bring different perspectives to the table, who respect different working styles, and who resolve conflicts along the way," says Tina Seelig, an expert in creativity. "Great teams also have a healthy dose of playfulness," she adds.[77]

**OBSERVE THE PRODUCTS AND SERVICES OF OTHER COMPANIES, ESPECIALLY THOSE IN COMPLETELY DIFFERENT MARKETS** Creative entrepreneurs often borrow ideas from companies that are in businesses totally unrelated to their own. Using pattern thinking, entrepreneurs look for underlying patterns in businesses that are totally different from their own and then apply those patterns to their own companies and industries. "Look outside your industry to see how others are solving problems," says Angela Benton, founder of NewME Accelerator. "Approaches that they think are routine might be out of the ordinary for you—and inspire great ideas."[78]

**ENTREPRENEURIAL PROFILE: Jerry Barber: Barber Wind Turbines** In 1971, Jerry Barber started Venture Ride Manufacturing, a company that produced amusement rides in Greenville, South Carolina. Over the course of the next 18 years, his small business grew to employ 70 people and earned many patents for its amusement ride designs. He sold the company in 1989 and became interested in wind turbines after having a conversation with an old friend who was delivering the gearbox assembly for a wind turbine. "I was shocked that the thing was the size of an SUV," he says. Drawing from his years of designing amusement rides, Barber came up with a design for a wind turbine that does not require a gearbox, which costs $250,000 and lasts for only 20 years. Barber's turbines have five blades (rather than the traditional three blades) inside a ring, and wheels on the edge of the ring, which are similar to those on a Ferris wheel, turn the generator to produce electricity. "This is a potential game-changer in the wind industry," says one industry expert.[79]

**RECOGNIZE THE CREATIVE POWER OF MISTAKES AND ACCIDENTS** Innovations sometimes are the result of serendipity, finding something while looking for something else, and sometimes they arise as a result of mistakes or accidents. Creative people recognize that even their errors may lead to new ideas, products, and services. "I would love to get to a place in my life where I can laugh at my failures," says one successful song writer, "because for every failed creative attempt, I'm closer to a successful one."[80] Louis Daguerre, a scene painter for the Paris Opera, was fascinated with lighting and in 1822 began conducting experiments with the effect of light on translucent screens. In 1829, Daguerre formed a partnership with Joseph Niecpe, who had invented a primitive version of photography called the heliograph in 1829. (The exposure time for Niecpe's first photograph was a mere eight hours!) The two men worked for years trying to capture photographic images on metal plates treated with silver iodide, but they made little progress before Niecpe died in 1833. One evening in 1835, Daguerre placed one of his treated plates in his chemical cupboard, intending to recoat it for other experiments. When he removed it later, he was surprised to see a photographic image with brilliant highlights. Excited but puzzled by the outcome, Daguerre finally discovered that mercury vapors from a broken thermometer in the cupboard had caused the photographic image to appear on the treated metal plate. Daguerre refined the process, naming it Daguerreotype after himself, and the world of modern photography was born—and an accident played a significant role.[81]

**BE POSITIVE** A negative outlook drains creative capacity and undermines the brain's ability to generate creative solutions. Research shows that positive emotions increase creativity and high-performance behavior. "Positive emotions expand awareness and attention," explains Barbara Fredrickson, a pioneer in this area of research. The good news: Entrepreneurs tend to be optimistic and resilient.

**NOTICE WHAT IS MISSING** Sometimes entrepreneurs spot viable business opportunities by noticing something, often very practical and simple, that is *missing*. The first step is to determine whether a market for the missing product or service actually exists (perhaps the reason it does not exist is that there is not market potential), which is one of the objectives of building a business plan.

**ENTREPRENEURIAL PROFILE: Shawn Boyer: Snagajob** Shawn Boyer was trying to help a friend who was finishing her doctorate in an obscure liberal arts field land an internship and noticed that existing job search sites focused on salaried jobs but offered no listings for people seeking internships or hourly jobs. As entrepreneurs are wont to do, Boyer decided to capitalize on the opportunity he spotted and launched Snagajob, a Web site that lists available full-time and part-time hourly jobs. He quit his job, cashed out his retirement account, and borrowed a significant chunk of money from his parents to start his business. Today, Snagajob has more than 40 million registered job seekers and 45,000 registered employers of all sizes and helps nearly 1 million people find hourly jobs each year.[82]

**PERIODICALLY ASK YOURSELF, "AM I ASKING THE RIGHT QUESTIONS?"** Sometimes creative flashes come when we change our perspective and ask questions that frame a problem or situation in a different light.

**ENTREPRENEURIAL PROFILE: Yuri Malina: SwipeSense** While Yuri Malina was a student at Northwestern University, he cofounded Design for America, an organization that helps students create solutions for various social problems, with two fellow students and a faculty member. Malina discovered that hospital acquired infections, most of which originate because of improper hand washing among health care professionals, cause more than 100,000 deaths each year in the United States. Although hospitals provide plenty of hand-sanitizing stations, health care professionals do not always use them. To solve the vexing problem, Malina and his team observed doctors and nurses at a local hospital and realized that physicians and nurses were so busy helping patients that they were constantly on the move. Malina realized that hospitals were asking the wrong question: "How can we convince health care professionals to comply with hand-washing requirements?" Malina and his team posed a different question: "How can we provide a nonintrusive solution to hand sanitizing that meshes with health care professionals' work habits and busy schedules?" That led Malina's team to develop SwipeSense, a smart phone-sized hand-sanitizing device that attaches to a health care professional's belt or waistband and allows busy doctors and nurses to clean their hands as they move from one patient to the next. Malina and his team acquired a patent for their device and raised $50,000 in seed capital and landed a spot in a health care–focused business incubator.[83]

**KEEP A JOURNAL HANDY TO RECORD YOUR THOUGHTS AND IDEAS** Creative ideas are too valuable to waste, so always keep a journal nearby to record them as soon as you get them. Leonardo da Vinci was famous for writing down ideas as they struck him. Patrick McNaughton invented the neon blackboards that restaurants use to advertise their specials. In addition to the neon blackboard, McNaughton has invented more than 30 new products, many of which are sold through the company that he and his sister, Jamie, own. McNaughton credits much of his creative success to the fact that he writes down every idea he gets and keeps it in a special folder. "There's no such thing as a crazy idea," he insists.[84]

**LISTEN TO OTHER PEOPLE** No rule of creativity says that an idea has to be your own! Sometimes the best business ideas come from someone else, but entrepreneurs are the ones to act on them.

**ENTREPRENEURIAL PROFILE: Cameron Roelofson: Splash Mobile Car Wash** Cameron Roelofson, owner of Splash Mobile Car Wash in Concord, Ontario, washes 2,500 tractor-trailer trucks per week during warm months but sales in his highly seasonal business fall to nothing during the frigid winters. On one cold winter day, Roelofson was talking with an acquaintance who asked if he would use his mobile truck wash equipment to put water into an outdoor skating rink. He agreed and quickly realized the potential for a business that would offset seasonality in the sales of his truck-washing business. Roelofson began advertising, and sales took off. For $1,000 to $2,000, Splash builds a frame with a reusable liner and then fills it with water. Three days later, frozen solid in Ontario's winter weather, the rink is ready for skating or hockey. In the spring, Splash returns to disassemble the rink and store it until the next winter.[85]

**GET ADEQUATE SLEEP** Sleep restores both our bodies and our brains. A study by the Mental Health Foundation shows a correlation between sound sleep and a person's ability to produce creative ideas and new insights.[86]

**WATCH A MOVIE** Great business ideas come from the strangest places, even the movies. As a child, Stanley Yang was fascinated by sci-fi movies such as *Star Wars*. That fascination led him to become an engineer so that he could transform his ideas into reality. Yang's company, NeuroSky, has developed headsets that allow people to control video games with their minds using biosensor technology, a concept used by an advanced alien race in the movie *Battle Los Angeles*. "Movies may spark an idea," says Yang, who still dreams of building a functional light saber.

**TALK TO A CHILD** As we grow older, we learn to conform to society's expectations about many things, including creative solutions to problems. Children place very few limitations on their thinking; as a result, their creativity is practically boundless. (Remember all of the games you and your friends invented when you were young?)

**ENTREPRENEURIAL PROFILE: Maxine Clark: Build-a-Bear Workshop** Maxine Clark was president of Payless ShoeSource when she took her best friend's young daughter, Katie Burkhardt, shopping. After a fruitless search for a Beany Baby she didn't already have, Katie picked up a Beany Baby and said to Clark, "We could make one." "She meant we could go home and make the small bears, but I heard something different," recalls Clark. "Her words gave me the idea to create a company that would allow people to create their own customized stuffed animals. I did some research and began putting together a plan. Build-a-Bear Workshop would be a theme park factory in a mall." Clark's plan proved to be successful. Today, the company she launched, Build-a-Bear Workshop, has 425 stores worldwide and generates annual sales of nearly $400 million.[87]

**DO SOMETHING ORDINARY IN AN UNUSUAL WAY** Experts say that simply doing something out of the ordinary can stimulate creativity. To stimulate his own creativity, Scott Jones, an entrepreneur who is known as "the guy who invented voice mail" (and many other items as well), often engages in what other people might consider bizarre behavior—eating without utensils, watching television sitting one foot away from the screen, or taking a shower with his eyes closed. "Anything I normally do, I'll do differently just to see what happens," says Jones.[88]

**KEEP A TOY BOX IN YOUR OFFICE**  Your box might include silly objects such as wax lips, a yo-yo, a Slinky, fortune cookie sayings, feathers, a top, a compass, or a host of other items. When you are stumped, pick an item at random from the toy box and think about how it relates to your problem.

**TAKE NOTE OF YOUR "PAIN POINTS": DO OTHER PEOPLE EXPERIENCE THEM AS WELL?** Entrepreneurs often create innovations to solve problems they themselves face. Observing "pain points" that result from missing products or services or flaws in existing products or services can be an excellent source of business ideas.

Payal Kadakia, founder of Classtivity.
*Source:* Stephanie Haller.

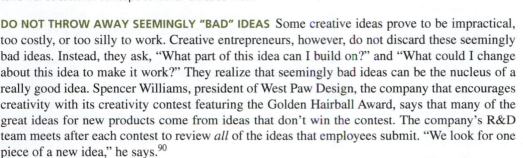

**ENTREPRENEURIAL PROFILE: Payal Kadakia: Classtivity**  While working at Warner Music Group in New York City, Payal Kadakia, who started dancing as a child, wanted to take a ballet class but could not find one at a convenient time that fit into her schedule. "I thought, 'This is ridiculous. This needs to be solved. There are so many classes being offered at this very moment, and I can't find one of them.'" Kadakia realized that this was a common problem and left her job to start Classtivity, a Web site that provides a searchable listing of classes, ranging from ballet and beer brewing to cooking and yoga, and their scheduled times and locations. Classtivity provides for classes much like OpenTable does for restaurants, offering users the convenience of easily finding the classes they seek and booking slots in them online, and charging the businesses that offer the classes a percentage (that ranges between 10 and 15 percent) of the class fee. Kadakia has included a social media component to the Classtivity Web site, expanded to San Francisco and Los Angeles, and has plans to take her successful concept to other cities as well.[89]

**DO NOT THROW AWAY SEEMINGLY "BAD" IDEAS**  Some creative ideas prove to be impractical, too costly, or too silly to work. Creative entrepreneurs, however, do not discard these seemingly bad ideas. Instead, they ask, "What part of this idea can I build on?" and "What could I change about this idea to make it work?" They realize that seemingly bad ideas can be the nucleus of a really good idea. Spencer Williams, president of West Paw Design, the company that encourages creativity with its creativity contest featuring the Golden Hairball Award, says that many of the great ideas for new products come from ideas that don't win the contest. The company's R&D team meets after each contest to review *all* of the ideas that employees submit. "We look for one piece of a new idea," he says.[90]

**READ BOOKS ON STIMULATING CREATIVITY OR TAKE A CLASS ON CREATIVITY**  Creative thinking is a technique that anyone can learn. Understanding and applying the principles of creativity can improve dramatically the ability to develop new and innovative ideas.

**TAKE SOME TIME OFF**  Relaxation is vital to the creative process. Getting away from a problem gives the mind time to reflect on it. It is often during this time, while the subconscious works on a problem, that the mind generates many creative solutions. One study reports that 35 percent of entrepreneurs say that they come up with their best ideas during down time, when they are away from work.[91] Research suggests that simply taking a walk outside, particularly in a garden or wooded area, can increase one's creativity.[92] One creativity expert claims that fishing is the ideal activity for stimulating creativity. "Your brain is on high alert in case a fish is around," he says, "but your brain is completely relaxed. This combination is the time when you have the 'Aha!' moment."[93]

**BE PERSISTENT**  Entrepreneurs know that one secret to success is persistence and a "don't quit" attitude. Twelve publishers rejected J. K. Rowling's manuscript about the adventures of a boy wizard and his friends, which she started writing at age 25 when she was a single mother trying to raise her children on welfare, before Bloomsbury, a small London publishing house, agreed to publish 1,000 copies of *Harry Potter and the Philosopher's Stone.* Rowling's seven-part Harry Potter book series went on to sell more than 450 million copies worldwide, making Rowling the first billionaire author.[94]

# How to Create a Culture of Creativity and Innovation

Creativity and innovation are important drivers of the global economy, allowing companies that use them well to prosper and providing consumers with products and services that make their lives better. A recent study by marketing communications firm MDC Partners reports that 98 percent of top executives say that creativity is critical to economic success; in addition, 76 percent of the managers believe that the world has entered an "imagination economy," in which companies' ability to harness the power of creativity determines their success. How can a company create a culture that promotes creativity among its employees and allows it to use innovation to gain a competitive advantage over its rivals? The following seven tips can help.

## Ignite passion

The philosopher Denis Diderot said, "Only passions, great passions, can elevate the soul to great things." So it is with creativity. The most basic ingredient for building a creative company culture is a passion to discover something new, to contribute to the betterment of society, and to make a difference. That passion starts at the top of an organization with the entrepreneur. Steve Jobs, cofounder of Apple Inc., often said that he wanted "to put a ding in the universe," an attitude that led his company to introduce many innovative products. When Jobs died in 2011, many observers noted how in his brief career he truly had changed the world. Your job as leader is to make sure that your passion for creativity spreads to everyone in your company.

## Celebrate creative ideas

In some companies, people who come up with new ideas learn quickly that the organization does not value creativity and risk taking and shies away from ideas that might fail. Smart entrepreneurs, however, recognize that the only way to move their companies forward is to take measured risks by implementing creative ideas that have potential. In fact, these entrepreneurs reward employees (and not just financially, although that helps) who develop creative ideas and innovative solutions to problems even if they fail. They understand that even though one idea fails, the next idea might be "the big one." Celebrating creative ideas with praise (both public and private), promotions, and cash send a clear signal to employees that a company values creativity.

## Foster autonomy

"The act of creativity is one of self-expression," says serial entrepreneur Josh Linkner. To be creative, employees must have the freedom to make decisions and call their own shots. Micromanaging saps creativity out of any organization. Smart entrepreneurs know that their job is to focus employees' efforts on the problems to solve and then to get out of their way and let them do it. "We challenge our employees to be their own CEOs," says Dan Satterwaithe, director of human resources at DreamWorks Animation, the animated filmmaker. Delegating authority and responsibility requires an atmosphere of trust, which increases the likelihood that employees are engaged in their work and buy into the company's mission. They key is letting employees know that you value their ideas, creativity, and judgment.

## Encourage courage

Some companies actually discourage creativity and innovation by punishing those who dare to take chances and fail. Businesses that succeed over time have cultures that encourage employees to be bold enough to take creative chances without fear of repercussions. At DreamWorks Animation, managers regularly solicit ideas from every employee—and not just those in the creative side of the business. Accountants, administrative assistants, lawyers—anyone—can (and do) submit ideas for everything from story lines for new movies to improving a business system.

## Fail forward

The most creative companies have built cultures that encourage people to try new ideas and recognize that many (perhaps most) of them will fail. Companies that punish failure end up with a cadre of employees who simply keep their heads down, never step out of line, and produce only mediocre results. "Failing forward means taking risks and increasing the rate of experimentation," says Josh Linkner. The key is to fail quickly, learn from the failure, make necessary adjustments, and try again.

## Ensure interaction

Creative managers know that one of the best ways to stimulate creativity is to ensure that employees interact with one another. At DreamWorks Animation, employees use cloud-computing technology to collaborate on projects, but managers also insist on face-to-face interactions, both formal and informal, because they know that's where many creative ideas originate. Many companies that cultivate creativity establish work spaces that encourage employees to interact with one another and talk about new ideas.

## Maximize diversity

Companies have discovered that hiring workers from different cultures, with varied backgrounds, and with diverse work experience enhances creativity. The 120 employees at Ziba, an innovation consulting firm in Portland, Oregon, come from 18 different countries and speak 26 different languages. "Genetic diversity breeds creativity, much like it does with biology," says Sohrab Vossoughi, the company's founder and CEO. To encourage creativity, Ziba implemented an "Ambassador Program," in which employees spend three months working in other areas of the company, which are known as tribes. "This helps create an understanding of another world," says Vossoughi.

1. Do you agree with the top managers in the MDC Partners survey who say that we have entered an "imagination economy"? Explain.

2. List and describe two additional steps that a company can take to create a culture of creativity and innovation.

*Sources:* Based on Josh Linkner, "7 Steps to a Culture of Innovation," *Inc.*, June 16, 2011, *www.inc.com/articles/201106/josh-linkner-7-steps-to-a-culture-of-innovation.html*; Anita Bruzzese, "DreamWorks Is Believer in Every Employee's Creativity," *USA Today*, *http://usatoday30.usatoday.com/money/jobcenter/workplace/bruzzese/story/2012-07-22/dreamworks-values-innovation-in-all-workers/56376470/1*; "MDC Partners and Allison and Partners Study Reveals Leading CEOs and CMOs View Creativity as a Critical Driver of the Global Economy," *Business Wire*, October 4, 2011, *www.businesswire.com/news/home/20111004005439/en/MDC-Partners-Allison-Partners-Study-Reveals-Leading*.

# The Creative Process

Although creative ideas may appear to strike as suddenly as a bolt of lightning, they are actually the result of the creative process, which involves seven steps:

Step 1. Preparation

Step 2. Investigation

Step 3. Transformation

Step 4. Incubation

Step 5. Illumination

Step 6. Verification

Step 7. Implementation

**6.** _____

Describe the steps in the creative process.

## Step 1. Preparation

This step involves getting the mind ready for creative thinking. Preparation might include a formal education, on-the-job training, work experience, and taking advantage of other learning opportunities. This training provides a foundation on which to build creativity and innovation. As one writer explains, "Creativity favors the prepared mind."[95] For example, Dr. Hamel Navia, a scientist at tiny Vertex Pharmaceuticals, was working on a promising new drug to fight the AIDS virus. His preparation included earning an advanced degree in the field of medicine and learning to use computers to create 3-D images of the protein molecules he was studying.[96] How can you prepare your mind for creative thinking?

- Adopt the attitude of a lifelong student. Realize that educating yourself is a never-ending process. Look at every situation you encounter as an opportunity to learn.

**ENTREPRENEURIAL PROFILE  Scientific Anglers: Sharkskin Fly Line** To develop a new fly line that reduces drag and allows anglers to cast flies more easily, researchers at Scientific Anglers studied how some insects can walk on the surface of the water, the leaves of the lotus plant can clean themselves, and geckoes can easily cling to almost any surface. Their research led them to develop a process that embosses the fly line, which they named Sharkskin, with a repeating geometric micropattern that mimics those found in nature and minimizes the line's contact with the rod's guides, greatly reducing friction and allowing a fisherman to cast more easily and to make longer casts. The line, which has a texture like sharkskin, is a radical departure from the traditional smooth-surface fly line that fly fisherman have used for decades.[97]

- Read—a lot—and not just in your field of expertise. Many innovations come from blending ideas and concepts from different fields in science, engineering, business, and the arts. Reading books, magazines, and papers covering a variety of subject matter is a great way to stimulate your creativity.

- Clip articles of interest to you and create a file for them. Over time, you will build a customized encyclopedia of information from which to draw ideas and inspiration.

- Take time to discuss your ideas with other people, including those who know little about it as well as experts in the field. Sometimes, the apparently simple questions an "unknowledgeable" person asks lead to new discoveries and to new approaches to an old problem. At Fahrenheit 212, an innovation consulting firm based in New York City, founder Mark Payne encourages employees to interact with one another to come up with new ideas and solutions to clients' problems. Almost every wall in the creative offices is made of glass, and markers are placed everywhere, allowing employees to sketch ideas as they discover them and to talk about them with coworkers. The work space follows an open design that encourages "wandering around" that leads to a "spontaneous combustion" of ideas, says Payne.[98]

- Join professional or trade associations and attend their meetings. There you have the chance to interact with others who have similar interests. Learning how other people have solved a particular problem may give you fresh insight into solving it.

- Develop listening skills. It's amazing what you can learn if you take the time to listen to other people—especially those who are older and have more experience. Try to learn something from everyone you meet.

- Eliminate creative distractions. Interruptions from telephone calls, e-mails, social media, and visitors can crush creativity. Allowing employees to escape to a quiet, interruption-free environment enhances their ability to be creative.

## Step 2. Investigation

This step requires one to develop a solid understanding of the problem, situation, or decision at hand. To create new ideas and concepts in a particular field, an individual first must study the problem and understand its basic components. Creative thinking comes about when people make careful observations of the world around them and then investigate the way things work (or fail to work). For example, Dr. Navia and another scientist at Vertex had spent several years conducting research on viruses and on a protein that blocks a virus enzyme called protease. His exploration of the various ways to block this enzyme paved the way for his discovery.

**ENTREPRENEURIAL PROFILE: Christopher Leamon: Endocyte** After earning his PhD in chemistry, Christopher Leamon began researching targeted anticancer therapy using molecules that tumors absorb as "Trojan horses" to deliver drugs that are lethal to them. Initially, Leamon had focused on the vitamin biotin, but after nine months of research and hard work, "it was a total failure," he says. One morning while sitting at the breakfast table with his wife, Leamon, a longtime cereal lover, was reading the ingredients on the nutrition panel of his box of Kellogg's Frosted Flakes. One of the items, folic acid, caught his attention. Leamon dashed off to the library and found a research paper on how folic acid enters a human cell. "I knew this was it," he recalls. Before long, Leamon had developed a technique for attaching cancer drugs to folic acid so that they would be absorbed and enable the cells to fight the disease in much the same way they battle infections. Leamon has licensed the promising therapy to a company called Endocyte, which plans to have drugs on the market within a few years. "There are lots of 'Eureka' moments in the lab," says Leamon. "None as great as the one with the folic acid though. That breakfast redefined my career and my life."[99]

## Step 3. Transformation

Transformation involves viewing the similarities and the differences among the information collected. This phase requires two types of thinking: convergent and divergent. **Convergent thinking** is the ability to see the *similarities* and the connections among various and often diverse data and events. "So much of innovation comes from connecting things where other people don't make connections," says Mark Rice, professor of technology entrepreneurship at Olin College.[100] Johannes Gutenberg made a connection between a common device of his day, the wine press, and a machine he invented that relied on the same principle to print books cheaply and efficiently using movable blocks of letters and graphics. His printing press is often cited as one of the most important inventions in the history of the world.

**ENTREPRENEURIAL PROFILE: Kate Szilagyi: Tempaper** Kate Szilagyi, a former set decorator in the film industry and window designer for Saks Fifth Avenue, knew all too well how difficult replacing traditional wallpaper is. Working with her nieces, Jennifer and Julia Biancella, Szilagyi combined the concepts of traditional wallpaper and Post-It Notes to develop wallpaper that uses a temporary adhesive (similar to the one used on Post-It Notes). The resulting wallpaper, which they call Tempaper, acts like a giant sticker and is easily removable and restickable. Installation involves peeling off a backing and sticking it on the wall. The entrepreneurs sell Tempaper through their New York City–based company, Lolliprops, for $75 to $85 for a 33-foot roll.[101]

**Divergent thinking** is the ability to see the *differences* among various data and events. While developing his AIDS-fighting drug, Dr. Navia studied the work of other scientists whose attempts at developing an enzyme-blocking drug had failed. He was able to see the similarities

WHERE EARL GETS HIS IDEAS

*Source:* Michael Crawford/The New Yorker Collection/*www.cartoonbank.com.*

and the differences in his research and theirs and to build on their successes while avoiding their failures.

How can you increase your ability to transform the information collected into a purposeful idea?

- Evaluate the parts of the situation several times, trying to grasp the big picture. Getting bogged down in the details of a situation too early in the creative process can diminish creativity. Look for patterns that emerge and for connections among things that on the surface do not appear to be connected, a process known as global processing.

- Rearrange the elements of the situation. By looking at the components of an issue in a different order or from a different perspective, you may be able to see the similarities and the differences among them more readily. Rearranging them also may help uncover a familiar pattern that had been masked by an unfamiliar structure. Engineers at Windtronics, a company in Muskegon, Michigan, rearranged the elements of a traditional power-generating wind turbine, moving them from the center to the outside of the blades. As a result, the blades of Windtronics turbines turn faster, operate more quietly and efficiently, and can generate electricity at wind speeds as low as two miles per hour, compared to six to eight miles per hour for traditional turbines. At just six feet in diameter, Windtronics turbines are suitable for industrial, commercial, and residential use. "We've turned traditional wind turbines inside out," says CEO Reg Adams.[102]

- Try using synectics (a term derived from the Greek words for "to bring together" and "diversity"), taking two seemingly nonsensical ideas and combining them. For instance, why not launch a bookstore with no physical storefront and no books—an accurate description of what Jeff Bezos did when he came up with the idea for Amazon.com.[103]

- Before locking into one particular approach to a situation, remember that several approaches might be successful. If one approach produces a dead end, don't hesitate to jump quickly to another. Considering several approaches to a problem or opportunity simultaneously would be like rolling a bowling ball down each of several lanes in quick succession. The more balls you roll down the lanes, the greater is the probability of hitting at least one strike. Resist the temptation to make snap judgments on how to tackle a problem or opportunity. The first approach may not be the best one.

## Step 4. Incubation

Often, ideas require a gestation period. The subconscious needs time to reflect on the information collected. To an observer, this phase of the creative process would be quite boring; it looks as though nothing is happening! In fact, during this phase, it may appear that the creative person is *loafing*. Incubation occurs while the individual is away from the problem, often engaging in some totally unrelated activity. Research shows that walking away from a problem to engage in routine tasks sparks creativity.[104] Dr. Navia's creative powers were working at a subconscious level even when he was away from his work, not even thinking about his research on AIDS-fighting drugs.

How can you enhance the incubation phase of the creative process, letting ideas marinate in your mind?

- Walk away from the situation. Time away from a problem is vital to enhancing creativity. A study by Wilson Brill, an expert on creativity, of how 350 great ideas became successful products shows that two-thirds of the ideas came to people while they were *away* from work—in the shower, in their cars, in bed, on a walk, and other nonwork situations.[105] Doing something totally unrelated to the problem gives your subconscious mind the chance to work on the problem or opportunity.

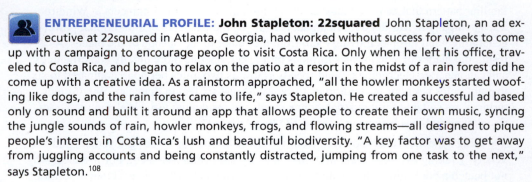

**ENTREPRENEURIAL PROFILE: Amy Baxter: Buzzy** For years, Amy Baxter, a physician and pain researcher, had been searching for a way to use cold to relieve the pain of children's vaccinations. While driving home from an all-night shift in the emergency room, she noticed that the steering wheel on her car was vibrating (her tires were badly misaligned). When she got out of her car, her hands were numb from the vibration. That's when the idea hit her: Combining vibration and cold temperatures could desensitize a vaccination site. To test her idea, she applied a frozen bag of peas and a vibrating massager to her son's arm and then rolled a small metal wheel used by neurologists over the area, and he could feel nothing. Baxter went on to invent Buzzy, a bee-shaped cold pack outfitted with a vibrating device that more than 500 hospitals and doctors' offices now use before administering vaccinations.[106]

- Take the time to daydream. Creative people build time into their schedules to allow their minds to wander. Although it may *look* as if you're doing nothing, daydreaming is an important part of the creative process. That's when your mind is most free from self-imposed restrictions on creativity. Research shows a connection between daydreaming and creativity; people who daydream are better at generating new ideas.[107] Feel free to let your mind wander, and it may just stumble onto a creative solution.

*Source:* bikeriderlondon/Shutterstock.

**ENTREPRENEURIAL PROFILE: John Stapleton: 22squared** John Stapleton, an ad executive at 22squared in Atlanta, Georgia, had worked without success for weeks to come up with a campaign to encourage people to visit Costa Rica. Only when he left his office, traveled to Costa Rica, and began to relax on the patio at a resort in the midst of a rain forest did he come up with a creative idea. As a rainstorm approached, "all the howler monkeys started woofing like dogs, and the rain forest came to life," says Stapleton. He created a successful ad based only on sound and built it around an app that allows people to create their own music, syncing the jungle sounds of rain, howler monkeys, frogs, and flowing streams—all designed to pique people's interest in Costa Rica's lush and beautiful biodiversity. "A key factor was to get away from juggling accounts and being constantly distracted, jumping from one task to the next," says Stapleton.[108]

- Relax—and play—regularly. Perhaps the worst thing you can do for creativity is to work on a problem or opportunity constantly. Soon enough, fatigue walks in, and creativity walks out! Great ideas often are incubated on the golf course, on the basketball court, on a hiking trail, or in the hammock.

**ENTREPRENEURIAL PROFILE: Aaron Lemieux: Tremont Electric** Aaron Lemieux was carrying a backpack while hiking the 1,500-mile Appalachian Trail when the idea for his business struck. Lemieux, trained as a mechanical and biomedical engineer, grew tired of purchasing disposable batteries along the way to power his portable devices and began to think about ways to capture the wasted kinetic energy generated by the movement of his backpack. Lemieux's hiking experience led him to launch Tremont Electric, a company that produces the nPower Personal Energy Generator, a small, lightweight electrical generator that produces enough energy to power personal electronic devices by simply harvesting kinetic energy from normal human movement, such as walking.[109]

- Dream about the problem or opportunity. "Dreams have been responsible for two Nobel prizes, the invention of a couple of major drugs, other scientific discoveries, several important political events, and innumerable novels, films, and works of visual art," says Harvard Medical School psychologists Dierdre Barrett.[110] Although you may not be able to dream on command, thinking about an issue just before you drift off to sleep can be an effective way to encourage your mind to work on it while you sleep, a process called lucid dreaming. Barrett's research suggests that about 50 percent of people can focus their dreams by contemplating a particular problem before they go to sleep, in essence "seeding" the subconscious to influence their dreams.[111] Arianna Huffington, founder of the *Huffington Post*, says that when she needs a creative solution, she goes to sleep. "There are many great ideas locked inside us," she says. "We just need to close our eyes to see them." To encourage creativity among her staff, Huffington has set up three "nap rooms" in the company's offices.[112]

- Work on the problem or opportunity in a different environment—somewhere other than the office. Take your work outside on a beautiful fall day or sit on a bench in a mall. The change of scenery will likely stimulate your creativity.

## Step 5. Illumination

This phase of the creative process occurs at some point during the incubation stage when a spontaneous breakthrough causes "the lightbulb to go on." It may take place after five minutes—or five years. Ben Baldwin, cofounder of ClearFit, a company that helps small companies find the best job candidates and predict their success, says that the idea for the company's business model "hatched in the back of my mind while I was driving 80 miles an hour, not thinking about work at all." Baldwin had been working on similar ideas for seven years before ClearFit's business model crystallized in his mind. "ClearFit wasn't the first company to help [companies] find employees, nor the first to predict job fit, nor the first company to make software that's easy for small businesses to use. However, it's the first to combine these in a way that's easy for anyone to find employees who fit."[113]

In the illumination stage, all of the previous stages come together to produce the "Eureka factor"—the creation of the innovative idea. In one study of 200 scientists, 80 percent said that at least once a solution to a problem had "just popped into their heads"—usually when they were away from the problem.[114] For Dr. Navia, the illumination stage occurred one day while he was reading a scientific journal. As he read, Dr. Navia says he was struck with a "hallucination" of a novel way to block protease.

Although the creative process itself may last for months or even years, the suddenness with which the illumination step occurs can be deceiving, making the process appear to occur much faster than it actually does. One night, Kent Murphy, an electrical engineer, began dreaming about what it would be like to be a photon of light. "I was riding a ray of light moving through the fiber," he recalls about his dream. Murphy, who holds 30 patents, used the insight from his dream to invent a fiber-optic gauge that monitors on a real-time basis the structural wear in airplanes.[115]

## Step 6. Verification

For entrepreneurs, validating an idea as realistic and useful may include conducting experiments, running simulations, test marketing a product or service, establishing small-scale pilot programs, building prototypes, and many other activities designed to verify that the new idea will work and is practical to implement. The goal is to subject the innovative idea to the test of cold, hard reality. At this phase, appropriate questions to ask include the following:

- Is it *really* a better solution to a particular problem or opportunity? Sometimes an idea that appears to have a bright future in the lab or on paper dims considerably when put to the test of reality.
- Will it work?

- Is there a need for it?
- If so, what is the best application of this idea in the marketplace?
- Does this product or service idea fit into our core competencies?
- How much will it cost to produce or to provide?
- Can we sell it at a reasonable price that will produce adequate sales, profit, and return on investment for our business?

Ramtron International Corporation, a maker of memory chips, uses a "product justification form" to collect information from the idea generator as well as from other departments in the company so that it can verify the potential of each idea.[116] To test the value of his new drug formulation, Dr. Navia used powerful computers at Vertex Pharmaceuticals to build 3-D Tinkertoy-like models of the HIV virus and then simulated his new drug's ability to block the protease enzyme. Subsequent testing of the drug verified its safety. "I was convinced that I had an insight that no one else had," he recalls.[117]

### Step 7. Implementation

The focus of this step is to transform the idea into reality. Plenty of people come up with creative ideas for promising new products or services, but most never take them beyond the idea stage. What sets entrepreneurs apart is that they *act* on their ideas. An entrepreneur's philosophy is "Ready, aim, fire," not "Ready, aim, aim, aim, aim." Innowattech, a company based in Ra'anana, Israel, has developed a variety of piezoelectric (PE) crystals that possess the ability to transform vibrations, motion, and temperature changes into clean energy. Like minigenerators, the pressure-sensitive ceramic crystals give off small electrical charges when "squeezed, squashed, bent, or slapped," says Markys Cain, a materials scientist. In a recent test, Innowattech placed PE generators two inches beneath a small section of Israel's busy Highway 4, where passing cars compressed the road, activated the tiny generators, and produced energy. The company estimates that placing the PE crystals under a half-mile stretch of highway would generate enough energy to supply 250 homes. Innowattech also has developed crystals for collecting clean energy from railways, airport runways, and pedestrian walkways. Pavegen Systems, a London-based company, has developed a similar technology for pedestrian walkways that captures the kinetic energy from passersby. Installed on a busy thoroughfare, the company's energy-absorbing pads (which are made from recycled material) can generate enough energy to power the area's lighting and signs.[118] The key to both companies' success is their ability to take a creative idea for a useful new product and turn it into a reality. As one creativity expert explains, "Becoming more creative is really just a matter of paying attention to that endless flow of ideas you generate, and learning to capture and act upon the new that's within you."[119]

For Dr. Navia and Vertex Pharmaceuticals, the implementation phase required testing the drug's ability to fight the deadly virus in humans. If it proved to be effective, Vertex would complete the process by bringing the drug to market. In this final phase of testing, Navia was so certain that he was on the verge of a major breakthrough in fighting AIDS that he couldn't sleep at night. Unfortunately, the final critical series of tests proved that Dr. Navia's flash of creativity was, as he now says, "completely, totally, and absolutely incorrect." Although his intuition proved to be wrong this time, Dr. Navia's research into fighting AIDS continues. Much of the current work at Vertex is based on Dr. Navia's original idea. Although it proved to be incorrect, his idea has served a valuable purpose: generating new ideas. "We are now applying a powerful technology in HIV research that wasn't used before, one inspired by a hunch," he says.[120]

## Conclusion

As you have seen, creativity and innovation are vital components to entrepreneurial success. "Innovation for a start-up is imperative," says Lisa Bodell, founder of futurethink, a global training company. "Small companies are often founded on a single, unorthodox idea." Successful entrepreneurs constantly push themselves and the people in their businesses to think bold new thoughts, come up with fresh new ideas, and question the status quo. The results of their efforts are innovative new products, services, and business models that benefit all of us and improve the quality of our lives.

# Chapter Review

1. Explain the differences among creativity, innovation, and entrepreneurship.
   - The entrepreneur's "secret" for creating value in the marketplace is applying creativity and innovation to solve problems and to exploit opportunities that people face every day. Creativity is the ability to develop new ideas and to discover new ways of looking at problems and opportunities. Innovation is the ability to apply creative solutions to those problems and opportunities to enhance or to enrich people's lives. Entrepreneurship is the result of a disciplined, systematic process of applying creativity and innovation to needs and opportunities in the marketplace.

2. Describe why creativity and innovation are such integral parts of entrepreneurship.
   - Entrepreneurs must always be on guard against paradigms—preconceived ideas of what the world is, what it should be like, and how it should operate—because they are logjams to creativity. Successful entrepreneurs often go beyond conventional wisdom as they ask "Why not?"
   - Success—even survival—in this fiercely competitive, global environment requires entrepreneurs to tap their creativity (and that of their employees) constantly.

3. Understand how the two hemispheres of the human brain function and what role they play in creativity.
   - For years, people assumed that creativity was an inherent trait. Today, however, we know better. Research shows that almost anyone can learn to be creative. The left hemisphere of the brain controls language, logic, and symbols, processing information in a step-by-step fashion. The right hemisphere handles emotional, intuitive, and spatial functions, processing information intuitively. The right side of the brain is the source of creativity and innovation. People can learn to control which side of the brain is dominant in a given situation.

4. Explain the 10 "mental locks" that limit individual creativity.
   - The number of potential barriers to creativity is limitless, but entrepreneurs commonly face 10 "mental locks" on creativity: searching for the one "right" answer, focusing on "being logical," blindly following the rules, constantly being practical, viewing play as frivolous, becoming overly specialized, avoiding ambiguity, fearing looking foolish, fearing mistakes and failure, and believing that "I'm not creative."

5. Understand how entrepreneurs can enhance the creativity of their employees as well as their own creativity.
   - Entrepreneurs can stimulate creativity in their companies by expecting creativity, expecting and tolerating failure, encouraging curiosity, viewing problems as challenges, providing creativity training, providing support, rewarding creativity, and modeling creativity.
   - Entrepreneurs can enhance their own creativity by using the following techniques: allowing themselves to be creative, giving their minds fresh input every day, keeping a journal handy to record their thoughts and ideas, reading books on stimulating creativity or taking a class on creativity, and taking some time off to relax.

6. Describe the steps in the creative process.
   - The creative process consists of seven steps. Step 1, preparation, involves getting the mind ready for creative thinking. Step 2, investigation, requires the individual to develop a solid understanding of the problem or decision. Step 3, transformation, involves viewing the similarities and the differences among the information collected. Step 4, incubation, allows the subconscious mind to reflect on the information collected. Step 5, illumination, occurs at some point during the incubation stage when a spontaneous breakthrough causes "the lightbulb to go on." Step 6, verification, involves validating the idea as accurate and useful. Step 7, implementation, involves transforming the idea into a business reality.

# Discussion Questions

3-1. Explain the differences among creativity, innovation, and entrepreneurship.

3-2. How are creativity, innovation, and entrepreneurship related?

3-3. Why are creativity and innovation so important to the survival and success of a business?

3-4. One entrepreneur claims, "Creativity unrelated to a business plan has no value." What does he mean? Do you agree?

3-5. Can creativity be taught, or is it an inherent trait? Explain.

3-6. How does the human brain function? What operations does each hemisphere specialize in? Which hemisphere is the "seat" of creativity?

3-7. Briefly outline the 10 "mental locks" that can limit individual creativity. Give an example of a situation in which you subjected yourself to one of these mental locks.

**3-8.** What can entrepreneurs do to stimulate their own creativity and to encourage it among workers?

**3-9.** Explain the steps of the creative process. What can an entrepreneur do to enhance each step?

**3-10.** Interview at least two entrepreneurs about their experiences as business owners. Where did their business ideas originate? How important are creativity and innovation to their success? How do they encourage an environment of creativity in their businesses?

**3-11.** Your dinner guests are to arrive in five minutes, and you've just discovered that you forgot to chill the wine! Wanting to maintain your reputation as the perfect host/hostess, you must tackle this problem with maximum creativity. What could you do? Generate as many solutions as you can in five minutes working alone. Then work with two or three students in a small group to brainstorm the problem.

**3-12.** Work with a group of your classmates to think of as many alternative uses for the commercial lubricant, WD-40, as you can. Remember to think *fluidly* (generating a quantity of ideas) and *flexibly* (generating unconventional ideas).

# CHAPTER 4

# Strategic Management and the Entrepreneur

## Learning Objectives

**On completion of this chapter, you will be able to:**

1. Understand the importance of strategic management to a small business.

2. Explain why and how a small business must create a competitive advantage in the market.

3. Develop a strategic plan for a business using the nine steps in the strategic planning process.

4. Discuss the characteristics of three basic strategies: low cost, differentiation, and focus.

5. Understand the importance of controls such as the balanced scorecard in the planning process.

*There is no competitive advantage in being just like everyone else.*

—Daniel Burrus

*Having a strategy in the first place is hard. Maintaining a strategy is even harder.*

—Michael Porter

**1.**

Understand the importance of strategic management to a small business.

Few activities in the life of a small business are as vital—or as overlooked—as that of developing a strategy for success. Too often, entrepreneurs brimming with optimism and enthusiasm launch businesses destined for failure because their founders never stop to define a workable strategy that sets them apart from their competition. Because entrepreneurs tend to be people of action, they often find the process of developing a strategy dull and unnecessary. Their tendency is to start a business, try several approaches, and see what works. Without a cohesive plan of action, however, these entrepreneurs have as much chance of building a successful business as a defense contractor attempting to build a jet fighter without blueprints. Companies lacking clear strategies may achieve success in the short run, but as soon as competitive conditions stiffen or an unanticipated threat arises, they usually "hit the wall" and fold. Without a strategy for differentiating itself from a pack of similar competitors, the best a company can hope for is mediocrity in the marketplace. "The worst [management] mistake—and the most common one—is not having a strategy at all," says strategy guru Michael Porter.[1]

In today's global, competitive environment, any business, large or small, that is not thinking and acting strategically is extremely vulnerable. Every business is exposed to the forces of a rapidly changing competitive environment, and in the future small business executives can expect even greater change and uncertainty. "The pace of disruption is roaring ahead," says one business writer. "Uncertainty has taken hold; chaotic disruption is rampant."[2] In 2007, three companies—Nokia, Research in Motion, and Motorola—accounted for 64 percent of the market for smart phones. Just five years later, smart phones from two different companies—Samsung and Apple—made up 60 percent of sales, reflecting the unprecedented level of turbulence in a major technology market.[3]

From more intense global competition and newly emerging international markets to sweeping political changes around the planet and rapid technological advances, the business environment has become more turbulent and challenging for entrepreneurs. Although this market turbulence creates many challenges for small businesses, it also creates opportunities for those companies that have in place strategies to capitalize on them. Small companies now have access to technology, tools, and techniques that once were available only to large companies, enabling them to achieve significant, sometimes momentous, results. To achieve those results, however, requires a business strategy that is stout enough to guide a company through normal turbulence but fluid enough to adapt to the sweeping changes wrought by the often chaotic uncertainty of the business environment.

Historically important, entrepreneurs' willingness to create change, experiment with new business models, and break traditional rules have become more important than ever. Rather than merely respond to the chaos in the environment, small companies that are prepared actually can *create* the disruptions that revolutionize their industries and gain a competitive edge. Just as sales of music CDs were at their peak, Steve Jobs's Apple Inc. revolutionized the music industry with the introduction of the iPod. Apple still commands more than 70 percent market share in the market for MP3 players more than a decade after introducing the iPod, and its iTunes Music Store became the world's leading music retailer within five years of its launch, having now sold more than 25 *billion* song downloads. In addition, Apple does not wait for rivals to render its products obsolete with better, more powerful versions; instead, the company disrupts its own products! Apple introduced the iPod Touch just 24 months after it released the highly successful iPod Nano and continues that pattern today with both the iPod and the iPhone.[4]

Perhaps the biggest change entrepreneurs face is still unfolding: the shift in the world's economy from a base of *financial to intellectual* capital. Intellectual capital is the knowledge and information a company acquires and uses to create a competitive edge in its market segment. "Knowledge is no longer just a factor of production," says futurist Alvin Toffler. "It is the *critical* factor of production."[5] Most small companies have significant stockpiles of valuable knowledge that can help them gain an edge in the marketplace *if* they put it to good use. Norm Brodsky, a serial entrepreneur who founded eight successful businesses, discovered the importance of intellectual capital early on in his business career, and it is a competitive advantage that he continues to rely on today. "I found that I could close a significantly higher percentage of sales than my competitors simply by knowing more than they did about the customer, its representatives, and every other aspect of the deal," he says. "That's still true today."

Brodsky explains what happens at his records storage business before a potential customer comes on site:

> We prepare thoroughly. Before the customer's people arrive, I go online and find out as much as I can about the organization's structure, mission, and history. My salespeople give me a full briefing on the visitors I'm about to meet—what they're like as individuals, whom else they're considering, how the decision will be made, and so on. I tailor my presentation accordingly.

The result of Brodsky's use of the knowledge in his company is a closing rate that exceeds 95 percent for all prospective customers who visit his company's facility.[6]

Unfortunately, much of the knowledge that resides in many small companies sits idle or is shared only by happenstance on an informal basis. This scenario is the equivalent of having a bank account without a checkbook or a debit card to access it! The key is learning how to utilize the knowledge a company accumulates over time as a strategic resource and as a competitive weapon. **Knowledge management** is the practice of gathering, organizing, and disseminating the collective wisdom and experience of a company's employees for the purpose of strengthening its competitive position. Because of their size and simplicity, small businesses have an advantage over large companies when it comes to managing knowledge. Knowledge management requires a small company to identify what its workers know, incorporate that knowledge into the business, distribute it where it is needed, and leverage it into more useful knowledge.

Today, a company's intellectual capital is likely to be the source of its competitive advantage in the marketplace. **Intellectual capital** is comprised of three components:[7]

1. *Human capital* includes the creativity, talents, skills, and abilities of a company's workforce and shows up in the innovative strategies, plans, and processes that the people in an organization develop and then passionately pursue.

2. *Structural capital* is the accumulated knowledge and experience in the industry and in business in general that a company possesses. It can take many forms including processes, software, patents, copyrights, and, perhaps most importantly, the knowledge and experience of the people in a company. "Don't let knowledge leave the premises when workers exit the building," advises one expert. "Some of it never returns."[8]

3. *Customer capital* is the established customer base, positive reputation, ongoing relationships, and goodwill a company builds up over time with its customers.

Increasingly, entrepreneurs are recognizing that the capital stored in these three areas forms the foundation of their ability to compete effectively and that they must manage this intangible capital base carefully. Every business uses all three components in its strategy, but the emphasis they place on each component varies.

**ENTREPRENEURIAL PROFILE: Joe Coulombe: Trader Joe's** Trader Joe's, founded by Joe Coulombe in 1967, is a highly successful grocery store chain with 372 stores in 33 states that relies on structural capital to create a significant competitive advantage. In an industry in which most companies treat their employees like interchangeable parts, Trader Joe's has built valuable structural capital by investing more in training, developing, compensating, and motivating its employees than its competitors. The company empowers every employee to do whatever it takes to make sure that customers have a "wow!" experience when they shop. The strategy works: Annual sales at Trader Joe's are nearly $10 billion and are growing at an impressive 12 percent a year. Zeynep Ton, a professor who has studied the retail industry and Trader Joe's, says that "highly successful retail chains not only invest heavily in store employees but also have the lowest prices in their industries, solid financial performance, and better customer service than their competitors."[9]

The rules of the competitive game of business are undergoing dramatic change. Entrepreneurs must recognize that the business forecast calls for continued chaos and disruption with the certainty of new opportunities and a slight chance of disaster. To be successful in this environment, entrepreneurs can no longer do things in the way they've always done them. They must learn to be initiators and agents of change. The late management guru Peter Drucker said that the key challenge for managers in the twenty-first century is leading change and that doing so successfully requires leaders "to abandon yesterday," leaving behind the products, services, management styles, marketing techniques, and other ideas that no longer work.[10]

Fortunately, successful entrepreneurs have at their disposal a powerful weapon to cope with a chaotic environment filled with disarray and constant disruptions: the process of strategic management. **Strategic management** is a process that involves developing a game plan to guide the company as it strives to accomplish its vision, mission, goals, and objectives and to keep it from straying off its desired course. The idea is to give the owner a blueprint for matching the company's strengths and weaknesses to the opportunities and threats in the environment.

## Building a Competitive Advantage

**2.**

Explain why and how a small business must create a competitive advantage in the market.

The goal of developing a strategic plan is to create for a small company a **competitive advantage**— the aggregation of factors that differentiates a small business from its competitors and gives it a unique and superior position in the market. From a strategic perspective, the key to business success is to develop a unique competitive advantage, one that creates value for customers, is sustainable, and is difficult for competitors to duplicate. No business can be everything to everyone. In fact, one of the biggest pitfalls many entrepreneurs stumble into is failing to differentiate their companies from the crowd of competitors. Entrepreneurs faced with the challenge of setting their companies apart from their larger, more powerful competitors (who can easily outspend them) use the creativity, speed, flexibility, and special abilities of their businesses as differentiators. Entrepreneurs should examine five aspects of their businesses to define their companies' competitive advantages:

**1.** *Products they sell.* What is unique about the products the company sells? Do they save customers time or money? Are they more reliable and more dependable than those that competitors sell? Do they save energy, protect the environment, or provide more convenience for customers? By identifying the unique customer benefits of their companies' products, entrepreneurs can differentiate their businesses.

**ENTREPRENEURIAL PROFILE: Mark Highland: Organic Mechanics Soil Company**  Mark Highland, who has a master's degree in public horticulture, transformed his specialized knowledge of compost into a successful business, Organic Mechanics Soil Company. Highland uses fertile compost rather than the peat moss mixture that other companies rely on to create an environmentally friendly potting soil that requires less watering and produces bigger flower blooms, fruit, and vegetable crops. Founded in 2006, Organic Mechanics Soil Company has expanded its product line to include nine items, which together generate more than $1 million in annual revenue. Despite competing in an industry dominated by several giant companies, Organic Mechanics Soil Company's unique line of products is profitable and growing fast.[11]

Mark Highland, founder of Organic Mechanics Soil Company.
*Source:* Natalie Brasington.

**2.** *Service they provide.* Many entrepreneurs find that the service they provide their customers is an excellent way to differentiate their companies. Because they are small, friendly, and close to their customers, small businesses are able to provide customer service that is superior to that which their larger competitors can provide. What services does the company provide (or which ones can it provide) to deliver added value and a superior shopping experience for customers?

**3.** *Pricing they offer.* As we will see later in this chapter, some small businesses differentiate themselves using price. Low prices can be a powerful point of differentiation but only if a business has the low-cost structure to drive them. However, offering the lowest prices is not always the best way to create a unique image. Small companies that do not offer the lowest prices must emphasize the value that their products offer.

**4.** *Way they sell.* Customers today want convenience when they shop, and companies that provide it (perhaps via the Internet) have a foundation for an important competitive advantage. Companies also can add value to customers' buying experience by creating fun, engaging places to shop that offer more than just products and services.

**ENTREPRENEURIAL PROFILE: Richard Howorth: Square Books** At Square Books, an independent bookstore started in 1979 in Oxford, Mississippi, owner Richard Howorth wants to create in his customers' eyes the image that his business is more than a bookstore by hosting a unique, live radio show, Thacker Mountain Radio, every week and sponsoring frequent author appearances. Howorth records the authors' readings and offers them as podcasts on the store's Web site. Square Books also offers a Signed Firsts Club that sells signed first-edition copies of books.

Howorth maximizes customers' convenience and sets his company apart from its competition by providing a free delivery service to any customer who lives within one mile of the city limits. "Amazon brags about how fast they can get books to you, but we can get ours out faster," he says.[12]

**5. *Values to which they are committed.*** The most successful companies exist for reasons that involve far more than merely making money. The entrepreneurs behind these companies understand that one way to connect with customers and establish a competitive edge is to manage their companies from a values-based perspective and operate them in an ethical and socially responsible fashion. In other words, they recognize that there is no inherent conflict between earning a profit and creating good for society and the environment.

Building a competitive advantage alone is not enough; the key to success over time is building a *sustainable* competitive advantage. In the long run, a company gains a sustainable competitive advantage through its ability to develop a set of core competencies that enable it to create value for its selected target customers better than its rivals. **Core competencies** are a unique set of capabilities that a company develops in key areas, such as superior quality, customer service, innovation, team building, flexibility, responsiveness, and others that allow it to vault past competitors. As the phrase suggests, they are central to a company's ability to compete successfully and are usually the result of important knowledge, skills, and lessons a business has learned over time (see Figure 4.1).

Typically, a company is likely to build core competencies in no more than three to five (sometimes fewer) areas. These core competencies form the nucleus of a company's competitive advantage and are usually quite enduring over time. Markets, customers, and competitors may change, but a company's core competencies are more durable, forming the building blocks for *everything* a company does. In fact, to be effective, these competencies must be sustainable over time. They also should be difficult for competitors to duplicate and must provide customers with a valuable perceived benefit. Small companies' core competencies often have to do with the advantages of their size—agility, speed, closeness to their customers, superior service, or ability to innovate. In short, they use their "smallness" to their advantage, doing things that their larger rivals cannot. The key to success is to build core competencies (or to identify the ones a company already has) and concentrate them on providing superior service and value for a company's target customers. Developing core competencies does *not* necessarily require a company to spend a great deal of money. It does, however, require an entrepreneur to use creativity, imagination, experience, and vision to identify or develop those things that the business does best and that are most important to its target customers.

Entrepreneurs should use their companies' core competencies to define a compelling **value proposition**, the value that the combination of goods and services that a business delivers to customers to create a sustainable competitive edge. Gaining a competitive advantage is not solely about outpacing one's rivals; it involves creating a meaningful value proposition for customers. Creating a meaningful value proposition necessitates identifying a company's target customers and understanding customers' needs, wants, behaviors, and buying motives. To be effective, a value proposition must be authentic, which means that a company should be able to identify tangible points of difference that are important to customers. A genuine value proposition should increase convenience, lower costs, or improve performance for customers. Ideally, a company can prove the validity of its value proposition with facts and back it up with customer testimonials.

Companies have three choices for defining their value propositions with an almost infinite number of variations on each one: product or service leadership, customer intimacy, and

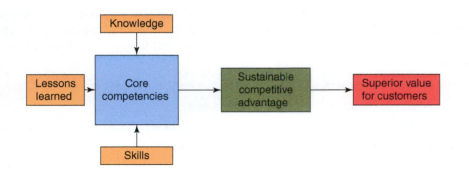

**FIGURE 4.1**

**Building a Sustainable Competitive Advantage**

operational excellence.[13] Successful businesses usually excel at one option and maintain acceptable levels of the other two. Companies that choose a product or service leadership value proposition tout their unique products or services as innovative solutions to customers' needs.

**ENTREPRENEURIAL PROFILE: Ren Ng: Lytro Inc.** Entrepreneur Ren Ng plans to build his company, Lytro, on a product leadership value proposition. Ng spent years studying light fields and optics and developed the Lytro, an easy-to-use camera that instantaneously captures not only the color and intensity of light rays in an image but also their direction. The result is a camera that needs no focusing and creates "living pictures." Photographers simply capture an image and then create an almost infinite number of variations of it by changing the focus and the perspective of any element in the photograph later.[14]

Businesses that use customer intimacy as the foundation of their value propositions develop close relationships with customers and set themselves apart by providing superior customer service and total solutions to customers' problems. Companies that differentiate themselves using operational efficiency excel at speed, selection, quality, availability, price, or some other important product or service characteristic. They set themselves apart by being the best at meeting customers' needs quickly and efficiently. For instance, Southwest Airlines has attracted a loyal following of customers with its low fares; simple check-in process; fast, efficient boarding; and enviable on-time record.

When it comes to developing a strategy for establishing a competitive advantage, small companies have a variety of natural advantages over their larger competitors. The typical small business has fewer product lines, a more clearly defined customer base, and a limited geographic market area. Entrepreneurs usually are in close contact with their customers, giving them valuable knowledge on how to best serve their customers' needs and wants. Because of the simplicity of their organization structures, small business owners are in touch with employees daily, often working side by side with them, allowing them to communicate strategic moves firsthand. Consequently, small businesses find that strategic management comes more naturally to them than to larger companies with their layers of bureaucracy and far-flung operations.

Strategic management can increase a small company's effectiveness, but entrepreneurs first must have a process designed to meet their needs and their business's special characteristics. The strategic management procedure for a small business should include the following features:

- Use a relatively short planning horizon—two years or less for most small companies.
- Be informal and not overly structured; a "shirt-sleeve" approach is ideal.
- Encourage the participation of employees and outside parties to improve the reliability and creativity of the resulting plan.
- Do not begin with setting objectives because extensive objective setting early on may interfere with the creative process of strategic management.
- Maintain flexibility; competitive conditions change too rapidly for any plan to be considered permanent.
- Focus on strategic *thinking*, not just planning, by linking long-range goals to day-to-day operations.

## The Strategic Management Process

**3.**

Develop a strategic plan for a business using the nine steps in the strategic planning process.

One of the most important tasks a business owner must perform is to look ahead—to peer into the future—and then devise a strategy for meeting the challenges and opportunities it presents. Strategic management, the best way to accomplish this vital task, is a continuous process that consists of nine steps:

**Step 1.** Develop a clear vision and translate it into a meaningful mission statement.

**Step 2.** Assess the company's strengths and weaknesses.

**Step 3.** Scan the environment for significant opportunities and threats facing the business.

**Step 4.** Identify the key factors for success in the business.

**Step 5.** Analyze the competition.

**Step 6.** Create company goals and objectives.

**Step 7.** Formulate strategic options and select the appropriate strategies.

**Step 8.** Translate strategic plans into action plans.

**Step 9.** Establish accurate controls.

## Step 1. Develop a Clear Vision and Translate It into a Meaningful Mission Statement

**VISION** Throughout history, the greatest political and business leaders have been visionaries. Whether the vision is as grand as Martin Luther King Jr.'s "I Have a Dream" speech or as simple as Ray Kroc's devotion to quality, service, cleanliness, and value at McDonald's, the purpose is the same: to focus everyone's attention and efforts on the same target. The vision touches everyone associated with the company—employees, investors, lenders, customers, and the community. It is an expression of what entrepreneurs believe in and the values on which they build their businesses. Highly successful entrepreneurs are able to communicate their vision and their enthusiasm about that vision to those around them. "Strategic planning is worthless unless there is first a strategic vision," says entrepreneur and author John Naisbitt.[15]

A vision statement addresses the question "What kind of company do we want to be?" In his book *Daring Visionaries: How Entrepreneurs Build Companies, Inspire Allegiance, and Create Wealth*, Ray Smilor describes the importance of vision:[16]

> Vision is the organizational sixth sense that tells us why we make a difference in the world. It is the real but unseen fabric of connections that nurture and sustain values. It is the pulse of the organizational body that reaffirms relationships and directs behavior.

A vision is the result of an entrepreneur's dream of something that does not exist yet and the ability to paint a compelling picture of that dream for everyone to see. A clearly defined vision helps a company in four ways:

1. *Vision provides direction.* Entrepreneurs who spell out the vision for their company focus everyone's attention on the future and determine the path the business will take to get there.

2. *Vision determines decisions.* The vision influences the decisions, no matter how big or how small, that owners, managers, and employees make every day in a business. This influence can be positive or negative, depending on how well defined the vision is. One writer explains, "Almost all workers are making decisions, not just filling out weekly sales reports or tightening screws. They will do what they think [is] best. If you want them to do as the company thinks best too, then you must [see to it that] they have an inner gyroscope aligned with the corporate compass."[17] That gyroscope's alignment depends on an entrepreneur's values and how well he or she transmits them throughout the company.

3. *Vision motivates people.* A clear vision excites and ignites people to action. People want to work for a company that sets its sights high and establishes targets that are worth pursuing.

4. *Vision allows a company to persevere in the face of adversity.* Small companies, their founders, and their employees face a multitude of challenges as they grow. Having a vision that serves as a "guiding star" inspires everyone in the company to work through challenging times.

Vision is based on an entrepreneur's values. Successful entrepreneurs build their businesses around a set of three to six core values, which might range from respect for the individual and encouraging innovation to creating satisfied customers and making the world a better place to live. These values become the foundation on which the entire company and its strategy are built. Even though the environment in which a company operates may be under turbulent disruptions and changes, the core values on which it is built remain constant. Truly visionary entrepreneurs see their companies' primary purpose as much more than just "making money." When Henry C. Turner started Turner Construction Company in 1902 in New York City, he identified three core values to guide his business: teamwork (people focused), integrity (highest ethical standards), and commitment (client driven). The company has grown into one of the largest construction and building services company in the United States, handling more than 1,600 construction projects around the world in a typical year, and the same principles on which Turner founded the company continue to guide it. Some of Turner Construction's most famous projects include Bloomingdales' Department Store, LaGuardia Airport, Rock and Roll Hall of Fame and Museum, and Ericcson Stadium.[18]

Danny Meyer, an author and the owner of New York City's Union Square Café, compares a company's core values to the banks of a river. "[Core values] are the riverbanks that guide us as we refine and improve our performance. A lack of riverbanks creates estuaries and cloudy waters that are confusing to navigate. I want a crystal-clear, swiftly flowing stream."[19] The best way to put an entrepreneur's core values into practice is to create a written mission statement that communicates the company's values to everyone it touches.

**MISSION STATEMENT** A mission statement addresses the first question of any business venture: "What business am I in?" Establishing the purpose of the business in writing must come first in order to give the company a sense of direction. The mission is the mechanism for making it clear to everyone the company touches "why we are here" and "where we are going." Because a mission statement reflects the company's core values, it helps create an emotional bond between a company and its stakeholders, especially its employees and its customers. Without a concise, meaningful mission statement, a small business risks wandering aimlessly in the marketplace, with no idea of where to go or how to get there.

**ENTREPRENEURIAL PROFILE: Jerry and Janie Murrell: Five Guys Burgers and Fries** Jerry Murrell and his wife Janie opened the first Five Guys Burger and Fries in Arlington, Virginia, in 1986, naming the business after their five sons. "I liked hamburgers and French fries—good ones," says Murrell. "We thought we could do it right, and people just took to it." The Murrell's original vision and mission statement still guides the company: "To sell the best quality burgers possible and provide the best customer service in the community. To fulfill these standards, we focus on quality, service, and cleanliness." Five Guys Burgers and Fries specializes in burgers made with fresh ground beef, fries cooked in peanut oil, fresh-baked buns, and free toppings, such as lettuce, tomato, sautéed mushrooms, jalapeno peppers, and others. The Murrells spent years perfecting their system and by 2001 had added five more locations in the Washington, D.C., metro area. In 2002, they began franchising their successful restaurant concept and now have more than 1,100 locations in 47 states and six Canadian provinces.[20]

*Elements of a Mission Statement* A sound mission statement need not be lengthy to be effective. Three key issues entrepreneurs and their employees should address as they develop a mission statement for their businesses include the following:

- The *purpose* of the company: What are we in business to accomplish?
- The *business* we are in: How are we going to accomplish that purpose?
- The *values* of the company: What principles and beliefs form the foundation of the way we do business?

A company's mission statement may be the most essential and basic communication that it puts forward. If the people on the plant, shop, retail, or warehouse floor don't know what a company's mission is, then, for all practical purposes, it does not have one! The mission statement expresses the company's character, identity, and scope of operations, but writing it is only half the battle, at best. The most difficult part is living that mission every day. *That's* how employees decide what really matters. To be effective, a mission statement must become a natural part of the organization, embodied in the minds, habits, attitudes, and decisions of everyone in the company every day.

A well-used mission statement serves as a strategic compass for a small company, guiding both managers and employees as they make decisions every day. Some companies use short, one- or two-sentence mission statements that are easy to remember and understand, and others create longer mission statements with multiple components. Consider the following examples:

- YouTube says that its mission is "to provide fast and easy video access and the ability to share videos frequently."[21]
- Starbucks' mission is to inspire and nurture the human spirit—one person, one cup, and one neighborhood at a time.[22]

- Zahner's Clothiers, a second-generation men's clothing store in Vernon, Connecticut, founded in 1951 by Manny Zahner and now operated by his son Scott, has a simple mission: "To provide quality merchandise with classic styling in a relaxed environment with professional service delivered by knowledgeable salespeople."[23]

- Trader Joe's mission is "to bring our customers the best food and beverage values and the information to make informed buying decisions."

- Gov Supply, a company that carries an inventory of more than 20,000 security items ranging from concrete barriers to bomb-resistant trash cans, says, "Our mission is to secure U.S. facilities and safeguard the lives of our citizens both domestically and abroad."[24]

A company may have a powerful competitive advantage, but it is wasted unless (1) the owner has communicated that advantage to workers, who, in turn, are working hard to communicate it to customers and potential customers and (2) customers are recommending the company to their friends because they understand the benefits they are getting from it that they cannot get elsewhere. *That's* the real power of a mission statement.

## Lessons from the Street-Smart Entrepreneur

# Thriving on Change

Having faced the worst economic recession since the 1930s, many entrepreneurs recognize that their customers' buying behavior, and, perhaps more important, attitudes have changed, perhaps permanently. A recent survey by Citibank reports that 53 percent of small business owners say that they have reinvented their businesses to stay afloat or to remain competitive. "Small-business owners are especially adept at reinvention, whether because of obstacles or new visions for growth," says Maria Veltre, managing director of Citi Small Business. "Change is never easy, but neither is starting and running a business. We see our small-business clients embracing change and reinventing themselves to secure a rewarding future." What are the keys to thriving on constant change? Consider these tips from the Street-Smart Entrepreneur:

### Tip 1. Get comfortable with chaos

The globalization of business, technology advancement, intense competition, and rapidly changing economic conditions mean that entrepreneurs can no longer expect long periods of stabilized economic prosperity. Instead, they must be prepared to face constant turbulence punctuated by opportunities for growth. Successful entrepreneurs make this important mental shift and are willing to reinvent their companies to capitalize on the opportunities that chaos creates. Chaos requires reinvention, and small companies are much more flexible and fleet-footed at reinventing themselves than their larger rivals.

### Tip 2. Play to win, not to avoid losing

You've seen it in sports: A team, often the underdog, gets an early lead over a stronger competitor by being aggressive and then later in the game changes its strategy to one of playing not to lose its lead. The result is almost always the same: a loss. Successful entrepreneurs play to win. In 2008, as economic conditions eroded, Randy Cohen, founder of TicketCity, a ticket brokering company in Austin, Texas, laid off workers, cut back

on marketing, and reduced managers' pay. Soon afterward, he came across a copy of an article that a local paper had published about his business. Its title: "Don't Be Afraid." Cohen realized that he had changed his strategy to one of avoiding a loss rather than striving for a win. He reenergized his company by hiring 10 new employees and pumping more money into marketing. Sales and profits increased immediately.

### Tip 3. Stay in contact with your customers

Businesses that constantly realign their product and service offerings to meet their customers' changing needs have a competitive edge. Small companies maintain closer contact with their customers than large businesses, which gives them the advantage. Entrepreneurs who listen to their customers, conduct surveys, and polls, and focus groups and simply just spend time with customers find it easy to stay in tune with their customers' needs, expectations, and demands. Ashton and Elaine Barrington started Elaine's as a gift shop in Clinton, South Carolina, a small town with a population of 10,000. After a few years, feedback from their customers prompted them to add a coffee shop inside their store. Before the Barringtons decided to expand the coffee business to include a sandwich shop, they tested the idea first on a small scale. Customers gave their overwhelming approval, and the Barringtons remodeled their store, making Jitters, their coffee shop and café, a larger part of their store. When a severe recession caused sales of gift items to plummet, the Barringtons' decision to reinvent their business proved to be a wise one. "Jitters has been the salvation of our business," says Ashton.

### Tip 4. Focus on providing value to your customers

In a severe recession, customers, even upscale ones, change their buying behavior and carefully evaluate every potential purchase, looking always for *value*. Companies that find creative ways to add value to their products and services and help their customers

*(continued)*

# Lessons from the Street-Smart Entrepreneur (continued)

solve problems will be the ones that succeed. A study by research firm Nielsen reports that customers' willingness to purchase innovative products and services in good and bad economic environments has remained constant over the last 30 years. Adding value does not have to be complex or expensive, nor does it require offering the lowest prices. Josh Davis and Bruno Tropeano, cofounders of Gelato Fiasco, have built a cult following for their luscious gelato by creating 32 unique flavors (cashew sea salt, hazelnut crunch, Maine wild blueberry, and others) each season in small, limited-edition batches compared to the five or six standard flavors its larger competitors offer. The Brunswick, Maine–based company sells its premium, all-natural gelato for $6.50 per pint through 110 independent shops and Whole Foods and generates annual sales of $1.1 million.

## Tip 5. Look for new markets

In a chaotic environment, game changing companies look for more than ways to cut costs; they look for new markets to enter. How can you change your existing business model to reach another market, perhaps one that exists with your current customers? When sales of low-end vinyl-lined pools declined during a recession, the family owners of Sparkle Pool, a small company in Weston, West Virginia, decided to exit that market even though the company had been in the business for three generations. General manager Bob Pirner says that the family decided to shift its pool business toward upscale customers who want custom-designed pools and "aquascapes," an area in which the youngest generation of family members had been developing expertise.

Sparkle Pool's unique installations now range from $50,000 to $300,000, a significant increase over the typical $12,000 to $16,000 installation for a vinyl pool. In spite of the recession, entering the new market has allowed the company to increase its annual sales by 30 percent to more than $1.2 million.

## Tip 6. Hitch a ride on a wave

Like a surfer catching the perfect wave, successful entrepreneurs constantly watch for meaningful trends (not fads) and find ways to capitalize on them. Shortly after Bob Wills and his wife, Beth Nachreiner, purchased her family's cheese business, Cedar Grove Cheese located in Plain, Wisconsin, in 1989, "the whole Wisconsin dairy industry seemed to be going out of business," recalls Wills. To keep the 133-year-old company going, Wills and Nachreiner decided to tap into the growing trend in organic, all-natural food. Cedar Grove Cheese produces basic organic cheeses and artisanal cheeses made from cow, goat, sheep, and water buffalo milk and makes a concerted effort to minimize its environmental impact. The now-thriving company has 35 employees and produces between 4 million and 5 million tons of cheese per year.

*Sources:* Based on "Percentage of U.S. Small Business Owners Reporting Positive Business Conditions Nearly Doubles Since 2010," *Citigroup News*, June 6, 2012, *www.citigroup.com/citi/news/2012/120606a.htm*; Verne Harnish, "Five Ways to Get Your Strategy Right," *Fortune*, April 11, 2011, p. 42; Elaine Pofeldt, "David v. Goliath," *Fortune*, November 7, 2011, p. 50; Chris Pentilla, "Evolve," *Entrepreneur*, May 2009, pp. 43–45; Suzanne Barlyn, "New and Improved," *Wall Street Journal*, April 23, 2009, p. R4; Gwen Moran, "Whey of the Future," *Entrepreneur*, November 2011, p. 70.

## Step 2. Assess the Company's Strengths and Weaknesses

Having defined the vision and the mission of the business, entrepreneurs can turn their attention to assessing company strengths and weaknesses. Competing successfully demands that a business create a competitive strategy that is built on and exploits its strengths and overcomes or compensates for its weaknesses. **Strengths** are positive internal factors that contribute to a company's ability to achieve its mission, goals, and objectives. **Weaknesses** are negative internal factors that inhibit a company's ability to achieve its mission, goals, and objectives.

An organization's strengths should originate in its core competencies because they are essential to its ability to remain competitive in each of the market segments in which it competes. The key is to build a successful strategy using the company's underlying strengths as its foundation and matching those strengths against competitors' weaknesses.

**ENTREPRENEURIAL PROFILE: Chad and Eleanor Laurans: SimpliSafe** SimpliSafe, a company cofounded by Chad and Eleanor Laurans that sells a simple yet effective wireless security system, relies on a strategy built on its strengths to compete successfully against much larger and more financially capable rivals in the home security industry. SimpliSafe's security systems offer customers significant benefits, including a low initial purchase price (starting at about $300), no long-term contracts (only a $15 pay-as-you-go monthly service fee), simple do-it-yourself installation, and a system that works with cell phones and requires no telephone line. The company, which promotes its "super secret formula: wireless technology + user-friendly product design + no contracts = happy customers who pay less and get more," generates more than $15 million in annual sales.[25]

One effective technique for taking a strategic inventory is to prepare a balance sheet of the company's strengths and weaknesses (see Table 4.1). The positive side should reflect important skills, knowledge, or resources that contribute to the company's success. The negative side should record honestly any limitations that detract from the company's ability

**TABLE 4.1** Identifying Company Strengths and Weaknesses

| Strengths (Positive Internal Factors) | Weaknesses (Negative Internal Factors) |
|---|---|
| | |
| | |
| | |
| | |
| | |

to compete. This balance sheet should analyze all key performance areas of the business—human resources, finance, production, marketing, product development, organization, and others. This analysis gives entrepreneurs a realistic perspective of their business, pointing out foundations on which they can build future strengths and obstacles that they must remove for the business to progress. This exercise can help entrepreneurs move from their current position to future actions.

## Step 3. Scan the Environment for Significant Opportunities and Threats Facing the Business

**OPPORTUNITIES** Once entrepreneurs have taken an internal inventory of company strengths and weaknesses, they must turn to the external environment to identify any opportunities and threats that might have a significant impact on the business. **Opportunities** are positive external options that the firm can exploit to accomplish its mission, goals, and objectives. The number of potential opportunities is boundless, but an entrepreneur should focus on only a limited number (probably two or three at most) of those that are grounded in the company's vision, core values, and mission. Otherwise, they may jeopardize their core business by losing focus and trying to do too much at once.

**ENTREPRENEURIAL PROFILE: Napoleon Barragan: Dial-a-Mattress** Napoleon Barragan launched Dial-a-Mattress in 1976 with a simple idea: to sell mattresses directly to customers (in those days with a toll-free telephone number). For three decades, the company grew steadily, eventually giving customers the option of buying online through the company's Web site. Annual sales reached $150 million, but in 2001, the company strayed from its core competency of direct sales and began opening retail stores. Unfortunately, Dial-a-Mattress managers lacked the skill and experience required to select the right retail locations. Although online and telephone sales continued to climb, the ill-fated foray into retail stores had plunged the company into debt, and Barragan was forced to sell his bankrupt company to rival Sleepy's.[26]

In essence, a good strategic plan helps entrepreneurs define what their companies will *not* do and determine which opportunities the company will *not* pursue.

When identifying opportunities, entrepreneurs must pay close attention to new potential markets. Are competitors overlooking a niche in the market? Is there a better way to reach customers? Are customers requesting new products or product variations? Are trends in the industry creating new opportunities to serve customers? Have environmental changes created new markets? Have technology innovations paved the way for new products?

**ENTREPRENEURIAL PROFILE: James Kerstein: Axion International** Axion International, a company based in New Providence, New Jersey, is using patented technology developed in labs at Rutgers University to build railroad cross-ties and I-beams for small bridges from recycled plastics. Founder James Kerstein sees the market for low-cost composite I-beams for bridges as an opportunity for his company because 11.5 percent of the bridges in the United States (more than 68,800 bridges) are "structurally deficient," according to the Federal Highway Administration. Not only do Axion's products divert hundreds of tons of plastics from landfills, but they also are strong, lightweight, durable, low maintenance, cost competitive, and never rust or corrode.[27]

**THREATS** Sixty-five million years ago, a giant asteroid or comet smashed into the earth, causing catastrophic damage to the environment that lasted for years and wiped out the dinosaurs. Today, astronomers monitor the heavens with their telescopes, watching for "near-earth objects" that pose the same threat to our planet today. In the same way, small businesses must be on the lookout for threats that could destroy their companies. **Threats** are negative external forces that hamper a company's ability to achieve its mission, goals, and objectives. Threats to the business can take a variety of forms, such as new competitors entering the local market, a government mandate regulating a business activity, an economic recession, rising interest rates, technology advances that make a company's product obsolete, bad weather, and many others. Brendan Harrison, owner of Down to Earth, a landscaping and lawn care business in St. Louis, Missouri, saw his company's sales shrivel when severe heat and drought devastated the Midwest. Harrison was able to keep his company going by adjusting his strategy to emphasize installations of permanent landscape features, such as retaining walls, rock gardens, patios, and others.[28]

Movie theater owners face serious threats to their business from a variety of sources, including increasingly sophisticated home-theater systems that contain DVD and Blu-Ray players, huge high-definition, 3-D televisions, and surround-sound systems; pay-per-view movies available on demand; thieves who distribute black-market copies of films (sometimes before the original is released); and other forms of entertainment, ranging from iPods and YouTube to video games such as *Guitar Hero* and the Internet. The result has been an overall decline in movie ticket sales. In 1946, the average person went to the movies 28 times per year; today, the average person goes to a movie theater only 4.1 times per year.[29] Although theater owners cannot directly control the threats their businesses face, they must prepare strategic plans to shield their businesses from these threats. Several small theater chains, including Muvico, Cinema de Lux, CineBistro, Cinépolis Luxury Theaters, and others, are changing their strategies to encourage movie fans to return to the big screen. These chains are creating luxury theaters, offering concierge services, fully stocked bars, and upscale dinners, such as sushi, limoncello-tossed shrimp, and duck quesadillas served by waitstaff. Approximately 350 theaters out of the 5,750 cinemas in the United States now offer full-service restaurants, but the number is growing fast. "These theaters are the future of movie-going," says industry veteran Jeffrey Katzenberg. In addition, the new theaters offer customers amenities such as online seat reservations, valet parking, stadium seating with plush reclining leather chairs with extra leg room, call buttons that summon waitstaff, digital systems that provide crisp images and superb sound (including subwoofers under each seat), interactive game rooms for children, and child care services. "We're competing with a million things for people's time," says Jeremy Welman, COO of CineBistro Theaters. "We have to give them an experience that's worth going out to."[30]

Table 4.2 provides a form that allows entrepreneurs to take a strategic inventory of the opportunities and threats facing their companies.

Table 4.3 provides an analytical tool that is designed to help entrepreneurs to identify the threats that pose the greatest danger to their companies.

### Step 4. Identify the Key Factors for Success in the Business

**KEY SUCCESS FACTORS** Every business is characterized by a set of controllable factors that determine the relative success of market participants. Identifying, understanding, and manipulating these factors allow a small business to gain a competitive advantage in its market segment. By focusing efforts to maximize their companies' performance on these key success factors,

**TABLE 4.2 Identifying Opportunities and Threats**

| Opportunities (Positive External Factors) | Threats (Negative External Factors) |
|---|---|
|  |  |
|  |  |
|  |  |
|  |  |
|  |  |

**TABLE 4.3  Identifying and Managing Major Threats**

Every business faces threats, but entrepreneurs cannot afford to be paranoid or paralyzed by fear when it comes to dealing with them. At the same time, they cannot afford to ignore threats that have the potential to destroy their businesses. The most productive approach to dealing with threats is to identify those that would have the most severe impact on a small company and those that have the highest probability of occurrence.

Research by Greg Hackett, president of management think tank MergerShop, has identified 12 major sources of risk that can wreak havoc on a company's future. The following table helps entrepreneurs determine the threats on which they should focus their attention.

| Source | Specific Threat | Severity (1 = Low, 10 = High) | Probability of Occurrence (0 to 1) | Threat Rating (Severity × Probability, Max = 10) |
|---|---|---|---|---|
| 1. Channels of distribution | | | | |
| 2. Competition | | | | |
| 3. Demographic changes | | | | |
| 4. Globalization | | | | |
| 5. Innovation | | | | |
| 6. Waning customer or supplier loyalty | | | | |
| 7. Offshoring or outsourcing | | | | |
| 8. Stage in product life cycle | | | | |
| 9. Government regulation | | | | |
| 10. Influence of special interest groups | | | | |
| 11. Influence of stakeholders | | | | |
| 12. Changes in technology | | | | |

Once entrepreneurs have identified specific threats facing their companies in the 12 areas (not necessarily all 12), they rate the severity of the impact of each one on their company on a 1-to-10 scale. Then they assign probabilities (between 0 and 1) to each threat. To calculate the Threat Score, entrepreneurs simply multiply the severity of each threat by its probability. (Maximum Threat Score is 10.) The higher is a threat's score, the more attention it demands. Typically, one or two threats stand out above all of the others, and those are the ones on which entrepreneurs should focus.

*Source:* Based on Edward Teach, "Apocalypse Soon," *CFO*, September 2005, pp. 31–32.

entrepreneurs can achieve dramatic strategic advantages over their competitors. Companies that understand these key success factors tend to be leaders of the pack, whereas those who fail to recognize them become also-rans.

**Key success factors** come in a variety of different patterns depending on the industry. Simply stated, they are the factors that determine a company's ability to compete successfully in an industry. Bruce Milletto, owner of Bellissimo Coffee Info-Group, a coffee business consulting firm, says that to be successful coffee shops must focus on three key success factors: high-quality coffee products, stellar customer service, and a warm, inviting ambience (with free wi-fi) that transforms a coffeehouse into a destination where people want to gather with their friends.

**ENTREPRENEURIAL PROFILE: Martin and Kerry Mayorga: Mayorga Coffee** Martin and Kerry Mayorga started a coffee roasting business in 1998 and then opened a retail coffee store in Silver Springs, Maryland, that focuses on specialty imported coffee beans. With these key success factors in mind, Mayorga created a shop that looks more like a lounge than a retail store with its plush leather family-style seating. The Mayorgas also have added an entertainment factor by including musical entertainment and allowing customers to view the entire roasting process on its custom-made bean roaster, attractive extras for customers looking for a way to relax after a busy day at work.[31]

Identifying the key success factors in an industry allows entrepreneurs to determine where they should focus their companies' resources strategically. It is unlikely that a company, even a

**TABLE 4.4 Identifying Key Success Factors**

List the key success factors that your business must possess if it is to be successful in its market segment.

| Key Success Factor | How Your Company Rates |
|:---:|:---|
| 1 | Low 1 2 3 4 5 6 7 8 9 10 High |
| 2 | Low 1 2 3 4 5 6 7 8 9 10 High |
| 3 | Low 1 2 3 4 5 6 7 8 9 10 High |
| 4 | Low 1 2 3 4 5 6 7 8 9 10 High |
| 5 | Low 1 2 3 4 5 6 7 8 9 10 High |
| **Conclusions:** | |

large one, can excel on every key success factor it identifies. Therefore, as they begin to develop their strategies, successful entrepreneurs focus on surpassing their rivals on one or two key success factors to build a sustainable competitive edge. As a result, key success factors become the cornerstones of a company's strategy. Simply stated, key success factors determine a company's ability to compete in the marketplace. For example, the owner of a pizza restaurant identifies the following key success factors for his business:

- Tight cost control (labor costs, 16 to 22 percent of sales, and food costs, 24 to 32 percent of sales)
- Waste minimization
- Convenient location
- Consistent food quality
- Affordable prices
- Clean restaurants
- Friendly and attentive service from a well-trained waitstaff

These controllable variables determine the ability of any restaurant in his market segment to compete. Pizzerias that lack these key success factors are not likely to survive, whereas those that build these factors into their strategies prosper. However, before entrepreneurs can build a strategy on the foundation of the industry's key success factors, they must identify them. Table 4.4 presents a form to help entrepreneurs identify the most important success factors and their implications for the company.

### Step 5. Analyze the Competition

Ask small business owners to identify the greatest challenge they face, and one of the most common responses is *competition*. Small retailers increasingly are under fire from larger, more powerful rivals, including general retailers such as Walmart and Amazon and specialty big-box stores such as Home Depot, PetSmart, and Office Depot. Figure 4.2 shows the results of a recent study of the small business sector's competitive health as measured by the Small Business Success Index, a composite of 28 measures of small business's ability to compete. Note that only 48 percent of small businesses are either marginally or highly competitive.

**ENTREPRENEURIAL PROFILE: Irving Shulman: Daffy's** Daffy's, a family-owned discount retail chain in the New York City metropolitan area, recently closed all 19 of its stores in the face in mounting competition. Founded in 1961 by Irving Shulman, Daffy's quickly became a popular shopping destination with high-traffic locations and its then-unique strategy of offering chic designer clothing at discount prices. Recently, the company's sales declined as competition in the discount market grew more intense. Discounters such as T.J. Maxx and Ross Stores, fast-fashion retailers such as Sara and H&M, and flash sales sites Gilt Group, Beyond the Rack, ideeli, and others expanded into Daffy's market, siphoning off much of the best merchandise and eroding the company's sales to the point that it became unprofitable. Daffy's "couldn't get access to products, and there were too many players," says an industry expert. "Everybody is fighting for the same customer, and competitors just ate their lunch."[32]

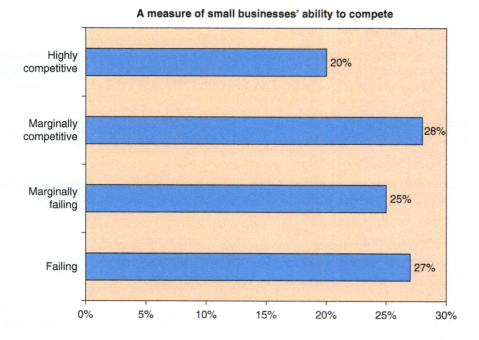

**A measure of small businesses' ability to compete**

**FIGURE 4.2**

**Small Business Success Index**

*Source:* Based on "The State of Small Business Report: January 2011 Survey of Small Business Success," February 9, 2011, Network Solutions and Robert H. Smith School of Business, University of Maryland.

Keeping tabs on rivals' strategic movements through competitive intelligence programs is a vital strategic activity. According to one small business consultant, "Like any general going into battle, entrepreneurs must know their competitors' strengths and weaknesses."[33] Tracking competitors allows business owners to reap the following benefits:

- Avoid surprises from existing competitors' new strategies and tactics
- Identify potential new competitors
- Anticipate rivals' next strategic moves
- Improve reaction time to competitors' actions
- Improve their ability to differentiate their companies' products and services from those of competitors
- Refine their companies' competitive edge

Unfortunately, most small companies fail to gather competitive intelligence because their owners mistakenly assume that it is too costly or simply unnecessary. In reality, the cost of collecting information about competitors typically is minimal, but it does require discipline.

**COMPETITOR ANALYSIS** Sizing up the competition gives entrepreneurs a more realistic view of the market and their companies' position in it. Yet not every competitor warrants the same level of attention in a strategic plan. *Direct competitors* offer the same products and services, and customers often compare prices, features, and deals from these competitors as they shop. *Significant competitors* offer some of the same products and services. Although their product or service lines may be somewhat different, there is competition with them in several key areas. *Indirect competitors* offer the same or similar products or services only in a small number of areas, and their target customers seldom overlap yours. Entrepreneurs should monitor closely the actions of their direct competitors, maintain a solid grasp of where their significant competitors are heading, and spend only minimal resources tracking their indirect competitors. For instance, two of Philadelphia's landmark businesses, Pat's King of Steaks and Geno's Steaks, are direct competitors in the market for Philly cheesesteaks. Their locations—across the street from one another in South Philadelphia—make it easy for each to keep track of the other. Pat's, founded in 1930, and Geno's, founded in 1966, have been fierce but good-natured competitors for decades and were featured in the original 1976 film *Rocky*. They charge the same prices for their sandwiches, and both claim to be the home of the original Philly cheesesteak sandwich.[34]

A competitive intelligence exercise enables entrepreneurs to update their knowledge of competitors by answering the following questions:

- Who are your major competitors, and where are they located? Bob Dickinson, president of Carnival Cruise Lines, considers his company's main competition to be land-based theme parks and casinos rather than other cruise lines. Why? Because 89 percent of American adults have never been on a cruise![35]
- What core competencies have they developed?
- How do their cost structures compare to yours? Their financial resources?
- How do they market their products and services?
- What do customers say about them? How do customers describe their products or services, their way of doing business, and the additional services they might supply?
- What are their key strategies?
- What are their strengths? How can your company surpass them?
- What are their primary weaknesses? How can your company capitalize on them?
- What messages are they communicating to their customers?
- Are new competitors entering the market?

A small business owner can collect a great deal of information about competitors through low-cost competitive intelligence methods, including the following:

- Read industry trade publications for announcements from competitors.
- Ask questions of customers and suppliers on what they hear competitors may be doing. In many cases, this information is easy to gather because some people love to gossip.
- Talk to employees, especially sales representatives and purchasing agents. Experts estimate that 70 to 90 percent of the competitive information a company needs already resides with employees who collect it in their routine dealings with suppliers, customers, and other industry contacts.[36]
- Attend trade shows and collect competitors' sales literature.
- Watch for employment ads from competitors; knowing what types of workers they are hiring can tell you a great deal about their future plans.
- Conduct patent searches for patents that competitors have filed. This gives important clues about new products they are developing.
- Environmental Protection Agency reports can provide important information about the factories of manufacturing companies, including the amounts and the kinds of emissions released. A private group, Environmental Protection, also reports emissions for specific plants.[37]
- Learn about the kinds and amounts of equipment and raw materials competitors are importing by studying the *Journal of Commerce Port Import Export Reporting Service (PIERS)* database. These clues can alert an entrepreneur to new products a competitor is about to launch.
- If appropriate, buy the competitors' products and assess their quality and features. Benchmark their products against yours. The owner of an online gift-basket company periodically places orders with his primary competitors and compares their packaging, pricing, service, and quality to his own.[38]
- Obtain credit reports on each of your major competitors to evaluate their financial condition. Dun & Bradstreet and other research firms also enable entrepreneurs to look up profiles of competitors that can be helpful in a strategic analysis.
- Investigate Uniform Commercial Code filings. Banks file these with the state whenever they make loans to businesses. These reports often include the amount of the loan and what it is for.
- Publicly held companies must file periodic reports with the Securities and Exchange Commission, including quarterly 10-Q and annual 10-K reports. These are available at the commission's Web site.
- Check out the resources of your local library, including articles and online databases. Press releases, which often announce important company news, can be an important source of

competitive intelligence. Many companies supply press releases through the *PR Newswire* (*www.prnewswire.com*). For local competitors, review back issues of the area newspaper for articles on and advertisements by competitors.

- Use the vast resources of the Internet to gather valuable competitive information at little or no cost. Entrepreneurs who use Google Alerts receive e-mails about articles, blogs, postings, or news stories about competitors. Entrepreneurs also have gained useful information by watching interviews on YouTube of managers from competing firms at trade shows and by viewing detailed PowerPoint presentations on SlideShare.

- Monitor competitors on social media. Perch, a social media tracking site, allows small business owners to monitor the events and promotions that local competitors are posting on social media sites.[39] In addition, employees often post informative work-related comments on Facebook, Twitter, LinkedIn, and other social media.

- Visit competing businesses periodically to observe their operations. Sam Walton, founder of Walmart, was famous for visiting competitors' operations to see what he could learn from them.

- Don't resort to unethical or illegal practices.

Using the information gathered, entrepreneurs should periodically evaluate their strongest competitors and develop strategic actions to improve their companies' competitive positions against each one.

Entrepreneurs can use the results of the competitive intelligence analysis to construct a competitive profile matrix for each market segment in which the firm operates. A **competitive profile matrix** allows entrepreneurs to evaluate their companies against major competitors on the key success factors for their market segments (refer to Table 4.4). The first step is to list the key success factors identified in step 4 of the strategic planning process and to attach weights to them reflecting their relative importance. Table 4.5 shows a sample competitive profile matrix for a small company. (For simplicity, the weights in this matrix sum add up to 1.00.) In this example, notice that product quality is the most important key success factor, which is why its weight (0.35) is the highest.

The next step is to identify the company's major competitors and to rate each one (and your company) on each of the key success factors:

| If factor is a: | Rating is: |
| --- | --- |
| Major weakness | 1 |
| Minor weakness | 2 |
| Minor strength | 3 |
| Major strength | 4 |

Once the rating is completed, the owner simply multiplies the weight by the rating for each factor to get a weighted score and then adds up each competitor's weighted scores to get a total weighted score. The results will show which company is strongest, which is the weakest, and

**TABLE 4.5 Sample Competitive Profile Matrix**

Key Success Factors (from Step 5)

| | Weight | Your Business Rating | Your Business Weighted Score | Competitor 1 Rating | Competitor 1 Weighted Score | Competitor 2 Rating | Competitor 2 Weighted Score |
| --- | --- | --- | --- | --- | --- | --- | --- |
| Ability to innovate | 0.20 | 2 | 0.40 | 1 | 0.20 | 1 | 0.20 |
| Customer service | 0.25 | 4 | 1.00 | 1 | 0.25 | 2 | 0.50 |
| Convenience | 0.10 | 3 | 0.30 | 3 | 0.30 | 4 | 0.40 |
| Product quality | 0.35 | 4 | 1.40 | 2 | 0.70 | 2 | 0.70 |
| Product selection | 0.10 | 2 | 0.20 | 4 | 0.40 | 3 | 0.30 |
| **Total** | **1.00** | | **3.30** | | **1.85** | | **2.10** |

which of the key success factors each one is best and worst at meeting. The matrix shows entre-preneurs how their companies "measure up" against competitors on the industry's key success factors and gives them an idea of which strategies they should employ to gain a competitive advantage over their rivals. For instance, the company in Table 4.5 should compete by emphasiz-ing its product quality and its customer service (both are major strengths for the company but are weaknesses for its rivals) and not its product selection (which is a minor weakness for the company but a significant strength for its rivals).

## Step 6. Create Company Goals and Objectives

Before entrepreneurs can build a comprehensive set of strategies, they must first establish busi-ness goals and objectives, which give them targets to aim for and provide a basis for evaluating their companies' performance. Without them, entrepreneurs cannot know where their businesses are going or how well they are performing. Creating goals and objectives is an essential compo-nent of motivating and engaging employees. Unfortunately, a survey by Metrus Group reports that only 14 percent of companies say that their employees have a good understanding of the businesses' goals and strategy.[40]

**GOALS** **Goals** are the broad, long-range attributes that a business seeks to accomplish; they tend to be general and sometimes even abstract. Goals are not intended to be specific enough for a manager to act on but simply state the general level of accomplishment sought. What level of sales would you like for your company to achieve in five years? Do you want to boost your market share? Does your cash balance need strengthening? Would you like to enter a new market or increase sales in a current one? Do you want your company to be the leader in its market segment? Do you want to improve your company's customer retention level? What return on your investment do you seek?

Setting too many goals is dangerous because an entrepreneur runs the risk of diluting the company's resources and people's time, focus, and energy.

**ENTREPRENEURIAL PROFILE: Tony Petrucciani: Single Source Systems** Tony Petrucciani, CEO of Single Source Systems, a software company in Fishers, Indiana, and his management team once set 15 annual goals in a planning session, but the company missed its sales target by 11 percent. "Nobody focused on any one thing," he says. The next year, convinced that setting so many goals distracted everyone, including himself, Petrucciani reduced the number of goals the com-pany pursued by 75 percent, and the company met its annual sales target.[41]

Researchers Jim Collins and Jerry Porras studied a large group of businesses and determined that one of the factors that set apart successful companies from unsuccessful ones was the for-mulation of very ambitious, clear, and inspiring long-term goals. Collins and Porras call them BHAGs ("Big Hairy Audacious Goals," pronounced "bee-hags") and say that their main benefit is to inspire and focus a company on important actions that are consistent with its overall mission. BHAGS are bold, daring, and exciting, and they operate on a long time frame, 10 to 30 years.[42] In their classic book *Built to Last: Successful Habits of Visionary Companies*, Collins and Porras, explain the role of BHAGs to a company:

> A true BHAG is clear and compelling and serves as a unifying focal point of effort and acts as a catalyst for team spirit. It has a clear finish line, so the organization can know when it has achieved the goal; people like to shoot for finish lines. A BHAG engages people—it reaches out and grabs them in the gut. It is tangible, energizing, highly focused.[43]

Figure 4.3 shows that effective BHAGs originate at the intersection of a company's mission, vi-sion, and values, its core competencies, and its key success factors.

Defining broad-based goals helps entrepreneurs to focus on the next phase—developing specific, realistic objectives.

**OBJECTIVES** **Objectives** are more specific targets of performance. They define the things that entrepreneurs must accomplish if they are to achieve their goals and overall mission. Common objectives address profitability, productivity, growth, efficiency, markets, financial resources, physical facilities, organizational structure, employee well-being, and social responsibility. The objectives a company sets determine the level of success it achieves. Establishing profitability

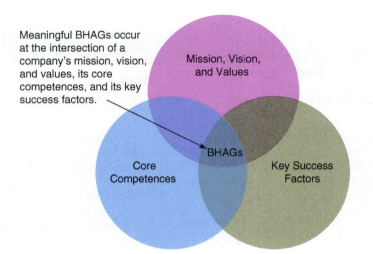

Meaningful BHAGs occur at the intersection of a company's mission, vision, and values, its core competences, and its key success factors.

**FIGURE 4.3**

**What Makes an Effective BHAG?**

targets alone is *not* sufficient. Instead, entrepreneurs must set objectives and measure performance in those critical areas that determine their companies' ability to be profitable—a concept that Collins calls a company's true economic denominators. These economic denominators might be the cost of acquiring a customer, sales per labor hour, the customer retention rate, the rate of inventory turnover, or some other factor. Unfortunately, Collins claims that fewer than 10 percent of all companies understand what their true economic denominators are. We will discuss the importance of identifying true economic denominators (also called **critical numbers**) in Chapter 7.

Because objectives in one area of the company might conflict with one another, entrepreneurs must establish priorities. Which objectives are most important? Arranging objectives in a hierarchy according to their priority can help business owners resolve conflicts when they arise. Well-written objectives have the following characteristics:

*They are specific.* Objectives should be quantifiable and precise. For example, "to achieve a healthy growth in sales" is not a meaningful objective, but "to increase retail sales by 12 percent and wholesale by 10 percent in the next fiscal year" is precise and spells out exactly what management wants to accomplish.

*They are measurable.* Entrepreneurs should be able to plot their companies' progress toward their objectives; this requires a well-defined reference point from which to start and a scale for measuring progress.

*They are assignable.* Unless an entrepreneur assigns responsibility for an objective to an individual, it is unlikely that the company will ever achieve it. Creating objectives without giving someone responsibility for accomplishing them is futile.

*They are realistic, yet challenging.* Objectives must be within the reach of the organization or motivation evaporates. However, entrepreneurs and their employees must set challenging objectives. One business expert says that good objectives are "out of reach but not out of sight."[44] (Remember the importance of BHAGs.) In other words, the more challenging an objective is (within realistic limits), the higher the performance will be. Set objectives that will test you, your business, and its employees; that's how companies become market leaders.

*They are timely.* Objectives must specify not only what is to be accomplished but also when it is to be accomplished. A time frame for achievement is important.

*They are written down.* This writing process does not have to be complex; in fact, entrepreneurs should make the number of objectives relatively small (from 5 to 15).

The strategic planning process works best when managers and employees are actively involved in jointly setting objectives. Developing a plan is top management's responsibility, but executing it falls to managers and employees; therefore, encouraging them to participate in the process broadens the plan's perspective and increases the motivation to make the plan work. In addition, managers and employees know a great deal about the organization and usually are willing to share their knowledge to make a company stronger.

## Entrepreneurship in Action

# Vizio: Disrupting Another Market

Before he turned 30, William Wang was a successful entrepreneur whose company, MAG Innovision, specialized in computer display screens. In 2002, Wang used $600,000 from the sale of MAG Innovision to launch Vizio Inc., which has surged past industry icons such as Sony, Sharp, and Samsung to become the fastest-growing maker of flat-panel televisions in North America. Wang's well-executed cost leadership strategy, much of which he developed from the mistakes he made at MAG Innovision, is the key to the company's success. When he started Vizio ("Where vision meets value"), high-definition televisions sold for $8,000, but Wang's vision was to offer quality products and to keep costs low, enabling his company to sell televisions at half the going price. "When I started this business, I believed we could do all of the things we're doing today," he says.

A lean operating strategy has been a hallmark of the Irvine, California–based company since its first day of operation. Outsourcing most functions, including tech support, warehousing, shipping, and research and development, and keeping its employee ranks lean hold operating costs well below the industry average. Vizio's overhead costs are less than 1 percent of its sales, far below the 10 percent of sales that those costs represent at its competition. "Every single dime counts," says Wang. Because concept development, marketing, and customer service are keys to success, Wang intentionally keeps them in-house. Vizio's distribution network is consistent with its low-cost strategy, relying on discount chains such as Sam's Club, Costco, and others to reach mass-market purchasers who tend to be price sensitive.

Wang recently extended Vizio's low-cost strategy to another maturing market that is ripe for a shake-up: personal computers. "If you rewind eight to ten years, the TV market looked similar to the PC market today," says Matt McRae, Vizio's chief technology officer. "It was a mature market with lots of companies. We did pretty well. We're now the number one TV company in the United States. We've done this before." Vizio introduced a line of computers and laptops that are as stylish as Apple's successful Macintosh line but run the Microsoft Windows software that drives 90 percent of the world's computers. The computers sport clean lines, machined lightweight aluminum bodies, and powerful, high-performance components. "PCs have become a sea of black plastic," says McRae. "We're building a product people want." What Vizio's computers don't include is the "bloatware," the preloaded software that clogs most other PCs, which means that Vizio's computers boot faster and run cleaner.

Maintaining consistency with its low price image, Vizio's computers are priced below Apple products and below competing PCs and laptops with prices that start at $898. The company's high-end computer, an all-in-one desktop with a crisp, 27-inch display, starts at just $1,098. "Our target audience is people who can't afford a $2,000 computer," says Wang. Vizio, which has a very small engineering staff, spent two years designing its line of computers and worked closely with key suppliers such as graphics card manufacturer Nvidia, chip maker Intel, and software designer Microsoft to optimize designs on the components and the systems that run them. "Vizio is doing a good job listening and taking advice from the experts on how to optimize hardware and software," says Steve Guggenheimer of Microsoft. Relying on experienced companies to assist in the design of its computers not only maximizes the machines' performance but also controls costs and allows Vizio to focus on providing a positive customer experience. Because the people who purchase computers are more likely to require technical support than those who purchase televisions, Vizio has decided to maintain all technical support services for computers in-house at its service center in Dakota Dunes, South Dakota. Vizio also keeps distribution costs under control by selling its computers through most of the same outlets that it uses to sell its popular line of televisions, including Walmart, Sam's Club, Amazon, Costco, and Target. The company also sells the computers through portable pop-up mini-stores made from old shipping containers that it sets up on college campuses, at music festivals, and other events. "If anyone says you can't disrupt a mature market, they're wrong," says McRae.

1. What challenges does Vizio face as it attempts to introduce a new line of products into a mature industry?

2. Use the resources of the Internet to learn more about Vizio. Describe the company's strengths and weaknesses. What opportunities and threats does the company face?

3. Which of the three strategies described in this chapter is Vizio using? Do you think that Vizio's strategy for competing in the PC and laptop market will be successful? Explain.

*Sources:* Based on Matt Krantz, "TV Maker Tuning in to Computers," *Greenville News*, May 27, 2012, p. 8E; Shara Tibken, "Vizio Launches First PCs; Pricing Starts at $898," *Wall Street Journal*, June 14, 2012, *http://online.wsj.com/article/BT-CO-20120614-716795.html*; Joanna Stern, "Vizio Aims to Stand Out in Laptop Market with Clean Software and Design," *ABC News*, June 15, 2012, *http://abcnews.go.com/Technology/vizio-aims-stand-laptop-market-clean-software-design/story?id=16571082*; Jason Gilbert, "Vizio Computer Prices Revealed, New Products to Be Released 'Imminently,'" *Huffington Post*, August 7, 2012, *www.huffingtonpost.com/2012/06/15/vizio-computer-thinlight-notebook-all-in-one_n_1599933.html*; Sara Wilson, "Picture It," *Entrepreneur*, July 2008, p. 43; Matt McClellan, "The Big Picture," *Smart Business Orange County*, June 2008, *www.sbonline.com/Local/Article/14706/77/0/The_big_picture.aspx*; "Vizio Announces Grand Opening of a New Customer Service Based Sales and Support Center," *Reuters*, May 14, 2009, *www.reuters.com/article/pressRelease/idUS137503+14-May-2009+PRN20090514*.

## Step 7. Formulate Strategic Options and Select the Appropriate Strategies

By this point in the strategic management process, entrepreneurs should have a clear picture of what their businesses do best and what their competitive advantages are. Similarly, they should know their companies' weaknesses and limitations as well as those of their competitors. The next step is to evaluate strategic options and prepare a game plan designed to achieve the company's mission, goals, and objectives.

**4.**

Discuss the characteristics of three basic strategies: low cost, differentiation, and focus.

**STRATEGY** A **strategy** is a road map an entrepreneur draws up of the actions necessary to fulfill a company's mission, goals, and objectives. In other words, the mission, goals, and objectives spell out the *ends*, and the strategy defines the *means* for reaching them. A strategy is the master plan that covers all of the major parts of the organization and ties them together into a unified whole. The plan must be action oriented—that is, it should breathe life into the entire planning process. Entrepreneurs must build a sound strategy based on the preceding steps that uses their company's core competencies as the springboard to success. Joseph Picken and Gregory Dess, authors of *Mission Critical: The 7 Strategic Traps That Derail Even the Smartest Companies*, write, "A flawed strategy—no matter how brilliant the leadership, no matter how effective the implementation—is doomed to fail. A sound strategy, implemented without error, wins every time."[45] A successful strategy is comprehensive and well integrated, focusing on establishing the key success factors that the entrepreneur identified in step 4.

**ENTREPRENEURIAL PROFILE: David Deigan: Advanced Flexible Materials** As a runner and former running coach, David Deigan knew that runners are susceptible to hypothermia after a race, particularly a marathon. In 1980, building on his work supplying insulating materials to the aerospace and window-film industries, Deigan launched Advanced Flexible Materials (AFM), to solve that problem. Today, AFM dominates its niche, making reflective insulation fabrics for products that range from gloves and sleeping bags to clothing and emergency blankets for consumer, commercial, and medical applications. However, AFM, with $5 million in annual sales, is best known for its market-leading Heatsheets that athletes in 400 triathlons, cycling events, and marathons (including the New York City, London, and Cincinnati Flying Pig marathons) receive when they cross the finish line.[46]

**THREE STRATEGIC OPTIONS** The number of strategies from which entrepreneurs can choose is infinite. When all of the glitter is stripped away, however, three basic strategies remain. In his classic book *Competitive Strategy*, Michael Porter defines these strategies: (1) cost leadership, (2) differentiation, and (3) focus.

*Cost Leadership* A company pursuing a **cost leadership strategy** strives to be the lowest-cost producer relative to its competitors in the industry. Many small companies attempt to compete by offering low prices, but low costs are a prerequisite for success. "You can't compete on price if you can't compete on cost," explains small business researcher Scott Shane.[47] Cost control on all fronts is paramount in companies that pursue this strategy. Economies of scale that are associated with large scale operations are a common source of a company's cost advantage (high volume = low per unit cost), which makes executing a successful cost leadership strategy difficult for small businesses. However, there are many ways to build a low-cost strategy. The most successful cost leaders know the areas in which they have cost advantages over their competitors and use them as the foundation for their strategies.

Low-cost leaders have a competitive advantage in reaching buyers whose primary purchase criterion is price, and they have the power to set the industry's price floor. This strategy works well when buyers are sensitive to price changes, when competing firms sell the same commodity products, and when companies can benefit from economies of scale. Not only is a low-cost leader in the best position to defend itself in a price war, but it also can use its power to attack competitors with the lowest price in the industry. "You have to be the lowest-cost producer in your patch," says the president of a small company that sells the classic commodity product—cement.[48]

**ENTREPRENEURIAL PROFILE: Neil Blumenthal, David Gilboa, Andrew Hunt, and Jeffrey Raider: Warby Parker** Neil Blumenthal, David Gilboa, Andrew Hunt, and Jeffrey Raider met at the University of Pennsylvania and discovered that they all preferred designer eyeglasses but were put off by the $500 prices they paid for them. They began researching the eyeglasses

Neil Blumenthal (l) and David Gilboa of Warby Parker.

*Source:* Corbis Images.

industry and discovered that it was dominated by a few giant companies and that the typical pair of glasses carried a markup of 20 times its cost. "There's no fundamental reason that glasses are so expensive," says Gilboa. "It's a couple of pieces of plastic and metal. It's technology that was invented several hundred years ago, and there's been little innovation on the product side or the distribution side." The young entrepreneurs decided to change that and launched Warby Parker, an online retailer of eyeglasses that designs and sells 50 styles of prescription glasses and sunglasses for as little as $95. "We thought there had to be a better way," says Blumenthal. Building their business on an e-commerce platform enables them to eliminate the costs associated with brick-and-mortar stores, and the foursome has become quite adept at low-cost, guerrilla marketing techniques. They promote Warby Parker using various social media tools, including Facebook, Pinterest, and Twitter. Recently, a free Instagram "photo walk" event that started at the company's New York City headquarters filled up quickly on Eventbrite, and the buzz it generated helped Warby Parker amass more than 19,000 Twitter followers, many of whom actively promote the brand. Creating their own stylish retro-inspired designs and outsourcing production enables the company to keep its production costs low. Warby Parker's low-cost strategy is disrupting the once-staid industry and has attracted a $12 million Series A round of venture capital funding. "They have developed great products and figured out new and cost-efficient ways to build and market them," says one investor. The entrepreneurs also include a social component in their business model, working with nonprofit agencies around the world to give a pair of glasses to someone in need for every pair they sell (more than 150,000 pairs and counting).[49]

Dangers exist in following a cost leadership strategy. Companies using this strategy are pursuing customers whose purchase decisions are driven almost exclusively by price and are not likely to be brand loyal. If another company dethrones a cost leader from its low-cost position, the former cost leader's customer base can evaporate quickly. Some companies attempt to compete on price even though their cost structure is not the lowest in the market. Other companies focus exclusively on lower manufacturing costs, without considering the impact of purchasing, distribution, or overhead costs. Another danger is misunderstanding a company's true cost drivers. For instance, one furniture manufacturer drastically underestimated its overhead costs and, as a result, was selling its products at a loss.

Pursuing a cost leadership strategy requires a company to constantly focus on controlling and lowering costs, but if executed properly, it can be an incredibly powerful strategic weapon.

**ENTREPRENEURIAL PROFILE: Gary Levitt: Mad Mimi** Before launching his e-mail marketing company, Mad Mimi, Gary Levitt was a professional skateboarder and a professional musician in his native South Africa. Eventually, he moved to New York City, where he started a small commercial music company that created jingles for a variety of clients, including the *Oprah Winfrey Show*, for which he created original music for six years. Accustomed to bootstrapping his music company, Levitt relied on e-mail marketing and e-newsletters to promote his business because they were low-cost methods. Intrigued by all that he had learned about developing e-mail marketing tools, Levitt decided to leave the music business to focus on providing price-conscious small businesses with effective, low-cost e-mail marketing tools and services. "I used to work from a coffee shop," he says. He raised $100,000 in start-up capital for Mad Mimi from friends and relatives and built a customer base by offering clients free advice and design work on newsletters and e-mail campaigns. As the company grew, Levitt retained his low-cost mind-set and a focus on simplicity. "I remember how painful and time consuming wrestling with complicated e-mail platforms was, so I built Mad Mimi with robust simplicity—something that is both simple and powerful." Mad Mimi, with 95,000 registered users and annual sales approaching $8 million, continues to keep costs low; all 24 employees telecommute from their homes, which allows the company to offer prices that start at just $8 per month.[50]

*Differentiation* A company following a **differentiation strategy** seeks to build customer loyalty by positioning its goods or services in a unique or different fashion. In other words, a company strives to be better than its competitors at something that its customers value. The primary benefit of successful differentiation is the ability to generate higher profit margins because of customers' heightened brand loyalty and reduced price sensitivity. There are many ways to create a differentiation strategy, but the key is to be special at something that is important to customers and offers them unique value such as quality, convenience, flexibility, performance, or style. "You'd better be on top of what it is your customers value and continually improve your offerings to better deliver that value," advises Jill Griffin, a strategic marketing consultant.[51] Any small company that can offer products or services that larger competitors do not, improve a product's or service's performance, reduce the customer's risk of purchasing it, or enhance the customer's status or self-esteem has the potential to differentiate.

Even in industries in which giant companies dominate, small companies that differentiate themselves can thrive even though they cannot compete effectively on the basis of price. For instance, the $20 billion pet food industry is dominated by large companies, but several small companies are achieving success with differentiation strategies that are designed to resonate with their target customers.

**ENTREPRENEURIAL PROFILE: Marie Moody: Stella and Chewy's** Taking a veterinarian's advice, Marie Moody put her recently adopted dog, Chewy, on a special diet of organic beef that she purchased every week from Whole Foods. Chewy's recovery was miraculous, and Moody noticed that her other adopted dog, Stella, was healthier, too. She believed that other pet owners might be interested in purchasing high-quality, wholesome, organic food for their pets rather than the cereal and meat by-product–based food sold by large companies. She began researching the market and learned that 81 percent of pet owners consider their pets to be full members of the family and that 46.3 million U.S. households own dogs. In 2003, Moody left her job in New York City's fashion industry and used a $50,000 loan from her father to launch from her apartment Stella and Chewy's, a company that sells pet food made from freeze-dried all-natural, hormone- and antibiotic-free meats and organic fruits and vegetables. Her business grew, and in 2007, Moody used a guarantee from the Small Business Administration to secure a $650,000 loan to open her own 12,000-square-foot factory in Muskego, Wisconsin. Recently, she expanded into a 50,000-square-foot factory in Milwaukee that produces more than 3 million pounds of natural dog food each year. Moody's differentiation strategy has been successful; Stella and Chewy's generates more than $20 million in annual sales and is profitable.[52]

Marie Moody with Stella and Chewy.
*Source:* Stella & Chewy's.

The key to a successful differentiation strategy is to build it on a core competency, something the small company is uniquely good at doing in comparison to its competitors. Common bases for differentiation include superior customer service, special product features, complete product lines, a custom-tailored product or service, instantaneous parts availability, absolute product reliability, supreme product quality, extensive product knowledge, and the ability to build long-term, mutually beneficial relationships with customers. To be successful, a differentiation strategy must create the perception of value to the customer. No customer will purchase a good or service that fails to produce a *perceived* value, no matter how *real* that value may be. One business consultant advises, "Make sure you tell your customers and prospects what it is about your business that makes you different. Make sure that difference is on the form of a true benefit to the customer."[53]

**ENTREPRENEURIAL PROFILE: Peter Keyes: Triton Logging** Satisfying global demand for lumber means that every year the world loses a patch of forest equivalent in size to the state of Delaware. In fact, the World Resources Institute estimates that the planet already has lost 80 percent of its forest cover. Triton Logging, a small company in Victoria, British Columbia, has developed a unique solution to the problem of deforestation: harvesting trees from the millions of acres of forests that lie submerged beneath the world's lakes, most of them the result of hydroelectric projects completed decades ago. Peter Keyes, Triton Logging's CEO, estimates that 300 million trees worth $50 billion lie underwater, available for harvesting with the right equipment, which Triton has developed. The company's SHARC system uses GPS, video, and sonar equipment to guide barges outfitted with a specially designed saw capable of cutting trees at depths of more than 80 feet. The company recently signed a 25-year contract with the government of Ghana, where the company is harvesting trees worth between $1 billion and $2 billion beneath Lake Volta, which was created by the construction of a dam in 1965.[54]

Pursuing a differentiation strategy includes risks. One danger is trying to differentiate a product or service on the basis of something that does not boost its performance or lower its cost to the buyer. Another pitfall is trying to differentiate on the basis of something that customers do

*Source:* CartoonStock.

not perceive as important. Business owners also must consider how long they can sustain a product's or service's differentiation; changing customer tastes makes the basis for differentiation temporary at best. Imitations and "knockoffs" from competitors also pose a threat to a successful differentiation strategy. For instance, designers of high-priced original clothing see much cheaper knockoff products on the market shortly after their designs hit the market. Another danger of this strategy is overdifferentiating and charging so much that a company prices its products out of its target customers' reach. The final risk is focusing only on the physical characteristics of a product or service and ignoring important psychological factors, such as status, prestige, and image, which can be powerful sources of differentiation.

*Focus* A **focus strategy** recognizes that not all markets are homogeneous. In fact, in any given market, there are many different customer segments, each having different needs, wants, and characteristics. The principal idea of this strategy is to select one (or more) segment(s); identify customers' special needs, wants, and interests; and approach them with a good or service designed to excel in meeting these needs, wants, and interests. Focus strategies build on *differences* among market segments. Using a focus strategy, entrepreneurs concentrate on serving a niche in the market rather than trying to reach the entire market.

A successful focus strategy depends on a small company's ability to identify the changing needs of its targeted customer group and to develop the skills required to serve them. That means the owner and everyone in the organization must have a clear understanding of how to add value to the product or service for the customer.

Rather than attempting to serve the total market, a small company pursuing a focus strategy specializes in serving a specific target segment or niche that larger companies do not serve or cannot serve profitably. A focus strategy is ideally suited to many small businesses, which often lack the resources to reach the overall market. Their goal is to serve their narrow target markets more effectively and efficiently than do competitors that pound away at the broad market. Common bases for building a focus strategy include zeroing in on a small geographic area, targeting a group of customers with similar needs or interests (e.g., left-handed people), or specializing in a specific product or service (e.g., petite clothing).

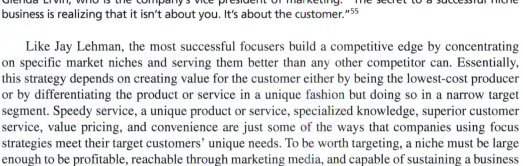

**ENTREPRENEURIAL PROFILE: Jay Lehman: Lehman's** In 1955, Jay Lehman opened a hardware store, Lehman's, in Kidron, Ohio, a town of fewer than 1,000 residents situated in the midst of Ohio's Amish country, designed to cater to the needs of the 40,000 Amish residents in the surrounding area. Because the Amish eschew most forms of modern technology and prefer a simple lifestyle, the products in Lehman's are decidedly "old-fashioned" and are designed to preserve the Amish way of life. The 45,000-square-foot store is made up of four pre–Civil War buildings and carries a unique product line, including wooden buckets and shoulder yokes for carrying them, a full line of canning supplies, hand-powered ice cream churns, oil lamps, woodstoves, washboards, handmade pottery, and thousands of other items that were readily available to shoppers 100 years ago. Lehman has extended the customer base for his "low-tech superstore" beyond the local Amish population to become a major supplier of historically accurate artifacts for television shows and films, including the *Pirates of the Caribbean* series. Lehman's also has become a popular stop for environmentalists, gardeners, cooks, tourists, and the chronically nostalgic, and customers from all over the world shop on its Web site. "If you think building a niche business can't work, think again," says Lehman's daughter, Glenda Ervin, who is the company's vice president of marketing. "The secret to a successful niche business is realizing that it isn't about you. It's about the customer."[55]

Jay Lehman, founder of Lehman's.
*Source:* Lehman's Hardware.

Like Jay Lehman, the most successful focusers build a competitive edge by concentrating on specific market niches and serving them better than any other competitor can. Essentially, this strategy depends on creating value for the customer either by being the lowest-cost producer or by differentiating the product or service in a unique fashion but doing so in a narrow target segment. Speedy service, a unique product or service, specialized knowledge, superior customer service, value pricing, and convenience are just some of the ways that companies using focus strategies meet their target customers' unique needs. To be worth targeting, a niche must be large enough to be profitable, reachable through marketing media, and capable of sustaining a business over time (in other words, not a passing fad). Many small companies thrive in small yet profitable niches, including the following:

- In 1975, J. M. Boswell started making pipes by hand and selling them at the retail store that he and his wife Gail operate in Chambersburg, Pennsylvania. With their signature fluted bowls, Boswell's pipes are functional works of art made from white heath briarwood, which he imports from Athens, Greece, and include a variety of styles, ranging from long-stemmed churchwarden pipes and shorter "nose warmer" pipes to fishing vest pipes and pipes made with deer antler accents. Today, Boswell's son Dan helps his father fill the more than 4,000 orders for pipes that the family-owned business receives from customers around the world. "All we do is make pipes," says J. M. "You've got to love it, and we do." Prices for the hand-crafted pipes range from $70 to $1,500. Some of Boswell's customers fly in for the day to shop and peruse the pipe museum located on the second floor of the retail store.[56]

- Rico Elmore's idea for a niche business came to him while he was on his honeymoon in 2004 and wanted to buy a pair of sunglasses. Elmore, who is six feet three inches tall and weighs 300 pounds, tried on about 300 pairs of sunglasses, but all of the frames were too small to fit his head. "I knew I couldn't be the only person in the world with this issue," he says. In 2005, Elmore launched Fatheadz, a company that markets a complete line of sunglasses and prescription glasses for customers with large heads. Based in his hometown of Indianapolis, Indiana, Fatheadz has 10 employees and generates more than $2 million in annual sales.[57]

- The Peerless Handcuff Company, located in Springfield, Massachusetts, specializes in manufacturing carbon-steel handcuffs for law enforcement and military agencies around the world. James Milton Gill founded the company in 1914 after purchasing the patent from inventor George Carney for a new "swing through" handcuff design that allowed officers to slap cuffs on suspects with one hand. Gill's great-grandson, Christopher Gill, now manages the 25-employee, family-owned business that continues its record of success by focusing on its niche.[58]

The rewards of dominating a niche can be huge, but pursuing a focus strategy does carry risks. Companies sometimes must struggle to capture a large enough share of a small market to be profitable. A niche must be big enough for a company to generate a profit. A successful focus strategy also brings with it a threat: invasion by competitors. If a small company is successful in its niche, there is the danger of larger competitors entering the market and eroding or controlling it. Sometimes a company with a successful niche strategy gets distracted by its success and tries to branch out into other areas. As it drifts farther away from its core strategy, it loses its competitive edge and runs the risk of confusing or alienating its customers. Muddying its image with customers puts a company in danger of losing its identity.

A successful strategic plan identifies a complete set of success factors—financial, operating, and marketing—that, taken together, produce a competitive advantage for a small business. The resulting action plan distinguishes the firm from its competitors by exploiting its competitive advantages. The focal point of this entire strategic plan is the customer. The customer is the nucleus of any business, and a competitive strategy will succeed only if it is aimed at serving customers better than competitors do. An effective strategy draws out the competitive advantage in a small company by building on its strengths and by making the customer its focus. It also defines methods for overcoming a company's weaknesses, and it identifies opportunities and threats that demand action.

## In the Entrepreneurial Spotlight

# Strategies for Success

Most entrepreneurs who launch businesses face established rivals with greater name recognition, more resources, bigger budgets, and existing customer bases. How can a small start-up company compete effectively against that? It all boils down to creating a winning strategy and then executing it well. The entrepreneurs profiled here developed strategies for their companies that set them apart from their rivals and gave them a competitive edge in their respective markets.

### Shaw & Tenney

Started in 1858 on the Stillwater River in Orono, Maine, by Frank Tenney, Shaw & Tenney is the one of the oldest manufacturers of marine products in the United States. Although owner Steve Holt, a former mechanical engineer, has added wooden masts, spars, flagpoles, and hand-woven baskets to its original product line of wooden paddles and oars, little else about the historic company has changed. "We are still manufacturing the same high quality products, using virtually unchanged designs," says Holt. "Some of the original machinery used in 1858 is still in operation today." Although the company's Web site generates some sales, the majority of Shaw & Tenney's sales originate from its existing base of satisfied customers who tell others about the superior quality of the company's signature paddles and oars and its passion for customer service. "We're known as an icon for our products," says Holt. "If you want a solid, one-piece, high-quality paddle or oar, you're going to end up calling us."

Holt credits much of the company's success to the master craftsmen who take great pride in producing the finest quality, hand-crafted wooden paddles and oars. "No one else in the world makes paddles and oars like this," says Holt. "Making these products takes a lot of eye–hand coordination. The key is the wood, but the craftsmen know how to respond to the wood." Because of the sheer beauty of Shaw and Tenney's paddles and oars, many customers treat them as works of art rather than tools for moving canoes and boats through water. "A lot of our paddles never touch the water," says Holt, noting that some customers purchase

*Source:* Jason P. Smith Photography.

them to hang on the walls of their homes, vacation getaways, or company board rooms. Shaw & Tenney sells about 3,000 paddles and oars each year to customers in all 50 states and through foreign distributors in Australia and Germany. The company recently partnered with another Maine icon, L.L.Bean, to create a line of limited-edition paddles in celebration of the centennial anniversary of Bean's founding. The paddles are made from spruce and pine trees, some of which are more than 500 years old, that were reclaimed from the bottom of Lake Quakish, where they sank on their way to sawmills in Millinocket more than 100 years ago. "L.L.Bean is an icon in the state," Holt says. "They're known all over the world. And in our little niche, Shaw & Tenney is known worldwide for making oars and paddles."

### The Resort at Paws Up

Larry Lipson and his family own a 37,000-acre working cattle ranch on the banks of the scenic Blackfoot River (that inspired the novel and the film *A River Runs Through It*) near Missoula, Montana. Recognizing that other people would enjoy the breathtaking views and outdoor activities their ranch offered, Lipson built 28 luxuriously appointed cabins to rent to guests. Building on the success of their cabins, in 2005, Lipson started The Resort at Paws Up, four luxury camps where guests stay in safari-style tents that include all of the appointments of a luxury hotel room (including electricity and twice-daily house-keeping services) but with more spectacular views of rivers, lush meadows, and majestic mountains than most hotels can offer. Guests who go "glamping" (a mashup of "glamorous camp-ing") at Paws Up "rough it like royalty," says Lipson. Guests sleep on king-size beds with designer linens; enjoy gourmet meals prepared by talented chefs; have access to a private mas-ter bathroom and Wi-Fi; sip cocktails while relaxing in comfort-able, rustic furniture; and can summon an attentive camp butler for anything they need. "We refer to it as 'nature served on a silver platter,'" he says. Although managing a ranch and a glamping resort can be challenging at times, Lipson says the benefits outweigh the costs. Revenues from Paws Up have in-creased each year even though nightly rates range from $875 to $3,275 per night. "We've discovered that there is very little price resistance among those who want to experience nature without giving up the creature comforts of a fine hotel," says

Lipson. "We've not only made each successive camp that we've built more luxurious than the last, but we've also increased the nightly rate. What truly differentiates Paws Up is that we are a very high-end *resort* situated on one of the most beautiful ranches in the west."

1. Which of the three strategies described in this chapter are these companies using? Explain.

2. What advantages does successful execution of their strate-gies produce for Shaw & Tenney and The Resort at Paws Up?

3. What are the risks associated with the strategies of these companies?

*Sources:* Based on Judith Ohikuare, "Behind the Scenes," *Inc.*, May 2012, pp. 16–17; "Shaw and Tenney Paddle Company Turns 150 This Year," *Canoe & Kayak*, April 30, 2008, *www.canoekayak.com/canoe/shawandtenneypaddles*; Nick McCrea, "Orono Company Offers New Line of Hand-Crafted Paddles for L.L. Bean's Centennial," *Bangor Daily News*, January 4, 2012, *http://bangordailynews.com/2012/01/04/business/orono-company-offers-new-line-of-handcrafted-paddles-for-l-l-beans-centennial*; John Holyoke, "Happy Birthday L.L. Bean," *Bangor Daily News*, February 22, 2012, *http://bangordailynews.com/2012/02/22/outdoors/happy-birthday-l-l-bean*; Laura Roberts, L.L. Bean Celebrates 100 Years with Help from Other Maine Businesses," *WABI TV5*, January 4, 2012 *www.wabi.tv/news/26510/l-l-bean-celebrates-100-years-with-help-from-other-maine-businesses*; Geoff Carter, "Camping's Extreme Makeover," *Entrepreneur*, August 2011, pp. 59–63; "FAQs," The Resort at Paws Up, *www.pawsup.com/faqs.php*.

## Step 8. Translate Strategic Plans into Action Plans

When it comes to strategic planning, entrepreneurs typically do not lack vision. Success, how-ever, requires matching vision with execution. No strategic plan is complete until it is put into action. Entrepreneurs must convert strategic plans into operating plans that guide their companies each day and become a visible, active part of their businesses. A small business cannot benefit from a strategic plan sitting on a shelf collecting dust.

**IMPLEMENT THE STRATEGY**    To make the plan workable, business owners should divide the plan into projects, carefully defining each one by the following:

*Purpose.*    What is the project designed to accomplish?

*Scope.*    Which areas of the company will be involved in the project?

*Contribution.*    How does the project relate to other projects and to the overall strategic plan.

*Resource requirements.*    What human and financial resources are needed to complete the project successfully?

*Timing.*    Which schedules and deadlines will ensure project completion?

Once entrepreneurs assign priorities to these projects, they can begin to implement the strate-gic plan. Involving employees and delegating adequate authority to them is essential because these projects affect them most directly. If an organization's people have been involved in the strategic management process to this point, they will have a better grasp of the steps they must take to achieve the organization's goals as well as their own professional goals. Early involvement of the workforce in the strategic management process is a luxury that larger busi-nesses cannot achieve. Commitment to reaching the company's objectives is a powerful force, but involvement is a prerequisite for achieving total employee commitment. The greater the level of involvement of those who implement a company's strategy (often those at the lower levels of an organization) in the process of creating the strategy (often the realm of those at the top of an organization), the more likely the strategy is to be successful. Without a team of committed, dedicated employees, a company's strategy, no matter how precisely planned, usually fails.

When putting their strategic plans into action, small companies must exploit all of the competitive advantages of their size by doing the following:

- Responding quickly to customers' needs.
- Remaining flexible and willing to change.
- Continually searching for new emerging market segments.
- Building and defending market niches.
- Erecting "switching costs" through personal service and special attention.
- Remaining entrepreneurial and willing to take risks.
- Acting with lightning speed to move into and out of markets as they ebb and flow.
- Constantly innovating.

Although it is possible for competitors to replicate a small company's strategy, it is much more difficult for them to mimic the way in which it implements and executes its strategy.

### Step 9. Establish Accurate Controls

So far, the planning process has created company objectives and has developed a strategy for reaching them, but rarely, if ever, will the company's actual performance match stated objectives. Entrepreneurs quickly realize the need to control actual results that deviate from plans.

**CONTROLLING THE STRATEGY** Planning without control has little operational value, and a sound planning program requires a practical control process. The plans created in this process become the standards against which actual performance is measured. It is important for everyone in the organization to understand—and to be involved in—the planning and controlling process.

Controlling projects and keeping them on schedule means that the owner must identify and track key performance indicators. The source of these indicators is the operating data from the company's normal business activity; they are the guideposts for detecting deviations from established standards. Accounting, production, sales, inventory, and other operating records are primary sources of data an entrepreneur can use for controlling activities. For example, on a customer service project, performance indicators might include the number of customer complaints, orders returned, on-time shipments, and a measure of order accuracy.

To evaluate the effectiveness of their strategies and to link them to everyday performance, many companies are developing **balanced scorecards**, a set of measurements unique to a company that includes both financial and operational measures and gives managers a quick yet comprehensive picture of the company's total performance against its strategic plan. The key to linking strategy and day-to-day organizational performance is identifying the right factors and measurements to be included on the scorecard. (Recall the discussion of the true economic denominators or critical numbers in step 6 of the strategic management process, creating goals and objectives.) One writer says that a balanced scorecard

> is a sophisticated business model that helps a company understand what's really driving its success. It acts a bit like the control panel on a spaceship—the business equivalent of a flight speedometer, odometer, and temperature gauge all rolled into one. It keeps track of many things, including financial progress and softer measurements—everything from customer satisfaction to return on investment—that need to be managed to reach the final destination: profitable growth.[59]

Rather than sticking solely to the traditional financial measures of a company's performance, the balanced scorecard gives managers a comprehensive view from _both a financial and an operational perspective._ The premise behind such a scorecard is that relying on any single measure of company performance is dangerous. Just as a pilot in command of a jet cannot fly safely by focusing on a single instrument, an entrepreneur cannot manage a company by concentrating on a single measurement. The complexity of managing a business demands that an entrepreneur be

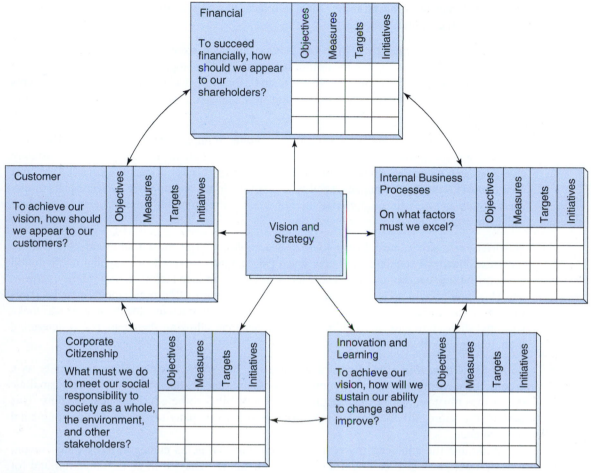

**FIGURE 4.4**

## The Balanced Scorecard

*Source:* Adapted from Robert S. Kaplan, David P. Norton, "The Balanced Scorecard—Measures that Drive Performance," Harvard Business Review, Jan./Feb. 1992.

able to see performance measures in several areas simultaneously. Those measures might include traditional standards such as financial ratios or cash flow performance and gauges of product innovation, customer satisfaction, retention, and profitability as well as measures of vendor performance and inventory management.

Properly used, an entrepreneur can trace the elements on the company's balanced scorecard back to its overall strategy and its mission, goals, and objectives. The goal is to develop a reporting system that does not funnel meaningful information to only a few decision makers but to make it available in a timely manner throughout the entire company, enabling employees at *all* levels to make decisions based on strategic priorities. A balanced scorecard reporting system should collect, organize, and display meaningful information that managers and employees need to make daily decisions that are congruent with the company's overall strategy, and it must do so in a concise, easy-to-read, timely manner. When creating a balanced scorecard for a company, the key is to establish goals for each critical indicator of company performance and then create meaningful measures for each one. Although some elements will apply to many businesses, a company's scorecard should be unique. The balanced scorecard looks at a business from five important perspectives (see Figure 4.4):[60]

*Customer Perspective* How do customers see us? Customers judge companies by at least four standards: speed (how long it takes the company to deliver a good or service), quality (how well a company's product or service performs in terms of reliability, durability, and accuracy), performance (the extent to which a good or service performs as expected), and service (how well a company meets or exceeds customers' expectations of value). Because customer-related goals are external, managers must translate them into measures of what the company must do to meet customers' expectations.

*Internal Business Perspective* On what factors must we excel? The internal factors that managers should focus on are those that have the greatest impact on customer satisfaction and retention and on company effectiveness and efficiency. Developing goals and measures for factors such as quality, cycle time, productivity, costs, and others that employees directly influence is essential.

*Innovation and Learning Perspective* Can we continue to improve and create value? This view of a company recognizes that the targets required for success are never static; they are constantly changing. If a company wants to continue its pattern of success, it cannot stand still; it must continuously improve. A company's ability to innovate, learn, and improve determines its future. These goals and measures emphasize the importance of continuous improvement in customer satisfaction and internal business operations.

*Financial Perspective* How do we look to shareholders? The most traditional performance measures, financial standards, tell how much the company's overall strategy and its execution are contributing to its bottom line. These measures focus on such factors as profitability, growth, and shareholder value. On balanced scorecards, companies often break their financial goals into three categories: survival, success, and growth. Companies use these measures to make sure that their strategies drive their budgets rather than allowing their budgets to determine their strategies.

*Corporate Citizenship* How well are we meeting our social responsibility to society as a whole, the environment, the community, and other external stakeholders? Even the smallest companies must recognize that they have a responsibility to be good business citizens. This part of the scorecard focuses on measuring a small company's social and environmental performance.

Although the balanced scorecard is a vital tool that helps managers keep their companies on track, it is also an important tool for changing behavior in an organization and for keeping everyone focused on what really matters. As conditions change, managers must make corrections in performances, policies, strategies, and objectives to get performance back on track. Increasingly, companies are linking performance on the metrics included in their balanced scorecards to employees' compensation. A practical control system is also economical to operate. Most small businesses have no need for a sophisticated, expensive control system. The system should be so practical that it becomes a natural part of the management process.

## Conclusion

The planning process outlined here is designed to be as simple as possible, but it does *not* end with the nine steps outlined here; it is an ongoing process that entrepreneurs repeat. "Plans aren't the secret to success; planning is," says John Jantsch, entrepreneur and author of *Duct Tape Marketing*. "It's the continuous process of planning, acting, measuring, and planning [again] that moves the organization in the direction of its goals."[61] With each round, the entrepreneur gains experience, and the steps become much easier.

This strategic planning process teaches entrepreneurs a degree of discipline that is important to their businesses' survival. It helps them to learn about their businesses, their competitors, and, most important, their customers. It forces them to recognize and evaluate their companies' strengths and weaknesses as well as the opportunities and threats facing them. It also encourages entrepreneurs to define how they will set their businesses apart from the competition. Although strategic planning cannot guarantee success, it does dramatically increase a small company's chances of survival in a hostile business environment.

# Chapter Review

1. **Understand the importance of strategic management to a small business.**
   Strategic planning, often ignored by small companies, is a crucial ingredient in business success. The planning process forces potential entrepreneurs to subject their ideas to an objective evaluation in the competitive market.

2. **Explain why and how a small business must create a competitive advantage in the market.**
   The goal of developing a strategic plan is to create for the small company a competitive advantage—the aggregation of factors that sets the small business apart from its competitors and gives it a unique position in the market. Every small firm must establish a plan for creating a unique image in the minds of its potential customers.

3. **Develop a strategic plan for a business using the nine steps in the strategic planning process.**
   Small businesses need a strategic planning process designed to suit their particular needs. It should be relatively short, be informal and not structured, encourage the participation of employees, and not begin with extensive objective setting. Linking the purposeful action of strategic planning to an entrepreneur's little ideas can produce results that shape the future.

   **Step 1.** Develop a clear vision and translate it into a meaningful mission statement. Highly successful entrepreneurs are able to communicate their vision to those around them. The firm's mission statement answers the first question of any venture: What business am I in? The mission statement sets the tone for the entire company.

   **Step 2.** Assess the company's strengths and weaknesses. Strengths are positive internal factors; weaknesses are negative internal factors.

   **Step 3.** Scan the environment for significant opportunities and threats facing the business. Opportunities are positive external options; threats are negative external forces.

   **Step 4.** Identify the key factors for success in the business. In every business, key factors that determine the success of the firms in it, so they must be an integral part of a company' strategy. Key success factors are relationships between a controllable variable (e.g., plant size, size of sales force, advertising expenditures, and product packaging) and a critical factor influencing the firm's ability to compete in the market.

   **Step 5.** Analyze the competition. Business owners should know their competitors almost as well as they know their own companies. A competitive profile matrix is a helpful tool for analyzing competitors, strengths, and weaknesses.

   **Step 6.** Create company goals and objectives. Goals are the broad, long-range attributes that the firm seeks to accomplish. Objectives are quantifiable and more precise; they should be specific, measurable, assignable, realistic, timely, and written down. The process works best when subordinate managers and employees are actively involved.

   **Step 7.** Formulate strategic options and select the appropriate strategies. A strategy is the game plan the firm plans to use to achieve its objectives and mission. It must center on establishing for the firm the key success factors identified earlier.

   **Step 8.** Translate strategic plans into action plans. No strategic plan is complete until the owner puts it into action.

   **Step 9.** Establish accurate controls. Actual performance rarely, if ever, matches plans exactly. Operating data from the business serve as guideposts for detecting deviations from plans. Such information is helpful when plotting future strategies.

   The strategic planning process does not end with these nine steps; rather, it is an ongoing process that the owner will repeat.

4. **Discuss the characteristics of three basic strategies: low-cost, differentiation, and focus.**
   Three basic strategic options are cost leadership, differentiation, and focus. A company pursuing a cost leadership strategy strives to be the lowest-cost producer relative to its competitors in the industry.

   A company following a differentiation strategy seeks to build customer loyalty by positioning its goods or services in a unique or different fashion. In other words, the firm strives to be better than its competitors at something that customers value.

   A focus strategy recognizes that not all markets are homogeneous. The principal idea of this strategy is to select one (or more) segment(s); identify customers' special needs, wants, and interests; and approach them with a good or service designed to excel in meeting these needs, wants, and interests. Focus strategies build on differences among market segments.

5. **Understand the importance of controls such as the balanced scorecard in the planning process.**
   Just as a pilot in command of a jet cannot fly safely by focusing on a single instrument, an entrepreneur cannot manage a company by concentrating on a single measurement. The balanced scorecard is a set of measurements unique to a company that includes both financial and operational measures and gives managers a quick yet comprehensive picture of the company's total performance.

# Discussion Questions

4-1. Why is strategic planning important to a small company?

4-2. What is a competitive advantage? Why is it important for a small business to establish one?

4-3. What are the steps in the strategic management process?

4-4. What are strengths, weaknesses, opportunities, and threats? Give an example of each.

4-5. What is knowledge management? What benefits does it offer a small company?

4-6. Explain the characteristics of effective objectives. Why is setting objectives important?

4-7. What are business strategies? Explain the three basic strategies from which entrepreneurs can choose. Give an example of each one.

4-8. Describe the three basic strategies available to small companies. Under what conditions is each most successful?

4-9. How is the controlling process related to the planning process?

4-10. What is a balanced scorecard? What value does it offer entrepreneurs who are evaluating the success of their current strategies?

# CHAPTER 5

# Choosing a Form of Ownership

## Learning Objectives

**On completion of this chapter, you will be able to:**

1. Discuss the issues that entrepreneurs should consider when evaluating different forms of ownership.

2. Describe the advantages and disadvantages of the sole proprietorship.

3. Describe the advantages and disadvantages of the partnership.

4. Describe the advantages and disadvantages of the corporation.

5. Describe the features of the S corporation.

6. Describe the features of the limited liability company.

7. Discuss the alternative options for corporate form, both for-profit and nonprofit, available to social entrepreneurs.

*Diligence is the mother of good luck.*

&mdash;Benjamin Franklin

*A man should never neglect his family for business.*

&mdash;Walt Disney

**1.**

Discuss the issues that entrepreneurs should consider when evaluating different forms of ownership.

One of the first decisions an entrepreneur faces when starting a business is selecting the form of ownership for the new venture. Too often, entrepreneurs give little thought to the decision, which can lead to problems because it has far-reaching implications for the business and its owners—from the taxes the company pays and how it raises money to the owner's liability for the company's debts and his or her ability to transfer the business to the next generation. Although the decision is not irreversible, changing from one form of ownership to another can be expensive, time consuming, and complicated.

There is no single "best" form of business ownership. Each form has its own unique set of advantages and disadvantages. The key to choosing the right form of ownership is to understand the characteristics of each business entity and to know how they affect an entrepreneur's business and personal circumstances. The good news is that the United States remains a relatively easy country in which to start a business no matter what form of business ownership is chosen. According to the World Bank, the United States is the 13th-easiest country in which to start a business out of the 185 countries ranked. On average, it takes about six days and six procedures to start a business.[1] Table 5.1 summarizes the typical business start-up process in the United States across all forms of business ownership.

The following are some of the most important issues an entrepreneur should consider when choosing a form of ownership:

- *Tax considerations.* Graduated tax rates, the government's constant modification of the tax code, and the year-to-year fluctuations in a company's income require an entrepreneur to calculate the firm's tax responsibility under each ownership option every year. Changes in federal or state tax codes may have a significant impact on a company's "bottom line" and an entrepreneur's personal tax exposure.

- *Liability exposure.* Certain forms of ownership offer business owners greater protection from personal liability from financial problems, faulty products, and a host of other difficulties. Entrepreneurs must evaluate the potential for legal and financial liabilities and decide the extent to which they are willing to assume personal responsibility for their companies' obligations. Individuals with significant personal wealth or a low tolerance for the risk of loss may benefit from forms of ownership that provide greater protection of their personal assets.

- *Start-up and future capital requirements.* The form of ownership can affect an entrepreneur's ability to raise start-up capital. Some forms of ownership are better when obtaining start-up capital, depending on how much capital is needed and the source from which it is to be obtained. As a business grows, capital requirements increase and some forms of ownership make it easier to attract outside financing.

- *Control.* Certain forms of ownership require an entrepreneur to relinquish some control over the company. Before selecting a business entity, entrepreneurs must decide how much control they are willing to sacrifice in exchange for resources from others.

### TABLE 5.1 Number of Days to Start a Business in the United States

| Activity | Time | Cost |
| --- | --- | --- |
| Reserve the company's business name (optional), file the company's articles of organization, and adopt the company's operating agreement | 1 day | $275 (USD $200 filing fee, $75 expedited service fee) |
| Apply for federal identification number (EIN) for tax and employer purposes | 1 day | no charge |
| Register to collect state sales tax | 1 day | no charge |
| Register as an employer with the Unemployment Insurance Division of the state Department of Labor | 1 day | no charge |
| Arrange for workers' compensation insurance and disability insurance | 1 day | no charge |
| Arrange for publication and submit certificate and affidavits of publication in local newspaper(s) | 1 day | $400 |

*Source:* "Ease of Doing Business in United States," *Doing Business 2013, www.doingbusiness.org/data/exploreeconomies/united-states/#starting-a-business.*

- *Managerial ability.* Entrepreneurs must assess their own ability to successfully manage their companies. If they lack skill or experience in certain areas, they may need to select a form of ownership that allows them to involve individuals who possess those needed skills or experience in the company.

- *Business goals.* The projected size and profitability of the business and any predetermined exit plans influence the form of ownership an entrepreneur chooses. Businesses often evolve into different forms of ownership as they grow, but moving from some formats can be complex and expensive. Legislation may change and make current ownership options no longer attractive.

- *Management succession plans.* When choosing a form of ownership, business owners must look ahead to the day when they will pass their companies on to the next generation or to a buyer. Some forms of ownership better facilitate this transition. In other cases, when the owner dies, so does the business.

- *Cost of formation.* Some forms of ownership are much more costly and involved to create. Entrepreneurs must weigh the benefits and the costs of the form they choose.

- *Cost of maintaining.* In addition to the cost of formation, there are ongoing fees and expenses associated with maintaining a business such as accounting and legal support that can vary based on the form of ownership the entrepreneur chooses.

Business owners can choose from five major forms of ownership: the sole proprietorship, the partnership, the C corporation, the S corporation, and the limited liability company. Social entrepreneurs also have choices in the form of business structure they choose for their ventures. This chapter describes the characteristics, advantages, and disadvantages of these forms of business ownership. Figure 5.1 provides an overview of the various forms of ownership.

## The Sole Proprietorship

The **sole proprietorship** is the simplest and most popular form of ownership. This form of business ownership is designed for a business owned and managed by one individual. The sole proprietor is the only owner and ultimate decision maker for the business. Its simplicity and ease of formation makes the sole proprietorship the most popular form of ownership, comprising 72 percent of all businesses in the United States.

**2.** _____

Describe the advantages and disadvantages of the sole proprietorship.

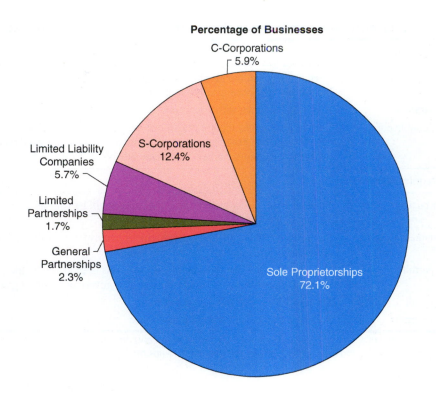

**Percentage of Businesses**

**FIGURE 5.1**

**Forms of Business Ownership**

*Source:* Based on "Number of Returns, Business Receipts, Net Income, and Deficit by Form of Business, Sector Tax Year 2008," Internal Revenue Service, 2012.

## Advantages of a Sole Proprietorship

**SIMPLE TO CREATE** One attractive feature of the sole proprietorship is the ease and speed of its formation. "Sole proprietorships are easy to set up and require very little legal work, outside of a business license," says Jason Deshayes, an Albuquerque-based CPA.[2] For example, if entrepreneurs want to form a business under their own names (J. Jolly Financial Consulting), they simply obtain the necessary business licenses from state, county, and/or local governments and begin operation. In many cases, an entrepreneur can complete all of the necessary steps in a single day because few barriers exist to creating a sole proprietorship. Table 5.2 summarizes the licenses and filings typical for most states and municipalities (specific requirements vary from state to state and city to city).

**LEAST COSTLY FORM OF OWNERSHIP TO ESTABLISH** In addition to being easy to set up, the sole proprietorship is generally the least expensive form of ownership to establish. There is no need to create and file the legal documents, such as those recommended for partnerships and required for corporations. An entrepreneur, for example, may simply contact the secretary of state's office, select a business name, identify the location, describe the nature of the business, and pay the appropriate fees and license costs. Paying these fees and license costs gives the entrepreneur the right to conduct business in that particular jurisdiction and avoids aggravating penalties.

In many jurisdictions, entrepreneurs planning to conduct business under a trade name are usually required to acquire a Certificate of Doing Business Under an Assumed Name (also known as a Doing Business As or Fictitious Business Name) from the secretary of state. Some sole proprietors use their own names as their company names, such as Bob Smith Towing Service. Others prefer to come up with creative company names as a way of distinguishing themselves in the market and creating the right impression with their target customers.

The fee for the Certificate of Doing Business Under an Assumed Name is usually nominal. Acquiring this certificate involves conducting a search to determine that the name chosen for the business is not already registered as a trademark or service mark with the secretary of state. Filing this certificate also notifies the state of the owners of the business. Additionally, most states now require notice of the trade name to be published in a newspaper serving the trading area of the business.

**TABLE 5.2 License and Other Filing Requirements for a Sole Proprietorship**

**State Requirements**

| | |
|---|---|
| State business license | Used to track and monitor businesses for tax purposes and are required for businesses to operate lawfully in the state |
| Tax registration | Required for states with a sales tax |
| Occupational licenses | Certain professions require practitioners to obtain licenses (doctors, lawyers, accountants, real estate agents, private security guards, funeral directors, private investigators, barbers, and many others) |

**Local Requirements**

| | |
|---|---|
| Register business name | Register with county clerk—the default name will be your name, but you can apply for "doing business as" |
| Local business licenses | License from the local government (city or county) to lawfully operate within their jurisdictions |
| Zoning permit | Demonstrates that the location of your business is approved by the city or county for your business' usage and can also govern permitted signage, etc. |
| Health permit | For businesses with food preparation |
| Building permits | Approval to remodel or build a new space |

*Source:* "State and Local Small Business Licenses for Start-Ups," *FindLaw.com, smallbusiness.findlaw.com/ starting-a-business/state-and-local-small-business-licenses-for-start-ups.html.*

**Lessons from the Street-Smart Entrepreneur**

# Get That Name Right!

Managers at Rise and Dine Restaurants, a chain of 15 breakfast and lunch restaurants based in Columbus, Ohio, decided to change the name of the business to Sunny Street Café. Market research showed that customers associated the name "Rise and Dine" with breakfast only and that many of them were unaware that the chain also was open for lunch. "We want our customers to know that we offer an extensive lunch menu with plenty of variety," says COO Joe Deavenport. "Our tagline, 'A Bright Spot for Breakfast and Lunch,' will resonate well with our target audience and capture the essence of our brand."

As Sunny Street Café's experience shows, choosing a memorable business name can be one of the most enjoyable—and most challenging—aspects of starting a business. Some entrepreneurs invest as much in the creation of their business names as they do in developing their business ideas. Ideally, a business name should convey the expertise, value, and uniqueness of the company and its products or services. Darrin Piotrowski saw a need for fast, affordable, reliable computer service in his native New Orleans, Louisiana; borrowed $300 from his mother; and started Rent-a-Nerd as a part-time business from his apartment. The clever name caught people's attention, and Piotrowski's customer service kept them coming back. The business grew quickly, and Piotrowski soon quit his job to run Rent-a-Nerd full-time.

Gerald Lewis, owner of CDI Designs, a brand consulting company that specializes in helping retail food businesses, says that the right name is essential. "In retailing, the market is so segmented that [a name must] convey very quickly what the customer is going after," he says. "For example, if it is a warehouse store, it has to convey that impression. If it's an upscale store selling high-quality food, it has to convey that impression. The name combined with the logo is very important in doing that."

Whatever the image you want to communicate to your customers, try the following process from the Street-Smart Entrepreneur:

1. Decide the most appropriate single quality of the business that you want to convey. Avoid sending a mixed or inappropriate message. Remember that a name is the first and single most visible attribute of a company. Your business's name will appear on all advertising and printed materials and, if done effectively, will portray its personality, stand out in a crowd, and stick in the minds of consumers. Remember: The more your name communicates about your business to your customers, the less effort you have to expend to educate them about what your company does.

2. Select a name that is short, attention getting, and memorable. Avoid names that are hard to spell, pronounce, or remember.

3. Be creative and have fun with a name but follow the guidelines of good taste. When Paul and Barbara Rasmussen started a store in Vancouver, British Columbia, that sells manufactured and custom-made sofas, they decided to name it Sofa So Good.

4. Make sure the name has longevity and does not limit your business. Although many small businesses operate locally, choosing a "local" name restricts a company that wants to expand its area of operation. For example, the name "Richmond Bakery" may not be suitable if the company wants to expand beyond the borders of Richmond.

5. Select a name that creates a positive image for your business. Is Rent-a-Wreck attractive because you think you will save money on a car rental, or does the name put you off because you question the reliability of their cars? Lord of the Fries is a Melbourne, Australia–based business that specializes in selling fresh, hand-cut fries topped with a variety of international sauces.

6. Once you have selected a name, try it out on friends and family. Does the name resonate, or does it create looks of bewilderment?

7. Once you are comfortable with your choice, conduct a name search to make sure that no one else in your jurisdiction has already claimed the name. This is an especially important task for companies whose Web site addresses use the company name. Registering a name with the proper office provides immediate protection.

Another useful tactic to coming up with a great name is to visualize your customers. What are your customers like? What are their ages, genders, lifestyles, and locations? What characteristics of your company are most important to your customers? Classic examples of companies that have used this approach include ServiceMaster, In-N-Out Burgers, and Value-Rite. According to Dave Batt, president of marketing consulting firm Everest Communications Inc. in Geneva, Illinois, "The more targeted your product or service is to a specific demographic, the more specific your name should be to appeal to that target."

The number of potential names for a company is almost limitless. Coming up with the right one can help you create a lasting brand image for your business. Choosing a name that is distinctive, memorable, and positive can go a long way toward helping you achieve success in your business venture. What's in a name? Everything!

*Sources:* Based on Andrew Raskin, "The Name of the Game," *Inc.*, February 2000, pp. 31–32; Rhonda Adams, "Sometimes Business Success Is All in the Name," *Business*, July 23, 2000, p. 3; Thomima Edmark, "What's in a Name?," *Entrepreneur*, October 1999, pp. 163–165; Steve Nubie, "Naming Names—Why a Good Business Plan Can Help You Name Your Company," *Entrepreneur*, May 2000, *www.entrepreneur.com/magazine/businessstartupsmagazine/2000/may/26080 .html*; "How to Name Your Business" *Entrepreneur*, April 23, 2005, *www .entrepreneur.com/startingabusiness/startupbasics/namingyourbusiness/ article21774.html*; "Rent-a-Nerd Life Story," Rent-a-Nerd, *www.rent-a-nerd.net/ about_us/about_us.shtml*.

**PROFIT INCENTIVE** One major advantage of operating as a sole proprietorship is that once the owner has paid all of the company's expenses, the entrepreneur keeps the remaining after tax profits. The profit incentive is a powerful one, and, among entrepreneurs, profits represent an excellent way of "keeping score" in the game of the business.

**TOTAL DECISION-MAKING AUTHORITY** Because sole proprietors are in total control of operations, they can respond quickly to changes. The ability to respond quickly is an asset in a rapidly shifting market, and the freedom to set the company's course of action is both a major motivational and a strategic force. For people who thrive on seeking new opportunities, the freedom of fast, flexible decision making is vital. The entrepreneur solely directs the operations of the business.

**NO SPECIAL LEGAL RESTRICTIONS** The proprietorship is the least regulated form of business ownership. In a time when government demands for information seem never-ending, this feature has merit.

**EASY TO DISCONTINUE** If an entrepreneur decides to discontinue operations, he or she can terminate the business quickly, even though he or she will still be personally liable for all of the business's outstanding debts and obligations.

Although these advantages of a proprietorship are extremely attractive to most individuals contemplating starting a new business, it is important to recognize that this form of ownership has some significant disadvantages.

## Disadvantages of the Sole Proprietorship

**UNLIMITED PERSONAL LIABILITY** The greatest disadvantage of a sole proprietorship is the unlimited personal liability of the owner; the sole proprietor is *personally* liable for all business debts. In the eyes of the law, the entrepreneur and the business are one in the same. The proprietor owns all of the business's assets, and if the business fails, creditors can force the sale of those assets to cover its debts. The company's debts are the owner's debts. If unpaid business debts remain, creditors can also force the sale of the proprietor's *personal* assets to cover repayment. State laws vary, but most states require creditors to leave the failed business owner a minimum amount of equity in a home, a car, and some personal items. The reality: *Failure of the business can ruin a sole proprietor financially.*

**LIMITED ACCESS TO CAPITAL** If the business is to grow and expand, a sole proprietor often needs additional financial resources. However, many proprietors already have invested their available resources into their businesses and may have used their personal assets as collateral on existing loans. Therefore, it may be difficult for sole proprietors to borrow additional funds. A sole proprietorship is limited to whatever capital the owner can contribute and whatever money the owner can borrow. Unless proprietors have substantial personal wealth, they may find it difficult to raise additional money while maintaining sole ownership. Most banks and other lending institutions have well-defined formulas for determining a borrower's eligibility.

**LIMITED SKILLS AND ABILITIES** A sole proprietor may not possess the full range of skills running a successful business requires. An entrepreneur's education, training, and work experiences may have taught him or her a great deal, yet there are areas in which their decision-making ability will benefit from the insight of others. Many business failures occur because owners lack skill, knowledge, and experience in areas that are vital to business success. Owners may tend to push aside problems they do not understand or do not feel comfortable with in favor of those they can solve more easily. Unfortunately, the problems they set aside seldom solve themselves.

**FEELINGS OF ISOLATION** Running a business alone allows an entrepreneur maximum flexibility, but it also creates feelings of isolation; there is no one to turn to for help in solving problems or getting feedback on a new idea. Most entrepreneurs report that they sometimes feel alone and frightened when they must make decisions knowing that they have nowhere to turn for advice or guidance. The weight of each critical decision rests solely on the proprietor's shoulders.

**LACK OF CONTINUITY FOR THE BUSINESS**  If the proprietor dies, retires, or becomes incapacitated, the business automatically terminates. Lack of continuity is inherent in a sole proprietorship. Unless a family member or employee can take over, the future of business could be in jeopardy. Because people look for secure employment and the opportunity for advancement, proprietorships often have trouble recruiting and retaining good employees. If no one is trained to run the business, creditors can petition the court to liquidate the assets of the dissolved business to pay outstanding debts.

A sole proprietorship is ideal for entrepreneurs who want to keep their businesses relatively small and simple. Some entrepreneurs, however, find that forming partnerships is one way to overcome the disadvantages of the sole proprietorship. For instance, a person who lacks specific managerial skills or has insufficient access to needed capital can compensate for those weaknesses by forming a partnership with someone who has complementary management skills or money to invest.

## Entrepreneurship in Action

# What's in a Name?

Clint Smith and Will Weaver were both veterans of the first generation of Internet start-ups. Even though the Internet bubble had burst a year before in 2000, both Clint and Will were confident that there were still opportunities. Realizing that small businesses needed to push out messages to their customers led Clint and Will to think about e-mail as a push-marketing medium. The e-mail services that they had used in previous businesses were not good products for small companies because they were designed for high-volume users and large companies.

They started to work on their new business in early 2002 and decided to name the product Emma. "Basically, EMMA is a quasi acronym for 'Email Marketing,'" says Clint. "There's no Great Aunt Emma, or Grandma Emma, or even Second Cousin Emma who inspired us to create the company. Instead, we chose the name because it was a tangible representation of what we were trying to do conceptually—take a fairly technical product and process and give it all a personable—even human—feel." They tried to secure the domain name emma.com, but it was already reserved by another company. Because they were unable to secure the domain name, they registered the domain name myemma.com instead.

The company experienced significant growth over the next decade, becoming one of the leading companies specializing in e-mail marketing for small business. They branded their product as "emma" and had a registered trademark for "emma" and their "emma" logo. However their domain name remained myemma.com.

MicroStrategy, headquartered in Tysons Corner, Virginia, had purchased the Web domain *www.emma.com* in the 1990s. Emma had approached MicroStrategy on multiple occasions to buy or lease the Web domain. Although MicroStrategy had not been actively using the domain name, Emma was not able to negotiate a deal with MicroStrategy.

In 2011, the conflict over the "emma" name escalated into legal action. Early in 2011, Emma registered with Apple Inc. to create an iPhone app for their e-mail marketing product. However, that same year, MicroStrategy launched its own Facebook products under the "emma" name. MicroStratey's Emma was an app that attaches Facebook credentials to classified listings so that both parties can more thoroughly know about each other when buying or selling merchandise and services. Emma filed a lawsuit claiming that MicroStrategy used the "emma" name in much the same way Emma's own trademark, using lowercase letters and a similar font. The suit claimed that MicroStrategy Inc. intentionally confused Emma's customers and irreparably damaged Emma's business through trademark infringement, trademark dilution, unfair competition, and unjust enrichment. MicroStrategy filed a counterclaim against Emma that claimed that its use of "emma" was not an infringement of Emma's trademark and that both companies should be able to continue to use their trademarks. However, a judge dismissed the counterclaim filed by MicroStrategy.

Internet domain name expert Andrew Allemann observed that Emma's cofounders could have avoided the problem in the first place. "I'm sure the company would prefer to have Emma.com," he said. "But if you don't have it, then you shouldn't brand your company as just 'Emma.' You should brand it as 'MyEmma.'"

1. Is selecting the right name for a business important to its success? Explain.

2. How important is matching a company's name to its domain name? Explain.

*Sources:* J. Wark and J. Cornwall, "EMMA," United States Association for Small Business and Entrepreneurship, *Proceedings*, 2010; Andrew Allemann, "Identity Crisis: Emma or MyEmma?," *Domain Name Wire*, December 1, 2008, *http://domainnamewire.com/2008/12/01/identity-crisis-emma-or-myemma*; James Nix, "E-Marketer Emma Sues Virginia Firm for Trademark Infringement," *The City Paper*, October 3, 2011, *http://nashvillecitypaper.com/content/city-news/e-marketer-emma-sues-virginia-firm-trademark-infringement*; *http://law.justia.com/cases/federal/district-courts/tennessee/tnmdce/3:2011cv00926/51565/36*.

## The Partnership

**3.**

Describe the advantages and disadvantages of the partnership.

A **partnership** is an association of two or more people who co-own a business for the purpose of making a profit. In a partnership, the co-owners (partners) legally share a business's assets, liabilities, and profits according to the terms of an established partnership agreement. The law does not require a written partnership agreement, also known as the articles of partnership, but it is wise to work with an attorney to develop an agreement that documents the exact status and responsibility of each partner. Partners may think they know what they are agreeing to, only to find that there was not a clear understanding about the role and obligation of each partner. The **partnership agreement** is a document that states all of the terms of operating the partnership for the protection of each partner involved. Every partnership should be based on a comprehensive written agreement. When problems arise between partners, the written document becomes invaluable. The partnership agreement should be developed *before* the business begins while everyone is getting along and there are no profits to squabble over.

When no partnership agreement exists, the Uniform Partnership Act, which will be discussed later in this chapter, governs the partnership, but its provisions may not be as favorable as a specific agreement drafted by the partners. Creating a partnership agreement is not necessarily costly. In most cases, the partners can review sample agreements and discuss each of the provisions in advance. Once they have reached an understanding, an attorney can draft the final document.

Banks often want to review the partnership agreement before lending the business money. Perhaps the most important benefit of a partnership agreement is that it addresses, in advance, sources of potential conflict that could result in partnership battles and the dissolution of a business that could have been successful. Documenting these details before they occur—especially for challenging issues such as profit splits, contributions, workloads, decision-making authority,

*Source:* CartoonStock.

dispute resolution, and others—helps avoid tension in a partnership that could lead to business failure or dissolution of the partnership.

A partnership agreement can include any terms the partners want (unless they are illegal). A standard partnership agreement includes the following information:

1. *Name of the partnership.*

2. *Purpose of the business.* What is the reason the partners created the business?

3. *Location of the business.*

4. *Duration of the partnership.* How long will the partnership last?

5. *Names of the partners and their legal addresses.*

6. *Contributions of each partner to the business, at the creation of the partnership and later.* This includes each partner's investment in the business. In some situations, a partner may contribute assets that are not likely to appear on the balance sheet. Experience, sales contracts, or a good reputation in the community may be some reasons for asking a person to join a partnership.

7. *Agreement on how the profits or losses will be distributed.*

8. *Agreement on salaries or drawing rights against profits for each partner.*

9. *Procedure for expansion through the addition of new partners.*

10. *Distribution of the partnership's assets if the partners voluntarily dissolve the partnership.*

11. *Sale of the partnership interest.* How can partners sell their interests in the business?

12. *Absence or disability of one of the partners.* If a partner is absent or disabled for an extended period of time, should the partnership continue? Will the absent or disabled partner receive the same share of profits as she did before her absence or disability? Should the absent or disabled partner be held responsible for debts incurred while unable to participate?

13. *Voting rights.* In many partnerships, partners have unequal voting power. The partners may base their voting rights on their financial or managerial contributions to the business.

14. *Decision-making authority.* When can partners make decisions on their own, and when must other partners be involved?

15. *Financial authority.* Which partners are authorized to sign checks, and how many signatures are required to authorize bank transactions?

16. *Handling tax matters.* The Internal Revenue Service requires partnerships to designate one person to be responsible for handling the partnership's tax matters.

17. *Alterations or modifications of the partnership agreement.* No document is written to last forever. Partnership agreements should contain provisions for making alterations or modifications. As a business grows and changes, partners often find it necessary to update their original agreement. In the event there is no written partnership agreement and a dispute arises, the courts apply the Uniform Partnership Act.

**ENTREPRENEURIAL PROFILE: Lin Miao, Andrew Bachman, Lucas Brown, and Lee Brown: Tatto Media** Lin Miao partnered with fellow Babson College students Andrew Bachman, Lucas Brown, and Lee Brown to build an Internet marketing company, Tatto Media, that fundamentally changed the way advertisers pay for display advertising. They came up with a plan to shift Web-based marketing from paying for impressions to paying for performance. Tatto Media grew from a self-funded, bootstrapped dorm room venture into the third-largest ad network in the world, with revenues of more than $100 million just four years after the business was founded. In 2011, the cofounders sold Tatto Media for more than $60 million. Bachman attributes much of their success to launching with college students who were eager to build a company and not tainted by years of working in a corporate setting. Bachman recommends finding partners who complement each other's skills. Tatto Media brought together Miao's ability to create a vision for each project, the design and engineering skills of Lucas and Lee Brown to build the project, and Bachman's ability to sell.[3]

## The Uniform Partnership Act

The **Uniform Partnership Act** (UPA) codifies the body of law dealing with partnerships in the United States. Under the UPA, the three key elements of any partnership are common ownership interest in a business, sharing the business's profits and losses, and the right to participate in managing the partnership. Under the act, each partner has the right to do the following:

1. Share in the management and operations of the business.
2. Share in any profits the business might earn from operations.
3. Receive interest on additional advances made to the business.
4. Be compensated for expenses incurred in the name of the partnership.
5. Have access to the business's books and records.
6. Receive a formal accounting of the partnership's business affairs.

The UPA also describes the partners' obligations. Each partner is obligated to do the following:

1. Share in any losses sustained by the business.
2. Work for the partnership without salary.
3. Submit differences that may arise in the conduct of the business to majority vote or arbitration.
4. Give the other partners complete information about all business affairs.
5. Give a formal accounting of the partnership's business affairs.

To meet these obligations, partners must abide by the following duties:

- *Duty of loyalty.* Each partner has a fiduciary responsibility to the partnership and, as such, must always place the interest of the partnership above his or her personal interest. This is a duty that must be upheld in every case.
- *Duty of obedience.* This duty requires each partner to adhere to the provisions of the partnership agreement and the decisions made by the partnership.
- *Duty of care.* As the name implies, each partner is expected to behave in ways that demonstrate the same level of care and skill that a reasonable manager in the same position would use under the same circumstances. Failure to perform up to these duties is considered negligence.
- *Duty to inform.* All information relevant to the management of the business must be made available to all partners.

Beyond what the law prescribes, a partnership is based on mutual trust and respect. Any partnership missing those elements is destined to fail. Like sole proprietorships, partnerships also have advantages and disadvantages.

## Advantages of the Partnership

**EASY TO ESTABLISH** Like the proprietorship, the partnership is relatively easy and inexpensive to establish. The owners must obtain the necessary business license and submit a minimal number of forms. In most states, partners must file a Certificate for Conducting Business as Partners if the business operates under a trade name.

**COMPLEMENTARY SKILLS** In successful partnerships, the parties' skills and abilities complement one another, strengthening the company's managerial foundation. The synergistic effect created when partners of equal skill and creativity collaborate effectively results in outcomes that reflect the contributions of all involved. In his book *The Illusions of Entrepreneurship*, Scott Shane says that businesses that are founded by teams of entrepreneurs (not necessarily partners) are more likely to succeed than those that are founded by a single entrepreneur.[4]

**ENTREPRENEURIAL PROFILE: Norm Brodksy and Sam Kaplan: CitiStorage** For years, Norm Brodsky, founder of CitiStorage, a document storage company in New York City, resisted taking on a partner because he knew that many partnerships fall apart. Finally, Brodsky brought his trusted friend Sam Kaplan in as a partner because he saw how Kaplan's values and philosophies were similar to his own and that Kaplan's strengths were skills that he lacked. With his strong background in finance, Kaplan had an immediate impact on the company. He took over the management of CitiStorage's finances and introduced systems and practices that were rare in a small company. "While I still think it's a bad idea to start a business with one, I've come to realize that ending with a partner is another matter—especially if the other person is someone like Sam," says Brodsky.[5]

**DIVISION OF PROFITS** There are no restrictions on how partners may distribute the company's profits as long as they are consistent with the partnership agreement and do not violate the rights of any partner. The partnership agreement should articulate the nature of each partner's contribution and proportional share of profits. If the partners fail to create an agreement, the UPA states that the partners share equally in the partnership's profits, regardless of the proportional amount of their original capital contributions.

**LARGER POOL OF CAPITAL** A partnership can significantly broaden the pool of capital available to a business. Each partner's asset base will support a larger borrowing capacity than either partner would have had alone. This may become a critical factor because undercapitalization is a common cause of business failures.

**ABILITY TO ATTRACT LIMITED PARTNERS** Not every partner need take an active role in the operation of a business. Partners who take an active role in managing a company and who share in its rewards, liabilities, and responsibilities are **general partners**. Every partnership must have at least one general partner (although there is no limit on the number of general partners a business can have). General partners have unlimited personal liability for the company's debts and obligations and are expected to take an active role in managing the business.

Limited partners are financial investors who do not want to participate in the day-to-day affairs of the partnership and seek to limit their risk. Limited partners cannot take an active role in the operation of the company and have limited personal liability for the company's debts and obligations. If the business fails, limited partners lose only what they have invested in the partnership itself and no more. If limited partners are "materially and actively" involved in a business— defined as spending more than 500 hours a year in the company—they will be treated as general partners and will lose their limited liability protection. Silent partners and dormant partners are special types of limited partners. **Silent partners** are not active in a business but generally are known to be members of the partnership. **Dormant partners** are neither active nor generally known to be associated with the business.

A limited partnership can attract investors by offering them limited liability and the potential to realize a substantial return on their investments if the business is successful. Many individuals find it profitable to invest in high-potential small businesses but *only* if they avoid the disadvantages of unlimited liability. We will discuss limited partnerships in greater detail later in this chapter.

**LITTLE GOVERNMENTAL REGULATION** Like the proprietorship, the partnership form of ownership is not burdened with reporting requirements.

**FLEXIBILITY** Although not as flexible as sole proprietorships, partnerships can react quickly to changing market conditions. In large partnerships, however, getting all partners' approval on key decisions can slow down a company's ability to react. Unless the partnership agreement states otherwise, each partner has a single vote in the management of the company no matter how large his or her contribution to the partnership is.

**TAXATION** The partnership itself is not subject to federal taxation. It serves as a conduit for the profit or losses it earns or incurs; its net income or losses are passed through the individual partners as personal income, and the partners, not the business, pay income tax on their distributive shares. The partnership, like the proprietorship, avoids the "double-taxation" disadvantage associated with the corporate form of ownership. Partners receive a K-1 tax return, which they file with their personal tax returns that shows their share of the partnership's income on which they must pay taxes. The K-1 also is issued to owners of S corporations and limited liability companies because they, too, are pass-through entities when it comes to income taxes.

## Lessons from the Street-Smart Entrepreneur

# How to Avoid a Business Divorce

Starting a business with another person or team of people offers many advantages, including a greater chance for success than starting a business solo. Ben Cohen and Jerry Greenfield (Ben & Jerry's Homemade), Larry Page and Sergey Brin (Google), Steve Jobs and Steve Wozniak (Apple), and Evan Williams and Biz Stone (Twitter) are examples of successful business partnerships. However, operating a business with others also presents challenges in the form of personality conflicts, differing business philosophies, workload expectations, and a variety of other important issues. Like marriage partners, business co-owners experience together happiness and heartbreak, good times and bad times, and success and failure. In addition, some business partnerships, like some marriages, fall apart. However, a failed business partnership is often much harder to untangle than a failed marriage. Before going into business with someone else, consider the following advice from the Street-Smart Entrepreneur on how to avoid a business divorce.

### Tip #1. Have shared vision and values

One of the biggest mistakes entrepreneurs make is jumping into a business with other people before they get to know their partners. Ideally, business co-owners should share a common vision for the business and common values on which they build the company's culture. Ben Cohen and Jerry Greenfield had so much success in building their company, Ben and Jerry's Ice Cream, as partners due in large part to their shared values. They made humanitarianism and philanthropy integral parts of their business. They found creative ways to combine profitability with social responsibility by creating a progressive approach to employee management.

### Tip #2. Divide responsibilities based on ability, experience, and interest

One of the greatest advantages of creating a company with others is the ability to create a whole that is greater than the sum of its parts. To do so, however, requires each cofounder to do what he or she is best at doing. Alicia Rockmore and Sarah Welch, cofounders of Buttoned Up, Inc., an online company that sells organizational products aimed specifically at women, worked together on and off for eight years in their respective corporate jobs before they decided to take the entrepreneurial plunge together. Each woman brings to the business a different skill set, but what ties them together is "respect for each other's business judgment," says Welch.

### Tip #3. Put it in writing

Before launching a business with someone else, take the time to put together an operating agreement in writing—whatever form of ownership you choose. The document should spell out the division of responsibilities and duties, the decision-making process and authority, the division of profits, compensation, exit strategies, and other important matters. Avoid the tendency to go into business with someone else, no matter how close you may be, with nothing more than a handshake and high hopes. Steve Hindy and Tom Potter, who founded Brooklyn Brewery in 1987, found that putting things in writing was a critical decision for their business partnership. "One important thing that we did at the beginning was to draw up a partnership agreement that defined it financially and also defined a buy-sell agreement, in case one of us wanted out or in case of disputes," says Hindy. The written agreement allowed them to part ways amicably with a clearly defined process when Potter decided to retire in 2004.

### Tip #4. Realize that conflicts will occur

Conflict is a natural part of any relationship. Co-owners will never agree on every aspect of operating a company. However, tempers tend to flare and disagreements arise when co-owners find themselves in a crucible, under pressure to make decisions or deal with a business crisis. The key is to have a mechanism such as an operating agreement in place for dealing with conflict when it does occur. The *worst* approach co-owners can take is to ignore or cover up the conflict. Unaddressed conflicts seldom resolve themselves.

### Tip #5. Keep the lines of communication open

The best way to deal with conflict is to talk and work through it. That requires co-owners to maintain open lines of communication with one another. When Dr. Shaparak Kemarei and Dr. Marjaneh Hedayat decided to become partners in a laser hair-removal practice, they often called each other after business hours to discuss issues, a procedure that imposed on their family time. Soon they established a better way of maintaining daily communication: Twice a day they set aside a designated time to devote to discussing business issues and regularly select management books to read and discuss together. "Even if we don't agree, we talk about everything, come to an understanding, and move on," says Dr. Hedayat. "That's how a business grows."

*Sources:* Based on Shelly Banjo, "Before You Tie the Knot," *Wall Street Journal*, November 26, 2007, p. R4; Alexander Stein, "Make Your Partnership Work," *FSB*, May 2009, p. 19; Stacy Perman, "Contemplating a Business Partnership?," *Bloomberg Businessweek*, November 21, 2008, www.businessweek.com/stories/2008-11-21/contemplating-a-business-partnership-businessweek-business-news-stock-market-and-financial-advice; "Ben Cohen & Jerry Greenfield: Caring Capitalists," *Entrepreneur*, October 10, 2008, www.entrepreneur.com/article/197626.

## Disadvantages of the Partnership

Business partnerships can be complicated and frustrating. Before taking on a partner, every entrepreneur should double-check the decision to be sure that the prospective business partner is adding value to the business. "I would never, ever, ever advise someone to go into a partnership unless it's necessary," says Clay Nelson, a Santa Barbara business adviser who works with partners.[6] For some entrepreneurs, taking on a partner *is* necessary; for others, it is a mistake. Before entering into a partnership, entrepreneurs must consider their disadvantages.

**UNLIMITED LIABILITY OF AT LEAST ONE PARTNER** At least one member of every partnership must be a general partner. The general partner has unlimited personal liability for the partnership's debts. In most states, certain property belonging to a proprietor or a general partner is exempt from attachment by creditors of a failed business. The most common is the homestead exemption, which allows the debtor's home to be sold to satisfy debt but stipulates that a certain dollar amount be reserved to allow the debtor to find other shelter. State laws commonly exempt certain personal property items from attachments by creditors. For example, household furniture (up to a specified amount), clothing and personal possessions, government or military pensions, and bonuses are protected and cannot be seized to satisfy an outstanding business debt.

**CAPITAL ACCUMULATION** Although the partnership form of ownership is superior to the sole proprietorship when it comes to attracting capital, it also presents limitations. The partnership is generally not as effective in raising funds as the corporate form of ownership, which can acquire capital by selling shares of ownership to outside investors.

**DIFFICULTY IN DISPOSING OF PARTNERSHIP INTEREST** Most partnership agreements restrict how partners can dispose of their shares of the business. Usually, a partner is required to sell his or her interest to the remaining partners. Even if the original agreement contains such a requirement and clearly delineates how the value of each partner's ownership will be determined, there is no guarantee that other partners will have the financial resources to buy the seller's interest. When the money is not available to purchase a partner's interest, the other partners may be forced to either accept a new partner or dissolve the partnership and distribute the remaining assets. Under previous versions of the UPA, when a partner withdrew from a partnership (an act called dissociation), the partnership automatically dissolved, which required the remaining partners to form a new partnership. Current provisions of the UPA, however, do not require dissolution and allow the remaining partners to continue to operate the business without the withdrawing partner. The withdrawing partner no longer has the authority to represent the business or to take part in managing it.

**POTENTIAL FOR PERSONALITY AND AUTHORITY CONFLICTS** In some ways, a partnership is similar to a marriage. The compatibility of partners' work habits, goals, ethics, and general business philosophies are an important ingredient in a successful relationship. Friction among partners is inevitable and can be difficult to control. The key is to have in place a comprehensive partnership agreement and open lines of communication. The demise of many partnerships can often be traced to interpersonal conflicts and the lack of a partnership agreement to resolve those conflicts. Knowing potential partners well and having a conflict resolution plan in place result in better outcomes when dealing with the inevitable conflicts that occur when there is a fundamental difference of opinion on one or more critical business decisions.

**PARTNERS ARE BOUND BY THE LAW OF AGENCY** Each partner acts as an agent for the business and can legally bind the other partners to a business agreement. This agency power requires all partners to exercise good faith and reasonable care in performing their responsibilities. For example, if a partner signs a three-year lease for new office space, dramatically increasing the operation costs of the business beyond what the business can afford, the partnership is legally bound to that agreement.

Some partnerships survive a lifetime; others experience difficulties and ultimately are dissolved. In a partnership, the continued exposure to personal liability for partners' actions may wear down the general partners. Knowing that they could lose their personal assets because of a partner's bad business decision is a fact of life in partnerships. Conflicts between or among partners can force a business to close. Unfortunately, few partnerships have a mutually agreed on means for conflict resolution, such as mediation or arbitration, which can help partners resolve underlying conflicts and keep the business operating. Without such a mechanism, disagreements can escalate to the point where the partnership is dissolved and the business ceases to operate.

Kathleen King, founder of
Kathleen's Bake Shop.

*Source:* Kathleen King.

**ENTREPRENEURIAL PROFILE: Kathleen King: Kathleen's Bake Shop** Kathleen King had worked for 23 years building her business, Kathleen's Bake Shop, in Southampton, New York. To help with the growing tasks and responsibilities created by the success of her business, King took on two brothers as business partners. All three had an equal ownership share. Six months later, the two brothers teamed up to get ownership of King's business. She went to work and was confronted by her partners blocking the door and holding paperwork that would evict her from her own bakery. When she returned the following day, armed security guards were guarding the business to keep her out. King filed a lawsuit against the brothers. When the lawsuit was settled, she had accumulated $200,000 in debt and was granted only the building the bakery was housed in. The brothers were granted the rights to keep the bakery's name and recipes. "They were allowed to use my recipes, but never once did they duplicate them in the quality and consistency that I did, so I felt in the big picture they really didn't have my recipes," says King. "They weren't interested in quality control—they were interested in the bottom line." In just a few more months, Kathleen's Bake Shop had accumulated $600,000 in debt and eventually had to shut down. "I never saw something so valuable get destroyed so fast," says King. "And as they were driving everything into debt, it was still my name on the business."[7]

## Limited Partnerships

A **limited partnership** is a modification of a general partnership. Limited partnerships are composed of at least one general partner and at least one limited partner. The general partner is treated, under law, in the same manner as in a general partnership, which means that he or she has unlimited personal liability for the partnership's debts. Limited partners are treated as *investors* in the business venture with limited liability and therefore can lose only the amount they have invested in the business. There is no limit on the number of limited partners in a limited partnership.

Most states recognize the ratified Revised Uniform Limited Partnership Act. To form a limited partnership, the partners must file a certificate of limited partnership in the state in which the partnership plans to conduct business. The certificate of limited partnership should include the following information:

- The name of the limited partnership.
- The general character of its business.
- The address of the office of the firm's agent authorized to receive summonses or other legal notices.
- The name and business address of each partner, specifying which ones are general partners and which are limited partners.
- The amount of cash contributions actually made and agreed to be made in the future by each partner.
- A description of the value of noncash contributions made or to be made by each partner.
- The times at which additional contributions are to be made by any of the partners.
- Whether and under what conditions a limited partner has the right to grant limited partner status to an assignee of his or her interest in the partnership.
- If agreed on, the time or the circumstances when a partner may withdraw from the firm (unlike the withdrawal of a general partner, the withdrawal of a limited partner does not automatically dissolve a limited partnership).
- If agreed on, the amount of or the method of determining the funds to be received by a withdrawing partner.
- Any right of a partner to receive distributions of cash or other property from the firm and the circumstances for such distributions.
- The time or circumstances when the limited partnership is to be dissolved.
- The rights of the remaining general partners to continue the business after the withdrawal of a general partner.
- Any other matters the partners want to include.

Although limited partners do not have the right to take an active role in managing the business, they can make management suggestions to general partners, inspect the business, and have access to and make copies of business records. A limited partner is, of course, entitled to a share of the business's profits (or losses) as agreed and specified in the certificate of limited partnership.

### Limited Liability Partnerships

Many states now recognize **limited liability partnerships** (LLPs), in which all partners in the business are limited partners, having only limited liability for the debts and obligations of the partnership. Most states restrict LLPs to certain types of professionals, such as attorneys, physicians, dentists, accountants, and others. Just as with any limited partnership, the partners must file a certificate of limited partnership in the state in which the partnership plans to conduct business. Just as with every partnership, an LLP does not pay taxes; its income is passed through to the limited partners, who pay personal taxes on their shares of the company's net income.

## The Corporation

The corporation is the most complex of the forms of business ownership. A **corporation** is an artificial legal entity created by the state that can sue or be sued in its own name, enter into and enforce contracts, hold title to and transfer property, and be found civilly and criminally liable for violations of the law.[8] The life of the corporation is independent of its owners, and shareholders can transfer their ownership in the business to others.

**4.**
Describe the advantages and disadvantages of the corporation.

Corporations, also known as **C corporations**, are creations of the state. When a corporation is founded, it accepts the regulations and restrictions of the state in which it is incorporated and any other state in which it chooses to conduct business. A corporation that conducts business in the state in which it is incorporated is a **domestic corporation**. When a corporation conducts business in another state, that state considers it to be a **foreign corporation**. Corporations that are formed in other countries and conduct business in the United States are referred to as **alien corporations**.

Corporations have the power to raise capital by selling shares of ownership to outside investors. Some corporations have thousands of shareholders, and others have only a handful of owners. **Publicly held corporations** have a large number of shareholders, and their stock is usually traded on one of the large stock exchanges. **Closely held corporations** have shares that are controlled by a relatively small number of people, often family members, relatives, or friends. Their stock is not traded on any stock exchange but instead is passed from one generation to the next. Many small corporations are closely held.

In general, a corporation must report annually its financial operations to its home state's secretary of state. These financial reports become public record. If the corporation's stock is sold in more than one state, the corporation must comply with federal regulations governing the sale of corporate securities and stringent reporting requirements. There are substantially more reporting requirements for a corporation than for the other forms of ownership.

### Requirements for Incorporation

Most states allow entrepreneurs to incorporate without the assistance of an attorney. Some states even provide incorporation kits to help in the incorporation process. Although it is less expensive for entrepreneurs to complete the process themselves, doing so may not be ideal because overlooking some provisions of the incorporation process creates legal and tax problems. In some states, the application process is complex, and the required forms are confusing. Entrepreneurs usually can find an attorney or an online service to help them incorporate their businesses for a reasonable fee.

Once the owners decide to form a corporation, they must choose the state in which to incorporate. If the business will operate in a single state, it usually makes sense to incorporate in that state. States differ—sometimes dramatically—in the requirements they place on the corporations they charter and in how they treat corporations chartered in other states. States also differ in the tax rates imposed on corporations, the restrictions placed on their activities, the capital required to incorporate, and the fees or organization tax charged to incorporate.

Every state requires a certificate of incorporation or charter to be filed with the secretary of state. The following information is generally required to be in the certificate of incorporation:

- *The corporation's name.* The corporations must choose a name that is not so similar to that of another firm in that state that it causes confusion or lends itself to deception. It must also include a term, such as *corporation, incorporated, company,* or *limited,* to notify the public that they are dealing with a corporation.

- *The corporation's statement of purpose.* The incorporators must state in general terms the intended nature of the business. The purpose must, of course, be lawful. An illustration might be "to engage in the sale of office furniture and fixtures." The purpose should be broad enough to allow for some expansion in the activities of the business as it develops.

- *The company's time horizon.* Most corporations are formed with no specific termination date and will continue "in perpetuity." However, it is possible to incorporate for a specific duration of time, for example, a period of 50 years.

- *Names and addresses of the incorporators.* The incorporators must be identified in the articles of incorporation and are liable under the law to attest that all information in this document is correct. In some states, one or more of the incorporators must reside in the state the corporation is being created.

- *Place of business.* The post office address of the corporation's principal office must be listed. This address, for a domestic corporation, must be in the state in which incorporation takes place.

- *Capital stock authorization.* The articles of incorporation must include the amount and class (or type) of capital stock the corporation wants to be authorized to issue. This is not the number of shares it must issue; a corporation must also define the different classification of stock and any special rights, preferences, or limits each class has.

- *Capital required at the time of incorporation.* Some states require a newly formed corporation to deposit in a bank a specific percentage of the stock's par value before incorporating.

- *Provisions for preemptive rights, if any, that are granted to stockholders.* If granted **preemptive rights** state that stockholders have the right to purchase new shares of stock before they are offered to the public.

- *Restrictions on transferring shares.* Many closely held corporations—those owned by a few shareholders, often family members—require shareholders interested in selling their stocks to offer it first to the corporation. Shares the corporation itself owns are called **treasury stock**. To maintain control over their ownership, many closely held corporations exercise this right, known as the **right of first refusal**.

- *Names and addresses of the officers and directors of the corporation.*

- *Rules under which the corporation will operate.* **Bylaws** are the rules and regulations the officers and directors establish for the corporation's internal management and operation.

Once the secretary of state of the incorporating state approves a request for incorporation and the corporation pays its fees, the approved articles of incorporation become its **corporate charter**. With the corporate charter as proof that the corporation legally exists, the next order of business is to hold an organizational meeting for the stockholders to formally elect directors, who, in turn, appoint the corporate officers.

Corporations account for the greatest proportion of sales and profits than other forms of ownership, but like the preceding forms of ownership, they have advantages and disadvantages.

## Advantages of the Corporation

**LIMITED LIABILITY OF STOCKHOLDERS** The primary reason most entrepreneurs choose to incorporate is to gain the benefit of limited liability, which allows investors to limit their liability to the total amount of their investments. This legal protection of personal assets outside the business is of critical concern to many investors. The shield of limited liability often is not impenetrable, however. Because start-up companies generally present higher levels of risk, lenders and other creditors usually require the owners to *personally* guarantee loans made to the corporation. Experts estimate that 95 percent of small business owners have to sign personal guarantees to get the financing they need. By making these guarantees, owners place their personal assets at risk (just as in a proprietorship) despite choosing the corporate form of ownership. The situation is similar to when a parent cosigns a loan for a child. Although the loan may be in the child's name and the child is responsible for making payments, the financial strength of the parent makes the loan possible. If the child defaults on the loan, the parent is responsible for paying back the loan as a result of the guarantee.

Court decisions have extended the personal liability of small corporation owners beyond the financial guarantees that banks and other lenders require, "piercing the corporate veil" more than

CHAPTER 5 • CHOOSING A FORM OF OWNERSHIP

ever before. Courts are increasingly holding corporate owners personally liable for environmental, pension, and legal claims against their corporations. Courts will pierce the corporate veil and hold owners liable for the company's debts and obligations if the owners deliberately commit criminal or negligent acts when handling corporate business. Corporate shareholders most commonly lose their liability protection, however, because owners and officers have commingled corporate funds with their own personal funds. Failing to keep corporate and personal funds separate is often a problem, particularly in closely held corporations.

Steps to avoid legal difficulties include the following:

- *File all of the reports and pay all of the necessary fees required by the state in a timely manner.* Most states require corporations to file reports with the secretary of state on an annual basis. Failing to do so will jeopardize the validity of your corporation and will open the door for personal liability problems for its shareholders.

- *Hold annual meetings to elect officers and directors.* In a closely held corporation, the officers elected may *be* the shareholders, but that does not matter. Corporations formed by an individual are not required to hold meetings, but the sole shareholder must file a written consent form.

- *Keep minutes of every meeting of the officers and directors, even if it takes place in the living room of the founders.* It is a good idea to elect a secretary who is responsible for recording the minutes.

- *Make sure that the corporation's board of directors makes all major decisions.* Problems arise in closely held corporations when one owner makes key decisions alone without consulting the elected board.

- *Make it clear that the business is a corporation by having all officers sign contracts, loan agreements, purchase orders, and other legal documents in the corporation's name rather than their own names.* Failing to designate their status as agents of the corporation can result in the officer's being held personally liable for agreements they think they are signing on the corporation's behalf.

- *Keep corporate assets and the personal assets of the owner's separate.* Few things make courts more willing to hold shareholder's personally liable for a corporation's debts than commingling corporate and personal assets. In some closely held corporations, owners have been known to use corporate assets to pay their personal expenses (or vice versa) or to mix their personal funds with corporate funds into a single bank account. Protecting the corporation's identity by keeping it completely separate from the owner's personal identities is critical.

**ENTREPRENEURIAL PROFILE: Richard Reinis: Krispy Kreme franchise** Richard Reinis was an experienced attorney who had helped many of his clients avoid the risks of signing a personal guarantee. When he decided to open a Krispy Kreme franchise, he needed financing from a bank to get the business started, and that loan came with the requirement of a personal guarantee. Reinis decided it was worth the risk of signing the personal guarantee. However, the business failed, and the bank called his personal guarantee. "I paid dearly in sleepless nights, guilt, and shame," said Reinis. "I don't know how many years of my life this emotional strain cost me, but I know how many years I'll have to work to make up the loss." Given the personal risks that come with guarantees, Reinis recommends being open and honest with your spouse about any guaranteed loans. "Tell your family the truth about the personal guarantee, upfront," urges Reinis. "You can't put your home and bank accounts on the hook without telling your spouse. You'd be amazed how few businessmen tell their wives when they do this."[9]

**ABILITY TO ATTRACT CAPITAL** Corporations have proved to be the most effective form of ownership for accumulating large amounts of capital largely due to the protection of limited liability. Restricted only by the number of shares authorized in its charter (which can be amended), the corporation can raise money to begin business and expand as opportunity dictates by selling shares of its stock to investors. A corporation can sell its stock to a limited number of private investors, called a **private placement**, or to the public, referred to as a **public offering**. In fact, the ability to generate financing is one of the most significant advantages of a corporation, especially those in need of major capital infusions. "If you're thinking about going public, there's no question that C corporations are the best vehicle," says Hillel Bennett, an attorney who specializes in corporate law.[10] Forming the business as a C corporation is best for businesses that plan to raise multiple rounds of venture capital funding, even if a public offering is not part of the plans for funding. "The C corporation is a venture capital firm's clear-cut choice for the type of entity in which to place their investment," says Ryan Roberts, a California attorney who specializes in technology startups. "When the to-be-venture-funded startup is a C corporation, various administrative and other burdens are minimized for the venture capital firm, which allows them (and their capital) to focus on developing the startup company's business."[11]

**ABILITY TO CONTINUE INDEFINITELY** As a separate legal entity, a corporation can continue indefinitely or in perpetuity unless limited by its charter. Unlike a proprietorship or partnership in which the death of a founder ends the business, the corporation lives beyond the lives of those who created it. This perpetual life gives rise to the next major advantage of the corporation: transferable ownership.

**TRANSFERABLE OWNERSHIP** If stockholders in a corporation are displeased with the business's progress, they can sell their shares to someone else. Millions of shares of stock representing ownership in companies are traded daily on the world's stock exchanges. Shareholders can also transfer their stock through inheritance to a new generation of owners. Throughout these transfers of ownership, the corporation seamlessly continues to conduct business as usual. Because only a small number of people, often company founders, family members, or employees, own the stock of closely held corporations, the resale market for shares is limited, and the transfer of ownership may be difficult.

## Disadvantages of the Corporation

**COST AND TIME INVOLVED IN THE INCORPORATION PROCESS** Corporations can be costly and time consuming to establish. As the owners give birth to this artificial legal entity, the gestation period can be prolonged. In some states, an attorney must handle the incorporation, but in most states, entrepreneurs can complete all of the required forms themselves. However, an entrepreneur must exercise great caution when incorporating without the help of an attorney. In addition to potential legal expenses, incorporating a business requires fees that do not apply to proprietorships or partnerships. Creating a corporation can cost between $500 and $3,000, with the average cost around $1,500.

**DOUBLE TAXATION** As a separate legal entity, a corporation must pay taxes on its net income to the federal, most state, and many local governments. Before stockholders receive any net income as dividends, a corporation must pay these taxes at the corporate tax rate. Then stockholders must pay taxes on the dividends they receive from these same profits at the individual tax rate. Thus, a corporation's profits are taxed twice—once at the corporate level and again at the individual level. This **double taxation** is a distinct disadvantage of the corporate form of ownership.

**POTENTIAL FOR DIMINISHED MANAGERIAL INCENTIVES** As corporations grow, they often require additional managerial expertise beyond that which the founder can provide. Because they created their companies and often have most of their personal wealth tied up in the business, entrepreneurs have an intense interest in ensuring their success and are willing to make sacrifices for their businesses. Professional managers an entrepreneur brings in to help run the business as it grows do not always have the same degree of dedication or loyalty to the company. As a result, the business may suffer without the founder's energy, care, and devotion. One way to minimize this potential problem is to link managers' (and even employees') compensation to the company's financial performance through profit-sharing or bonus plans. The corporation can directly tie managers' and employees' performances to the value of the firm by establishing **stock option** plans that allow employees to buy stock at discounted prices. Corporations also can stimulate managers' and employees' incentive on the job by creating an **employee stock ownership plan** in which managers and employees become part of the whole owners in the company.

**LEGAL REQUIREMENTS AND REGULATORY RED TAPE** Corporations are subject to more legal and financial requirements than other forms of ownership. Entrepreneurs must meet stringent requirements to accurately record and report business transactions in a timely manner. They must hold annual meetings and consult the board of directors about major decisions that are beyond day-to-day operations. Managers may be required to submit major decisions to the stockholders for approval. Corporations that are publicly held must also file quarterly and annual reports with the Securities and Exchange Commission. Failure to follow state and federal regulations has led to problems for many corporations and their founders.

**POTENTIAL LOSS OF CONTROL BY THE FOUNDERS** When entrepreneurs sell shares of ownership in their companies, they relinquish some degree of control. In corporations that require large capital infusions, entrepreneurs may have to give up a significant amount of control, so much, in fact, that they become minority shareholders. Losing majority ownership—and therefore control—of their companies leaves founders in a precarious position. They no longer have the power to determine the company's direction; "outsiders" do. The founders' shares may become so diluted that majority shareholders may vote them out of their jobs. One study of the "founder's dilemma" reports that 52 percent of business founders have been replaced as CEO by the time they receive the third round of venture capital financing (and in 73 percent of the replacements, the board fired the founder).[12]

## Professional Corporations

A **professional corporation** offers professionals, such as lawyers, doctors, dentists, accountants, and others, the advantages of the corporate form of ownership. Corporate ownership is ideally suited for licensed professionals, who must always be concerned about malpractice lawsuits, because it offers limited liability. For example, if three doctors form a professional corporation, none of them would be liable for the malpractice of the other. (Of course, each would be liable for his or her own actions.) Professional corporations are created in the same way as regular corporations. They often are identified by the abbreviation P.C. (professional corporation), P.A. (professional association), or S.C. (service corporation).

## The S Corporation

The Internal Revenue Service Code created the Subchapter S corporation in 1954. Now known as the S corporation, this form of ownership has undergone modifications in its legal requirements. An **S corporation** is a distinction that is made only for federal income tax purposes and is, in terms of its legal characteristics, no different from any other corporation. Small businesses seeking S corporation status must meet the following criteria:

**5.** ———————
Describe the features of the S corporation.

1. It must be a domestic (U.S.) corporation.
2. It cannot have a nonresident alien as a shareholder.
3. It can issue only one class of common stock, which means that all shares must carry the same distribution or liquidation rights. Voting rights, however, may differ. In other words, an S corporation can issue voting and nonvoting common stock.
4. It must limit its shareholders to individuals, estates, and certain trusts, although tax-exempt entities, such as employee stock ownership plans and pension plans, can be shareholders.
5. It cannot have more than 100 shareholders (increased from 75).
6. No more than 25 percent of the corporation's gross revenues during three successive tax years can be from passive investment income.

By increasing the number of shareholders allowed in S corporations to 100, the new law makes succession planning easier for business owners. Founders now can pass their stock on to their children and grandchildren without worrying about exceeding the maximum allowable number of owners. The larger number of shareholders also gives S corporations greater ability to raise capital by attracting more investors.

The new law also allows S corporations to own subsidiary companies. Previously, the owners of S corporations had to establish separate businesses if they wanted to launch new ventures, even those closely related to the S corporation. This change is especially beneficial to entrepreneurs with several businesses in related fields. They can establish an S corporation as the "parent"

**FIGURE 5.2**

**Tax Rate Comparison of C Corporation Versus S Corporation or LLC**

| | | Net Income $500,000 | | | |
|---|---|---|---|---|---|
| **C Corporation** | | | **S Corporation or LLC** | | |
| | Corporate Tax Rates | | | | Individual Tax Rates |
| $-000 | 15% | | | $-000 | 10% |
| $50,000 | 25% | | | $16,700 | 15% |
| $75,000 | 34% | | | $67,900 | 25% |
| $100,000 | 39% | | | $137,050 | 28% |
| $335,000 | 34% | | | $208,850 | 33% |
| $10,000,000 | 35% | | | $372,950 | 35% |
| $15,000,000 | 38% | | | | |
| $18,333,333 | 35% | | | | |

| Corporate | Tax Bill $170,000 | Shareholder | Tax Bill $175,000 |
|---|---|---|---|
| | | Tax burden is split among owners based on percentage of ownership and paid with their personal tax returns. | |
| Dividend | $330,000 | | |
| Individual Tax Bill | $49,500 | | |
| Total | $219,500 | Tax savings by using S Corporation or LLC | $44,500 |

company and then set up multiple subsidiaries as either S or C corporations as "offspring" under it. Because they are separate corporations, the liabilities of one business cannot spill over and destroy the assets of another.

Violating any of the requirements for an S corporation automatically terminates a company's S status. If a corporation meets the criteria for an S corporation, its shareholders must elect to be treated as one. (The corporation must have been eligible for S status for the entire year.) To make the election of S status effective for the current tax year, an entrepreneur must file Internal Revenue Service (IRS) Form 2553 within the first 75 days of the tax year. *All* shareholders must consent to have the corporation treated as an S corporation. Figure 5.2 demonstrates the tax implications of an S corporation (or limited liability company) and a C corporation.

## Advantages of an S Corporation

S corporations retain all of the advantages of a regular corporation, including continuity of existence, transferability of ownership, and limited personal liability for its owners. The most notable provision of the S corporation is that it passes all of its profits or losses through to the *individual* shareholders, and its income is taxed only *once* at the individual tax rate. Thus, electing S corporation status avoids the double taxation disadvantage of a C corporation. In essence, the tax treatment of an S corporation is exactly like that of a partnership; its owners report their shares of the company's profits on their individual income tax returns and pay taxes on those profits at the individual rate, even if they never take the money out of the business.

Another advantage of the S corporation is that it avoids the tax C corporations pay on the assets that have appreciated in value and are sold. S corporations owners also enjoy the ability to make year-end payouts to themselves when net income is high. To minimize their tax bills, some S corporation owners pay themselves minimal salaries, which are subject to Social Security and Medicare taxes, and instead make large dividend distributions, which are not subject to those taxes, to themselves. In C corporations, owners have no such luxury because the IRS watches for excessive compensation to owners and managers. However, the IRS is trying to eliminate this loophole, arguing that it costs the U.S. Treasury billions of lost revenue annually.

### Disadvantages of an S Corporation

Although tax implications should not be the sole criterion when choosing a form of ownership, they are important to business owners. Congress's constant tinkering with the tax code means that the tax advantages that the S corporation offers may not be permanent. S corporations lose their attractiveness if either personal income tax rates rise above those of C corporation rates or if C corporation rates fall below personal income tax rates.

In addition to the tax implications of choosing an S corporation, owners should consider the following factors in their decision:

- The size of the company's net profits
- The tax rates of its shareholders
- Strategic plans and their timing to sell the company or transition ownership
- The impact of the C corporation's double-taxation penalty on income distributed as dividends

### When Is an S Corporation a Wise Choice?

Choosing S corporation status is usually beneficial to start-up companies that anticipate net losses and to highly profitable firms with substantial dividends to pay out to shareholders. In these cases, the owner can use the loss to offset other income or is in a lower tax bracket than the C corporation, thus reducing his or her tax bills. Companies that plan to reinvest most of their earnings to finance growth also find S corporation status favorable. Small business owners who intend to sell their companies in the future prefer S status over C status because the capital gains tax on the sale of the assets of an S corporation is lower than those on the sale of a C corporation.

Small companies with the following characteristics are *not* likely to benefit from S corporation status:

- Highly profitable companies with large numbers of shareholders in which most of the profits are passed on to shareholders as compensation or retirement benefits
- Shareholders who pay marginal tax rates that are higher than the marginal tax rates that C corporations pay
- Fast-growing companies that must retain most of their earnings to finance growth and capital spending
- Corporations in which the cost of employee benefits to shareholders exceeds the tax savings that S status produces

## The Limited Liability Company

Like an S corporation, the limited liability company (LLC) is a hybrid structure that features elements of a partnership and a corporation. Because of the advantages it offers and its flexibility, the LLC is the fastest-growing form of business ownership. LLCs provide owners with many of the benefits of S corporations but are not subject to the restrictions imposed on S corporations. For instance, an LLC offers its owners limited liability without imposing any requirements on their characteristics or any ceiling on their numbers. LLCs do not restrict their members' ability to become involved in managing the company, unlike a limited partnership, which prohibits limited partners from participating in day-to-day management of the business.

Although an LLC can have just one owner, most have multiple owners (called *members*). LLCs offer its members the advantages of limited liability and avoiding the double taxation imposed on C corporations. Like an S corporation, an LLC does not pay income taxes; its income flows through to the members, who are responsible for paying income taxes on their shares of the LLC's net income. LLCs permit their members to divide income and thus tax liability as they see fit, just as in a partnership.

Creating an LLC is much like creating a corporation. Forming an LLC requires an entrepreneur to file the articles of organization with the secretary of state. The LLC's **articles of organization**, similar to the corporation's articles of incorporation, establish the company's name, its method of management (board managed or member managed), its duration, and the names and addresses of each organizer. In most states, the company's name must contain the words *limited liability company*, *limited company*, or the letters LLC or LC. LLCs can have a defined term of

**6.** ───────────────

Describe the features of the limited liability company.

duration, or it can elect to be an "at-will" LLC that has no specific term of duration. However, the same factors that would cause a partnership to dissolve also cause an LLC to dissolve before its charter expires.

Although an operating agreement is not required by law, it is essential for entrepreneurs who form LLCs to create one. The LLC **operating agreement** is similar to a corporation's bylaws and outlines the provisions governing the way the LLC will conduct business by defining members' voting rights and power, their percentages of ownership, how profits and losses are distributed, and other important matters. To ensure that an LLC is classified as a partnership for tax purposes, an entrepreneur must carefully draft the operating agreement. The operating agreement must create an LLC that has more characteristics of a partnership than of a corporation to maintain this favorable tax treatment. Specifically, an LLC cannot have any more than two of the following four corporate characteristics:

1. *Limited liability.* Limited liability exists if no member of the LLC is personally liable for the debts or claims against the company. Because entrepreneurs choosing this form of ownership usually get limited liability protection, the operating agreement almost always contains this characteristic.

2. *Continuity of life.* Continuity of life exists if the company continues to exist despite changes in stock ownership. To avoid continuity of life, any LLC member must have the power to dissolve the company. Most entrepreneurs choose to omit this characteristic from their LLC's operating agreements. Thus, if one member of an LLC resigns, dies, or declares bankruptcy, the LLC automatically dissolves and all remaining members must vote to keep the company going.

3. *Free transferability of interest.* Free transferability of interest exists if each LLC member has the power to transfer his or her ownership to another person without the consent from other members. To avoid this characteristic, the operating agreement must state the recipient of a member's LLC stock cannot become a substitute member without the consent of the remaining members.

4. *Centralized management.* Centralized management exists if a group that does not include all LLC members has the authority to make management decisions and to conduct company business. To avoid this characteristic, the operating agreement must state that the company elects to be "member managed."

Despite their universal appeal to entrepreneurs, LLCs present some disadvantages. For example, they can be expensive to create. Although LLCs may be ideally suited for an entrepreneur launching a new company, it may pose problems for business owners who are considering converting an existing business to an LLC. Switching to an LLC from a general partnership, a limited partnership, or a sole proprietorship reorganizing to bring in new owners is usually not a problem. However, owners of corporations and S corporations can incur large tax obligations if they convert their companies to LLCs.

Table 5.3 summarizes the key features of the sole proprietorship, the partnership, the C corporation, the S corporation, and the LLC.

**TABLE 5.3 Characteristics of the Major Forms of Ownership**

| Characteristic | Sole Proprietorship | General Partnership | Limited Partnership | C Corporation | S Corporation | Limited Liability Company |
|---|---|---|---|---|---|---|
| Definition | A for-profit business owned and operated by one person | A for-profit business jointly owned and operated by two or more people | One general partner and one or more partners with limited liability and no rights of management | An artificial legal entity separate from its owners and formed under state and federal laws | An artificial legal entity that is structured like a C corporation but taxed by the federal government like a partnership | A business entity that provides limited liability like a corporation but is taxed like a partnership. Owners are referred to as members |

**TABLE 5.3** (continued)

| Characteristic | Sole Proprietorship | General Partnership | Limited Partnership | C Corporation | S Corporation | Limited Liability Company |
|---|---|---|---|---|---|---|
| Ease of formation | Easiest form of business to set up. If necessary, acquire licenses and permits, register fictitious name, and obtain taxpayer identification | Easy to set up and operate. A written partnership agreement is highly recommended. Must acquire an employer ID number. If necessary, register fictitious name | File a Certificate of Limited Partnership with the secretary of state. Name must show that business is a limited partnership. Must have written agreement, and must keep certain records | File articles of incorporation and other required reports with the secretary of state. Prepare bylaws and follow corporate formalities | Must meet all criteria to file as an S corporation. Must file timely election with the IRS (within two and a half months of first taxable year) | File articles of organization with the secretary of state. Adopt operating agreement and file necessary reports with secretary of state. The name must show it is a limited liability company |
| Owner's personal liability | Unlimited | Unlimited for general partners, limited for limited partners | Limited | Limited | Limited | Limited |
| Number of owners | One | Two or more | At least one general partner and any number of limited partners | Any number | Maximum of 100 with restrictions as to who they are | One (a few states require two or more) |
| Tax liability | Single tax: personal tax rate | Single tax: partners pay on their proportional shares at their individual rate | Same as general partnership | Double tax: corporation pays tax and shareholders pay tax on dividends distributed | Single tax: owners pay on their proportional shares at individual rate | Single tax: members pay on their proportional shares at individual rate |
| Current maximum tax rate | 39.6% | 39.6% | 39.6% | 39% corporate plus 39.6% individual | 39.6% | 39.6% |
| Transferability of ownership | Fully transferable through sale or transfer of company assets | May require consent of all partners | Same as general partnership | Fully transferable | Transferable (but transfer may affect S status) | Usually requires consent of all members |
| Continuity of the business | Ends on death or insanity of proprietor or upon termination by proprietor | Dissolves on death, insanity, or retirement of a general partner (business may continue) | Same as general partnership | Perpetual life | Perpetual life | Perpetual life |
| Cost of formation | Low | Moderate | Moderate | High | High | High |
| Liquidity of the owner's investment in the business | Poor to average | Poor to average | Poor to average | High | High | High |
| Ability to raise capital | Low | Moderate | Moderate to high | Very high | High | High |
| Formation procedure | No special steps required other than buying necessary licenses | No written partnership agreement required (but highly advisable) | Must comply with state laws regarding limited partnership | Must meet formal requirements specified by state law | Must follow same procedures as C corporation, then elect S status with IRS | Must meet formal requirements specified by state law |

## Social Enterprises

**7.**

Discuss the alternative options for corporate form, both for-profit and nonprofit, available to social entrepreneurs.

Traditionally, social enterprises were established as nonprofit corporations. However, today we see social entrepreneurs setting up for-profit social ventures, funneling any excess cash and profits into the social cause they are supporting. We also see nonprofits setting up sister for-profit businesses that can generate profits that directly benefit the nonprofit. New forms of organization address the changing nature of the philanthropic sector of the economy. This section provides an overview of the various organizational forms available to social entrepreneurs.

Gabrielle Palermo, Susanna Young and Clay Tyler launched their award winning social enterprise, G3Box, out of the Arizona State University incubator SkySong.
*Source:* ASU SkySong.

## In the Entrepreneurial Spotlight

# From the Life on the Street to Running a Business

Magdalene is a residential program for women who have survived lives of prostitution, trafficking, addiction, and life on the streets. An unlikely entrepreneur, Reverend Becca Stevens, an Episcopal priest who serves as Chaplain at St. Augustine's at Vanderbilt University, is Magdalene's founder.

Residents can remain at Magdalene for two years, where they receive housing, food, medical and dental needs, therapy, education, and job training. The program does not charge the residents and receives no government funding. Residents live in six homes that are run by residents without the assistance of any live-in staff. The residents, who are women ranging from age 20 to 50, come to Magdalene from prison and from the streets.

"I met this guy that was a pimp, and he took me under his wing; he took real good care of me, fed me with dope, and gave me clothes, a place to live, and I thought I was just in heaven," says Tara, a resident who was a prostitute from the age of 17 to 33 before being forced to live on the street. "And then one day he told me, 'hit the block.'"

Magdalene has high success rates, with 72% percent of the women remaining clean and sober two and a half years after beginning the program. After four months, the women find work,

return to school and/or enter Magdalene's job training program called Thistle Farms.

Thistle Farms is a social enterprise that is run by the women of Magdalene. The name is symbolic for the women who work at Thistle Farms. "Thistles [are] weeds that people despise; we take them and make something beautiful," says Reverend Stevens. The women of Thistle Farms create handmade, natural bath and body products. One of the goals for Thistle Farms is to make body products that are as good for the earth as they are for the body. Purchases of the products directly benefit the women working in Thistle Farms by helping them earn a living wage. Thistle Farms employs more than 40 Magdalene residents or graduates who learn skills in manufacturing, packaging, marketing and sales, and administration. Thistle Farms is housed in an 11,000-square-foot sales and manufacturing facility. Its products are available in more than 200 stores across the country.

Reverend Stevens is launching another social enterprise to help support her work with the residents of Magdalene: the Thistle Stop Café, which will be located adjacent to the Thistle Farms building. Like Thistle Farms, Thistle Stop Café will give survivors of trafficking, prostitution, and addiction an opportunity to learn valuable job skills to help them move toward financial independence. Thistle Stop Café will offer a welcoming atmosphere while serving coffees, teas, sandwiches, wraps, and baked goods that are healthy, local, and fair trade. A stage and a professional quality sound system will be included, offering a platform for the women and community members to share their poetry, music, and stories. Sharing stories of healing, hope, and love is a vital part of the Magdalene and Thistle Farms community. "A story in every cup," the Café's mantra, is highlighted by a collection of donated teacups, each with a personal story behind it. These beautiful contributions will be commemorated in a special coffee-table book, including a photograph and the story behind each teacup.

"To watch all this stuff happening around you is wonderful, and to watch all the transformation in women's lives, who I think a lot of people gave up on," says Reverend Stevens, who was one of 15 people named as Champions of Change by President Obama in 2011. "You don't have to worry about changing the world. The idea of loving the whole world one person at a time is a great way to live your life. Don't worry about big or small. I'm okay being a drop in the bucket, and I love the idea of a thousand more people with us being drops in the bucket too. I want the women here to be employed, to have financial security, and to be able to change their lives."

1. How do the social enterprises founded by Reverend Becca Stevens create a "triple bottom line" as a social venture? Explain.

2. What are the advantages to creating social enterprises like Thistle Farms and Thistle Stop Café that rely on earned income for their financial viability? Explain.

3. What are the limitations of using an earned income model for social enterprises like Thistle Farms and Thistle Stop Café?

4. What recommendations would you make to Becca Stevens about the future growth of her social enterprises? What opportunities do you see for growth? What cautions would you offer her about growing and expansion?

*Sources:* Molly Theobald, "Thistle Farms Cultivates a Better Alternative to Life on the Streets," *Christian Science Monitor*, February 8, 2012, *www.csmonitor.com/World/Making-a-difference/Change-Agent/2012/0208/Thistle-Farms-cultivates-a-better-alternative-to-life-on-the-streets*; Melinda Clark, "Magdalene and Thistle Farms Offer Prostitutes a Chance for Regrowth," *Huffington Post*, April 26, 2011, *www.huffingtonpost.com/2011/04/26/magdalene-and-thistle-farms_n_854130.html*; Rob Simbeck, "Divinity Grads Aim to Compensate for the Chaos in Contemporary Society," *Vanderbilt Magazine*, Fall 2010, *www.vanderbilt.edu/magazines/vanderbilt-magazine/2010/12/acts-of-faith*; *www.thistlefarms.org*.

## Nonprofit Organizations

A nonprofit organization uses its revenues to pursue social value rather than to create personal value for investors. A nonprofit is essentially a public good, which is not owned by any individuals. Its purpose is to serve the public good by providing services for specific purposes. Churches, public schools, public charities, public clinics and hospitals, political organizations, legal aid societies, volunteer services organizations, labor unions, professional associations, research institutes, and museums are examples of nonprofit organizations. Nonprofit organizations are organized under state law but are granted tax-exempt status through the IRS. Nonprofit organizations generate most of their revenues from grants from foundations and government agencies, as well as from tax-deductible donations from individuals.

Social entrepreneurs establishing nonprofits should follow these steps when forming their organizations:

- ***File the certificate of incorporation.*** Just like a for-profit entity, a nonprofit corporation must file with the state to become a legal entity. The major difference is that a nonprofit corporation must include a **purpose clause**, which defines the social purpose that the nonprofit will pursue as its mission. There is a delicate balance with defining the purpose clause because founders should state the goals of the organization broadly enough to provide program flexibility in the future but not be so broad as to include goals the nonprofit will not purse.

Nonprofit organizations, such as Habitat for Humanity, exist to create social value and enjoy tax-exempt status. Habitat for Humanity has grown to become on of the top-ten homebuilders in the United States.
*Source:* © bawinner/Fotolia.

- *Select individuals to serve on the board of directors.* The members of a nonprofit board must be passionate about the purpose of the organization. It is best if they have previous nonprofit board experience so that they know what to expect and what is expected from them. Board members should be well respected and well connected in the local community to help attract other board members and help in fund-raising efforts. It is also beneficial to add board members with specific expertise in areas such as banking, real estate, nonprofit law, and accounting to help reduce the need to pay for this expertise.

- *Develop a mission statement.* The mission statement should clearly capture the organization's beliefs and values and define its overriding purpose that will guide the daily operation of the organization.

- *Establish bylaws and board policies.* The bylaws are the legal rules that define how the organization will operate, particularly the rules that the board and the executive leadership will follow as they guide the organization. The board policies set up specific rules for board members, such as conflict of interest policies, attendance policies, and financial oversight policies.

- *File required forms with the IRS.* Form SS-4 filed with the IRS gives the IRS the official name of the organization and leads to the issuance of an employer identification number, which is the corporate version of a social security number. Form 1023 is used to request tax-exempt status under Section 501(c)(3) with the IRS. It can take up to six months for the IRS to grant a nonprofit's tax-exempt status, which allows donors to deduct gifts to the organization on their personal tax returns and is required status to receive many grants.

- *Develop a fund-raising plan.* Since the Great Recession, fund-raising has been a major challenge for nonprofits. A nonprofit's fund-raising plan should be diversified with a combination of grants, donations, and even earned-income opportunities.

**FOR-PROFIT SOCIAL VENTURES** Rather than deal with the challenges of starting and maintaining a nonprofit, many social entrepreneurs are forgoing nonprofit status and setting up their organizations as traditional corporations or LLCs. Although their primary goal is creating social value, the for-profit structure requires financial viability by paying attention to the financial objectives that guide any corporation. The dual focus of these entities is known as a **double bottom line**—both social and financial objectives guide decision making and define true success.

Tom's Shoes is an example of a for-profit social enterprise. Profits from the sale of its shoes in the United States are used to give free shoes to needy children in developing countries around the globe.
*Source:* © adrian lourie/Alamy.

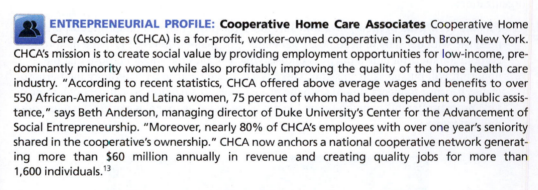

**ENTREPRENEURIAL PROFILE: Cooperative Home Care Associates** Cooperative Home Care Associates (CHCA) is a for-profit, worker-owned cooperative in South Bronx, New York. CHCA's mission is to create social value by providing employment opportunities for low-income, predominantly minority women while also profitably improving the quality of the home health care industry. "According to recent statistics, CHCA offered above average wages and benefits to over 550 African-American and Latina women, 75 percent of whom had been dependent on public assistance," says Beth Anderson, managing director of Duke University's Center for the Advancement of Social Entrepreneurship. "Moreover, nearly 80% of CHCA's employees with over one year's seniority shared in the cooperative's ownership." CHCA now anchors a national cooperative network generating more than $60 million annually in revenue and creating quality jobs for more than 1,600 individuals.[13]

Just like any for-profit corporation, for-profit social enterprises are subject to market forces. A disadvantage of these entities is that if they are not successful in achieving their financial objectives, the "other bottom line" of their social mission suffers. For example, ShoreBank Corporation was organized in Chicago, Illinois, as a for-profit bank holding company. Its mission was to demonstrate that a commercial bank could profitably invest in inner-city neighborhoods that other financial institutions were neglecting. ShoreBank defined its "triple bottom line" of economically improving inner-city communities, promoting environmental health, and operating profitably. Unfortunately, the bank suffered the fate of many commercial banks during the Great Recession, and after mounting losses and an inability to raise more funding, the Federal Deposit Insurance Corporation closed ShoreBank and transferred its assets to Chicago's Urban Partnership Bank.[14]

**TABLE 5.4** The L3C Versus the Traditional LLC and Nonprofit

| Type of Corporation | Organizational Purpose | Potential ROI | Private Sector Resources |
|---|---|---|---|
| LLC | Financial | 5% or more | Market driven; making money and building wealth |
| L3C | Financial and mission related | Between 0% and 5% | Philanthropic source invests with a lower than market rate of return; philanthropic investment lowers the risk and raises potential ROI for subsequent investors |
| Nonprofit | Mission related | 0% to negative 100% | Market incentives inadequate or nonexistent |

*Source:* Americans for Community Development, *www.americansforcommunitydevelopment.org.*

**NEW FORMS OF SOCIAL VENTURES** The low-profit limited liability company (L3C) is a new form of organization that is a cross between a nonprofit and a for-profit LLC. The L3C was first approved in Vermont in 2008 and is now an option for social entrepreneurs in eight other states. The L3C builds on the structure of the existing LLC; it provides the liability protection of a corporation, can sell shares of ownership, and is not tax exempt. Unlike an LLC, L3Cs are specifically formed to pursue a social mission. The L3C is meant to integrate the best of both the nonprofit and the for-profit LLC by creating a market for investments in financially risky but socially beneficial activities. Table 5.4 compares the traditional LLC and nonprofit organizations with the L3C.

# Chapter Review

1. Discuss the issues that entrepreneurs should consider when evaluating different forms of ownership.
   - The key to choosing the "right" form of ownership is to understand the characteristics of each from and knowing how they affect an entrepreneur's personal and business circumstances.
   - Factors to consider include tax implications, liability expense, start-up and future capital requirements, control, managerial ability, business goals, management succession plans, and cost of formation.
2. Describe the advantages and disadvantages of the sole proprietorship.
   - A sole proprietorship is a business owned and managed by one individual and is the most popular form of ownership.
   - Sole proprietorships offer these advantages:
     - Simple to create
     - Least costly to begin
     - Owner has total decision-making authority
     - No special reporting requirement or legal restriction
     - Easy to discontinue
   - Sole proprietorships suffer from these disadvantages:
     - Unlimited personal liability of owner
     - Limited managerial skills and capabilities
     - Limited access to capital
     - Lack of continuity

3. Describe the advantages and disadvantages of the partnership.
   - A partnership is an association of two or more people who co-own a business for the purpose to make a profit.
   - Partnerships offer these advantages:
     - Easy to establish
     - Complementary skills of partners
     - Division of profits
     - Large pool of capital available
     - Ability to attract limited partners
     - Little government regulation
     - Flexibility
     - Tax advantages
   - Partnerships impose these disadvantages:
     - Unlimited liability of at least one partner
     - Difficulty in disposing of partnership interest
     - Lack of continuity
     - Potential for personal and authority conflicts
     - Partners are bound by the law of agency
4. Describe the advantages and disadvantages of the corporation.
   - A limited partnership operates like any other partnership except that it allows limited partners—primary investors who cannot take an active role in managing the business—to become owners without subjecting themselves to unlimited personal liability of the company's debts.

- A corporation is a separate legal entity and the most complex of the three basic forms of ownership.
- To form a corporation an entrepreneur must file the articles of incorporation with the state in which the company will incorporate.
- Corporations offer these advantages:
  - Limited liability of stockholder
  - Ability to attract capital
  - Ability to continue indefinitely
  - Transferable ownership
- Corporations suffer from theses disadvantages:
  - Cost and time involved in incorporation
  - Double taxation
  - Potential for diminished managerial incentives
  - Legal requirement and regulatory red tape
  - Potential loss of control by the founders

5. Describe the features of the S corporation.
   - An S corporation offers its owners limited liability protection but avoids the double taxation of C corporations.
   - S corporations retain all of the advantages of a regular corporation, including continuity of existence, transferability of ownership, and limited personal liability for its owners.

6. Describe the features of the limited liability company.
   - A limited liability company (LLC), like an S corporation, is a cross between a partnership and a corporation and offers many of the advantages of each. However, it operates without the restrictions imposed on an S corporation. To create an LLC, an entrepreneur must file the articles of organization and the operating agreement with the secretary of state.
   - LLCs can be expensive to create.

7. Discuss the alternative options for corporate form, both for-profit and nonprofit, available to social entrepreneurs.
   - Traditionally, social enterprises were established as nonprofit corporations.
   - Social entrepreneurs have begun to set up for-profit social ventures, funneling any excess cash and profits into the social cause they are supporting. Nonprofits are setting up sister for-profit businesses that can generate profits that directly benefit the nonprofit.
   - A new form of organization called a low-profit limited liability company (L3C) has been introduced in nine states. It blends the advantages of both a nonprofit and an LLC for social entrepreneurs.

# Discussion Questions

**5-1.** What factors should an entrepreneur consider before choosing a form of ownership?

**5-2.** Why are sole proprietorships the most popular form of ownership?

**5-3.** How does personal conflict affect partnerships? What steps might partners take to minimize personal conflict?

**5-4.** Why are the articles important to a successful partnership? What issues should the articles of partnership address?

**5-5.** Can one partner commit another to a business deal without the other's consent? Why and what are the potential ramifications?

**5-6.** Explain the differences between a domestic corporation, a foreign corporation, and an alien corporation.

**5-7.** What issues should the Certificate of Incorporation cover?

**5-8.** How does an S corporation differ from a regular corporation?

**5-9.** What role do limited partners play in a partnership? What will happen if a limited partner takes an active role in managing the business?

**5-10.** What advantages does a limited liability company offer over an S corporation? Over a sole proprietorship?

**5-11.** How is an LLC created? How does this differ from creating an S corporation?

**5-12.** What criteria must an LLC meet to avoid double taxation?

**5-13.** What are the advantages to organizing as a nonprofit for a social entrepreneur? What are the critical steps a social entrepreneur must take to launch a nonprofit?

**5-14.** How can a for-profit pursue a social mission? What is meant by a "double bottom line" for such an organization?

**5-15.** What is an L3C? How is it similar to and how is it different than an LLC?

# CHAPTER 6
# Franchising and the Entrepreneur

*With franchising, you don't have to reinvent the wheel; you just roll the wheel.*

**—Angelo Crowell, former National Football League player and current owner of two Jersey Mike's Subs franchises**

*Good judgment comes from experience. Experience comes from bad judgment.*

**—Bob Packwood**

## Learning Objectives

**On completion of this chapter, you will be able to:**

1. Explain the importance of franchising in the U.S. and global economy.

2. Define the concept of franchising.

3. Describe the different types of franchises.

4. Describe the benefits of buying a franchise.

5. Describe the limitations of buying a franchise.

6. Describe the legal aspects of franchising, including the protection offered by the Federal Trade Commission's Trade Regulation Rule.

7. Explain the right way to buy a franchise.

8. Describe a typical franchise contract and its primary provisions.

9. Explain current trends that are shaping franchising.

10. Describe the potential of franchising a business as a growth strategy.

**1.**

Explain the importance of franchising in the U.S. and global economy.

Miles Blauvelt began working in his father's Jiffy Lube franchise when he was just 14 years old. He started at the bottom of the organization and worked his way up to a management position in the business while earning his business degree from the University of Maryland at College Park. At the age of 23, Blauvelt, already an experienced manager, took over ownership of the franchise and became the youngest franchisee in the history of the Jiffy Lube chain. "I am thrilled to carry on the family tradition by taking over the business my father worked so hard to build," he says. Blauvelt already has implemented several new ideas that have increased the franchises' sales, including creating a business presence in social media, using direct mail advertisements, and supporting local charities and school sports programs to raise the company's visibility. "The thing I enjoy most about being a franchisee is owning my own business," says Blauvelt. "There is nothing more rewarding than being your own boss. I am accountable for all business-related issues to ensure that the center is operating smoothly."[1]

Franchises like Miles Blauvelt's are an important part of the American business system. Much of franchising's popularity arises from its ability to offer those who lack business experience the chance to own and operate a business with a high probability of success. Franchising's reach now extends far beyond the traditional fast-food outlets and auto dealerships. Shoppers can buy nearly every kind of good or service imaginable through franchises—from insurance and health care to hardware and pet waste pickup (see Figure 6.1). More than 757,000 franchise outlets operate in the United States, generating more than $802 billion in total economic output. Franchised businesses make up less than 3 percent of all businesses, but they employ more than 8.2 million people, generate $304 billion in annual payroll, and add more than $460 billion to the nation's gross domestic product.[2]

Franchising also has a significant impact on the global economy as well. American franchisors are expanding globally to reach their growth targets. A survey by the International Franchise Association reports that 61 percent of its members operate in international markets and that 74 percent of franchisors plan to accelerate the growth of their global franchised units in the near future. In addition, 32 percent of the units of the 200 largest U.S. franchisors are located outside the United States.[3] Countries that are attracting the greatest attention for international expansion among franchisors include Brazil, Russia, India, China, and nations in the Middle East and North

**FIGURE 6.1**

**Franchised Businesses by Product or Service Line**

*Source:* 2012 Franchised Business Economic Outlook, International Franchising Association, January 2012, p. 2.

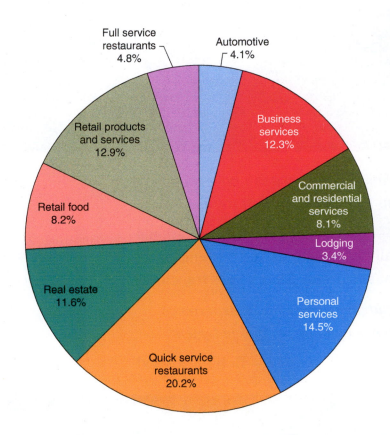

- Full service restaurants 4.8%
- Automotive 4.1%
- Business services 12.3%
- Commercial and residential services 8.1%
- Lodging 3.4%
- Personal services 14.5%
- Quick service restaurants 20.2%
- Real estate 11.6%
- Retail food 8.2%
- Retail products and services 12.9%

Africa region. With their fast-growing populations, rising levels of disposable income, spreading urbanization, and keen interest in American brands, these nations offer prime growth opportunities for U.S. franchisors.

## What Is a Franchise?

In **franchising**, semi-independent business owners (franchisees) pay fees and royalties to a parent company (franchisor) in return for the right to become identified with its trademark, to sell its products or services, and often to use its business format and system. Franchisees do not establish their own autonomous businesses; instead, they buy a "success package" from the franchisor, who shows them how to use it. Franchisees, unlike independent business owners, don't have the freedom to change the way they run their businesses—for example, shifting advertising strategies or adding new products—but they do have access to a formula for success that the franchisor has worked out. Fundamentally, when they buy their franchises, franchisees are purchasing a successful business model. The franchisor provides a business system and the expertise to make it work; the entrepreneur brings the investment, spirit, and drive necessary to implement the system successfully.

> **2.**
> _____
> Define the concept of franchising.

Many franchisees say that buying a franchise is like going into business *for* yourself but not *by* yourself. Although franchisees own their own outlets, they must operate them according to the system that the franchisor has developed. One writer explains,

> The science of franchising is an exacting one; products and services are delivered according to tightly-wrapped operating formulas. There is no variance. A product is developed and honed under the watchful eye of the franchisor, then offered by franchisees under strict quality standards. The result: a democratization of products and services. Hamburgers that taste as good in Boston as in Beijing. Quick lubes available to everyone, whether they drive a Toyota or a Treblinka.[4]

Franchising is built on an ongoing relationship between a franchisor and a franchisee. The franchisor provides valuable services such as a proven business system, training and support, name recognition, and many other forms of assistance; in return, the franchisee pays an initial franchise fee as well as an ongoing percentage of his or her outlet's sales to the franchisor as a royalty and agrees to operate the outlet according to the franchisor's terms. Because franchisors develop the business systems their franchisees use and direct their distribution methods, they maintain substantial control over their franchisees. Entrepreneurs who insist on doing things their own way usually do not make good franchisees. Successful franchisors claim that failing to follow the formula that they have developed is one of the main reasons that franchisees fail. "First and foremost, franchising demands that you 'follow the system,'" says Nicholas Bibby, a franchise consultant. "Whether the business is a major food brand or a home-based franchise, you must be a team player who is willing to follow the rules. If changing the order of things is among your favorite pastimes, think seriously about another form of self-employment. The best franchises simply have the best systems."[5] In other words, successful franchisees tend to follow the franchisor's business recipe. This standardized, formulaic approach lies at the core of franchising success.

*Source:* ZITS © 2011 Zits Partnership, Dist. By King Features.

## Types of Franchising

**3.**

Describe the different types of franchises.

Franchising includes three basic types of systems: trade-name franchising, product distribution franchising, and pure franchising. Each of these forms of franchising allows franchisees to benefit from the parent company's identity.

**Trade-name franchising** involves being associated with a brand name, such as True Value Hardware or Western Auto. In trade-name franchising, a franchisee purchases the right to become identified with the franchisor's trade name without distributing particular products exclusively under the manufacturer's name.

**Product distribution franchising** involves licensing the franchisee to sell specific products under the manufacturer's brand name and trademark through a selective, limited distribution network. This system is commonly used to market automobiles (General Motors and Toyota), gasoline products (Exxon Mobil and Chevron), soft drinks (Pepsi Cola and Coca-Cola), and other products.

**Pure franchising** (or **comprehensive franchising** or **business format franchising**) involves providing franchisees with a complete business format, including a license for a trade name, products or services to be sold, store or building design, methods of operation, a marketing plan, a quality control process, and a network of business support services. The franchisee purchases the right to use all the elements of a fully integrated business operation. Business format franchising is the most common and is the fastest growing of the three types of franchising. It is common among restaurants, hotels, business service firms, car rental agencies, automotive service and repair shops, and many other types of businesses. Business format franchises account for nearly 95 percent of all franchised outlets.[6]

## The Benefits of Buying a Franchise

**4.**

Describe the benefits of buying a franchise.

The primary reason for franchising's success is the mutual benefits it offers both franchisors and franchisees. The ideal franchising relationship is a partnership based on trust and a willingness to work together for mutual success (see Figure 6.2). The most successful franchisors are the ones that see their franchisees as business partners. They recognize that *their* success depends on their *franchisees'* success.

**FIGURE 6.2**

**The Franchising Relationship**

*Source:* Adapted from Economic Impact of Franchised Businesses: A Study for the International Franchise Association, National Economic Consulting Practice of PriceWaterhouseCoopers (New York: IFA Educational Foundation, 2004), pp. 3, 5.

| Element | The Franchisor | The Franchisee |
|---|---|---|
| Site selection | Oversees and approves; may choose site | Chooses site with franchisor's approval |
| Design | Provides prototype design | Pays for and implements design |
| Employees | Makes general recommendations and training suggestions | Hires, manages, and fires employees |
| Products and services | Determines product or service line | Modifies only with franchisor's approval |
| Prices | Can only recommend prices | Sets final prices |
| Purchasing | Establishes quality standards; provides list of approved suppliers; may require franchisees to purchase from the franchisor | Must meet quality standards; must purchase only from approved suppliers; must purchase from supplier if required |
| Advertising | Develops and coordinates national ad campaign; may require minimum level of spending on local advertising | Pays for national ad campaign; complies with local advertising requirements; gets franchisor's approval on local ads |
| Quality control | Sets quality standards and enforces them with inspections; trains franchisees | Maintains quality standards; trains employees to implement quality systems |
| Support | Provides support through an established business system | Operates business on a day-to-day basis with franchisor's support |

Franchisees get the opportunity to own a small business relatively quickly, and, because of the identification with an established product and brand, a franchise often reaches the break-even point faster than an independent business would. Still, most new franchise outlets don't break even for at least six to 18 months.

**ENTREPRENEURIAL PROFILE: Allie and Hung Lam: Children's Lighthouse Learning Center** Copreneurs Allie and Hung Lam invested more than $2 million to open a Children's Lighthouse Learning Center, a franchise that provides educational child care for children from six weeks to 12 years old, in Richmond, Texas. Their substantial investment covered the cost of franchise fees, land, building and furnishings, and hiring 35 staff members. The Lam's center was so successful that it reached its break-even point in just four months, prompting the couple to open a second center in Katy, Texas. Their second center reached its break-even point in just one month![7]

Franchisees also benefit from the franchisor's business experience. In fact, *experience* in the form of a proven business system is, in essence, what a franchisee buys from a franchisor. The franchisor's knowledge, expertise, and experience in the industry provide a competitive advantage for franchisees. Given the thin margin for error in a start-up business, independent entrepreneurs cannot afford to make too many mistakes. In a franchising arrangement, the franchisor already has worked out the kinks in the system, often by trial and error, and franchisees benefit from that experience. Franchisors already have climbed up the learning curve and share with their franchisees the secrets to success that they have learned. This ability to draw on the franchisor's experience and benefit from their support acts as a safety net for entrepreneurs as they build their businesses.

**ENTREPRENEURIAL PROFILE: Patrick Sinclair: Kona Ice** After Patrick Sinclair opened an independent shaved-ice shop in the Garden Oaks neighborhood in Houston, Texas, he saw an opportunity for a mobile shaved-ice business that he could take to customers. Rather than build his own truck, however, Sinclair decided to rely on the experience of a franchise. He researched franchise opportunities and found Kona Ice, a shaved-ice truck franchise based in Kentucky, and signed on to operate 10 trucks within the next several years. "I could have spent $600,000 and gone through four or five prototypes," he says, "but there's value in skipping past a thousand mistakes. Kona Ice had already made those mistakes and ironed them out."[8]

Before jumping into a franchise, an entrepreneur should ask, "What can a franchise do for me that I cannot do for myself?" The answer depends on one's particular situation and is just as important as a systematic evaluation of any franchise opportunity. After careful deliberation, an entrepreneur may conclude that a franchise offers nothing that he or she cannot do on his or her own; on the other hand, it may turn out that a franchise is the key to success for an entrepreneur.

**ENTREPRENEURIAL PROFILE: David Ambinder: Mr. Handyman** David Ambinder worked as an executive on Wall Street for 25 years before being laid off from Lehman Brothers just before the financial services company went bankrupt. Rather than take a chance on another corporate layoff, Ambinder decided to create his own job security by owning his own business. For Ambinder, the structure, support, and safety net of a franchise was ideal. "For me, it's the right move," he says. After investigating several franchise options, Ambinder opened a Mr. Handyman franchise, a company that provides skilled repairmen for a variety of home repair jobs, in Union, New Jersey.[9]

Ambinder is one of many corporate castoffs and dropouts who have discovered that franchising offers them the ideal blend of corporate support to which they are accustomed and the freedom of entrepreneurship.

Let's explore the advantages of buying a franchise.

## A Business System

One major benefit of joining a franchise is gaining access to a tested business system. Tariq Faird, founder and CEO of franchisor Edible Arrangements, says that he learned the importance of a solid business system when he started working for McDonald's at age 15. "I loved the system," he says. When Faird started Edible Arrangements, he put into place the same types of systems that he learned to appreciate many years before at McDonald's and credits those with his company's and his 1,130 franchisees' success.[10] In many cases, the systems that franchisors have developed over time allow entrepreneurs to get their businesses up and running much faster, more efficiently, and more effectively than if they launched their own independent companies. Using the franchisor's business system as a guide, franchisees can be successful even though they may have little or no experience in the industry. Mark Daly, media director for Anytime Fitness, a franchise based in Hastings, Minnesota, that operates nearly 2,000 franchises in 49 states and 10 countries, says, "Previous experience in the fitness industry is not needed to own a successful club. All you need is the passion to help people and to follow the business model."[11]

## Management Training and Support

Franchisors want to give their franchisees a greater chance for success than independent businesses and offer management training programs to franchisees prior to opening a new outlet. Many franchisors, especially the well-established ones, also provide follow-up training and consulting services. This service is vital because most franchisors do not require a franchisee to have experience in the business. These programs teach franchisees the details they need to know for day-to-day operations as well as the nuances of running their businesses successfully. "Just putting a person in business, giving him a trademark, patting him on the [back], and saying, 'Good luck,' is not sufficient," says one franchise consultant.[12]

Training programs often involve both classroom and on-site instruction to teach franchisees the basic operations of the business—from producing and selling the goods or services to purchasing raw materials and completing paperwork. McDonald's is famous for Hamburger University, where franchisees and their employees go to learn the proper systems and procedures for operating a restaurant successfully. Training involves classroom instruction from 19 faculty members from around the world, hands-on activities, simulations of events that franchisees are likely to encounter, and computerized e-learning modules at one of seven Hamburger University centers around the world. More than 275,000 people have graduated from Hamburger University, earning their degrees in Hamburgerology.[13] Additional training takes place in existing McDonald's restaurants over 12 to 24 months.

Franchisees at Zaxby's, a fast-casual chain of chicken restaurants, receive six weeks of training in a variety of venues before opening their stores. The first component of the program involves classroom training at Zaxby's headquarters, where they learn about the company's culture and expectations. Then franchisees go into Zaxby's restaurants, where they learn the details of daily operations from existing franchisees. For the final part of their training, franchisees return to headquarters to learn about Zaxby's franchise support system and to take a final written and hands-on test.[14] Although these training programs are beneficial to running a successful franchise, franchisees should not expect a two- to five-week program to make them management experts. The necessary management skills for any business are too complex to learn in any single course.

Many franchisors supplement their start-up training programs with ongoing instruction and support to ensure franchisees' continued success. Franchisors often provide field support to franchisees in customer service, quality control, inventory management, and general management. Franchisors may assign field consultants to guide new franchisees through the first week or two of operation after the grand opening. Zaxby's offers its franchisees a Web-based Learning Center, where they can take refresher courses, view videos, listen to podcasts, participate in discussion boards, and access an online library.[15]

Hamburger University, the training ground for McDonald's franchisees.

*Source:* Mark Peterson/Corbis.

The support system that franchisees provide often is the key to franchisees' success.

**ENTREPRENEURIAL PROFILE: Katie Reinisch: Red Mango** Although Katie Reinisch had no experience in the yogurt business, she left her job as communications director in the Colorado legislature to open a Red Mango franchise in Denver with her husband. "We'd always wanted to own something instead of just getting a paycheck," she says. After researching several franchise options, the couple settled on Red Mango, and the support system the franchisor offers was one of the deciding factors. "The company held my hand, gave me manuals, and gave me guidance every step of the way," says Reinish. Including assisting the couple in finding a high-traffic location that is drawing a highly diverse customer base. "It's been hard and challenging and terrific," she admits, "but this is the perfect job for me. It's like hosting a party all of the time."[16]

## Brand-Name Appeal

Franchisees purchase the right to use a known and advertised brand name for a product or service, giving them the advantage of identifying their businesses with a widely recognized name. Customers recognize the identifying trademark, the standard symbols, the store design, and the products of an established franchise. In fact, a basic tenet of franchising is cloning the franchisor's success. Customers can be confident that the quality and content of a meal at McDonald's in Fort Lauderdale will be consistent with a meal at a San Francisco McDonald's. Because of a franchise's name recognition, franchisees who have just opened their outlets often discover a ready supply of customers eager to purchase their products or services. Entrepreneurs who launch independent businesses may have to work for years and spend many thousands of dollars in advertising to build a customer base of equivalent size. One franchising expert explains, "The day you open a McDonald's franchise, you have instant customers. If you choose to open [an independent] hamburger restaurant, you'd have to spend a fortune on advertising and promotion before you'd attract [that many] customers."[17]

## Standardized Quality of Goods and Services

Many entrepreneurs choose to operate franchises because of the quality and selection of products and services that the franchisor has developed, a task that could take many years to accomplish independently. Amy McAnarney, president of retail client services for H&R Block, a tax preparation franchise with more than 4,500 locations across the United States, says that franchisees are drawn to the company because of its well-known brand and "the products and services that H&R Block brings." Franchisees have access to the latest tax code software, expert advice from the company's Tax Institute, and extensive, ongoing training for all tax preparers. In addition, the company provides its franchisees with a full complement of revenue-enhancing products, including prepaid debit cards, savings accounts, and lines of credit.[18]

Because a franchisee purchases a license to sell the franchisor's product or service for the privilege of using the associated brand name, the quality of the goods or service franchisees sell determines the franchisor's reputation. Building a sound reputation in business can be a slow process, but destroying a good reputation takes no time at all. If some franchisees are allowed to operate at substandard levels, the image of the entire chain suffers irreparable damage; therefore, franchisors demand strict compliance with uniform standards of quality and service throughout the chain. Many franchisors conduct periodic inspections of local facilities to assist in maintaining acceptable levels of performance. Maintaining quality is so important that most franchisors retain the right to terminate the franchise contract and to repurchase the outlet if the franchisee fails to comply with established standards.

## National Advertising Programs

An effective advertising program is essential to the success of virtually all franchise operations. Marketing a brand-name product or service over a wide geographic area requires a far-reaching advertising campaign. A regional or national advertising program benefits all franchisees, and most franchisors have one. In fact, one study reports that 79 percent of franchisors require franchisees to contribute to a national advertising fund (the average amount is 2 percent of sales).[19] Typically, these advertising campaigns are organized and controlled by the franchisor, but franchisees actually pay for the campaigns. In fact, they are financed by each franchisee's contribution of a percentage of monthly sales, usually 1 to 5 percent, or a flat monthly fee. For example, Subway franchisees pay 4.5 percent of gross revenues to the Subway national advertising program. The franchisor pools these funds to create a cooperative advertising program, which has more impact than if the franchisees spent the same amount of money separately. The result is that franchisees associated with a well-developed system do not have to struggle for recognition in the local marketplace as much as an independent owner might.

Many franchisors also require franchisees to spend a minimum amount on local advertising. In fact, 41 percent of franchisors require their franchisees to invest in local advertising (once again, the average amount is 2 percent of sales).[20] To supplement Wendy's national advertising efforts (to which franchisees contribute 3.25 percent of gross sales), Wendy's requires franchisees to spend at least 0.75 percent of gross sales on local and regional advertising. Some franchisors assist franchisees in designing and producing local advertising. Many companies help franchisees create promotional plans and provide press releases, advertisements, and special materials, such as signs and banners for grand openings and special promotions.

## Financial Assistance

Purchasing a franchise can be just as expensive (if not more so) than launching an independent business. Although franchisees typically invest a significant amount of their own money in their businesses, most of them need additional financing. According to a recent study by the International Franchise Association, more than 80 percent of franchisors say that limited access to credit has slowed their ability to expand.[21] The study estimates the funding gap between the capital that franchises need to grow and the capital that lenders actually provide at between 20 and 23 percent per year for the last several years (see Figure 6.3). In the most recent year analyzed, franchises requested $26.5 billion in new lending capital, but lenders provided only $23.9 billion, leaving a significant funding gap that represents about 6,400 franchises that were not created.[22] Some franchisors are willing to provide at least a portion of that additional financing through their own internal financing programs. A basic principle of franchising is to use franchisees' money to grow the franchisor's business, but some franchisors realize that because start-up costs have reached breathtakingly high levels, they must provide financial help for franchisees. In fact, a study by

**FIGURE 6.3**

**Franchise Lending Activity**

*Source:* Based on data from Small Business Lending Matrix and Analysis, FRANdata, Volume V, March 2013, p. 18.

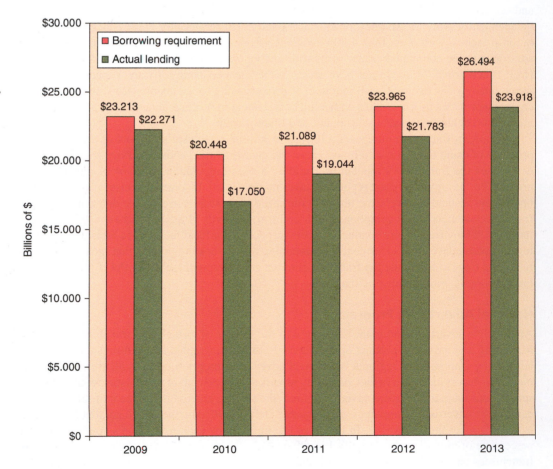

FRANdata, a franchising research company, reports that 20 percent of franchisors offer direct financing to their franchisees.[23] Small franchise systems are more likely to provide direct financial assistance to franchisees than are larger, established franchisors. Once a franchisor locates a suitable prospective franchisee, it may offer the qualified candidate direct financial assistance in the form of financing for equipment or inventory purchases or even the franchise fee. To make their franchises more affordable to prospective franchisees, some franchisors have reduced their fees and waived royalty payments for the first few months of a new franchise's operation. Huddle House, a restaurant chain founded in Decatur, Georgia, in 1964 by John Sparks, recently started a program that cuts $5,000 from the initial franchise fee (which ranges from $12,500 to $25,000) and contributes $5,000 to help new franchisees with their marketing efforts.[24]

Traditionally, financial assistance from franchisors takes a form other than direct loans, leases, or short-term credit. Franchisors usually assist qualified franchisees with establishing relationships with banks, nonbank lenders, and other sources of funds. The support and connections from the franchisor enhance a franchisee's credit standing because lenders recognize the lower failure rate among established franchises. Tight credit standards in the last several years have made this benefit all the more important to prospective franchisees. "Today, if franchisors want to keep their growth engines humming, they must work with lenders to help their franchisees receive loan approvals to open new stores," says Lex Lane, a top manager at United Capital Business Lending.[25]

The International Franchise Association and the Consumer Bankers Association have created the Franchise Registry, a program that is designed to increase franchise lending by providing bank financing and loan guarantees to franchisees through the Small Business Administration (SBA) (more on the SBA's loan guarantee programs is provided in Chapter 17). The Franchise Registry streamlines and expedites the loan application process for franchisees who pass the screening tests at franchises that are members of the Registry. More than 3,000 franchises ranging from AAMCO Transmissions (automotive repair) to Zaxby's (fast-food chicken restaurants) participate in the Franchise Registry program. Approximately 6.3 percent of all SBA loan guarantees go to franchisees, and the amount typically ranges from $250,000 to $500,000.[26]

BoeFly offers an online service for fees that range from $100 to $500 that matches franchisees' loan request with more than 2,200 national, regional, and local lenders. Mohammed Azam recently used BoeFly's loan matching service to connect with eight potential lenders and acquire an SBA-guaranteed loan to finance the purchase of his first Great Clips hair salon franchise.[27]

## Proven Products and Business Formats

A franchisee is purchasing the franchisor's experience, expertise, products, and support. A franchise owner does not have to build a business from scratch. Rather than relying solely on personal ability to establish a business and attract a clientele, the franchisee can depend on the methods and systems of an established business. These standardized procedures and operations greatly enhance the franchisee's chances of success and avoid the most inefficient type of learning— trial and error. "When we say 'Do things our way,' it's not just an ego thing on the part of the franchisor," says an executive at Subway Sandwiches and Salads. "We've proven it works."[28]

Reputable franchisors also invest resources in researching and developing new products and services, improving on existing ones, and tracking market trends that influence the success of its product line. Many franchisees cite this as another key benefit of the franchising arrangement.

## Centralized Buying Power

Some franchisees have a significant advantage over independent small businesses because of their franchisors' centralized and large-volume buying power. If franchisors sell goods and materials to franchisees—and not all do—they may pass on to franchisees any cost savings through volume discounts. Other franchisors negotiate quantity discounts with vendors on behalf of their franchisees. For example, 7-Eleven, the largest operator of convenience stores in the world with more than 50,000 outlets, is able to negotiate discounts for its franchisees with suppliers that the owner of a single, independently operated convenience store could not match.

## Site Selection and Territorial Protection

A proper location is critical to the success of any small business, and franchises are no exception. In fact, franchise experts consider the three most important factors in franchising to be *location*,

*location*, and *location*. Becoming affiliated with a franchise may be the best way to get into prime locations. McDonald's, for example, is well known for its ability to obtain prime locations in high-traffic areas for its restaurants. Although choosing a location is the franchisee's responsibility, the franchisor reserves the right to approve the final site. Many franchisors will conduct an extensive location analysis for new outlets (usually for a fee). A thorough demographic and statistical analysis of potential locations is essential to selecting the site that offers the best potential for success. You will learn more about this in Chapter 18.

Some franchisors offer territorial protection, which gives the franchisee the right to exclusive distribution of brand-name goods or services within a particular geographic area. Under such an agreement, a franchisor agrees not to sell another franchised outlet or to open a company-owned unit within the franchisee's defined territory. The size and description of a franchisee's territory varies from one franchise to another. For example, one restaurant franchise agrees not to license another franchisee within a three-mile radius of existing locations. The purpose of this protection is to prevent an invasion of existing franchisees' territories and the accompanying dilution of sales. The owner of a fast-food franchise saw his store's sales decline from $15,000 per week to $8,000 per week when another franchisee opened a second outlet in the same small Connecticut town. Because the franchisor offered no territorial protection, however, the owner of the original franchise could do nothing about his nearby competitor from the same chain.[29]

Unfortunately for franchisees, fewer franchisors now offer their franchisees territorial protection, and franchise owners may find that they are in close proximity to each other. As competition for top locations escalates, disputes over the placement of new franchise outlets have become a source of friction between franchisors and franchisees. Existing franchisees charge that franchisors are encroaching on their territories by granting new franchises in such close proximity that their sales are diluted. Franchise experts consistently cite territorial encroachment as the number one threat to franchisees.

## Increased Chance for Success

Investing in a franchise is not risk free. New franchise companies enter the market each year, and many do not survive. Not surprisingly, the failure rate for young franchise systems is higher than that of older, more established ones.[30] A study by The Coleman Report of SBA loans to more than 580 franchises shows that the failure rate of franchisees in these systems over a recent 10-year period averaged 17.2 percent but ranged from 0 to 94 percent, depending on the chain.[31] Despite the fact that franchising offers no guarantees of success, experts contend that franchising is less risky than building a business from the ground up. The tradition of success for franchises is attributed to the broad range of services, assistance, guidelines, and the comprehensive business system the franchisor provides. "Every franchisor has its products, services, marketing, and business systems in place," says a top small business lender at TD Bank. "If you plug a franchisee into that model, he or she has a better chance of success than a non-franchised business start-up."[32] A recent study of franchises reports that the success rate of franchisees is higher when a franchise system does the following:

- Requires franchisees to have prior industry experience
- Requires franchisees to actively manage their stores (no "absentee" owners)
- Has built a strong brand name
- Offers training programs designed to improve franchisees' knowledge and skills[33]

**ENTREPRENEURIAL PROFILE: Kerry Kramp: Sizzler** Sizzler, a steakhouse chain started in 1958 in Culver City, California, that had 650 franchised outlets at its peak, filed for Chapter 11 bankruptcy in 1996, reorganized, and limped along for the next decade. Kerry Kramp purchased the company in 2008 and instituted a turnaround program aimed at restoring the chain to its original glory by focusing on its roots. "We went through our menu archives and found our original steak seasoning, our cheese toast, and other classics," says Kramp. Kramp simplified the Sizzler menu, trimming it by 25 percent, reintroduced fresh-cut meats, upgraded kitchens, and introduced standardized operating procedures. He also added modern menu items, including hot wings, Asian slaw, Greek salads, and an ultimate value menu, and worked with franchisees to renovate their restaurants to make them brighter and more modern. Sizzler is once again selling franchises and has 180 locations across the United States and Puerto Rico.[34]

The risk involved in purchasing a franchise is two-pronged: success—or failure—depends on the franchisee's managerial skills and motivation and on the franchisor's business experience, system, and support. Many franchisees are convinced that franchising has been the key to their success in business.

# Drawbacks of Buying a Franchise

The benefits of franchising can mean the difference between success and failure for some entrepreneurs. However, prospective franchisees must understand the disadvantages of franchising before choosing this method of doing business. Perhaps the biggest drawback of franchising is that a franchisee must sacrifice some freedom to the franchisor. Other disadvantages are discussed in the following sections.

## Franchise Fees and Ongoing Royalties

Virtually every franchisor imposes some type of fees and demands a share of franchisees' sales revenue in return for the use of the franchisor's name, products or services, and business system. The fees and the initial capital requirements vary among the different franchisors. The total investment required for a franchise varies from around $3,000 for some home-based service franchises to $13.5 million or more for hotel and motel franchises. For example, Jan-Pro, a commercial cleaning franchise, requires a capital investment that ranges from just $3,145 to $50,405, and Snap Fitness, a 24-hour fitness center, estimates that the total cost of opening a franchise ranges from $76,100 to $361,700. Sonic Drive In Restaurants, a chain that sells a variety of fast-food items that range from breakfast dishes and hot dogs to hamburgers and slushies in the retro atmosphere of a 1950s curbside diner, requires an investment of $1.1 million to $3.05 million, depending on land acquisition and building construction costs.

Financial requirements that franchisors stipulate often create a stumbling block for many would-be franchisees. Franchisors do not want their franchisees to take on so much debt that their franchises are not sustainable; therefore, minimum requirements for net worth and available cash can be extremely high for franchises that require significant up-front investments. Hardees, the quick service hamburger chain with an estimated total investment that ranges from $1.2 million to $1.6 million, requires franchisees to have a minimum net worth of $1 million and available cash of $300,000.

Start-up costs for franchises often include a variety of fees. Most franchises impose a franchise fee up front for the right to use the company name. The average up-front fee that franchisors charge is $25,147.[35] Sonic Drive In Restaurants, the fast-food chain, charges a franchise fee of $45,000, and Subway's franchise fee is $15,000. Other franchise start-up costs might include a location analysis, site purchase and preparation, construction, signs, fixtures, equipment, management assistance, and training. Some franchise fees include these costs, but others do not. Before signing any contract, a prospective franchisee should determine the total cost of a franchise, something every franchisor is required to disclose in its Franchise Disclosure Document (see the "Franchising and the Law" section later in this chapter).

Franchisors also impose continuing royalty fees as revenue-sharing devices. The royalty usually involves a percentage of gross sales with a required minimum or a flat fee levied on the franchise. (In fact, 82 percent of franchisors charge a royalty based on a percentage of franchisees' sales.[36]) Royalty fees range from 1 to 11 percent, and the average royalty rate is 6.7 percent.[37] Subway charges franchisees a royalty of 8 percent of gross sales, which is payable weekly, and Snap Fitness charges a flat royalty of $449 per month. These ongoing royalties increase a franchisee's overhead expenses significantly. Because the franchisor's royalties and fees (the total fees the average franchisor collects amount to 8.4 percent of a franchisee's sales) are calculated as a percentage of a franchisee's sales, the franchisor gets paid—even if the franchisee fails to earn a profit.[38] Sometimes unprepared franchisees discover (too late) that a franchisor's royalties and fees are the equivalent of the normal profit margin for a franchise. To avoid this problem, prospective franchisees should determine exactly how much their fees will be and then weigh the benefits of the services the fees cover. One of the best ways to do this is to itemize what you are getting for your money and then determine whether the cost is reasonable. Getting details on all expenses—the amount, the time of payment, and the financing arrangements—is important. It is critical that entrepreneurs find out which items, if any, are included in the initial franchise fee and which fees represent additional expenditures.

**5.** _____

Describe the limitations of buying a franchise.

## Strict Adherence to Standardized Operations

Although franchisees own their businesses, they do not have the autonomy of independent owners. Franchisors must ensure the quality and integrity of their brands and require franchisees to abide by the terms of the franchise agreement that governs the franchisor–franchisee relationship. That agreement requires franchisees to operate their outlets according to the principles spelled out in the franchisor's operations manual. Typical topics covered in the manual include operating hours, dress codes, operating policies and procedures, product or service specifications, and confidentiality requirements. At times, strict adherence to franchise standards may become a burden to some franchisees.

To protect their public image, franchisors require their franchisees to maintain certain operating standards. If a franchise consistently fails to meet the minimum standards established for the business, the franchisor may terminate its license. Many franchisors determine compliance with standards by using periodic inspections and mystery shoppers. Mystery shoppers work for a survey company and, although they look like any other customer, are trained to observe and then later record on a checklist a franchise's performance on key standards such as cleanliness, speed of service, employees' appearances and attitudes, and others. Michael Mershimer owns a company that employs an army of 300,000 freelance mystery shoppers and works for many franchises. Mershimer once caught a franchisee of a large ice cream chain who purchased tubs of cheaper ice cream and used a hot iron on the containers to transfer the products to the official franchisor's branded tubs. Franchises that detect franchisees who are violating the company's standardized operations typically send a "notice to cure" the problem. If the franchisee fails to comply, the franchisor sends a letter demanding that the franchisee comply with standards within 10 days. If the franchisee refuses, the franchisor sends notice that the franchisee's contract is terminated.[39]

## Restrictions on Purchasing

To maintain quality standards, franchisors sometimes require franchisees to purchase products, supplies, or special equipment from the franchisor or from approved suppliers. For example, KFC requires that franchisees use only seasonings blended by a particular company because a poor image for the entire franchise could result from some franchisees using inferior products to cut costs. The franchise contract spells out the penalty for using unapproved suppliers, which usually is termination of the franchise agreement.

Before signing with a franchisor, prospective franchisees should investigate the prices that the franchisor and approved suppliers charge for supplies.

**ENTREPRENEURIAL PROFILE: Marty Tate: Quiznos** Several franchisees in the Quiznos sandwich chain filed a class-action lawsuit against the franchisor alleging that the company requires franchisees to buy practically all of their supplies—including the meat and the cheese for sandwiches, bathroom soap, payroll and accounting systems, and even the piped-in music—from the franchisor or its approved suppliers at inflated prices, which caused their stores to be unprofitable. "We can't make money," says Marty Tate, a franchisee who owns a Quiznos outlet in Pennsylvania. He claims that 40 percent of his sales go to cover food costs, the ongoing royalty, and franchise advertising fee.[40]

For many years, franchisors could legally set the prices they charge for the products they sell to franchisees but could not control the retail prices franchisees charge for products. However, a 1997 Supreme Court decision opened the door for franchisors to establish maximum prices that franchisees can charge. Many franchisors do not impose maximum prices, choosing instead to provide franchisees with suggested prices, but some do establish price limits. For instance, Burger King requires franchisees to charge no more than $1 for items on its Value Menu. Franchisees filed a lawsuit against the franchisor, claiming that Burger King did not have the right to dictate maximum prices under the franchise agreement. Franchisees argued that being forced to sell a double cheeseburger for $1 caused them to lose more than 10 cents per sandwich. A federal court judge ruled that the franchisor did have the right to set maximum prices for the products its franchisees sell. In response to franchisees' concerns, Burger King removed the double cheeseburger from the Value Menu, which allowed franchisees to raise its price to $1.19, and replaced it with the BK Dollar Double, a sandwich that has two beef patties but only one slice of cheese.[41]

Franchisors also influence the prices that their franchisees charge in other ways. A common technique is to offer discount coupons that franchisees must honor. One sandwich company's franchisees complained that the franchisor's discount coupons were cutting into their profit margins so severely that they could not make a profit on sales of the discounted items. "This company never saw a discount it didn't like," says one franchisee. "Those great discounts are financed solely by franchisees."[42]

## Limited Product Line

In most cases, the franchise agreement stipulates that franchisees can sell only those products approved by the franchisor. Franchisees must avoid selling any unapproved products through their outlets unless they are willing to risk cancellation of their franchise licenses. Franchisors strive for standardization in their product lines so that customers, wherever they may be, know what to expect. Some companies allow franchisees to modify their product or service offerings to suit regional or local tastes, but only with the franchisor's approval.

The idea for the Joey Junior burrito, one of the most popular items on Moe's Southwest Grill's menu, came from one of the company's franchisee's, Laura Leigh Drake.

*Source:* Boston Globe/Getty Images.

**ENTREPRENEURIAL PROFILE: Laura Leigh and Kealon Drake: Moe's Southwest Grill** Laura Leigh Drake and her husband Kealon invested in a Moe's Southwest Grill franchise in Birmingham, Alabama. After hearing many of her customers rave about the food but complain that they could not finish a regular burrito, Laura Leigh developed a burrito that was larger than a child's burrito but smaller than the company's huge "regular" burrito. She pitched her new product idea, which she named the Joey Junior, to the company's new owner, who agreed to test the smaller burrito across the chain. The Joey Junior went on to become one of the best-selling items on the Moe's menu.[43]

A franchise may be required to carry an unpopular product or be prevented from introducing a desirable one by the franchise agreement. Some franchises discourage franchisees from deviating from the standard "formula" in any way, including experimenting with new products and services. However, other franchisors encourage and even solicit new ideas and innovations from their franchisees.

**ENTREPRENEURIAL PROFILE: Herb Peterson: McDonald's** Santa Barbara, California, McDonald's franchisee Herb Peterson created the highly successful Egg McMuffin in 1972 while experimenting with a Teflon-coated egg ring that gave fried eggs rounded corners and a poached appearance. Peterson put his round eggs on English muffins, adorned them with Canadian bacon and melted cheese, and showed his creation to McDonald's CEO, Ray Kroc. Even though Kroc had just eaten lunch, he devoured two of them and was sold on the idea. The catchy name came about later when the Krocs were having dinner with another McDonald's executive, Fred Turner, and his wife, Patty, who suggested the Egg McMuffin name. In 1975, McDonald's became the first fast-food franchise to open its doors for breakfast, and the Egg McMuffin became a staple on the breakfast menu, which accounts for 15 percent of McDonald's sales. McDonald's franchisees also came up with the ideas for the Big Mac and the Happy Meal.[44]

## Market Saturation

Franchisees in fast-growing systems reap the benefits of the franchisor's expanding reach, but they also may encounter the downside of a franchisor's aggressive growth strategy: market saturation. As the owners of many fast-food, sandwich shops, and yogurt and ice cream franchises have discovered, market saturation is a very real danger. One researcher has determined that only one place in the contiguous 48 states, a high plain in northwestern Nevada, is more than 100 miles from a McDonald's restaurant.[45] Fast-growing franchises in particular run the risk of having outlets so close together that they cannibalize sales from one another. Franchisees of one fast-growing ice cream chain claim that the franchisor's rapid expansion has resulted in oversaturation in some markets, causing them to struggle to reach their break-even points. Some franchisees saw their sales drop precipitously and were forced to close their outlets.

Although some franchisors offer franchisees territorial protection, others do not. Territorial encroachment has become a hotly contested issue in franchising as growth-seeking franchisors have exhausted most of the prime locations and are now setting up new franchises in close proximity to existing ones. In some areas of the country, franchisees are upset, claiming that their markets are oversaturated and their sales are suffering.

**TABLE 6.1 A Franchise Evaluation Quiz**

Taking the emotion out of buying a franchise is the goal of this self-test developed by Franchise Solutions, Inc., a franchise consulting company in Portsmouth, New Hampshire. Circle the number that reflects your degree of certainty or positive feelings for each of the following 12 statements: 1 is low; 5 is high.

| | Low High |
|---|---|
| **1.** I would really enjoy being in this kind of business. | 1 2 3 4 5 |
| **2.** This franchise will meet or exceed my income goals. | 1 2 3 4 5 |
| **3.** My people-handling skills are sufficient for this franchise. | 1 2 3 4 5 |
| **4.** I understand fully my greatest challenge in this franchise, and I feel comfortable with my abilities. | 1 2 3 4 5 |
| **5.** I have met with the company management and feel compatible. | 1 2 3 4 5 |
| **6.** I understand the risks with this business and am prepared to accept them. | 1 2 3 4 5 |
| **7.** I have researched the competition in my area and feel comfortable with the potential market. | 1 2 3 4 5 |
| **8.** My family and friends think this is a great opportunity for me. | 1 2 3 4 5 |
| **9.** I have had an adviser review the disclosure documents and the franchise agreement. | 1 2 3 4 5 |
| **10.** I have contacted a representative number of the existing franchisees; they were overwhelmingly positive. | 1 2 3 4 5 |
| **11.** I have researched this industry and feel comfortable about the long-term growth potential. | 1 2 3 4 5 |
| **12.** My background and experience make this franchise an ideal choice. | 1 2 3 4 5 |

The maximum score on the quiz is 60. A score of 45 or below means that either the franchise opportunity is unsuitable or that you need to do more research on the franchise you are considering.

*Source:* Roberta Maynard, "Choosing a Franchise," *Nation's Business*, October 1996, p. 57.

## Limited Freedom

When franchisees purchase their franchises and sign their contracts, they agree to sell the franchisor's product or service by following its prescribed formula. When McDonald's rolls out a new national product, for instance, all franchisees put it on their menus. Franchisors want to ensure success, and most monitor their franchisees' performances closely. Strict uniformity is the rule rather than the exception. This feature of franchising is the source of the system's success, but it also gives many franchisees the feeling that they are reporting to a "boss." Entrepreneurs who want to be their own bosses and to avoid being subject to the control of others most likely will be frustrated as franchisees. "It's their system, so they get to write the rule book," says Joe Libava, The Franchise King. "If you spend $200,000 on a franchise and think you're going to be an independent entrepreneur, you're going to be disappointed."[46] In short, highly independent, "go-my-own-way" individuals probably should not choose the franchise route to business ownership, which requires playing by someone else's rules. Table 6.1 offers a Franchise Evaluation Quiz designed to help potential franchisees decide whether a franchise is right for them.

## No Guarantee of Success

As some failed franchisees have learned, purchasing a franchise does not provide a guarantee of success. Franchise systems that are built on poorly conceived and untested business models, that do not screen prospective franchisees properly, or that provide inadequate training and support for their franchisees are not likely to succeed. Any new business venture, including a franchise, involves some level of risk. However, by carefully evaluating franchisors using the procedure outlined in this chapter, prospective franchisees can select a franchisee that increases the probability that they will succeed.

**6.**
---
Describe the legal aspects of franchising, including the protection offered by the Federal Trade Commission's Trade Regulation Rule.

## Franchising and the Law

The franchising boom of the late 1950s brought with it many prime investment opportunities. However, the explosion of legitimate franchises also ushered in with it numerous fly-by-night franchisors who defrauded their franchisees. By the 1970s, franchising was rife with fraudulent practitioners. Thousands of people lost millions of dollars to criminals and unscrupulous operators who sold flawed business concepts and phantom franchises to unsuspecting investors. In an effort to control the rampant fraud in the industry and the potential for deception inherent in a franchise relationship, California in 1971 enacted the first Franchise Investment Law. This law and those of 14 other states* that have since passed similar laws requires franchisors to register their franchises and file a **Franchise Disclosure Document** (FDD) with the state and deliver a copy to prospective franchisees before any offer or sale of a franchise. In October 1979, the Federal Trade Commission (FTC) adopted similar legislation at the national level that established full disclosure guidelines on 20 topics for any company selling franchises and was designed to give potential franchisees the information they needed to protect themselves from unscrupulous franchisors.

In 2008, the FTC revised the requirements of the FDD to include specific information on 23 topics. All franchisors must disclose this detailed information on their operations at least 14 days before a franchisee signs a contract or pays any money. The FDD applies to all franchisors, even those in the 35 states that lack franchise registration laws. The purpose of the regulation is to assist potential franchisees' investigations of a franchise deal and to introduce consistency into the franchisor's disclosure statements. The FTC also established a "plain English" requirement for the FDD that prohibits legal and technical jargon and makes a document easy to read and understand. The FTC's philosophy is not so much to prosecute abusers as to provide information to prospective franchisees and help them to make intelligent decisions. Although the FTC requires each franchisor to provide a potential franchisee with this information, it does not verify its accuracy. Prospective franchisees should use this document only as a starting point for their investigations.

In its FDD, a franchisor must include a sample franchise contract, audited financial statements for three years, and information on the following 23 items:

1. Information identifying the franchisor and its affiliates and describing the franchisor's business experience and the franchises being sold.

2. Information identifying and describing the business experience of each of the franchisor's officers, directors, and managers responsible for the franchise program. Prospective franchisees should be wary of franchises whose executives lack franchise experience.

3. A description of the lawsuits in which the franchisor and its officers, directors, and managers have been involved. Although most franchisors have been involved in some type of litigation, an excessive number of lawsuits, particularly if they relate to the same problem, is alarming. Another red flag is an excessive number of lawsuits brought against the franchisor by franchisees. "The history of the litigation will tell you the future of your relationship [with the franchisor]," says the founder of a maid-service franchise.[47]

4. Information about any bankruptcies in which the franchisor and its officers, directors, and managers have been involved.

5. Information about the initial franchise fee and other payments required to obtain the franchise, the intended use of the fees, and the conditions under which the fees are refundable.

6. A table that describes all of the other fees that franchisees are required to pay after start-up, including royalties, service fees, training fees, lease payments, advertising or marketing charges, and others. The table also must include the due dates for the fees.

7. A table that shows the components of a franchisee's total initial investment. The categories covered are preopening expenses, the initial franchise fee, training expenses, equipment, opening inventory, initial advertising fee, signs, real estate (purchased or leased), equipment, opening inventory, security deposits, business licenses, initial advertising fees, and other expenses, such as working capital, legal and accounting fees. Also included is an estimate of amount of working capital a franchisee should have on hand to sustain the company in its first three months of operation. (Franchisees should be aware that the actual amount of capital required to keep a franchise going until it generates positive cash flow is probably much higher.) These estimates, usually stated as a range, give prospective franchisees an idea of how much their total start-up costs will be.

---

* The 15 states requiring franchise registration are California, Hawaii, Illinois, Indiana, Maryland, Michigan, Minnesota, New York, North Dakota, Oregon, Rhode Island, South Dakota, Virginia, Washington, and Wisconsin.

8. Information about quality requirements of goods, services, equipment, supplies, inventory, and other items used in the franchise and where franchisees may purchase them, including required purchases from the franchisor. When interviewing existing franchisees, prospective franchisees should ask whether the prices they pay for products and services are reasonable.

9. A cross-reference table that shows the location in the FDD and in the franchise contract of the description of the franchisee's obligations under the franchise contract.

10. A description of the financial assistance (if any) that is available from the franchisor in the purchase of the franchise. Although many franchisors do not offer direct financial assistance to franchisees, they may have special arrangements with lenders who may provide franchisees with financing.

11. A description of all obligations the franchisor must fulfill to help a franchisee prepare to open and operate a unit, including site selection, advertising, computer systems, pricing, training (a table describing the length and type of training is required), and other forms of assistance provided to franchisees. This list and description of the support services the franchisor provides usually is the longest section of the FDD.

12. A description of any territorial protection that the franchise receives and a statement as to whether the franchisor may locate a company-owned store or other franchised outlets in that territory. The franchisor must specify whether it offers exclusive or nonexclusive territories. Given the controversy in many franchises over market saturation, franchisees should pay close attention to this section. Prospective franchisees should recognize the risks associated with purchasing a franchise that provides no territorial protection or exclusive territories.

13. All relevant information about the franchisor's trademarks, service marks, trade names, logos, and commercial symbols, including where they are registered. Prospective franchisees should look for a strong trade or service mark that is registered with the U.S. Patent and Trademark Office.

14. Similar information on any patents, copyrights, and proprietary processes the franchisor owns and the rights franchisees have to use them.

15. A description of the extent to which franchisees must participate personally in the operation of the franchise. Many franchisors look for "hands-on" franchisees and discourage or even prohibit "absentee owners."

16. A description of any restrictions on the goods or services that franchises are permitted to sell and with whom franchisees may deal. The agreement usually restricts franchisees to selling only those items that the franchisor has approved.

17. A table that describes the length of the franchise contract, the conditions under which the franchise may be repurchased or refused renewal by the franchisor, transferred to a third party by the franchisee, and terminated or modified by either party. This section also addresses the methods established for resolving disputes, usually either mediation or arbitration, between franchisees and the franchisor.

18. A description of the involvement of celebrities and public figures in the franchise. Less than 1 percent of franchise systems use public figures as part of their promotional strategies.[48]

19. A complete statement of the basis for any financial performance claims made to the franchisee, including the percentage of existing franchises that have actually operated at or above the averages that the franchisor provides. Franchisors that make financial performance claims must include them in the FDD, and the claims must "have a reasonable basis" at the time they are made. However, franchisors are *not* required to make any financial performance claims at all; in fact, about 80 percent of franchisors do not, primarily because of liability concerns about committing their numbers to writing.[49]

20. A table that displays system-wide statistical information about the expansion or the contraction of the franchise over the last three years. This section allows prospective franchisees to determine whether a franchise is growing or shrinking and how fast. A large number of closures may indicate that the franchisor's products or service have fallen out of

favor with customers. The tables in this section show the current number of franchises, the number of franchises projected for the future and the states in which they are to be sold, the number of franchises terminated, the number of agreements the franchisor has not renewed, the number of franchises that have been sold to new owners, the number of outlets the franchisor has repurchased, and a list of the names and addresses (organized by state) of other franchisees in the system and of those who have left the system within the last year. Contacting some of the franchisees who have left the system can alert would-be franchisees to potential problems with the franchise.

**21.** The franchisor's audited financial statements. Prospective franchisees can use this information to determine how stable the franchisor is.

**22.** A copy of all franchise and other contracts (leases, purchase agreements, and others) that the franchisee will be required to sign.

**23.** A standardized, detachable "receipt" to prove that the prospective franchisee received a copy of the FDD. The FTC now allows franchisors to provide the FDD to prospective franchisees electronically.

The typical FDD can be several hundred pages long, but every potential franchisee should read and understand it. Unfortunately, many do not, which often results in unpleasant surprises for franchisees. The information contained in the FDD does not fully protect potential franchisees from deception, nor does it guarantee success. The FDD does, however, provide enough information to begin a thorough investigation of the franchisor and the franchise deal, and prospective franchisees should use it to their advantage.

## Entrepreneurship in Action

# After the Cheering Stops

Jamal Mashburn beat the odds. Just 1.2 percent of college basketball players end up playing professional basketball, but Mashburn (whose nickname was "Monster Mash") made the leap from the University of Kentucky to the National Basketball Association (NBA), playing for the Dallas Mavericks and the New Orleans Hornets, where he was selected to play in the All Star Game. Since retiring from the NBA, Mashburn has beaten the odds again; 60 percent of professional basketball players (and 78 percent of professional football players) are bankrupt within two years of retiring from the game.

Not Mashburn, who was already thinking about his exit plan when he entered the NBA. His exit strategy included investing in franchises with a group of investors, including his former college coach, Rick Pitino. Just six years after retiring from professional basketball, Mashburn is a co-owner of 37 Papa John's restaurants, 34 Outback Steakhouses, three Dunkin' Donuts shops, and the largest Toyota dealership in Kentucky. Other professional athletes who have found success in franchising include Drew Brees (Super Bowl MVP and quarterback for the New Orleans Saints), Junior Bridgeman (former NBA player for the Milwaukee Bucks), Keyshawn Johnson (former wide receiver, Super Bowl champion, and Panera Bread franchisee), Reggie Bush (National Football League [NFL] star and Panera Bread franchisee), and Venus Williams (tennis professional and Jamba Juice franchisee).

Brees owns three Jimmy John's Gourmet Sandwiches outlets in New Orleans and plans to open more. He first learned about the franchise in Indiana where he was attending Purdue University (he started as a walk-on member of the football team) and

enjoyed eating there. After arriving in New Orleans to play for the Saints, Brees says that he "missed Jimmy John's so much" that he decided to introduce the city to the pleasures of Jimmy John's sandwiches. Although Brees has full-time managers in his restaurants, he often stops by to make sure things are running smoothly and to do some bootstrap marketing. He recently caused a traffic jam outside his first franchise when he tweeted to his nearly 1.2 million followers that he was going to eat lunch there.

Michael Stone, who played in the NFL for seven years, believes that franchising is an ideal fit for professional athletes and formed the Professional Athletes Franchise Initiative, an organization that encourages athletes to explore franchising as a postsports career. Stone says that franchising is a good fit for retired professional athletes because it requires many of the same skills to succeed. Athletes implement the game plan that their coaches create to win a game. Similarly, franchisees must execute the franchiser's game plan to operate their outlets successfully. Junior Bridgeman's experience lends credibility to Stone's observation. After a 12-year career in the NBA, Bridgeman invested in several Wendy's restaurants. Today, Bridgeman is the owner of 162 Wendy's and 121 Chili's restaurants that generate $507 million in annual sales.

Because their playing (and earning) time is relatively short (the average professional football player's career lasts just 3.5 years), professional athletes must plan for their second careers as soon as they sign their professional contracts. "Before they know it, they're out of the league, and their income drops significantly," says Robert Luna, a financial adviser to several athletes. "Unlike a young physician who will be making a lot more money

*(continued)*

# Entrepreneurship in Action *(continued)*

10, 20, or 30 years down the road, [a professional athlete] is getting it all up front.

Steve Caldeira, president of the International Franchise Association, sees athletes as a good fit for franchising. "[They] are strong leaders in the ultra-competitive sports arena, so they inherently understand the importance of working as a team and as part of a system to achieve success." Angelo Crowell, who played in the NFL for the Buffalo Bills for seven years before injuries ended his career, became a Jersey Mike's sandwich shop franchisee, opening two outlets in Tallahassee, Florida. Crowell had been a fan of the chain since he was a teenager in high school. When he discovered that the territory near his home was available, Crowell and his wife Kim decided to purchase the rights to develop it. Crowell says that as the owner, he is involved in the daily operations of the franchise.

1. What benefits does franchising offer professional athletes such as those described here?

2. Do you agree with Michael Stone that franchising is a good fit for athletes? Explain.

3. What steps should prospective franchisees, whether they are athletes or not, take to ensure that franchising is the right path to business ownership for them and that they select the right franchise?

*Sources:* Jason Daley, "Playing for Keeps," *Entrepreneur*, February 2012, pp. 82–87; Jan Norman, "Franchising Courts Pro Athletes," *Orange County Register*, November 10, 2011, *www.ocregister.com/articles/franchising-326406-athletes-franchise.html*; "The All Franchising Team," *Franchise Help*, October 17, 2011, *www.franchisehelp.com/blog/top-professional-athletes-who-own-franchises*; Russ Wiles, "Pro Athletes Often Fumble the Financial Ball," *USA Today*, April 22, 2012, *www.usatoday.com/sports/story/2012-04-22/Pro-athletes-and-financial-trouble/54465664/1*; Susan Langenhenning, "Drew Brees Hungry to Expand Jimmy John's Sandwich Shop's Reach into Local Market, *Times-Picayune*, July 1, 2012, *www.nola.com/dining/index.ssf/2012/07/drew_brees_takes_a_run_at_sand.html*; Michael Stone, "Angelo and Kim Crowell Implement the Jersey Mike's Game Plan," *Professional Athletes Franchise Initiative*, *www.thepafi.org/2010/11/angelo-and-kim-crowell-implement-the-jersey-mikes-gameplan.*

## The Right Way to Buy a Franchise

**7.**
_____

Explain the right way to buy a franchise.

The FDD can help potential franchisees to identify and avoid dishonest franchisors. The best defenses a prospective entrepreneur has against making a bad investment decision or against unscrupulous franchisors are preparation, common sense, and patience. A thorough investigation before investing in a franchise reduces the risk of being hoodwinked into a nonexistent franchise or a system that is destined to fail. Asking the right questions and resisting the urge to rush into an investment decision helps potential franchisees avoid unscrupulous franchisors.

Despite existing disclosure requirements, dishonest franchisors are still in operation, often moving from one state to another just ahead of authorities. Potential franchisees must beware. Franchise fraud has destroyed the dreams of many hopeful franchisees and has robbed them of their life savings. Because dishonest franchisors tend to follow certain patterns, well-prepared franchisees can avoid getting burned. The following clues should arouse the suspicion of an entrepreneur about to invest in a franchise:

- Claims that the franchise contract is "the standard one" and that "you don't need to read it." There is no standard franchise contract.

- A franchisor who fails to give you a copy of the required disclosure document, the FDD, at your first face-to-face meeting.

- A marginally successful prototype store or no prototype at all.

- A poorly prepared operations manual outlining the franchise system or no manual (or system) at all.

- An unsolicited testimonial from "a highly successful franchisee." Scam artists will hire someone to pose as a successful franchisee, complete with a rented luxury car and expensive-looking jewelry and clothing, to "prove" how successful franchisees can be and to help close the sale. Use the list of franchisees in item 20 of the FDD to find real franchisees and ask them plenty of questions.

- An unusual amount of litigation brought against the franchisor. In this litigious society, companies facing lawsuits is a common situation. However, too many lawsuits are a sign that something is amiss. This information is found in item 3 of the FDD.

- Verbal promises of large future earnings without written documentation. Remember: If franchisors make financial performance claims, they *must* document them in item 19 of the FDD.

- A high franchisee turnover rate or a high termination rate. This information is described in item 20 of the FDD.

- Attempts to discourage you from allowing an attorney to evaluate the franchise contract before you sign it.

- No written documentation to support claims and promises.

- A high pressure sale—sign the contract now or lose the opportunity. This tactic usually sounds like this: "Franchise territories are going fast. If you hesitate, you are likely to miss out on the prime spots."

- Claiming to be exempt from federal laws requiring complete disclosure of franchise details in a FDD. If a franchisor has no FDD, run—don't walk—away from the deal.

- "Get-rich-quick schemes," promises of huge profits with only minimum effort.

- Reluctance to provide a list of present franchisees for you to interview.

- Evasive, vague answers to your questions about the franchise and its operation.

Not every franchise "horror story" is the result of dishonest franchisors. In fact, most franchising problems are due to franchisees buying legitimate franchises without proper research and analysis. They end up in businesses they do not enjoy and that they are not well suited to operate. The steps outlined in the following sections will help any potential franchisee make the right franchise choice.

## Evaluate Yourself

Henry David Thoreau's advice to "know thyself" is excellent advice for prospective franchisees. Before looking at any franchise, entrepreneurs should study their own traits, goals, experience, likes, dislikes, risk orientation, income requirements, time and family commitments, and other characteristics. Knowing how much you can afford to invest in a franchise is important, but it is not the only factor to consider. The following are valuable questions for the entrepreneur to ask:

- Will you be comfortable working in a structured environment?

- What kinds of franchises fit your desired lifestyle?

- Do you want to sell a product or a service?

- Do you enjoy working with the public?

- Do you like selling?

- What hours do you expect to work?

- Do you want to work with people, or do you prefer to work alone?

- Which franchise concepts mesh best with your past work experience?

- What activities and hobbies do you enjoy?

- What income do you expect a franchise to generate?

- How much can you afford to invest in a franchise?

- Will you be happy with the daily routine of operating the franchise?

Most franchise contracts run for 10 years or more, making it imperative that prospective franchisees conduct a complete inventory of their interests, likes, dislikes, and abilities before buying a franchise.

## Research the Market

Entrepreneurs should research the market in the areas they plan to serve before shopping for a franchise:

- How fast is the surrounding area growing?

- In which areas is that growth occurring fastest?

- Is the market for the franchise's product or service growing or declining?

- How strong is the competition?

- Who are your potential customers?

- What are their characteristics?

- What are their income and education levels?

- What kinds of products and services do they buy?
- What gaps exist in the market?

Investing time in the local library or on the Internet to determine whether an area has a sufficient number of the franchise's target customers is essential to judging an outlet's potential for success.

Solid market research should tell a prospective franchisee whether a particular franchise is merely a passing fad or a long-term trend. Steering clear of fads and into long-term trends is a key to sustained success in franchising. The secret to distinguishing between a fad that will soon fizzle and a meaningful trend that offers genuine opportunity is finding products or services that are consistent with fundamental demographic and lifestyle patterns of the population. That requires sound market research that focuses not only on local market opportunities but also on the "big picture." For instance, a growing number of aging Baby Boomers is creating an opportunity for franchises that provide cleaning, in-home care, and home improvement services.

### Consider Your Franchise Options

Tracking down information on prospective franchise systems is easier now than ever before. Franchisors publish information about their systems on the Internet. These listings can help potential franchisees find a suitable franchise within their price ranges. Many cities host franchise trade shows throughout the year, where hundreds of franchisors gather to sell their franchises. Many business magazines such as *Entrepreneur, Inc.*, and others devote at least one issue and a section of their Web sites to franchising, where they often lists hundreds of franchise opportunities. Another useful resource is *Bond's Franchise Guide* (Source Book Publications), which provides detailed profiles of nearly 900 North American franchisors and lists of franchise attorneys, consultants, and service providers.

### Get a Copy of the FDD and Study It

Once you narrow down your franchise choices, contact each franchise and get copy of the FDD. Then read it! The FDD is an important tool in your search for the right franchise. When Ali Saifi was looking for a franchise, he reviewed disclosure documents from 130 different franchises before selecting Subway. Today, Saifi owns 390 Subway restaurants that employ 4,000 people and generate more than $200 million in annual sales.[50]

When evaluating a franchise opportunity, what should a potential franchisee look for? Although there is no guarantee of success, the following characteristics make a franchisor stand out:

- *A unique concept or marketing approach.* "Me-too" franchises are no more successful than "me-too" independent businesses. Pizza franchisor Papa John's has achieved an impressive growth rate by emphasizing the quality of its ingredients, whereas Domino's is known for its fast delivery.

- *A profitable business model.* A franchisor should have a track record of profitability, and so should its franchisees. If a franchisor is not profitable, its franchisees are not likely to be either. Franchisees who follow the business format should expect to earn a reasonable rate of return after paying all franchise royalties, fees, and advertising contributions.

- *A solid brand name and a registered trademark.* Name recognition is difficult to achieve without a well-known, protected, and federally registered trademark. "Having a federally registered, recognized, protected brand name is one of the most critical factors for any franchise," says the director of a franchise consulting and law firm.[51]

- *A business system that works.* A franchisor should have in place a system that is efficient and is well documented in its manuals. After all, a proven business system lies at the heart of what a franchisee purchases from a franchisor.

- *A solid training program.* One of the most valuable components of a franchise system is the training it offers franchisees. The system should be relatively easy to learn.

- *Affordability.* A franchisee should not have to take on an excessive amount of debt to purchase a franchise. Being forced to borrow too much money to open a franchise outlet can doom a business from the outset. Respectable franchisors verify prospective franchisees' financial qualifications as part of the screening process.

- *A positive relationship with franchisees.* The most successful franchises are those that see their franchisees as partners—and treat them accordingly. "You want companies that award franchises, not sell them," says one franchise consultant.[52] One indication of a positive franchisor–franchisee relationship is the existence of a franchisee advisory council, a group of franchisees selected by their peers to provide advice to the franchisor on topics ranging from marketing strategies and new products to operating procedures and training.

The FDD covers the 23 items discussed earlier and includes a copy of the company's franchise agreement and any contracts accompanying it. Although the law requires a FDD to be written in plain English rather than "legalese," it is best to have an attorney with franchise experience to review the FDD and discuss its provisions with you. The franchise contract summarizes the details that will govern the franchisor–franchisee relationship over its life. The contract outlines exactly the rights and the obligations of each party and sets the guidelines that govern the franchise relationship. Franchise contracts typically are long term; 50 percent run for 15 years or more, making it is extremely important for prospective franchisees to understand their terms before they sign a contract.

Particular items in the FDD that entrepreneurs should focus on include the franchisor's experience (items 1 and 2), the current and past litigation against the franchisor (item 3), the fees and total investment (items 5, 6, and 7), and the franchisee turnover rate for the previous three years (item 20). The **franchisee turnover rate**, the rate at which franchisees leave the system, is one of the most revealing items in the FDD. If the turnover rate is less than 5 percent, the franchise probably is sound; however, a rate approaching 20 percent is a sign of serious, underlying problems in a franchise. Although virtually every franchisor has been involved in lawsuits, an excessive amount of litigation against a franchisor over a particular matter should alert a prospective franchisee to potential problems down the road. Determining what the cases were about and whether they have been resolved is important.

## Talk to Existing Franchisees

Although the FDD contains valuable information, it is only the starting point for researching a franchise opportunity thoroughly. Perhaps the best way to evaluate the reputation of a franchisor is to interview (in person) several franchise owners who have been in business at least one year about the positive and the negative aspects of the agreement and the franchisor–franchisee relationship and whether the franchisor delivered what it promised. Knowing what they know now, would they buy the franchise again? Another useful technique is to monitor franchisees' blogs, where prospective franchisees can learn the "real story" of running a franchise.

Another revealing exercise is to spend an entire day with at least one (preferably more) franchisee to observe firsthand what it is like to operate a franchise unit. Some prospective franchisees work in an existing outlet, sometimes without pay, to get a sense of what the daily routine is like. Item 20 of the FDD lists all of a company's current franchisees and former franchisees who have left the system within the last year and their contact information, which makes it easy for potential franchisees to contact them. It is wise to interview former franchisees to get their perspectives on the franchisor–franchisee relationship. Why did they leave?

Table 6.2 provides some important questions to ask current franchisees.

## Ask the Franchisor Some Tough Questions

Take the time to visit the franchisor's headquarters and ask plenty of questions about the company and its relationship with its franchisees. You will be in this relationship a long time, and you need to know as much about it as possible beforehand. Many franchisors offer "discovery days," events to which they invite prospective franchisees to their headquarters to meet face-to-face and to see the franchisor's operation in action firsthand. Important questions to ask include the following:

- What skills does a successful franchisee need? (Then consider how you measure up.)
- What is the franchisor's philosophy concerning the franchisor–franchisee relationship?
- How do franchisees and the franchisor resolve conflicts? (Ask for specific examples.)
- What are the most common causes of the problems that franchisees encounter?
- How would you describe the company's culture?

**TABLE 6.2 Questions to Ask Existing Franchisees**

A key ingredient in any prospective franchisee's evaluation of a franchise opportunity is visiting existing franchisees and asking them questions about their relationship with the franchisor. "What you need to know from franchisees is what the franchisor does that makes it worth the fees," says one franchise consultant. The following questions will reveal how well the franchisor supports its franchisees and the nature of the franchisor–franchisee relationship.

- How much did it cost to start your franchise? Did you encounter unexpected costs?
- How much training did you receive at the outset? How helpful was it?
- How prepared were you when you opened your franchise?
- Does the franchisor provide you with adequate ongoing support? How much? Are you pleased with the level of support you receive? What is the nature of this support?
- Is the company available to answer your questions? How often do you contact the company? What is the typical response?
- How much marketing assistance does the franchisor provide? Is it effective? How can you tell?
- Do franchisees have input into the development of new products or services?
- Which of your expectations has the franchisor met? Failed to meet?
- How often does someone from the franchise check on your operation? What is the purpose of those visits?
- What is a "typical day" like for you? How do you spend most of your time?
- Which day-to-day tasks do you enjoy performing most? Least?
- How much did your franchise generate in sales last year? How much do you expect it to generate in sales this year? What has been the pattern of your outlet's sales since you started?
- Is your franchise making a profit? If so, how much? What is your net profit margin?
- How long did you operate before your outlet began to earn a profit? Is your outlet consistently profitable?
- What is your franchise's break-even point? How long did it take for your franchise to reach the break-even point?
- Has your franchise met your expectations for return on investment?
- Is there a franchisee association? Do you belong to it? What is its primary function?
- Does the franchisor sponsor system-wide meetings? Do you attend? Why?
- Does the franchisor listen to franchisees?
- What changes would you recommend the franchisor make in its business system?
- Where do you purchase supplies, equipment, and products for your franchise? Are the prices you pay reasonable?
- How much freedom do you have to run your business?
- Does the franchisor encourage franchisees to apply their creativity to running their businesses, or does it frown on innovation in the system?
- Has the franchisor given you the tools you need to compete effectively?
- How much are your royalty payments and franchise fees? What do you get in exchange for your royalty payments? Do you consider it to be a good value?
- Are you planning to purchase additional territories or franchises? Why?
- Has the franchisor lived up to its promises?
- Looking back, what portions of the franchise contract would you change?
- What are communications with the franchisor like?
- How would you describe franchisees' relationship with the franchisor? How would you describe your relationship with the franchisor?
- Are most franchisees happy with the franchise system? With the franchisor?
- What advice would you give to someone considering purchasing a franchise from this franchisor?
- Knowing what you know now, would you buy this franchise again?

*Sources:* Based on Carol Tice, "How to Research a Franchise," *Entrepreneur*, January 2009, pp. 112–119; Andrew A. Caffey, "Analyze This," *Entrepreneur*, January 2000, pp. 163–167; Roger Brown, "Ask More Questions of More People Before Deciding, Then Plan to Work Very Hard," *Small Business Forum*, Winter 1996/1997, pp. 91–93; Roberta Maynard, "Choosing a Franchise," *Nation's Business*, October 1996, pp. 56–63; Andrew A. Caffey, "The Buying Game," *Entrepreneur*, January 1997, pp. 174–177; Julie Bawden Davis, "A Perfect Match," *Business Start-Ups*, July 1997, pp. 44–49.

- How much input do franchisees have into the system?
- What are the franchisor's future expansion plans? How will they affect your franchise?
- Are you entitled to an exclusive territory?
- What kind of earnings can you expect? (If the franchisor made no earnings claims in item 19 of the FDD, why not?)
- Has the franchisor terminated any franchisee's contracts? If so, why?
- How many franchisees have failed? Why?
- Does the franchisor have a well-formulated strategic plan?

## Make Your Choice

The first lesson in franchising is "Do your homework before you get out your checkbook." Only after conducting a thorough analysis of a franchise opportunity can you make an informed choice about which franchise is right for you. Then it is time to put together a solid business plan to serve as your road map to success with the franchise you have selected. The plan also is a valuable tool for attracting financing to purchase your franchise. We will discuss the process of creating a business plan in Chapter 8.

 **ENTREPRENEURIAL PROFILE: Rocco Valluzo: Microtel Inn and Suites** Rocco Valluzo, a second-generation McDonald's franchisee, decided to make the leap from the restaurant business to the hotel business after his wife stayed at a Microtel Inns and Suites and marveled at the smoothly operating business system. Before signing on with Microtel, Valluzo did his homework. In addition to evaluating the local market and conducting a location analysis, Valluzo says that he "toured properties and looked at the franchise cost and what the service fees would be." His preparation has paid off. His hotel reached its break-even point within six months of opening, and he already is making plans to open three more locations. "The key to success is having the support of the franchisor," he says.[53]

## Lessons from the Street-Smart Entrepreneur

# Make Sure You Select the Right Franchise

Bill Adams spent 21 years in the U.S. Special Operatives ("the Green Berets") division of the military. After retiring from the armed forces, Adams started two businesses and sold them before he and his wife Lysa purchased an iFly franchise, a company that operates high-speed wind tunnels in which customers can practice their skydiving technique or just fly around on a column of air. Adams's first experience with a wind tunnel occurred during his training as a Green Beret when the concept was considered top secret. After a week of training, he recalls thinking, "That's the most fun I've ever had. Someone should perfect that technology." Lysa, also an experienced skydiver, reveled in her first indoor skydiving experience. "Everyone should have one of these in their backyard," she thought. The couple's research led them to iFly, and after months of work that included finding new financing after their original lender backed out, the Adamses opened their $10 million iFly indoor skydiving franchise in Seattle, Washington. Their business has been so successful that the Adamses are planning to open one new iFly franchise in carefully selected locations across the United States every 18 months.

Bill and Lysa Adams found their ideal franchise, but finding the right franchise is no easy task. The results are well worth the effort—*if* you make the right choice. The Street Smart

Entrepreneur identifies the most common mistakes that first-time franchisees make:

**Mistake 1. Not knowing what they want in a franchise.** Start by evaluating your personal and business interests. What type of work and activities do you enjoy? Which ones do you dislike? What are your financial expectations? Failing to define your goals increases the chance you will make the wrong choice.

**Mistake 2. Buying a franchise they cannot afford.** Franchises can be expensive, and you must know how much you can afford to spend before you go shopping for a franchise. A surefire recipe for failure is buying a franchise that breaks your budget. Franchises are available in a myriad of price ranges, from just a few thousand dollars to several million dollars. Determine the price range that best fits your budget before you begin reviewing franchise packages.

**Mistake 3. Failing to ask current and former franchisees about the franchise.** One of the best ways to determine what your franchise experience will be is to talk with current and former franchisees. Item 20 of the FDD provides the necessary information for you to contact these people.

*(continued)*

# Lessons from the Street-Smart Entrepreneur *(continued)*

Visit their operations and ask them *lots* of questions about the franchise system and how well it works, the franchisor, and the franchisor–franchisee relationship. This is one of the best ways to get the *real* story about how well a franchise system works.

**Mistake 4. Failing to read the fine print.** The FDD is a valuable document for potential franchisees but only for those who actually read it and use it to make a franchising decision. After you narrow down your potential franchise choices, get their FDDs and review them. Many potential franchisees find it helpful to go through the FDD and the franchise contract with an experienced franchise attorney who can point out potential problem areas.

**Mistake 5. Failing to get professional help.** Inexperienced franchise shoppers believe that paying attorneys and accountants to help them understand the FDD and the franchise contract is a waste of money. Wrong! The franchise contract governs the franchisor–franchisee relationship, and most contracts run for at least 10 years. Make sure you understand its terms clearly before you sign a franchise contract.

**Mistake 6. Buying in too early.** Buying into a new franchise concept offers advantages (refer to Figure 6.4). However, doing so involves some risk because some new franchise operations have not worked the "bugs" out of their business systems or are not prepared to teach their systems effectively to franchisees. Established franchises have proven track records of success and typically involve less risk, but that security comes at a higher price. If you are considering buying into a new franchise, be extra diligent in your investigation of the opportunity.

**Mistake 7. Neglecting the signs of a struggling franchise system.** Buying a franchise is no guarantee of success, and prospective franchisees must watch for indications that a franchise is struggling to avoid buying into a system that is floundering. Telltale signs include a high franchisee turnover rate, franchisees who cannot generate reasonable profits under the franchisor's system, a franchise system that constantly changes (usually an indication that the system does not work), and sour relationships between franchisees and the franchisor.

**Mistake 8. Falling for exaggerated earnings claims.** One question of paramount interest to potential franchisees is

"How much money can I expect to earn from a franchise?" Item 19 of the FDD includes a statement of the basis for any earnings claims that franchisors make. Any financial representations that a franchisor makes must represent the earnings that an average franchisee can expect, not the results of the top-performing franchise. However, the FDD does not require franchisors to make earnings claims. In fact, fewer than 20 percent of franchisors make any earnings claims in their FDDs. "An earnings claim is an opportunity to showcase your company," says Charlie Simpson, a top manager at Great Clips, a hairstyling franchise with more than 2,700 salons. "[Doing so] provides instant credibility with a candidate." Remember: Any earnings claims franchisors make must be backed by *facts*. If a franchise does not provide any information on franchisees' expected earnings, what is the reason? Potential franchisees need access to statistics on expected earnings so that they can assemble reasonable financial forecasts for their business plans.

**Mistake 9. Neglecting to check the escape clause.** Most franchise contracts include options for getting out of the franchise relationship for both the franchisor and the franchisee. Under what circumstances can the franchisor end the relationship? Under what circumstances can you end the relationship? What is the cost associated with terminating the franchise agreement?

**Mistake 10. Assuming that the franchise will run itself.** Some franchisees buy franchises with the expectation that they will be able to write a check to the franchisor, put the franchise system in place, and then sit back and watch the money roll in. It doesn't work that way! Building a successful franchise takes just as much hard work as building a successful independent business. "I work six days a week," says Rick Warman, who owns a business that operates 31 outlets of multiple franchise concepts, including Papa John's, Schlotzsky's Deli's, and Jenny Craig.

*Sources:* Based on Jason Daley, "Blowin' in the Wind," *Entrepreneur*, February 2012, p. 116; "Rich Warman," *Empire Builders TV*, www.franchising.com/empirebuilders/franchisees/rich_warman; Eddy Goldberg and Kerry Pipes, "How Much Can I Earn?," Franchising.com, August 18, 2008, www.franchising.com/articles/385; Andrew A Caffey, "Watch Your Step," *Entrepreneur B.Y.O.B.*, August 2002, p. 82, adapted from Todd D. Maddocks, "Write the Wrong," *Entrepreneur B.Y.O.B.*, January 2001, pp. 152–155; Kerry Pipes, "Franchisee Lifestyles, Franchise Update, www.franchise-update.com/fuadmin/articles/article_Franchise Lifestyles5.htm; "Franchise How-To Guides: The Paper Trail," *Entrepreneur*, www.entrepreneur.com/franchises/buyingafranchise/howtoguides/article36392-4.html.

## Franchise Contracts

**8.**
_____

Describe a typical franchise contract and its primary provisions.

Franchising's popularity as a business system has created growing pains that have resulted in an increase in the number of franchise-related lawsuits. "Litigation sends a signal to the franchisor and others that something is wrong," says a franchise industry analyst.[54] A common source of much of this litigation is the interpretation of the franchise contract's terms. Most often, difficulties arise after the agreement is in operation. Because a franchisor's attorney prepares franchise contracts, the provisions favor the franchisor, giving minimal protection to franchisees. Franchise contracts typically include arbitration clauses, which require disputes to go to arbitration and restrict franchisees' ability to file lawsuits. A franchise contract summarizes the details that will govern the franchisor–franchisee relationship over its life. It outlines exactly the rights and the obligations of each party and sets the guidelines that govern the franchise relationship. To protect potential franchisees from having to rush into a contract without clearly understanding it, the FTC requires that franchisees receive a completed contract with all revisions at least five business days before signing it.

Every potential franchisee should have an attorney evaluate the franchise contract and review it with the investor before he signs anything. Many franchisees don't discover unfavorable terms in their contracts until *after* they have invested in a franchise. By then, however, it's too late to negotiate changes. Although most large, established franchisors are not willing to negotiate the franchise contract's terms ("The contract is what it is"), many smaller franchises will negotiate some terms, especially for highly qualified candidates. Figure 6.4 describes the advantages and the disadvantages of buying a new versus an established franchise.

Although franchise contracts cover everything from initial fees and continuing payments to training programs and territorial protection, three terms are responsible for most franchisor–franchisee disputes: termination of the contract, contract renewal, and transfer and buyback provisions.

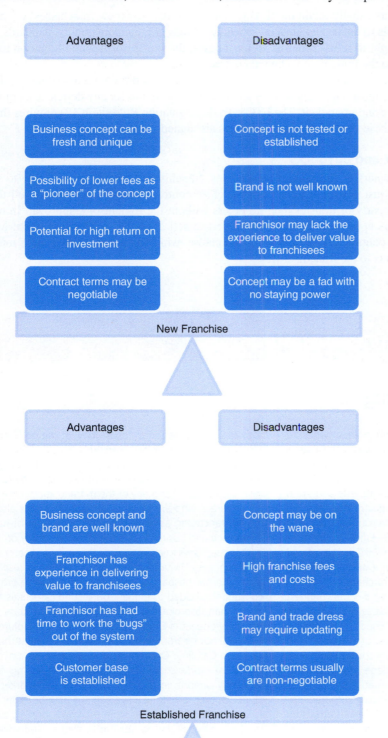

**FIGURE 6.4**

**Advantages and Disadvantages of Buying and New vs. an Established Franchise**

### Termination

One of the most litigated subjects of a franchise agreement is the termination of the contract by either party. Most contracts prevent franchisees from terminating the agreement but allow franchisors to terminate the agreement "with or without cause." Therefore, prospective franchisees must be sure they know exactly under what circumstances the franchisor can terminate the contract. Generally, the franchisor has the right to cancel a contract if a franchisee fails to abide by the terms of the agreement, declares bankruptcy, fails to make required payments on time, or fails to maintain quality standards.

### Renewal

Franchisors usually retain the right to renew or refuse to renew franchisees' contracts. If a franchisee fails to make payments on schedule or does not maintain quality standards, the franchisor has the right to refuse renewal. In most cases, the franchisor has no obligation to offer contract renewal to the franchisee when the contract expires.

When a franchisor grants renewal, the two parties draw up a new contract. Frequently, the franchisee must pay a renewal fee and may be required to fix any deficiencies of the outlet or to modernize and upgrade it. The FTC's Trade Regulation Rule (item 17) requires the franchisor to disclose these terms before any contracts are signed.

### Transfer and Buybacks

Unlike owners of independent businesses, franchisees typically are not free to sell their businesses to just anyone. Under most franchise contracts, franchisees cannot sell their franchises to a third party or transfer them to others without the franchisor's approval. In most instances, franchisors approve a franchisee's request to sell an outlet to another person. Many franchise contracts contain a right of first refusal clause, which means that franchisees must offer to sell their outlets to the franchisor first.

## In the Entrepreneurial Spotlight

# The Allure of Franchising

Neil Erlich knew that he wanted to be an entrepreneur when he helped start a contracting business when he was just 14 years old. During his junior year at Sonoma State University, Erlich, with help from his father, a corporate executive, began investigating franchise options that would suit his interests and skills. They honed in on the automotive service industry and reviewed the FDDs of several franchises, including Meineke, Jiffy Lube, and Midas, before settling on Express Oil Change. Erlich was particularly impressed with the support that Express Oil Change offered its franchisees. When Erlich graduated with a business degree, his father put up $375,000 to help him purchase and set up the $1.5 million franchise operation. Erlich, who is the youngest franchisee in the Express Oil Change system, sees the franchisor's support as one of the greatest benefits of choosing to open a franchise rather than an independent business of his own. "[The franchisor] is there for you," he says. "It's very comforting."

Like Erlich, a growing number of college graduates and twenty-something adults who are disenchanted with the prospects of a dull job in the corporate grind are looking to franchising as a promising career choice. Indeed, franchising is attracting people of all ages and backgrounds, from corporate dropouts and military veterans to retired Baby Boomers and corporate cast-offs. "People say, 'I put 20 years into a company, and because

they ran into some tough times, they let me go,'" explains Ray Titus, head of the United Franchise Group. "They think, 'Do I want to put myself into a position where I may get laid off again?' Instead, they take control of their future by running their own businesses." For many of them, franchising is the perfect fit.

Retirees who are looking for second careers also are turning to franchising as well. "They've got school-of-hard-knocks experience and business skills that they can apply on day one at a franchise," says Michael Shay of the International Franchise Association. Judy Divita, a retired corporate human resources manager, and her husband Charlie, a retired college professor and consultant, decided to embark on second careers as franchisees rather than stop working. After researching franchise opportunities, they opened a Firehouse Subs franchise in Columbia, South Carolina, not far from where Charlie had taught at the University of South Carolina. Over the next nine years, the Divitas opened five more sandwich shops in Columbia, including one on the university campus. In addition to their built-in market of college students, they target the players on the athletic teams that come to campus to participate in more than 400 sporting events ranging from baseball and football to basketball and volleyball each year. The Divitas have won Firehouse Subs's National Franchisee of the Year Award and the MVP Award Winner for Innovation from *Multi-Unit Franchisee* magazine. Their nine outlets generate $4.5 million in annual sales, and the couple's goal is to have 13 Firehouse Subs locations within 10 years. "The franchise gives you the basic things to put you in business pretty quickly," says Charlie. "You have to take it beyond that and be creative to come up with novel ways of doing things that are particular to your company and your community."

In 1984, at age 19, Atour Eyvazian escaped his war-torn homeland of Iran across a range of rugged mountains, only to be arrested as he crossed into neighboring Turkey. After spending 40 days in jail, he was able to bribe his captors with money that his mother had sewed into his jeans. He emigrated to the United States, learned to speak English, and took a job as a janitor at a Jack in the Box franchise in California. After just two years, Eyvazian's ability and work ethic enabled him to become a manager of the quick-service restaurant and to earn an undergraduate and a master's degree in business administration. Over the next several years, he climbed the corporate ranks to become the company's manager of guest service systems with responsibility for more than 700 restaurants. In 2007, 42-year-old Eyvazian and his family moved to Houston, Texas, where he had the opportunity to become a franchisee of Jack in the Box. Today, the award-winning franchisee owns 109 Jack in the Box franchises in the Houston area, making him the largest individual operator in the chain.

Franchising can be the ideal path to owning a business for people in almost any phase of professional life, whether they are retirees looking for a new direction and extra income or recent college graduates who are ready to embark on exciting careers. "Boosted by a brand name, training, advertising, and an established business plan, a franchise can ease the struggle and the risk of opening a business and still let you call some shots," says one business writer.

1. These examples show people at different stages of their professional lives choosing to become business owners with the help of a franchise. What conclusions can you draw from their stories about the appeal of franchising?

2. What are the advantages and the disadvantages of investing in a franchise?

3. Suppose that one of your friends who is about to graduate is considering purchasing a franchise. What advice would you offer him or her before signing the franchise contract?

*Sources:* Based on Helen Bond, Home Field Advantage, *Multi-Unit Franchisee*, Issue III, 2012, pp. 18–24; Helen Bond, "A Life of Service," *Multi-Unit Franchisee*, Issue III, 2012, pp. 32–36; Deborah L. Cohen, "Young Entrepreneurs Bypass Corporate Rat Race," *Reuters*, August 20, 2009, www.reuters.com/article/deborahCohen/idUSTRE57J2XS20090820; Allison Ross, "Unemployed Pinning Hopes on Franchise Ventures," *Palm Beach Post*, May 11, 2009, pp. 1F, 6F.

## Trends in Franchising

Franchising has experienced three major growth waves since its beginning. The first wave occurred in the early 1970s when fast-food restaurants used the concept to grow rapidly. The fast-food industry was one of the first to discover the power of franchising, but other businesses soon took notice and adapted the franchising concept to their industries. The second wave took place in the mid-1980s as the U.S. economy shifted heavily toward the service sector. Franchises followed suit, springing up in every service business imaginable—from maid services and copy centers to mailing services and real estate. The third wave began in the early 1990s and continues today. It is characterized by new, low-cost franchises that focus on specific market niches. In the wake of major corporate downsizing and the burgeoning costs of traditional franchises, these new franchises allowed would-be entrepreneurs to get into proven businesses faster and at lower costs. These companies feature start-up costs that range from $3,000 to $250,000 and span a variety of industries—from leak detection in homes and auto detailing to day care and cost-reduction consulting. Other significant trends in franchising include the following:

**9.** _____
Explain current trends that are shaping franchising.

### Changing Face of Franchisees

Franchisees today are a more diverse group than in the past, providing business ownership opportunities for minorities, women, and veterans. The International Franchise Association reports that minorities own 20.5 percent of franchises, compared to 14.2 percent of nonfranchised businesses.[55] Many franchisors have established diversity programs to encourage members of minority groups to become franchisees and to help them overcome the obstacles they face to business ownership, particularly access to capital. In 2006, Domino's Pizza, now with nearly 10,000 stores in more than 70 countries, established its Delivering the Dream program, which offers minority entrepreneurs financial grants, reduced franchise fees, and guarantees on loans up to $250,000 through GE Franchise Finance. Al Daniels, an African-American navy veteran, was one of the early beneficiaries of the Delivering the Dream program and now owns eight Domino's locations and plans to open more.[56]

Modern franchisees also are better educated, are more sophisticated, have more business acumen, and are more financially secure than those of just 20 years ago. People of all ages and backgrounds are choosing franchising as a way to get into business for themselves. Franchising also is attracting skilled, experienced businesspeople who are opening franchises in their second careers and whose goal is to own multiple outlets that cover entire states or regions. Many of them are former corporate managers—either corporate castoffs or corporate dropouts—looking for a new start on a more meaningful and rewarding career. They have the financial resources, management skills and experience, and motivation to operate their franchises successfully. Experts estimate that 35 to 40 percent of new franchisees are people who have experienced a layoff or some type of job displacement.[57]

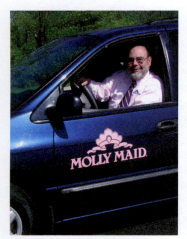

Harry Young, Molly Maid franchisee.

*Source:* Molly Maid Inc.

**ENTREPRENEURIAL PROFILE: Harry and Emelie Young: Molly Maid** Harry Young and his wife Emelie moved to Austin, Texas, where he took a job in information technology at a large corporation. Traveling 300 days a year was beginning to take its toll on Harry, and the Youngs decided to purchase a Molly Maid housecleaning services franchise. Harry kept his corporate job for a few more years while Emelie managed the franchise. "We set up a system right out of the corporate world," says Harry, and Emelie followed the Molly Maid franchise model meticulously. When Harry decided to leave the corporate world to join the franchise, Emelie had built it into an operation with $1.2 million in annual sales. Today, the Young's Molly Maid franchise employs 100 people and generates $4 million in annual sales.[58]

## Multiple-Unit Franchising

Thirty years ago, the typical franchisee operated a single outlet. Today, however, modern franchisees strive to operate multiple franchise units. In **multiple-unit franchising**, a franchisee opens more than one unit in a broad territory within a specific time period. According to the International Franchise Association, 20 percent of franchisees are multiple-unit owners, a number that is expected to continue to grow over the next several years. These multiple-unit franchisees own 55 percent of all franchise units. Although the typical multiple-unit franchise owns 4.5 outlets, it is no longer unusual for a single franchisee to own 25, 75, or even 100 units.[59]

**ENTREPRENEURIAL PROFILE: Tommy Haddock: Bojangles** Tommy Haddock, who purchased his first Bojangles restaurant franchise in 1980, recently opened his forty-seventh Bojangles outlet and has number 48 under construction. Even though Bojangles outlets cost $1.4 to $1.6 million to build, they typically generate $1.7 million in annual sales. "I'm opening stores at a faster pace now than ever before," he says.[60]

Franchisors have discovered that multiple-unit franchising is an efficient way to do business. For a franchisor, the time and cost of managing 10 franchisees each owning 12 outlets are much less than managing 120 franchisees each owning one outlet. A multiple-unit strategy also accelerates a franchise's growth rate. Michael Ansley, who started his career in franchising as a partner in a Buffalo Wild Wings restaurant shortly after graduating from college, now owns 22 Buffalo Wild Wings franchises in Michigan and Florida. He recently signed an area development agreement with the fast-growing franchise to open 16 more locations over the next several years.[61] Not only is multiple-unit franchising an efficient way to expand quickly, but it also is effective for franchisors who are targeting foreign markets, where having experienced local representatives who know the territory is essential.

The popularity of multiple-unit franchising has paralleled the trend toward increasingly experienced, sophisticated franchisees who set high performance goals that a single outlet cannot meet. Michael Ansley, the Buffalo Wild Wings franchisee, says that owning multiple units was part of his plan "from day one. One restaurant was not going to be enough," he says. "I'm not wired to stay in one place. I'm always looking for the next challenge."[62] For franchisees, multiple-unit franchising offers the opportunity to achieve rapid growth without leaving the safety net of the franchise. In addition, franchisees may be able to build fast-growing companies at bargain prices when franchisors offer discounts on their standard fees for buyers who purchase multiple units.

Although operating multiple units offers advantages for both franchisors and franchisees, there are dangers. Operating multiple units requires franchisors to focus more carefully on selecting the right franchisees—those who are capable of handling the additional requirements of multiple units. The impact of selecting the wrong franchise owners is magnified when they operate multiple units and can create huge headaches for the entire chain. Franchisees must be aware of the dangers of losing their focus and becoming distracted if they take on too many units. In addition, operating multiple units means more complexity because the number of business problems franchisees face also is multiplied.

## International Opportunities

One of the major trends in franchising is the internationalization of American franchise systems. Increasingly, franchising is becoming a major export industry for the United States; in fact, two-thirds of the members of the International Franchise Association say that international markets will be important to the success of their franchise operations.[63] Franchises based in the United States are expanding rapidly into international markets to boost sales and profits as the domestic market becomes increasingly saturated. Currently, about 3,000 of Dunkin' Donuts's 10,000 outlets are located in foreign markets, but the company has plans to increase the number of foreign outlets to 10,000 over the next few years. Reflecting the views of many U.S.-based franchisors, Nigel Travis, CEO of Dunkin' Brands Group, the parent company of Dunkin' Donuts, says, "We will grow faster internationally than domestically." The company is targeting India and China, where it currently operates 80 stores that sell more than coffee and doughnuts, including savory bagels with toppings such as spinach, roasted red peppers, and garlic mayonnaise. In China, Dunkin' Donuts sells a green tea–flavored Mochi Ring Donut made from sticky rice. Yum! Brands, the parent company of Taco Bell, Pizza Hut, KFC, A&W All-American Food, and Long John Silver's, has more than 38,000 franchised restaurants in 120 countries. The company, which derives more than 70 percent of its profit from international locations, already has a significant presence in China and plans to expand its operations there and in India.[64]

As they venture into foreign markets, franchisors have learned that *adaptation* is one key to success. Although they keep their basic systems intact, franchises that are successful in foreign markets quickly learn how to change their concepts to adjust to local cultures and to appeal to local tastes. "We're not naïve enough to replicate a U.S. Hampton [hotel] and plop it into country X," says Phil Cordell, a global manager for the fast-growing hotel chain that has locations in Europe, Asia, and South America.[65] Fast-food chains in other countries often must make adjustments to their menus to please locals' palates. In India, a nation that is predominantly Hindu and Muslim and reveres cows, beef-based sandwiches do not appear on menus. Instead, fast-food franchises sell sandwiches made from chicken, lamb, and vegetable patties, and some franchises' Indian menus are strictly vegetarian. Venezuelan diners prefer mayonnaise with their french fries, and in Chile, customers want avocado on their hamburgers. In Japan, McDonald's (known as "Makudonarudo") franchises sell shrimp burgers (Ebi Filet-O), rice burgers, seaweed soup, vegetable croquette burgers, and katsu burgers (cheese wrapped in a roast pork cutlet topped with katsu sauce and shredded cabbage) in addition to their traditional American fare. In the Philippines, the McDonald's menu includes a spicy Filipino-style burger, spaghetti, and chicken with rice. In France, McDonald's, known as "McDo" to locals, sells the McBaguette, a specialty burger made of Charolais beef topped with local Emmental cheese and mustard on a baguette. In Spain, the chain's menu includes gazpacho, a tomato-based vegetable soup that originated in the southern province of Andalusia. In some countries in Europe, McDonald's franchises sell beer. In China, Burger King offers localized menu items such as pumpkin porridge, deep-fried twisted dough sticks called *you tiao*, and *shaobing*, a toasted sesame seed cake that is a traditional Chinese snack.

## In the Entrepreneurial Spotlight

# The Middle East: A Hot Spot for Franchising

As franchisors in the United States have found wringing impressive growth rates from the domestic market increasingly difficult, they have begun to export their franchises to international markets. A severe recession and a slow recovery have made foreign markets all the more attractive to U.S. franchisors. One of the fastest-growing areas for U.S. franchisors is the Middle East and North Africa region (MENA). With residents of many countries enjoying the wealth generated by rich oil reserves and the region's strong interest in U.S. brands, MENA offers both experienced and new franchisors excellent expansion opportunities. The area's oppressive desert heat compels the population to spend a great deal of time inside, and large shopping malls are a popular destination for many because they serve as social hubs.

"It's a very social culture, and going to malls and socializing is a big part of people's day," says Jonathan Spiel, who sold the first franchise of his Brooklyn, New York–based Tea Lounge to a franchisee in Kuwait. "The malls there are unbelievable. Every brand you can think of is there."

Most U.S. franchisors' first foray into international markets is in either Canada or Mexico because of the countries' proximity and ease of doing business, but others have bravely entered fast-growing, less familiar regions such as the Middle East. Candace Nelson opened Sprinkles Cupcakes, a cupcakes-only bakery in Beverly Hills, California, in 2005 and over the next seven years expanded to 10 company-owned locations in five states. In 2012, Nelson signed a franchise agreement to open 34 outlets in

*(continued)*

# In the Entrepreneurial Spotlight *(continued)*

the Middle East with M.H. Alshaya Company, a leading international retail franchise operator of more than 55 brands, including Starbucks, P.F. Changs, H&M, Cheesecake Factory, Pinkberry, Shake Shack, and Pottery Barn. The agreement will take Sprinkles into 10 countries across the region, including Bahrain, Egypt, Jordan, Kuwait, Lebanon, Morocco, Oman, Qatar, Saudi Arabia, and the United Arab Emirates. "Our cupcakes are a sophisticated update on an American classic and have developed a strong international fan base overseas," says Nelson.

Hans Hess started Elevation Burger, a restaurant that serves high-quality, organic hamburgers and hand-cut fries cooked in olive oil, in 2002 in Falls Church, Virginia, and began franchising in 2008. Hess had sold just 12 franchises in the United States when he received an inquiry from Ali Askkanani, CEO of TABCo International Food Catering, about opening an Elevation Burger franchise in Kuwait. Although Hess had not intended to take his franchise into international markets quite so soon, he realized that this was a golden opportunity. In the fall of 2010, Askkanani opened the first international location of Elevation Burger in the Avenues Mall, Kuwait's largest mall (more than 3 million square feet), located in one of the Middle East's premier retail and leisure destinations. Askkanani has opened a second Elevation Burger location in Kuwait's Al Hamra Mall, which features more than 100 stores, including other U.S.-based franchises. "We will be expanding throughout Kuwait," he says. Hess has signed several more franchising deals in other countries in the Middle East, where he says Elevation Burger's restaurant sales are more than double those of their counterparts in the United States.

The Middle East is drawing established franchisors as well. Mike Shattuck, CEO of Focus Brands International, which owns Auntie Anne's Pretzels, Carvel (ice cream), Cinnabon (cinnamon rolls), Moe's Southwest Grill (Mexican), and Schlotzsky's Deli (sandwiches), is developing franchisees in the Middle East. Walid Hajj learned about Focus Brands's franchises while he was a student at Harvard University. After graduating, Hajj returned to Dubai to work in the family business, a company that handles distribution for U.S.- and European-based franchises. When he learned that Focus Brands was planning to expand into the Middle East, he "jumped at the opportunity." Hajj formed a company, Cravia, that operates 32 Cinnabon locations, most of which are cobranded outlets that include Seattle's Best Coffee.

As in every global market, franchisors must adapt their products to suit local tastes and customs. "With proper due diligence and research on the countries you want to go into, changes are usually minor," says Jeff Abbott of iFranchise. In the Middle East, for example, food items must be *halal*, compliant with Islamic dietary requirements, and most companies make sure that their supply chains meet the standards. Subway, the sandwich chain, has experienced rapid growth in the number of outlets in the MENA region and, other than promoting its meat products as *halal*, has made only minor changes to its menu.

Some U.S. franchisors' products are somewhat foreign to residents of the Middle East, but the people there are willing to experiment with new concepts and have a strong affinity for U.S. brands. Cravia's Hajj faced some challenges when he introduced Cinnabon's cinnamon rolls to customers in Dubai. "We had to educate the locals with heavy sampling," he says. "There is already a local taste for cinnamon; it was something the locals were accustomed to." Hajj also worked with the

A Cinnabon outlet in Dubai.
*Source:* Bloomberg/Getty Images.

chefs at Cinnabon to launch Datebon, a roll made from dates, which are a popular treat in the region. "It's done really well, which shows that we are in touch with local tastes," says Hajj. "There's a huge value in making minor modifications [to the product line]."

When targeting international markets, Popeye's, a quick-service chicken franchise with a Cajun bent, prefers to expand into countries in which people have a propensity for spicy flavors, which also makes the Middle East an attractive region. "We actually look at the cayenne pepper index, the propensity of a country to eat cayenne pepper," says CEO Cheryl Bachelder. Popeye's already has locations in Dubai, Abu Dhabi, Kuwait, Saudi Arabia, and Turkey and is planning for further expansion.

1. What steps should U.S.-based franchisors take when establishing outlets in foreign countries?

2. Describe the opportunities and the challenges U.S. franchisors face when entering global markets such as the countries of the MENA region.

3. Use the Web as a resource to develop a list of at least five suggestions that will help new franchisors looking to establish outlets in the MENA region.

*Sources:* Based on "Jason Daley, "New Market Opportunities," *Entrepreneur*, March 2012, pp. 88–97; Mark Brandau, "Middle East Seen as a Hot Growth Market," *Nation's Restaurant News*, June 13, 2012, *http://nrn.com/article/restaurants-see-middle-east-hot-growth-market*; Jeremiah McWilliams, "Fast Food Chains Heading Overseas, Fast," *Atlanta Journal-Constitution*, April 29, 2010, *www.ajc.com/news/business/fast-food-chains-heading-overseas-fast/nQfc2*; Brenda Urban, "Sprinkles Cupcakes to Open at 34 Locations in the Middle East," *Business Wire*, June 19, 2012, *www.businesswire.com/news/home/20120619006452/en/Sprinkles-Cupcakes-Open-34-Locations-Middle-East*; "Elevation Burger to Open in Kuwait," *Franchise Wire*, June 22, 2010, *www.franchisewire.com/article.php?id=5100*; "Elevation Burger Opens Second Location in Kuwait," *FranSmart*, June 8, 2012, *http://fransmart.com/news/70/59/Elevation-Burger-Opens-2nd-Location-In-Kuwait.html*; Diane Brady, "Small U.S. Franchises Head to the Middle East," *Bloomberg Business Week*, June 21, 2012, *www.businessweek.com/articles/2012-06-21/small-u-dot-s-dot-franchises-head-to-the-middle-east*.

## Smaller, Nontraditional Locations

Given the challenges of finding financing and the high cost of building full-scale locations, franchisors are searching out nontraditional locations in which to build smaller, less expensive outlets. Based on the principle of **intercept marketing**, the idea is to put a franchise's products or services directly in the paths of potential customers, wherever that may be. Franchises are putting scaled-down outlets on college campuses, in sports arenas, in museums and hospitals, on airline flights, and in zoos. Customers are likely to find a mini-Wendy's inside the convenience store at a Mobil gas station, a Subway sandwich shop in a convenience store, a Dunkin' Donuts outlet in the airport, or a Red Mango kiosk at a sports stadium or arena. Subway has more than 8,000 franchises in nontraditional locations that range from airports and military bases to college campuses and convenience stores. The company has restaurants located in a Goodwill store in Greenville, South Carolina, and inside the True Bethel Baptist Church in Buffalo, New York. Perhaps Subway's most unusual location was a temporary restaurant that served only the construction workers building the skyscraper at 1 World Trade Center in New York City. As work progressed on the 105-story building, a hydraulic lift elevated the restaurant, which was housed inside 36 shipping containers welded together.[66]

Many franchisees have discovered that the sales volume per square foot at smaller outlets in nontraditional locations often exceeds that at full-sized outlets at just a fraction of the cost. Doc Popcorn, a franchise that sells flavored popcorn (including "sinfully cinnamon" and "hoppin' jalapeno") offers franchisees the option of opening full-scale stores, mall kiosks, or mobile carts at price points that range from $70,000 to $150,000 and that can accommodate a variety of potential locations.[67] Dunkin' Donuts recently opened 10 locations on college campuses across the United States. The outlets range from full retail stores to small kiosks that fit into small spaces in campus centers, students unions, dining commons, and other high-traffic areas.[68] Establishing outlets in innovative locations will be a key to continued franchise growth in the domestic market.

## Conversion Franchising

The trend toward **conversion franchising**, in which owners of independent businesses become franchisees to gain the advantage of name recognition, will continue. In a franchise conversion, the franchisor gets immediate entry into new markets and experienced operators; franchisees get increased visibility and often experience a significant sales boost. It is not unusual for entrepreneurs who convert their independent stores into franchises to experience an increase of 20 percent or more in sales because of the instant name recognition the franchise offers.

## Refranchising

Another trend that has emerged over the last several years is franchises selling their company-owned outlets to franchisees. Known as **refranchising**, the goal is to put outlets into the hands of operators, who tend to run their franchises more efficiently than the franchisor can. Since 2007, McDonald's has reduced the percentage of company-owned stores in the chain from 23 to 19 percent. Burger King recently sold 96 company-owned restaurants in Orlando, Florida, to longtime franchisee Guillermo Perales, bringing the total number of outlets that Perales owns to 172.[69] Burger King's goal is to have all of its restaurants owned by franchisees, and the sale means that 92 percent of its outlets are franchise operations. Refranchising not only increases franchisors' profitability because it generates more royalty income for franchisors but also provides capital to finance their international expansion.

## Area Development and Master Franchising

Driving the trend toward multiple-unit franchising are area development and master franchising. Under an **area development** arrangement, a franchisee earns the exclusive right to open multiple outlets in a specific area within a specified time. Pizza Patrón, a Dallas-based chain of pizza restaurants aimed at the Hispanic market, recently announced an area development agreement with one of its most successful franchisees, SA Pizza Inc., to develop eight new outlets in San Antonio, Texas, within 31 months. SA Pizza has been a Pizza Patrón franchisee for nine years, has won the company's Patrón of the Year award for excellence twice, and has been a leader in innovation, building the franchise's first stand-alone outlet and its first double drive-through store. Pizza Patrón operates 104 franchises in seven states and has more than 80 outlets under development.[70]

A **master franchise** (or **subfranchise**) gives a franchisee the right to create a semi-independent "subfranchising" operation in a particular territory to recruit, sell, and support other franchisees. A master franchisee buys the right to develop subfranchises within a territory or, sometimes, an entire country. Like multiple-unit franchising, subfranchising "turbo-charges" a franchisor's growth. Many franchisors use master franchising to open outlets in international markets because the master franchisees understand local laws and the nuances of selling in local markets. Papa Murphy's International recently signed a master franchise agreement with MAM Foodco LLC, a food company in Dubai, United Arab Emirates, owned by Mohamed Aaly Maghrabi, to manage the opening of 100 Papa Murphy's Take N' Bake Pizza outlets in the Middle East. The master franchise deal is the company's first foray outside of North America.[71]

## Cobranding

Some franchisors also are discovering new ways to reach customers by teaming up with other franchisors selling complementary products or services. A growing number of companies are **cobranding** (or **combination franchising**) outlets—combining two or more distinct franchises under one roof. This "buddy system" approach works best when the two franchise ideas are compatible and appeal to similar customers. At one location, a Texaco gasoline station, a Pizza Hut restaurant, and a Dunkin' Donuts, all owned by the same franchisee, work together in a piggyback arrangement to draw customers. Focus Brands, which owns the Schlotzsky's Deli, Cinnabon, Carvel Ice Cream, Cold Stone Creamery, Auntie Anne's Pretzels, and Moe's Southwest Grill, has had success pairing one of its restaurant franchises with a dessert franchise. The company also is expanding its tribranded locations that combine Schlotzsky's Deli (sandwiches), a Cinnabon (cinnamon buns), and a Carvel (ice cream) into a single location. Franchisees who operate cobranded outlets find that sales throughout various day parts are more consistent than single-brand franchises that see significant swings from peak to nonpeak times.[72] Cobranding does increase the operational complexity of an operation, but if properly selected, cobranded franchises can magnify many times over the sales and profits of separate, self-standing outlets.

Combination (co-branded) franchise—two franchises in one location.

*Source:* © Helen Sessions/Alamy.

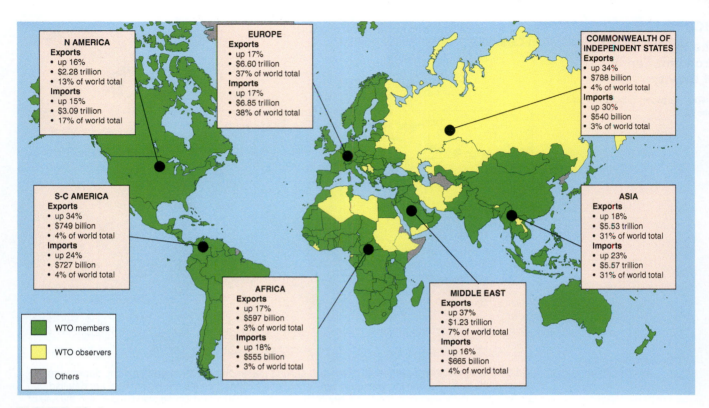

**FIGURE 12.1**

**Merchandise Exports and Imports by Region of the World, 2011**

*Source:* World Trade Organization, 2012, *http://www.wto.org/english/news_e/pres12_e/pr658_e.htm.*

high-tech employees. In 2011, Wilson, Maybank, and Susan Lyne, the company's CEO, expanded the company's global presence significantly when they began offering Gilt Groupe Web sites that are customized to appeal to shoppers in each of 90 countries. Wilson and Maybank expect international sales to accelerate their company's growth and have created mobile apps for various platforms that allow global shoppers to make purchases from their smart phones, tablets, and other mobile devices. Now with 5 million members, Gilt Groupe conducts 156 flash sales each week of products that range from clothing and home décor to food and wine.[3]

Just a few decades ago, military might governed world relationships; today, commercial trade and economic benefit have become the forces that drive global interaction. Since 1948, the value of world merchandise exports has risen from $58.0 billion to $18.4 *trillion* (see Figure 12.1).[4] Countries at every stage of development are reaping the benefits of increased global trade. The economies of emerging markets such as China and India are growing faster than those of mature markets such as the United States and Germany. The International Monetary Fund (IMF) predicts that the countries whose economies will grow the fastest over the next several years are China, India, and the ASEAN 5, which includes the Philippines, Indonesia, Malaysia, Thailand, and Vietnam.[5] The IMF estimates that China, where economic growth has been among the fastest in the world, will boast the largest gross domestic product (GDP) in the world by 2016.[6] China also will become one of the world's largest consumer markets by 2025.[7] Indeed, the world economic center of gravity, which is calculated adjusting each country's geographic center by its global economic influence (measured by its GDP), has shifted from the mid-Atlantic in 1970 to a point between Bucharest, Romania, and Helsinki, Finland because of Asia's rapid economic growth. By 2050, the world economic center of gravity will be located on the border between China and India (see Figure 12.2).[8] The message is clear: Global markets present a tremendous opportunity for entrepreneurs who are prepared to tap into them.

Advances in technology have cut the cost of long-distance communications and transactions so much that conducting business globally often costs no more than doing business locally. Even the smallest companies are using their Web sites to sell in foreign markets at minimal costs. Small businesses are buying raw materials and services from all over the globe, wherever the deals are best, and selling their products and services to domestic and international customers. Jack Stack, CEO of Springfield Remanufacturing Corporation, a Springfield, Missouri-based company that refurbishes automotive engines and parts, was surprised when he learned that the company was

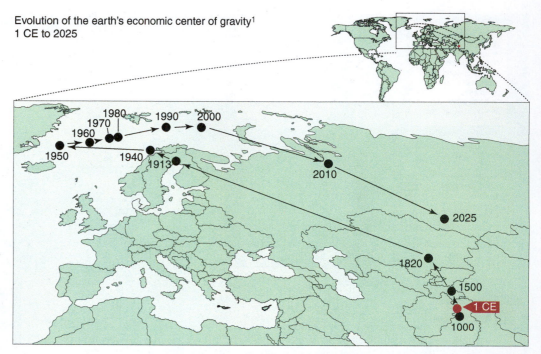

Evolution of the earth's economic center of gravity[1]
1 CE to 2025

[1]Calculated by weighting national GDP by each nation's geographic center of gravity; a line drawn from the center of the earth through the economic center of gravity locates it on the earth's surface. For detailed analysis, see the appendix in the McKinsey Global Institute (MGI) report *Urban world: Cities and the rise of the consuming class.*

purchasing parts from suppliers in 56 different countries! "Here we were, minding our business in Springfield, Missouri," says Stack, "and suddenly we discover that we've gone global."[9]

Entrepreneurs are seeing new markets emerge around the world as the ranks of the middle class surge. These business owners realize that the size of these fast-growing markets is small today compared to their potential in the near future. Changes such as these are creating instability for businesses of *any* size going global, but they also are creating tremendous opportunities for those small companies ready to capitalize on them.

**ENTREPRENEURIAL PROFILE: Tim Link: Skirts Plus** Tim Link, the second-generation owner of Skirts Plus, a small company based in Shakopee, Minnesota, that markets rubber skirts used in fishing lures, conducts business globally. Skirts Plus creates its skirt designs in Minnesota, works with a company in Vietnam to manufacture them, and sells about 250,000 rubber skirts per week to wholesale customers around the world. The company benefits from the quality rubber skirts and lower prices its Vietnamese supplier provides. Link says that "building trust" with international suppliers and customers is essential to his company's success. "When we first started manufacturing in Vietnam, I traveled there every other month for two to three weeks at a time," he says. "Today, I visit about once a year, and that's really important. We've had the same [manufacturing] partner for 10 years, and the trust and understanding we have established makes all the difference."[10]

## Why Go Global?

**1.**

Explain why "going global" has become an integral part of many small companies' strategies.

Small companies can no longer consider themselves to be strictly domestic businesses in this hotly competitive global environment. Approximately 95 percent of the world's population lives outside the United States, and more than 70 percent of the world's purchasing power lies beyond the borders of the United States. In addition, 80 percent of economic growth through 2016 will take place outside the United States.[11] Companies also face stiff foreign competition. "In the global economy, the competitor six time zones away is potentially as serious a threat as the competitor six blocks away," says one expert.[12] For companies across the world, going global is a matter of survival, not preference. No matter where a company's home base is, competitors are forcing it to think globally. "There are an awful lot of people in the rest of the world who think they are pretty good at doing your business," warns Lester Thurow.[13] Companies that fail to see the world as a global marketplace risk being blindsided in their markets both at home and abroad. "Just being part of the domestic market and depending on that source of revenue isn't cutting it anymore," says Maryann Stein, director of a development agency in Erie, Pennsylvania, that helps small companies break into global markets. "We haven't really had to explore other markets because U.S. companies have been OK just selling domestically. That's not the case anymore."[14]

Failure to cultivate global markets can be a lethal mistake for modern businesses—whatever their size. In short, to thrive in today's economy, small businesses must take their place in the world market. Today, the potential for doing business globally for businesses of all sizes means that where a company's goods and services originate or where its headquarters is located is insignificant. To be successful, companies must consider themselves to be businesses without borders.

Going global can put a tremendous strain on a small company, but entrepreneurs who take the plunge into global business can reap many benefits, including the ability to offset sales declines in the domestic market and the opportunity to increase sales and profits. "When a small business owner expands internationally, it becomes less dependent on the ebb and flow of one particular country's economic cycle," says Shan Nair, an international business consultant. "This helps the owner build a profitable alternative revenue stream." Other benefits include the ability to improve the quality of their products to meet the stringent demands of foreign customers, lower the manufacturing cost of their products by spreading fixed costs over a larger number of units, and enhance their competitive positions to become stronger businesses. Expanding a business beyond its domestic borders actually enhances a small company's overall performance, particularly when the owner transfers the lessons learned from competing in international markets to the entire business. Several studies have concluded that small companies that export are 20 percent more productive, produce 20 percent more job growth, earn more money, grow faster, create higher paying jobs, and are more likely to survive than their purely domestic counterparts. One study shows that 64 percent of small and medium companies saw a positive financial return within two years of launching an export initiative; 34 percent of them generated positive financial returns within six months.[15] Another study conducted by CompTIA of small and medium-size businesses that export reports that 64 percent of owners say that doing business globally has made their companies significantly more competitive. In addition, 86 percent of these business owners say that their companies' export sales are growing faster than their domestic sales.[16]

Unfortunately, many entrepreneurs have not learned to view their companies from a global perspective. Indeed, learning to *think globally* may be the first—and most threatening—obstacle an entrepreneur must overcome on the way to creating a truly global business. One British manager explains,

> If you are operating in South America, you'd better know how to operate in conditions of hyperinflation. If you're operating in Africa, you'd better know a lot about government relations and the use of local partners. If you're operating in Germany, you'd better understand the mechanics of codetermination and some of the special tax systems that one finds in that country. If you're operating in China, it's quite useful in trademark matters to know how the People's Court of Shanghai works. . . . If you're operating in Japan, you'd better understand the different trade structure.[17]

Gaining a foothold in newly opened foreign markets or maintaining a position in an existing one is no easy task, however. Until an entrepreneur develops the attitude of operating a truly global company rather than a domestic company that happens to be doing business abroad, achieving success in international business is difficult. That attitude starts at the top in the executive's office. Success in the global economy also requires constant innovation; staying nimble enough to use speed as a competitive weapon; maintaining a high level of quality and constantly improving it; being sensitive to foreign customers' unique requirements; adopting a more respectful attitude toward foreign habits and customs; hiring motivated, multilingual employees; and retaining a desire to learn constantly about global markets. In short, the path to success requires businesses to become "insiders" who see the world as their market rather than mere "exporters."

Before venturing into the global marketplace, an entrepreneur should consider six questions:

1. Is there a profitable market in which our company has the potential to be successful over the long run? Table 12.1 shows a country screening matrix designed to help entrepreneurs decide which countries offer the best opportunities for their products.

2. Do we have and are we willing to commit adequate resources of time, people, and capital to a global campaign?

## TABLE 12.1 A Country Screening Matrix

For an entrepreneur considering launching a global business venture, getting started often is the hardest step. "The world is such a big place! Where do I start?" is a typical comment from entrepreneurs considering global business. The following matrix will help you narrow down your options. Based on preliminary research, select three to five countries that you believe have the greatest market potential for your products. Then, use the following factors to guide you as you conduct more detailed research into these countries and their markets. Rate each factor on a scale of 1 (lowest) to 5 (highest). Based on your ratings, which country has the highest score?

| Market Factor | Country 1 Rating | Country 2 Rating | Country 3 Rating |
|---|---|---|---|
| **Demographic/physical environment** | | | |
| • Population size, growth, density | | | |
| • Urban and rural distribution | | | |
| • Climate and weather variations | | | |
| • Shipping distance | | | |
| • Product-significant demographics | | | |
| • Physical distribution and communication network | | | |
| • Natural resources | | | |
| **Political environment** | | | |
| • System of government | | | |
| • Political stability and continuity | | | |
| • Ideological orientation | | | |
| • Government involvement in business | | | |
| • Attitudes toward foreign business (trade restrictions, tariffs, nontariff barriers, bilateral trade agreements) | | | |
| • National economic and developmental priorities | | | |
| **Economic environment** | | | |
| • Overall level of development | | | |
| • Economic growth: gross domestic product, industrial sector | | | |
| • Role of foreign trade in the economy | | | |
| • Currency: inflation rate, availability, controls, stability of exchange rate | | | |
| • Balance of payments | | | |
| • Per capita income and distribution | | | |
| • Disposable income and expenditure patterns | | | |
| **Social/cultural environment** | | | |
| • Literacy rate, educational level | | | |
| • Existence of middle class | | | |
| • Similarities and differences in relation to home market | | | |
| • Language and other cultural considerations | | | |
| **Market access** | | | |
| • Limitations on trade: high tariff levels, quotas | | | |
| • Documentation and import regulations | | | |
| • Local standards, practices, and other nontariff barriers | | | |
| • Patents and trademark protection | | | |
| • Preferential treaties | | | |
| • Legal considerations for investment, taxation, repatriation, employment, code of laws | | | |
| **Product potential** | | | |
| • Customer needs and desires | | | |
| • Local production, imports, consumption | | | |
| • Exposure to and acceptance of product | | | |
| • Availability of linking products | | | |
| • Industry-specific key indicators of demand | | | |
| • Attitudes toward products of foreign origin | | | |
| • Competitive offerings | | | |
| **Local distribution and production** | | | |
| • Availability of intermediaries | | | |
| • Regional and local transportation facilities | | | |
| • Availability of manpower | | | |
| • Conditions for local manufacture | | | |
| **Total score** | | | |

Source: Adapted from "International Business Plan," *Breaking into the Trade Game: A Small Business Guide* (Washington, DC: U.S. Small Business Administration Office of International Trade, 2001), *www.sba.gov/oit/info/Guide-To-Exporting/trad6.html.*

3. Are we considering going global for the right reasons? Are domestic pressures forcing our company to consider global opportunities? Will going global make our company stronger and enhance our competitive advantage?

4. Do we understand the cultural differences, history, economics, values, opportunities, and risks of conducting business in the country(s) we are considering?

5. Do we have a viable exit strategy for our company if conditions change or the new venture does not succeed?

6. Can we afford *not* to go global?

## Going Global: Strategies for Small Businesses

The globalization of business actually *favors* small businesses because it creates an abundance of niche markets that are ideal for small companies to serve. "In this global economy, the competitive edge is swiftness to market and innovation," says John Naisbitt, trend-spotting author of *The Global Paradox*, and those are characteristics that are hallmarks of entrepreneurs.[18] Their agility and adaptability gives small firms the edge in today's highly interactive, fast-paced global economy. "The bigger the world economy, the more powerful its smallest players," concludes Naisbitt.[19]

**2.** _____

Describe the nine principal strategies small businesses can use to go global.

Becoming a global business depends on instilling a global culture throughout the organization that permeates *everything* the company does. Entrepreneurs who conduct international business successfully have developed a global mind-set for themselves and their companies. As one business writer explains,

> The global [business] looks at the whole world as *one market*. It manufactures, conducts research, raises capital, and buys supplies wherever it can do the job best. It keeps in touch with technology and market trends around the world. National boundaries and regulations tend to be irrelevant, or a mere hindrance. [Company] headquarters might be anywhere.[20]

As cultures across the globe become increasingly interwoven, companies' ability to go global will determine their degree of success. Small companies pursuing a global presence have nine principal strategies available: creating a presence on the Web, relying on trade intermediaries, establishing joint ventures, engaging in foreign licensing arrangements, franchising, using countertrading and bartering, exporting products or services, establishing international locations, and importing and outsourcing (see Figure 12.3).

### Creating a Presence on the Web

The simplest and least expensive way for a small business to reach the 95 percent of the world's consumers who live outside the United States is to establish a Web site. The Internet gives small businesses tremendous marketing potential all across the globe without having to incur the expense of opening international locations. With a well-designed Web site, a small company can extend its reach to customers anywhere in the world—without breaking the budget! A Web site is available to anyone, anywhere in the world and provides 24-hour-a-day exposure to a company's products or services, making global time differences meaningless. "You don't have to go out the door to be global," says Susan Anthony, a patent attorney. "If you have a Web site, you're global."[21]

**FIGURE 12.3**

**Nine Strategies for Going Global**

**FIGURE 12.4**

**World Internet Users by Region**

*Source:* "Internet Usage Statistics: The Big Picture," Internet World Stats 2012, *http://www.internetworldstats. com/stats.htm.*

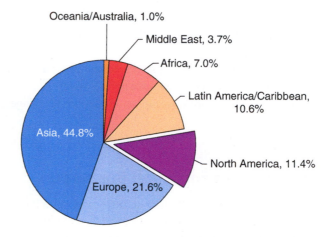

Establishing a presence on the Web is an essential ingredient in the strategies of small companies trying to reach customers outside the borders of the United States. Although Internet usage varies greatly by region of the world (see Figure 12.4), the number of Internet users is growing extremely fast—nearly 570 percent worldwide since 2000. Other important factors for U.S. entrepreneurs to note are that almost 89 percent of the estimated 2.4 billion Internet users worldwide live *outside* of North America and that less than 27 percent of Internet users speak English.[22]

Before the advent of the Internet, small businesses usually took incremental steps toward becoming global businesses. They began selling locally, and, then, after establishing a reputation, expanded regionally and perhaps nationally. Only after establishing their businesses domestically did entrepreneurs begin to think about selling their products or services internationally. The Internet makes that business model obsolete because it provides small companies with a low-cost global distribution channel that they can utilize from the day they are launched. Designed properly, a Web site can be a powerful and engaging global marketing tool. "Thanks to the Internet and mobile technologies, an entire world of entrepreneurs can participate in global trade and bring products to world markets," says a senior manager at eBay. "For the first time in history, global trade is open to every business, regardless of its size."[23]

**ENTREPRENEURIAL PROFILE: David Greenberg: Parliament Tutors** After graduating from New York University in 2008 with a degree in economics, David Greenberg could not find a job in the financial industry, which was in the midst of a severe crisis. Greenberg borrowed $5,000 from his mother to launch Parliament Tutors, a Web-based company that matches in-home tutors with students who need private tutoring and preparation for standardized tests. In its first month of operation, Parliament Tutors generated $8,000 in revenue. Today, the company has four full-time employees who coordinate more than 600 tutors and generates revenues of $50,000 per month. Greenberg now offers online tutoring as well as in-home tutoring in 27 states and recently decided to expand internationally, targeting students in London, Paris, Montreal, Shanghai, and Tel Aviv whose goal is to attend schools in the United States. The global expansion has been successful, but Greenberg says that he should have "made a Web site for each country instead of just one Web site for our whole international operation."[24]

Entrepreneurs who do not want to take the time to set up their own Web sites can still sell to international customers through the Internet giant eBay, which has a wide global reach of 116 million active users. eBay handles an average of $2,100 worth of transactions every second, and 57 percent of all eBay transactions take place outside the United States.[25] eBay's international sales are growing twice as fast as its domestic sales. In fact, a recent study reports that 97 percent of eBay commercial sellers, most of which are small businesses, sell their products internationally. More than 80 percent of eBay sellers export to five or more foreign countries.

**ENTREPRENEURIAL PROFILE: Elizabeth Bennett and Sara Luther: AfricaDirect** In 1997, Elizabeth Bennett and Sara Luther started AfricaDirect, a company that specializes in selling unique items such as clay pots, textiles, jewelry, bead work, carvings, and other items created by crafters in Africa. Bennett heard about a business owner selling beads on eBay and decided to see whether AfricaDirect's products would sell on an eBay store. "At first, I was like, "Wow! We made $50 this week [on eBay]," she recalls. Today, AfricaDirect has seven employees, pumps more than $500,000 into the economies of small African villages, and provides a valuable marketplace for the hand-crafted products produced by local artisans. The company generates the majority of its $1.2 million in annual sales through eBay, Etsy, and the AfricaDirect Web site. "I never would have guessed that we could grow our business into what it is today," says Bennett.[26]

Rather than merely counting on international customers to stumble onto their Web sites, small companies can take a proactive approach by creating sites that are customized for specific countries. Business owners can determine which countries to target by using Web analytics to identify the countries in which their existing online customers live. Hiring someone who understands the nuances of the language, culture, and business practices of the target countries to create the site is the safest strategy and avoids embarrassing cultural blunders. An entrepreneur won't have much luck listing "tennis shoes" for sale on a Web site aimed at customers in the United Kingdom; customers there would search for "plimsolls" or "daps." Google Global Market Finder is a free market research tool that shows entrepreneurs how many times people around the world use particular key words in online searches in 56 different languages. Business owners can use the Global Market Finder to test the international appeal of key words on their Web sites and to isolate the key words that are likely to produce the best results in their search engine optimization strategies.

 **In the Entrepreneurial Spotlight**

## Going Global One Step at a Time

Like most small businesses, Couch Guitar Straps, a company based in Signal Hill, California, that makes high-quality guitar straps used by famous and not-so-famous guitarists, received its first international order through its Web site from a customer in Japan. "I had no idea how much it was going to cost to ship or whether the customer would really pay," recalls Dan Perkins, the company's owner. Perkins, who started Couch Guitar Straps in his garage in 1999, filled that first international order in 2004. Today, international sales account for 35 percent of the company's sales, and that percentage is growing. "Technology erases boundaries and makes it convenient to conduct business globally," says Laurel Delaney, an international business expert and consultant. For Couch Guitar Straps, selling to international customers came naturally as growing numbers of them found the company's Web site and placed orders. "Having a Web site flattens the globe," says Perkins, who also discovered the importance of a sound search engine optimization (SEO) strategy. "SEO is like the new Yellow Pages," he says. "If you can get listed high in search results, you're in the world's phone book."

Delaney encourages her small business clients with global aspirations to use social media to attract and connect with international customers. "Market via every imaginable platform—blogs, Facebook, YouTube, Twitter, and LinkedIn," she says. "Keep a conversation going worldwide about what's great about your company." That strategy proved to be quite successful for Couch Guitar Straps, whose Web site, blog, and e-mail newsletters profile the uniqueness of its products (which include a vegan guitar strap) and the musicians who use them, including Beck, The White Stripes, and Keith Urban. One of Couch's four employees always includes a hand-written thank you note in every order. Couch also keeps shipping as simple as possible, relying on the U.S. Postal Service and postage software from DYMO Endicia to keep shipping costs low and to allow customers to track their packages.

Ensuring that international customers pay is a common concern among small companies that sell globally because they cannot afford to incur the burdensome costs of writing off bad debts. Selling on open account to international customers is the most risky option, and collecting cash in advance is the least risky but can severely limit the pool of international customers. On small orders, companies can accept payments through PayPal or credit cards. Larger orders may require a company to work with its bank's international department on a letter of credit or to purchase credit insurance from a private insurer or the Export-Import Bank.

A decade after making its first international sale, Couch Guitar Straps has developed a sizable pool of global customers. The company continues to sell guitar straps to individual customers around the world through its Web site, to 70 retail outlets in the United States and around the world, and to distributors in Japan, Austria, and Germany. When working with international distributors, Perkins says, "just like in the United States, we start out with a small order and see how it goes."

Small companies such as Couch Guitar Straps prove that even really small businesses can go global. "It's like getting the first olive out of the jar, and then the rest tumble out," says Delaney. "Once you get that first [international] market or customer, you'll want to do more. There's never been a better time to go global," she says. "You have nothing to lose and everything to gain."

1. How does the Internet enable entrepreneurs to create global businesses at start-up? Has this always been the case?

2. What lessons can you draw from Dan Perkins's experience with international sales at Couch Guitar Straps?

*Sources:* Based on Rieva Lesonsky, "Taking Your Business Global," *Success,* October 2012, *www.success.com/articles/1053-taking-your-business-global;* "About Us," Couch Guitar Straps, *www.couchguitarstraps.com/about_us.html.*

### Relying on Trade Intermediaries

Another alternative for low-cost and low-risk entry into international markets is to use a trade intermediary. Trade intermediaries are domestic agencies that serve as distributors in foreign countries for domestic companies of all sizes. They rely on their networks of contacts, their extensive knowledge of local customs and markets, and their experience in international trade to market products effectively and efficiently all across the globe. Trade intermediaries serve as export departments for small businesses. Although a broad array of trade intermediaries is available, the following are ideally suited for small businesses:

**EXPORT MANAGEMENT COMPANIES** **Export management companies** (EMCs) are an important channel of foreign distribution for small companies just getting started in international trade or for those lacking the resources to assign their own people to foreign markets. Most EMCs are merchant intermediaries, working on a buy-and-sell arrangement with domestic small companies. They provide small businesses with a low-cost, efficient, independent international marketing department, offering services ranging from market research on foreign countries and advice on patent protection to arranging financing and handling shipping. More than 1,000 EMCs of all sizes operate across the United States, and many of them specialize in particular products or product lines. The chief advantage of using an export management company is that a small business's products get international exposure without having to tie up its own resources excessively.

**ENTREPRENEURIAL PROFILE: Michigan Maple Block Company** Dorian Drake International, an EMC founded in 1947 in New York City, specializes in exporting goods to more than 100 countries around the world for companies in four industries—automotive, food service, lawn and garden, and environmental. Since 1999, Dorian Drake has managed global sales for the Michigan Maple Block Company, a small business in Petoskey, Michigan, owned by members of the same family for 125 years that manufactures solid-wood, commercial-grade cutting tables used in food preparation.[27]

The greatest benefits that EMCs offer small companies are ready access to global markets and an extensive knowledge base on foreign trade, both of which are vital for entrepreneurs who are inexperienced in conducting global business. In return for their services, EMCs usually earn an extra discount on the goods they buy from their clients or, if they operate on a commission rate, a higher commission than domestic distributors earn on what they sell. EMCs charge commission rates of about 10 percent on consumer goods and 15 percent on industrial products. Although EMCs rarely advertise their services, finding one is not difficult. The Federation of International Trade Associations provides useful information for small companies about global business and trade intermediaries on its Web site (*http://fita.org*), including a *Directory of Export Management Companies*. Industry trade associations and publications and the U.S. Department of Commerce's Export Assistance Centers[*] also can help entrepreneurs to locate EMCs and other trade intermediaries.

**EXPORT TRADING COMPANIES** Another tactic for getting into international markets with a minimum of cost and effort is through export trading companies, which have been important vehicles in international trade throughout history. The Hudson's Bay Company and the East India Company were dominant powers in world trade in the sixteenth, seventeenth, and eighteenth centuries.

**Export trading companies** (ETCs) are businesses that buy and sell products in a number of countries, and they typically offer a wide range of services such as exporting, importing, shipping, storing, distributing, and others to their clients. Unlike EMCs, which tend to focus on exporting, ETCs usually perform both import and export trades across many countries' borders. However, like EMCs, ETCs lower the risk of exporting for small businesses. Some of the largest trading companies in the world are based in the United States and Japan. In fact, many businesses that have navigated successfully Japan's complex system of distribution have done so with the help of ETCs.

In 1982, Congress passed the Export Trading Company Act to allow producers of similar products to form ETC cooperatives without the fear of violating antitrust laws. The goal was to encourage U.S. companies to export more goods by allowing businesses in the same industry to band together to form export trading companies to increase their export efficiency.

---

[*]A searchable list of the Export Assistance Centers is available at the *Export.gov* Web site *www.export.gov/eac/index.asp*.

**MANUFACTURER'S EXPORT AGENTS** **Manufacturer's export agents** (MEAs) act as international sales representatives in a limited number of markets for various noncompeting domestic companies. Unlike the close, partnering relationship formed with most EMCs, the relationship between an MEA and a small company is a short-term one in which the MEA typically operates on a commission basis.

**EXPORT MERCHANTS** **Export merchants** are domestic wholesalers who do business in foreign markets. They buy goods from many domestic manufacturers and then market them in foreign markets. Unlike MEAs, export merchants often carry competing lines, which means they have little loyalty to suppliers. Most export merchants specialize in particular industries—office equipment, computers, industrial supplies, and others.

**RESIDENT BUYING OFFICES** Another approach to exporting is to sell to a **resident buying office**, a government-owned or privately-owned operation established in a country for the purpose of buying goods made there. Many foreign governments and businesses have set up buying offices in the United States. Selling to them is just like selling to domestic customers because the buying office handles all the details of exporting.

**FOREIGN DISTRIBUTORS** Some small businesses work through foreign distributors to reach international markets. Domestic small companies export their products to these distributors who handle all of the marketing, distribution, and service functions in the foreign country.

**ENTREPRENEURIAL PROFILE: Peter Cole: Gamblin Artists Colors** In 2007, when Peter Cole took over Gamblin Artists Colors, a company that makes hand-crafted oil paints, varnishes, and other artists' supplies, international sales accounted for less than 5 percent of the company's revenue. Cole realized that foreign markets represented a significant opportunity for the company's high-quality products and traveled to several countries that basic market research helped managers select as prime targets. Logging more than 80,000 miles in less than one year, Cole established relationships with foreign distributors in Israel, Australia, Mexico, Great Britain, and Spain. Gamblin Artists Colors now generates more than $5 million in annual sales, and international sales account for 10 percent (and growing) of the total.[28]

## The Value of Using Trade Intermediaries

Trade intermediaries such as these are becoming increasingly popular among businesses attempting to branch out into world markets because they make that transition much faster and easier. Most small business owners simply do not have the knowledge, resources, or confidence to go global alone. Intermediaries' global networks of buyers and sellers allow their small business customers to build their international sales much faster and with fewer hassles and mistakes. Entrepreneurs who are inexperienced in global sales and attempt to crack certain foreign markets quickly discover just how difficult the challenge can be. However, with their know-how, experience, and contacts, trade intermediaries can get small companies' products into foreign markets quickly and efficiently. The primary disadvantage of using trade intermediaries is that doing so requires entrepreneurs to surrender control over their foreign sales. Maintaining close contact with intermediaries and evaluating their performance regularly help to avoid major problems, however.

The key to establishing a successful relationship with a trade intermediary is conducting a thorough screening to determine which type of intermediary—and which one in particular—will serve a small company's needs best. An entrepreneur looking for an intermediary should compile a list of potential candidates using some of the sources listed in Table 12.2. In addition, entrepreneurs can find reliable intermediaries by using their network of contacts in foreign countries and by attending international trade shows while keeping an eye out for potential candidates. After compiling the list, entrepreneurs should evaluate each one using a list of criteria to narrow the field to the most promising ones. Interviewing a principal from each intermediary on the final list should tell entrepreneurs which ones are best able to meet their companies' needs. Finally, before signing any agreement with a trade intermediary, it is wise to conduct thorough background and credit checks. Entrepreneurs with experience in global trade also suggest entering short-term agreements of about a year with new trade intermediaries to allow time to test their ability and willingness to live up to their promises. Many entrepreneurs begin their global business initiatives with trade intermediaries and then venture into international business on their own as their skill and comfort levels increase.

**TABLE 12.2 Resources for Locating a Trade Intermediary**

Trade intermediaries make doing business around the world much easier for small companies, but finding the right one can be a challenge. Fortunately, several government agencies offer a wealth of information to businesses interested in reaching into global markets with the help of trade intermediaries. Entrepreneurs looking for help in breaking into global markets should contact the International Trade Administration, the U.S. Commerce Department, and the Small Business Administration first to take advantage of the following services:

- **Agent/Distributor Service.** Provides customized searches to locate interested and qualified foreign distributors for a product or service. (Search cost, $250 per country)
- **Commercial Service International Contacts List.** Provides contact and product information for more than 82,000 foreign agents, distributors, and importers interested in doing business with U.S. companies.
- **Country Directories of International Contacts List.** Provides the same kind of information as the CSIC List but is organized by country.
- **Industry Sector Analyses.** Offer in-depth reports on industries in foreign countries, including information on distribution practices, end users, and top sales prospects.
- **International Market Insights.** Include reports on specific foreign market conditions, upcoming opportunities for U.S. companies, trade contacts, trade show schedules, and other information.
- **Trade Opportunity Program.** Provides up-to-the-minute, prescreened sales leads around the world for U.S. businesses, including joint venture and licensing partners, direct sales leads, and representation offers.
- **International Company Profiles.** Commercial specialists will investigate potential partners, agents, distributors, or customers for U.S. companies and will issue profiles on them.
- **Commercial News USA.** A government-published magazine that promotes U.S. companies' products and services to 400,000 business readers in 176 countries at a fraction of the cost of commercial advertising. Small companies can use *Commercial News USA* to reach new customers around the world for as little as $499.
- **Gold Key Service.** For a small fee, business owners wanting to target a specific country can use the Department of Commerce's Gold Key Service, in which experienced trade professionals arrange meetings with prescreened contacts whose interests match their own.
- **Platinum Key Service.** The U.S. Commercial Service's Platinum Key Service is more comprehensive than its Gold Key Service, offering business owners long-term consulting services on topics such as building a global marketing strategy, deciding which countries to target, and how to reach customers in foreign markets.
- **Matchmaker Trade Delegations Program.** This program helps small U.S. companies establish business relationships in major markets abroad by introducing them to the right contacts.
- **Multi-State/Catalog Exhibition Program.** The Department of Commerce presents companies' product and sales literature to hundreds of interested business prospects in foreign countries for as little as $450.
- **Trade Fair Certification Program.** This service promotes U.S. companies' participation in foreign trade shows that represent the best marketing opportunities for them.
- **Economic Bulletin Board.** Provides online trade leads and valuable market research on foreign countries compiled from a variety of federal agencies.
- **U.S. Export Assistance Centers.** The Department of Commerce has established 19 export centers in major metropolitan cities around the country to serve as one-stop shops for entrepreneurs who need export help. (*www.sba.gov/aboutsba/sbaprograms/internationaltrade/useac/index.html*)
- **Trade Information Center.** The center helps locate federal export assistance, provides export assistance, and offers a 24-hour automated fax retrieval system that gives entrepreneurs free information on export promotion programs, regional market information, and international trade agreements. Call USA-TRADE.
- **Office of International Trade.** Through the Office of International Trade, the Small Business Administration works with other government and private agencies to provide a variety of export development assistance, how-to publications, online courses, and information on foreign markets.
- **Export-U.com.** This Web site (*www.export-u.com*) offers free export webinars to business owners on topics that range from the basics, "Exporting 101," to more advanced topics such as export financing arrangements. The site also provides links to many useful international trade Web sites.
- **U.S. Commercial Service.** The U.S. Commercial service, a division of the International Trade Administration (*www.trade.gov*), provides many of the services listed in this table. Its Web site (*www.buyusa.gov*) is an excellent starting point for entrepreneurs who are interested in exporting.
- **Export.gov.** This Web site from the U.S. Commercial Service is an excellent gateway to myriad sources for entrepreneurs who are interested in learning more about exporting. This site includes market research, trade events, trade leads, and much more.
- **Federation of International Trade Associations.** The FITA Global Trade Portal (*www.fita.org*) is an excellent source for international import and export trade leads and events and provides links to about 8,000 Web sites related to international trade.

shops in Moscow by 2017. The franchisor was drawn to Novikov because of his extensive experience in food service and his deep knowledge of the local market, culture, and customs.[41]

▪ **Master franchising** is the most popular strategy for companies entering international markets. In a master franchising deal, a franchisor sells to a franchisee the right to develop subfranchises within a broad geographic area or, sometimes, an entire foreign country. In short, master franchising turbocharges a franchisor's growth. Many franchisors use this method to open outlets in international markets more quickly and efficiently because their master franchisees understand local laws and the nuances of selling in local markets. Although master franchising simplifies a franchisor's expansion into global markets, it gives franchisors the least amount of control over their international franchisees. Started in 1987, Tasti D-Lite, a company that sells tasty, low-calorie, frozen desserts made from natural ingredients, began franchising in 2008 and has grown rapidly. Tasti D-Lite used master franchising to enter Australia and Central America and recently created a master franchise agreement with Al-Himmah International Limited to open locations in six Middle Eastern countries, including Saudi Arabia, Bahrain, Kuwait, Qatar, Lebanon, and Jordan.[42]

 **Entrepreneurship In Action**

## Growing Beyond the Borders

### Johnny Rockets

Ronn Teitelbaum started Johnny Rockets, a restaurant with a retro 1950s theme that serves classic American fare such as burgers, hot dogs, fries, onion rings, milkshakes, and floats, on Melrose Avenue in Los Angeles in 1986. Today, the company operates 300 company-owned or franchised restaurants, 223 of which are located in the United States and the remainder in 16 countries. Like many franchises, Johnny Rockets is expanding rapidly in international markets; the company recently opened its first outlets in the Dominican Republic, Indonesia, Nigeria, Russia, Brazil, Pakistan, and Morocco. John Fuller, the company's CEO, says that Johnny Rockets's American theme resonates well with customers in international markets. "Internationally, we sell Americana," he says. "The currency we use is burgers, shakes, and fries."

Fuller wants to open more international franchises but says that finding the right franchisees poses a significant challenge. The company has identified China and India as markets with tremendous growth potential for its products but has been stymied by the inability to find qualified franchisees to operate its restaurants.

### Wing Zone

In 1991, University of Florida students Matt Friedman and Adam Scott grew weary of ordering pizza to fuel their late-night study sessions and decided that chicken wings would provide a tasty alternative. Late at night, they would take over the kitchen of the fraternity house where they lived and experiment until they had perfected their special sauces and the process of cooking wings. They began selling their delectable wings to other students and knew that they had a hit when they sold out their first two nights in business. Friedman and Scott soon opened their first Wing Zone store in Gainesville, Florida, to target the population of hungry students. The company, which began franchising its restaurants in

1999, is now based in Atlanta, Georgia, and has 100 units, most of which are located in college towns, in 20 states.

A few years ago, Friedman, the company's CEO, evaluated the U.S. franchise market and saw that it was crowded with competition and was not likely to provide significant growth opportunities. "We realized that, although our stores were performing well, our domestic expansion was going to be limited," he says. "We started considering other growth avenues we could follow." That led Wing Zone to investigate establishing international franchises, something that Friedman and his management team did not take lightly. They knew that international expansion would test the integrity of their franchise system, would require a significant investment of capital and time, and would require many months of research to determine which international markets offer the greatest promise for the Wing Zone concept. In addition, they realized that finding the right franchisees was one key to success. Friedman and his management team realized that international expansion would require a significant financial investment, one that would not likely produce a return for at least two or three years.

Friedman and his management team established the criteria for the ideal international market: a culture that had a taste for the company's spicy wings, an acceptance of home delivery (one of Wing Zone's core concepts), a high level of poultry consumption, and a growing middle class with adequate purchasing power. They settled on Panama as the location of their first international outlet. The team's research paid off, enabling the company to adapt its first international location to the local culture. They expanded the size of the restaurant to include seating for up to 60 customers (the chain's domestic stores are take-out and delivery only) and modified the menu slightly to please local palates. The adaptations were successful, and the store set a new company sales record in its first week. Wing Zone has since opened locations in the Bahamas, the Dominican Republic,

*(continued)*

## Entrepreneurship in Action *(continued)*

Malaysia, the United Arab Emirates, and Saudi Arabia. Friedman also is negotiating with potential franchisees in England, Ireland, Scotland, and Japan.

1. Why are franchises such as Johnny Rockets and Wing Zone expanding into international markets? What are the risks and the rewards of doing so?

2. John Fuller says that finding the right franchisees to operate Johnny Rockets restaurants in foreign countries is a challenge. How do you recommend that the company locate qualified franchisees?

3. Use the Internet to research other countries that would be good target markets for Johnny Rockets and Wing Zone. Explain your reasoning.

4. Develop at least three suggestions for a small franchisor that is interested in opening its first international outlet.

*Sources:* Based on Lisa Jennings, "Johnny Rockets Expands Overseas," *Nation's Restaurant News*, June 20, 2012, *http://nrn.com/latest-headlines/johnny-rockets-expands-overseas*; "About Us," Johnny Rockets, *www.johnnyrockets.com/about-us/our-company.html*; Jason Daley, "Despite the Slowdown at Home, U.S. Franchises Expand Abroad," *Entrepreneur*, April 26, 2011, *www.entrepreneur.com/article/219493*; "Company Information," Wing Zone, *www.wingzone.com/company.html*.

### Countertrading and Bartering

As business becomes increasingly global, companies are discovering that attracting customers is just one part of the battle. Another problem global businesses face when selling to some countries is that their currencies are virtually worthless outside their borders, so getting paid in a valuable currency is a real challenge! Companies wanting to reach these markets must countertrade or barter. A **countertrade** is a transaction in which a company selling goods and services in a foreign country agrees to help promote investment and trade in that country. The goal of the transaction is to help offset the capital drain from the foreign country's purchases. As entrepreneurs enter more developing nations, they will discover the need to develop skill at implementing this global trading strategy.

Countertrading does suffer from numerous drawbacks. Countertrade transactions can be complicated, cumbersome, and time consuming. They also increase the chances that a company will get stuck with useless merchandise that it cannot move. They can lead to unpleasant surprises concerning the quantity and quality of products required in the countertrade. Still, countertrading offers one major advantage: Sometimes it's the only way to make a sale!

Entrepreneurs must weigh the advantages against the disadvantages for their companies before committing to a countertrade deal. Because of its complexity and the risks involved, countertrading is not the best choice for a novice entrepreneur looking to break into the global marketplace.

**Bartering**, the exchange of goods and services for other goods and services, is another way of trading with countries lacking convertible currency. In a barter exchange, a company that manufactures electronics components might trade its products for the coffee that a business in a foreign country processes, which it then sells to a third company for cash. Barter transactions require finding a business with complementary needs, but they are much simpler than counter-trade transactions.

### Exporting

**3.** _____
Explain how to build a successful export program.

For years, small businesses in the United States could afford the luxury of conducting business at home in the world's largest market, never having to venture outside its borders. However, a growing number of small companies, realizing the profit potential that exporting offers, are making exporting part of their business models. A recent study by CompTIA reports that small and medium-size companies that export generate on average 12 percent of their revenues from exports.[43]

Large companies continue to dominate export sales, however. Only about 1 percent of the 27 million businesses in the United States export their goods and services, a percentage that is significantly lower than that in other developed nations. Although small and medium-size companies account for 98 percent of the 293,000 U.S. businesses that export goods and services, they generate less than one-third of the nation's export sales. In addition, 58 percent of small businesses that sell internationally export to just one country.[44] Their impact is significant, however; small companies generate $1.8 billion each day in export sales. Small businesses that export are bigger, more productive, and more profitable than their strictly domestic counterparts.[45] Other studies show that exporters grow faster, are less likely to fail, and produce higher employment growth.[46]

Many more small companies are capable of exporting but are not doing so. One of the biggest barriers facing companies that have never exported is not knowing where or how to start

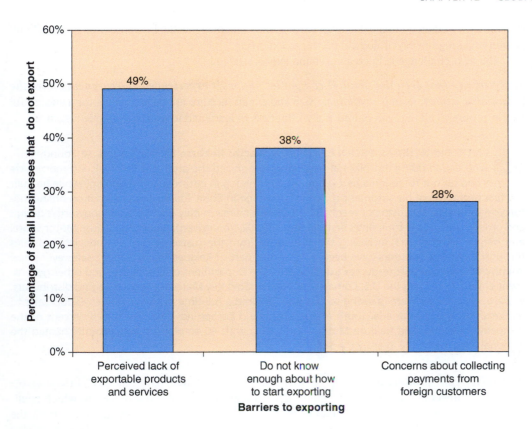

**FIGURE 12.6**

**Barriers to Exporting—Among Small Companies That Do Not Export**

*Source:* Based on NSBA/SBEA Small Business Exporting Survey, 2010.

(see Figure 12.6). Paul Hsu, whose company sells ginseng across the globe, explains, "Exporting starts with a global mind-set, which unfortunately, is not all that common among owners of small- and medium-sized businesses in the United States. Most entrepreneurs in the United States envision markets only within domestic and sometimes even state borders, while foreign entrepreneurs look at export markets first."[47]

Breaking the psychological barrier to exporting is the first—and most difficult—step in setting up a successful program. The U.S. Commercial Service's *Export Programs Guide* provides entrepreneurs with a comprehensive list of federal programs designed to help U.S. exporters. The U.S. Commercial Service Web site (*www.buyusa.gov*) is an excellent starting point for entrepreneurs who are looking for international business partners to help their companies expand into global markets. Another valuable source of information are the U.S. Export Assistance Centers (*http://www.export.gov/eac/*), which serve as single contact points for information on the multitude of federal export programs that are designed to help entrepreneurs who want to start exporting. Entrepreneurs who want to learn more about exporting should investigate *A Basic Guide to Exporting* (*http://export.gov/basicguide*). The U.S. Small Business Administration (SBA) publishes the *Export Business Planner*, a comprehensive set of worksheets that guides users through the process of building an export business plan and is available to download for free (*www.sba.gov/exportbusinessplanner*). The SBA's Web site (*www.sba.gov*) also includes a section that is dedicated to exporting and importing. The U.S. government export portal, *www.export.gov*, gives entrepreneurs access to valuable information about exporting in general (finance, shipping, documentation, and others) as well as details on individual nations (market research, trade agreements, statistics, and more). Export-U (*www.export-u.com/exportu4*), a Web site created by the Export Assistance Center in Atlanta and the Georgia Small Business Development Center's International Trade Center, offers a series of Webinars ranging from "Are You Ready to Export?" to "Managing Global Risk." The Census Bureau (*www.census.gov/foreign-trade/aes/exporttraining/videos/index.html*) provides several short videos on export-related topics. *The Trade Finance Guide*, a publication from the International Trade Administration (*http://export.gov/tradefinanceguide/index.asp*), helps entrepreneurs learn the basics of trade finance, including the various methods of payments that exporters use and the source of export financing that are available. Shipping giant UPS International offers a Web site (*www.international.ups.com*) aimed at business owners who want to take part in global trade, including both exporting and importing. Learning more about exporting and realizing that it is within the realm of possibility for small companies—even *very* small companies—is the first and often most difficult step in breaking the psychological barrier to exporting.

The next challenge is to create a sound export strategy.

**1. *Recognize that even the smallest companies and least experienced entrepreneurs have the potential to export; help is available.*** Size and experience are not prerequisites for a successful export program; all that is required is a willingness to learn and to utilize available resources.

Al Youngwerth, founder of Rekluse Motor Sports.
*Source:* Rekluse Motorsports.

**ENTREPRENEURIAL PROFILE: Al Youngwerth: Rekluse Motor Sports** Al Youngwerth, who began riding dirt bikes at age eight, recognized the problems with existing motorcycle clutches and set out to design a better one. He kept his job in information technology while he built the first prototype of his automatic clutch in his garage in Boise, Idaho, and posted it on online motorcycle forums to get customer feedback. A business owner in Italy discovered Youngwerth's design and ordered one of the company's first clutches. In 2002, Youngwerth launched Rekluse Motor Sports and began filling orders, including the first order from the customer in Italy. International sales through foreign distributors have been a significant part of Rekluse Motor Sports's sales ever since. Youngwerth used export resources from the SBA, the Department of Commerce, and other government entities, including the U.S. Commercial Services Gold Key Matching Service, to find distributors. In 2010, export sales were growing so fast that he hired a full-time export manager. Export sales to markets that include Canada, South Africa, Brazil, and Europe now account for 26 percent of the company's revenue, and Rekluse Motor Sports, now with 40 employees, was recently named the National Exporter of the Year by the SBA.[48]

**2. *Analyze your product or service.*** Is it special? New? Unique? High quality? Priced favorably due to lower costs or exchange rates? Does it appeal to a particular niche? In which countries would there be sufficient demand for it? In many foreign countries, products from the United States are in demand because they have an air of mystery about them. Exporters also quickly learn the value that foreign customers place on quality. In some cases, entrepreneurs must modify their existing products and services slightly to suit foreign customers' lifestyles, housing needs, body sizes, traditions, and cultures. When Peter Cole, CEO of Gamblin Artists Colors, the company that makes hand-crafted oil paints, varnishes, and other artists' supplies, began exporting to Australia, he quickly realized the importance of modifying the size of the products. "In Australia, they want larger sizes of paints—sizes we had not contemplated for the U.S. market," says Cole. "People tend to paint bigger and thicker."[49] Making modifications such as these often spells the difference between success and failure in the global market. In other cases, products destined for export need little or no modification. Experts estimate that one-half of exported products require little modification, one-third require moderate modification, and only a few require major changes.

**3. *Analyze your commitment.*** Are you willing to devote the time and the energy to develop export markets? Does your company have the necessary resources to capitalize on market opportunities? In any international venture, patience is essential. Laying the groundwork for an export operation can take from six to eight months (or longer), but entering foreign markets isn't as tough as most entrepreneurs think. "One of the biggest misconceptions people have is that they can't market overseas unless they have a big team of lawyers and specialists," says one export specialist. "That just isn't true."[50] Table 12.3 summarizes key issues managers must address in making the "export or not" decision.

**4. *Research markets and pick your target market.*** Before investing in a costly sales trip abroad, entrepreneurs should use the vast resources available for exporters online to research potential markets that are most promising for their products. Armed with research, small business owners can avoid wasting time and money pursuing markets with limited potential for their products and can concentrate on those with the greatest promise. Entrepreneurs usually are most comfortable starting their export efforts in nations with which the United States has trade agreements and where English is the accepted language of business. A study by UPS International reports that small exporters have had the most success selling their products in Canada, the United Kingdom, Australia, and Mexico.[51] Figure 12.7 shows the top five countries to which small and medium-size businesses plan to export within the next two years. Table 12.4 offers questions to guide entrepreneurs as they conduct international market research. Weber-Stephen, a privately held

## TABLE 12.3 Management Issues in the Export Decision

### I. Experience

1. With what countries has your company already conducted business (or from what countries have you received inquiries about your product or service)?
2. Which product lines do foreign customers ask about most often?
3. Have you prepared a list of sales inquiries for each buyer by product and by country?
4. Is the trend of inquiries or sales increasing or decreasing?
5. Who are your primary domestic and foreign competitors?
6. What lessons has your company learned from past export experience?

### II. Management and Personnel

1. Who will be responsible for the export entity's organization and staff? (Do you have an export "champion"?)
2. How much top management time
   a. should you allocate to exporting?
   b. can you afford to allocate to exporting?
3. What does management expect from its exporting efforts? What are you company's export goals and objectives?
4. What organizational structure will your company require to ensure that it can service export sales properly? (Note the political implications, if any.)
5. Who will implement the plan?

### III. Production Capacity

1. To what extent is your company using its existing production capacity? Is there any excess? If so, how much?
2. Will filling export orders hurt your company's ability to make and service domestic sales?
3. What will additional production for export markets cost your company?
4. Are there seasonal or cyclical fluctuations in your company's workload? When? Why?
5. Is there a minimum quantity foreign customers must order for a sale to be profitable?
6. To what extent must your company modify its products, packaging, and design specifically for its export targets? Is your product quality adequate for foreign customers?
7. What pricing structure will your company use? Will your prices be competitive?
8. How will your company collect payment on its export sales?

### IV. Financial Capacity

1. How much capital will your company need to begin exporting? Where will it come from?
2. How will you allocate the initial costs of your company's export effort?
3. Does your company have other expansion plans that would compete with an exporting effort?
4. By what date do you expect your company's export program to pay for itself?
5. How important is establishing a global presence to your company's future success?

*Source:* Based on *A Basic Guide to Exporting* (Washington, DC: U.S. Department of Commerce, 1986), p. 3.

family business in Palatine, Illinois, that makes the famous Weber grill that is a mainstay in millions of backyards in the United States (where 70 percent of the population owns a grill), has achieved success exporting its iconic grills to other parts of the world, including Europe, New Zealand, Australia, and South Africa. Weber-Stephen discovered that the smallest version of its grill, the 14½-inch Smokey Joe, appeals to customers in China and India, where living quarters and available outdoor spaces are much smaller than in the United States.[52]

**5.** *Develop a distribution strategy.* Should you use an export intermediary or sell directly to foreign customers? As you learned earlier in this chapter, many small companies just entering international markets prefer to rely on trade intermediaries or a joint venture partner to break new ground. Using intermediaries or joint ventures often makes sense until an entrepreneur has the chance to gain experience in exporting and to learn the ground rules of selling in foreign lands. Figure 12.8 illustrates the various distribution strategies that micro-size companies (those

**FIGURE 12.7**

**Countries to Which Small Businesses Intend to Export Within the Next Two Years**

*Source:* Based on *Perceptions of Global Trade,* UPS International, 2011, p. 21.

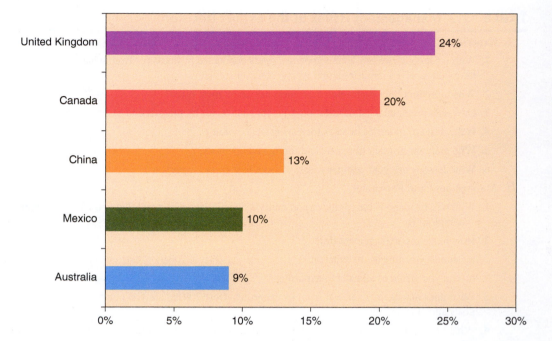

### TABLE 12.4  Questions to Guide International Market Research

- Is there an overseas market for your company's products or services?
- Are there specific target markets that look most promising?
- Which new markets abroad are most likely to open up or expand?
- How big is the market your company is targeting, and how fast is it growing?
- What are the major economic, political, legal, social, technological, and other environmental factors affecting this market?
- What are the demographic and cultural factors affecting this market, such as disposable income, occupation, age, gender, opinions, activities, interests, tastes, and values?
- Who are your company's present and potential customers abroad?
- What are their needs and desires? What factors influence their buying decisions: price, credit terms, delivery terms, quality, brand name, and so on?
- How would they use your company's product or service? What modifications, if any, would be necessary to sell to your target customers?
- Who are your primary competitors in the foreign market?
- How do competitors distribute, sell, and promote their products? What are their prices?
- What are the best channels of distribution for your product?
- What is the best way for your company to gain exposure in this market?
- Are there any barriers such as tariffs, quotas, duties, or regulations to selling your product in this market? Are there any incentives?
- Are there any potential licensing or joint venture partners already in this market?

*Source:* Based on *A Basic Guide to Exporting* (Washington, DC: U.S. Department of Commerce, 1986), p. 11.

with less than $1 million in annual sales) and small companies (those with annual sales between $1 million and $20 million) use to export their products and services.

**6. *Find your customer.*** Small businesses can rely on a host of export specialists to help them track down foreign customers. (Refer to Table 12.1 for a list of some of the resources available from the government.) The U.S. Department of Commerce and the International Trade Administration should be the first stops on any entrepreneur's agenda for going global. These agencies have the market research available for locating the best target markets for a particular company and specific customers in those markets. Industry Sector Analyses, International Market Insights, and Customized Market Analyses (CMAs) are just some of the reports and services global entrepreneurs

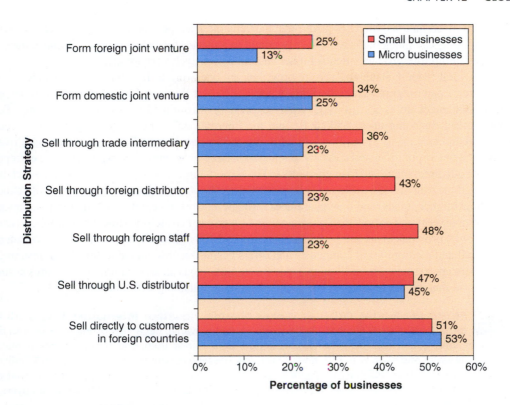

**FIGURE 12.8**

**Distribution Strategies for Exporting by Company Size**

*Source:* Based on Small and Medium Size Business Export Insights and Opportunities, CompTIA, 2010, p. 8.

find most useful. These agencies also have knowledgeable staff specialists experienced in the details of global trade and in the intricacies of foreign cultures. Michigan State University's GlobalEDGE (*http://globaledge.msu.edu*), an international trade information portal, also offers useful information on doing business in more than 200 countries, including directories, tutorials, online courses, and diagnostic tools designed to help companies determine their potential for conducting global business. The International Finance Corporation's Enterprise Surveys (*www .enterprisesurveys.org*) give entrepreneurs useful profiles of the business environments in 135 countries, including overviews of basic infrastructure and business regulations to corruption and business obstacles. Through its Gold and Platinum Key services, the U.S. Commercial Service provides entrepreneurs who want to take their companies global with a list of prescreened distributors and potential customers and arranges face-to-face meetings with them.

One of the most efficient and least expensive ways for entrepreneurs to locate potential customers for their companies' products and services is to participate in a trade mission. These missions usually are sponsored by either a federal or a state economic development agency or an industry trade association for the purpose of cultivating international trade by connecting domestic companies with prescreened potential trading partners overseas. A trade mission may focus on a particular industry or may cover several industries but target a particular country. "We set up meetings for them with distributors, suppliers, manufacturers, customers, accountants, law firms, the whole gamut, to be able to provide them with the necessary resources to get into that market," says Christian Bartley, president of the World Trade Center Wisconsin, an organization that regularly sponsors trade missions to foreign countries for Wisconsin entrepreneurs who are interested in exploring export markets.[53] On a recent trade mission trip to China sponsored by the Maine International Trade Center, representatives from 13 small companies from diverse industries participated in 77 matchmaking meetings with potential customers and distributors in just one week. Previous trade missions had resulted in sales increases from $3 million to $8 million for the small companies involved. Lighthouse Imaging, a company based in Portland, Maine, that manufactures optical equipment for the medical industry, participated in the trade mission because China is the second-largest market for medical devices in the world. "We are looking forward to developing the Chinese market for the optical medical products that we manufacture and export," says Lighthouse Imaging chief technology officer Dennis Leiner. "I expect great things to happen."[54]

**7. *Find financing.*** One of the biggest barriers to small business exports is lack of financing. The trouble is that bankers and other sources of capital don't always understand the intricacies of international sales and view financing them as highly risky ventures. In addition, among major industrialized nations, the U.S. government spends the least per capita to promote exports. Access to adequate financing is a crucial ingredient in a successful export program because the cost of generating foreign sales often is higher and collection cycles are longer.

Several federal, state, and private programs are operating to fill this export financing void, however. Loan programs from the SBA include its Export Working Capital program (90 percent loan guarantees up to $5 million), Export Express (a streamlined approach to obtaining SBA-guaranteed financing up to $500,000), and the International Trade Loan program (90 percent loan guarantees up to $5 million). In addition, the Export-Import Bank, the Overseas Private investment Corporation, and a variety of state-sponsored programs offer export-minded entrepreneurs both direct loans and loan guarantees. The Export-Import Bank (*www.exim.gov*), which has financed the sale of $456 billion in U.S. exports since 1934, provides small exporters with export credit insurance, loans, and loan guarantees through its working capital line of credit and a variety of preexport and export loan programs. The Overseas Private Investment Corporation (*www.opic.gov/*) provides loans and loan guarantees up to $250 million to support foreign investments by small and medium-sized companies and offers businesses discounted political risk insurance. The Bankers Association for Foreign Trade (*www.baft.org*) is an association of 150 banks around the world that matches exporters needing foreign trade financing with interested banks.

**ENTREPRENEURIAL PROFILE: Vankee Sharma: Aquatech International** Aquatech International, a small company in Canonsburg, Pennsylvania, began exporting in 1994 with the help of loan guarantees from the Export-Import Bank. Since then, the company, which makes industrial water and wastewater treatment products, has seen its export sales increase from $1 million annually to more than $42 million. "Ex-Im Bank support of our exports gives us opportunities that we otherwise would not have," says CEO Vankee Sharma. "The Ex-Im Bank allows us to serve buyers in many different countries. Exports now make up 40 to 60 percent of our business."[55]

**8. *Ship your goods.*** Export novices usually rely on international freight forwarders and custom-house agents—experienced specialists in overseas shipping—for help in navigating the bureaucratic morass of packaging requirements and paperwork demanded by customs. These specialists, also known as transport architects, are to exporters what travel agents are to passengers and normally charge relatively small fees for a valuable service. They move shipments of all sizes to destinations all over the world efficiently, saving entrepreneurs many headaches. Good freight forwarders understand U.S. export regulations, foreign import requirements, shipping procedures (such as packing, labeling, documenting, and insuring goods), customs processes, and maintaining proper records for paying tariffs. In addition, because they work for several companies, freight forwarders can aggregate payloads to negotiate favorable rates with shippers. "[A freight forwarder] is going to be sure that his client conforms with all the government regulations that apply to export cargo," explains the owner of an international freight forwarding business. "He acts as an agent of the exporter, and, in most circumstances, is like an extension of that exporter's traffic department." The Johnston Sweeper Company, a manufacturer of street sweepers, ships its 20,000-pound pieces of equipment worldwide with the help of an international freight forwarder.[56] Exporters can find an online directory of more than 1,000 freight forwarders located in 140 countries at Freightbook (*www.freightbook.net*). Another useful resource is the National Customs Brokers and Forwarders Association of America (*www.ncbfaa.org*), which represents 940 freight forwarders and customs brokers who work with more than 250,000 exporters and importers. Small businesses also can use fulfillment companies such as Shipwire, Amazon Fulfillment, and others that store and ship companies' products anywhere in the world. Table 12.5 features common international shipping terms and their meaning.

**9. *Collect your money.*** Collecting foreign accounts can be more complex than collecting domestic ones; however, by picking their customers carefully and checking their credit references closely, entrepreneurs can minimize bad-debt losses. Businesses engaging in international sales can use four primary payment methods (ranked from least risky to most risky): cash in advance, a letter of credit, a bank (or documentary) draft, and an open account. Collecting cash in advance is the safest method of selling to foreign customers because it eliminates the risk of collection problems and provides immediate cash flow. However, requiring cash payments up front may limit severely a small company's base of foreign customers.

One tool that small exporters can use to minimize the risk of bad-debt losses on foreign sales is export credit insurance, which protects a company against the nonpayment of its open accounts due to commercial and political problems. The cost of export credit insurance usually is a very

**TABLE 12.5  Common International Shipping Terms and Their Meaning**

| Shipping Term | Seller's Responsibility | Buyer's Responsibility | Shipping Method(s) Used |
|---|---|---|---|
| FOB ("Free on Board") Seller | Deliver goods to carrier and provide export license and clean on-board receipt. Bear risk of loss until goods are delivered to carrier. | Pay shipping, freight, and insurance charges. Bear risk of loss while goods are in transit. | All |
| FOB ("Free on Board") Buyer | Deliver goods to the buyer's place of business and provide export license and clean on-board receipt. Pay shipping, freight, and insurance charges. Bear risk of loss until goods are delivered to buyer. | Accept delivery of goods after documents are tendered. | All |
| FAS ("Free Along Side"), vessel | Deliver goods alongside ship. Provides an "alongside" receipt. | Provide export license and proof of delivery of the goods to the carrier. Bear risk of loss once goods are delivered to the carrier. | Ship |
| CFR ("Cost and Freight") | Deliver goods to carrier, obtain export licenses, and pay export taxes. Provide buyer with clean bill of lading. Pay freight and shipping charges. Bear risk of loss until goods are delivered to buyer. | Pay insurance charges. Accept delivery of goods after documents are tendered. | Ship |
| CIF ("Cost, Insurance, and Freight") | Same as CFR plus pay insurance charges and provide buyer with insurance policy. | Accept delivery of goods after documents are tendered. | Ship |
| CPT ("Carriage Paid to . . .") | Deliver goods to carrier, obtain export licenses, and pay export taxes. Provide buyer with clean transportation documents. Pay shipping and freight charges. | Pay insurance charges. Accept delivery of goods after documents are tendered. | All |
| CIP ("Carriage and Insurance Paid to . . .") | Same as CPT plus pay insurance charges and provide buyer with insurance policy. | Accept delivery of goods after documents are tendered. | All |
| DDU ("Delivered Duty Unpaid") | Obtain export license, pay insurance charges, and provide buyer documents for taking delivery. | Take delivery of goods and pay import duties. | All |
| DDP ("Delivered Duty Paid") | Obtain export license and pay import duty, pay insurance charges, and provide buyer documents for taking delivery. | Take delivery of goods. | All |

Source: Based on *Guide to the Finance of International Trade*, edited by Gordon Platt (HBSC Trade Services, Marine Midland Bank, and the Journal of Commerce), *http://infoserv2.ita.doc.gov/efm/efm.nsf/503d177e3c63f0b48525675900112e24/6218a8703573b32985256759004c41f3/$FILE/Finance_.pdf*, pp. 6–10.

small percentage of the sale that the company is insuring. Private insurers and the Export-Import Bank offer export credit insurance. The Ex-Im Bank provides more than $6 billion in export credit insurance annually to small businesses.

**ENTREPRENEURIAL PROFILE: Martin Weinberg: Xamax Industries** Xamax Industries, a small company in Seymour, Connecticut, that makes specialty paper, plastics, and nonwoven fabrics, uses export credit insurance from the Ex-Im Bank to lower the risk associated with its foreign sales. Prior to purchasing insurance from the Ex-Im Bank, Xamax Industries restricted its export sales because of the risk it incurred on open account sales to foreign customers. Then Xamax's president, Martin Weinberg, learned about the Ex-Im Bank's export insurance that protects against nonpayment on international sales and quickly signed on. "The Ex-Im Bank policy lets us sell products where we otherwise could not have sold them," says Weinberg. "We have added sales in China, Spain, Mexico, Canada, and Malaysia—all sales that would not have happened without [Ex-Im Bank] insurance."[57]

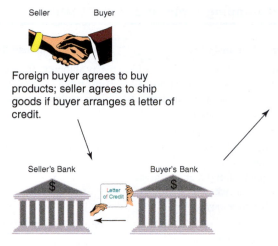

**FIGURE 12.9**

**How a Letter of Credit Works**

Seller        Buyer

Foreign buyer agrees to buy products; seller agrees to ship goods if buyer arranges a letter of credit.

Seller ships goods to buyer according to letter of credit's terms and submits shipping documents to bank issuing letter of credit.

Seller's Bank        Buyer's Bank

Buyer requests that his bank grant a letter of credit, which assures exporter payment if she presents documents proving goods were actually shipped. Bank makes out letter of credit to seller and sends it to seller's bank (called the confirming bank).

Buyer's bank makes payment to seller's (confirming) bank. Confirming bank then pays seller amount specified in letter of credit.

Financing foreign sales often involves special credit arrangements, such as letters of credit and bank (or documentary) drafts. A **letter of credit** is an agreement between an exporter's bank and the foreign buyer's bank that guarantees payment to the exporter for a specific shipment of goods. In essence, a letter of credit reduces the financial risk for the exporter by substituting a bank's creditworthiness for that of the purchaser (see Figure 12.9). A **bank draft** is a document the seller draws on the buyer's bank, requiring the bank to pay the face amount (the purchase price of the goods) either on sight (a sight draft) or on a specified date (a time draft) once the goods are shipped. Bank drafts lower international sellers' risk because the issuing bank guarantees payment for the buyer's purchase. Rather than use letters of credit or bank drafts, some exporters simply sell to foreign customers on open account. In other words, they ship the goods to a foreign customer without any guarantee of payment. This method is riskiest because collecting a delinquent account from a foreign customer is even more difficult than collecting past-due payments from a domestic customer. The parties to an international deal should always come to an agreement in advance on an acceptable method of payment.

 **Lessons from the Street-Smart Entrepreneur**

# Finding Your Place in the World

For 20 years, Steve McMenamin designed and sold luxury goods such as luggage, jewelry, watches, and eyewear for the legendary Porsche Design Group. McMenamin was inspired to create eyeglasses made from wood rather than plastic with bold designs that would provide their wearers with a more comfortable fit and started iWood Eco Design. Based in Louisville, Kentucky, iWood Eco Design manufactures its unique glasses by hand in the midwestern United States from reclaimed wood that is used to decorate the interior of luxury private jets. McMenamin purchases the scraps of exotic wood, including zebrawood, bamboo, bubinga,

and Makassar ebony, from local wood laminators that otherwise would go to waste but are ideal for making iWood Eco Design's glasses. Each pair of sunglasses is meticulously sanded by hand and assembled with optical-quality lenses by Carl Zeiss and imported Italian temple grips. Feather-light and perfectly balanced, they look and fit like no other eyewear and are stronger and lighter than glasses made from plastic frames.

McMenamin recognized the potential to sell his company's stylish, unique, and eco-friendly glasses globally. "Many products on the market claim to be 'eco-friendly,' yet they are not," he says.

A pair of iWood Eco Design's wood-framed glasses.
*Source:* Newscom.

"That's where we have a competitive advantage. Our products are Forest Stewardship Council certified, harvested by sustainable methods, and use glue and protective coatings that are formaldehyde free and emit no VOCs." The young company had never sold its products internationally, however, and McMenamin's first task was to identify the countries that would be most interested in eco-friendly, high-fashion products. As an international newcomer, he preferred to work through foreign distributors but didn't know how to find reliable distributors in foreign countries.

Fortunately, McMenamin discovered the U.S. Commercial Service office in nearby Indianapolis, Indiana, and asked the global trade experts there for help. iWood Eco Design qualified for the Commercial Service's Trade Show Assistance Program, which provides financing to small companies to attend international trade shows. With the Commercial Service's help, McMenamin identified the Premiere Classe Show in Paris, France, as the ideal venue for establishing relationships with international vendors and distributors of fashion accessories. The U.S. Commercial Service office in Paris helped iWood Eco Design land an invitation to the trade show and helped promote the company among global fashion companies such as Hermes and Louis Vuitton before the show opened. At the Paris trade show, the company landed deals with distributors in France and in the United Kingdom. When McMenamin returned home, he began receiving orders from distributors across Europe and in Russia, Australia, and the Middle East. "I was excited that our product had even stronger potential in Europe than in the United States," he says. "The U.S. Commercial Service in Indiana worked with us all the way, providing counseling on European Union tariffs and taxes, distribution methods, and providing market intelligence."

iWood Eco Design is now a global business, selling its unique glasses to customers in France, the United Kingdom, Russia, New Zealand, Australia, China, Canada, Spain, Italy, Germany, Denmark, and other nations. "The majority of our sales are international," says McMenamin, "and we expect tremendous growth in international sales. "Exporting has provided us with a steady stream of business through the economic downturn [in the United States]." The company also is planning to expand its reach into global markets by introducing new product lines that include earrings, necklaces, bracelets, and rings made from the same exotic, reclaimed wood from which its glasses are made.

What lessons can other entrepreneurs learn from iWood Eco Design's successful foray into international markets?

- ***Analyze foreign markets carefully to determine which ones offer the most promising opportunities for your products or services.*** Start by conducting secondary research to develop a short list of countries before investing in more intensive research, travel time, and money to conduct primary research on the few countries on your short list. Research showed iWood Eco Designs that global demand existed for its products but that customers in Germany and Japan were extremely interested in their eco-fashion products.

- ***Focus on a single market or very small number of similar markets at the outset.*** Entering global markets requires a company to invest its resources, including people's time. Don't make the mistake of taking a broad "shotgun" approach, trying to enter a large number of markets at once. Instead, focus your resources on the most promising country first, learn from your mistakes, and establish a foothold there before entering other markets.

- ***Learn everything you can about your target country.*** The business practices, customs, and tastes of a country are unique and reflect its culture. Make sure that you invest the necessary time to learn how people in the country expect to do business. Is calling other business executives by their first names acceptable? Do potential business partners expect to build relationships with your through informal dinners where no "business" is discussed or attending social events before negotiating a contract? Are certain gestures considered taboo in a culture? Is gift giving appropriate? If so, what kinds of gifts are suitable?

- ***Discover whether you must modify your product or service to suit local tastes.*** Many companies have discovered that to be successful in foreign markets, they must modify the size of their products, their packages' colors, labels, and other characteristics to suit local customers' preferences. Usually, the required modifications are not extensive, but making them is one key to success and requires research.

- ***Take steps to protect your company.*** Small companies incur risks such as nonpayment, a customer's bankruptcy, goods that are not delivered, and many others when doing business with domestic customers. Those same risks apply to international sales as well, but their challenges are exacerbated by distance. Small companies that export their goods and services can use standard business tools, such as letters of credit, bank drafts, and export credit insurance, to minimize their risk of loss.

- ***Attend a trade show.*** One of the best ways to reach a large number of potential distributors or customers in another country is to attend a trade show that focuses on your industry. The Premiere Classe Show in Paris was the key to opening doors to international markets for iWood Eco Design. Be sure to thoroughly investigate the profile of the show's attendees before signing on, however, to make sure that they are your target customers.

- ***Use the resources that are available to small businesses as they go global.*** Steve McMenamin relied on the expertise of the people at the U.S. Commercial Service to help his company navigate the intricacies of the global market. "The Commercial Service has been instrumental in providing us with information and support for our exporting efforts," he says. As you learned in this chapter, there are many helpful resources available; use them!

*Sources:* Based on "Export Success Stories: iWood Eco Design," *Export.gov*, January 11, 2013, *http://new.export.gov/community/users/export-success-stories/posts/183-success-story-iwood-eco-design*; Tony Baker, "Special Report: Ten Mistakes Exporters Make and Ways to Avoid Them," Market Access Worldwide, *www.maww.com/Articles/MistakesReport-04-09-27.pdf*.

## Establishing International Locations

Once established in international markets, some small businesses set up permanent locations there. Establishing an office or a factory in a foreign land can require a substantial investment reaching beyond the budgets of many small companies. In addition, setting up an international office can be an incredibly frustrating experience in some countries. Business infrastructure is in disrepair or is nonexistent. Getting a telephone line installed can take months in some places, and finding reliable methods to ship goods to customers is challenging. Securing necessary licenses and permits from bureaucrats often takes more than filing the necessary paperwork; in some nations, bureaucrats expect payments to "grease the wheels of justice." According to Ernst and Young's Global Fraud Survey, 39 percent of executives in 43 nations report that bribery or corrupt practices occur frequently in their countries. Alarmingly, 15 percent of respondents say that they are prepared to make cash payments to win or retain business.[58] The Foreign Corrupt Practice Act, passed in 1977, considers bribing foreign officials to be a criminal act. One study by the World Bank of "grease payments" made for the purpose of minimizing the red tape imposed by foreign regulations concludes that the payments do *not* work; in fact, companies that make them actually experience *greater* government scrutiny and red tape in their international transactions.[59] Finally, finding the right person to manage an international office is crucial to success; it also is a major challenge, especially for small businesses. Small companies usually have lean management staffs and cannot afford to send key people abroad without running the risk of losing their focus.

Small companies that establish international locations can reap significant benefits. Start-up costs are lower in some foreign countries (but not all!), and lower labor costs can produce significant savings as well. In addition, by locating in a country, a business learns firsthand how its culture influences business and how it can satisfy customers' demands most effectively. In essence, the business becomes a local corporate citizen. Clothing retailer J. Crew, which has only one store outside the United States in Toronto, Canada, recently began implementing plans to open stores in key cities in Europe and Asia. Although the company sold only to online customers in the United States, Canada, and Japan, 10 percent of the traffic on its Web site is from outside North America. With its "Hello, World" campaign, J. Crew began testing the potential for its products in foreign countries by shipping its clothing to online customers in 107 countries, ranging from China and Brazil to Latvia and Estonia. Determining where its online orders originate will tell managers where to open international J. Crew retail locations, reducing the risk of the company's international expansion.[60]

## Importing and Outsourcing

In addition to selling their goods in foreign markets, small companies also buy goods from distributors and manufacturers in foreign markets. In fact, the intensity of price competition in many industries—from textiles and handbags to industrial machinery and computers—means that more companies now shop the world market, looking for the lowest prices they can find. In the United States alone, businesses import $2.7 billion worth of goods and services annually.[61] Because labor costs in countries such as Thailand, Vietnam, Bangladesh, India, and China are far below those in other nations, businesses there can produce goods and services at very low prices. Increasingly, these nations are home to well-educated, skilled workers who are paid far less than comparable workers in the United States or northern and western Europe (see Figure 12.10). For instance, a computer programmer in the United States might earn $75,000 a year, but in Latvia, a computer programmer doing the same work earns $15,000 a year or less. As a result, many companies either import goods or outsource work directly to manufacturers in countries where costs are far lower than they would be domestically. According to TPI, a leading outsourcing consulting firm, global outsourcing is a $464 billion per year industry (up from $232 billion in 2000).[62]

**ENTREPRENEURIAL PROFILE: Hussein and Hassan Iddrissu: Roadstarr Motorsports**
Twin brothers Hussein and Hassan Iddrissu, immigrants from Ghana, left their corporate jobs and used personal savings and investments from family members to start Roadstarr Motorsports, a Los Angeles–based company that imports high-performance cars from Europe and customizes them to suit the tastes of their upscale owners. Roadstarr Motorsports offers a wide array of customizing options, including sporty wheels, upscale interiors, fancy paint jobs, trim kits, multimedia packages, and almost anything else that customers can imagine. The brothers have generated plenty of "buzz"

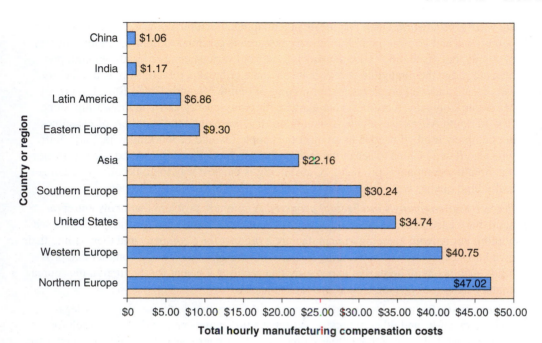

**FIGURE 12.10**

**Total Hourly Manufacturing Compensation Costs for Selected Countries and Regions**

*Source:* Based on *International Labor Comparisons,* Bureau of Labor Statistics, 2012.

for their company by creating unique, customized vehicles for several rap stars, professional basketball players, and international royalty and using social media such as Facebook and Twitter to show off their latest designs. Buoyed by their success in the United States, the Iddrissus are planning to take Roadstarr Motorsports to Moscow, Russia, which has the highest concentration of billionaires in the world.[63]

Finding the right international suppliers and manufacturers has a direct impact on a small company's reputation and financial performance. Web sites such as *Alibaba.com*, *MadeInChina.com*, and *GlobalSources.com* are good places to start. Entrepreneurs who are considering importing goods and service or outsourcing their service or manufacturing jobs to foreign countries should follow these steps:

- *Make sure that importing or outsourcing is right for your business.* Even though foreign manufacturers often can provide items at significant cost savings, using them may not always be the best business decision. Entrepreneurs sometimes discover that achieving the lowest price may require a tradeoff of other important factors such as quality and speed of delivery. When Patrick Kruse, owner of Ruff Wear, the business that sells dog booties, began outsourcing many of his company's products to Chinese factories, he discovered that the quality of the goods was poor. "We actually had to refuse some shipments, which really hurt our business," he says.[64] In addition, some foreign manufacturers require sizeable minimum orders, perhaps $100,000 or more, before they produce a product.

- *Establish a target cost for your product.* Before setting off on a global shopping spree, entrepreneurs first should determine exactly what they can afford to spend on manufacturing a product and make a profit on it. Given the low labor costs of many foreign manufacturers, products that are the most labor intensive make good candidates for outsourcing.

- *Do your research before you leave home.* Investing time in basic research about the industry and potential suppliers in foreign lands is essential before setting foot on foreign soil. Useful resources are plentiful, and entrepreneurs should use them. Refer to Table 12.2 for a list of some of the most popular sources of information on foreign countries and the companies that are based there.

- *Be sensitive to cultural differences.* When making contacts, setting up business appointments, or calling on prospective manufacturers in foreign lands, make sure you understand what is accepted business behavior and what is not. Once again, this is where your research pays off; be sure to study the cultural nuances of doing business in the countries you will visit.

- *Do your groundwork.* Once you locate potential manufacturers, contact them to set up appointments and go visit them. Preliminary research is essential to finding reliable sources of supply, but "face time" with representatives from various companies allows entrepreneurs to judge the intangible factors that can make or break a relationship. Is the factory safe, clean, and well organized? After months of online research, Cathy Raff, founder of My Stone Company, a business that markets religious jewelry and The Friendship Stone, flew to South Africa to evaluate several mines that were potential suppliers of the stones her company used. "I needed to go meet the people I would be working with," says Raff, who also flew to China to select the factory that produces the embroidered suede pouches that hold her company's products. "Outsourcing is the best way to go because you can get really high quality work from these countries at much lower rates," she says.[65]

- *Protect your company's intellectual property.* A common problem that many entrepreneurs have encountered with outsourcing is "knockoffs." Some foreign manufacturers see nothing wrong with agreeing to manufacture a product for a company and then selling their own knockoff version of it. Securing a nondisclosure agreement and a contract that prohibits such behavior helps, but experts say that securing a patent for the item in the source country itself (not just the United States) is a good idea.

- *Select a manufacturer.* Using quality, speed of delivery, level of trust, degree of legal protection, costs, and other factors, select the manufacturer that can do the best job for your company. Be aware that delivery times may be longer—sometimes much longer—for outsourced goods. Items that domestic suppliers can supply within a week or two may take months to arrive from some foreign countries.

- *Provide an exact model of the product you want manufactured.* Providing a manufacturer with an actual model of the item to be manufactured will save lots of time, mistakes, and problems. One entrepreneur learned this lesson the hard way when he submitted a rough prototype of a product to a Chinese factory with which he had contracted for production. When the first shipment of the products arrived, he was shocked to see that they were exact duplicates—including imperfections and flaws—of the prototype that he had submitted!

- *Stay in constant contact with the manufacturer and try to build a long-term relationship.* Communication is a key to building and maintaining a successful relationship with a foreign manufacturer. Weekly teleconferences, e-mails, and periodic visits are essential to making sure that your company gets the performance you expect from a foreign manufacturer.

Going global by employing one or more of these nine strategies can put tremendous strain on a small company, but the benefits of cracking international markets can be significant. Not only does going global offer attractive sales and profit possibilities, but it also strengthens the company's competitive skills and enhances its overall reputation. Pleasing tough foreign customers also keeps companies on their competitive toes.

## Barriers to International Trade

**4.**

Discuss the major barriers to international trade and their impact on the global economy.

Governments have always used a variety of barriers to block free trade among nations in an attempt to protect businesses within their own borders. The benefit of protecting their own companies, however, comes at the expense of foreign businesses, which face limited access to global markets. Ultimately, customers in nations that restrict free trade pay the price in the form of higher prices and smaller supplies of goods available. Numerous trade barriers—both domestic and international—restrict the freedom of businesses in global trading. Despite these barriers, international trade has grown to more than $17.8 trillion.[66]

### Domestic Barriers

Sometimes the biggest barriers potential exporters face are right here at home. Three major domestic roadblocks are common: attitude, information, and financing. Perhaps the biggest barrier to small businesses exporting is the attitude: "I'm too small to export. That's just for big corporations." The first lesson of exporting is "Take nothing for granted about who can export and what you can and cannot export." The first step to building an export program is recognizing that the opportunity to export exists.

Another reason entrepreneurs neglect international markets is a lack of information about how to get started. The key to success in international markets is choosing the correct target market and designing the appropriate strategy to reach it. That requires access to information and research. Although a variety of government and private organizations make volumes of exporting and international marketing information available, many small business owners never use it. A successful global marketing strategy also recognizes that not all international markets are the same. Companies must be flexible and willing to make adjustments to their products and services, promotional campaigns, packaging, and sales techniques.

Another significant obstacle is the lack of export financing available. A common complaint among small exporters is that they lose export business simply because they cannot get the financing to support it. Financial institutions that serve small companies often do not have experience in conducting international business and simply deny loans for international transactions as being too risky.

## International Barriers

Domestic barriers are not the only ones that export-minded entrepreneurs must overcome. Trading nations also erect obstacles to free trade. Two types of international barriers are common: tariff and nontariff.

**TARIFF BARRIERS** A **tariff** is a tax, or duty, that a government imposes on goods and services imported into that country. Imposing tariffs raises the price of the imported goods—making them less attractive to consumers—and protects the makers of comparable domestic products and services. Established in the United States in 1790 by Alexander Hamilton, the tariff system generated the majority of federal revenues for about 100 years. Today, the *Harmonized Tariff Schedule*, which sets tariffs for products imported into the United States, includes 37,000 categories of goods. The United States imposes tariffs on thousands of items ranging from brooms and fish fillets to costume jewelry and fence posts. American tariffs vary greatly depending on the type of product. For instance, women's bathing suits made from synthetic fibers carry a 24.9 percent tariff, but the tariff on women's bathing suits made from other materials is 13.2 percent.[67] The average tariff on goods imported into the United States is 1.8 percent (compared to the global average of 2.7 percent), but the U.S. International Trade Commission (ITC) estimates that eliminating tariffs would expand U.S. exports by $9 billion and increase imports by $11.5 billion.[68] Nations across the globe rely on tariffs to protect local manufacturers of certain products, and tariff rates vary greatly among nations. Singapore, Switzerland, and Hong Kong impose no tariffs at all on imported goods, but Bermuda has the highest average tariff rate in the world at 26.1 percent.[69] When a small company's products are subject to a country's high tariffs, exporting to that nation becomes much more difficult because remaining price competitive with products made by local manufacturers is virtually impossible.

**NONTARIFF BARRIERS** Many nations have lowered the tariffs they impose on products and services brought into their borders, but they rely on other nontariff structures as protectionist trade barriers.

*Quotas* Rather than impose a direct tariff on certain imported products, nations often use quotas to protect their industries. A **quota** is a limit on the amount of a product imported into a country. The United States imposes quotas on sugar imports from 40 countries, limiting the amount of sugar they can sell in the U.S. each year. The result of these trade restrictions is that in the United States, sugar sells for 69 cents per pound, but the international market price is just 26 cents per pound, 62 percent lower.[70] Other countries impose quotas on everything from shoes to movies in an attempt to protect domestic industries. For instance, China allows only 34 foreign films to be released each year. In addition, foreigners can invest in Chinese cinemas, but they can own no more than 49 percent of the joint venture.[71]

*Embargoes* An **embargo** is a total ban on imports of certain products or all products from a particular nation. The motivation for embargoes is not always economic, but it also can involve political differences, environmental disputes, terrorism, and other issues. For instance, the United States imposes embargoes on products from nations it considers to be adversarial, including Cuba, Iran, Iraq, and North Korea, among others. An embargo on trade with Cuba, begun in 1962 when Fidel Castro nationalized all U.S. businesses on the island nation and formed an alliance with the Soviet Union, still exists today. In 1994, the United States lifted a total trade embargo against Vietnam that had stood since 1975, when Saigon fell into communist hands at the end of the Vietnam War. Today, the United States imports $18.5 billion worth of goods from Vietnam and exports goods worth $4.2 billion.[72]

*Dumping*  In an effort to grab market share quickly, some companies have been guilty of **dumping** products, selling large quantities of them in foreign countries at prices that are below those in the home country. The United States has been a dumping target for steel, televisions, tires, barbed wire, shoes, and computer chips in the past. Under the U.S. Antidumping Act, a company must prove that the foreign company's prices are lower here than in the home country and that U.S. companies are directly harmed. In response to a complaint from U.S.-based companies, the ITC recently ruled that manufacturers in Taiwan and Vietnam were dumping wire garment hangers illegally in the United States at unfairly low prices and, as a result, were damaging the ability of U.S. producers to compete. The ITC imposed tariffs ranging from 70 to 125 percent on wire hangers imported from Taiwan and Vietnam.[73]

*Piracy*  Another barrier to conducting business globally is the threat that counterfeit and pirated products pose to businesses and their customers. The World Customs Organization estimates that 5 to 7 percent of goods traded globally are counterfeit, costing the global economy $600 billion per year.[74] Pirates and counterfeiters ply their illegal, unethical trade to almost every kind of product, from designer handbags and smart phones to birth control pills and industrial equipment. Not only do counterfeit products erode the profitability of the companies that make the "genuine" articles, but they also can be dangerous or even deadly to consumers who purchase them. In the United States, the most commonly seized counterfeit goods (based on value) are handbags, watches and jewelry, apparel, consumer electronics, and footwear. China is the source of 72 percent of the counterfeit goods that are seized in the United States.[75]

## Political Barriers

Entrepreneurs who go global quickly discover a labyrinth of political tangles. Although many American business owners complain of excessive government regulation in the United States, they are often astounded by the complex web of governmental and legal regulations and barriers they encounter in foreign countries.

Companies doing business in politically risky lands face the very real dangers of government takeovers of private property; attempts at coups to overthrow ruling parties; kidnappings, bombings, and other violent acts against businesses and their employees; and other threatening events. Companies' investments of millions of dollars may evaporate overnight in the wake of a government coup or the passage of a law nationalizing an industry (giving control of an entire industry to the government). In 2005, Jeff Ake, owner of Equipment Express, was kidnapped by militants in Iraq while installing bottling equipment that his Laporte, Indiana, company manufactured. His kidnappers called his wife to demand a ransom, and a video of Ake being held at gunpoint appeared on Arabic television network Al-Jazeera. His wife and four children still do not know what happened to Ake.[76]

## Business Barriers

American companies doing business internationally quickly learn that business practices and regulations in foreign lands can be quite different from those in the United States. Simply duplicating the practices they have adopted (and have used successfully) in the domestic market and using them in foreign markets is not always a good idea. Perhaps the biggest shock comes in the area of human resources management, where international managers discover that practices common in the United States, such as overtime, women workers, and employee benefits, are restricted, disfavored, or forbidden in other cultures. Business owners new to international business sometimes are shocked at the wide range of labor costs they encounter and the accompanying wide range of skilled labor available. In some countries, what appear to be "bargain" labor rates turn out to be excessively high after accounting for the quality and productivity of the labor force and the mandated benefits their governments impose—from company-sponsored housing, meals, and clothing to required profit sharing and extended vacations. For instance, in many European

Counterfeit goods being destroyed.
*Source:* Frank Perry/Getty Images.

nations, laws mandate that companies provide a minimum of 20 paid vacation days in addition to paid holidays, giving workers an average of nearly 35 days off a year.[77]

## Cultural Barriers

The **culture** of a nation includes the beliefs, values, views, and mores that its inhabitants share. Differences in cultures among nations create another barrier to international trade. The diversity of languages, business philosophies, practices, and traditions make international trade more complex than selling to the business down the street. Entrepreneurs who want to do business in international markets must have a clear understanding and appreciation of the cultures in which they plan to do business. Consider the following examples:

- A U.S. entrepreneur, eager to expand into Europe, arrives at his company's potential business partner's headquarters in France. Confidently, he strides into the meeting room, enthusiastically pumps his host's hand, slaps him on the back, and says, "Tony, I've heard a great deal about you; please, call me Bill." Eager to explain the benefits of his product, he opens his briefcase and gets right down to business. The French executive politely excuses himself and leaves the room before negotiations ever begin, shocked by the American's rudeness and ill manners. Rudeness and ill manners? Yes—from the French executive's perspective.

- Another American business owner flies to Tokyo to close a deal with a Japanese executive. He is pleased when his host invites him to play a round of golf shortly after he arrives. He plays well and manages to win by a few strokes. The Japanese executive invites him to play again the next day, and again he wins by a few strokes. Invited to play another round the following day, the American asks, "But when are we going to start doing business?" His host, surprised by the question, says, "But we *have* been doing business."

- The CEO of a successful small company is in China negotiating with several customers on deals, any of which would be significant to the company. On the verge of closing one deal, the CEO sends in his place to the negotiation a young sales representative, thinking that the only thing that remained is to sign the contract. At the meeting, the manager of the Chinese company remarks, "Ah, you are about the same age as my son." Much to the U.S. entrepreneur's surprise, the deal falls through.[78]

When American businesspeople enter international markets for the first time, they often are amazed at the differences in foreign cultures' habits and customs. In the first scenario described, for instance, had the entrepreneur done his homework, he would have known that the French are very formal (back slapping is *definitely* taboo!) and do not typically use first names in business relationships (even among longtime colleagues). In the second scenario, a global manager would have known that the Japanese place a tremendous importance on developing personal relationships before committing to any business deals. Thus, he would have seen the golf games for what they really were: an integral part of building a business relationship. In the final scenario, the U.S. entrepreneur did not understand that status (*shehui dengji*) is extremely important to the Chinese. The Chinese executive would consider negotiating a deal with an executive whose rank in the organization did not at least equal his to be a great insult. That deal was doomed the minute the lower-level salesperson walked into the room.

Understanding and heeding these often subtle cultural differences is one of the most important keys to international business success. "There's more to business than just business," says one writer, "particularly when confronting the subtleties of deeply ingrained cultural customs, conventions, and protocols that abound in today's global marketplace."[79] Conducting a business meeting with a foreign executive in the same manner as one with an American business person could doom the deal from the outset. Business customs, behaviors, and even gestures that are acceptable—even expected—in this country may be taboo in others. For instance, the hand gesture that Americans routinely use to indicate "OK" is considered rude and offensive in many countries in the Middle East and in Brazil.

Entrepreneurs who fail to learn the differences in the habits and customs of the cultures in which they hope to do business are at a distinct disadvantage. When it comes to conducting international business, a lack of understanding of cultures and business practices can be as great a barrier to structuring and implementing a business transaction as an error in the basic assumptions of the deal. Consider, for instance, the American who was in the final stages of contract negotiations with an Indonesian company. Given the size of the contract and his distance from home, the American business executive was nervous. Sitting across from his Indonesian counterpart, the American propped his feet up. Obviously angered, the Indonesian business owner stormed out of the room, refusing to sign the contract and leaving the American executive totally bewildered. Only later did he discover that exposing the soles of one's shoes to an Indonesian is an insult. Profuse apologies and some delicate negotiations salvaged the deal.[80]

Inaccurate translations of documents into other languages often pose embarrassing problems for companies conducting international business. In other cases, mistranslated ads have left foreign locals scratching their heads, wondering why a company's advertising message would say *that*! For example, when an ad for Kentucky Fried Chicken that was supposed to say "Finger lickin' good" was translated into Chinese, it came out as "Eat your fingers off." An ad for the Parker Pen Company that was supposed to say "Avoid embarrassment" in Spanish actually said "Avoid pregnancy," leaving Parker Pen executives quite embarrassed themselves.[81] Nike issued an apology to customers in Ireland after the company marketed an athletic shoe named the "Black and Tan," not realizing that in Ireland, the Black and Tans refers to a paramilitary group that massacred civilians during the Irish war for independence from Great Britain.[82]

## International Trade Agreements

**5.**

Describe the trade agreements that have the greatest influence on foreign trade.

In an attempt to boost world trade, nations have created a variety of trade agreements over the years. The United States has 20 trade agreements with other nations.[83] Although hundreds of agreements are paving the way for free trade across the world, the following stand out with particular significance: the World Trade Organization, the North American Free Trade Agreement, and the Dominican Republic-Central American Free Trade Agreement.

### World Trade Organization

The World Trade Organization (WTO) was established in January 1995 and replaced the General Agreement of Tariffs and Trade (GATT), the first global tariff agreement, which was created in 1947 and designed to reduce tariffs among member nations. The WTO, currently with 158 member countries, is the only international organization that establishes rules for trade among nations. Its member countries represent 97 percent of all world trade. The rules and agreements of the WTO, called the multilateral trading system, are the result of negotiations among its members. The WTO actively implements the rules established by the Uruguay Round negotiations of GATT from 1986 to 1994 and continues to negotiate additional trade agreements. The ninth round of negotiations, the Doha Development Agenda, began in 2001 and is still under way. Through the agreements of the WTO, members commit themselves to nondiscriminatory trade practices and to reducing barriers to free trade. Member countries receive guarantees that their exports will be treated fairly and consistently in other member countries' markets. The WTO's General Agreement on Trade in Services addresses specific industries, including banking, insurance, telecommunications, and tourism. In addition, the WTO's intellectual property agreement, which covers patents, copyrights, and trademarks, defines rules for protecting ideas and creativity across borders.

In addition to the development of agreements among members, the WTO is involved in the resolution of trade disputes among members. The WTO system is designed to encourage dispute resolutions through consultation. If this approach fails, the WTO has a stage-by-stage procedure that can culminate in a ruling by a panel of experts.

## North American Free Trade Agreement

The North American Free Trade Agreement (NAFTA) created the world's largest free trade zone among Canada, Mexico, and the United States. A **free trade zone** is an association of countries that have agreed to eliminate trade barriers—both tariff and nontariff—among partner nations. Under the provisions of NAFTA, these barriers were eliminated for trade among the three countries, but each remained free to set its own tariffs on imports from nonmember nations.

NAFTA forged a unified U.S.–Canada–Mexico market of 478 million people with a total annual output of more than $19.2 trillion of goods and services. This important trade agreement binds together the three nations on the North American continent into a single trading unit stretching from the Yukon to the Yucatan. NAFTA has made trade less cumbersome and more profitable for companies of all sizes and has opened new export opportunities for many businesses. Since NAFTA's passage, trade among the three nations has more than tripled.

## The Dominican Republic-Central America Free Trade Agreement

The Dominican Republic-Central America Free Trade Agreement (CAFTA-DR) is to Central America what NAFTA is to North America. The agreement, which was implemented in stages between 2006 and 2008, is designed to promote free trade among the United States and six Central American countries: Costa Rica, El Salvador, Guatemala, Honduras, the Dominican Republic, and Nicaragua. Annual trade between the United States and these Central American countries has grown from $35 billion before CAFTA to $56 billion today.[84] In addition to reducing tariffs among these nations, CAFTA-DR protects U.S. companies' investments and intellectual property in the region, simplifies the export process for U.S. companies, and provides easier access to Central American markets.

**ENTREPRENEURIAL PROFILE: Wilma Castro: International Export Sales** Lower tariffs and the elimination of other trade barriers through CAFTA-DR allowed International Export Sales, a small company in Santa Rose, Louisiana, to increase sales of its light industrial refrigeration and supermarket equipment to Central America. "Our business with Central America has increased 100 percent since CAFTA-DR took effect," says sales manager Wilma Castro. Because its exports sales have increased, the company has expanded its workforce from four employees to eight.[85]

## Conclusion

For a rapidly growing number of small businesses, conducting business on a global basis is the key to future success. A small company going global exposes itself to certain risks, but, if planned and executed properly, a global strategy can produce huge rewards. To remain competitive, businesses of all sizes must assume a global posture. Global effectiveness requires managers to be able to leverage workers' skills, company resources, and customer know-how across borders and throughout cultures across the world. Managers also must concentrate on maintaining competitive costs structures and focus on the core of every business—the *customer*! Robert G. Shaw, CEO of International Jensen Inc., a global maker of home and automobile stereo speakers, explains the importance of retaining that customer focus as his company pursues its global strategy: "We want [our customers] to have the attitude of [our] being across the street. If we're going to have a global company, we have to behave in that mode—whether [the customer is] across the street—or seven miles, seven minutes, or 7,000 miles away."[86]

Few businesses can afford the luxury of defining their target markets solely as the customers who live within the boundaries of their company's home borders. The manager of one global business who discourages the use of the word domestic among his employees says, "Where's 'domestic' when the world is your market?"[87] Although there are no surefire rules for going global, small businesses wanting to become successful international competitors should observe these guidelines:

- Make yourself at home in all three of the world's key markets—North America, Europe, and Asia. This triad of regions is forging a new world order in trade that will dominate global markets for years to come. Small companies that focus on business opportunities in the fast-growing economies of Brazil, Russia, India, and China are likely to benefit most because forecasts call for these four nations to account for 45 percent of global GDP by 2030, a significant increase from the 18 percent of global GDP that they currently produce.[88]

- Appeal to the similarities within the various regions in which you operate but recognize the differences in their specific cultures. Although the European Union, which produces 25.8 percent of global GDP, is a single trading bloc comprised of 27 countries with a combined population of 503 million people, smart entrepreneurs know that each country has its own cultural uniqueness and do not treat them as a unified market.[89]

- Be willing to commit the necessary resources to make your global efforts successful. Going global requires an investment of time, talent, money, and patience.

- Develop new products for the world market. Make sure your products and services measure up to world-class quality standards.

- Use the many resources available, such as the U.S. Commercial Service and the International Trade Administration, to research potential markets and to determine the ideal target market for your products.

- Familiarize yourself with foreign customs and languages; constantly scan, clip, and build a file on the cultures of countries where you are likely to do business—their lifestyles, values, customs, and business practices.

- Learn to understand your customers from the perspective of *their* culture, not your own. Bridge cultural gaps by being willing to adapt your business practices to suit their preferences and customs.

- "Glocalize." Make global decisions about products, markets, and management but allow local employees to make tactical decisions about packaging, advertising, and service. Building relationships with local companies that have solid reputations in a region or a country can help overcome resistance, lower risks, and encourage residents to think of them as local companies.

- Make positive and preferably visible contributions to the local community. A company's social responsibility does not stop at the borders of its home country. Seattle-based Starbucks enhances its reputation in the Chinese communities in which it does business by donating coffee and snacks for local celebrations such as the Autumn Moon Festival. Once, when a group of protesters approached the U.S. embassy in Beijing, they stopped at a nearby Starbucks café to buy coffee. Rather than being the object of a protest, the branch actually saw sales climb![90]

- Train employees to think globally, send them on international trips, and equip them with state-of-the-art communications technology.

- Hire local managers to staff foreign offices and branches.

- Do whatever seems best wherever it seems best, even if people at home lose jobs or responsibilities.

- Consider using partners and joint ventures to break into foreign markets you cannot penetrate on your own.

- Be patient. International business often takes time to cultivate. "Selling to the world does not happen overnight," says Laurel Delaney, an international business expert and author. "It is a slow process that requires thought, discipline, and lots of hard work. However, go global today, and you could fulfill your own version of the American dream."[91]

By its very nature, going global can be a frightening experience for an entrepreneur considering the jump into international markets. Most of those who have already made the jump, however, have found that the benefits outweigh the risks and that their companies are much stronger because of it.

# Chapter Review

1. **Explain why "going global" has become an integral part of many entrepreneurs marketing strategies.**
   - Companies that move into international business can reap many benefits, including offsetting sales declines in the domestic market' increasing sales and profits, extending their products' life cycles, lowering manufacturing costs, improving competitive position, raising quality levels, and becoming more customer oriented.

2. **Describe the nine principal strategies for going global.**
   - Perhaps the simplest and least expensive way for a small business to begin conducting business globally is to establish a site on the Web. Companies wanting to sell goods on the Web should establish a secure ordering and payment system for online customers.
   - Trade intermediaries, such as export management companies, export trading companies, manufacturer's export agents, export merchants, resident buying offices, and foreign distributors, can serve as a small company's "export department."
   - In a domestic joint venture, two or more U.S. small companies form an alliance for the purpose of exporting their goods and services abroad. In a foreign joint venture, a domestic small business forms an alliance with a company in the target area.
   - Some small businesses enter foreign markets by licensing businesses in other nations to use their patents, trademarks, copyrights, technology, processes, or products.
   - Over the last decade, a growing number of franchises have been attracted to international markets to boost sales and profits as the domestic market has become increasingly saturated with outlets and much tougher to wring growth from. International franchisors sell virtually every kind of product or service imaginable in global markets. Most franchisors have learned that they must modify their products and services to suit local tastes and customs.
   - Some countries lack a hard currency that is convertible into other currencies, so companies doing business there must rely on countertrading or bartering. A countertrade is a transaction in which a business selling goods in a foreign country agrees to promote investment and trade in that country. Bartering involves trading goods and services for other goods and services.
   - Although small companies account for 97 percent of the companies involved in exporting, they generate only one-third of the nation's export sales. However, small companies, realizing the incredible profit potential it offers, are making exporting an ever-expanding part of their marketing plans.
   - One established in international markets, some small businesses set up permanent locations there. Although they can be very expensive to establish and maintain, international locations give businesses the opportunity to stay in close contact with their international customers.

3. **Explain how to build a thriving export program.**
   - Building a successful export program takes patience and research. Steps include the following: realize that even the tiniest firms have the potential to export, analyze your product or service, analyze your commitment to exporting, research markets and pick your target, develop a distribution strategy, find your customer, find financing, ship your goods, and collect your money.

4. **Discuss the major barriers to international trade and their impact on the global economy.**
   - Three domestic barriers to international trade are common: the attitude that "we're too small to export," lack of information on how to get started in global trade, and a lack of available financing.
   - International barriers include tariffs, quotas, embargoes, dumping, and political business, and cultural barriers.

5. **Describe the trade agreements that will have the greatest influence on foreign trade into the twenty-first century.**
   - Created in 1947, the GATT, the first global tariff agreement, was designed to reduce tariffs among member nations and to facilitate trade across the globe.
   - The WTO was established in 1995 and replaced GATT. The WTO has 158 member nations and represents over 97 percent of all global trade. The WTO is the governing body that resolves trade disputes among members.
   - NAFTA created a free trade area among Canada, Mexico, and the United States. The agreement created an association that knocked down trade barriers, both tariff and nontariff, among these partner nations.

# Discussion Questions

**12-1.** Why must entrepreneurs learn to think globally?

**12-2.** What forces are driving small businesses into international markets?

**12-3.** Outline the nine strategies that small businesses can use to go global.

**12-4.** Describe the various types of trade intermediaries small business owners can use. Explain the functions they perform.

**12-5.** What is a domestic joint venture? A foreign joint venture? What advantages does taking on an international partner through a joint venture offer? Disadvantages?

**12-6.** What mistakes are first-time exporters most likely to make? Outline the steps a small company should take to establish a successful export program.

**12-7.** What are the benefits of establishing international locations? Disadvantages?

**12-8.** Describe the barriers businesses face when trying to conduct business internationally. How can a small business owner overcome these obstacles?

**12-9.** What is a tariff? A quota? What impact do they have on international trade?

**12-10.** Thirty furniture makers in the United States recently asked the ITC to impose high tariffs on Chinese makers of wooden bedroom furniture for dumping their products in the U.S. market at extremely low prices. The U.S. manufacturers claimed that the Chinese imports single-handedly sent their industry into a deep tailspin. The Chinese factory owners contend that their low-cost furniture is the result of taking a labor-intensive product and building it with low-priced workers in high-tech modern factories. Identify the stakeholders in this trade dispute. What are the consequences for each stakeholder likely to be if the ITC were to impose tariffs on Chinese furniture? What impact do tariffs have on international trade? If you served on the ITC, what factors would you consider in making your decision? How would you vote in this case? Explain.

**12-11.** What impact have the WTO and NAFTA had on small companies wanting to go global? What provisions are included in these trade agreements?

**12-12.** What advice would you offer an entrepreneur interested in launching a global business effort?

# CHAPTER 13

# E-Commerce and Entrepreneurship

## Learning Objectives

**On completion of this chapter, you will be able to:**

1. Understand the factors an entrepreneur should consider before launching into e-commerce.

2. Explain the 10 myths of e-commerce and how to avoid falling victim to them.

3. Explain the basic strategies entrepreneurs should follow to achieve success in their e-commerce efforts.

4. Learn the techniques of designing a killer Web site.

5. Explain how companies track the results from their Web sites.

6. Describe how e-businesses ensure the privacy and security of the information they collect and store from the Web.

*Like China, the Internet is a huge new market. It's up to you to figure out what to do with it: use it as a prospecting tool, make connections with people, add value for your existing customers.*

—Larry Chase

*In the mental geography of e-commerce, distance has been eliminated. There is only one economy and one market.*

—Peter Drucker

E-commerce has transformed the way that entrepreneurs conduct business, enabling them to connect to vendors, suppliers, and customers via technology in ways that have never been possible before. The result is a new method of doing business that is turning traditional methods of commerce and industry on their heads. The most successful small companies are embracing the Internet, not merely as another advertising medium or marketing tool but as a mechanism for transforming their companies and changing *everything* about the way they do business. As these companies discover new, innovative ways to use the Internet and communications technology to connect with their vendors and suppliers and to serve their customers better, they are creating a new industrial order. Companies are using the Internet to lower their costs of doing business, to broaden their base of reliable suppliers of quality products and services, and to tap into new markets, some of which are in foreign lands. The Internet allows innovative entrepreneurs to create new business models that they can test, improve, and implement in record time. E-commerce has launched a business revolution. Just as in previous revolutions in the business world, some old players are ousted, and new leaders emerge. The winners are discovering new business opportunities, new ways of serving their customers, and new ways of organizing and operating their businesses.

Perhaps the most visible impact of the Internet is in the world of retailing. Nearly 2.5 billion people around the world are Internet users, creating a huge potential customer base for businesses that are prepared to capitalize on the opportunity. In the United States alone, e-commerce sales total $385 billion, and the growth rate of online sales continues to outpace the growth rate of in-store sales.[1] Although e-commerce will not replace traditional retailing, no retailer, from the smallest corner store to industry giant Wal-Mart, can afford to ignore the impact of the Internet on their businesses. Most shoppers still prefer to make their purchases in brick-and-mortar stores, but the convenience of e-commerce means that online sales are growing faster than in-store sales. Customers also are utilizing the Internet to change the way they shop, going into retail outlets where they test products before using their mobile devices to comparison shop for the best prices online. Known as **showrooming**, this trend poses a threat to retailers, particularly those who sell luxury items and consumer electronics, which are the items that customers most commonly showroom. Studies show that 7 percent of shoppers are habitual showroomers and that 50 percent of online sales are driven by showrooming.[2] Entrepreneurs are discovering that a cross-channel approach—meeting customers where they want to buy, whether in-store, online, from a mobile device such as a smart phone or a tablet, or some combination of these—is essential to combating showrooming.

Online companies can take orders at the speed of light from anywhere in the world and at any time of day. The Internet enables companies to collect more information on customers' shopping and buying habits than any other medium in history. This ability means that companies can focus their marketing efforts like never before—for instance, selling garden supplies to customers who are most likely to buy them and not wasting resources trying to sell to those who have no interest in gardening. The capacity to track customers' Web-based shopping habits allows companies to personalize their approaches to marketing and to realize the benefits of individualized (or one-to-one) marketing. Ironically, the same Web-based marketing approach that allows companies to get so personal with their customers also can make shopping extremely impersonal. Entrepreneurs who set up shop on the Internet will likely never meet their customers face-to-face or even talk to them. Yet those customers, who can live anywhere in the world, will visit the online store at all hours of the day or night and expect to receive individual attention and superior customer service. Making an online business model succeed requires a business to strike a balance, creating an e-commerce strategy that capitalizes on the strengths and efficiency of the Internet while meeting customers' expectations of convenience and service.

In this fast-paced world of e-commerce, size no longer matters as much as speed and flexibility do. One of the Internet's greatest strengths is its interactive, social nature and the ability to provide companies with instantaneous customer feedback, giving them the opportunity to learn and to make necessary adjustments. Businesses, whatever their size, that are willing to experiment with different approaches to reaching customers and are quick to learn and adapt will grow and prosper; those that cannot will fall by the wayside.

E-commerce is redefining even the most traditional industries such as the pizza business. Papa John's, Domino's, and Pizza Hut have surpassed the $3 billion mark in online pizza sales. Online pizza sales are growing so fast that it took Papa John's seven years to reach its first billion

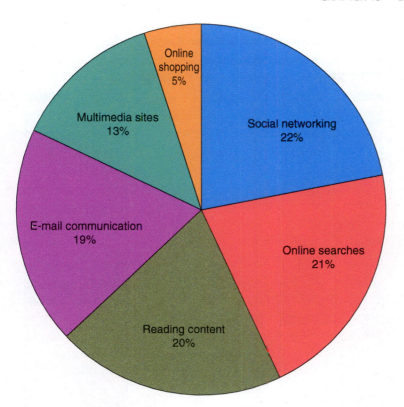

**FIGURE 13.1**

**How People Spend Their Time Online**

*Source:* Based on "How People Spend Their Time Online," SocialMedia Today, May 9, 2012, *http://socialmediatoday.com/node/504064.*

in online sales but only two years to achieve its second billion and just one year to reach its third billion. Online sales now account for more than 35 percent of Papa John's sales, but for some franchisees online sales account for more than 50 percent of sales. On a recent Super Bowl Sunday (the busiest single day in the pizza business), Domino's, where online sales account for more than 30 percent of total sales, took more than 160,000 orders online, and more than 1,000 customers *per minute* were placing online orders just before kickoff.[3] Jonathan Kaplan, founder of The Melt, a restaurant with 14 locations in California that specializes in grilled cheese sandwiches and soups, offers customers the convenience of online ordering and speedy pickup by scanning a quick-response (QR) code at the counter.[4]

Globally, people spend 35 *billion* hours online per month. The average global Internet user spends 16 hours online per month, half the average time spent by Internet users in the United States. Figure 13.1 shows how people spend their time online. Although shopping accounts for just 5 percent of Internet users' time online, global e-commerce sales total $1.3 trillion and are growing rapidly (see Figure 13.2).[5] In 2011, 167 million people in the United States (53 percent of the U.S. population) made an online purchase; by 2016, 192 million people (56 percent of the U.S. population will make an online purchase. Their average online spending will increase from $1,207 per person in 2011 to $1,738 per person in 2016.[6] The items that customers purchase most often online are apparel, books, and computer hardware and software.[7] However, companies can—and do—sell practically anything online, from antiques and pharmaceuticals to popcorn and drug-free urine. Even businesses that, at first glance, do not appear to be suited for conducting business online have been able to build successful e-commerce business models.

**ENTREPRENEURIAL PROFILE: Mary Helen Bowers: Ballet Beautiful** Shortly after Mary Helen Bowers, a former dancer for the New York City Ballet, started Ballet Beautiful, a company that provides clients with dance training and fitness routines, in New York City, actress Natalie Portman asked her to help Portman prepare for her leading role as a ballet dancer in the film Black Swan (for which Portman would win an Oscar). Although the job would cement Bowers's reputation as a dance and fitness trainer, it demanded almost constant travel, which would require her to put her successful business on hold. Rather than giving up her business, however, Bowers decided to move her training and fitness business online. She put together a team of programmers, videographers, and Web designers; spent $40,000 to build a proprietary videoconferencing application that syncs with Skype; and began offering live, interactive, streaming classes for her students. Within a year of launching the online class, Ballet Beautiful's client base had grown by more than 400 percent to 10,000 customers in 50 countries. Bowers has since opened a studio in Manhattan to accommodate

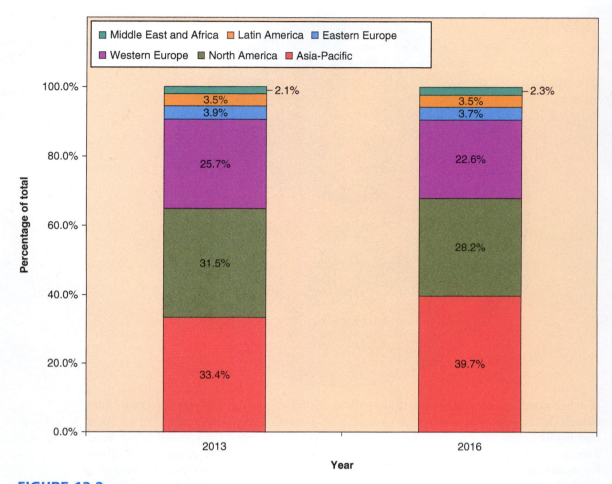

**FIGURE 13.2**

**Global B2C E-Commerce Sales by Region: Percentage of Global Total**

*Source:* "E-Commerce Sales Topped $1 Trillion for the First Time in 2012," Marketer, February 5, 2013, *http://www.emarketer.com/ Article/Ecommerce-Sales_Topped-1-Trillion-First-Time-2012/1009649.*

local clients, but 75 percent of her sales are generated online. She also generates online sales with DVDs and streaming videos of her workouts. "Online is the future of the fitness industry, and we can grow a lot bigger from here," says Bowers.[8]

Consumers have adopted the Internet much more quickly than any other major innovation in the past. The Internet reached an audience of 50 million people in just four years, compared to 38 years for radio and 13 years for television. One of the Internet's most popular sites, Facebook, reached 50 million users in just two years.[9] Online sales now account for 8 percent of total retail sales in the United States.[10] In addition, Jupiter Research predicts that online research will influence 52 percent of total retail spending in the United States by 2016, up from 27 percent in 2005 (see Figure 13.3).[11] Although the rapid growth rate of online sales will not last indefinitely, the Web represents a tremendous opportunity for both online and offline sales that small businesses cannot afford to ignore. Successful entrepreneurs are learning to engage their customers across multiple platforms, including their companies' Web sites, mobile sites, social media sites, and apps that give customers easy, convenient access for making purchases.

**1.**

Understand the factors an entrepreneur should consider before launching into e-commerce.

## Factors to Consider Before Launching into E-Commerce

Despite the many benefits the Web offers, not every small business owner has embraced e-commerce. According to a study by advertising and marketing firm Ad-ology, 82 percent of small companies have Web sites, but many of those businesses do not engage in e-commerce

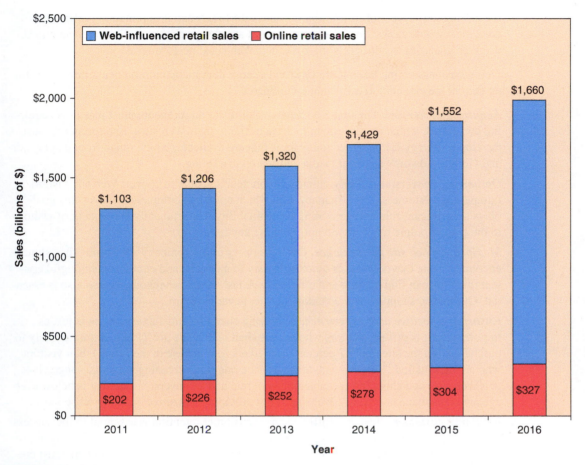

**FIGURE 13.3**

## U.S. Online and Web-Influenced Retail Sales, 2011–2016 (in Billions of $)

*Source:* Based on Forrester Research Web Influenced Retail Sales Forecast, 2012.

because their Web sites cannot accept payments.[12] Why are so many small companies hesitant to embrace e-commerce? For many entrepreneurs, the key barrier is not knowing where or how to start an e-commerce effort, whereas for others cost concerns are a major issue. Other roadblocks include the fear that the Web site will not draw customer traffic and the problems associated with ensuring online security.

Whatever the size of their companies, entrepreneurs must realize that establishing a Web presence is a necessity. "A Web site is your ticket to get into the game," says the CEO of one high-tech company. "If you don't have one, you might as well not even name your business."[13] However, before launching an e-commerce effort, business owners should consider the following important issues:

- Success requires a company to develop a plan for integrating the Web into its overall strategy. The plan should address issues such as site design and maintenance, creating and managing a brand name, marketing and promotional strategies, sales, and customer service.

- How a company exploits the Internet's interconnectivity and the opportunities it creates to transform relationships with its suppliers and vendors, its customers, and others is crucial to its success. Integrating social media into a company's Web presence can produce a significant payoff, but engaging customers through social media requires time and resources.

- Developing deep, lasting relationships with customers takes on even greater importance on the Internet. Attracting online customers costs money, and companies must be able to retain them to make their Web sites profitable.

- Creating a meaningful presence on the Internet requires an ongoing investment of resources—time, money, energy, and talent. Establishing an attractive Web site is only the beginning.

- Measuring the success of its Web-based sales effort is essential to remaining relevant to customers whose tastes, needs, and preferences are always changing. Entrepreneurs must use Web analytics to constantly improve their Web sites' performance.

Doing business online takes more time and energy than many entrepreneurs think. The following factors are essential to achieving e-commerce success:

- *Acquiring customers.* The first e-commerce skill that entrepreneurs must master is acquiring customers, which requires them to drive traffic to their Web sites. Entrepreneurs must develop a strategy for using the many tools that are available, which range from display ads and Google Adwords to social media and search marketing.

- *Optimizing conversions.* Every online entrepreneur's goal is to convert Web site visitors into paying customers. The efficiency with which an online company achieves this goal plays a significant role in determining its profitability. Unfortunately, 98 percent of visitors to the typical online retail site do not purchase anything.

- *Maximizing Web site performance.* Once shoppers find a company's Web site, they should encounter a site that downloads quickly, is easy to navigate, and contains meaningful content that they can find quickly and efficiently. A fast, simple checkout process also is essential. Otherwise, shoppers will abandon the site, never to return.

- *Ensuring a positive user experience.* Achieving customer satisfaction online is just as important as it is offline. Visitors who are satisfied with a site are 71 percent more likely to purchase from the site (and 67 percent more likely to purchase in the future) than visitors who are dissatisfied.[14] An above-average bounce rate (the percentage of single-page visits to a Web site) and shopping cart abandonment rate and a conversion rate that is below average are signs that a company's Web site is not providing a positive customer experience.

- *Retaining customers.* Just as in offline stores, customer retention is essential to the success of online businesses. One study reports that increasing customer retention by 2 percent produces the same financial impact as reducing costs by 10 percent.[15] Entrepreneurs must create an online shopping experience that engages customers, offers them value, and provides them with convenience.

- *Use Web analytics as part of a cycle of continuous improvement.* Entrepreneurs have a multitude of Web analytics tools (many of them free) that they can use to analyze the performance and the effectiveness of their Web sites. A Web site is never really "finished"; it is always a work in progress, and analytics tools provide the data for driving continuous improvement. Unfortunately, a survey conducted by the Small Business Authority reports that 63 percent of small business owners do not use analytics tools to track customers' shopping patterns on their Web sites.[16]

We will explain how to achieve these six goals in the "Strategies for E-Success" section of this chapter.

## Ten Myths of E-Commerce

**2.**

Explain the 10 myths of e-commerce and how to avoid falling victim to them.

Although many entrepreneurs have boosted their businesses with e-commerce, setting up shop on the Web is no guarantee of success. Scores of entrepreneurs have plunged unprepared into the world of e-commerce only to discover that there is more to it than merely setting up a Web site and waiting for the orders to start pouring in. Make sure that you do not fall victim to the following e-commerce myths.

### Myth 1. If I Launch a Site, Customers Will Flock to It

Some entrepreneurs think that once they set up their Web sites, their expenses end there. Not true! Without promotional support, no Web site will draw enough traffic to support a business. With more than 634 million Web sites already in existence and more being added every day, getting a site noticed is becoming increasingly difficult.[17] Listing a site with popular Web search engines does not guarantee that online customers will find a small company's Web site. Just like traditional retail stores seeking to attract customers, online companies have discovered that drawing sufficient traffic to a Web site requires promotion—and lots of it! "No one will know you're on the Web unless you tell them and motivate them to visit," explains Mark Layton, owner of a Web-based distributor of computer supplies and author of a book on e-commerce.[18]

Entrepreneurs with both physical and online stores must promote their Web sites at every opportunity by printing their URLs on everything related to their physical stores—on signs, in print and broadcast ads, in store windows, on shopping bags, on merchandise labels, on employees' uniforms, and anywhere else their customers will see them. QR codes allow smart phone users to go directly to the appropriate Web page without having to type in a long URL. Entrepreneurs also use social media such as Facebook, Twitter, and Pinterest to drive traffic to their Web sites. A recent survey by VerticalResponse reports that 43 percent of small business owners spend at least six hours a week on social media, mainly on Facebook and Twitter. "My posts and tweets are little messages that tap my clients on the shoulder and remind them to get back in the game," says Johnny Shelby, owner of Third Coast Training, an exercise and training facility in Houston, Texas.[19]

**ENTREPRENEURIAL PROFILE:** **John Goscha, Jeff Avallon, and Morgen Newman: IdeaPaint** IdeaPaint, a company founded in 2002 that sells paint that converts almost any surface into a whiteboard, relies on an innovative, comprehensive approach using social media to promote its Web site and engage its customers. The welcome page on IdeaPaint's Web site includes numerous hot spots on which visitors can click to access the company's social media sites and its blog. IdeaPaint's Facebook page includes links to its other social media sites and videos that show potential customers how to install its whiteboard paint. Its Facebook page encourages customers to post comments on the company's wall and includes photographs and videos of installations from customers. In addition to a "like" button, the Facebook page also includes a "send" button that visitors can use to send the company's link to their friends. IdeaPaint also hosts a YouTube channel that includes its "how-to" videos as well as videos that feature the creative ways in which customers use its product. The company repeats this strategy on its Pinterest page. IdeaPaint also sponsors a makeover competition and uses social media to attract applicants and to allow people to vote on a winner. IdeaPaint also engages customers on Twitter. One customer recently tweeted about transforming the front of his family's refrigerator into a whiteboard using IdeaPaint's product and included a photograph and product endorsement. The idea is not only to engage customers through social media but also to encourage satisfied customers to help sell the product by explaining its benefits.[20]

IdeaPaint.
*Source:* IdeaPaint.

Virtual shop owners should consider buying ads in traditional advertising media as well as using banner ads, banner exchange programs, and cross-marketing arrangements with companies that sell complementary products on their own Web sites. Other techniques include interacting with customers through a blog, sending Web-based or e-mail newsletters, posting videos about the company's products on YouTube, writing or posting articles that link to the company's site, offering a live chat option that allows customers to interact with company personnel, incorporating customer-generated reviews, or sponsoring a contest.

Blogs are easy to create using software such as WordPress, TypePad, Squarespace, or Blogger, but they require regular updating with fresh content to attract visitors. One recent survey reports that 55 percent of small businesses have blogs; however, 65 percent of business owners say that they have not updated their blogs in at least one year.[21] Blogs can be an effective way to draw potential customers, but with 42 million blogs online, they must contain fresh, thoughtful, useful, and entertaining content and a (very) soft-sell approach.

**ENTREPRENEURIAL PROFILE:** **Danny Wegman: Wegmans** Wegmans, a family-owned chain of 81 grocery stores founded in 1916 in Rochester, New York, has had tremendous success with its blog, FRESH STORIES: AN INSIDE LOOK AT ALL THINGS WEGMANS. Company employees make regular blog posts about a variety of topics, ranging from the operation of the company's organic research garden and how Wegmans's products get to market to nutritional tips and how the company recycles old employee uniforms into insulation. In an early blog entry, CEO Danny Wegman wrote, "This blog is for you. We'd love to hear what you'd like us to share. So join in and let us know what you've been wondering about." Wegman's blog has become extremely popular with customers and is an important sales driver for the company, which, with $6.3 billion in annual sales, is one of the largest private companies in the United States and has consistently appeared on *Fortune's* list of the 100 Best Companies to Work For.[22]

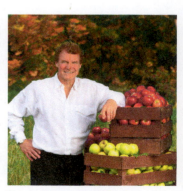

Danny Wegman, CEO of Wegmans.
*Source:* Wegmans.

The keys to promoting a Web site successfully is networking—building relationships with customers, bloggers, social media, trade associations, online directories, and other Web sites a company's customers visit—and interacting with current and potential customers online and through social media outlets.

## Myth 2. Online Customers Are Easy to Please

Customers who shop online today tend to be experienced Internet users whose expectations of their online shopping experiences are high and continue to rise. Experienced online shoppers tend to be unforgiving, quickly clicking to another site if their shopping experience is subpar or they cannot find the products and information they want. In a recent study by 1&1 Internet, 65 percent of Web users say that they are regularly inconvenienced by faulty Web sites; in addition, 68 percent of users say that they are more critical and less tolerant of Web site errors than they were five years ago.[23] Because Web shoppers are becoming more discriminating, companies are finding that they must constantly improve their Web sites to attract and keep their customers.

Although online shoppers rarely encounter a live salesperson, they still have high expectations of customer service in their online purchases. A recent study by comScore and UPS reports that customer satisfaction with online shopping is high; 86 percent of customers express satisfaction with their online shopping experiences. However, e-commerce companies have room for improvement, particularly when it comes to offering free or discounted shipping, easy returns, the variety of products offered, and the ability to track shipments online.[24]

**ENTREPRENEURIAL PROFILE: Heikki Haldre and Paul Pällin: Fits.me** Fits.me, a London-based company launched in 2010 by Heikki Haldre and Paul Pällin, provides online retailers with a virtual fitting room designed to combat online clothing retailers' biggest problem: Customers cannot try on garments before they purchase them. Fits.me's goal is to enhance online shoppers' experience by providing e-commerce clothing companies with a virtual fitting room that shows how specific garments look on a robotic mannequin with the exact dimensions of the shopper's body. Fits.me created the robotic mannequins, which can shift shapes and sizes to replicate nearly 100,000 body types, by using 30,000 three-dimensional body scans of real people. Online clothing retailers who have adopted Fits.me's virtual fitting room have seen the conversion rates on their Web sites double, their sales increase by 6 percent, and their returns decrease by 8 percent.[25]

To be successful online marketers, small companies must create Web sites with the features that appeal to experienced Web shoppers, such as simple navigation, customer reviews, rock-solid security, and quick access to product information, videos, and blogs. Many small businesses outsource most (sometimes all) of the activities associated with conducting business online to companies that specialize in e-commerce services. These companies prefer to focus on their core competencies—product design, marketing, extending a brand, manufacturing, and others—and hire other companies whose core competencies reside in e-commerce to handle Web site design, hosting, order processing, and order fulfillment ("pick, pack, and ship"). Rather than make constant investments in technology that may not produce a reasonable return, these small companies preserve their capital and their energy and focus them on the aspects of business that they do best. Other entrepreneurs prefer to keep the design and operation of their Web sites in house.

## Myth 3. Making Money on the Web Is Easy

Promoters who hawk "get-rich-quick" schemes on the Internet lure entrepreneurs with the promise that making money online is easy. It isn't. Doing business online *can* be quite lucrative, but it takes a well-designed strategy and proper execution. Attracting potential customers to a Web site can be challenging; the average Internet user in the United States views 2,750 Web pages per month.[26] As hundreds of new Web sites spring up every day, getting a company's site noticed requires more effort and marketing muscle than ever before.

Entrepreneurs engaging in e-commerce recognize the power that the Internet gives customers. Pricing, for example, is no longer as simple as it once was for companies because entrepreneurs can no longer be content to take into account only local competitors when setting their own prices. With the Internet, price transparency is the rule of the day. With a few mouse clicks, customers can compare the prices of the same or similar products and services from companies across the globe. In this wired and connected economy, the balance of power has shifted to customers, and new business models recognize this fact.

## Myth 4. Privacy Is Not an Important Issue on the Web

The Internet allows companies to gain access to almost unbelievable amounts of information about their customers. Many sites offer visitors "freebies" in exchange for information about themselves. Companies then use this information to learn more about their target customers and how to market to them most effectively. Concerns over the privacy of and the use of this information have become the topic of debate by many interested parties, including government agencies, consumer watchdog groups, customers, and industry trade associations. The TRUSTe Privacy Index reports that 90 percent of adults in the United States worry about their privacy online.[27]

Companies that collect information from their online customers have a responsibility to safeguard their customers' privacy, to protect it from unauthorized use, and to use it responsibly. That means that businesses should post a privacy statement on their Web sites, explaining to customers how they intend to use the information they collect. One of the surest ways to alienate online customers is to experience a security breach that allows their personal information to be stolen, to abuse the information collected from them by selling it to third parties, or to spam customers with unwanted solicitations. A recent survey by online security firm TRUSTe reports that 89 percent of Internet users avoid doing business with companies that they believe do not respect their privacy online.[28] BBBOnLine offers a data security guide (*www.bbb.org/data-security*) that is designed to help business owners maintain proper security over the data they collect from customers.

Businesses that publish privacy policies and then adhere to them build trust among their customers, an important facet of doing business on the Web. According to John Briggs, director of e-commerce for Yahoo!, customers "need to trust the brand they are buying and believe that their online purchases will be safe transactions. They need to feel comfortable that [their] personal data will not be sold and that they won't get spammed by giving their e-mail address. They need to know about shipping costs, product availability, and return policies up front."[29] Privacy *does* matter on the Web, and businesses that respect their customers' privacy win their customers' trust. Trust is the foundation on which companies build the long-term customer relationships that are so crucial to success online. Perhaps the best way for an e-commerce company to prove its trustworthiness to potential customers is to have its data collection, debit and credit card handling procedures, and privacy policies and practices certified by companies such as TRUSTe, BBBOnLine, McAfee, or ControlScan.

## Myth 5. "Strategy? I Don't Need a Strategy to Sell on the Web! Just Give Me a Web Site, and the Rest Will Take Care of Itself"

Building a successful e-business is no different than building a successful brick-and-mortar business, and that requires a well-thought-out strategy. Building a strategy means that an entrepreneur must first develop a clear definition of the company's target customers and have a thorough understanding of their needs, wants, likes, and dislikes. To be successful, a Web site must be appealing to the customers it seeks to attract just as a traditional store's design and decor must draw foot traffic. Entrepreneurs must build their Web sites with their customers in mind. How do they expect the site to work? How should the site be organized to allow customers to find the products they want most efficiently? What content should the site contain to keep customers coming back? What image should the site create for the business in customers' minds?

Recall from Chapter 4 that one goal of developing a strategy is to set a business apart from its competitors. The same is true for creating a strategy for conducting business online. It is just as important, if not more important, for an online business to differentiate itself from the competition if it is to be successful. Unlike customers in a retail store, who must exert the effort to go to a competitor's store if they cannot find what they want, online customers only have to make a mouse click or two to go to a rival Web site. Therefore, competition online is fierce, and to succeed, a company must have a sound strategy.

**ENTREPRENEURIAL PROFILE: Alex Zhardanovsky and Joe Speiser: PetFlow** Serial entrepreneur Alex Zhardanovsky's inspiration for his latest e-commerce business came from his tendency to run out of food for his beloved dog. Zhardanovsky teamed up with Joe Speiser to launch PetFlow, an online company that sells healthy pet food, supplies, and toys. Recalling that another online pet supply company, *Pets.com*, began operations in 1998 and burned through $110 million of investors' money before flaming out and shutting down, Zhardanovsky and Speiser developed a simple e-commerce strategy. PetFlow offers customers a subscription service that allows them to receive regular deliveries of pet food, which enables Zhardanovsky and Speiser to minimize their inventory investment, negotiate favorable terms with suppliers, build long-term relationships with customers, and maintain steady cash flow. "It's the best business model you can ever have," says Zhardanovsky. "I already know how many bags of dog food I've sold in the next 60 days." PetFlow, which required an initial investment of just $50,000 (excluding inventory), takes 35,000 orders per month, sells 1.5 million pounds of dog food each month, and is growing at a rate of 10 percent per month.[30]

## Myth 6. The Most Important Part of Any E-Commerce Effort Is Technology

Technology advances have reduced significantly the cost of launching an e-commerce business. Brian Walker, an e-commerce expert at Forrester Research, says that a decade ago, the cost to launch an online retail business was three to five times higher than it is today. "The technology to run the site, the physical warehouse, site hosting, and staff required a significant investment before the site even went live," says Walker.[31] Modern e-commerce entrepreneurs can build a Web site for next to nothing, outsource the tasks of storing and shipping products, lease space on a server, and rent cloud-computing software to operate their online businesses—all of which lower the cost and the complexity of starting an online company. Julie Wainwright says that building the e-commerce company that she helped launch in 1998 cost between $7 million and $10 million (not including the cost of inventory). Wainwright recently launched an online luxury clothing marketplace called TheRealReal at a cost of only $25,000 to $30,000.[32]

As important as having the right technology to support an e-commerce business is, it is *not* the most crucial ingredient in the recipe for success. What matters most is the ability to understand the underlying business and to develop a workable business model that offers customers something of value at a reasonable price and produces a profit for the company. The entrepreneurs who are proving to be most successful in e-commerce are those who know how their industries work inside and out and then build an e-business around that knowledge. They know that they can hire Web designers, database experts, and fulfillment companies to create the technical aspects of their online businesses but that nothing can substitute for a solid understanding of inner workings of their industry, their target market, and the strategy needed to pull the various parts together. The key is seeing the Web for what it really is: another way to reach and serve customers with an effective business model and to minimize the cost of doing business.

Some entrepreneurs tackle e-commerce by focusing on technology first and then determine how that technology fits their business idea. "If you start with technology, you're likely going to buy a solution in search of a problem," says Kip Martin, program director of META Group's Electronic Business Strategies. Instead, he suggests, "Start with the business and ask yourself what you want to happen and how you'll measure it. *Then* ask how the technology will help you achieve your goals. Remember: Business first, technology second."[33]

## Myth 7. On the Web, Customer Service Is Not as Important as It Is in a Traditional Retail Store

The Internet offers the ultimate in shopping convenience. Numerous studies report that convenience and low prices are the primary drivers of online shopping. In fact, customers say that convenience is more important than getting the lowest prices when shopping online.[34] With just a few mouse clicks or taps on the screen of a smart phone or tablet, people can shop for practically anything anywhere in the world and have it delivered to their doorsteps within days. As convenient as online shopping is, customers still expect high levels of service. Unfortunately, some e-commerce companies treat customer service as an afterthought, an attitude that costs businesses in many ways, including lost customers and a diminished public image.

The average conversion rate for e-commerce sites is just 2.1 percent.[35] In other words, out of 1,000 visitors to the typical company's Web site, only 21 of them actually make a purchase! Sites that are difficult to navigate, slow to load, offer complex checkout systems, or confuse shoppers will turn customers away quickly, never to return. Only 22 percent of e-commerce companies are satisfied with their conversion rates.[36]

**ENTREPRENEURIAL PROFILE: Michael Gotfredson: Roadrunner Sports** Roadrunner Sports, a small chain of stores with locations in 11 states that Michael Gotfredson started in his garage in 1983, sells running shoes, apparel, and equipment. The company's Web site offers shoppers a unique tool called Shoe Dog that "fetches" specific shoe recommendations based on their responses to questions about their running habits, including their arch type, body frame, weekly mileage, type of terrain, and specific injuries they may have experienced. The breadth and depth of Roadrunner Sports's inventory allows shoppers who may not know exactly which style of brand of shoe they need to make the right selection. The result: satisfied customers, a high customer retention rate, and an above-average conversion rate.[37]

There is plenty of room for improvement in customer service on the Web. More than 65 percent of Web shoppers who fill their online shopping carts abandon them without checking out, and the average value of the goods in their carts is $117.[38] The most common reasons for leaving a site without purchasing include the following: (1) unexpected shipping and handling charges (70 percent), (2) insufficient product information (56 percent), (3) lack of trust or security concerns about the site (50 percent), and (4) difficulty navigating the Web site to find the right product (46 percent).[39] One tool that increases a company's conversion rate and reduces its cart abandonment rate is live help. In fact, a study by Oracle reports that 57 percent of customers say that live help is one of the most important features that a Web site can offer.[40] For reasonable fees, companies can hire virtual assistants: employees who work remotely to answer online shoppers' questions or to offer advice (e.g., whether an item's sizes tend to run small) in real time. Even small companies that cannot afford to staff a live chat center can incorporate customer-responsive chat options into their Web sites by using virtual chat agents. Loaded onto a company's site, these avatar-like creations can step in at the appropriate time to interact with customers, answering their questions or giving them the extra nudge they need, such as an offer of free shipping, to close the deal.

When customers do abandon their online shopping carts, companies often can close a significant percentage of those sales by sending a prompt follow-up e-mail designed to win back the customer. One study reports that just 26 percent of e-commerce companies send follow-up e-mails to customers who have abandoned their shopping carts.[41] The benefits from doing so can be significant, however. Seventy percent of the companies that send follow-up e-mails to customers who abandon their carts produce increased their sales (and 19 percent reported a large increase in sales).[42] The faster a company sends the e-mail when a customer abandons a cart, the higher the probability that the customer completes the transaction. Including the company's name and some information about the product(s) that are in the cart in the e-mail's subject line also increases the probability of a completed transaction.[43]

**ENTREPRENEURIAL PROFILE: Lisa Mann: Boot Barn** Boot Barn, a company based in Irvine, California, sells western boots, clothing, and accessories through its 87 stores located in 10 states and through its Web site (*www.bootbarn.com*). E-commerce marketing manager Lisa Mann noticed that Boot Barn's cart abandonment rate was too high and developed a triggered e-mail campaign designed to recover those lost sales. Just 20 minutes after abandoning a cart, a customer would receive a customer service e-mail ("Howdy [customer name]. Oops! Was there a problem?") inviting the customer to contact a customer service representative. If that e-mail failed to produce results, the customer received two more e-mails, the first one "emphasizing trust factors that set us apart," says Mann, and the second one nudging the customer to complete the transaction. Boot Barn's e-mail strategy worked well, generating a 12 percent increase in revenue.[44]

The lesson for e-commerce entrepreneurs is simple: invest time, energy, and money to develop a functional mechanism for providing superior customer service. Those companies that do will build a sizable base of loyal customers who keep coming back. Perhaps the most significant actions online companies can take to bolster their customer service efforts are to provide a quick, intuitive online checkout process; create a well-staffed and well-trained customer response team; offer a simple return process; and provide an easy order-tracking process so customers can check the status of their orders at any time.

## Myth 8. Flashy Web Sites Are Better Than Simple Ones

Businesses that fall into this trap pour significant amounts of money into designing flashy Web sites with all of the "bells and whistles." The logic is that to stand out on the Web, a site really has to sparkle. That logic leads to a "more is better" mentality when designing a site. In e-commerce, however, "more" does *not* necessarily equate to "better." A Web site that includes a simple design, easy navigation, clear calls to action on every page, and consistent color schemes shows that a company is putting its customers first. "Form over functions is always a recipe for disaster," says one Web design expert.[45] A site that performs efficiently and loads quickly is a far better selling tool than one that is filled with "cornea gumbo," slow to download, and confusing to shoppers. Sites that download slowly usually never have the chance to sell because customers click to another site. A study by Akamai reports that 47 percent of online shoppers expect a Web page to load within two seconds and that 40 percent of online shoppers will abandon a Web site that takes more than three seconds to load.[46] (Shoppers using mobile devices are more patient, saying that they are willing to wait 6 to 10 seconds for a page to load before abandoning it.) The study also shows that a one-second delay in a Web page loading results in a 7 percent decrease in the number of conversions.[47] "Businesses do not understand the impact of poor site performance," warns Brian Walker, an analyst at Forrester Research. "Customers not only will bail out on a session or a [shopping] cart, but they also may not return." Walker points out that the company's research shows that more than 25 percent of customers are less likely to shop at a company's brick-and-mortar store if they have a bad experience online.[48] The lesson: keep the design of your site simple so that pages download in no more than two seconds and make sure that the site's navigation is easy and intuitive.

### Myth 9. It's What's Up Front That Counts

Designing an attractive Web site is important to building a successful e-business. However, designing the back office, the systems that take over once a customer places an order on a Web site, is just as important as designing the site itself. If the behind-the-scenes support is not in place or cannot handle the traffic from the Web site, a company's entire e-commerce effort will come crashing down. Although e-commerce can lower many costs of doing business, it still requires a basic infrastructure somewhere in the channel of distribution to process orders, maintain inventory, fill orders, and handle customer service. Many entrepreneurs hoping to launch virtual businesses are discovering the need for a "clicks-and-mortar" approach to provide the necessary infrastructure to serve their customers. "The companies with warehouses, supply-chain management, and solid customer service are going to be the ones that survive," says Daryl Plummer, head of the Gartner Group's Internet and new media division.[49]

To customers, a business is only as good as its last order, and some e-companies are not measuring up. Many small e-tailers' Web sites do not offer real-time inventory lookup, which gives online shoppers the ability to see whether an item they want to purchase is actually in stock. In addition, many have not yet linked their Web sites to an automated back office, which means that processing orders takes longer and that errors are more likely. As software to integrate Web sites with the back office becomes easier to use and more affordable, more small businesses are using them to offer these features.

Web-based entrepreneurs often discover that the greatest challenge their businesses face is not necessarily attracting customers on the Web but creating a workable order fulfillment strategy. Order fulfillment involves everything required to get goods from a warehouse into a customer's hands and includes order processing, warehousing, picking and packing, shipping, and billing. Some entrepreneurs choose to handle order fulfillment in-house with their own employees, whereas others find it more economical to hire specialized fulfillment houses to handle these functions. **Virtual order fulfillment** (or drop shipping) suits many e-tailers perfectly. When a customer orders a product from its Web site, the company forwards the order to its wholesaler or distributor, which then ships the product to the customer with the online merchant's label on it. Although e-tailers avoid the risks and problems associated with managing inventory, they lose control over delivery times and service quality. In addition, for some small businesses, finding a fulfillment house willing to handle a relatively small volume of orders at a reasonable price can be difficult. Major fulfillment providers that focus on small companies include Amazon, Federal Express, UPS, DHL, Shipwire, Webgistix, and WeFullfillIt. When Zhardanovsky and Joe Speiser launched PetFlow, they outsourced the company's storage and shipping operations to a company that specializes in that area at a cost of just $4 to $5 per order. (With 35,000 orders rolling in per month, however, the company recently began shipping its own orders from a 65,000-square-foot warehouse that it leases in New Jersey.) PetFlow's annual sales recently passed the $30 million mark.[50]

### Myth 10. My Business Doesn't Need a Web Site

Nearly one in five small businesses does not have a Web site, and many of those that do have sites lack the ability to make sales online. To online shoppers, especially, these businesses might as well be invisible because doing business online and offline are inextricably connected. Today's shoppers prefer to purchase from companies that offer a multichannel approach, particularly those that offer in-store pickup for online orders and in-store returns for online purchases.[51] A multichannel approach pays big dividends. One recent survey reports that 91 percent of shoppers have gone into a store as a result of an online encounter with a business.[52] When looking to purchase products locally, many shoppers go online to conduct research first. Others prefer the convenience of making online purchases after having a positive encounter with a company's physical location. In addition, customers routinely share their opinions online about products and their shopping experience with companies. These trends point to the need for businesses to use a multichannel approach to selling their products and services that includes the Internet as one option. The key is to meet customers *wherever* they want to do business.

One fact of e-commerce is the importance of speed. Companies doing business on the Internet have discovered that those who reach customers first often have a significant advantage over their slower rivals. "The lesson of the Web is not how the big eat the small, but how the fast eat the slow," says a manager at a venture capital firm specializing in Web-based companies.[53] Succumbing to this myth often leads entrepreneurs to make a fundamental mistake once they finally decide to go online: They believe they have to have a "perfect" site before they can launch it. Few businesses get their sites "right" the first time. In fact, the most successful e-commerce sites are works in progress; entrepreneurs are constantly changing them, removing what does not work and experimenting with new features to see what does work. Successful Web sites are much like a well-designed flower garden, constantly growing and improving yet changing to reflect the climate of each season. Their creators worry less about creating the perfect site at the outset than about getting a site online and then using Web analytics to fix it, tweak it, and update it to meet changing customer demands.

## Strategies for E-Success

The typical Internet user in the United States spends an average of 104 hours per month online (see Figure 13.4). However, converting these Web users into paying customers requires a business to do more than merely set up a Web site and wait for the hits to start rolling up. Doing business from a Web site is like setting up shop on a dead-end street or a back alley. You may be

**3.** _____

Explain the basic strategies entrepreneurs should follow to achieve success in their e-commerce efforts.

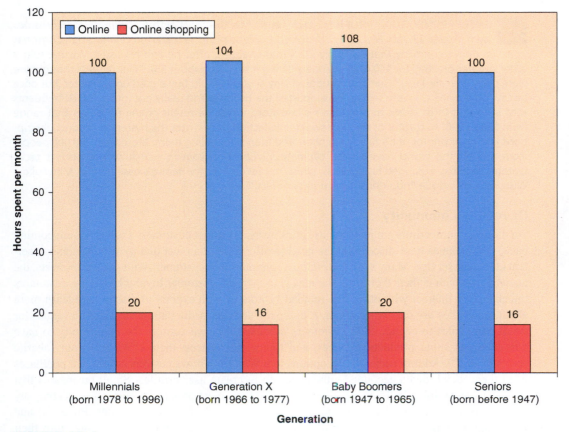

**FIGURE 13.4**

**Average Time Americans Spend Online and Shopping Online per Month**

*Source:* Based on WSL/Strategic Retail, 2013.

ready to sell, but no one knows you are there! Building sufficient volume for a site takes energy, time, money, creativity, and, perhaps most important, a well-defined strategy.

Although the Internet is a unique medium for creating a company, launching an e-business is not much different from launching a traditional offline company. The basic drivers of a successful business are the same on the Internet as they are on Main Street. To be successful, both off-line and online companies require a sound business model and a well-formulated strategy that emphasizes customer service. The goals of e-commerce are no different from traditional off-line businesses—to increase sales, improve efficiency, and generate a profit. How a company integrates the Internet into its overall business strategy determines how successful it ultimately will become. Following are some guidelines for building a successful Web strategy for a small e-company.

### Focus on a Niche in the Market

Like Curly, the crusty old trail boss in the movie *City Slickers*, who said that the secret to happiness was "one thing," many small businesses are finding success on the Internet by focusing on one thing. Rather than compete head-to-head with the dominant players in e-commerce who have the resources and the name recognition to squash smaller competitors, smart entrepreneurs focus on serving the market niches that make up the "long tail" of the market. Because of the efficiency and low cost the Internet offers, small companies can profitably tap into almost microscopic niches that in pre-Internet days would have been too difficult to reach. Small companies' limited resources usually are better spent serving niche markets than trying to be everything to everyone (recall the discussion of the focus strategy in Chapter 4). Niches exist in every industry and can be highly profitable given the right strategy for serving them. A niche can be defined in many ways, including by geography, by customer profile, by product, by product usage, and many other variables.

The Internet allows small businesses to attract niche customers that would have been impossible to reach in sufficient volume without it.

Jack McCarthy, cofounder of UltimateUglyChristmas.
*Source:* Jack McCarthy.

**ENTREPRENEURIAL PROFILE: Jack and Martha McCarthy: *UltimateUglyChristmas*
.com** At age 17, Jack McCarthy discovered a unique niche. Jack started *UltimateUglyChristmas.com*, an online company that sells ugly Christmas sweaters, after he and his sister, Martha, sold a tacky sweater on eBay for $50 (they were expecting it to go for about $5). "Our parents thought we were crazy," recalls Jack. "Our Dad wondered why anyone would buy a used ugly sweater, but once he saw how many we were selling, he supported the business and really got into it." Jack frequents yard sales and thrift stores to purchase his inventory, which he resells online for prices that range from $20 to $50. As curator of the ugly sweater collection, Jack writes the hysterical product descriptions and takes photos of his family members and friends modeling them. More than 200,000 people from around the world have visited *UltimateUglyChristmas.com* in search of the perfect tacky sweater. Jack has expanded his business, which has taken over the family's basement in Milwaukee, Wisconsin, to include "non-Christmas" ugly sweaters.[54]

### Develop a Community

On the Web, competitors are just a mouse click away. To attract customers and keep them coming back, e-companies have discovered the need to offer more than just quality products and excellent customer service. Many seek to develop a community of customers with similar interests, the nucleus of which is their Web site. The idea is to increase customer loyalty by giving customers the chance to interact with other like-minded visitors or with experts to discuss and learn more about topics they are passionate about. A company's social media outlets are natural avenues for small companies to engage their customers because they give visitors the opportunity to have conversations about products, services, and topics that interest them ("What is your favorite sports drink?"). Adding social log-in options to a Web site allows customers to make purchases from their social media accounts without having to create user profiles. Small businesses that are most successful at building a community enlist their most passionate customers as company evangelists through social media outlets such as Facebook, LinkedIn, Twitter, Pinterest, and Instagram. Companies that successfully create a community around their Web sites turn their customers into loyal fans who keep coming back and, better yet, invite others to join them.

Utilizing social media not only creates brand advocates by giving customers a venue to share their experiences with a company but also improves a company's ability to listen to its customers for praise, criticism, and suggestions for improvement. Recently, L.L. Bean, the famous retailer of outdoor gear based in Freeport, Maine, noticed that customers were criticizing one of its top-selling products, Supima cotton sheets, in online customer reviews. After investigating the problem, Bean discovered that a supplier had mistakenly added a wrinkle-resistant treatment to the fabric that was causing it to unravel. Managers acted quickly, offering new sheets (without the treatment) to all 6,300 customers who had purchased them and created a positive buzz online, transforming what could have been a marketing nightmare into a trust-building, customer service victory.[55]

## Attract Visitors by Giving Away "Freebies"

One of the most important words on the Internet is "free." Many successful e-merchants have discovered the ability to attract visitors to their site by giving away something free and then selling them something else. One e-commerce consultant calls this cycle of giving something away and then selling something "the rhythm of the Web."[56] The "freebie" must be something that customers value, but it does *not* have to be expensive, nor does it have to be a product. In fact, one of the most common giveaways on the Internet is *information*. Creating a free online or e-mail newsletter with links to your company's site, of course, is one of the most effective ways of attracting potential customers. Meaningful content presented in a clear, professional fashion is a must. Experts advise keeping online newsletters short—no more than about 600 words.

**ENTREPRENEURIAL PROFILE: Tammy Rosen: Fur-Get Me Not** In 2000, Tammy Rosen left her job in corporate information technology and started Fur-Get Me Not, a pet-sitting service that she ran out of her home. Over time, she added pet training, day care, and taxi services. Today, Fur-Get Me Not is a full-service pet service center and retail shop in Arlington, Virginia. Wanting to stay connected to her customers and keep them informed about her company's special events, Rosen began sending plain-text e-mails but soon realized their limitations. She switched to an HTML-based e-mail campaign and added a monthly newsletter that offers customers news about upcoming events, special sales, and new products in addition to training and health care tips and spotlight features of customers' pets and her employees. Fur-Get Me Not has expanded its e-mail list to more than 1,800 and enjoys an above-average open rate of 35.2 percent. "The e-mails we send help instill loyalty in our customers," says Rosen. "I know that what I'm sending makes a difference when I see them clicking through to the Web site or when I receive 'thank you's' from customers in response to a newsletter."[57]

Fur-Get Me Not.
*Source:* Fur-Get Me Not.

## Make Creative Use of E-Mail, but Avoid Becoming a "Spammer"

As Tammy Rosen's experience proves, when used properly and creatively, e-mail can be an effective, low-cost way to drive traffic to a Web site. The average e-mail **open rate**, the percentage of recipients who actually open a marketing e-mail, is 20.1 percent; the average e-mail **click-through rate**, the percentage of recipients who open an e-mail and click on the link to the company's Web site, is 5.2 percent.[58] Marketing e-mails sent on Thursdays have the highest combination of open and click-through rates.[59] An extensive study of open and click-through rates by GetResponse shows that the best time of day to send marketing e-mails is 8 A.M. to 9 A.M. and 3 P.M. to 4 P.M.[60]

Just as with newsletters, an e-mail's content should offer something of value to recipients. Customers welcome well-constructed permission e-mail that directs them to a company's site for information or special deals. Unfortunately, spam, those unsolicited and universally despised e-mail messages (which rank below postal "junk mail" and telemarketing calls as the worst form of junk advertising), limits the effectiveness of companies' e-mail legitimate marketing efforts. Spam is a persistent problem for online marketers; Internet security firm Symantec reports that 68.4 percent of e-mails sent are spam.[61] Companies must comply with the CAN-SPAM Act, a law passed in 2003 that regulates commercial e-mail and sets standards for commercial e-mail messages. (The penalties can be as much as $16,000 per e-mail for companies that violate the law.)

To avoid having their marketing messages become part of that electronic clutter, companies rely on permission e-mails, collecting customers' and visitors' e-mail addresses (and their permission to send them e-mail messages) when they register on a site to receive a "freebie." The most successful online retailers post e-mail opt-in messages prominently throughout their Web sites and on their social media pages as well. **Triggered e-mails**, those that are triggered by a particular event, such as a customer signing up to receive a newsletter, downloading a white paper, abandoning a shopping cart, placing an order, and others, generate open and click-through rates that are twice those of conventional e-mail. When customers sign up to receive permission e-mails, a company should send them "welcome" e-mails immediately. More than one-third of retailers do not despite research showing that welcome e-mails can generate as much as six times the revenue that standard broadcast e-mails do.[62]

**ENTREPRENEURIAL PROFILE: Jim Broadhurst: SmileyCookie**  Jim Broadhurst, founder of SmileyCookie, a gourmet cookie retailer in Pittsburgh, Pennsylvania, recently implemented a triggered e-mail campaign that sends customers a discount coupon when they sign up. If the customer fails to make a purchase within six days, he or she receives a reminder e-mail. Customers who abandon their SmileyCookie shopping carts also receive up to three e-mails encouraging them to complete their purchases.[63]

To be successful at collecting a sufficient number of e-mail addresses, a company must make clear to customers that they will receive messages that are meaningful to them and that the company will not sell e-mail addresses to others (which should be part of its posted privacy policy). Once a business has a customer's permission to send information in additional e-mail messages, it has a meaningful marketing opportunity to create a long-term customer relationship and to build customer loyalty. Table 13.1 includes a spam test to which every company should submit its e-mail campaigns.

## Sell the "Experience"

When shoppers enter a retail store, they are courted by an attractive layout, appealing decor, and eye-catching merchandise displays and perhaps are greeted by a salesperson who can offer them information and advice about its products and services. Although e-commerce businesses lack this ability to have face-to-face contact with customers, they can still engender loyalty by creating an engaging and enjoyable online shopping experience. Sites that offer shoppers easy navigation, a simple and fast checkout process, and thorough product descriptions with quality images can provide the same positive shopping experience that the best retail stores do. Athleta, a chain with retail stores in 18 states that sells athletic-inspired apparel and accessories for women, has designed its Web site to replicate the shopping experience that customers enjoy when they walk into one of its retail outlets. A simple layout with high-quality product images and comprehensive product descriptions that include sizing details and laundering tips allow customers

**TABLE 13.1 Does Your E-Mail Measure Up to the Anti-Spam Test?**

1. Is the content of your e-mail appropriate for your audience? Are recipients likely to be interested in the offers or articles you are sending? The biggest problem with sales-oriented e-mails and the primary cause of low open and click-through rates is irrelevant content.

2. Does the e-mail offer something of value to recipients—an invitation to a special sale, a free newsletter filled with useful information, or something similar? Sending frivolous e-mails that pack little or no value to customers is one surefire way to send your company's click-through rate plummeting.

3. Has your e-mail provider been blacklisted by spam screening tools?

4. Have the recipients on your e-mail list opted into your e-mail list? Trolling Internet user lists for e-mail addresses is *not* an acceptable way to build a recipient list.

5. Does the subject line include your company's name? Is the subject line accurate and not misleading? Do *not* include "$$$" in the subject line as so many spam messages do.

6. Is the e-mail readable? Some e-mails sent in HTML format can appear garbled and unreadable on some computers.

7. Is the frequency of the e-mail appropriate? Customers do not appreciate being hammered by 20 e-mails from a company in one week.

8. Is the timing of your e-mail appropriate? Monday mornings, when people are returning to work from the weekend and their in-boxes are full of messages, is *not* the best time to send an e-mail.

9. Can recipients opt out of your e-mail list if they choose to?

10. Does the e-mail contain your company's valid mailing address? In 2003, Congress passed the CAN-SPAM Act, which did not ban spam but put limitations on how marketers can use e-mail as part of their marketing tools. This is one of the act's requirements.

to find exactly the items they want. One section of the site displays complete coordinated outfits with links to pages that feature every item included, ready to be added to a shopping cart with one click.[64]

## Make Sure Your Web Site Says "Credibility"

Many studies have concluded that trust and security issues are the leading inhibitors of online shopping. Unless a company can build among customers *trust* in its Web site, selling is virtually impossible. Visitors begin to evaluate the credibility of a site as soon as they arrive. In fact, a recent study reports that Internet users judge the credibility of a Web site within the first twenty-fifth of a second (40 milliseconds, or 0.04 seconds)![65] "Windows of opportunity, especially in the online environment, close very quickly," says Jay Bower, president of Crossbow Group, a digital marketing company.[66] Does the site look professional? Are there misspelled words and typographical errors? If the site provides information, does it note the sources of that information? If so, are those sources legitimate? Are they trustworthy? Is the presentation of the information fair and objective, or is it biased? Has the site been updated recently? Does the company include a privacy policy posted in an obvious place?

One of the simplest ways to establish credibility with customers is to use brand names they know and trust. Whether a company sells nationally recognized brands or its own well-known private brand, using those names on its site creates a sense of legitimacy. People buy brand names they trust, and online companies can use that to their advantage. Another effective way to build customer confidence is by joining an online seal program, such as McAfee, TrustWave, TRUSTe, Norton, BBBOnLine, or others. The online equivalent of the Underwriter Laboratories stamp or the Good Housekeeping Seal of Approval, these seals mean that a company meets certain standards concerning the privacy of customers' information and the resolution of customer complaints. Posting a privacy policy (more on this later in this chapter) is another key ingredient in building trust. Including customer reviews, which Internet users say they believe more than product descriptions from a business, on product Web pages increases customer loyalty and trust in an online business. Testimonials, either in writing or on video, from real customers enhance a company's online credibility, especially among first-time customers. Businesses that are the subject of media coverage should include a "media" or "featured in" page with links to articles or videos about the company so that they can magnify the benefits of publicity. Links to the company's social media accounts using "follow" buttons also lends credibility to an online business. Finally, providing a street address, an e-mail address, and a toll-free telephone number sends a subtle message to shoppers that a legitimate business is behind the Web site. Many small companies include photographs of their brick-and-mortar stores and of their founders and employees to combat the Web's anonymity and to let shoppers know that they are supporting a friendly small business.

## Make the Most of the Internet's Global Reach

The Internet has reduced dramatically the cost of launching a global business initiative; even the smallest business can engage in international business with a well-designed Web site. Still, despite the Web's reputation as an international marketplace, many Web entrepreneurs fail to utilize fully its global reach. Nearly 90 percent of the 2.4 billion people around the world who use the Internet live outside the United States. Only 26.8 percent of Web users speak English.[67] Limiting a Web site to just a small percentage of the world because of a language barrier makes no sense. Figure 13.5 shows the T-Index, a statistical index that measures a nation's online sales potential using the number of Internet users and gross domestic product per capita.

E-companies aiming to generate sales from foreign markets must design their sites with customers from other lands and cultures in mind. Global shoppers are much more likely to buy from Web sites that are written in their native languages. A common mechanism is to include several "language buttons" on the opening page of a site that take customers to pages in the language of their choice. However, e-commerce companies often find that setting up dedicated Web sites with country-specific domain names attracts more international customers. Companies trying to establish a foothold in foreign markets by setting up Web sites dedicated to them run the same risk that companies setting up physical locations there do: offending international visitors by using the business conventions and standards they are accustomed to using in the United States. Business practices, even those used on the Web, that are acceptable and even expected in the United States,

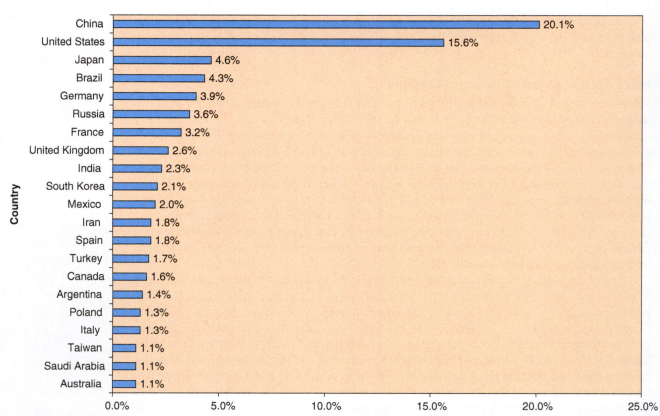

**FIGURE 13.5**

**Markets with the Highest Online Sales Potential**

*Source:* Based on *Translated.net*, 2012.

may be taboo in other countries. Even color schemes are important. Selecting the "wrong" colors and symbols on a site targeting people in a particular country can hurt sales and offend visitors. A little research into the subtleties of a target country's culture and business practices can save a great deal of embarrassment and money! Creating secure, simple, and reliable payment methods for foreign customers also increases sales. International delivery services offer software that small companies can incorporate into their Web sites that calculate the final "landed cost" (including relevant tariffs and duties) of orders and estimate delivery dates.

**ENTREPRENEURIAL PROFILE: Jarrod Rogers: MotoSport** MotoSport, an online retailer of motorcycle parts and accessories based in Portland, Oregon, received its first international order from a customer in Canada and filled it promptly. The sale fell through when the shipping company demanded that the customer pay an additional $100 in tariffs about which Jarrod Rogers, MotoSport's director of marketing, was unaware. "The tariff was more than the price of the item," he says. Recognizing the potential of international sales for its product line, MotoSport hired Fifty-One Global Ecommerce, a company that specializes in international shipping and logistics, to integrate software into MotoSport's Web site that calculates country-specific taxes, tariffs, and shipping charges. Although MotoSport has not yet translated its Web site into its international customers' languages, it now sells to customers in 84 countries.[68]

When translating the content of their Web pages into other languages, entrepreneurs must use extreme caution. This is *not* the time to pull out their notes from an introductory Spanish course and begin their own translations. Hiring professional translation and localization services to convert a company's Web content into other languages minimizes the likelihood of a company unintentionally offending foreign customers.

**Lessons from the Street-Smart Entrepreneur**

# How to Make Your Business Ready for Global E-Commerce

In 1999, Robert Beaver and his sons, Bobby and Jeff, created Zazzle, a Redwood City, California–based business that allows customers to create their own customized products—from T-shirts and coffee mugs to posters and postage stamps. Although Zazzle has been shipping its products to customers in 70 countries for several years, the company only recently made a serious effort to increase sales in specific global markets. The Beavers combed through the company's Web analytics to identify the nations from which its foreign traffic and sales originated and targeted the top 15 nations. Then they developed an Internet platform that they could easily adapt to suit local customers' shopping habits, tastes, and payment preferences. The Beavers invested in translating each country-specific Web site into its native language, changed its frequently-asked-questions (FAQ) section to match the specific concerns of customers in each nation, and hired multilingual customer support teams. The payoff has been significant; international sales have propelled the company's growth rate.

Not so long ago, tapping global markets was not a realistic possibility for small companies such as Zazzle because of the resources required to go global, but the Internet has changed all of that, making global markets available to even the smallest of businesses. Almost 89 percent of the estimated 2.4 billion Internet users worldwide live *outside* of North America, and less than 27 percent of Internet users speak English. China, for instance, has 242 million online shoppers (45 percent more than the United States), more than any nation in the world, and they spend an average of $40,000 per second! No e-commerce company, whatever its size, can afford to ignore the market potential of global markets. Generating e-commerce sales in global markets requires a company to develop an appropriate global e-commerce strategy. Small business can increase the probability of success by following these tips from the Street-Smart Entrepreneur:

- *Study the culture of the countries you are targeting.* To be successful, e-commerce entrepreneurs must learn the habits, customs, and traditions of doing business in a country just as if they were opening a physical location there. Incorporating the lessons you learn into your company's Web site makes international customers feel welcome and increases their willingness to buy and become repeat customers. JRS Consulting, a marketing and management consulting firm, invested months learning about the business culture of France before building a Web site devoted to landing customers there. The effort produced a 95 percent return on investment, and 15 percent of the company's annual revenue now comes from France.
- *Translate your company's Web site into the local language.* Online customers are more likely to buy from Web sites written in their native languages. Skyscanner, an airline flight price comparison Web site, translated its site into the languages of the 23 countries it targeted and saw

its international orders skyrocket. International sales now make up 70 percent of the company's revenue. In Russia alone, the number of Skyscanner users increased from 30,000 to 1 million in just 18 months after the company created a dedicated site for Russian customers.

- *Tailor your company's Web site to meet the expectations of customers in each country.* Although Google's search engine dominates the market in the United States, shoppers in other nations often use other search engines to find the products they want to purchase online. For example, companies that want to sell to customers in China should know that Baidu is the leading search engine there and optimize their Web sites for maximum performance on it. Key terms must match the local language. A customer in North America is most likely to use a search engine to look for "pants," but a shopper in Australia would use the term "trousers."
- *Incorporate country-specific pricing.* Product pages should display prices in international shoppers' local currencies, including any tariffs, duties, and taxes that may apply. You can hire companies that specialize in international business transactions to set up this portion of your Web site in exchange for a fee or a percentage of each sale.
- *Provide payment options that international customers expect to use.* In many countries (as in the United States), most customers use credit cards to pay for online purchases. Shoppers in some countries prefer to use other methods of payment. In the Netherlands, direct debit transactions account for 60 percent of online payments. In the Czech Republic, 50 percent of online sales are cash on delivery. In Germany, nearly half of customers use online banking transfers.
- *Display shipping options, charges, and delivery dates up front.* Small companies, in particular, benefit by outsourcing international shipping to companies that specialize in the field. Some exported items are subject to tariffs and taxes that can create nasty surprises for customers and lost sales for companies that are unaware of them. When managers at *DrJays.com*, a retailer of hip-hop clothing aimed at young adults with outlets in New York City, reviewed the company's Web analytics, they discovered that shoppers in Russia were browsing the DrJays Web site. DrJays hired i-parcel LLC, a company that specializes in international shipping services, to handle all of the specifics of shipping its international orders. DrJays has since worked with i-parcel to begin shipping to customers in 20 more countries. In just one year, DrJays's international sales have doubled.
- *Post your company's return policy and customer service information.* You can increase the appeal of your products to international customers by addressing a potential stumbling block to making a sale: your company's return policy. In addition, be sure to tell customers for

*(continued)*

# Lessons from the Street-Smart Entrepreneur *(continued)*

whom the FAQ section of your company's Web site is not sufficient how to reach customer service representatives with their questions.

- ● ***Incorporate the nuances of a country's business culture into your Web site.*** Your Web site should show customers that you understand how business works in each country. For instance, asking customers in Ireland to input a ZIP code on an order form is pointless; outside of Dublin, Ireland does not use ZIP codes. Displaying product sizes in local measurements also increases a site's conversion rate.

*Sources:* Based on Steven Millward, "China Now Has 242 Million E-Commerce Shoppers Spending $40,000 per Second," *TechInAsia*, January 18, 2013, *www.techinasia.com/china-ecommerce-242-million-online-shoppers-2013-stats*; "Internet Usage Statistics: The Internet Big Picture," *Internet World Stats*, June 30, 2012, *www.internetworldstats.com/stats.htm*; Christian Arno, "Take Your Online Presence Global: Five Foreign-Language Online Marketing Tips," *Marketing Profs*, November 4, 2011, *www.marketingprofs.com/articles/2011/6316/take-your-online-presence-global-five-foreign-language-online-marketing-tips*; Ryan Underwood, "Clicks from Around the World," *Inc.*, December 2010/January 2011, pp. 146–147; Chris Bishop, "Seven Tips for Global E-commerce," Econsultancy, March 22, 2012, *http://econsultancy.com/us/blog/9387-7-tips-for-global-ecommerce*; Paul Demery, "*DrJays.com* Opens Foreign Doors with i-parcel," *Internet Retailer*, February 26, 2013, *www.internetretailer.com/2013/02/26/drjayscom-opens-foreign-doors-i-parcel*.

## Go Mobile

More people now access the Internet with a mobile device such as a smart phone or a tablet device than with a desktop computer.[69] More than 55 percent of U.S. adults (about 126 million people) own smart phones, and 25 percent of adults own tablets.[70] These mobile users continue to increase the frequency with which they make online purchases from their devices (m-commerce). In fact, the average amount per order for smart phones ($97.82) and tablets ($96.84) is larger than the average amount per order for desktop computers ($91.76). However, conversion rates for mobile devices (1.01 percent for smart phones and 3.12 percent for tablets) are lower than those for desktop computers (3.28 percent).[71] Despite the rapid growth of m-commerce (see Figure 13.6), 74 percent of small businesses have not developed a version of their Web sites that is viewable on smart phones, and 86 percent of small companies have not developed a version of their Web sites that is viewable on tablets.[72] The payoff for companies that cater to mobile shoppers is significant; 84 percent of the companies that have created dedicated mobile Web sites say that they have experienced increased sales.[73]

Because mobile devices have smaller screens than desktop PCs, they cannot display traditional Web sites properly. One recent survey reports that 96 percent of mobile shoppers have encountered Web sites that were not designed for mobile devices. In addition, 61 percent of mobile users say that they quickly move on to other sites when they cannot navigate a site and find the items they want to purchase. Conversely, 67 percent of mobile users say that when they visit a mobile-friendly site, they are *more* likely to make a purchase from the company.[74] By investing a little more time and money to create **responsive Web sites**, those that conform naturally and seamlessly to the size and resolution of the screen on which they are displayed, small companies can accommodate customers on *any* device from which they want to shop. A responsive Web design eliminates the necessity of creating multiple versions of a Web site for various platforms and moves a company's Web site higher in Google's all-important search engine rankings. When designing mobile Web sites, companies must be aware that speed is important (although mobile customers are somewhat more forgiving than those who use desktop PCs). Three seconds is the magic download time for mobile Web sites; nearly 60 percent of mobile users expect a Web site to download in three seconds or less, and 40 percent of them say that they abandon sites that require more than three seconds to load.[75]

**ENTREPRENEURIAL PROFILE: Deb Palacio and Terri Hunsinger: Webundies** In 1999, Deb Palacio and Terri Hunsinger started Webundies, an online specialty retailer that sold novelty boxer shorts in 15 designs. Today, Webundies has expanded its product line to include 1,500 styles of men's, women's, and children's underwear, loungewear, and robes and recently launched a dedicated mobile commerce Web site to reach the growing number of shoppers who access the Internet from mobile devices. The company's mobile sales account for 5.4 percent of its $3.1 million in annual sales and are growing rapidly. To build its mobile site, Webundies relied on vendors who specialize in m-commerce. "It was so easy," says Hunsinger. "Vendors are so much better at these things than we are. I recognize where our strengths are and where they are not." Webundies' next move is to strengthen its mobile site's search feature to allow shoppers to find the items they want more easily.[76]

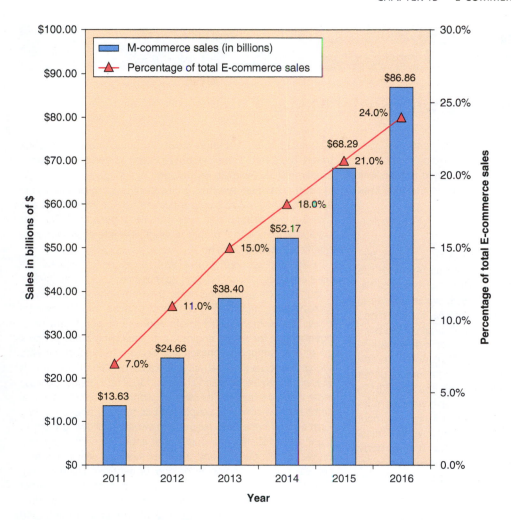

**FIGURE 13.6**

**U.S. Mobile Commerce Sales**

*Source:* Based on eMarketer, January 2013.

## Promote Your Web Site Online and Offline

E-commerce entrepreneurs have to use every means available—both online and offline—to promote their Web sites and to drive traffic to it. Cross promotions in which a physical store promotes the Web site and the Web site promotes the physical store can boost sales in both venues. In addition to using traditional online techniques such as registering with search engines, creating banner ads, and joining banner exchange programs, Web entrepreneurs must promote their sites offline as well. Ads in other media such as direct mail or newspapers that mention a site's URL will bring customers to it. It is also a good idea to put the company's Web address on *everything* a company publishes, from its advertisements and letterhead to shopping bags and business cards. A passive approach to generating Web site traffic is a recipe for failure. On the other hand, entrepreneurs who are as innovative at promoting their e-businesses as they are at creating them can attract impressive numbers of visitors to their sites.

## Use Social Media Tools to Attract and Retain Customers

Online companies are harnessing the power of social media sites such as Facebook, LinkedIn, Twitter, YouTube, Pinterest, and others to drive traffic to their Web sites. Social media and other online tools recognize that shoppers, especially young ones, expect to take an interactive role in their shopping experience by writing (and reading) product reviews, asking questions, posting comments on social media sites, and engaging in other interactive behavior. Approximately 67 percent of adult Internet users participate in social networking sites, 85 percent watch online videos, and 33 percent read blogs.[77] Small businesses are responding to the opportunity to connect with their customers online by adding the following social media to their e-commerce strategies:

- *Mashups.* A **mashup** is a Web site or an application that combines content from multiple sources into a single Web service. For example, Twitzu is a mashup that allows users to manage

**Entrepreneurship in Action**

# Enhancing E-Commerce with Social Media

Entrepreneurs who use social media to drive traffic to their companies' Web sites can generate impressive returns on their investments. The following companies successfully used two popular social media tools—Facebook and Pinterest—to enhance their e-commerce efforts.

## Toll Booth Saddle Shop

Toll Booth Saddle Shop (TBSS), a tack shop located in Eastampton, New Jersey, has built a solid e-commerce business with the help of a creative Facebook strategy. Patricia Janssen and her mother Rose Hunter are co-owners of TBSS, which opened in 1974, but Janssen credits her daughter, Andrea, for the shop's Facebook success. Andrea created the shop's original Facebook page and then taught her mother how to use it as a marketing tool. The site's home page includes a "Follow Us" section with highly visible links to the company's social media pages on Facebook, Twitter, Pinterest, LinkedIn, and YouTube. TBSS's Facebook page is appealing to horse enthusiasts because it includes posts and comments that contain useful tips on proper equine care, reviews of equipment, and answers to visitors' questions about their horses. It also features a photo contests, horse jokes, and horse trivia. Employees frequently engage customers with questions such as "What is your favorite barn boot?" or "What is your favorite cowboy quotation?" The goal is twofold: to engage customers in conversation and to create a page that serves as a valuable source of useful information so that customers keep coming back. "We know our customers pretty well," says Janssen, "and we try to make it fun." TBSS gives visitors an incentive to "like" the company: a 10 percent discount on any purchase from the online store. The Facebook page also has a clickable link, "Shop Now," that takes customers directly to a landing page on the company's Web site and an invitation to sign up for the TBSS e-mail newsletter. One of the most popular features of the TBSS Facebook page is the home-made video that the company posts every Wednesday featuring Harold the Hero Horse, the shop's mascot. (One recent episode featured Harold and his canine sidekick JR, Janssen's Jack Russell Terrier, dreaming that they are shopping for a gift for Harold's girlfriend, Miranda, on the TBSS Web site.) Customers who follow TBSS on Twitter receive tweets announcing the latest videos. TBSS's creative use of Facebook has allowed the company to amass nearly 2,000 likes and to increase its e-commerce sales.

## Souchi

Suzi Johnson started Souchi in 1998 to sell a line of luxury cashmere sweaters to upscale women. Within a few months, her sweaters had appeared in national magazines such as *Elle*, *InStyle*, *People*, *Vogue*, and *Seventeen* as well as on characters in several popular television shows, including *Friends*. Johnson's brand benefited from celebrities such as Jennifer Aniston, Cameron Diaz, Gwenyth Paltrow, and Kim Kardashian appearing in Souchi cashmere sweaters. Johnson invested several thousand dollars building a Web site to showcase her line of sweaters and tops but was disappointed with the sales it generated. She was confident that, with a proper redesign, the site could generate significant sales for Souchi.

Johnson worked with a Web developer to review the site's analytics, navigation, and appearance. Looking at the site through Souchi's customers' eyes, they redesigned it, simplifying its navigation, improving its content with better product descriptions, adding high-quality photographs, incorporating a blog, optimizing it for search engines, and employing a pay-per-click advertising campaign. Johnson also decided to support the Web site with a social media strategy. Because her target customer is virtually all female, Johnson chose to focus on Pinterest because more than 90 percent of its users are women. Pinterest is a virtual pinboard that connects people with common interests ranging from art and hobbies to recipes and sweaters, allowing them to organize and share photographs that appeal to or inspire them. People use Pinterest to find the latest fashions, learn new recipes, share ideas on home decorating, or get tips on landscaping. Johnson saw Pinterest as the ideal way to connect with her target customers and to encourage them to promote Souchi's product line, which now includes a full line of women's clothing, and added a "Pin It" button that allows users to share photos of her fashions on Pinterest. The results amazed Johnson. Almost immediately, customers began pinning Souchi product photographs to Pinterest. Traffic to the Souchi Web site increased by an incredible 5,700 percent, which resulted in an impressive increase in sales for the company.

1. Conduct an online search for tips on integrating social media into a company's e-commerce strategy. Select a social media tool such as Facebook, Pinterest, Twitter, LinkedIn, or others and develop a list of at least five suggestions that entrepreneurs can use to implement it into their e-commerce strategies.

2. Work with a team of your classmates to select a local small business and develop a plan for adding or enhancing the integration of social media into its e-commerce effort.

*Sources:* Based on Phil Mershon, "9 Facebook Marketing Success Stories You Should Model," *Social Media Examiner*, September 13, 2011, *www.socialmediaexaminer .com/9-facebook-marketing-success-stories-you-should-model*; Rose Krebs, "Eastampton Saddle Shop Making a Name for Itself Online," *Philly Burbs*, August 12, 2011, *www.phillyburbs.com/news/local/burlington_county_times_news/eastampton-saddle-shop-making-a-name-for-itself-online/article_3fcef6ed-f772-59ed-ac5a-6ba81f41feb4.html*; Joe Kutchera, "The Power of Pinterest: Small Business Case Study of Souchi.com," *JoeKutchera.com*, November 6, 2012, *http://joekutchera .com/the-power-of-pinterest-small-business-case-study-of-souchi-com*.

invitations and responses to events. They invite their Twitter followers to an event—the grand opening of a new location, for example—and then receive responses from guests on Twitter.

- *Really Simple Syndication.* **Really Simple Syndication** (RSS) is an application that allows subscribers to aggregate content from their favorite Web sites into a single feed that is delivered automatically whenever the content is updated. RSS is ideal for companies whose customers are information junkies.

- *Social Media.* Many online businesses attract potential customers to their Web sites through their Facebook and Pinterest pages, Twitter posts, and LinkedIn accounts. They use Web sites as a "hub" supported by the "spokes" of social media. Web sites that include a social sign-in feature, which allows social media users to bypass creating accounts and passwords when they log into a company's Web site, create a seamless integration between a company's Web site and social media. Just 24 percent of small businesses integrate social media in a strategic and structured way, but those that do often see big payoffs.[78] In a recent survey by Manta, 36 percent of small business owners say that at least half of the new customers they acquired in the previous year originated with social media.[79]

**ENTREPRENEURIAL PROFILE: Jake Godby and Sean Vahey: Humphrey Slocombe** Humphrey Slocombe, a 14-seat ice cream shop in San Francisco co-owned by Jake Godby and Sean Vahey, has built a large following of dedicated customers almost exclusively using Twitter. "We started using Twitter because we have zero money for any kind of advertising and promotion," says Vahey. The entrepreneurs, who are known for their sometimes bizarre flavors, including Peanut Butter Curry, Secret Breakfast (corn flakes and bourbon), Butter-Beer (butter, molasses, and oatmeal stout), and government cheese (Mimolette, sour cream, cinnamon, and cayenne), keep their 300,000 Twitter followers updated on the latest featured flavors. "As soon as we put it on Twitter, it moves," says Vahey.[80]

Other companies find that encouraging customers to post their favorite products to their Pinterest or Facebook pages increases sales and can create an army of brand ambassadors.

- *Wikis.* A **wiki** is a dynamic collection of Web pages that allows users to add to or edit their content. The most popular wiki is Wikipedia, the user-created online encyclopedia for which users provide the content. Some companies use wikis to encourage customers to participate in the design of their products, a process called **co-creation**.

- *Widgets.* Another tool that small companies use to attract attention on the Web is **widgets** (also known as **gadgets**), low-cost applications that appear like small television screens on Web sites, blogs, or computer desktops and perform specific functions. Entrepreneurs can create their own widgets or purchase them from developers and customize them, adding their own names, brands, and logos. Customers and visitors can download the widget to their desktops or, perhaps, post it to their Facebook pages, where other Web users see it, and the social nature of the Web exposes the company to thousands of potential customers. A popular widget not only drives customers to a site but also can improve a company's ranking on major search engines. "It's a great way to continually remind people that you exist," says Ivan Pope, CEO of widget developer Snipperoo.[81] Many companies create shopping widgets that alert customers to special deals and allow them to shop the company's Web site directly from the widget.

## Capture Local Traffic

A well-designed Web site not only opens global markets for a company but also is an important tool for attracting local customers to its storefront. According to the Pew Internet and American Life Project, 51 percent of U.S. adults get information about local businesses on the Internet.[82] Small companies should include their physical addresses and telephone numbers on their Web sites (60 percent of small businesses do not) and should use geographically specific keywords in pages titles, header tags, and content that search engines will pick up.[83] Establishing a presence in online directories such as *YellowPages.com*, Yelp, and Google Places also attracts local shoppers.

## Develop an Effective Search Engine Optimization Strategy

**Search engine optimization** (SEO) strategies have become an essential part of online companies' success. With more than 246 million domain names in existence, it is no surprise that Internet shoppers use search engines extensively. Search engines are the most common tool that

*Source:* CartoonStock.

*"Why is my site always the caboose on every search engine?"*

people use to find the products and services they want; 89 percent of shoppers say that they use search engines to find information about the products and services for which they are shopping.[84] As a result, companies are devoting more of their marketing budgets to search engine listings that are focused on landing their Web sites at or near the top of the most popular search engines. For a company engaged in e-commerce, a well-defined SEO strategy is an essential component in its business model. Search engines drive more traffic to e-commerce sites (32.0 percent) than either e-mail (4.3 percent) or social media (1.9 percent) and generate higher average order values ($90.40) than either e-mail ($82.72) or social media ($64.19).[85]

One of the biggest challenges facing e-commerce entrepreneurs is maintaining the effectiveness of their search engine marketing strategies. Because the most popular search engines are constantly updating and refining their algorithms, the secretive formulas and methodology search engines use to find and rank the results of Web searches, Web entrepreneurs also must evaluate and refine constantly their search strategies.

**ENTREPRENEURIAL PROFILE: Andrew Strauss: Oh My Dog Supply LLC** Andrew Strauss, owner of Oh My Dog Supply LLC, an online company based in San Francisco that sells a full range of dog supplies, says that 70 percent of his customers found his company's Web site through natural listings on search engines. His company almost always appeared in the top results list on search engine giant Google. Then Google engineers changed the algorithm used in searches, and Oh My Dog Supply LLC virtually disappeared from its search results. Strauss watched helplessly as his company's search engine traffic plunged by 96 percent and his sales decline by more than 60 percent. "We're completely crippled now," he says.[86]

A company's Web search strategy must incorporate the two basic types of search engine results: natural or organic listings and paid or sponsored listings. Although shoppers more often click on organic listings (70 percent vs. 30 percent for paid listings), research shows that shoppers are more likely to purchase from a particular Web site that ranks high in both organic and paid or sponsored listings.[87] **Natural or organic listings** often arise as a result of "spiders," powerful programs search engines use to crawl around the Web, analyzing sites for keywords, links, and other data. Based on what they find, spiders index Web sites so that a search engine can display a listing of relevant Web sites when a person enters a keyword in the engine to start a search. Some search engines use people-powered searches rather than spider-powered ones to assemble their indexes. With natural listings, an entrepreneur's goal is to get his or her Web site displayed at or near the top of the list of search results. SEO involves managing the content, keywords, titles, tags, features, and design of a Web site so that it appears at or near the top of Internet search results. The reason that SEO is so important: 75 percent of search engine users never go beyond the first page of organic search results.[88] (In fact, 53 percent of users click on the first result listed, 15 percent on the second result, and 9 percent on the third result.[89]) "The difference between being seen on page 1 and page 2 of search results can mean thousands, even millions, of dollars for a business in revenue," says Martin Falle, CEO of SEO Research, a search engine marketing company.[90] A useful resource for entrepreneurs is SEO Book, a search engine optimization site (*www.seobook.com*) that offers both free tools and more than 100 training modules on a variety of SEO topics for a fee.

Companies can use the following tips to improve their search placement results:

- Conduct brainstorming sessions to develop a list of keywords and phrases that searchers are likely to use when using a search engine to locate a company's products and services and then use those words and phrases on your Web pages. Usually, simple terms are better than industry jargon.

- Use Google's AdWords Keyword Tool to determine how many monthly searches users conduct globally and locally for a keyword or phrase. More specific, lower-volume keywords and phrases usually produce higher search rankings because they provide potential customers the more focused results they are seeking.

- Use these keywords in the title tags (meta tags, which are limited to 140 characters) and headlines of your Web pages. Most search engines are geared to pick them up. For best results, you should focus each page of your site on one specific keyword or phrase, which should appear in the page's title. Placing keywords in these critical locations can be tedious, but it produces search results for the companies that take the time to do it.

- Create the content of each Web page with your customers in mind. Each page should contain between 500 and 1,500 words that are relevant to the keyword used in the title tag. Organize the text into well-structured paragraphs and include photographs (that have file names that match the keyword of that page) and videos.

- Visit competitors' sites for keyword ideas but avoid using the exact phrases. Simply right-clicking on a competitor's Web page and choosing "View Source" will display the keywords used in the meta tags on the site.

- Consider using less obvious keywords and brand names. For instance, rather than use just "bicycles," a small bicycle retailer should consider keywords such as "racing bikes," "road racing bike," or "LeMond" to draw customers.

- Ask customers which words and phrases they use when searching for the products and services the company sells.

- Use data analysis tools to find the words and phrases (and the search engines) that brought visitors to the company's Web site.

- Check blogs and bulletin boards related to the company's products and services for potential key terms.

- Don't forget about misspellings; people often misspell the words they type into search engines. Include them in your list.

- Hire services such as Wordtracker that monitor and analyze Web users' search engine tendencies.

- Block irrelevant results with "negative keywords," those that are excluded in a search.

- Land links to your Web site on high-profile Web sites. Search engines rank sites that have external links to high-volume sites higher than those that do not.

- Start a blog. Well-written blogs not only draw potential customers to your site but also tend to attract links from other Web sites. Blogs also allow entrepreneurs to use key words strategically and frequently, which moves their sites up in search result rankings.

- Post videos on your site. In addition to uploading them to video sites such as YouTube, companies can wait for organic listings to appear, or they can submit their videos to search engines for listing. Forrester Research estimates that a properly submitted video is 50 times more likely to achieve a first-page listing on Google than any text-based page.[91]

Because organic listings can take months to materialize, many e-commerce companies rely on paid listings, which give them an immediate presence in search engines. **Paid or sponsored**

**listings** are short text advertisements with links to the sponsoring company's Web site that appear on the results pages of a search engine when a user types in a keyword or phrase. Entrepreneurs use paid search listings to accomplish what natural listings cannot. Fortunately, just four search engines—Google, Microsoft Bing, Yahoo!, and AOL—account for more than 98 percent of the searches conducted in the United States.[92] Google, the most popular search engine with 67 percent of all searches, displays paid listings as "sponsored links" at the top and down the side of each results page, and Yahoo! shows "sponsored results" at the top and the bottom of its results pages. Advertisers bid on keywords to determine their placement on a search engine's results page. On Google, an ad's placement in search results is a function of the ad's relevance (determined by a quality score of 1 to 10 that Google assigns) and the advertiser's bid on the keyword. The ad that gets the most prominent placement (at the top) of the search engine's results page when a user types in that keyword on the search engine is the one with the highest combination of quality score and bid price. An advertiser pays only when a shopper clicks through to its Web site from the search engine. For this reason, paid listings also are called pay-for-placement, pay-per-click, and pay-for-performance ads. On Google's Adwords program, the minimum keyword bid is 5 cents, but some words can cost $75 or more!* The average cost for a pay-per-click keyword has risen from 39 cents in 2004 to 53 cents today.[93] Although paid listings can be expensive, they allow advertisers to evaluate their effectiveness using the statistical reports the search engine generates. Pay-per-click advertisers can control costs by geo-targeting their ads, having them appear only in certain areas, and by setting a spending limit per day.

Using generic terms results in large numbers of searches but often produces very small conversion rates and very little in sales; normally, entrepreneurs get better results bidding on more precise, lower-volume keywords. Rather than compete with much larger companies for 5 or 10 common keywords, a more effective strategy is to bid on 200 less popular keywords.

**ENTREPRENEURIAL PROFILE: Suzanne Golter: Happy Hound** Suzanne Golter, owner of Happy Hound, a doggy day care, boarding, and spa located in a renovated warehouse in Oakland, California, credits Google Adwords for her company's rapid growth. Golter began using Adwords shortly after she started her company, bidding on common keywords such as "dog boarding," "dog walking," and "dog day care." The keyword strategy was successful, attracting large numbers of customers, but as Golter learned more about paid advertising, she began to focus her bidding strategy on a larger number of more focused, geographically specific keywords. Golter's company now cares for more than 120 dogs a day, employs more than 30 employees, and is looking to open new locations. "The doors are packed with dog noses waiting to get into Happy Hound," she says. "Life is great."[94]

One problem facing companies that rely on paid listings to generate Web traffic is **click fraud**, which occurs when a company pays for clicks that are generated by someone with no interest in or intent to purchase a product or service. "Clickbots," programs that can generate thousands of phony clicks on a Web site, are a common source of click fraud. Experts estimate that the pay-per-click fraud rate is 19 percent.[95] Web analytics software can help online merchants detect click fraud, which can be quite costly. Large numbers of visitors who leave within seconds of arriving at a site, computer IP addresses that appear from all over the world, and pay-per-click costs that rise without any corresponding increase in sales are clues that a company is a victim of click fraud.

## Designing a Killer Web Site

**4.**

Learn the techniques of designing a killer Web site.

Web users are not a patient lot. They sit before their computers, their fingers poised on their mouse buttons, daring any Web site to delay them with files that take too long to load. Slow-loading sites or sites that are confusing and poorly designed cause Web users to move on faster than a bolt of lightning can strike. With more than 634 million Web sites online and more added every day, how can an entrepreneur design a Web site that captures and holds potential customers' attention long enough to make a sale? What can they do to keep customers coming back on a regular basis? There is no surefire formula for stopping online customers in their tracks, but the following suggestions will help.

---

* An online merchant's cost per sale = cost per click ÷ merchant's conversion rate. For example, a merchant with a 1 percent conversion rate who submits a keyword bid of 10 cents per click is paying $10 per sale ($0.10 ÷ 0.01 = $10).

## Decide How to Bring Your Site to Life

Merely building a Web site and building a Web site that produces results are not the same. Entrepreneurs who are not technologically savvy should turn to e-commerce hosting companies that provide one-stop services, including site design, built-in shopping carts, security filters, Web analytics, and, in some cases, credit card processing. Many of these services offer customizable templates that allow entrepreneurs to update and modify their sites very easily using "wizards." Other entrepreneurs choose to hire Web site designers to create a customized Web site. Still others decide to build their sites themselves. Whatever option they choose, entrepreneurs must pay a monthly hosting fee, which can be a flat amount, an amount per transaction, or a percentage of sales. When it comes to e-commerce, the lesson for entrepreneurs is this: focus your efforts on the core competencies that your company has developed, whether they reside in "traditional" business practices or online, and outsource all of the other aspects of doing business online to companies that have the expertise to make your e-commerce business successful.

## Start with Your Target Customer

Before creating their Web sites, entrepreneurs must paint a clear picture of their target customers. How would they organize your company's Web site? The goal is create a design in which customers see themselves when they visit. Creating a site in which customers find a comfortable fit requires a careful blend of market research, sales know-how, and aesthetics. A good Web site demonstrates brand, message, and design consistency throughout. For instance, a Web site selling discount office supplies will have a different look and feel than one selling upscale kitchen appliances. The challenge for a business with a physical presence is to create online the same image, style, and ambiance in its online presence as in its offline stores. Table 13.2 shows a breakdown of the online activities by generation for Internet users.

## Give Customers What They Want

The main reason that people shop online is *convenience*. Online companies that fail to provide a fast, efficient, and flawless shopping experience for their customers will not succeed. A well-designed Web site is intuitive, leading customers to a series of actions that are natural and result in a sale. Sites that provide customers with meaningful content and allow them to find what they are looking for easily and to pay for it conveniently and securely keep customers coming back. High-quality images of products with alternative views that allow customers to zoom in for detail, rotate them 360 degrees, and see color changes showcase a company's products and increase sales. Product descriptions should be simple, detailed, and jargon free. Videos that show product details or the product in use not only increase customer traffic but also produce higher conversion rates. One of the reasons *Amazon.com* has become the largest online retailer is that its five-point strategy is designed to give online shoppers exactly what they want: low prices, wide selection, product availability, shopping convenience, and extensive information about the products it sells.[96]

A recent survey by the Boston Consulting Group reports that the improvements to customers' online shopping experience that would motivate them to shop more online are free shipping (74 percent), lower prices (56 percent), free returns (35 percent), more secure Web sites (25 percent), and better views of virtual products (25 percent).[97] Warby Parker, an online store that sells vintage-inspired eyeglasses for as little as $95 per pair, offers free shipping and returns on up to five pairs of glasses so that customers can try them on. Many customers take photos of themselves wearing the glasses, post them to Facebook, and solicit feedback from their friends, not only increasing the probability that they will purchase at least one pair but also promoting Warby Parker. In its second year of operation, the company's sales quintupled, and it had to move its headquarters four times to accommodate its rapid growth.[98]

## Select an Intuitive Domain Name

Choose a domain name that is consistent with the image you want to create for your company and register it. Entrepreneurs should never underestimate the power of the right domain name or Uniform Resource Locator (URL), which is a company's address on the Internet. It not only tells Web users where to find a company, but it also should suggest something about the company and what it does. The ideal domain name should be as follows:

- *Short.* Short names are easy for people to remember, so the shorter a company's URL is, the more likely potential customers are to recall it.

### TABLE 13.2 Online Activities by Generation

| Millennials Ages 18–33 | Gen X Ages 34–45 | Younger Boomers Ages 46–55 | Older Boomers Ages 56–64 | Silent Generation Ages 65–73 | G.I. Generation Age 74+ |
|---|---|---|---|---|---|
| Email | Email | Email | Email | Email | Email |
| Search | Search | Search | Search | Search | Search |
| Health info | Health info | Health info | Health info | Health info | Health info |
| Social network sites | Get news | Get news | Get news | Get news | Buy a product |
| Watch video | Govt website | Govt website | Govt website | Travel reservations | Get news |
| Get news | Travel reservations | Travel reservations | Buy a product | Buy a product | Travel reservations |
| Buy a product | Watch video | Buy a product | Travel reservations | Govt website | Govt website |
| IM | Buy a product | Watch video | Bank online | Watch video | Bank online |
| Listen to music | Social network sites | Bank online | Watch video | Financial info | Financial info |
| Travel reservations | Bank online | Social network sites | Social network sites | Bank online | Religious info |
| Online classifieds | Online classifieds | Online classifieds | Online classifieds | Rate things | Watch video |
| Bank online | Listen to music | Listen to music | Financial info | Social network sites | Play games |
| Govt website | IM | Financial info | Rate things | Online classifieds | Online classifieds |
| Play games | Play games | IM | Listen to music | IM | Social network sites |
| Read blogs | Financial info | Religious info | Religious info | Religious info | Rate things |
| Financial info | Religious info | Rate things | IM | Play games | Read blogs |
| Rate things | Read blogs | Read blogs | Play games | Listen to music | Donate to charity |
| Religious info | Rate things | Play games | Read blogs | Read blogs | Listen to music |
| Online auction | Online auction | Online auction | Online auction | Donate to Charity | Podcasts |
| Podcasts | Donate to charity | Donate to Charity | Donate to Charity | Online auction | Online auction |
| Donate to charity | Podcasts | Podcasts | Podcasts | Podcasts | Blog |
| Blog | Blog | Blog | Blog | Blog | IM |
| Virtual worlds | Virtual worlds | Virtual worlds | Virtual worlds | Virtual worlds | Virtual worlds |

| | |
|---|---|
| 90–100% | 40–49% |
| 80–89% | 30–39% |
| 70–79% | 20–29% |
| 60–69% | 10–19% |
| 50–59% | 0–9% |

*Key:* % of internet users in each generation who engage in this online activity.

*Source:* Kathryn Zickuhr, *Generations 2010*, Pew Internet & American Life Project, December 16, 2010, p. 13.

- *Memorable.* Not every short domain name is necessarily memorable. Some business owners use their companies' initials as their domain name (e.g., *www.sbfo.com* for Stanley Brothers Furniture Outlet). The problem with using initials for a domain name is that customers rarely associate the two, which makes a company virtually invisible on the Web.

- *Indicative of a company's business or business name.* Perhaps the best domain name for a company is one that customers can guess easily if they know the company's name. For instance, mail order catalog company L.L. Bean's URL is *www.llbean.com*, and New Pig, a maker of absorbent materials for a variety of industrial applications, uses *www.newpig.com* as its domain name. (The company carries this concept over to its toll-free number, which is 1-800-HOT-HOGS.)

- *Easy to spell.* Even though a company's domain name may be easy to spell, it is usually wise to buy several variations of the correct spelling simply because some customers are not good spellers!

Just because entrepreneurs come up with the perfect URL for their companies' Web sites does not necessarily mean that they can use it. Domain names are given on a first-come, first-served basis. Before business owners can use a domain name, they must ensure that someone else has not already taken it. The simplest way to do that is to go to one of the accredited domain name registration services such as Network Solutions at *www.networksolutions.com*, NetNames at *www.netnames.com*, or Go Daddy at *www.godaddy.com* to conduct a name search. Entrepreneurs who find the domain name they have selected already registered to someone else have two choices: They can select another name, or they can try to buy the name from the original registrant.

With 100 million ".*com*" domain names currently registered, finding a relevant, unregistered domain name can be a challenge, but several new top-level domain (TLD) names recently became available: .aero (airlines), .biz (any business site), .coop (business cooperatives), .info (any site), .museum (museums), .name (individuals' sites), and .pro (professionals' sites). The Internet Corporation for Assigned Names and Numbers, the organization officially in charge of domain names worldwide, also has authorized the use of generic TLDs, such as .app, .joy, .beauty, .pizza, and others, increasing the number of TLDs from about two dozen to thousands.[99] Once an entrepreneur finds an unused name that is suitable, he or she must register it (plus any variations of it)—and the sooner, the better! Registering is quite easy: simply use one of the registration services listed above to fill out a form and pay the required fee. Although not required, registering the domain name with the U.S. Patent and Trademark Office at a cost of $275 provides maximum protection for a company's domain name. The office's Web site (*www.uspto.gov*) not only allows users to register a trademark online but also offers useful information on trademarks and the protection they offer.

## Make Your Web Site Easy to Navigate

Research shows that the leading factor in convincing online shoppers to make a purchase from a Web site is its ease of navigation. The starting point for evaluating a site's navigability is to conduct a user test. Find several willing shoppers, sit them in front of a computer, and watch them as they cruise through the company's Web site to make a purchase. It is one of the best ways to get meaningful, immediate feedback on the navigability of a site. Watching these test customers as they navigate the site also is useful. Where do they pause? Do they get lost in the site? Are they confused by the choices the site gives them? Is the checkout process too complex? Are the navigation buttons from one page of the site to another clearly marked, and do they make sense? Patterns that entrepreneurs discern from a site's Web analytics also reveal valuable insights about its navigability.

Because many visitors do not start from a Web site's home page, the starting point for easy navigability involves creating the right **landing pages**, the pages on which visitors land after they click on a sponsored link in a search engine, e-mail ad, or online ad. Ideally, a landing page should have the same marketing message as the link that led to it; otherwise, customers are likely to abandon the site immediately (an occurrence that is measured by a site's **bounce rate**, the percentage of visits in which customers leave a site from the landing page). A good landing page also allows customers to search or to dig deeper into the company's Web site to the products or services that they are seeking.

Successful Web sites recognize that shoppers employ different strategies to make a purchase. Some shoppers want to use a search tool, others want to browse through product categories, and still others prefer a company to make product recommendations. Effective sites accommodate all three strategies in their design. Shoppers at Gourmet Gift Baskets, an online retailer of gift baskets based in Kingston, New Hampshire, can use an internal search engine to find a gift basket, or they can browse collections of baskets organized by price range, occasion, theme, or popularity.

### Provide Customer Ratings and Reviews

Customer ratings and reviews have become extremely important to online shoppers. The Global Consumer Shopping Habits Survey reports that 90 percent of online shoppers read reviews from other shoppers and that 83 percent say that the reviews influence whether they actually make a purchase.[100] Allowing customers to post product reviews and ratings enhances a site's credibility and leads to increased sales.

### Offer Suggestions for Related Products

Many online merchants increase sales with the help of recommendation engines, which match keywords that shoppers enter into a site's internal search engine with complementary or supplementary items that the company sells. The goal is to increase total sales by cross-selling. For example, a customer who enters the word "French cuff shirt" into a company's search tool might see a link to the company's selection of cufflinks and ties in addition to all of the French cuff shirts that appear. *Amazon.com* is famous for the success of its product recommendations, which appear as "customers who bought this item also bought . . ." product suggestions.

### Add Wish List Capability

Giving customers the ability to create wish lists of products and services they want and then connect other people to those lists not only boosts a company's sales but also increases its visibility.

### Create a Gift Idea Center

Online retailers have discovered that one of the most successful tools for improving their conversion rates is to offer a gift idea center. A gift idea center is a section of a Web site that includes a variety of gift ideas where shoppers can browse for ideas based on price, gender, or category. Gift centers can provide a huge boost for e-tailers, particularly around holidays, because they offer creative suggestions for shoppers looking for the perfect gift. Other variations of this approach that have proved to be successful for e-commerce entrepreneurs include suggested items pages, bargain basement sale pages, and featured sale pages.

### Establish the Appropriate Call to Action on Each Page

Every page of a Web site should have a purpose, steering customers to take a specific action—place an order, review the company's services, sign up for a newsletter, request information, read customer testimonials, and more. Make sure that the call to action on every page is highly visible and appropriate.

### Build Loyalty by Giving Online Customers a Reason to Return to Your Web Site

Just as with brick-and-mortar retailers, e-tailers that constantly have to incur the expense of attracting new customers find it difficult to remain profitable because of the extra cost required to acquire customers. One of the most effective ways to encourage customers to return to a site is to establish an incentive program that rewards them for repeat purchases. "Frequent-buyer" programs that offer discounts or points toward future purchases, giveaways such as T-shirts emblazoned with a company's logo, or special sales only for loyal customers are common elements of incentive programs. Incentive programs that are properly designed with a company's target customer in mind really work. Business Supply, an online office products company, periodically sends its most frequent and highest spending customers a thank-you e-mail that includes a $10 coupon. The promotion produces a 400 percent return on investment.[101]

### Establish Hyperlinks with Other Businesses, Preferably Those Selling Products or Services That Complement Yours

Listing the Web addresses of complementary businesses on your company's site and having them list your site's address on their sites offers customers more value and can bring traffic to your site that you otherwise would have missed. For instance, the owner of a site selling upscale kitchen gadgets should consider a cross-listing arrangement with sites that feature gourmet recipes, wines, and kitchen appliances.

## Include an E-Mail Option, an Address, and a Telephone Number on Your Site

Customers appreciate the opportunity to communicate with your company, and you should give them many options for doing so. If you include e-mail access on your site, however, be sure to respond to it promptly. Nothing alienates customers faster than a company that is slow to respond or fails to respond to their e-mail messages. Also be sure to include an address and a toll-free telephone number for customers who prefer to write or call with their questions. Unfortunately, many companies either fail to include their telephone numbers on their sites or bury them so deeply within the sites' pages that customers never find them.

## Give Shoppers the Ability to Track Their Orders Online

Many customers who order items online want to track the progress of their orders. One of the most effective ways to keep a customer happy is to send an e-mail confirmation that your company received the order and another e-mail notification when you ship the order. The shipment notice should include the shipper's tracking number and instructions on how to track the order from the shipper's site. Order and shipping confirmations instill confidence in even the most Web-wary shoppers.

## Offer Web-Only Specials

Give Web customers a special deal that you don't offer in any other advertising piece. Change your specials often (weekly, if possible) and use clever "teasers" to draw attention to the offer. Regular special offers available only on the Web give customers an incentive to keep visiting a company's site.

## Use the Power of Social Media

Make it easy for customers to connect with your company on social media such as Facebook, Pinterest, Twitter, and others by including social media sharing links and links to your company's social media pages on your Web site.

## Use Customer Testimonials

Customer testimonials about a company and its products and services lend credibility to a site, but the testimonials must be genuine and believable. Video testimonials can be even more powerful than written ones.

**ENTREPRENEURIAL PROFILE: Charlie and Eddie Bakhash: American Pearl** American Pearl, a company that sells pearls from its Fifth Avenue showroom in New York City and its Web site (*www.americanpearl.com*), reinforces the owners' extensive knowledge of and dedication to pearls with a Web page dedicated to customer testimonials. Explaining the importance of the testimonial page, Eddie Bakhash, whose father, Charlie, started the company in 1950, says, "We understand that purchasing an expensive strand of pearls for a loved one on the Internet can require courage." The highly successful company also instills confidence in customers by offering an unconditional 30-day, money-back guarantee.[102]

## Follow a Simple Design

Catchy graphics and photographs are important to snaring customers, but designers must choose them carefully. Designs that are overly complex take a long time to download, and customers are likely to move on before they appear. Web Site Garage (*http://thewebsitegarage.com*), a Web site maintenance company, offers companies a free 21-point inspection of their Web sites and a report that describes problems ranging from slow download speeds to search engine optimization and their potential solutions.

Specific design tips include the following:

• Avoid clutter, especially on your site's home page. "The homepage is like a store's display window, minus the mannequins," explains a report on proper Web design.[103] The best designs are simple and elegant with a balance of both text and graphics. "The minimalist approach makes a site appear more professional," says one design expert.[104]

- Use less text on your site's home page, landing pages, and initial product or service pages. Although including detailed, text-heavy content deeper in your site is acceptable and even desirable, incorporating too much text early on dissuades customers. Allow customers to drill down to more detailed product and service descriptions.

- Avoid huge graphic headers that must download first, prohibiting customers from seeing anything else on your site as they wait (or, more likely, *don't* wait). Use graphics judiciously so that the site loads quickly; otherwise, impatient customers will abandon the site.

- Include a menu bar at the top of every page that makes it easy for customers to find their way around your site.

- Make the site easy to navigate by including easy-to-follow navigation buttons at the bottom of pages that enable customers to return to the top of the page or to the menu bar. This avoids "the pogo effect," where visitors bounce from page to page in a Web site looking for what they need. Without navigation buttons or a site map page, a company runs the risk of customers getting lost in its site and leaving. Organizing a Web site into logical categories also helps.

- Minimize the number of clicks required for a customer to get to any particular page in the site. Long paths increase the likelihood of customers bailing out before they reach their intended destination.

- Incorporate meaningful content in the site that is useful to visitors, well organized, easy to read, and current. The content should be consistent with the message a company sends in the other advertising media it uses. Although a Web site should be designed to sell, providing useful, current information attracts visitors, keeps them coming back, and establishes a company's reputation as an expert in the field.

- Include a FAQ section. Adding a searchable FAQ section to a site can reduce dramatically the number of telephone calls and e-mails customer service representatives must handle. FAQ sections typically span a wide range of issues—from how to place an order to how to return merchandise—and cover topics that customers most often want to know about.

- Be sure to include privacy and return policies as well as product guarantees the company offers.

- Avoid fancy typefaces and small fonts because they are too hard to read.

- Be vigilant for misspelled words, typographical errors, formatting mistakes, and dead links; they destroy a site's credibility in no time and send customers fleeing to competitors' sites.

- Don't put small fonts on "busy" backgrounds; no one will read them!

- Use contrasting colors of text and graphics. For instance, blue text on a green background is nearly impossible to read.

- Be careful with frames. Using frames that are so thick that they crowd out text makes for a poor design.

- Test the site on different Web browsers and on different size monitors. A Web site may look exactly the way it was designed to look on one Web browser and be a garbled mess on another. Sites designed to display correctly on large monitors may not view well on small ones.

- Use your Web site to collect information from visitors but don't tie up customers with a tedious registration process. Most will simply leave the site never to return. Offers for a free e-mail newsletter or a contest giveaway can give visitors enough incentive to register with a site.

- Incorporate a search function that allows shoppers to type in the items they want to purchase. Unlike in-store shoppers, who might browse until they find the item, online shoppers usually want to go straight to the products they seek. Ideally, the search function acknowledges common misspellings of key terms, avoiding the dreaded "No Results Found" message.

- Include company contact information and an easy-to-find customer service telephone number.

- Avoid automated music that plays continuously and cannot be cut off.

- Make sure the overall look of the site is consistent and appealing. "When a site is poorly designed, lacks information, or cannot support customer needs, that [company's] reputation is seriously jeopardized," says one expert.[105]

- Remember: Simpler usually is better.

## Assure Customers That Online Transactions Are Secure

If you are serious about doing business on the Web, make sure that your site includes the proper security software and encryption devices. Computer-savvy customers are not willing to divulge their credit card numbers on sites that are not secure. Unfortunately, 60 percent of small companies do not tell their customers about the precautions they take to protect customers' data.[106] E-commerce companies also should avoid storing their customers' credit card information. With attacks from hackers increasingly prevalent, the risk is just too high.

## Post Shipping and Handling Charges Up Front

A common gripe among online shoppers is that some e-tailers fail to reveal their shipping and handling charges early in the checkout process. Responsible online merchants keep shipping and handling charges reasonable and display them early on in the buying process—before shoppers adds items to a cart. When customers' orders qualify for free shipping, the site should automate this step rather than require customers to input a free shipping code. Providing shoppers with multiple shipping options and their associated costs increases a site's conversion rate. At checkout, Gourmet Gift Baskets, the online retailer of gift baskets, displays delivery dates, shipping methods, and their associated costs, enabling shoppers to easily select the shipping option that best suits their needs.[107]

## Create a Fast, Simple Checkout Process

One surefire way to destroy an online company's conversion rate is to impose a lengthy, convoluted checkout process that requires customers to wade through pages of forms to fill out just to complete a purchase. When faced with a lengthy checkout process, customers simply abandon a site and make their purchases elsewhere. The fewer the steps required for customers to check out, the more successful will be the site at generating sales.

## Provide Customers Multiple Payment Options

In the United States, credit cards remain the most popular method of payment online (preferred by 69 percent of shoppers).[108] However, because some customers are skittish about using their credit cards online, online merchants should offer other payment options, such as Paypal, Google Checkout, or some other payment service.

## Confirm Transactions

Order-confirmation e-mails, which a company can generate automatically, let a customer know that the company received the online order and can be an important first line of defense against online fraud. If the customer claims not to have placed the order, the company can cancel it and report the transaction and the credit card information as suspicious. Order confirmation e-mails should include shipping information and a tracking number that allows customers to view the status of their orders.

## Keep Your Site Fresh

Customers want to see something new when they visit stores, and they expect the same when they visit virtual stores as well. Regularly add new content such as videos, blogs, customer testimonials, or information-rich articles to your site. Delete any hyperlinks that have disappeared and keep the information on your Web site current. One sure way to run off customers on the Web is to continue to advertise your company's "Christmas Special" in August! On the other hand, fresh information and new specials keep customers coming back.

## Rely on Analytics to Improve Your Site

Web analytics (see the following section) provide a host of useful information ranging from the keywords that shoppers use to find your site and how long they stay on it to the number of visitors and their locations. The best way to increase a site's conversion rate is to use analytics to determine which techniques work best and integrate them throughout the site. Analytics also are useful for determining what's *not* working on a Web site. Above-average bounce and shopping cart abandonment rates, low traffic counts, and slow-moving inventory are signs that a Web site is in need of an overhaul.

## Test Your Site Often

Smart e-commerce entrepreneurs check their sites frequently to make sure they are running smoothly and are not causing customers unexpected problems. A good rule of thumb is to check your site at least monthly—or weekly if its content changes frequently.

### Consider Hiring a Professional Designer

Pros can do it a lot faster and better than you can. However, don't give designers free rein to do whatever they want to with your site. Make sure it meets your criteria for an effective site that can sell.

Entrepreneurs must remember that on the Web every company, no matter how big or small it is, has the exact same screen size for its site. What matters most is not the size of your company but how you put that screen size to use.

 ## In the Entrepreneurial Spotlight

# Web Site Makeovers

## Favi Entertainment

In 2006, Jeremy Yakel launched Favi Entertainment, a provider of electronic devices and accessories including televisions, projection systems, wireless keyboards, and screens that use the latest technology. The company, headquartered in Macomb, Michigan, targets professionals, educators, and home enthusiasts with its high-performing yet affordable devices and generates $2.6 million in annual sales. Favi Entertainment's Web site contributed only a paltry $6,000 to the company's annual sales, and Yakel knew that the site was underperforming because it was disorganized and cluttered. "We had grown into a premier manufacturer of consumer electronics, and our site just didn't say that to our customers," admits Yakel.

Yakel and his team of 12 employees undertook a complete overhaul to fix the Web site's problems. The overriding goals were to make the site cleaner and easier to navigate and to improve customers' shopping experience. They started by studying the existing site's Google Analytics report to determine what customers were looking for and how they moved around the Web site. The team improved the site's content, adding more descriptive product explanations and product videos, and used Google's Keyword Tool to upgrade the site's metatags to include the terms that electronics shoppers enter most frequently into the search engine. They also added a foreign currency conversion tool to make shopping easier for customers outside the United States to make purchases. The team's next step was to integrate an e-commerce platform that provides international shoppers with shipping costs, delivery dates, and multilingual customer support and invoices.

Yakel spent $3,900 revamping the Favi Entertainment Web site, an investment that has paid off well. The company's shopping cart abandonment rate declined 43 percent almost immediately, and the site was on track to generate sales of $244,000 in the first year.

## SKLZ

John Sarkasian started Pro Performance Sports in 2002 to market the Hit-A-Way baseball swing training device that he had developed. In 2005, Sarkasian began marketing a line of athletic training products under the SKLZ brand through its own Web site and through sporting goods retailers around the United States. He then launched an interactive, online training program under the SKLZ label to teach athletes how to get the greatest benefit from the company's training products. The training program includes postworkout snacks and techniques that help injuries heal faster. Sarkasian wanted to differentiate his company by emphasizing the unique value that the combination of its training devices and online training program provided customers and saw the SKLZ Web site as the ideal place to start. "We're delivering not only hardware—the training devices—but also content for the athlete," he says. His goal is to make SKLZ a destination site for athletes who want the equipment and the skills to train properly.

Sarkasian knew that he would have to overhaul the SKLZ Web site to accomplish his goal. The first change was beefing up the content of the site to include more custom text rather than generic descriptions of the equipment the company sells. Shoppers can browse the site by sport or by specific skills they want to improve. Those who sign up to receive the SKLZ e-mail newsletter receive a 10 percent discount on their online purchases. SKLZ also added video content, creating videos that show customers how to use 83 of its top-selling pieces of equipment. Sarkasian's team also added QR codes on all of its product packaging that customers in retail stores can scan with their smart phones or tablets to access Web pages that contain detailed information and instructional videos about a particular piece of equipment.

Sarkasian invested "hundreds of thousands of dollars" on the Web site overhaul but says that "it's been absolutely worth it." Sales of performance training tools are running 41 percent higher than the company's forecast, and SKLZ total revenue have increased 140 percent since the site relaunched. Sarkasian says that revamping the Web site was essential to the company's long-term success.

1. What lessons about developing the proper e-commerce strategy can you learn from Favi Entertainment and SKLZ?

2. What advice can you offer the management teams at Favi Entertainment and SKLZ as they continue to develop their e-commerce strategies? What additional steps can they take to stay connected to their customers and to keep their customers coming back to their Web sites?

*Sources:* Based on Gwen Moran, "System Rebuild," *Entrepreneur*, February 2012, p. 45; Gwen Moran, "They've Got SKLZ," *Entrepreneur*, January 2012, p. 43; Tanya Mannes, "SKLZ Aims to Help Amateur Athletes Improve Skills," *U-T San Diego*, September 3, 2011, *www.utsandiego.com/news/2011/sep/03/sklz-aims-to-help-amateur-athletes-improve-skills.*

# Tracking Web Results

## Software Solutions

Web sites offer entrepreneurs a treasure trove of valuable information about how well their sites are performing—if they take the time to analyze it. **Web analytics**, tools that measure a Web site's ability to attract customers, generate sales, and keep customers coming back, help entrepreneurs to know what works—and what doesn't—on their sites. Online companies that use Web analytics have an advantage over those that do not. Their owners can review the data collected from their customers' Web site activity, analyze them, make adjustments to the Web site, and then start the monitoring process over again to see whether the changes improve the site's performance. In other words, Web analytics give entrepreneurs the ability to apply the principles of continuous improvement to their sites. In addition, the changes these e-business owners make are based on facts (the data from the Web analytics) rather than on mere guesses about how customers interact with a site. Avi Steinlauf, president of automotive guide publisher *Edmunds.com*, uses an app on his iPad to track the company's Web analytics on the go, giving him the ability to monitor its Web site's performance at any time from anywhere.[109] There are many Web analytics software packages, but effective ones offer the following types of information:

5.

Explain how companies track the results from their Web sites.

- *Commerce metrics.* These are basic analytics such as sales revenue generated, number of items sold, which products are selling best (and which are not), and others.
- *Visitor segmentation measurements.* These measurements provide entrepreneurs valuable information about online shoppers and customers, including whether they are return customers or new customers, how they arrived at the site (e.g., via a search engine or a pay-per-click ad), which search terms they used (if they used a search engine), and others.
- *Content reports.* This information tells entrepreneurs which products customers are looking for and which pages they view most often (and least often), how they navigate through the site, how long they stay, which pages they are on when they exit, and more. Using this information, an entrepreneur can get an idea of how effective the site's design is.
- *Process measurements.* These metrics help entrepreneurs understand how their Web sites attract visitors and convert them into customers. Does the checkout process work smoothly? How often do shoppers abandon their carts? At what point in the process do they abandon them? These measures can lead to higher conversion rates for an online business.

Other common measures of Web site performance include the following:

- The **click-through rate** (CTR) is the proportion of people who see a company's online ad and actually click on it to reach the company's Web site. Each time an ad is displayed is called an impression:

$$CTR = \text{number of clicks} \div \text{number of impressions}$$

  For instance, if a company's ad is displayed 500 times in one day and 12 people clicked on it, the CTR is $12 \div 500 = .024 = 2.4\%$.

- The **conversion or browse-to-buy rate** is the proportion of visitors to a site who actually make a purchase. It is one of the most important measures of Web success and is calculated as follows:

  Conversion rate = number of customers who make a purchase ÷ number of visitors to the site

  Conversion rates vary dramatically across industries but usually range from 1 to 4 percent. The average conversion rate is 2.1 percent.[110] In other words, out of every 1,000 people who visit a Web site, on average 21 of them actually make a purchase.

- The **average number of visits per visitor** (AVPV) measures how many visitors return to a site and how many times they return. It is calculated as follows:

$$AVPV = \text{total number of visitors} \div \text{number of unique visitors}$$

  The AVPV is most meaningful when measured over time.

- The **cost per acquisition** (CPA) is the cost a company incurs to generate each purchase (or customer registration):

$$CPA = \text{Total cost of acquiring a new customer} \div \text{number of new customers}$$

For example, if a company purchases an advertisement in an e-magazine for $200 and it yields 15 new customers, then the cost of acquisition is $200 ÷ 15 = $13.33.

- Other important metrics include landing and exit page data, keywords used, and referring URLs. Landing pages are important because not every shopper arrives via a site's home page. Are your site's landing pages producing a suitable conversion rate? Exit page data tell entrepreneurs where in the Web site shoppers tend to leave. If the same pages show up consistently, entrepreneurs should redesign them. Keywords data tell entrepreneurs which words shoppers typed into a search engine to find the site and can be a valuable tool in refining a company's SEO strategy. Referring URL data tell entrepreneurs how people arrive at the company's site. Do they type in the company's URL directly, use a search engine, or arrive from a social media site?

## Ensuring Web Privacy and Security

### Privacy

**6.**

Describe how e-businesses ensure the privacy and security of the information they collect and store from the Web.

The Web's ability to track customers' every move naturally raises concerns over the privacy of the information companies collect. E-commerce gives businesses access to tremendous volumes of information about their customers, creating a responsibility to protect that information and to use it wisely. The potential for breaching customers' privacy is present in any e-business, and the results of a data breach can be devastating. A recent survey by online security firm TRUSTe reports that 89 percent of online adults avoid doing business with companies that fail to protect their privacy.[111] To make sure they are using the information they collect from visitors to their Web sites legally and ethically and safeguarding it adequately, companies should take the steps outlined in the following sections.

**TAKE AN INVENTORY OF THE CUSTOMER DATA COLLECTED** The first step to ensuring proper data handling is to assess exactly the type of data the company is collecting and storing. How are you collecting the information? Why are you collecting it? How are you using it? Do visitors know how you are using the data? Should you get their permission to use the data in this way? Do you use all of the data you are collecting?

**DEVELOP A COMPANY PRIVACY POLICY FOR THE INFORMATION YOU COLLECT** A **privacy policy** is a statement explaining the type of information a company collects online, what it does with that information, and the recourse customers have if they believe the company is misusing the information. *Every* online company should have a privacy policy, but many do not. A survey by Symantec and the National Cyber Security Alliance reports that 60 percent of small business's Web sites have no privacy policy.[112]

Several online privacy firms, including TRUSTe (*www.truste.org*), BBBOnline (*www.bbbonline.com*), and BetterWeb (*www.betterweb.com*), offer Web "seal programs," the equivalent of a Good Housekeeping seal of privacy approval. To earn a privacy seal of approval, a company must adopt a privacy policy, implement it, and monitor its effectiveness. Many of these privacy sites also provide online policy wizards, automated questionnaires that help e-business owners create comprehensive privacy statements.

**POST YOUR COMPANY'S PRIVACY POLICY PROMINENTLY ON YOUR WEB SITE AND FOLLOW IT** Creating a privacy policy is not sufficient; posting it in a prominent place on the Web site (accessible from every page on the site) and then abiding by it make a policy meaningful. Whether a company has a privacy policy posted prominently often determines whether customers will do online business with it. Shoppers are more likely to purchase from online merchants who have sound privacy policies and post them. One of the worst mistakes a company can make is to publish its privacy policy online and then fail to follow it. Not only is this unethical, but it also can lead to serious damage awards if customers take legal action against the company.

### Security

Concerns about security and fraud present the greatest obstacles to the growth of e-commerce. A study by Kikscore reports that 90 percent of online shoppers have terminated a transaction because of security concerns.[113] Indeed, cybercrime has become big business, affecting 1.5 million victims each day and costing consumers and companies around the world $110 billion annually.[114] Ninety-six percent of the data that cybercriminals target involves customer records. The companies most often targeted are in the retail, food and beverage, and hospitality industries.[115] Every company with a Web site—no matter how small—is a potential target for hackers and other cybercriminals; an alarming 36 percent of online attacks target small businesses.[116] Hackers and attackers have become more sophisticated, which makes Web site security a top priority for *every* company doing business online.

A company doing business on the Web faces two conflicting goals: to establish a presence on the Web so that customers can have access to its site and the information maintained there and to preserve a high level of security so that the business, its site, and the information it collects from customers are safe from hackers and intruders intent on doing harm. According to a survey by the National Cyber Security Alliance and Symantec, 76 percent of small business owners believe that their companies are either somewhat safe or very safe from cybersecurity breaches, yet 83 percent of them have no formal cybersecurity plan (and 69 percent have no informal cybersecurity plan).[117] Companies have a number of safeguards available to them, but hackers with enough time, talent, and determination usually can beat even the most sophisticated safety measures. If hackers manage to break into a system, they can do irreparable damage, stealing programs and sensitive customer data, modifying or deleting valuable information, changing the look and content of sites, or crashing sites altogether. Sixty percent of small companies that experience a cyberattack close within six months.[118] In the largest data breach to date, hackers broke into the database at one retail company and stole information that included more than 45 million debit and credit card numbers.[119] One band of cyberthieves attacked 53 small and medium-size businesses in Seattle, Washington, over a two-year period, stealing data and causing $3 million in damages to the companies and their customers.[120] Delayed detection of cybercrimes is typical; the average time between a breach and its discovery is 210 days.[121] In addition to the actual losses scams cause, another real danger is that they erode customers' confidence in e-commerce, posing real threats to every online entrepreneur.

Security threats are real for companies of every size, and entrepreneurs must contend with that reality. To minimize the likelihood of invasion by hackers and viruses, e-companies rely on several tools, including virus detection software, intrusion detection software, and firewalls. At the most basic level of protection is **virus detection software**, which scans computer drives for viruses, nasty programs written by devious hackers and designed to harm computers and the information they contain. The severity of viruses ranges widely, from relatively harmless programs that put humorous messages on a user's screen to those that erase a computer's hard drive or cause the entire system to crash. Because hackers are *always* writing new viruses to attack computer systems, entrepreneurs must keep their virus detection software up to date and must run it often. An attack by one virus can bring a company's entire e-commerce platform to a screeching halt in no time!

**Intrusion detection software** is essential for any company doing business on the Web. These packages constantly monitor the activity on a company's network server and sound an alert if they detect someone breaking into the company's computer system or if they detect unusual network activity. Intrusion detection software not only can detect attempts by unauthorized users to break into a computer system while they are happening but also can trace the hacker's location. Most packages also have the ability to preserve a record of the attempted break-in that will stand up in court so that companies can take legal action against cyberintruders. Web security companies such as McAfee provide software, such as ScanAlert, that scans a small business's Web site daily to certify that it is "Hacker Safe." Online companies using the software are able to post a certification mark signifying that their sites are protected from unauthorized access.

A **firewall** is software that operates between the Internet and a company's computer network that allows authorized data from the Internet to enter a company's network and the programs and data it contains but keeps unauthorized data, such as viruses, spyware, and other malware, out. The equivalent of the lock on a small company's front door, a firewall serves as the lock on its computer network's front door. Establishing a firewall is essential for any company operating on the Web, but entrepreneurs must make sure that their firewalls are set up properly. Otherwise, they are useless! Even with all of these security measures in place, it is best for a company to run its Web site on a separate server from the network that runs the business. If hackers break into the Web site, they still do not have access to the company's sensitive data and programs.

Increasing the security of a computer system requires using properly installed security tools, perhaps in multiple layers, and making sure that they function properly and are up to date. Even though 65 percent of small businesses store customer data on their computer systems, only 44 percent of small companies check their virus detection software and firewalls weekly to ensure that they are up to date (and 14 percent *never* check them).[122] The National Cyber Security Alliance (*http://staysafeonline.org*) and the Computer Security Institute (*http://gocsi.com*) offer articles, information, and seminars to help business owners maintain computer security. *Information Security Magazine* (which can be found at *http://searchsecurity.techtarget.com*) also offers helpful advice on maintaining computer security.

In e-commerce just as in traditional retailing, sales do not matter unless a company gets paid! On the Web, customers demand transactions they can complete with ease and convenience, and the simplest way to allow customers to pay for e-commerce transactions is with credit cards. From a Web customer's perspective, however, one of the most important security issues is the security of his or her credit card information. To ensure the security of their customers' credit card information, online retailers typically use **Secure Sockets Layer technology** to encrypt customers' transaction information as it travels across the Internet. By using secure shopping cart features from storefront-building services or Internet service providers, even the smallest e-commerce stores can offer their customers secure online transactions.

Processing credit card transactions requires a company to obtain an Internet merchant account from a bank or financial intermediary. Setup fees for an Internet merchant account typically range from $500 to $1,000, but companies also pay monthly access and statement fees of between $40 and $80 plus a transaction fee of 10 to 60 cents per transaction. Once an online company has a merchant account, it can accept credit cards from online customers.

Online credit card transactions also pose a risk for merchants; online companies lose $3.4 billion a year to online payment fraud each year, 1 percent of their sales revenue (see Figure 13.7), 41 percent of it from **charge-backs**, or online credit card transactions that customers

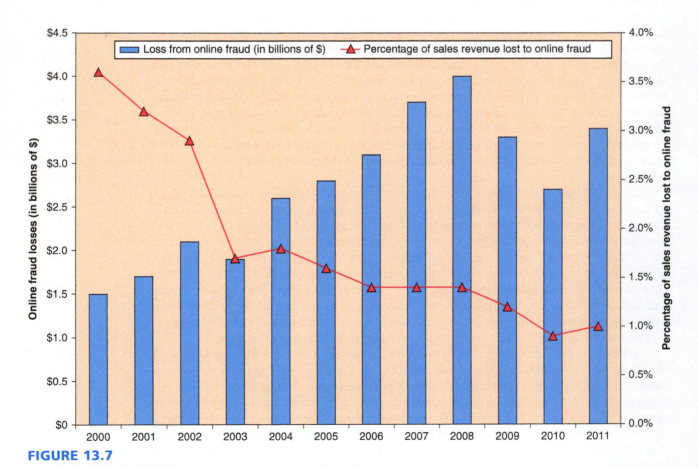

**FIGURE 13.7**

**Losses to Online Fraud**

*Source:* Based on Online Fraud Report: Thirteenth Annual Edition, Cybersource Corporation, Mountain View, California: 2012, p. 1.

dispute.[123] Good customer service minimizes the number of legitimate charge-backs. Illegitimate charge-backs usually are the result of thieves stealing credit card numbers and then using them to make online purchases. Unlike credit card transactions in a retail store, those made online ("card not present" transactions) involve no signatures, and Internet merchants incur the loss (and usually a fine from the credit card company) when a customer disputes the transaction.

**ENTREPRENEURIAL PROFILE: Jamon Robinson: Sun Tints, Inc.** Jamon Robinson, president of Sun Tints, Inc., a company that sells automotive accessories online and from a store in Bountiful, Utah, was frustrated that one out of every 100 online purchases resulted in a charge-back. Robinson recently signed up at *BadCustomer.com*, a Web site that allows merchants to search for customers who have a history of charge-backs, before completing a credit card sale. In the first three months since he began using the service, Robinson had refused several credit card transactions and has not had any charge-backs.[124]

One way to prevent fraud is to ask customers for their card verification value (CVV, CID, or CVV2), the three-digit number above the signature panel on the back of the credit card, as well as their card number and expiration date. Online merchants also can subscribe to a real-time credit card processing service that authorizes credit card transactions, but the fees can be high. Sending confirmation e-mails that include the customer's shipping information after receiving an order also reduces the likelihood of a charge-back. In addition, using a shipper that provides the ability to track shipments so that online merchants can prove that the customer actually received the merchandise can help minimize the threat of payment fraud.

# Chapter Review

E-commerce is creating a new economy, one that is connecting producers, sellers, and customers via technology in ways that have never been possible before. In this fast-paced world of e-commerce, size no longer matters as much as speed and flexibility do. The Internet is creating a new industrial order, and companies that fail to adapt to it will fall by the wayside.

1. Understand the factors an entrepreneur should consider before launching into e-commerce.
   - Before launching an e-commerce effort, business owners should consider the following important issues:
     - How a company exploits the Web's interconnectivity and the opportunities it creates to transform relationships with its suppliers and vendors, its customers, and other external stakeholders is crucial to its success.
     - Web success requires a company to develop a plan for integrating the Web into its overall strategy. The plan should address issues such as site design and maintenance, creating and managing a brand name, marketing and promotional strategies, sales, and customer service.
     - Developing deep, lasting relationships with customers takes on even greater importance on the Web. Attracting customers on the Web costs money, and companies must be able to retain their online customers to make their Web sites profitable.
     - Creating a meaningful presence on the Web requires an ongoing investment of resources—time, money, energy, and talent. Establishing an attractive Web site brimming with catchy photographs of products is only the beginning.

   - Measuring the success of Web-based sales efforts is essential to remaining relevant to customers whose tastes, needs, and preferences are always changing.

2. Explain the 10 myths of e-commerce and how to avoid falling victim to them.
   - The 10 myths of e-commerce are the following:
     Myth 1. If I launch a site, customers will flock to it.
     Myth 2. Making money on the Web is easy.
     Myth 3. Privacy is not an important issue on the Web.
     Myth 4. "Strategy? I don't need a strategy to sell on the Web! Just give me a Web site, and the rest will take care of itself."
     Myth 5. The most important part of any e-commerce effort is technology.
     Myth 6. On the Web, customer service is not as important as it is in a traditional retail store.
     Myth 7. Flash makes a Web site better.
     Myth 8. It's what's up front that counts.
     Myth 9. E-commerce will cause brick-and-mortar retail stores to disappear.
     Myth 10. My business doesn't need a Web site.

3. Explain the basic strategies entrepreneurs should follow to achieve success in their e-commerce efforts.
   - Following are some guidelines for building a successful Web strategy for a small e-company:
     - Consider focusing on a niche in the market.
     - Develop a community of online customers.
     - Attract visitors by giving away "freebies."
     - Make creative use of e-mail, but avoid becoming a "spammer."
     - Make sure your Web site says "credibility."

- Consider forming strategic alliances with larger, more established companies.
- Make the most of the Web's global reach.
- Promote your Web site online and off-line.

4. Learn the techniques of designing a killer Web site.
- There is no surefire formula for stopping surfers in their tracks, but the following suggestions will help:
  - Select a domain name that is consistent with the image you want to create for your company and register it.
  - Be easy to find.
  - Give customers what they want.
  - Establish hyperlinks with other businesses, preferably those selling products or services that complement yours.
  - Include an e-mail option and a telephone number in your site.
  - Give shoppers the ability to track their orders online.
  - Offer Web shoppers a special all their own.
  - Follow a simple design for your Web page.
  - Assure customers that their online transactions are secure.
  - Keep your site updated.
  - Consider hiring a professional to design your site.

5. Explain how companies track the results from their Web sites.
- Web analytics, tools that measure a Web site's ability to attract customers, generate sales, and keep customers coming back, help entrepreneurs to know what works—and what doesn't—on their sites. Information that Web analytics software provide include: commerce metrics, customer segmentation measurements, content reports, and process measurements.

6. Describe how e-businesses ensure the privacy and security of the information they collect and store from the Web.
- To make sure they are using the information they collect from visitors to their Web sites legally and ethically, companies should take the following steps:
  - Take an inventory of the customer data collected.
  - Develop a company privacy policy for the information you collect.
  - Post your company's privacy policy prominently on your Web site and follow it.
  - To ensure the security of the information they collect and store from Web transactions, companies should rely on virus and intrusion detection software and firewalls to ward off attacks from hackers.

## Discussion Questions

**13-1.** How has the Internet and e-commerce changed the ways companies do business?

**13-2.** Explain the benefits a company earns by selling on the Web.

**13-3.** Discuss the factors entrepreneurs should consider before launching an e-commerce site.

**13-4.** What are the 10 myths of e-commerce? What can an entrepreneur do to avoid them?

**13-5.** What strategic advice would you offer an entrepreneur about to start an e-company?

**13-6.** What design characteristics make for a successful Web site?

**13-7.** Explain the characteristics of an ideal domain name.

**13-8.** Describe the techniques that are available to e-companies for tracking results from their Web sites. What advantages does each offer?

**13-9.** What steps should e-businesses take to ensure the privacy of the information they collect and store from the Web?

**13-10.** What techniques can e-companies use to protect their banks of information and their customers' transaction data from hackers?

**13-11.** Why does evaluating the effectiveness of a Web site pose a problem for online entrepreneurs?

**13-12.** When Matt Buchan and Alex Garcia purchased a struggling hair salon in Seattle, Washington, their turnaround strategy included using the Internet as a key component of their business and marketing strategies. What advice can you offer these entrepreneurs for integrating the Web into their hair salon to enhance their customers' experience?

CHAPTER 14

# Creating a Solid Financial Plan

## Learning Objectives

**On completion of this chapter, you will be able to:**

1. Understand the importance of preparing a financial plan.

2. Describe how to prepare financial statements and use them to manage a small business.

3. Create projected financial statements.

4. Understand the basic financial statements through ratio analysis.

5. Explain how to interpret financial ratios.

6. Conduct a break-even analysis for a small company.

*Success is a lousy teacher. It seduces smart people into thinking they can't lose.*

—Bill Gates

*The only thing we know about the future is that it is going to be different.*

—Peter F. Drucker

**1.**
_____

Understand the importance
of preparing a financial
plan.

One of the most important steps in launching a new business venture is fashioning a well-designed, practical, realistic financial plan. Potential lenders and investors expect to see a financial plan before putting their money into a start-up company. More important, however, a financial plan is a vital tool to help entrepreneurs manage their businesses more effectively, steering their way around the pitfalls that cause failures. By understanding the assumptions that drive their financial models, entrepreneurs can better anticipate deviations from their financial forecast and take corrective actions quickly and effectively. Entrepreneurs who ignore the financial aspects of their businesses run the risk of watching their companies become another failure statistic. Many empirical studies have verified the positive correlation between the degree of planning (including financial planning) that entrepreneurs engage in and the success of their new ventures. These studies also show a significant positive relationship between formal planning by small companies and their financial performances.[1] One financial expert says of small companies, "Those that don't establish sound controls at the start are setting themselves up to fail."[2]

However, both research and anecdotal evidence suggests that a significant percentage of entrepreneurs run their companies without any kind of financial plan and never analyze their companies' financial statements as part of the decision-making process. They generate financial statements weeks after the end of each month and pay little attention to what they tell them about their company's performance. Why is the level of financial planning and analysis so low among entrepreneurs? The primary reason is the lack of financial know-how. One survey of small business owners by Greenfield Online found that accounting was the most intimidating part of managing their businesses and that more than half had no formal financial training at all.[3] To reach profit objectives, entrepreneurs cannot afford to be intimidated by financial management and must be aware of their companies' overall financial position and the changes in financial status that occur over time. Brian Hamilton, CEO of the financial data firm Sageworks, sees another reason why many entrepreneurs avoid accounting. "Small-business owners tend to hate accounting because it's boring. The mistake they make is not thinking about how they can use certain numbers as tools to better manage where their business is headed tomorrow."[4] Norm Brodsky, a veteran entrepreneur and author, says, "When you learn the basics of accounting, you realize that the numbers aren't as complicated as you feared and that you're developing the knowledge you need to be in control of your company."[5]

This chapter focuses on some very practical tools that help entrepreneurs to develop workable financial plans, keep them focused on their company's financial plans, and enable them to create a plan for earning a profit. They can use these tools to anticipate changes and plot an appropriate profit strategy to meet them head-on. These profit planning techniques are not difficult to master, nor are they overly time consuming. We will discuss the techniques involved in preparing projected (pro forma) financial statements, conducting ratio analysis, and performing break-even analysis.

## Basic Financial Reports

**2.**
_____

Describe how to prepare
financial statements and
use them to manage a small
business.

Before we begin building projected financial statements, it will be helpful to review the basic financial reports that measure a company's overall financial position: the balance sheet, the income statement, and the statement of cash flows. Every business, no matter how small, will benefit from preparing these basic financial statements. Building them is the first step toward securing a small company's financial future. Most accounting experts advise entrepreneurs to use one of the popular computerized small business accounting programs, such as Intuit's Quickbooks, Sage 50 (or the cloud version called Sage One), or one of the other products available to manage routine record-keeping tasks that form the underlying framework of these financial statements. A survey by Microsoft, however, reports that less than half of small companies use dedicated accounting software; most use a combination of homemade spreadsheets and paper records to handle their accounting needs.[6] Accounting software reduces the number of errors in calculations that occur when entrepreneurs try to keep records on their own. The software also easily creates reports and analyses that help improve decision making based on solid financial data. Working with an accountant to set up a smoothly functioning accounting system at the outset and then having an employee or a part-time bookkeeping service enter the transactions is most efficient for the businesses that use these packages.

## The Balance Sheet

Like a digital camera, the balance sheet takes a "snapshot" of a business, providing owners with an estimate of the company's worth on a given date. Its two major sections show the assets a business owns and the claims creditors and owners have against those assets. The balance sheet is usually prepared on the last day of the month and at the end of each fiscal year. Figure 14.1 shows the balance sheet for a small business, Sam's Appliance Shop, for the year ended December 31, 2015.

The balance sheet is built on the fundamental accounting equation Assets = Liabilities + Owner's equity. Any increase or decrease on one side of the equation must be offset by an equal increase or decrease on the other side, hence the name *balance sheet*. It provides a baseline from which to measure future changes in assets, liabilities, and equity (or net worth). The first section of the balance sheet lists the company's **assets** (valued at the original cost, not actual market value) and shows the total cost value of everything the business owns. **Current assets** consist of cash and items to be converted into cash within one year or within the normal operating cycle of the company, whichever is longer, such as accounts receivable and inventory. **Fixed assets** are those acquired for long-term use in the business, such as equipment, furnishings, and buildings. **Intangible assets** include items that, although valuable, do not have tangible value, such as goodwill, copyrights, and patents.

**FIGURE 14.1**

**Balance Sheet, Sam's Appliance Shop**

For Year Ending December 31, 2015.

| Assets | | |
|---|---:|---:|
| **Current Assets** | | |
| Cash | | $49,855 |
| Accounts Receivable | $179,225 | |
| Less Allowance for Doubtful Accounts | $6,000 | $173,225 |
| Inventory | | $455,455 |
| Prepaid Expenses | | $8,450 |
| Total Current Assets | | $686,985 |
| | | |
| **Fixed Assets** | | |
| Land | | $59,150 |
| Buildings | $74,650 | |
| Less Accumulated Depreciation | $7,050 | $67,600 |
| Equipment | $22,375 | |
| Less Accumulated Depreciation | $1,250 | $21,125 |
| Furniture and Fixtures | $10,295 | |
| Less Accumulated Depreciation | $1,000 | $9,295 |
| Total Fixed Assets | | $157,170 |
| | | |
| Intangibles (Goodwill) | | $3,500 |
| Total Assets | | $847,655 |
| **Liabilities** | | |
| **Current Liabilities** | | |
| Accounts Payable | | $152,580 |
| Notes Payable | | $83,920 |
| Accrued Wages/Salaries Payable | | $38,150 |
| Accrued Interest Payable | | $42,380 |
| Accrued Taxes Payable | | $50,820 |
| Total Current Liabilities | | $367,850 |
| | | |
| Long-term Liabilities | | |
| Mortgage | | $127,150 |
| Note Payable | | $ 85,000 |
| Total Long-term Liabilities | | $212,150 |
| **Owner's Equity** | | |
| Sam Lloyd, Capital | | $267,655 |
| | | |
| Total Liabilities and Owner's Equity | | $847,655 |

The second section shows the business's **liabilities**—the creditors' claims against the company's assets. **Current liabilities** are those debts that must be paid within one year or within the normal operating cycle of the company, whichever is longer. **Long-term liabilities** are those that come due after one year. This section of the balance sheet also shows the **owner's equity**, the value of the owner's investment in the business. It is the balancing factor on the balance sheet, representing all of the owner's capital contributions to the business plus all accumulated earnings not distributed to the owner(s).

## The Income Statement

The **income statement** (or profit and loss statement) compares expenses against revenue over a certain period of time to show the firm's net income or loss. Like a digital video recorder, the income statement provides a "moving picture" of a company's profitability over time. The annual income statement reports the bottom line of the business over the fiscal or calendar year. Figure 14.2 shows the income statement for Sam's Appliance Shop for the year ended December 31, 2015.

To calculate net income or loss, business owners record sales revenue for the year, which includes all income that flows into the business from the sale of goods and services. Income from other sources (rent, investments, interest, and others) also must be included in the revenue section of the income statement. To determine net revenue, owners subtract the value of returned items and refunds from gross revenue. **Cost of goods sold** represents the total cost of purchasing (including shipping) the merchandise that the company sells during the year. Wholesalers, manufacturers, and retailers calculate cost of goods sold by adding purchases to beginning inventory and subtracting ending inventory. Service companies typically have no cost of goods sold.

Subtracting the cost of goods sold from net sales revenue results in a company's **gross profit**. Allowing the cost of goods sold to get out of control whittles away a company's gross profit, virtually guaranteeing a net loss at the bottom of the income statement. Dividing gross profit by net sales revenue produces the **gross profit margin**, a percentage that every entrepreneur should watch closely. If a company's gross profit margin slips too low, it is likely that it will operate at a loss (negative net income). A declining gross profit margin also restricts a company's ability to invest in revenue-generating activities such as marketing, advertising, and business development.

Many business owners whose companies are losing money mistakenly believe that the problem is inadequate sales volume; therefore, they focus on pumping up sales at any cost. In many

"Take this and have a masseuse massage the numbers until they fit into our proposed profit projections."

| | | |
|---|---:|---:|
| Net Sales Revenue | | $1,870,841 |
| Cash Sales | $561,252 | |
| Credit Sales | $1,309,589 | |
| | | |
| Cost of Goods Sold | | |
| Beginning Inventory, 1/1/15 | $805,745 | |
| + Purchases | $939,827 | |
| Goods Available for Sale | $1,745,572 | |
| – Ending Inventory, 12,31/15 | $455,455 | |
| Cost of Goods Sold | | $1,290,117 |
| | | |
| Gross Profit | | $580,724 |
| | | |
| Operating Expenses | | |
| Advertising | $139,670 | |
| Insurance | $46,125 | |
| Depreciation | | |
| Building | $18,700 | |
| Equipment | $9,000 | |
| Salaries | $224,500 | |
| Travel | $4,000 | |
| Entertainment | $2,500 | |
| Total Operating Expenses | | $444,495 |
| | | |
| General Expenses | | |
| Utilities | $5,300 | |
| Telephone | $2,500 | |
| Postage | $1,200 | |
| Payroll Taxes | $25,000 | |
| Total General Expenses | | $34,000 |
| | | |
| Other Expenses | | |
| Interest Expense | $39,850 | |
| Bad Check Expense | $1,750 | |
| Total Other Expenses | | $41,600 |
| | | |
| Total Expenses | | $520,095 |
| | | |
| Net Income | | $60,629 |

**FIGURE 14.2**

**Income Statement, Sam's Appliance Shop**

For Year Ending December 31, 2015.

cases, however, the losses are due to an inadequate gross profit margin, and pumping up sales only deepens their losses! Repairing a poor gross profit margin requires a company to raise prices, cut manufacturing or purchasing costs, refuse orders with low profit margins, or add new products with more attractive profit margins. *Increasing sales will not resolve the problem.* One business owner admits that he fell victim to this myth of profitability. His company was losing money, and in an attempt to correct the problem, he focused his efforts on boosting sales. His efforts were successful, but the results were not. The costs he incurred to add sales produced withering gross profit margins, and by the time he deducted operating costs, the business incurred an even greater net loss! Cash flow suffered, the business could not pay its bills on time, and the owner ended up filing for Chapter 11 bankruptcy. Now a successful business owner, this entrepreneur says, "Ever since, I've tracked my gross [profit] margins like a hawk."[7] Monitoring the gross profit margin over time and comparing it to those of other companies in the same industry are important steps to maintaining a company's long-term profitability.

**Operating expenses** include those costs that contribute directly to the manufacture and distribution of goods. General expenses are indirect costs incurred in operating the business. "Other expenses" is a catchall category covering all other expenses that don't fit into the other two categories. Total revenue minus total expenses gives the company's **net income (or loss)**. Reducing expenses increases a company's net income, and even small reductions in expenses can add up to big savings.

**ENTREPRENEURIAL PROFILE: Peter Jupp: Infocore**  Peter Jupp, owner of direct-marketing firm Infocore, was facing huge losses in 2008 due to the financial downturn and accounting mistakes that had occurred over the previous three years. "When your financial basis is threatened, and you start to wonder about the viability of the business you own and run, everything seems bleak," said Jupp. He decided to "face the headwinds and deal with it." Judd cut Infocore's expenses across the board, including reducing his staff by half and slashing travel and client entertainment budgets (Infocore's biggest cost categories). Judd was able to reduce his operating costs by 34 percent, thus saving the company and positioning it for future, more profitable growth.[8]

Business owners must be careful when embarking on cost-cutting missions, however. Although minimizing costs can improve profitability, entrepreneurs must be judicious in their cost cutting, taking a strategic approach rather than imposing across-the-board cuts. Brad Smith, CEO of Intuit, a company that makes software and provides business services for small businesses, knows that research and development and product innovation are keys to the company's success. "We're not going to cut innovation," he vows. "For 25 years, this company has been fueled by new product innovation. We're protecting the innovation pipeline so that [our future] is strong."[9] Cutting costs in areas that are vital to a company's success—such as a retail jeweler cutting its marketing budget during a recession—can inhibit its ability to compete and do more harm than good. In fact, a study by McGraw-Hill Research reports that companies that advertise consistently even during recessions perform better in the long run; companies that advertised aggressively during a recent recession generated sales that were 256 percent higher than those that did not advertise consistently.[10]

In other cases, entrepreneurs on cost-cutting vendettas alienate employees and sap worker morale by eliminating nitpicking costs that affect employees but retaining expensive perks for themselves. One business owner enraged employees by cutting the budget for the company Christmas party to $5 (for the whole event) and encouraging employees not to skip lines on interoffice envelopes (which, one worker calculated, cost the company $0.0064 per skipped line). Although his reasons for cutting costs were valid, this CEO lost all credibility because employees knew that when he traveled, he stayed only at upscale, butler-serviced hotels and had a chauffeur drive him to work every day![11]

## The Statement of Cash Flows

The **statement of cash flows** shows the changes in a company's working capital from the beginning of the accounting period by listing the sources of funds and the uses of these funds. Many small businesses never need such a statement; instead, they rely on a cash budget, a less formal managerial tool that tracks the flow of cash into and out of a company over time. (We will discuss cash budgets in Chapter 15.) Sometimes, however, creditors, lenders, investors, or business buyers may require this information.

To prepare the statement of cash flows, owners must assemble the balance sheets and the income statements summarizing the year's operations. They begin with the company's net income for the accounting period (from the income statement). Then they add the sources of funds—borrowed funds, owner contributions, decreases in accounts payable, decreases in inventory, depreciation, and any others. Depreciation is listed as a source of funds because it is a noncash expense that is deducted as a cost of doing business. Because the owners have already paid for the item being depreciated, its depreciation is a source of funds. Next the owners subtract the uses of these funds—plant and equipment purchases, dividends to owners, repayment of debt, increases in accounts receivable, decreases in accounts payable, increases in inventory, and so on. The difference between the total sources and the total uses of funds is the increase or decrease in working capital. By investigating the changes in their companies' working capital and the reasons for them, owners can create a more practical financial plan of action for the future.

These statements are more than just complex documents used only by accountants and financial officers. When used in conjunction with the analytical tools described in the following sections, they can help entrepreneurs map their companies' financial future and actively plan for profit. Merely preparing these statements is not enough, however; entrepreneurs and their employees must *understand and use* the information contained in them to make their businesses more effective and efficient.

# Creating Projected Financial Statements

Creating projected financial statements helps entrepreneurs transform their business goals into reality. These projected financial statements answer questions such as the following: What profit can the business expect to earn? If the founder's profit objective is $x$ dollars, what sales level must the business achieve? What fixed and variable expenses can the owner expect at that level of sales? The answers to these and other questions are critical in formulating a successful financial plan for the small business.

> **3.** _____
>
> Create projected financial statements.

This section focuses on creating projected income statements and balance sheets for a small business. These projected (pro forma) statements estimate the profitability and the overall financial condition of the business in the immediate future. They are an integral part of convincing potential lenders and investors to provide the financing needed to get the company off the ground or to expand. In addition, because these statements forecast a company's financial position, they help entrepreneurs plan the route to improved financial strength and healthy business growth. In other words, they lay the foundation for a pathway to profitability.

Because an established business has a history of operating data from which to construct projected financial statements, the task is not nearly as difficult as it is for a brand-new business. When creating projected financial statements for a business start-up, entrepreneurs often rely on published statistics summarizing the operation of similar-size companies in the same industry. These statistics are available from a number of sources (described later), but this section draws on information found in *RMA's Annual Statement Studies*, published by the Risk Management Association (RMA), a compilation of financial data on thousands of companies across hundreds of industries (organized by North American Industry Classification (NAICS) and Standard Industrial Classification (SIC) codes). However, developing a sound business model and business plan (discussed in Chapter 8) helps an entrepreneur develop a realistic financial plan for the specific market segment in which he or she is launching a business. Entrepreneurs should use published industry financial data as a guide for validating their own financial projections. Because conditions and markets change so rapidly, entrepreneurs developing financial forecasts for start-ups should focus on creating projections for two years into the future. Investors mainly want to see that entrepreneurs have realistic expectations about their companies' income and expenses and when they expect to start earning a profit.

## Projected Statements for the Small Business

One of the most important tasks confronting an entrepreneur is to determine the capital required to launch the business and to keep going until it begins to generate positive cash flow. The amount of money needed to begin a business depends on the type of operation, its location, inventory requirements, sales volume, credit terms, and other factors. Every new company must have enough capital to cover all start-up costs, including funds to rent or buy plant, equipment, and tools, as well as to pay for employees' salaries and wages, advertising, licenses, insurance, utilities, travel, and other expenses. In addition, the entrepreneur must maintain a reserve of capital to carry the company until it begins to produce positive cash flow. Too often, entrepreneurs are overly optimistic in their financial plans and fail to recognize that expenses initially exceed income for most start-ups, which creates a drain on their cash flow. This period of net losses and the resulting cash drain is normal and may last from just a few months to several years. During this time, entrepreneurs must be able to meet payroll, maintain adequate inventory, take advantage of cash discounts, pay all other business expenses, grant customer credit, and meet their personal obligations. Figure 14.3 provides a model that shows the connections among the various financial forecasts (income statement, balance sheet, and cash flow) entrepreneurs should include in their business plans.

**THE PROJECTED INCOME STATEMENT** When creating a projected income statement, the first step is to create a sales forecast. An entrepreneur has two options: develop a sales forecast and work down or set a profit target and work up. Many entrepreneurs prefer to use the latter method—targeting a profit figure and then determining the sales level they must achieve to reach it. This approach allows entrepreneurs to better match the size of the businesses to their goals and aspirations, both financial and lifestyle. Of course, it is important to compare this sales target against the results of the marketing plan to determine whether it is realistic. Although all financial

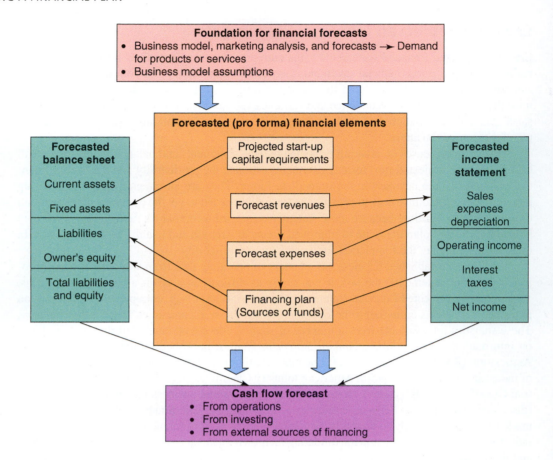

**FIGURE 14.3**

**Financial Forecasting Model**

*Source:* Adapted from Benjamin B. Gaunsel, "Toward a Framework of Financial Planning in New Venture Creation," presented at the annual meeting of United States Association for Small Business and Entrepreneurship, January 2005, Palm Springs, California, *www.sbaer.uca.edu/research/usasbe/2005/pdffiles/papers/25.pdf*.

forecasts are projections, they must be based in reality; otherwise, they are nothing more than hopeless dreams. This is why it is so important to test the business model with real customers to develop **proof of concept** for a new venture.

The next step is to estimate all of the expenses the business will incur to generate those sales. In any small business, the resulting profit must be large enough to produce a return for the time the owners spend operating the business and a return on their financial investment in the business. Ideally, a small company's net income after taxes should be at least as much as the owner could earn by working for someone else. An adequate profit must also include a reasonable return on the owner's total financial investment in the business. If a would-be owner has $200,000 and can invest it in securities that earn 8 percent, pouring the money into a small business that yields only 3 percent may not be the best course of action.

An entrepreneur's target income is the sum of a reasonable salary for the time spent running the business and a normal return on the amount invested in the firm. Determining this amount is the first step in creating the pro forma income statement.

The next step is to translate this target profit into a sales estimate for the forecasted period. To calculate net sales from a target profit, the owner needs published statistics for this type of business. Suppose an entrepreneur wants to launch a small retail flower shop and has determined that his target net income is $30,000 for the upcoming year. Interviews with entrepreneurs already in the industry and through statistics gathered from the *RMA Annual Statement Studies* show that the typical florist's net profit margin (Net profit ÷ Sales) is 7.2 percent. Using this information, he can compute the sales level required to produce a net profit of $30,000:

$$\text{Net profit margin} = \frac{\text{Net profit}}{\text{Sales (annual)}}$$

Solving for net sales produces the following result:

$$\text{Sales} = \frac{\$30,000}{0.072}$$

$$= \$416,667$$

Now the entrepreneur knows that to earn a net profit of $30,000 (before taxes), he must achieve annual sales of $416,667. To complete the projected income statement, he simply applies the appropriate statistics from the *RMA Annual Statement Studies* to the annual sales figure. Because the statistics for each income statement item are expressed as percentages of sales, he merely multiplies the proper statistic by the annual sales figure to obtain the desired value. For example, cost of goods sold usually comprises 46.6 percent of sales for the typical small flower shop. The owner of this new flower shop expects the cost of goods sold to be the following:

$$\text{Cost of goods sold} = \$416,667 \times 46.6\% = \$194,167$$

The flower shop's complete projected income statement is shown as follows:

| | | |
|---|---|---|
| Net sales | (100%) | $416,667 |
| −Cost of goods sold | (46.6%) | 194,167 |
| Gross profit margin | (53.4%) | $222,500 |
| −Operating expenses | (46.2%) | 192,500 |
| Net income (before taxes) | (7.2%) | $30,000 |

At this point, the business appears to be a lucrative venture. But remember that this income statement represents a goal that the entrepreneur may not be able to attain. The next step is to determine whether this required sales volume is reasonable. One useful technique is to break down the required annual sales volume into daily sales figures. Assuming that the shop will be open six days per week for 52 weeks (312 days), the owner must average $1,335 per day in sales:

$$\text{Average daily sales} = \frac{\$416,667}{312 \text{ days}}$$

$$= \$1,335/\text{day}$$

We can break down this estimate even further. If the store will be open 10 hours a day, the owner must average $133.50 in sales every hour the store is open. If the average customer spends $20, the store must average about 7 customers per hour ($133.50 sales per hour ÷ $20 spent per customer = 6.675. This calculation gives the owner a better perspective of the sales required to yield an annual profit of $30,000.

To determine whether the profit expected from the business will meet or exceed the entrepreneur's target income, the prospective owner should create an income statement based on a realistic sales estimate. The previous analysis showed this entrepreneur the sales level necessary to reach the desired profit of $30,000. But what happens if sales are lower or higher? To answer that question, he must develop a reliable sales forecast using the market research techniques described in Chapter 9.

Suppose that by gathering information from the industry trade association and conducting a marketing survey of local customers, the prospective florist projects first-year sales for the proposed business to be only $395,000. Using this expected sales figure to develop a pro forma income statement yields the following result:

| | | |
|---|---|---|
| Net sales | (100%) | $395,000 |
| −Cost of goods sold | (46.6%) | 184,070 |
| Gross profit margin | (53.4%) | 210,930 |
| −Operating expenses | (46.2%) | 182,490 |
| Net income (before taxes) | (7.2%) | $28,440 |

Based on sales of $395,000, this entrepreneur should expect a net income (before taxes) of $28,440. If this amount is acceptable as a return on the investment of time and money in the business, he should proceed with his planning.

At this stage in developing the financial plan, the entrepreneur should create a more detailed picture of the company's expected operating expenses. One method is to use the statistics found in publications such as *Dun & Bradstreet's Cost of Doing Business* or reports from industry trade associations. These publications document selected operating expenses (expressed as a percentage of net sales) for different lines of businesses. Although publications such as these offer valuable guidelines for preparing estimates of expenses, the most reliable estimates of a start-up company's expenses are those that entrepreneurs develop for their particular locations. Expenses such as rent, wages, salaries, benefits, utilities, and others vary dramatically from one part of the nation to another, and entrepreneurs must be sure that their forecasted expenses reflect the real cost of operating their particular businesses. Internet searches and a few telephone calls usually produce the necessary cost estimates.

To ensure that they have overlooked no business expenses in preparing their business plans, entrepreneurs should list all of the initial expenses they will incur and have an accountant review the list. Figures 14.4 and 14.5 show two useful forms designed to help assign dollar values to anticipated expenses. Totals derived from this list of expenses should approximate the total expense figures calculated from published statistics. Naturally, an entrepreneur should be more confident of the total from his or her own list of expenses because this reflects his or her particular set of circumstances.

Entrepreneurs who follow the top-down approach to building an income statement—developing a sales forecast and working down to net income—must be careful to avoid falling into the trap of excessive optimism. Many entrepreneurs using this method overestimate their anticipated revenues and underestimate their actual expenses, and the results can be disastrous. To avoid this problem, some experts advise that entrepreneurs use the rule that many venture capitalists apply when they evaluate business start-ups: Divide revenues by two, multiply expenses by two, and, if the business can still make it, it's a winner!

**THE PROJECTED BALANCE SHEET** In addition to projecting the small company's net profit or loss, the entrepreneur must develop a pro forma balance sheet outlining the fledgling company's assets and liabilities. Most entrepreneurs' primary focus is on the potential profitability of their businesses, but the assets their businesses use to generate profits are no less important. In many cases, small companies begin life on weak financial footing because their owners fail to determine their firms' total asset requirements. To prevent this major oversight, the entrepreneur should prepare a projected balance sheet listing every asset the business will need and all the claims against these assets.

**ASSETS** Cash is one of the most useful assets the business owns; it is highly liquid and can quickly be converted into other tangible assets. But how much cash should a small business have at its inception? Obviously, there is no single dollar figure that fits the needs of every small firm. One practical rule of thumb, however, suggests that the company's cash balance should cover its operating expenses (less depreciation, a noncash expense) for one inventory turnover period. Using this rule, we can calculate the cash balance for the small flower shop as follows:

Operating expenses = \$182,490 (from projected income statement)

Less Depreciation (1.9% of annual sales) = \$7,505 (a noncash expense)

Equals Cash expenses (annual) = \$174,985

$$\text{Cash requirement} = \frac{\text{Cash expenses}}{\text{Average inventory turnover ratio}}$$

$$= \frac{\$174,985}{13.6^*}$$

$$= \$12,867$$

*from the *RMA Annual Statement Studies*

Notice the inverse relationship between a small company's average inventory turnover ratio and its cash requirements. The faster a business turns its inventory, the shorter the time its cash is tied up in inventory and the smaller is the amount of cash at start-up the company requires. For instance, if this florist could turn its inventory 17 times per year, its cash requirement would be \$10,293 (\$174,985 ÷ 17).

| Estimated Monthly Expenses | Your estimate of monthly expenses based on sales of $_____ per year. | Your estimate of how much cash you need to start your business. (See column 3.) | What to put in column 2. (These figures are typical for one kind of business. You will have to decide how many months to allow for in your business.) |
|---|---|---|---|
| **ITEM** | **COLUMN 1** | **COLUMN 2** | **COLUMN 3** |
| Salary of owner-manager | $ | $ | 2 times column 1 |
| All other salaries and wages | | | 3 times column 1 |
| Rent | | | 3 times column 1 |
| Advertising | | | 3 times column 1 |
| Delivery expense | | | 3 times column 1 |
| Supplies | | | 3 times column 1 |
| Telephone and telegraph | | | 3 times column 1 |
| Other utilities | | | 3 times column 1 |
| Insurance | | | Payment required by insurance company |
| Taxes, including Social Security | | | 4 times column 1 |
| Interest | | | 3 times column 1 |
| Maintenance | | | 3 times column 1 |
| Legal and other professional fees | | | 3 times column 1 |
| Miscellaneous | | | 3 times column 1 |
| Start-up costs you have to pay only once | | | Leave column 2 blank |
| Fixtures and equipment | | | Fill in worksheet 3 and put the total here |
| Decorating and remodeling | | | Talk it over with a contractor |
| Installation of fixtures and equipment | | | Talk to suppliers from whom you buy these |
| Starting inventory | | | Suppliers will probably help you estimate this |
| Deposits with public utilities | | | Find out from utilities companies |
| Legal and professional fees | | | Lawyer, accountant, and so on |
| Licenses and permits | | | Find out from city offices what you have to have |
| Advertising and promotion for opening | | | Estimate what you'll use |
| Accounts receivable | | | What you need to buy more stock until credit customers pay |
| Cash | | | For unexpected expenses or losses, special purchases, etc. |
| Other | | | Make a separate list and enter total |
| Total Estimated Cash You Need to Start | | $ | Add up all the numbers in column 2 |

**FIGURE 14.4**

## Anticipated Expenses

*Source:* U.S. Small Business Administration, *Checklist for Going into Business*, Small Marketers Aid No. 71 (Washington, DC: Government Printing Office, 1982), pp. 6–7.

**List of Furniture, Fixtures, and Equipment**

| Leave out or add items to suit your business. Use separate sheets to list exactly what you need for each of the items below. | If you plan to pay cash in full, enter the full amount below and in the last column. | If you are going to pay by installments, fill out the columns below. Enter in the last column your down payment plus at least one installment. | | | Estimate of the cash you need for furniture, fixtures, and equipment. |
|---|---|---|---|---|---|
| | | Price | Down payment | Amount of each installment | |
| Counters | $ | $ | $ | $ | $ |
| Storage shelves and cabinets | | | | | |
| Display stands, shelves, tables | | | | | |
| Cash register | | | | | |
| Safe | | | | | |
| Window display fixtures | | | | | |
| Special lighting | | | | | |
| Outside sign | | | | | |
| Delivery equipment if needed | | | | | |
| Total Furniture, Fixtures, and Equipment (enter this figure also in worksheet 2 under Starting Costs You Have to Pay Only Once) | | | | | $ |

**FIGURE 14.5**

**Anticipated Expenditures for Fixtures and Equipment**

*Source:* U.S. Small Business Administration, *Checklist for Going into Business*, Small Marketers Aid No. 71 (Washington, DC: Government Printing Office, 1982), pp. 6–7.

*Inventory* Another decision facing the entrepreneur is how much inventory the business should carry. An estimate of the inventory needed can be calculated from the information found on the projected income statement and from published statistics:

$$\text{Cost of goods sold} = \$184,070 \text{ (from projected income statement)}$$

$$\text{Average inventory turnover} = \frac{\text{Cost of goods sold}}{\text{Inventory level}} = 13.6 \text{ times/year}$$

Rearranging the equation to solve for inventory level produces the following:

$$\text{Inventory level} = \frac{\$184,070}{13.6 \text{ times/year}} = \$13,535$$

The entrepreneur also includes $1,800 in miscellaneous current assets.
Suppose the estimate of fixed assets is as follows:

| | |
|---|---|
| Fixtures (including refrigeration units) | $54,500 |
| Office equipment | 5,250 |
| Computers/cash register | 5,125 |
| Signs | 7,200 |
| Miscellaneous | 1,500 |
| | $73,575 |

**LIABILITIES** To complete the projected balance sheet, the owner must record all of the small company's liabilities, the claims against the assets. The florist was able to finance 50 percent of inventory and fixtures ($34,018) through suppliers and has a short-term note payable of $3,750. The only other major claim against the store's assets is a note payable to the entrepreneur's father-in-law for $25,000. The difference between the company's total assets ($101,776) and its

| Assets | | Liabilities | |
|---|---|---|---|
| **Current Assets** | | **Current Liabilities** | |
| Cash | $12,867 | Accounts Payable | $34,018 |
| Inventory | 13,535 | Note Payable | 3,750 |
| Miscellaneous | 1,800 | | |
| Total Current Assets | $28,201 | Total Current Liabilities | $37,768 |
| | | | |
| **Fixed Assets** | | **Long-term Liabilities** | |
| Fixtures | $54,500 | Note Payable | $25,000 |
| Office equipment | 5,250 | | |
| Computers/Cash register | 5,125 | Total Liabilities | $62,768 |
| Signs | 7,200 | | |
| Miscellaneous | 1,500 | | |
| Total Fixed Assets | $73,575 | **Owner's Equity** | $39,008 |
| Total Assets | $101,776 | **Total Liabilities and Owner's Equity** | $101,776 |

**FIGURE 14.6**

**Projected Balance Sheet for a Small Flower Shop**

total liabilities ($62,768) represents the owner's investment in the business (owner's equity) of $39,008.

The final step is to compile all of these items into a projected balance sheet, as shown in Figure 14.6.

## Ratio Analysis

Would you be willing to drive a car on an extended trip without being able to see the dashboard displays showing fuel level, engine temperature, oil pressure, battery status, or the speed at which you were traveling? Not many people would! Yet many small business owners run their companies exactly that way. They never take the time to check the vital signs of their businesses using their "financial dashboards." The result: Their companies develop engine trouble, fail, and leave them stranded along the road to successful entrepreneurship.

Smart entrepreneurs know that once they have their businesses up and running with the help of a solid financial plan, the next step is to keep the company moving in the right direction with the help of proper financial controls. Establishing these controls—and using them consistently— is one of the keys to keeping a business vibrant and healthy. Business owners who don't do so often are shocked to learn that their companies are in serious financial trouble, *and they never knew it.*

A smoothly functioning system of financial controls is essential to achieving business success. These systems serve as an early warning device for underlying problems that could destroy a young business. They allow an entrepreneur to step back and see the big picture and to make adjustments in the company's strategic direction when necessary. According to one writer,

A company's financial accounting and reporting system will provide signals, through comparative analysis, of impending trouble, such as:

- Decreasing sales and falling profit margins.
- Increasing overhead.
- Growing inventories and accounts receivable.

These are all signals of declining cash flows from operations, the lifeblood of every business. As cash flows decrease, the squeeze begins:

- Payments to vendors become slower.
- Maintenance on production equipment lags.
- Raw material shortages appear.
- Equipment breakdowns occur.

**4.**

Understand the basic financial statements through ratio analysis.

All of these begin to have a negative impact on productivity. Now the downward spiral has begun in earnest. The key is hearing and focusing on the signals.[12]

What are these signals, and how does an entrepreneur go about hearing and focusing on them? One extremely helpful tool is ratio analysis. **Ratio analysis**, a method of expressing the relationships between any two accounting elements, provides a convenient technique for performing financial analysis. When analyzed properly, ratios serve as barometers of a company's financial health. Using ratios as benchmarks allows entrepreneurs to determine, for example, whether their companies are carrying excessive inventory, experiencing heavy operating expenses, collecting payments from their customers slowly, managing to pay their debts on time and to answer other questions relating to the efficient operation of their businesses. Unfortunately, few business owners actually compute financial ratios and use them in managing their businesses!

Clever business owners use financial ratio analysis to identify problems in their businesses while they are still problems, not business-threatening crises. Tracking these ratios over time permits an owner to spot a variety of "red flags" that are indications of these problem areas. This is critical to business success because an entrepreneur cannot solve problems he or she does not know exist! Business owners also can use ratio analysis to increase the likelihood of obtaining bank loans. By analyzing their financial statements with ratios, entrepreneurs can anticipate potential problems and identify important strengths in advance. When evaluating a business plan or a loan request, lenders often rely on ratio analysis to determine how well managed a company is and how solid its financial footing is.

How many ratios should a small business manager monitor to maintain adequate financial control over the firm? Only the number of accounts recorded on the company's financial statements limits the number of ratios an entrepreneur can calculate. However, tracking too many ratios only creates confusion and saps the meaning from an entrepreneur's financial analysis. The secret to successful ratio analysis is *simplicity*, focusing on just enough ratios to provide a clear picture of a company's financial standing.

## 12 Key Ratios

In keeping with the idea of simplicity, this section describes 12 key ratios that enable most business owners to monitor their companies' financial position without becoming bogged down in financial details. This chapter presents examples and explanations of these ratios based on the balance sheet and the income statement for Sam's Appliance Shop shown in Figures 14.1 and 14.2. We will group them into four categories: liquidity ratios, leverage ratios, operating ratios, and profitability ratios.

**LIQUIDITY RATIOS** **Liquidity ratios** tell whether a small business will be able to meet its maturing obligations as they come due. These ratios can forewarn entrepreneurs of impending cash flow problems. A small company with solid liquidity not only is able to pay its bills on time but also is in a position to take advantage of attractive business opportunities as they arise. Liquidity ratios measure a company's ability to convert its assets into cash quickly and without a loss of value to pay its short-term liabilities. The two most common measures of liquidity are the current ratio and the quick ratio.

*1. Current Ratio* The **current ratio** measures a small company's solvency by showing its ability to pay current liabilities from current assets. It is calculated in the following manner:

$$\text{Current ratio} = \frac{\text{Current assets}}{\text{Current liabilities}}$$

$$= \frac{\$686,985}{\$367,850}$$

$$= 1.87:1$$

Sam's Appliance Shop has $1.87 in current assets for every $1 it has in current liabilities.

Current assets are those that an entrepreneur expects to convert into cash in the ordinary business cycle and normally include cash, notes or accounts receivable, inventory, and any other short-term marketable securities. Current liabilities are short-term obligations that come due within one year and include notes or accounts payable, taxes payable, and accruals.

The current ratio is sometimes called the working capital ratio and is the most commonly used measure of short-term solvency. Typically, financial analysts suggest that a small business maintain a current ratio of at least 2:1 (i.e., two dollars of current assets for every one dollar of current liabilities) to maintain a comfortable cushion of working capital. Generally, the higher a company's current ratio, the stronger its financial position, but a high current ratio does not guarantee that the company's assets are being used in the most profitable manner. For example, a business maintaining excessive balances of idle cash or overinvesting in inventory would likely have a high current ratio.

With its current ratio of 1.87:1, Sam's Appliance Shop could liquidate its current assets at 53.5% (1 ÷ 1.87 = 53.5%) of book value and still manage to pay its current creditors in full.

**2. Quick Ratio** The current ratio can sometimes be misleading because it does not show the quality of a company's current assets. For instance, a company with a large number of past-due receivables and stale inventory could boast an impressive current ratio and still be on the verge of financial collapse. The **quick ratio** (or the **acid test ratio**) is a more conservative measure of a firm's liquidity because it shows the extent to which its most liquid assets cover its current liabilities. This ratio includes only a company's "quick assets"—those assets that a company can convert into cash immediately if needed—and excludes the most illiquid asset of all, inventory. It is calculated as follows:

$$\text{Quick ratio} = \frac{\text{Quick assets}}{\text{Current liabilities}}$$

$$= \frac{\$686{,}985 - \$455{,}455}{\$367{,}850}$$

$$= 0.63{:}1$$

Sam's has 63 cents in quick assets for every $1 of current liabilities.

The quick ratio is a more rigorous test of a company's liquidity. It expresses capacity to re-pay current debts if all sales income ceased immediately. Generally, a quick ratio of 1:1 is considered satisfactory. A ratio of less than 1:1 indicates that the small company is overly dependent on inventory and on future sales to satisfy short-term debt. A quick ratio of more than 1:1 indicates a greater degree of financial security.

**LEVERAGE RATIOS** **Leverage ratios** measure the financing supplied by a company's owners against that supplied by its creditors; they show the relationship between the contributions of investors and creditors to a company's capital base. Leverage ratios serve as gauges of the depth of a company's debt. These ratios show the extent to which an entrepreneur relies on debt capital (rather than equity capital) to finance the business. Leverage ratios provide one measure of the degree of financial risk in a company. Generally, small businesses with low leverage ratios are less affected by economic downturns, but the returns for these firms are lower during economic booms. Conversely, small firms with high leverage ratios are more vulnerable to economic slides because their debt loads consume cash flow; however, they have greater potential for large profits. "Leverage is a double-edged sword," says one financial expert. "If it works for you, you can really build something. If you borrow too much, it can drag a business down faster than anything."[13]

Companies that end up declaring bankruptcy most often take on more debt than the business can handle.

**ENTREPRENEURIAL PROFILE: Andy Wiederhorn: Fatburger** Andy Wiederhorn, CEO and owner of Fatburger, had struggled to turn the 40-location restaurant chain around from the time he purchased the business in 2003. However, by 2009, the combination of a recession, a weak management team, and $35 million in debt forced Wiederhorn to file for Chapter 11 bankruptcy for his business. Wiederhorn closed the thirty stores that were not profitable. As a result of the reorganization that occurred while in bankruptcy, the company was able to reduce its debt to $8 million, renegotiate leases for its remaining stores, and work out new payment terms with its suppliers. He reorganized Fatburger as a franchise company, which reduced his operating expenses and stabilized cash flow. The company was able generate enough cash to reinvest $23 million in restructuring and operating expenses and become cash flow positive. By 2013, Fatburger had grown to 120 franchised locations around the globe.[14]

The following ratios help entrepreneurs keep their debt levels manageable.

*3. Debt Ratio* A small company's **debt ratio** measures the percentage of total assets financed by its creditors. The debt ratio is calculated as follows:

$$\text{Debt ratio} = \frac{\text{Total debt (or liabilities)}}{\text{Total assets}}$$

$$= \frac{\$367,850 + \$212,150}{847,655}$$

$$= 0.68:1$$

Sam's creditors have claims of 68 cents against every $1 of assets that Sam's Appliance Shop owns, which means that creditors have contributed twice as much to the company's asset base as the company's owners have.

Total debt includes all current liabilities and any outstanding long-term notes and bonds. Total assets represent the sum of the firm's current assets, fixed assets, and intangible assets. A high debt ratio means that creditors provide a large percentage of the firm's total financing and, therefore, bear most of its financial risk. Owners generally prefer higher leverage ratios; otherwise, business funds must come either from the owners' personal assets or from taking on new owners, which requires them to surrender more control over the business. In addition, with a greater portion of the firm's assets financed by creditors, the owner is able to generate profits with a smaller personal investment. However, creditors typically prefer moderate debt ratios because a lower debt ratio indicates a smaller chance of creditor losses in case of liquidation. To lenders and creditors, high debt ratios mean a high risk of default.

*4. Debt to Net Worth Ratio* A small company's **debt to net worth ratio** also expresses the relationship between the capital contributions from creditors and those from owners. This ratio compares what the business "owes" to "what it is worth." It is a measure of a company's ability to meet both its creditor and its owner obligations in case of liquidation. The debt to net worth ratio is calculated as follows:

$$\text{Debt to net worth ratio} = \frac{\text{Total debt (or liabilities)}}{\text{Tangible net worth}}$$

$$= \frac{\$367,850 + \$212,150}{\$267,655 - \$3,500}$$

$$= 2.20:1$$

Sam's Appliance Shop owes creditors $2.20 for every $1 of equity that Sam owns.

Total debt is the sum of current liabilities and long-term liabilities, and tangible net worth represents the owners' investment in the business (capital + capital stock + earned surplus + retained earnings) less any intangible assets (e.g., goodwill) the company shows on its balance sheet.

The higher this ratio, the lower the degree of protection afforded creditors if the business fails. A high debt to net worth ratio means that the firm has less capacity to borrow; lenders and creditors see the firm as being "borrowed up." In addition, carrying high levels of debt limits a company's options and restricts managers' flexibility. Quite simply, there isn't much "wiggle room" with a debt-laden balance sheet. Metro-Goldwyn-Mayer (MGM), the venerable Hollywood movie studio that has produced many legendary movies since the 1920s, including *The Wizard of Oz* and *A Christmas Story*, has amassed so much debt and the resulting interest expense that it lacks the cash to produce significant numbers of films. In one recent year, MGM released only one film and had to count on DVD sales from its archive of 4,100 titles for revenue. As sales slipped, the

Businesses that turn their inventories more rapidly than average require a smaller inventory investment to produce a particular sales volume. That means that these companies tie up less cash in inventory that sits idly on shelves. For instance, if Sam's could turn its inventory four times each year instead of just two, the company would require an average inventory of just $322,529 instead of the current level of $630,600 to generate sales of $1,870,841. Increasing the number of inventory turns would free up more than $308,000 currently tied up in excess inventory! Sam's would benefit from improved cash flow and higher profits.

**ENTREPRENEURIAL PROFILE: Jonathan and James Murrell: MyDormFood and Candy Galaxy** Managing inventory has been one of the biggest challenges facing Jonathan and James Murrell as they try to scale their online businesses MyDormFood and Candy Galaxy. Their inventory, all of which is perishable, grew from $15,000 to more than $100,000 in just six months. This rapid increase in inventory caused two major problems. First, they did not have a system for reordering and constantly ran out of their best-selling items. "When our inventory was small, we could do daily spot checks," said Jonathan Murrell, "but once we grew and moved into a warehouse, our spot-checking system was no longer adequate." The second major challenge was slow turnover. "I never really understood why companies ran large sales until I found myself sitting on $10,000 of inventory that was nearing expiration and had not turned over in six months," said Murrell. "Cash was tight, and I did not have enough money to keep my hot-selling items in stock because so much money was tied up in slow-moving product." After identifying their slow-moving items, the Murrells ran a sale to help clear them out their slow-moving inventory and generate cash to invest in their faster-moving products.[20]

The inventory turnover ratio can be misleading, however. For example, an excessively high ratio could mean that the firm has a shortage of inventory and is experiencing stockouts. Similarly, a low ratio could be the result of planned inventory stockpiling to meet seasonal peak demand. Another problem is that the ratio is based on an inventory balance calculated from two days out of the entire accounting period. Thus, inventory fluctuations due to seasonal demand patterns are ignored, which may bias the resulting ratio. There is no universal, ideal inventory turnover ratio. Financial analysts suggest that a favorable turnover ratio depends on the type of business, its size, its profitability, its method of inventory valuation, and other relevant factors. The most meaningful basis for comparison is other companies of similar size in the same industry (more on this later in this chapter). For instance, the typical drugstore turns its inventory about 12 times per year, but a retail shoe store averages just 2.5 inventory turns a year.

**7. Average Collection Period Ratio** A small company's **average collection period ratio** (or **days sales outstanding** [DSO]) tells the average number of days it takes to collect accounts receivable. To compute the average collection period ratio, you must first calculate the firm's receivables turnover. Given that Sam's *credit* sales for the year were $1,309,589 (out of the total sales of $1,870,841), the company's receivables turnover ratio is as follows:

$$\text{Receivables turnover ratio} = \frac{\text{Credit sales (or net sales)}}{\text{Accounts receivable}}$$

$$= \frac{\$1,309,589}{\$179,225}$$

$$= 7.31 \text{ times/year}$$

Sam's Appliance Shop turns its receivables 7.31 times per year. This ratio measures the number of times a company's accounts receivable turn over during the accounting period. The higher a company's receivables turnover ratio, the shorter the time lag between making a sale and collecting the cash from it.

Use the following formula to calculate a company's average collection period ratio:

$$\text{Average collection period ratio} = \frac{\text{Days in accounting period}}{\text{Receivables turnover ratio}}$$

$$= \frac{365 \text{ days}}{7.31}$$

$$= 50.0 \text{ days}$$

Sam's accounts receivable are outstanding for an average of 50 days. Typically, the higher a company's average collection period ratio, the greater is its chance of bad debt losses. Sales don't count unless a company collects the revenue from them!

One of the most useful applications of the collection period ratio is to compare it to the industry average and to the firm's credit terms. This comparison indicates the degree of the small company's control over its credit sales and collection techniques. Perhaps the most meaningful analysis is to compare the collection period to the company's credit terms. One rule of thumb suggests that a company's collection period ratio should be no more than one-third greater than its credit terms. For example, if a small company's credit terms are "net 30," its average collection period ratio should be no more than 40 days (30 + 30 × 1/3). For this company, a ratio greater than 40 days would indicate poor collection procedures, such as sloppy record keeping or failure to send invoices promptly.

**ENTREPRENEURIAL PROFILE: Paul Burns and Eric Edelson: Fireclay Tile** Eric Edelson joined Paul Burns as a partner in Fireclay Tile, located in San Jose, California, which manufactures ceramic tile using recycled materials. Edelson noticed that the company's accounts receivable balance was more than $100,000. "At first, I thought it was kind of neat since we could count on all that cash coming in," Edelson said. "But after I started digging into it, I noticed a lot of stale accounts that were more than six months overdue." The partners tightened up their credit policy by requiring customers to pay for all previous orders before they could get credit for new orders. This change reduced their outstanding accounts receivables to less than $30,000, all of it current and more likely to be paid.[21]

Just as Eric Edelson has learned, slow payers represent great risk to small businesses. Many entrepreneurs proudly point to rapidly rising sales only to find that they must borrow money to keep their companies going because credit customers are paying their bills in 45, 60, or even 90 days instead of 30. Slow receivables often lead to a cash crisis that can cripple a business. Table 14.1 shows how lowering its average collection period ratio can save a company money.

*8. Average Payable Period Ratio*  The converse of the average collection period ratio, the **average payable period ratio** (or **days payables outstanding** [DPO]), tells the average number of days it takes a company to pay its accounts payable. Like the average collection period, it is measured in

---

**TABLE 14.1 How Lowering Your Average Collection Period Can Save You Money**

Too often, entrepreneurs fail to recognize the importance of collecting their accounts receivable on time. After all, collecting accounts is not as glamorous or as much fun as generating sales. Lowering a company's average collection period ratio, however, can produce tangible—and often significant—savings. The following formula shows how to convert an improvement in a company's average collection period ratio into dollar savings:

$$\text{Annual savings} = \frac{(\text{Credit sales} \times \text{Annual interest rate} \times \text{Number of days average collection period is lowered})}{365}$$

where

credit sales = company's annual credit sales in dollars,

annual interest rate = the interest rate at which the company borrows money,

and number of days average collection period is lowered = the difference between the previous year's average collection period ratio and the current one.

**Example**

The average collection period ratio for Sam's Appliance Shop is 50 days. Suppose that the previous year's average collection period ratio was 58 days, an eight-day improvement. The company's credit sales for the most recent year were $1,309,589. If Sam borrows money at 8.75 percent, this six-day improvement has generated the following savings for Sam's Appliance Shop:

$$\text{Savings} = \frac{\$1,309,589 \times 8.75\% \times 8 \text{ days}}{365 \text{ days}} = \$2,512$$

By collecting his accounts receivable just eight days faster on the average, Sam has saved his business more than $2,500! Of course, if a company's average collection period ratio increases, the same calculation will tell the owner how much that change costs.

*Source:* Based on "Days Saved, Thousands Earned," *Inc.*, November 1995, p. 98.

days. To compute this ratio, first calculate the payables turnover ratio. Sam's payables turnover ratio is as follows:

$$\text{Payables turnover ratio} = \frac{\text{Purchases}}{\text{Accounts payable}}$$

$$= \frac{\$939,827}{\$152,580}$$

$$= 6.16 \text{ times/year}$$

To find the average payable period, we use the following computation:

$$\text{Average payable period ratio} = \frac{\text{Days in accounting period}}{\text{Payables turnover ratio}}$$

$$= \frac{365 \text{ days}}{6.16}$$

$$= 59.3 \text{ days}$$

Sam's Appliance Shop takes an average of about 59 days to pay its accounts with vendors and suppliers.

An excessively high average payable period ratio may indicate that a company is enjoying extended credit terms from its suppliers, or it may be a sign of a significant amount of past-due accounts payable. Although sound cash management calls for business owners to keep their cash as long as possible, slowing payables too drastically can severely damage a company's credit rating.

Ideally, the average payable period would match (or exceed) the time it takes to convert inventory into sales and ultimately into cash. In this case, the company's vendors are financing its inventory and its credit sales. *Amazon.com* reaps the benefits of this situation. On average, it does not pay its vendors until 15 days *after* it collects payment from its customers.[22]

To make this comparison, an entrepreneur subtracts the company's average collection period (DSO) from its average collection period ratio (DPO) to calculate the company's float, the net number of days of cash that flows into or out of a company. The float for Sam's Appliance Shop is the following:

$$\text{Float} = \text{DPO} - \text{DSO} = 59.3 - 50.0 \text{ days} = 9.3 \text{ days}$$

A positive value for float is desirable because it means that cash will accumulate in a company over time. Multiplying float by a company's average daily sales tells Sam how much the company's cash balance will change over the course of the year as a result of its collection and payable processes. For Sam's Appliance Shop, this is calculated as follows:

$$\text{Change in cash position} = \$1,870,841 \div 365 \text{ days} \times 9.3 \text{ days} = \$47,668$$

Another meaningful comparison for this ratio is against the credit terms offered by suppliers (or an average of the credit terms offered). If the average payable period ratio slips beyond vendors' credit terms, it is an indication that the company is suffering from cash shortages or a sloppy accounts payable procedure and that its credit rating is in danger. If this ratio is significantly lower than vendors' credit terms, it may be a sign that a business is not using its cash most effectively.

*9. Net Sales to Total Assets Ratio* A small company's **net sales to total assets ratio** (also called the **total assets turnover ratio**) is a general measure of its ability to generate sales in relation to its assets. It describes how productively a company employs its assets to produce sales revenue. The total assets turnover ratio is calculated as follows:

$$\text{Total assets turnover ratio} = \frac{\text{Net sales}}{\text{Net total assets}}$$

$$= \frac{\$1,870,841}{\$847,655}$$

$$= 2.21:1$$

Sam's Appliance Shop generates $2.21 in sales for every dollar of assets.

The denominator of this ratio, net total assets, is the sum of all of the firm's assets (cash, inventory, land, buildings, equipment, tools—everything it owns) less depreciation. This ratio is meaningful only when compared to that of similar firms in the same industry category. A total assets turnover ratio below the industry average suggests that a small company is not generating an adequate sales volume for its asset size. In a recent National Federation of Independent Businesses survey, 19 percent of small businesses report poor sales as their number one problem.[23] If a company's sales fall too far, it operates below its break-even point and cannot stay in business for long.

**PROFITABILITY RATIOS** **Profitability ratios** indicate how efficiently a small company is being managed. They provide the owner with information about a company's ability to generate a profit. They focus on a company's "bottom line"; in other words, they describe how successfully the business is using its resources to generate a profit.

*10. Net Profit on Sales Ratio* The **net profit on sales ratio** (also called the **profit margin on sales** or the **net profit margin**) measures a company's profit per dollar of sales. This ratio (which is expressed as a percentage) shows the number of cents of each sales dollar remaining after deducting all expenses and income taxes. The profit margin on sales is calculated as follows:

$$\text{Net profit on sales ratio} = \frac{\text{Net income}}{\text{Net sales}} \times 100\%$$

$$= \frac{\$60,629}{\$1,870,841} \times 100\%$$

$$= 3.24\%$$

Sam's Appliance Shop keeps 3.24 cents in profit out of every dollar of sales it generates.

A recent study by *Inc.* magazine and Sageworks shows that the average net profit margin for privately held companies normally falls between 5 and 6.5 percent, but this ratio varies from one industry to another. The retail industry typically produces a net profit on sales ratio that falls between 2 and 4 percent, but profit margins in the health care field range between 10 and 16 percent.[24]

If a company's profit margin on sales is below the industry average, it is a sign that its prices are relatively low, that its costs are excessively high, or both.

A Jellio light fixture.
*Source:* Jellio Inc.

**ENTREPRENEURIAL PROFILE: Mario Marsicano and Chris Lenox: Jellio** Mario Marsicano and Chris Lenox, cofounders of Jellio, which manufactures whimsical home furnishings, found that although their company's revenues were growing fast (doubling in just one year to nearly $900,000), profits were not following suit. The company makes products such as four-foot tall gummy-bear lamps, Rubik's Cube tables, and cupcake chairs. Because the owners made each product one at a time, the company's production and material costs were high and its profit margins were low. Marsicano and Lenox began to focus on higher-priced products that had the strongest demand, found ways to reduce the amount of materials they needed to make their products without diminishing their quality, and discovered a way to speed up and simplify manufacturing. The company now generates more than $1 million a year in sales with solid profits.[25]

Recall that if a company's net profit on sales ratio is excessively low, the owner should check the gross profit margin (net sales minus cost of goods sold expressed as a percentage of net sales). However, a reasonable gross profit margin varies from industry to industry. For instance, a service company may have a gross profit margin of 75 percent, whereas a manufacturer's may be 35 percent. If this margin slips too low, it puts the company's ability to generate a profit and stay in business in jeopardy.

*11. Net Profit to Assets Ratio* The **net profit to assets ratio** (also known as the **return on assets** [ROA]) ratio tells how much profit a company generates for each dollar of assets that it owns. This ratio describes how efficiently a business is putting to work all of the assets it owns to generate a profit. It tells how much net income an entrepreneur is squeezing from each dollar's worth of the company's assets. It is calculated as follows:

$$\text{Net profit to assets ratio} = \frac{\text{Net profit}}{\text{Total assets}} \times 100\%$$

$$= \frac{\$60,629}{\$847,655} \times 100\%$$

$$= 7.15\%$$

Sam's Appliance shop earns a return of 7.15 percent on its asset base. This ratio provides clues about the asset intensity of an industry. Return on assets ratios that are below 5 percent are indicative of asset-intense industries that require heavy investments in assets to stay in business (e.g., manufacturing companies). Return on assets ratios that exceed 20 percent tend to occur in asset-light industries, such as business or personal services (e.g., advertising agencies and computer services). A net profit to assets ratio that is below the industry average suggests that a company is not using its assets very efficiently to produce a profit. Another common application of this ratio is to compare it to the company's cost of borrowed capital. Ideally, a company's return on assets ratio should exceed the cost of borrowing money to purchase those assets. Companies that experience significant swings in the value of their assets over the course of a year often use an average value of the asset base over the accounting period to get a more realistic estimate of this ratio.

**12. Net Profit to Equity Ratio** The **net profit to equity ratio** (or the **return on net worth ratio**) measures the owners' rate of return on investment. Because it reports the percentage of the owners' investment in the business that is being returned through profits annually, it is one of the most important indicators of a company's profitability or management's efficiency. The net profit to equity ratio is computed as follows:

$$\text{Net profit to equity ratio} = \frac{\text{Net income}}{\text{Owners' equity (or net worth)}} \times 100\%$$

$$= \frac{\$60,629}{\$267,655} \times 100\%$$

$$= 22.65\%$$

This ratio compares profits earned during the accounting period with the amount the owners have invested in the business during that time. If this interest rate on the owners' investment is excessively low, some of this capital might be better employed elsewhere. For instance, a business should produce a rate of return that exceeds its cost of capital.

 **In the Entrepreneurial Spotlight**

# Pitcher Strikes Out While Trying to Hit a Home Run

Curt Schilling had great success in major league baseball as a right-handed pitcher, including a record of 3–1 in the World Series while playing for three different teams. Besides his passion for baseball, Shilling also was an avid video gamer. After retiring from baseball, Shilling decided to pursue a second career as a video game entrepreneur.

In 2006, Shilling formed his video game company 38 Studios LLC (named after his jersey number) in Massachusetts. The company purchased existing video game companies to add their titles to the company's offerings, hoping to speed up its growth and accelerate its ability to launch a blockbuster video game. 38 Studio hired some of the best executives and developers in the gaming industry, and Shilling invested $50 million of his own money, most of which he had saved up from his days playing baseball, to fund the company.

Four years after the launch of the company, the Rhode Island Economic Development Corporation approved a $75 million loan guarantee to lure 38 Studios LLC from Massachusetts to Rhode Island. 38 Studios promised that they would bring more than 400 new jobs to Rhode Island within the next two years. "We need to make a statement . . . this gives us the ability to be a real player in the digital-media area," said then Rhode Island Governor Donald Carcieri, who served as chairman of board of the Economic Development Corporation. Under the terms of the deal, 38 Studios was responsible for repaying the money, but if it defaulted, the state would be responsible for paying back all guaranteed loans.

38 Studio was betting the $133 million invested into the company on the success of its game "Kingdoms of Amalur: Reckoning," which had to sell at least 2 million copies just to

*(continued)*

# In the Entrepreneurial Spotlight (continued)

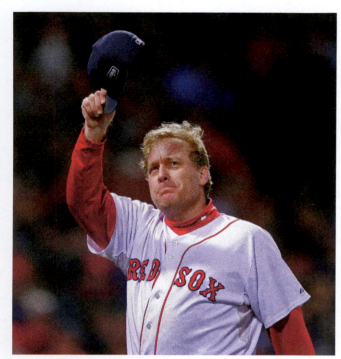

Curt Schilling.
*Source:* Getty Images.

cover the development costs and reach its breakeven point. However, the game achieved only modest success, selling a little more than 1 million copies. While its first big game introduction was failing, the company continued to pour millions into developing what 38 Studios executives hoped would be its second big game title, "Copernicus." However, "Copernicus" never made it to market.

In May 2012, 38 Studio was unable to make a $1.1 million loan payment to the state. The company soon laid off more than 400 employees, citing the burden of millions in state debt that it was unable to pay due to the poor performance of its first major video game launch.

38 Studio ultimately filed for Chapter 7 bankruptcy (liquidation). Court documents indicated that the studio owed $150 million to more than 1,000 entities. The largest creditor was the Rhode Island Economic Development Corporation. At the time of its bankruptcy filing, 38 Studio had less than $22 million in assets. Rhode Island taxpayers were left owing the balance of the $75 million in guaranteed loans to 38 Studios.

Because Shilling personally guaranteed many of the loans to 38 Studio, he was forced to sell the property he used as collateral for those loans. Among the assets he was forced to sell to help cover his personal loan guarantees were his most cherished mementos from his baseball career, including the famed "bloody sock" he wore while pitching in game 2 for the Red Sox in the 2004 World Series and a cap worn by Lou Gehrig. Shilling also was forced to sell most of his personal real estate holdings.

Shilling and other 38 Studio executives faced investigation for fraud and could face further legal actions by state and federal authorities for covering up advance knowledge that the company was failing and would be unable to pay its debts.

1. What factors contributed to the financial collapse of 38 Studio?

2. If you had advised Curt Shilling at the time he launched 38 Studio, what advice would you have offered that might have helped avoid the financial distress that both he and his company experienced?

3. Which ratios and key performance indicators would you have used to manage 38 Studio to help avoid its financial collapse?

4. Why are businesses that require high levels of investment inherently more risky? How could 38 Studio have avoided some of that risk?

*Sources:* Andy Smith, "Curt Schilling's Video-Game Company Gets $75-Million Loan to Come to R.I.," *Providence Journal*, July 27, 2010, *http://web.archive.org/web/20100731001844* and *www.projo.com/news/content/38_Studios_vote__07-27-10_JIJB71G_v18.3dd3796.html*; Michael del Castillo, "Failed Entrepreneur Curt Schilling's Bloody Sock on the Auction Block," *Upstart Business Journal*, January 18, 2013, *http://upstart.bizjournals.com/companies/startups/2013/01/18/38-studios-curt-schilling-selling-sock.html*; Erik Kain, "Is It Game Over for Curt Schilling's 38 Studios?," *Forbes*, May 25, 2012, *www.forbes.com/sites/erikkain/2012/05/25/is-it-game-over-for-curt-schillings-38-studios*.

## Interpreting Business Ratios

**5.**

Explain how to interpret financial ratios.

Ratios are useful yardsticks when measuring a small company's performance and can point out potential problems before they develop into serious crises. However, calculating these ratios is not enough to ensure proper financial control. In addition to knowing how to calculate these ratios, the owner must understand how to interpret them and apply them to managing the business more effectively and efficiently.

Not every business measures its success with the same ratios. In fact, key performance ratios vary dramatically across industries and even within different segments of the same industry. Entrepreneurs must know and understand which ratios are most crucial to their companies' success and focus on monitoring and controlling those. Many successful entrepreneurs identify or develop ratios that are unique to their own operations to help them achieve success. Known as **key performance indicators** (KPIs), these barometers of business success measure financial and operational aspects of a company's performance. When these KPIs are headed in the right direction, a business is on track to achieve its objectives.

**ENTREPRENEURIAL PROFILE: Dawn Gluskin: SolTec** In 2008, Dawn Gluskin founded SolTec Electronics, a company that sells highly specialized electronic circuit board components to the electronic manufacturing and aerospace industries, from her living room. She financed her business with her savings and retirement accounts. Within two years, the company had grown to almost $3 million in sales. "We tripled our staff size, moved from the home office, added a lab, and were spending, spending, spending on equipment," says Gluskin. When the management team met to go over the final-quarter results from 2010, Gluskin learned that the company suffered its first-ever loss. She hired a consultant who helped develop a financial dashboard to track relevant financial results and financial ratios. The dashboard includes net account receivables, net worth, net sales, gross profit margin, and operating profit margin. Gluskin now reviews all of SolTec's critical numbers every two weeks to stay on top of her company's performance.[26]

Examples of KPIs at other companies include the following:

- The load factor, the number of seats filled with passengers, on a luxury bus targeting business travelers with daily trips from downtown Boston to midtown Manhattan.[27]

- The number of cases shipped per employee at a food distributor.

- Food costs as a percentage of sales for a restaurant. To maintain profitability, many restaurateurs strive to keep their food costs between 22 and 30 percent of sales.[28] At Dos Caminos, a Mexican restaurant in New York City, chef Ivy Stark's goal is to keep the restaurant's food cost at or below 26 percent of sales. Stark relies on a five-page spreadsheet generated each morning to keep food costs under control.[29]

- Subscriber renewal rates at a magazine.

- Room occupancy rates at a hotel. Although a particular hotel's break-even occupancy rate depends on its cost structure, the average occupancy rate required for hotels to break even ranges from 62 to 65 percent. Other critical numbers in the hospitality industry include the average daily room rate and the revenue per available room.[30]

- Page rank for Internet searches on major search engines for a retailer's Web site.

- Response time in seconds for retail mobile app sites.[31]

KPIs may be different for two companies in the same industry, depending on their strategies. The key is identifying *your* company's KPIs, monitoring them, and then driving them in the right direction. That requires communicating the importance of KPIs to employees, explaining to them *why* these numbers are important, and giving them feedback on how well the business is achieving them.

**ENTREPRENEURIAL PROFILE: Norm Brodsky: CitiStorage** Over time, Norm Brodsky, owner of CitiStorage, a highly successful records-storage business in New York City that targets law firms, accounting firms, and hospitals, discovered that his company's critical number was the number of new boxes put into storage each week, so he began tracking it closely. "Tell me how many new boxes came in during [a month]," he says, "and I can tell you our overall sales figure for [that month] within 1 or 2 percent of the actual figure." That particular critical number surprised Brodsky because new boxes account for only a small percentage of total sales, yet new-box count was the key to allowing Brodsky to forecast his company's future. Once, during a period of rapid growth (about 55 percent a year), Brodsky saw on his Monday morning report that the new-box count had fallen by 70 percent in the previous week. Alarmed, Brodsky temporarily stopped expanding the company's workforce to see whether the drop was an aberration or the beginning of a business slowdown. A few weeks later, he knew that the market had changed and that sales growth indeed had slowed to 15 percent. By using his company's critical number, Brodsky avoided excessive labor costs, a nasty cash crisis, and a morale-destroying layoff and was able to keep his company on track.[32]

One of the most valuable ways to utilize ratios is to compare them with those of similar businesses in the same industry. By comparing the company's financial statistics to industry averages, an entrepreneur can identify problem areas and develop a plan to improve them. "By themselves, these numbers are not that meaningful," says one financial expert of ratios, "but when you compare them to [those of] other businesses in your industry, they suddenly come alive because they put your operation in perspective."[33]

The principle behind calculating these ratios and other KPIs and then comparing them to industry norms is the same as that of basic medical tests in the health care profession. Just as a healthy person's blood pressure and cholesterol levels should fall within a range of normal values, so should a financially healthy company's ratios. A company cannot deviate too far from these normal values and remain successful for long. When deviations from "normal" do occur (and they will), an entrepreneur should focus on determining the cause of the deviations. In some cases, deviations are the result of sound business decisions, such as building up inventory in preparation for the busy season, investing heavily in new technology, and others. In other cases, however, ratios that are out of the normal range for a particular type of business are indicators of what could become serious problems for a company. When comparing a company's ratios to industry standards, entrepreneurs should ask the following questions:

- Is there a significant difference in my company's ratio and the industry average?
- If so, is this a *meaningful* difference?
- Is the difference good or bad?
- What are the possible causes of this difference? What is the most likely cause?
- Does this cause require that I take action?
- What action should I take to correct the problem?

Properly used, ratio analysis can help owners identify potential problem areas in their businesses early on—*before* they become crises that threaten their very survival. Several organizations regularly compile and publish operating statistics, including key ratios, summarizing the financial performance of many businesses across a wide range of industries. The local library should subscribe to most of these publications and databases:

*BizMiner.* The resource provides industry financial analysis for almost 5,500 different industries, including detailed industry profit-and-loss statements, summary balance sheets, sources and uses of funds summaries, and 33 industry financial ratios.

*RMA Annual Statement Studies.* The Risk Management Association publishes its *Annual Statement Studies*, showing ratios and other financial data drawn from more than 280,000 companies' financial statements for more than 800 different industrial, construction, wholesale, retail, and service categories.

*Dun & Bradstreet's Key Business Ratios.* Since 1932, Dun & Bradstreet has published *Key Business Ratios*, which provides 30 ratios for more than 800 business categories.

*Almanac of Business and Industrial Financial Ratios.* This handy guide provides key ratios and financial data in 50 areas organized by company size for nearly 200 industries.

*Industry Spotlight.* Published by Schonfeld & Associates, this publication, which covers more than 250 industries, contains financial statement data and 17 key ratios from more than 95,000 tax returns. *Industry Spotlight* also provides detailed financial information for both profitable companies and those with losses.

*Standard and Poor's Industry Surveys.* In addition to providing information on financial ratios and comparative financial analysis, these surveys also contain useful details on how the industry operates, current industry trends, key terms in the industry, and others.

*Online resources.* Many companies publish comparative financial resources online. Some require subscriptions, but others are free:

- BizStats publishes common-size financial statements and ratios for 95 business categories for sole proprietorships, S corporations, and corporations.
- Reuters provides an overview of many industries that includes industry trends and news as well as financial ratios.
- A subscription to Lexis/Nexis allows users to view detailed company profiles, including financial reports and analysis, for publicly held companies.

*Industry trade associations.* Virtually every type of business is represented by a national trade association that publishes detailed financial data compiled from its membership. For example, the owner of a small coffee shop could consult the National Coffee Association (and its newsletter, *The Coffee Reporter*), the Specialty Coffee Association of America, the International Coffee Organization, or a variety of state coffee associations for financial statistics relevant to his operation.

***Government agencies.*** Several government agencies (Federal Trade Commission, Interstate Commerce Commission, Department of Commerce, Department of Agriculture, and Securities and Exchange Commission) offer a great deal of financial operating data on a variety of industries, although the categories are more general. In addition, the Internal Revenue Service (IRS) annually publishes *Statistics of Income*, which includes income statement and balance sheet statistics compiled from income tax returns. The IRS also publishes the *Census of Business*, which gives a limited amount of ratio information.

## What Do All These Numbers Mean?

Learning to interpret financial ratios just takes a little practice! This section and Table 14.2 shows you how it's done by comparing the ratios from the operating data already computed for Sam's Appliance Shop to those taken from *BizMiner* for retail appliance stores that are of a comparable size to Sam's Appliance Shop. Calculating the variance from the industry average ((company ratio − industry average) ÷ industry average) helps entrepreneurs identify the areas in which the company is out of line with the typical company in the industry.

When comparing ratios for their individual businesses to published statistics, entrepreneurs must remember that the comparison is made against averages. Owners should strive to achieve ratios that are at least as good as these average figures. The goal should be to manage the business so that its financial performance is *better* than the industry average. As owners compare financial performance to those covered in the published statistics, they inevitably will discern differences between them. They should note those items that are substantially out of

## TABLE 14.2 Ratios: Sam's Appliance Shop Versus the Industry Averages

| Ratio | Sam's Appliance Shop | Industry Average | Variance |
|---|---|---|---|
| *Liquidity ratios* tell whether a small business will be able to meet its maturing obligations as they come due. | | | |
| 1. Current ratio | 1.87:1 | 1.69:1 | 10.70% |
| **Explanation:** Sam's Appliance Shop falls short of the rule of thumb of 2:1, but its current ratio is above the industry average by a significant amount. Sam's should have no problem meeting its short-term debts as they come due. By this measure, the company's liquidity is solid. | | | |
| 2. Quick ratio | 0.63:1 | 0.81:1 | −22.20% |
| **Explanation:** Sam's is below the rule of thumb of 1:1 and below industry standards. This may mean that Sam's has too much of its current assets tied up in inventory. Sam's relies on selling inventory to satisfy short-term debt (as do most appliance shops). If sales slump, the result could be liquidity problems for Sam's. | | | |
| *Leverage ratios* measure the financing supplied by the company's owners against that supplied by its creditors and serve as a gauge of the depth of a company's debt. | | | |
| 3. Debt ratio | 0.68:1 | 0.71:1 | −4.20% |
| **Explanation:** Creditors provide 68 percent of Sam's total assets, slightly below the industry average of 71%. Although Sam's does not appear to be overburdened with debt and is quite close to the industry average, the company might have difficulty borrowing additional money, especially from conservative lenders. | | | |
| 4. Debt to net worth ratio | 2.20:1 | 2.51:1 | −12.40% |
| **Explanation:** Sam's Appliance Shop owes $2.20 to creditors for every $1.00 the owners have invested in the business (compared to $2.51 in debt to every $1.00 in equity for the typical business). Although this is not an exorbitant amount of debt by industry standards, many lenders and creditors see Sam's as "borrowed up." Borrowing capacity is somewhat limited because creditors' claims against the business are more than twice those of the owners. | | | |

*(continued)*

**TABLE 14.2** *(continued)*

| Ratio | Sam's Appliance Shop | Industry Average | Variance |
|---|---|---|---|
| 5. Times interest earned | 2.52:1 | 9.44:1 | −73.30% |

*Explanation:* Sam's earnings are high enough to cover the interest payments on its debt by a factor of 2.52, which is right at the typical marginal threshold that bankers want to see of 2.5. The typical firm in the industry has a much higher coverage ratio of more than nine times. Sam's Appliance Shop should be able to meet its interest payments, but bankers like to see a larger cushion than Sam's has. Sam's bank will be keeping a close eye on this ratio!

*Operating ratios* evaluate a company's overall performance and show how effectively it is putting its resources to work.

| Ratio | Sam's Appliance Shop | Industry Average | Variance |
|---|---|---|---|
| 6. Average inventory turnover | 2.05 times/year | 4.3 times/year | −52.33% |

*Explanation:* Inventory is moving through Sam's at a very slow pace-half the industry average. Whereas the typical business in its industry turns its inventory over about every three months, Sam's turns its over every six months. The company has a problem with slow-moving items in its inventory and, likely, too much inventory. Which items are they, and why are they slow moving? Does Sam need to drop some product lines?

| Ratio | Sam's Appliance Shop | Industry Average | Variance |
|---|---|---|---|
| 7. Average collection period | 50.0 days | 26.9 days | 85.90% |

*Explanation:* Sam's Appliance Shop collects the average accounts receivable after 50 days, compared with the industry average of about 27 days, nearly twice as long. A more meaningful comparison is against Sam's credit terms; if credit terms are net 30 (or anywhere close to that), Sam's has a dangerous collection problem, one that drains cash and profits and demands immediate attention!

| Ratio | Sam's Appliance Shop | Industry Average | Variance |
|---|---|---|---|
| 8. Average payable period | 59.3 days | 25.5 days | 132.50% |

*Explanation:* Sam's payables are *significantly* slower than those of the typical firm in the industry. Stretching payables too far could seriously damage the company's credit rating, causing suppliers to cut off future trade credit. This could be a sign of cash flow problems or a sloppy accounts payable procedure. This problem, which indicates that the company suffers cash flow problems, also demands immediate attention.

| Ratio | Sam's Appliance Shop | Industry Average | Variance |
|---|---|---|---|
| 9. Net sales to total assets | 2.21:1 | 4.3:1 | −48.60% |

*Explanation:* Sam's Appliance Shop is not generating enough sales given the size of its asset base. This could be the result of a number of factors—improper inventory (as indicated by the inventory turnover ratio above), inappropriate pricing, poor location, poorly trained sales personnel, and many others. The key is to find the cause—fast!

*Profitability ratios* measure how efficiently a firm is operating and offer information about its bottom line.

| Ratio | Sam's Appliance Shop | Industry Average | Variance |
|---|---|---|---|
| 10. Net profit on sales | 3.24% | 3.60% | −10.00% |

*Explanation:* After deducting all expenses, 3.24 cents of each sales dollar remains as profit for Sam's—10% below the industry average. Sam should review his company's gross profit margin and investigate its operating expenses, checking them against industry standards and looking for those that are out of balance.

| Ratio | Sam's Appliance Shop | Industry Average | Variance |
|---|---|---|---|
| 11. Net profit to assets | 7.15% | 15.28% | −53.20% |

*Explanation:* Sam's generates just a return of 7.15% for every $1 in assets, which is less than half the industry average. This is consistent with the previous ratio that indicated profits that are weaker than the industry average.

| Ratio | Sam's Appliance Shop | Industry Average | Variance |
|---|---|---|---|
| 12. Net profit to equity | 22.65% | 53.40% | −57.60% |

*Explanation:* Sam's Appliance Shop's owners are earning 22.65% on the money they have invested in the business. This yield is half of the industry average, which indicates that the company's profits are below average.

line from the industry average. However, a ratio that varies from the average does not necessarily mean that a small business is in financial jeopardy. Instead of making drastic changes in financial policy, entrepreneurs must explore why the figures are out of line. Steve Cowan, co-owner of Professional Salon Concepts, a wholesale beauty products distributor, routinely performs such an analysis on his company's financial statements. "I need to know whether the variances for expenses and revenues for a certain period are similar," he says. "If they're not, are the differences explainable? Is an expense category up just because of a decision to spend more, or were we just sloppy?"[34]

In addition to comparing ratios to industry averages, owners should analyze their firms' financial ratios over time. By themselves, these ratios are "snapshots" of the firm's finances at a single instant, but by examining these trends over time, the owner can detect gradual shifts that otherwise might go unnoticed until a financial crisis is looming.

 ## Lessons from the Street-Smart Entrepreneur

# Gaining a Competitive Edge

### Do You Know How Your Company Will Make Money?

When they launch their businesses, entrepreneurs instinctively know that their companies must make a profit to survive. However, many entrepreneurs never take the time to examine the factors in their business models that drive their companies' profitability. The following model is a useful tool for visualizing these factors, analyzing their impact on a company's profits, and identifying strategies for improving them so that a business can improve its profitability. Four factors determine a company's ability to produce an attractive profit: revenue drivers, margins, operating leverage, and volumes (see Figure 1).

**Revenue drivers** include all of the ways a company generates revenue. For instance, an automobile dealership revenue drivers may be new cars sales, used cars sales, auto leases, service, parts, and short-term rentals. For instance, one small jewelry store identified its revenue generators as new jewelry, estate jewelry, watches, and gift items. Small companies with extensive inventories, such as hardware stores, can organize their revenue-generating product lines into a manageable number of major categories—for example, power tools, hand tools, lawn and garden, home repair, plumbing, electrical, and others. The next step is to assess the impact of each of the company's revenue drivers on total sales and their interaction with one another. For instance, an auto dealer may discover that the business generates more sales from used cars than from new cars.

Entrepreneurs must then consider how much control they have over pricing their revenue drivers. Pricing may be either fixed or flexible. A company relies on fixed pricing if it sells goods or services at standard prices without negotiation or variation— for example, the items on the menu of a restaurant. Flexible pricing means that a company can offer different prices depending on when customers make a purchase, how many items they purchase, whether other items are bundled into the purchase, and other variables. Even though a restaurateur may be limited to fixed pricing on the menu, he or she would be able to use

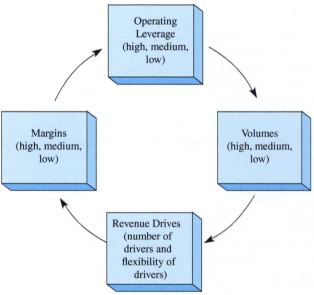

**FIGURE 1**

**Four Key Elements of a Firm's Economic Model**

flexible pricing on catering jobs. Flexible pricing gives entrepreneurs greater ability to maximize total revenue (and profitability).

**Margins** reflect how much each revenue driver contributes to the profitability of a company. Margins are the price that a customer pays minus the cost to the company of providing that good or service. A small company can increase its margins either by raising its prices or by improving its efficiency and providing goods and services at lower costs. The goal is to determine which revenue drivers are capable of generating the greatest profit. For instance, an auto dealership may find that its profit margin on used cars is much higher than new cars and that the margin on auto repairs is higher still.

**Volumes** are another important determinant of a company's profitability. A small company's volume depends on the

*(continued)*

# Lessons from the Street-Smart Entrepreneur (continued)

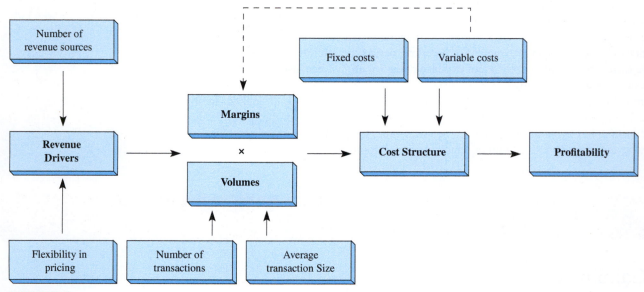

**FIGURE 2**

## Keys to Profitability

number of sales transactions it generates over a given time period and the value of each transaction. For instance, a fast-food restaurant counts on selling a large number of relatively low-priced meals, but an upscale restaurant generates revenue from a smaller number of meals at much higher average prices. At the fast-food restaurant, the average check may be $5.18, but at the upscale restaurant, the average check may be $45.80.

**Operating leverage** is the impact that a change in a company's sales volume has on its net income. If a small company achieves positive operating leverage, its expenses as a percentage of sales revenues flatten or even decline as sales increase. As a result, the company's net profit margin will increase as it grows. Operating leverage is a function of a business's cost structure. Companies that have high levels of fixed costs have high operating leverage; conversely, companies that have high levels of variable costs have low operating leverage. Profits are more volatile when a company has high operating leverage because slight changes in revenue cause dramatic swings in profits as the company's sales fluctuate above and below its break-even point.

Once entrepreneurs have analyzed the four components of a company's profitability, they can formulate strategies to enhance them (see Figure 2). For instance, if a company's current business model is characterized by a single revenue driver, low margins, low volumes, and high operating leverage, it is not likely to be a highly profitable venture. The entrepreneur in this

situation, however, might change the business model to make it more profitable using the following questions:

- Can I add more revenue drivers to my business?
- How can I increase the number of transactions and/or the average transaction size that make up our volume?
- What can I do to reduce the level of fixed costs in my company?
- Can I change to a flexible pricing strategy and move away from a fixed pricing strategy?
- How can I improve the efficiency with which my company provides products and services to customers?
- In what other ways can I improve my company's profit margins?

Ron Towry, owner of Truck Gear SuperCenter, a small-truck accessories business, was able to increase his company's sales by 25 percent and profits by 32 percent after making a strategic decision to begin selling his products at wholesale to truck and auto dealerships in addition to selling to his traditional retail customers. Although the company's wholesale prices and profit margins were lower, wholesale customers purchased in higher volumes, and Towry's company could sell to them at a lower cost per transaction, resulting in higher sales and profits.

*Sources:* Adapted from April Murdoch and Michael Morris, "Is Your Economic Model Working?," *Orange Entrepreneur*, Fall 2006, pp. 16–19; Ron Stodghill, "Bolt Down Those Costs," *FSB*, May 2006, pp. 85–87.

## Break-Even Analysis

**6.**

Conduct a break-even analysis for a small company.

Another key component of every sound financial plan is a break-even analysis (or cost-volume-profit analysis). A small company's **break-even point** is the level of operation (sales dollars or production quantity) at which it neither earns a profit nor incurs a loss. At this level of activity, sales revenue equals expenses—that is, the company "breaks even." A business that generates sales that are greater than its break-even point will generate a profit, but one that operates below its break-even point will incur a net loss. The break-even point is the single most important financial figure for an entrepreneur to understand because it is the point at which his or her business is able to sustain itself through generating revenues. It is the point at which the business generates enough revenues to pay all of its bills *and* provide the entrepreneur with a paycheck!

**ENTREPRENEURIAL PROFILE: Todd Campbell: E.B. Capital Markets** Todd Campbell's business, E.B. Capital Markets, provides research on the stock market to portfolio managers. When the recession hit in 2008, he realized that he had to keep better track of his company's finances to ensure that he could meet its financial obligations, such as payroll for his employees. The company's monthly expenses were $20,000, and its gross profit margin was 50 percent. To calculate the company's breakeven point, he divided $20,000 by 50 percent. Campbell knew that his business had to sell $40,000 per month to break even. "It is the single best indicator because it helps you see if the canary in the coal mine is getting woozy," Campbell says. "Now I know what decisions I have to make today so that I don't have to panic a few months from now."[35]

By analyzing expenses using break-even analysis, an entrepreneur can calculate the minimum level of activity required to keep a business in operation. These techniques can then be refined to project the sales needed to generate a desired level of profit. Most potential lenders and investors require entrepreneurs to prepare a break-even analysis so that they can judge the earning potential of a new business and the likelihood that it will be successful. In addition to its being a simple, useful screening device for financial institutions, break-even analysis can serve as a planning device for entrepreneurs. It can show an entrepreneur who might have unreasonable expectations about a business idea just how unprofitable a proposed business venture is likely to be.

## Calculating the Break-Even Point

A small business owner can calculate a firm's break-even point by using a simple mathematical formula. To begin the analysis, the owner must determine fixed costs and variable costs. **Fixed expenses** are those that do not vary with changes in the volume of sales or production (e.g., rent, depreciation expense, insurance, salaries, lease or loan payments, and others). **Variable expenses**, on the other hand, vary directly with changes in the volume of sales or production (e.g., raw material purchases, sales commissions, hourly wages, and others).

Some expenses cannot be neatly categorized as fixed or variable because they contain elements of both. These semivariable expenses change, although not proportionately, with changes in the level of sales or production (electricity would be one example). These costs remain constant up to a particular production or sales volume and then climb as that volume is exceeded. To calculate the break-even point, an entrepreneur must separate these expenses into their fixed and variable components. A number of techniques can be used (which are beyond the scope of this text), but a good cost accounting system can provide the desired results.

Here are the steps an entrepreneur must take to compute the break-even point using an example of a typical small business, the Magic Shop:

**Step 1.** *Determine the expenses the business can expect to incur.* With the help of a budget, an entrepreneur can develop estimates of sales revenue, cost of goods sold, and expenses for the upcoming accounting period. The Magic Shop expects net sales of $950,000 in the upcoming year, with a cost of goods sold of $646,000 and total expenses of $236,500.

**Step 2.** *Categorize the expenses estimated in step 1 into fixed expenses and variable expenses and separate semivariable expenses into their component parts.* From the budget, the owner anticipates variable expenses (including the cost of goods sold) of $705,125 and fixed expenses of $177,375.

**Step 3.** *Calculate the ratio of variable expenses to net sales.* For the Magic Shop, this percentage is $705,125 ÷ $950,000 = 74 percent. So the Magic Shop uses $0.74 out of every sales dollar to cover variable expenses, leaving $0.26 ($1.00 − 0.74) as a contribution margin to cover fixed costs and make a profit.

**Step 4.** *Compute the break-even point by inserting this information into the following formula:*

$$\text{Break-even sales (\$)} = \frac{\text{Total fixed cost}}{\text{Contribution margin expressed as a percentage of sales}}$$

For the Magic Shop,

$$\text{Break-even sales} = \frac{\$177,375}{0.26}$$

$$= \$682,212$$

Thus, the Magic Shop will break even with sales of $682,212. At this point, sales revenue generated will just cover total fixed and variable expense. The Magic Shop will earn no profit and will incur no loss. To verify this, make the following calculations:

| | |
|---|---:|
| Sales at break-even point | $682,212 |
| − Variable expenses (74% of sales) | −504,837 |
| Contribution margin | 177,375 |
| − Fixed expenses | −177,375 |
| Net income (or net loss) | $          0 |

Some entrepreneurs find it more meaningful to break down their companies' annual break-even point into a daily sales figure. If the Magic Shop will be open 312 days per year, then the average daily sales it must generate just to break even is $682,212 ÷ 312 days = $2,187 per day.

### Adding a Profit

What if the Magic Shop's owner wants to do *better* than just break even? His analysis can be adjusted to consider such a possibility. Suppose the owner expects a reasonable profit (before taxes) of $80,000. What level of sales must the Magic Shop achieve to generate this? He can calculate this by treating the desired profit as if it were a fixed cost. In other words, he modifies the formula to include the desired net income:

$$\text{Sales (\$)} = \frac{\text{Total fixed expenses } + \text{ Desired net income}}{\text{Contribution margin expressed as a percentage of sales}}$$

$$= \frac{\$177,375 + \$80,000}{0.26}$$

$$= \$989,904$$

To achieve a net profit of $80,000 (before taxes), the Magic Shop must generate net sales of $989,904. Once again, if we transform this sales annual volume into a daily sales volume, we get $989,904 ÷ 312 days = $3,173 per day.

### Break-Even Point in Units

Some small businesses may prefer to express the break-even point in units produced or sold instead of in dollars. Manufacturers often find this approach particularly useful. The following formula computes the break-even point in units:

$$\text{Break-even volume} = \frac{\text{Total fixed costs}}{\text{Sales price per unit } - \text{ Variable cost per unit}}$$

For example, suppose that Trilex Manufacturing Company estimates its fixed costs for producing its line of small appliances at $390,000. The variable costs (including materials, direct labor, and factory overhead) amount to $12.10 per unit, and the selling price per unit is $17.50. Thus, Trilex computes its contribution margin as follows:

$$\text{Contribution margin} = \text{Price per unit } - \text{ Variable cost per unit}$$

$$= \$17.50 \text{ per unit } - \$12.10 \text{ per unit}$$

$$= \$5.40 \text{ per unit}$$

Thus, Trilex's break-even volume is as follows:

$$\text{Break-even volume (units)} = \frac{\text{Total fixed costs}}{\text{Per unit contribution margin}}$$

$$= \frac{\$390,000}{\$5.40 \text{ per unit}}$$

$$= 72,222 \text{ units}$$

To convert this number of units to break-even sales dollars, Trilex simply multiplies it by the selling price per unit:

$$\text{Break-even sales} = 72{,}222 \text{ units} \times \$17.50 = \$1{,}263{,}889$$

Trilex could compute the sales required to produce a desired profit by treating the profit as if it were a fixed cost:

$$\text{Sales (units)} = \frac{\text{Total fixed costs} + \text{Desired net income}}{\text{Per unit contribution margin}}$$

For example, if Trilex wanted to earn a $60,000 profit, its required sales would be as follows:

$$\text{Sales (units)} = \frac{\$390{,}000 + \$60{,}000}{5.40} = 83{,}333 \text{ units}$$

## Constructing a Break-Even Chart

The following outlines the procedure for constructing a graph that visually portrays the firm's break-even point (that point where revenues equal expenses):

**Step 1.** ***On the horizontal axis, mark a scale measuring sales volume in dollars (or in units sold or some other measure of volume).*** The break-even chart for the Magic Shop shown in Figure 14.7 uses sales volume in dollars because it applies to all types of businesses, products, and services.

**Step 2.** ***On the vertical axis, mark a scale measuring income and expenses in dollars.***

**Step 3.** ***Draw a fixed expense line intersecting the vertical axis at the proper dollar level parallel to the horizontal axis.*** The area between this line and the horizontal axis represents the firm's fixed expenses. On the break-even chart for the Magic Shop shown in Figure 14.7, the fixed expense line is drawn horizontally beginning at $177,375 (point A). Because this line is parallel to the horizontal axis, it indicates that fixed expenses remain constant at all levels of activity.

**Step 4.** ***Draw a total expense line that slopes upward beginning at the point at which the fixed cost line intersects the vertical axis.*** The precise location of the total expense line is determined by plotting the total cost incurred at a particular sales volume. The total cost for a given sales level is found by the following formula:

$$\text{Total expenses} = \text{Fixed expenses} + \text{Variable expenses expressed as a percentage of sales} \times \text{Sales level}$$

Arbitrarily choosing a sales level of $950,000, the Magic Shop's total costs would be as follows:

$$\text{Total expenses} = \$177{,}375 + (0.74 \times \$950{,}000)$$

$$= \$880{,}375$$

Thus, the Magic Shop's total cost is $880,375 at a net sales level of $950,000 (point B). Connecting points A and B creates the variable cost line. The area between the total cost line and the horizontal axis measures the total costs the Magic Shop incurs at various levels of sales. For example, if the Magic Shop's sales are $850,000, its total costs will be $806,375.

**Step 5.** ***Beginning at the graph's origin, draw a 45-degree revenue line showing where total sales volume equals total income.*** For the Magic Shop, point C shows that sales = income = $950,000.

**Step 6.** ***Locate the break-even point by finding the intersection of the total expense line and the revenue line.*** If the Magic Shop operates at a sales volume to the left of the break-even point, it will incur a loss because the expense line is higher than the revenue line over this range. The triangular section labeled "Loss Area" shows this. On the other hand, if the firm operates at a sales volume to the right of the break-even point, it will earn a profit because the revenue line lies above the expense line over this range. The triangular section labeled "Profit Area" shows this.

**FIGURE 14.7**

**Break-Even Chart, the Magic Shop**

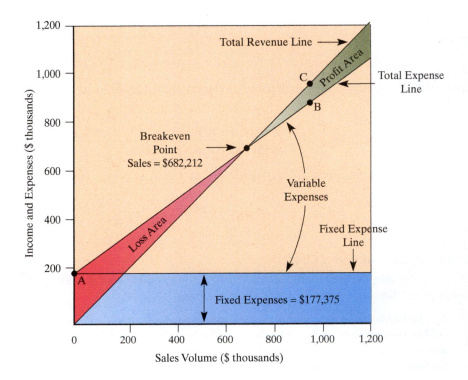

## Using Break-Even Analysis

Break-even analysis is a useful planning tool for entrepreneurs, especially when approaching potential lenders and investors for funds. It provides an opportunity for integrated analysis of sales volume, expenses, income, and other relevant factors. Break-even analysis is a simple, preliminary screening device for the entrepreneur faced with the business start-up decision. It is easy to understand and use. With just a few calculations, an entrepreneur can determine the minimum level of sales needed to stay in business as well as the effects of various financial strategies on the business. It is a helpful tool for evaluating the impact of changes in investments and expenditures.

**ENTREPRENEURIAL PROFILE: Fergus McCann: LimoLiner** Before launching LimoLiner, a company that provides luxury bus service with full amenities aimed at businesspeople traveling between downtown Boston and midtown Manhattan, entrepreneur Fergus McCann calculated his venture's break-even point. Knowing that it would take a while to build a solid base of customers, McCann determined that to break even, his buses had to be only half full on each one-way trip. A LimoLiner trip is priced at $89, which is $20 less than Amtrak's Acela Express and $120 less than a full-fare airline ticket. Satisfied that he would be able to generate at least $483 per one-way trip within a short time of opening, McCann launched LimoLiner.[36]

Break-even analysis does have certain limitations. It is too simple to use as a final screening device because it ignores the importance of cash flows. In addition, the accuracy of the analysis depends on the accuracy of the revenue and expense estimates. Finally, the assumptions pertaining to break-even analysis may not be realistic for some businesses. Break-even calculations make the following assumptions: Fixed expenses remain constant for all levels of sales volume, variable expenses change in direct proportion to changes in sales volume, and changes in sales volume have no effect on unit sales price. Relaxing these assumptions does not render this tool useless, however. For example, the owner could employ nonlinear break-even analysis using a graphical approach.

**In the Entrepreneurial Spotlight**

# Open Book Management

In 1982, Jack Stack led a management buyout of a failing division of International Harvester that refurbished engines. In one of the most highly leveraged buyouts in corporate history, the managers invested $100,000 of their own money and borrowed $9 million to purchase the business, leaving the company, Springfield Remanufacturing Company (SRC), with an incredible debt to equity ratio of 90 to 1! Facing a huge debt load and a short time horizon to turn SRC around, Stack and his team of managers knew that one key to success was to ignite a passion for the company among its employees. Stack's idea was to give everyone in the factory, from cam rod grinders to purchasing agents, access to SRC's financial statements and to teach them how to read, analyze, and understand the company's critical numbers.

Managers met with teams of employees in weekly meetings to discuss the numbers, answer questions, and solicit ideas about how to improve them in a process he called open book management, a revolutionary concept at the time. The idea behind open book management, says Stack, "is to get employees to start approaching their jobs as if they owned the place, which, in fact, they might." Some companies that practice open book management, including SRC, share ownership of the business with their employees through employee stock ownership plans. "Our goal was to teach our employees to think and act like owners," says Stack. "We started by trying to improve their financial literacy by turning topics like accounting into a game. We played this game with real money, however, and the game's pieces were each and every employee's quality of life. We called it The Great Game of Business."

Using The Great Game of Business, managers transformed employees into owners of every line of the company's balance sheet, income statement, and cash flow statement, enabling workers at every level of operation to understand how they could move the numbers in the right direction. "Rather than having some engineer with a stopwatch trying to get people to work faster for less money, open book management gives everyone the chance to see what they need to do to succeed," says Stack. In its first full year of operation, SRC lost $60,500 on sales of $16 million. Within 10 years, the company was earning a profit of $1.3 million on sales of $66 million. Today, SRC is the leading success story of open book management, having evolved into a collection of 37 employee-owned businesses that employ more than 1,200 workers and make everything from race car engines to home furnishings.

Stack's daughter, who owns a small upscale clothing store in Missouri, learned the lessons of open book management from her father. She operates her small business using open book management with her seven employees. "She now has seven people who think like she does," observes Stack. "They now understand inventory turns and [profit margins] and the relationship between the two."

A growing number of privately owned businesses are taking open book management to another level with a system called open enterprise. Whereas open book management provides access to relevant information that employees need to do their jobs better, the open enterprise movement opens up *all* information within the business to all employees. For example, SumAll, a data-analytics company, posts information online about investor agreements, company financials, performance appraisals, hiring decisions, and employee pay and bonuses for all employees to see. Peer Insight, a consulting company, provides information on salaries, bonuses, and performance appraisals to all employees. Peer Insight employees can also view detailed financial information, including the current cash balance in the bank.

1. Use online resources to identify the management principles on which traditional open book management is based.

2. What benefits does traditional open book management offer a company and its employees? Do these benefits also apply to firms that take the "open enterprise" approach?

3. Conduct an online search for a company that uses open book management or the open enterprise approach and write a one-page summary of its experience with this technique. Identify at least two keys to using open book management or open enterprise successfully.

4. What limits should be placed on opening information to employees? What are the risks to taking the "open enterprise" approach to managing a small business? What limits to opening up information would you implement within your business? Would you be willing to follow the practices of SumAll and Peer Insight and share everything with everyone in your company? Explain.

*Sources:* Based on Jack Stack, "Introducing 'Open the Books: Why Would Anyone Do This?," *New York Times,* December 15, 2009, *http://boss.blogs.nytimes .com/2009/12/15/introducing-open-the-books-why-would-anyone-do-this*; Jack Stack, "The Great Game of Business," *Institute for Entrepreneurial Excellence,* April 10, 2010, *www.entrepreneur.pitt.edu/eventfiles/1010.pdf*; Darren Dahl, "Open Book Management Lessons for Detroit," *New York Times,* May 21, 2009, *www .nytimes.com/2009/05/21/business/smallbusiness/21open.html*; Laura Lorber, "An Open Book," *Wall Street Journal,* February 23, 2009, p. R8; Jack Stack, "Open Wide," *Inc.,* January/February 2009, p. 76; Rachel Silverman, "Psst . . . This Is What Your Co-Worker Is Paid," *Wall Street Journal,* January 30, 2013, p. B6.

# Chapter Review

1. Understand the importance of preparing a financial plan.
   - Launching a successful business requires an entrepreneur to create a solid financial plan. Not only is such a plan an important tool in raising the capital needed to get a company off the ground, but it also is an essential ingredient in managing a growing business.
   - Earning a profit does not occur by accident; it takes planning.

2. Describe how to prepare the basic financial statements and use them to manage the small business.
   - Entrepreneurs rely on three basic financial statements to understand the financial conditions of their companies:
     1. The balance sheet. Built on the accounting equation: Assets = Liabilities + Owner's equity (capital), it provides an estimate of the company's value on a particular date.
     2. The income statement. This statement compares the firm's revenues against its expenses to determine its net income (or loss). It provides information about the company's bottom line.
     3. The statement of cash flows. This statement shows the change in the company's working capital over the accounting period by listing the sources and the uses of funds.

3. Create projected financial statements.
   - Projected financial statements are a basic component of a sound financial plan. They help the manager plot the company's financial future by setting operating objectives and by analyzing the reasons for variations from targeted results. In addition, the small business in search of start-up funds will need these pro forma statements to present to prospective lenders and investors. They also assist in determining the amount of cash, inventory, fixtures, and other assets the business will need to begin operation.

4. Understand the basic financial statements through ratio analysis.
   - The 12 key ratios described in this chapter are divided into four major categories: liquidity ratios, which show the small firm's ability to meet its current obligations; leverage ratios, which tell how much of the company's financing is provided by owners and how much by creditors; operating ratios, which show how effectively the firm uses its resources; and profitability ratios, which disclose the company's profitability.
   - Many agencies and organizations regularly publish such statistics. If there is a discrepancy between the small firm's ratios and those of the typical business, the owner should investigate the reason for the difference. A below-average ratio does not necessarily mean that the business is in trouble.

5. Explain how to interpret financial ratios.
   - To benefit from ratio analysis, the small company should compare its ratios to those of other companies in the same line of business and look for trends over time.
   - When business owners detect deviations in their companies' ratios from industry standards, they should determine the cause of the deviations. In some cases, such deviations are the result of sound business decisions; in other instances, however, ratios that are out of the normal range for a particular type of business are indicators of what could become serious problems for a company.

6. Conduct a break-even analysis for a small company.
   - Business owners should know their firm's break-even point, the level of operations at which total revenues equal total costs; it is the point at which companies neither earn a profit nor incur a loss. Although just a simple screening device, break-even analysis is a useful planning and decision-making tool.

# Discussion Questions

14-1. Why is it important for entrepreneurs to develop financial plans for their companies?

14-2. How should a small business manager use the ratios discussed in this chapter?

14-3. Outline the key points of the 12 ratios discussed in this chapter. What signals does each give a business owner?

14-4. Describe the method for building a projected income statement and a projected balance sheet for a beginning business.

14-5. Why are pro forma financial statements important to the financial planning process?

14-6. How can break-even analysis help an entrepreneur planning to launch a business? What information does it give an entrepreneur?

# CHAPTER 15

# Managing Cash Flow

## Learning Objectives

**On completion of this chapter, you will be able to:**

1. Explain the importance of cash management to the success of a small business.

2. Differentiate between cash and profits.

3. Understand the five steps in creating a cash budget and use them to build a cash budget.

4. Describe the fundamental principles involved in managing the "big three" of cash management: accounts receivable, accounts payable, and inventory.

5. Explain how bootstrapping can help a small business avoid a cash crunch.

*The three most important things you need to measure in a business are customer satisfaction, employee satisfaction, and cash flow.*

—Jack Welch

*Beware of little expenses; a small leak will sink a great ship.*

—Benjamin Franklin

Cash—a four-letter word that has become a curse for many small businesses. Lack of this valuable asset has driven countless small companies into bankruptcy. Unfortunately, many more firms will become failure statistics because their owners have neglected the principles of cash management, which can spell the difference between success and failure. One small business consultant says that a serious mistake that entrepreneurs make is trying to run their businesses without accurate cash flow projections. "This is like driving along on the freeway at 70 miles per hour with a blindfold on. It's not a question of whether you are headed for an accident. It's a question of how serious the accident will be and whether or not you will survive it."[1]

Developing cash forecasts is important for every small business but is essential for new businesses in particular because early sales levels usually do not generate sufficient cash to keep the company afloat. Too often, entrepreneurs launch their companies with insufficient cash to cover their start-up costs and the cash flow gap that results while expenses outstrip revenues. The result is business failure. Controlling the financial aspects of a business with the profit-planning techniques described in the previous chapter is immensely important; however, by themselves, these techniques are insufficient to achieve business success. Entrepreneurs are prone to focus on their companies' income statements—particularly sales and profits. The balance sheet and the income statement, of course, show an important part of a company's financial picture, but it is just that: only part of the total picture. It is entirely possible for a business to have a solid balance sheet and to make a profit and still go out of business by *running out of cash*. Even if a company's revenue exceeds its expenses for a given period, the cash flow from that revenue may not arrive in time to pay the company's cash expenses. Managing cash effectively requires an entrepreneur to look beyond the "bottom line" and focus on what keeps a company going—cash.

## Cash Management

*Source:* CartoonStock.

**1.**
Explain the importance of cash management to the success of a small business.

Managing cash flow is a struggle for many business owners. In fact, research by the National Federation of Independent Businesses (NFIB) shows that managing cash flow consistently ranks among the top 10 problems that small business owners face. Surveys by American Express OPEN Small Business Monitor and Visa show similar concerns: Cash flow management ranks as the number one issue facing small business owners. Figure 15.1 shows the most common cash flow challenges that business owners encounter.

**Cash management** involves forecasting, collecting, disbursing, investing, and planning for the cash a company needs to operate smoothly. For a start-up business, managing cash depends on the accuracy of the financial forecasts that come from a well-developed business model and business plan. These forecasts guide fund-raising for the new venture. For an operating small

"I'll covet this trophy right up to the time
I sell it to meet my payroll."

In recent surveys, at least 50 percent of small business owners report experiencing cash flow problems. The most common challenges they encounter are as follows:

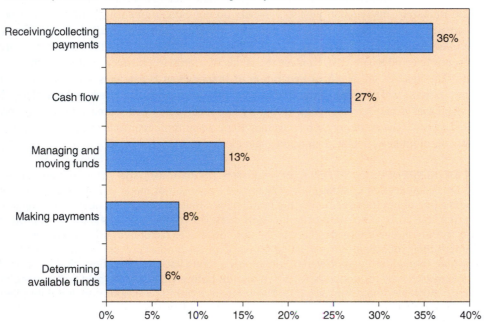

**FIGURE 15.1**

**Cash Flow Challenges**

*Source:* Visa 2012 Small Business Cash Management Survey, September 26, 2012.

business, managing cash is a matter of timing—gaining control over when a company collects cash and when it pays it out. Managing cash is an important task because cash is the most important yet least productive asset that a small business owns. A business must have enough cash to meet its obligations as they come due, or it will eventually experience bankruptcy. The Small Business Administration recommends that business owners have enough cash on hand to cover at least six months of operating expenses, and many experts recommend up to a year's worth during a slow economy. Creditors, employees, and lenders expect to be paid on time no matter how tough the economy may get, and cash is the required medium of exchange to meet these expectations.

Proper cash management permits entrepreneurs to adequately meet the cash demands of their businesses, to avoid retaining unnecessarily large cash balances, and to stretch the profit-generating power of each dollar their companies own. Entrepreneurs must have the discipline to manage cash flow from the business's first day of operation.

**ENTREPRENEURIAL PROFILE: Henry Ford: Ford Motor Company** Shortly after he launched his new company on June 16, 1903, entrepreneur Henry Ford ran headlong into a cash crisis that nearly wiped out the Ford Motor Company. Start-up expenses (including $10,000 to the Dodge brothers for engines and other parts and $640 to the Hartford Rubber Works for 64 tires) quickly soaked up Ford's $28,000 in start-up capital he and eleven associates invested, and by July 10, the company's cash balance had fallen a mere $223.65. Another payroll and more parts orders were just around the corner, and the 25-day-old company was already on the brink of a financial collapse. On July 11, an investor saved the day with a $5,000 contribution. Four days later the Ford Motor Company sold its first car to Dr. E. Pfennig of Chicago, pushing the company's cash balance to $6,486.44. From this shaky financial beginning grew one of the largest automakers in the world![2]

Although cash flow problems afflict companies of all sizes and ages, young businesses are prone to suffering cash shortages because they act like "cash sponges," soaking up every available dollar and then some. The reason is that their cash-generating "engines" have not had the opportunity to "rev up" to full speed and cannot generate sufficient power to produce the cash necessary to cover rapidly climbing expenses.

Owners of fast-growing businesses also must pay particular attention to cash management because the greatest potential threat to cash flow occurs when a company is experiencing rapid growth. If a company's sales are rising, the owner also must hire more employees, expand plant capacity, develop new products, increase the sales force and customer service staff, build inventory, and incur other drains on the firm's cash supply. In addition to these cash demands, collections from sales often slip as a company grows, and the result is a cash crisis.

Unfortunately, many small business owners do not engage in cash planning. One study of 2,200 small businesses found that 68 percent performed no cash flow analysis at all![3] The result is that many successful, growing, and profitable businesses fail because they become insolvent; they do not have adequate cash to meet the needs of a growing business with a booming sales volume. The head of the National Federation of Independent Businesses says that many small business owners "wake up one day to find that the price of success is no cash on hand. They don't understand that if they're successful, inventory and receivables will increase faster than profits can fund them."[4] The resulting cash crisis may force an entrepreneur to lose equity control of the business or, ultimately, declare bankruptcy and close.

**ENTREPRENEURIAL PROFILE: Peter Justen: MyBizHomepage** After 94 years in business, Cerf Brothers Bag Company, a family-owned business that made duffle, cargo, and storage bags and a line of outdoor gear under the brand names Hideaway Hunting Gear and Camp Inn, fell victim to a cash crisis. In an attempt to lower its costs, the company shifted most of its production from its three manufacturing operations in the United States to factories in Asia. When these vendors accelerated their collection terms, insisting on payment for products when Cerf Brothers placed an order rather than after it was delivered, the company found itself in a cash flow bind. [Our vendors] were asking us to pay for goods three to five months before we would be paid by our customers," says Jerry Michelson, the company's CEO. The company's cash flow evaporated and debt piled up, forcing its owners to declare bankruptcy and sell the once-successful business.[5]

Table 15.1 describes the five key cash management roles every entrepreneur must fill.

The first step in managing cash more effectively is to understand the company's **cash flow cycle**—the time lag between paying suppliers for merchandise and receiving payment from customers (see Figure 15.2). The longer this cash flow cycle, the more likely the business owner is to encounter a cash crisis. Preparing a cash forecast that recognizes this cycle, however, helps avoid a crisis.

**ENTREPRENEURIAL PROFILE: John Fernsell: Ibex Outdoor Clothing** John Fernsell recognizes the importance of cash management because of the length of his company's cash flow cycle. Fernsell, a former stockbroker, is the founder of Ibex Outdoor Clothing, a company that makes outdoor clothing from high-quality European wool. Ibex's sales are growing rapidly, but cash is a constant problem because of its lengthy cash flow cycle. Fernsell orders wool from his European suppliers in February and pays for it in June. The wool then goes to garment makers in California,

### TABLE 15.1 Five Cash Management Roles of the Entrepreneur

*Role 1: Cash Finder.* This is your first and foremost responsibility. You must make sure that there is enough capital to pay all present (and future) bills. This is not a one-time task; it is an ongoing job.

*Role 2: Cash Planner.* As cash planner, you make sure that your company's cash is used properly and efficiently. You must keep track of its cash, make sure that it is available to pay bills, and plan for its future use. Planning requires you to forecast your company's cash inflows and outflows for the months ahead with the help of a cash budget (discussed later in this chapter).

*Role 3: Cash Distributor.* This role requires you to control the cash needed to pay the company's bills and the priority and the timing of those payments. Forecasting cash disbursements accurately and making sure that the cash is available when payments come due is essential to keeping your business solvent.

*Role 4: Cash Collector.* As cash collector, your job is to make sure that your customers pay their bills on time. Too often, entrepreneurs focus on pumping up sales while neglecting to collect the cash from those sales. Having someone in your company responsible for collecting accounts receivable is essential. Uncollected accounts drain a small company's pool of cash very quickly.

*Role. 5: Cash Conserver.* This role requires you to make sure that your company gets maximum value for the dollars it spends. Whether you are buying inventory to resell or computer systems to keep track of what you sell, it is important to get the most for your money. Avoiding unnecessary expenditures is an important part of this task. The goal is to spend cash so that it produces a return for the company.

*Source:* Based on Bruce J. Blechman, "Quick Change Artist," *Entrepreneur*, January 1994, pp. 18–21.

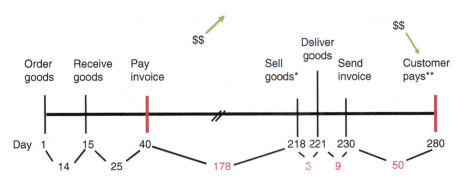

**FIGURE 15.2**

**The Cash Flow Cycle**

Cash flow cycle = 240 days

* Based on average inventory turnover:

$$\frac{365 \text{ days}}{2.05 \text{ times/year}} = 178 \text{ days}$$

** Based on average collection period:

$$\frac{365 \text{ days}}{7.31 \text{ times/year}} = 50 \text{ days}$$

who ship finished clothing to Ibex in July and August, when Fernsell pays for the finished goods. Ibex ships the clothing to retailers in September and October but does not get paid until November, December, and sometimes January! Ibex's major cash outflows are from June to August, but its cash inflows during those months are virtually nil, making it essential for Fernsell to manage the company's cash balances carefully.[6]

The next step in effective cash management is to begin whittling down the length of the cash flow cycle. Reducing the cycle from 240 days to, say, 180 days would free up incredible amounts of cash that this company could use to finance growth and dramatically reduce its borrowing costs. What steps do you suggest that the owner of the business whose cash flow cycle is illustrated in Figure 15.2 take to reduce the cycle's length?

## Cash and Profits Are Not the Same

When analyzing cash flow, entrepreneurs must understand that cash and profits are not the same. Both are important financial concepts for entrepreneurs, but they measure very different aspects of a business. **Profit** (or net income) is the difference between a company's total revenue and its total expenses. It is an accounting concept designed to measure how efficiently a business is operating. On the other hand, cash is the money that is readily available to use in a business. **Cash flow** measures a company's liquidity and its ability to pay its bills and other financial obligations on time by tracking the flow of cash into and out of the business over a period of time. Many factors determine a company's cash flow, including its sales patterns, the timing of its accounts receivable and accounts payable, its inventory turnover rate, its debt repayment schedule, and its schedule of capital expenditures (e.g., fixtures, equipment, facilities expansion, and others).

**2.**

Differentiate between cash and profits.

**ENTREPRENEURIAL PROFILE: Anne-Marie Faiola: Bramble Berry** Anne-Marie Faiola founded Bramble Berry, a soap-making supply company, in 1998. From the beginning, Faiola grew her company by aggressively introducing new products. However, even though Bramble Berry was showing a profit on its income statement, the business never seemed to have any cash at the end of the month. The problem was that the money that Faiola spent on product development outpaced her ability to earn it back with increased cash flow from sales. Faiola had to use credit cards and drawing on her company's line of credit to fund the gap in cash flow. "If you do that for too many years, you will find yourself heavily in debt—while still being profitable—and wondering why you can't seem to get ahead," says Faiola. Once she recognized that more money was going out than was coming in, Faiola slowed spending on new products for period of time to generate positive cash flow that she could use to pay down her debt. Bramble Berry now offers more than 2,500 products to thousands of customers across the country.[7]

Anne-Marie Faiola, founder of Bramble Berry.

*Source:* BrambleBerry Inc.

**FIGURE 15.3**

**Cash Flow**

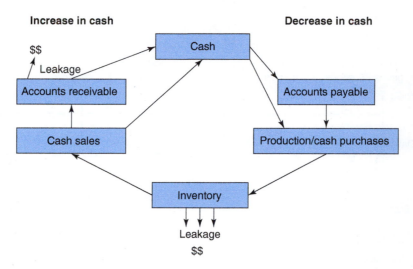

Figure 15.3 shows the flow of cash through a typical small business. Decreases in cash occur when a business purchases, on credit or for cash, goods for inventory or materials for use in production. The company sells the goods either for cash or on credit. When it takes in cash or collects accounts receivable, a company's cash balance increases. Notice that purchases for inventory and production *lead* sales; that is, these bills typically must be paid *before* sales materialize. However, collection of accounts receivable *lags* behind sales; that is, customers who purchase goods on credit may not pay until a month or more later.

As important as earning a profit is, no business owner can pay creditors, employees, and lenders in profits; that requires *cash*! "Cash flow is more important than earnings," says Evan Betzer, founder of a financial services firm.[8] A company can operate in the short run with a net loss showing on its income statement, but if its cash flow becomes negative, the business is in trouble. It can no longer pay suppliers, meet payroll, pay its taxes, or any other bills. In short, the business is out of business!

 **In the Entrepreneurial Spotlight**

# Cash Flow and Pass-Through Entities

Jean Young was excited about the first full year of operations of the company that she and her sister Susan had started just a year and a half ago. The Young sisters had started their fashion and jewelry boutique, Young Fashion, in the summer of 2011 as a limited liability company (LLC). Although the first few months were rather slow, their store picked up business during the holiday season. At the end of 2011, they had sold enough so that they had broken even during their company's first partial year of operation. Not a bad start for a new store!

The momentum they had gained in 2011 carried over into 2012. Like many retailers, they broke even for the first four quarters of the year. Their store's second holiday season was a phenomenal success. When they ran the year-end financial statements for 2012, they showed a profit of a little more than $80,000. Even better was the fact that they had earned that much profit even after paying themselves very modest salaries throughout the year.

Excited about their success, Jean and Susan decided to use the extra cash they had built up for three things. First, they expanded their company's inventory. With a bit of careful planning, they determined that Young Fashion could easily hold quite a bit more inventory on the floor without making it too crowded.

Second, they bought new racks and display cases to give the store a better look. They had bootstrapped the start-up and had bought a variety of used and even discarded equipment to keep their initial costs down. Now that they had cash on hand, they wanted to replace that equipment with new, more professional-looking displays. Third, because they launched their business right out of college, neither of them had much money to invest. They had to borrow the money from their parents and other family members to cover the start-up costs for Young Fashion. Thus, they used most of the rest of their business's excess cash to pay down that debt to their family. They kept enough cash on hand to cover day-to-day needs.

In early April, they met with the accountant who prepared the tax returns for Young Fashion. "You certainly had a great year," he said. "But, as you know, with that success you are going to owe a bit to Uncle Sam in taxes."

"I am not sure I understand," said Susan with more than a bit of worry. "How much to we owe?"

"The $80,000 profit will be split between the two of you, so I will issue each of you a K-1 tax form that you will include with your personal tax returns. Each of you owes taxes on an additional $40,000 above the salaries you earned. At your tax rate, each of you will probably owe at least another $10,000 in taxes in a couple of weeks."

"But we don't have any extra cash," said Jean. "We put it all back into the business!"

What Jean and Susan are facing is not an unusual situation for new business owners. Because they set the business up as an LLC, it is treated as a pass-through entity. Therefore, any profit from the business is not taxed at the corporate rate but rather passes directly through to each of the owners based on their shares of ownership.

Jean and Susan had spent excess cash on items that did not increase the business's profits. They bought inventory, which merely exchanged one asset, cash, for another asset, inventory, which does not become an expense until it is sold. They bought equipment, which they will depreciate over time as an expense, but in the short run also trades one asset for another. Finally, they paid down debt, which decreases cash and decreases a liability on the balance sheet. None of these transactions had an impact on the company's income statement. Thus, even though they spent the cash, their business still showed a profit.

Experienced entrepreneurs learn to manage cash more strategically. Many use the 1/3-1/3-1/3 rule of thumb. One-third of cash flow from profits is set aside for the taxes that owners will owe when profits flow through to their personal tax returns. Whereas some business owners build this up throughout the year and then distribute it at tax time, others distribute cash to cover taxes each quarter based on the profits for those three months. At that point, the business has done what it is

responsible for—paying out the cash to cover the tax liability. If any of the owners decide to spend it rather than save it for taxes, that is their responsibility!

Entrepreneurs keep the second third of cash from profits in the business to support growth. They use it to build up inventory, buy equipment, upgrade fixtures, and so forth, or they can simply hold it to build up cash reserves (for that eventual "rainy day).

They use the final third of cash from profits to pay down the principle on any debt that the business owes. If the business has no debt, this final third can be distributed to the owners as dividends. Because the business already has paid taxes on the earnings from which the dividends originate, owners of pass-through entities do not pay taxes on them.

By following this approach to managing cash created by the profits of a business, entrepreneurs should never face the kind of surprise that Jean and Susan did when they met with their accountant.

1. Why is it so important for owners of pass-through entities to pay attention to personal income taxes even if they did not receive dividends or distributions of earnings?

2. If the owners of a pass-through entity are personally responsible for pay the taxes for the profits of their businesses, why is it advisable to choose and LLC or S corporation for a small business?

3. Identify and explain at least three recommendations can you make to Jean and Susan that would help them manage their company's cash flow more effectively.

## Preparing a Cash Budget

The need for a reliable cash forecast arises because in every business, the cash flowing in is rarely "in sync" with the cash flowing out. This uneven flow of cash creates periodic cash surpluses and deficits, making it necessary for entrepreneurs to track the flow of cash through their businesses so that they can project realistically the pool of cash that is available throughout the year. Many owners operate their businesses without knowing the pattern of their cash flows, believing that the process is too complex or time consuming. In reality, entrepreneurs simply cannot afford to ignore cash management. They must ensure that an adequate but not excessive supply of cash is on hand to meet their companies' operating needs.

How much cash is enough? What is suitable for one business may be totally inadequate for another, depending on each company's size, sales, collections, expenses, and other factors. Entrepreneurs should prepare a **cash budget**, which is nothing more than a "cash map" showing the

**3.**
Understand the five steps in creating a cash budget and use them to build a cash budget.

Preparing a Cash Budget.
*Source:* Rido/Shutterstock.

amount and the timing of the cash receipts and the cash disbursements week by week or month by month. Entrepreneurs use it to predict the amount of cash they will need to cover expenses, operate smoothly, and grow the business over time, making it a valuable tool in managing a company successfully.

 **Lessons from the Street-Smart Entrepreneur**

# A Short Season

Dennis and Steve Vourderis, owners of Deno's Wonder Wheel Amusement Park on the boardwalk at New York's famous Coney Island, know that their business has to make the most of its revenue generating potential when the time is right. The company, started by their parents and home to the Wonder Wheel, a famous Ferris wheel built in 1920, generates all of its sales in the six month stretch from April to October. Years of experience have taught them that the business must be operating profitably by the July 4 holiday, or the company will struggle. Operating a highly seasonal business is a challenge in many ways. "You have to budget carefully to make sure you don't overspend," says Dennis. "Maintenance, taxes, and equipment financing are based on a 12-month year. You need to know that you'll have enough funding to cover those expenses during the time you have no cash flow." During the winter months, the Vourderis brothers are busy preparing for the next season. They and their staff disassemble the seats and other parts of the rides, inspect and refurbish them, and store them until the spring. Every year, they also repaint the Wonder Wheel, which stands 150 feet tall and weighs 400,000 pounds.

"A seasonal business is infinitely more difficult to manage than most other businesses," says Les Charm, who teaches entrepreneurship at Babson College. How can business owners whose companies face highly seasonal sales patterns manage the uneven cash flow? The Street-Smart Entrepreneur offers the following tips:

- *Be financially disciplined.* Seasonal business owners must establish a realistic budget, stick to it, and avoid the temptation to spend lavishly when cash flow is plentiful. Teevan McManus, owner of the Coronado Surfing Academy in San Diego, California, failed to heed this advice in his first year of business. "I burned through everything I made in the summer and was living off of my business line of credit before the next season came around," he recalls. "I barely made it to the next June."

- *Manage your time and your employees' time carefully.* During the busy season, employees may be working overtime to serve the rush of customers; during the off-season, a business owner may cut back to 20-hour workweeks or operate with a skeleton crew.

- *Use permanent employees sparingly.* Many owners of seasonal businesses use a small core of permanent employees and then hire part-time workers or student interns during their busy season. Planning for the right number of seasonal employees and recruiting them early ensures that a business will be able to serve its customers properly.

- *Put aside cash in a separate account that you use only for the lean months of your seasonal business.* Creating a separate account imposes a degree of discipline and discourages excess spending when a company is flush with cash.

- *Maximize your productivity in the off-season.* Use the slow season to conduct market research, perform routine maintenance and repairs, revise your Web site, and stay in touch with customers. Steve Kopelmam's company, *HauntedHouse.com*, earns all of its $2.6 in annual revenue in a six-week period leading up to Halloween. Starting in November, Kopelman surveys his customers so that he can refine his marketing efforts for the next season and solicit suggestions for improvement. He visits trade shows to look for the latest technology and gadgets to keep his haunted houses fresh and exciting for his customers. Kopelman also negotiates leases on properties for the next season and studies his competition by visiting every haunted house Web site that he can find.

- *Use the off-season to reconnect with customers.* The off-season is the ideal time to catch up on all of the small but important customer service tasks that you do not have time to perform during the height of the busy season. The owner of one small company increased his company's annual sales and reduced customer turnover by 75 percent when he set up one-on-one meetings with clients during the slow season with the purpose of discovering their needs and getting feedback about how his company could serve them better.

- *Keep inventory at minimal levels during the off-season.* As you learned in this chapter, holding inventory unnecessarily merely ties up valuable cash uselessly.

- *Offer off-peak discounts.* Doing so may generate some revenue during slow periods.

- *Consider starting a complementary seasonal business.* Jan Axel, founder of Delphinium Design Landscaping in South Salem, New York, sees her business slow down considerably during the winter and decided to launch a holiday decorating service that generates cash flow when landscape sales evaporate.

- *Create a cash flow forecast.* Perhaps one of the most important steps that seasonal business owners can take is to develop a forecast of their companies' cash flow. Doing so allows them to spot patterns and trends and to make plans for covering inevitable cash shortages. Make sure that you include a pessimistic or worst-case scenario in your cash forecast.

- *Establish a bank line of credit.* The line of credit should be large enough to cover at least three months' worth of expenses. Use your cash flow forecast to show the banker how and when your company will be able to repay the loan. "[A good cash forecast] shows the banker that you know exactly where the peaks and valleys are and what your cash needs are," says one banker.

1. What impact do highly seasonal sales have on a small company's cash flow?

2. What other advice can you offer owners of seasonal businesses about coping with the effects of their companies'

highly irregular sales patterns? About managing cash flow in general?

*Sources:* Based on John Grossman, "A Tourist-Dependent Business Decides to Reboot," *New York Times,* July 18, 2012, *http://boss.blogs.nytimes.com/2012/07/18/ a-tourist-dependant-business-decides-to-reboot*; John Grossman, "A Seasonal Business Aims to Survive the Off-Season," *New York Times,* July 11, 2012, p. B9; "Make the Most of the Slow Season," *Marketing Profs,* May 28, 2009, pp. 1–2; Rich Mintzer, "Running a Seasonal Business," *Entrepreneur,* March 16, 2007, *www .entrepreneur.com/management/operations/article175954.html*; Sarah Pierce, "Surviving a Seasonal Business," *Entrepreneur,* July 15, 2008, *www.entrepreneur.com/ startingabusiness/businessideas/article195680.html*; Rich Mintzer, "Running a Seasonal Business," *Entrepreneur,* March 16, 2007, *http://www.entrepreneur.com/ management/operations/article175954.html.*

Typically, a small business owner should prepare a projected monthly cash budget for at least one year and quarterly estimates one or two years beyond that. To be effective, a cash budget must cover all seasonal sales fluctuations. The more variable a company's sales pattern, the shorter its planning horizon should be. For example, a firm whose sales fluctuate widely over a relatively short time frame might require a weekly cash budget rather than a monthly one. The key to managing cash flow successfully is to monitor not only the amount of cash flowing into and out of a company but also the *timing* of those cash flows.

Regardless of the time frame selected, a cash budget must be in writing for an entrepreneur to visualize a company's cash position. Creating a written cash plan is not an excessively time-consuming task and can help the owner avoid unexpected cash shortages, a situation that can cause a business to fail. One financial consultant describes "a client who won't be able to make the payroll this month. His bank agreed to meet the payroll for him—but banks don't like to be surprised like that," he adds.[9] Preparing a cash budget will help business owners avoid unpleasant surprises such as that. It will also let owners know whether they are keeping excessive amounts of cash on hand. Computer spreadsheets, such as Excel, make the job fast and easy to complete and allow for instant updates and "what-if" analysis. In addition, many accounting software packages also have effective cash management tools integrated into their reports.

A cash budget is based on the cash method of accounting, which means that cash receipts and cash disbursements are recorded in the forecast only when the cash transaction is expected to take place. For example, credit sales to customers are not reported until the company expects to receive the cash from them. Similarly, purchases made on credit are not recorded until the owner expects to pay them. Because depreciation, bad debt expense, and other noncash items involve no cash transfers, they are omitted entirely from the cash budget.

A cash budget is nothing more than a forecast of a company's cash inflows and outflows for a specific time period, and it will never be completely accurate. However, it does give a small business owner a clear picture of a company's estimated cash balance for the period, pointing out where external cash infusions may be required or where surplus cash balances may be available for investing. A good cash budget serves as an early warning system for cash flow challenges. In addition, by comparing actual cash flows with projections, an entrepreneur can revise his or her forecast so that future cash budgets will be more accurate. "Watch your income on a daily basis until you fully understand your revenue and expenses," says Robin Wilson, CEO of Robin Wilson Home. "Make sure your bookkeeper is your partner and never settle for being told 'everything is handled.'"[10]

Formats for preparing a cash budget vary depending on the pattern of a company's cash flow. Table 15.2 shows a monthly cash budget for a small retail store over a four-month period. Each monthly column should be divided into two sections—estimated and actual (not shown)—so that subsequent cash forecasts can be updated according to actual cash transactions. There are five steps to creating a cash budget:

1. Determining an adequate minimum cash balance

2. Forecasting sales

3. Forecasting cash receipts

4. Forecasting cash disbursements

5. Estimating the end-of-month cash balance.

### Step 1: Determining an Adequate Minimum Cash Balance

What is considered an excessive cash balance for one small business may be inadequate for another, even though the two firms are in the same industry. Some suggest that a company's cash balance should equal at least one-fourth of its current liabilities, but this simple guideline does not work for all small businesses. The most reliable method of deciding cash balance is based on past experience. Past operating records should indicate the proper cash cushion needed to cover any unexpected expenses after all normal cash outlays are deducted from the month's cash receipts. For example, past records may indicate that it is desirable to maintain a cash balance equal to five days' sales. Seasonal fluctuations may cause a company's minimum cash balance to change. For example, the desired cash balance for a retailer in December may be greater than in June.

### Step 2: Forecasting Sales

The heart of the cash budget is the sales forecast. It is the central factor in creating an accurate picture of a company's cash position because sales ultimately are transformed into cash receipts and cash disbursements. For most businesses, sales constitute the primary source of the cash flowing into the business. Similarly, sales of merchandise require entrepreneurs to use

### TABLE 15.2 Cash Budget for Small Department Store

*Assumptions:*

Cash balance on December 31 = $12,000

Minimum cash balance desired = $10,000

Sales are 75% credit and 25% cash.

Credit sales are collected in the following manner:

- 60% collected in the first month after the sale.
- 30% collected in the second month after the sale.
- 5% collected in the third month after the sale.
- 5% are never collected.

| Sales Forecasts Are as Follows: | Pessimistic | Most Likely | Optimistic |
|---|---|---|---|
| October (actual) | | $300,000 | |
| November (actual) | | 350,000 | |
| December (actual) | | 400,000 | |
| January | $120,000 | 150,000 | $175,000 |
| February | 160,000 | 200,000 | 250,000 |
| March | 160,000 | 200,000 | 250,000 |
| April | 250,000 | 300,000 | 340,000 |

The store pays 70% of sales price for merchandise purchased and pays for each month's anticipated sales in the preceding month.

Rent is $2,000 per month.

An interest payment of $7,500 is due in March.

A tax prepayment of $50,000 must be made in March.

A capital addition payment of $130,000 is due in February.

Utilities expenses amount to $850 per month.

Miscellaneous expenses are $70 per month.

Interest income of $200 will be received in February.

Wages and salaries are estimated to be

January—$30,000

February—$40,000

March—$45,000

April—$50,000

**TABLE 15.2** *(continued)*

**Cash Budget—Pessimistic Sales Forecast**

| | Oct. | Nov. | Dec. | Jan. | Feb. | Mar. | Apr. |
|---|---|---|---|---|---|---|---|
| *Cash Receipts:* | | | | | | | |
| Sales | $300,000 | $350,000 | $400,000 | $120,000 | $160,000 | $160,000 | $250,000 |
| Credit Sales | 225,000 | 262,500 | 300,000 | 90,000 | 120,000 | 120,000 | 187,500 |
| *Collections:* | | | | | | | |
| 60%—1st month after sale | | | | $180,000 | $ 54,000 | $ 72,000 | $ 72,000 |
| 30%—2nd month after sale | | | | 78,750 | 90,000 | 27,000 | 36,000 |
| 5%—3rd month after sale | | | | 11,250 | 13,125 | 15,000 | 4,500 |
| Cash Sales | | | | 30,000 | 40,000 | 40,000 | 62,500 |
| Interest | | | | 0 | 200 | 0 | 0 |
| Total Cash Receipts | | | | $300,000 | $197,325 | $154,000 | $175,000 |
| *Cash Disbursements:* | | | | | | | |
| Purchases | | | | $112,000 | $112,000 | $175,000 | $133,000 |
| Rent | | | | 2,000 | 2,000 | 2,000 | 2,000 |
| Utilities | | | | 850 | 850 | 850 | 850 |
| Interest | | | | 0 | 0 | 7,500 | 0 |
| Tax Prepayment | | | | 0 | 0 | 50,000 | 0 |
| Capital Addition | | | | 0 | 130,000 | 0 | 0 |
| Miscellaneous | | | | 70 | 70 | 70 | 70 |
| Wages/Salaries | | | | 30,000 | 40,000 | 45,000 | 50,000 |
| Total Cash Disbursements | | | | $144,920 | $284,920 | $280,420 | $185,920 |
| *End-of-Month Balance:* | | | | | | | |
| Cash (beginning of month) | | | | $ 12,000 | $167,080 | $ 79,485 | $ 10,000 |
| +Cash Receipts | | | | 300,000 | 197,325 | 154,000 | 175,000 |
| − Cash Disbursements | | | | 144,920 | 284,920 | 280,420 | 185,920 |
| Cash (end of month) | | | | 167,080 | 79,485 | (46,935) | (920) |
| Borrowing/Repayment | | | | 0 | 0 | 56,935 | 10,920 |
| Cash (end of month [after borrowing]) | | | | $167,080 | $ 79,485 | $ 10,000 | $ 10,000 |

**Cash Budget—Most Likely Sales Forecast**

| | Oct. | Nov. | Dec. | Jan. | Feb. | Mar. | Apr. |
|---|---|---|---|---|---|---|---|
| *Cash Receipts:* | | | | | | | |
| Sales | $300,000 | $350,000 | $400,000 | $150,000 | $200,000 | $200,000 | $300,000 |
| Credit Sales | 225,000 | 262,500 | 300,000 | 112,000 | 150,000 | 150,000 | 225,000 |
| *Collections:* | | | | | | | |
| 60%—1st month after sale | | | | $180,000 | $ 67,500 | $ 90,000 | $ 90,000 |
| 30%—2nd month after sale | | | | 78,750 | 90,000 | 33,750 | 45,000 |
| 5%—3rd month after sale | | | | 11,250 | 13,125 | 15,000 | 5,625 |
| Cash Sales | | | | 37,500 | 50,000 | 50,000 | 75,000 |
| Interest | | | | 0 | 200 | 0 | 0 |
| Total Cash Receipts | | | | $307,500 | $220,825 | $188,750 | $215,625 |
| *Cash Disbursements:* | | | | | | | |
| Purchases | | | | $140,000 | $140,000 | $210,000 | $175,000 |
| Rent | | | | 2,000 | 2,000 | 2,000 | 2,000 |

*(continued)*

**TABLE 15.2** *(continued)*

**Cash Budget—Most Likely Sales Forecast**

|  | Oct. | Nov. | Dec. | Jan. | Feb. | Mar. | Apr. |
|---|---|---|---|---|---|---|---|
| Utilities |  |  |  | 850 | 850 | 850 | 850 |
| Interest |  |  |  | 0 | 0 | 7,500 | 0 |
| Tax Prepayment |  |  |  | 0 | 0 | 50,000 | 0 |
| Capital Addition |  |  |  | 0 | 130,000 | 0 | 0 |
| Miscellaneous |  |  |  | 70 | 70 | 70 | 70 |
| Wages/Salaries |  |  |  | 30,000 | 40,000 | 45,000 | 50,000 |
| Total Cash Disbursements |  |  |  | $172,920 | $312,920 | $315,420 | $227,920 |
| *End-of-Month Balance:* |  |  |  |  |  |  |  |
| Cash [beginning of month] |  |  |  | $ 12,000 | $146,580 | $ 54,485 | $ 10,000 |
| +Cash Receipts |  |  |  | 307,500 | 220,825 | 188,750 | 215,625 |
| − Cash Disbursements |  |  |  | 172,920 | 312,920 | 315,420 | 227,920 |
| Cash (end of month) |  |  |  | 146,580 | 54,485 | (72,185) | (2,295) |
| Borrowing/Repayment |  |  |  | 0 | 0 | 82,185 | 12,295 |
| Cash (end of month [after borrowing]) |  |  |  | $146,580 | $ 54,485 | $ 10,000 | $ 10,000 |

**Cash Budget—Optimistic Sales Forecast**

|  | Oct. | Nov. | Dec. | Jan. | Feb. | Mar. | Apr. |
|---|---|---|---|---|---|---|---|
| *Cash Receipts:* |  |  |  |  |  |  |  |
| Sales | $300,000 | $350,000 | $400,000 | $175,000 | $250,000 | $250,000 | $340,000 |
| Credit Sales | 225,000 | 262,500 | 300,000 | 131,250 | 187,500 | 187,500 | 255,000 |
| *Collections:* |  |  |  |  |  |  |  |
| 60%—1st month after sale |  |  |  | $180,000 | $ 78,750 | $112,500 | $112,500 |
| 30%—2nd month after sale |  |  |  | 78,750 | 90,000 | 39,375 | 56,250 |
| 5%—3rd month after sale |  |  |  | 11,250 | 13,125 | 15,000 | 6,563 |
| Cash Sales |  |  |  | 43,750 | 62,500 | 62,500 | 85,000 |
| Interest |  |  |  | 0 | 200 | 0 | 0 |
| Total Cash Receipts |  |  |  | $313,750 | $244,575 | $229,375 | $260,313 |
| *Cash Disbursements:* |  |  |  |  |  |  |  |
| Purchases |  |  |  | $175,000 | $175,000 | $238,000 | $217,000 |
| Rent |  |  |  | 2,000 | 2,000 | 2,000 | 2,000 |
| Utilities |  |  |  | 850 | 850 | 850 | 850 |
| Interest |  |  |  | 0 | 0 | 7,500 | 0 |
| Tax Prepayment |  |  |  | 0 | 0 | 50,000 | 0 |
| Capital Addition |  |  |  | 0 | 130,000 | 0 | 0 |
| Miscellaneous |  |  |  | 70 | 70 | 70 | 70 |
| Wages/Salaries |  |  |  | 30,000 | 40,000 | 45,000 | 50,000 |
| Total Cash Disbursements |  |  |  | $207,920 | $347,920 | $343,420 | $269,920 |
| *End-of-Month Balance:* |  |  |  |  |  |  |  |
| Cash [beginning of month] |  |  |  | $ 12,000 | $117,830 | $ 14,485 | $ 10,000 |
| + Cash Receipts |  |  |  | 313,750 | 244,575 | 229,375 | 296,125 |
| − Cash Disbursements |  |  |  | 207,920 | 317,920 | 343,120 | 269,920 |
| Cash (end of month) |  |  |  | 117,830 | 14,485 | (99,560) | 36,205 |
| Borrowing/Repayment |  |  |  | 0 | 0 | 109,560 | 0 |
| Cash (end of month [after borrowing]) |  |  |  | $117,830 | $ 14,485 | $ 10,000 | $ 36,205 |

cash to replenish inventory. As a result, the cash budget is only as accurate as the sales forecast from which it is derived; an accurate sales forecast is essential to producing a reliable cash flow forecast.

For an established business, the sales forecast can be based on past sales, but entrepreneurs must be careful not to be excessively optimistic in projecting sales. Economic swings, inflation, increased competition, fluctuations in demand, and other factors can drastically alter sales patterns. A good cash budget must reflect the seasonality of a company's sales. Simply deriving a realistic annual sales forecast and then dividing it by 12 does *not* produce a reliable monthly sales forecast. Most businesses have sales patterns that are "lumpy" and not evenly distributed throughout the year. For instance, Super Bowl Sunday is the single-largest revenue-generating day of the year for most pizzerias (and ranks second only to Thanksgiving as the largest food consumption day). David Evans, owner of EasySeat, an online ticket broker for concerts and sporting events, knows about the challenges of owning a seasonal business. "With opening day of Major League Baseball over, I breathe a deep sigh of relief as a ticket broker," says Evans. "It means my company has started shipping all of the baseball tickets that it has been purchasing for the last 7 months. That means cash flow will soon turn positive again."[11] Highly seasonal sales patterns such as these can make managing cash flow a challenge for entrepreneurs.

The task of forecasting sales for a new firm is difficult but not impossible. For example, an entrepreneur might conduct research on similar firms and their sales patterns in the first year of operation to come up with a forecast. The local chamber of commerce and industry trade associations also collect such information. Publications such as *BizMiner* and the Risk Management Association's *Annual Statement Studies*, which profile financial statements for companies of all sizes in many industries, also are useful tools. Other potential sources that may help predict sales include Census Bureau reports, newspapers, radio and television customer profiles, polls and surveys, and local government statistics. Talking with owners of similar businesses (outside the local trading area, of course) can provide entrepreneurs with realistic estimates of start-up sales. Table 15.3 provides an example of how one entrepreneur used a variety of marketing information to derive a sales forecast for his first year of operation in the automotive repair business.

No matter what techniques entrepreneurs use to forecast cash flow, they must recognize that even the best sales estimates will be wrong. Many financial analysts suggest that entrepreneurs create *three estimates*—a most likely, an optimistic, and a pessimistic sales estimate—and then make a separate cash budget for each forecast (a very simple task with a computer spreadsheet).

## TABLE 15.3 Forecasting Sales for a Business Start-Up

Robert Adler wants to open a repair shop for imported cars. The trade association for automotive garages estimates that the owner of an imported car spends an average of $485 per year on repairs and maintenance. The typical garage attracts its clientele from a trading zone (the area from which a business draws its customers) with a 20-mile radius. Census reports show that the families within a 20-mile radius of Robert's proposed location own 84,000 cars, of which 24 percent are imports. Based on a local market consultant's research, Robert believes he can capture 9.9 percent of the market this year. Robert's calculations to estimate of his company's first year's sales are as follows:

| | |
|---|---|
| Number of cars in trading zone | 84,000 autos |
| × Percent of imports | × 24% |
| = Number of imported cars in trading zone | 20,160 imports |
| Number of imports in trading zone | 20,160 |
| × Average expenditure on repairs and maintenance | × $485 |
| = Total import repair sales potential | $9,777,600 |
| Total import repair sales potential | $9,777,600 |
| × Estimated share of market | ×9.9% |
| = Sales estimate | $967,982 |

Now Robert Adler can convert this annual sales estimate of $967,982 into monthly sales estimates for use in his company's cash budget.

This dynamic forecast enables entrepreneurs to determine the range within which their business's sales and cash flows will likely fall as the year progresses. By using the forecast that most closely reflects their sales patterns, entrepreneurs can project their companies' cash flow more accurately.

### Step 3: Forecasting Cash Receipts

As noted earlier, sales constitute the major source of cash receipts. When a company sells goods and services on credit, the cash budget must count for the delay between the sale and the actual collection of the proceeds. Remember: You cannot spend cash you haven't collected yet! For instance, a commercial carpet cleaning company might not collect the cash from carpets they clean in hotels and restaurants in February until March or April (or even later), and the cash budget must reflect this delay. To project accurately a firm's cash receipts, entrepreneurs must analyze their companies' accounts receivable to determine their collection pattern. For example, an entrepreneur may discover that 20 percent of sales are for cash, 50 percent are paid in the month following the sale, 20 percent are paid two months after the sale, 7 percent are paid after three months, and 3 percent are never collected. In addition to cash and credit sales, a cash budget must include any other cash the company receives, such as interest income, rental income, dividends, and others.

Some small business owners never discover the hidden danger in accounts receivable until it is too late for their companies. Receivables act as cash sponges, tying up valuable dollars until an entrepreneur collects them.

**ENTREPRENEURIAL PROFILE: Mary and Phil Baechler: Baby Jogger Company** When Mary and Phil Baechler started Baby Jogger Company to make strollers that would enable parents to take their babies along on their daily runs, Mary was in charge of the financial aspects of the business and watched its cash flow closely. As the company grew, the couple created an accounting department to handle its financial affairs. Unfortunately, the financial management system could not keep up with the company's rapid growth and failed to provide the necessary information to keep its finances under control. As inventory and accounts receivable ballooned, the company headed for a cash crisis. To ensure Baby Jogger's survival, the Baechlers were forced to reduce their company's workforce by half. Then they turned their attention to the accounts receivable and discovered that customers owed the business almost $700,000! In addition, most of the accounts were past due. Focusing on collecting the money owed to their company, the Baechlers were able to steer clear of a cash crisis and get Baby Jogger back on track.[12]

Figure 15.4 demonstrates how vital it is to act promptly once an account becomes past due. Notice how the probability of collecting an outstanding account diminishes the longer the account is delinquent. Table 15.4 illustrates the high cost of failing to collect accounts receivable on time.

Many banks now offer cash management tools designed to speed up the collection of invoices to small companies that once were reserved only for large businesses. Once set up with a bank, **electronic (or Automated Clearing House, ACH) collections** automatically deduct invoice amounts from a customer's account and deposit them into the seller's account within 24 hours. Businesses can use electronic collections for single or periodic transactions, but they are ideal for recurring transactions. **Remote deposit** allows businesses to scan customers' checks and deposit them from anywhere using a smart phone or portable scanner, a computer, and an Internet connection. Scanned checks create an online, digital deposit that eliminates time-consuming runs to the bank. Banks typically charge a monthly fee and a charge for each scanned check to provide the remote deposit service. Entrepreneurs should compare the benefits and the costs of these services at various banks, which should be able to provide a daily list of transactions to allow entrepreneurs to reconcile payments with their accounts receivable records.

### Step 4: Forecasting Cash Disbursements

Most owners of established businesses have a clear picture of a company's pattern of cash disbursements. In fact, many cash payments, such as rent, salaries, loan repayments, and insurance premiums, are fixed amounts due on specified dates. The key factor in forecasting disbursements for a cash budget is to *record them in the month in which they will be* paid, *not*

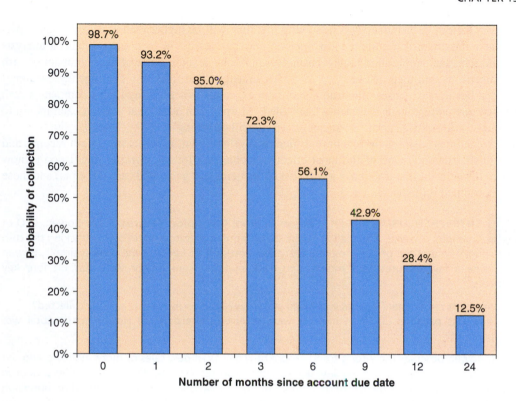

**FIGURE 15.4**

**Probability of Collecting Accounts Receivable**

*Source:* Based on Commercial Collection Agency Section of the Commercial Law League of America.

## TABLE 15.4  Managing Accounts Receivable

Are your customers who purchase on credit paying late? If so, these outstanding accounts receivable probably represent a significant leak in your company's profits. Regaining control of these late payers will likely improve your company's profits and cash flow.

Slow-paying customers, in effect, are borrowing money from your business interest free! They are using your money without penalty while you forgo opportunities to put it to productive use in your company or to place it in interest-bearing investments. Exactly how much are poor credit practices costing you? The answer may surprise you.

The first step is to compute the company's average collection period ratio, which tells the number of days required to collect the typical account receivable. Then you compare this number to your company's credit terms. The following example shows how to calculate the cost of past-due receivables for a company whose credit terms are "net 30":

| | |
|---|---|
| Average collection period | 65 days |
| Less: credit terms | −30 days |
| Excess in accounts receivable | 35 days |
| Average daily sales of $21,500 × 35 days excess* | $752,500 |
| Normal rate of return on investment | ×5% |
| Annual cost of excess | $37,625 |

Slow paying customers are costing this company nearly $38,000 per year. If your business is highly seasonal, quarterly or monthly figures may be more meaningful than annual ones.

* Average daily sales = $\dfrac{\text{Annual sales}}{365} = \dfrac{\$7,847,500}{365} = \$21,500$

*when the debt or obligation is incurred.* Of course, the number and type of cash disbursements varies with each particular business, but the following disbursement categories are standard: purchases of inventory or raw materials, wages and salaries, rent, taxes, loan repayments, interest, marketing and selling expenses, Internet and Web site expenses, utility expenses, and miscellaneous expenses.

When preparing a cash budget, one of the worst mistakes entrepreneurs can make is to underestimate cash disbursements, which can result in a cash crisis. To prevent this, wise entrepreneurs cushion their cash disbursements, assuming that they will be higher than expected. This is particularly important for entrepreneurs opening new businesses. In fact, some financial analysts recommend that people starting new businesses make the best estimates of their companies' cash disbursements and then add another 25 to 50 percent of that total as a contingency, recognizing that business expenses often run higher than expected. When setting up his company's cash budget, one entrepreneur included a line called "Murphy," an additional amount each month to account for Murphy's Law ("What can go wrong will go wrong").

Sometimes business owners have difficulty developing initial forecasts of cash receipts and cash disbursements. One of the most effective techniques for overcoming the "I don't know where to begin" hurdle is to make a *daily* list of the items that generated cash (receipts) and those that consumed it (disbursements).

**ENTREPRENEURIAL PROFILE: Susan Bowen: Champion Awards** Susan Bowen, CEO of Champion Awards, a $9 million T-shirt screen printer, monitors cash flow by tracking the cash that flows into and out of her company every day. Focusing on keeping the process simple, Bowen sets aside a few minutes each morning to track updates from the previous day on four key numbers:

Accounts receivable: (1) What was billed yesterday? (2) How much was actually collected?
Accounts payable: (3) What invoices were received yesterday? (4) How much in total was paid out?

If Bowen observes the wrong trend—more new bills than new sales or more money going out than coming in—she makes immediate adjustments to protect her cash flow. The benefits produced (not the least of which is the peace of mind knowing no cash crisis is looming) more than outweigh the 10 minutes she invests in the process every day. "I've tried to balance my books every single day since I started my company in 1970," says Bowen.[13]

## Step 5: Estimating the End-of-Month Cash Balance

To estimate a company's final cash balance for each month, entrepreneurs first must determine the cash balance at the beginning of each month. The beginning cash balance includes cash on hand as well as cash in checking and savings accounts. The cash balance at the *end* of one month becomes the *beginning* balance for the following month. Next, the owner simply adds to that balance the projected total cash receipts for the month and then subtracts projected total cash disbursements to obtain the end-of-month balance before any borrowing takes place. A positive balance indicates that the business has a cash surplus for the month, but a negative balance shows that a cash shortage will occur unless the entrepreneur is able to collect, raise, or borrow additional cash.

Normally, a company's cash balance fluctuates from month to month, reflecting seasonal sales patterns. These fluctuations are normal, but entrepreneurs must watch closely any increases and decreases in the cash balance over time. A trend of increases indicates that the small firm has ample cash that could be placed in some income-earning investment. On the other hand, a pattern of cash decreases should alert the owner of an impending cash crisis.

Preparing a cash budget not only illustrates the flow of cash into and out of the small business but also allows a business owner to *anticipate* cash shortages and cash surpluses. By planning cash needs ahead of time, an entrepreneur is able to do the following:

- Increase the amount and the speed of cash flowing into the company.
- Reduce the amount and the speed of cash flowing out of the company.
- Develop a sound borrowing and repayment program.
- Impress lenders and investors with a plan for repaying loans or distributing dividends.
- Reduce borrowing costs by borrowing only when necessary.
- Take advantage of money-saving opportunities, such as cash discounts.
- Make the most efficient use of the cash available.
- Finance seasonal business needs.
- Provide funds for expansion.
- Improve profitability by investing surplus cash.

The message is simple: Managing cash flow means survival for a business. Businesses tend to succeed when their owners manage cash effectively. Entrepreneurs who neglect cash flow management techniques are likely to see their companies fold; those who take the time to manage their cash flow free themselves of worrying about their companies' solvency to focus on what they do best: taking care of their customers and ensuring their companies' success.

## Entrepreneurship in Action

# Rowena's Cash Budget

Rowena Rowdy had been in business for slightly more than two years, but she had never taken the time to develop a cash budget for her company. Based on a series of recent events, however, she knew the time had come to start paying more attention to her company's cash flow. The business was growing fast, with sales more than tripling from the previous year, and profits were rising. However, Rowena often found it difficult to pay all of the company's bills on time. She didn't know why exactly, but she knew that the company's fast growth was requiring her to incur higher levels of expenses.

Last night, Rowena attended a workshop on managing cash flow sponsored by the local chamber of commerce.

Much of what the presenter said hit home with Rowena. "This fellow must have taken a look at my company's financial records before he came here tonight," she said to a friend during a break in the presentation. On her way home from the workshop, Rowena decided that she would take the presenter's advice and develop a cash budget for her business. After all, she was planning to approach her banker about a loan for her company, and she knew that creating a cash budget would be an essential part of her loan request. She started digging for the necessary information, and this is what she came up with:

| | |
|---|---|
| Current cash balance | $10,685 |
| Sales pattern | 63% on credit and 37% in cash |
| Collections of credit sales | 61% in 1 to 30 days; |
| | 27% in 31 to 60 days; |
| | 8% in 61 to 90 days; |
| | 4% never collected (bad debts). |

Sales forecasts:

| | Pessimistic | Most Likely | Optimistic |
|---|---|---|---|
| January (actual) | — | $24,780 | — |
| February (actual) | — | $20,900 | — |
| March (actual) | — | $21,630 | — |
| April | $19,100 | $23,550 | $25,750 |
| May | $21,300 | $24,900 | $27,300 |
| June | $23,300 | $29,870 | $30,000 |
| July | $23,900 | $27,500 | $29,100 |
| August | $20,500 | $25,800 | $28,800 |
| September | $18,500 | $21,500 | $23,900 |

| | |
|---|---|
| Utilities expenses | $950 per month |
| Rent | $2,250 per month |
| Truck loan | $427 per month |

The company's wages and salaries (including payroll taxes) estimates are as follows:

| | | | |
|---|---|---|---|
| April | $3,550 | July | $6,255 |
| May | $4,125 | August | $6,060 |
| June | $5,450 | September | $3,525 |

*(continued)*

# Entrepreneurship in Action *(continued)*

The company pays 66 percent of the sales price for the inventory it purchases, an amount that it actually pays in the following month. (Rowena has negotiated "net 30" credit terms with her suppliers.)

Other expenses include the following:

| | |
|---|---|
| Insurance premiums | $1,200, payable in April and September |
| Office supplies | $125 per month |
| Maintenance | $75 per month |
| Uniforms/cleaning | $80 per month |
| Office cleaning service | $85 per month |
| Internet and computer service | $225 per month |
| Computer supplies | $75 per month |
| Advertising | $450 per month |
| Legal and accounting fees | $250 per month |
| Miscellaneous expenses | $95 per month |

A tax payment of $3,140 is due in June.

Rowena has established a minimum cash balance of $1,500.

If Rowena must borrow money, she uses her line of credit at the bank, which charges interest at an annual rate of 10.25 percent. Any money that Rowena borrows must be repaid the next month.

1. Help Rowena put together a cash budget for the six months beginning in April.
2. Does it appear that Rowena's business will remain solvent, or could the company be heading for a cash crisis?
3. What suggestions can you make to help Rowena improve her company's cash flow?

## The "Big Three" of Cash Management

**4.**

Describe the fundamental principles involved in managing the "big three" of cash management: accounts receivable, accounts payable, and inventory.

It is unrealistic for entrepreneurs to expect to trace the flow of every dollar through their businesses. However, by concentrating on the three primary causes of cash flow problems, they can dramatically lower the likelihood of experiencing a devastating cash crisis. The "big three" of cash management are accounts receivable, accounts payable, and inventory. When it comes to managing cash flow, entrepreneurs' goals should be to accelerate their companies' accounts receivable and to carefully manage their accounts payable. Business owners also must monitor inventory carefully to avoid tying up valuable cash in an excess inventory. Figure 15.5 illustrates the interaction of the "big three" (inventory, accounts receivable, and accounts payable) in a company's cash conversion cycle and a measure for each one (days' inventory outstanding, days sales' outstanding, and days' payable outstanding).

### Accounts Receivable

Selling merchandise and services on credit is a necessary evil for most small businesses. Many customers expect to buy on credit, and entrepreneurs extend it to avoid losing customers to competitors. However, selling to customers on credit is expensive; it requires more paperwork, more

**FIGURE 15.5**

**The Cash Conversion Cycle**

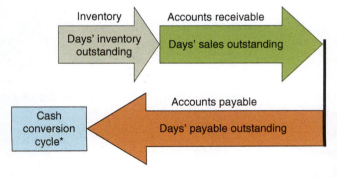

*Cash conversion cycle = Days' inventory + Days' sales outstanding − Days' payable

staff, and *more cash* to service accounts receivable. In addition, because extending credit is, in essence, lending money, the risk involved is higher. Every business owner who sells on credit will encounter customers who pay late or, worst of all, who never pay at all.

**ENTREPRENEURIAL PROFILE: Trish and Richard Wolfe: Artisan Shutter Co.** Trish and Richard Wolfe, co-owners of Artisan Shutter Co., felt the pinch of late payments by customers on accounts receivable. Their company makes custom shutters for high-end residential and commercial buildings. In the aftermath of the real estate collapse that was part of the Great Recession, half of Artisan Shutter's customers were late on their payments, which was a dramatic increase from the 5 percent late payments the company experienced before the real-estate decline started. "The bigger they are, the less they want to give us up front," says Trish. At one point, a large architecture firm called to say it couldn't pay the $40,000 balance it owed for $180,000 worth of shutters it had purchased for a high-end hotel development. Artisan Shutter was forced to lay off about 15 percent of its employees.[14]

According to a survey by Decipher Inc. and software publisher Intuit, the average small business has $1,500 in past-due accounts receivable per month. The same survey also reports an average of $1,900 in bad debt losses each year for the typical small business, which adds up to a total annual loss of $42 billion for all small businesses![15] As you can imagine, this revenue leakage can be the source of severe cash flow problems for a small business. Much like a leak in a water pipe, revenue leakages from undisciplined collection procedures can become significant over time and cause serious damage. One expert estimates that revenue leakages rob companies of 2 percent of their sales. Health care and Web service providers, for instance, typically lose 5 to 10 percent of their revenues each year.[16]

Selling on credit is a common practice in business. "Extending credit is a [double]-edged sword," says Robert Smith, president of his own public relations firm in Rockford, Illinois. "I give credit so more people can afford my publicity services. I also have people who still owe me money—and who will probably never pay."[17]

Because so many entrepreneurs sell on credit, an assertive collection program is essential to managing a company's cash flow. A credit policy that is too lenient can destroy a business's cash flow, attracting nothing but slow-paying and "deadbeat" customers. On the other hand, a carefully designed credit policy can be a powerful selling tool, attracting customers and boosting cash flow. "A sale is not a sale until you collect the money," warns the head of the National Association of Credit Management. "Receivables are the second most important item on the balance sheet. The first is cash. If you don't turn those receivables into cash, you're not going to be in business very long."[18]

**ENTREPRENEURIAL PROFILE: Steve Goldberg: TLS International LLC** Steve Goldberg, co-owner of the winter-cap company TLS International LLC, sells about $1 million in caps each year. After about 15 of his customers became more than 100 days behind in their payments, his business got into a cash flow bind. "It's very difficult for us," said Goldberg. "We have bills that we need to pay, and now we fall into the cycle of paying our bills late."[19]

**HOW TO ESTABLISH A CREDIT AND COLLECTION POLICY** The first step in establishing a workable credit policy that preserves a company's cash flow is to screen customers carefully before granting credit. Unfortunately, few small businesses conduct any kind of credit investigation before selling to a new customer. According to one study, nearly 95 percent of small firms that sell on credit sell to anyone who wants to buy.[20] If a debt becomes past due and a business owner has gathered no information about the customer, the odds of collecting the account are virtually nil.

The first line of defense against bad debt losses is a detailed credit application. Before selling to any customer on credit, a business owner should have the customer complete a customized application designed to provide the information needed to judge the potential customer's creditworthiness. At a minimum, this credit profile should include the following information about customers:

- Name, address, Social Security number, and telephone number
- Form of ownership (proprietorship, S corporation, LLC, corporation, and so on) and number of years in business
- Credit references (e.g., other suppliers), including contact names, addresses, and telephone numbers
- Bank and credit card references

After collecting this information, entrepreneurs should use it by checking the potential customer's credit references! The savings from lower bad debt expenses can more than offset the cost of using a credit reporting service. Companies such as Dun & Bradstreet (*www.dnb.com*), Experian (*www.experian.com*), Equifax (*www.equifax.com*), and TransUnion (*www.transunion.com*) enable entrepreneurs to gather credit information on potential customers. For entrepreneurs who sell to other business, Dun & Bradstreet offers many useful services for evaluating the credit risk of new and existing businesses. The National Association of Credit Management (*www.nacm.org*) is another important source of credit information because it collects information on many small businesses that other reporting services ignore. The cost to check a potential customer's credit at reporting services such as these starts at $119, a small price to pay when a small business is considering selling thousands of dollars worth of goods or services to a new customer. Before Terri Wilson, a top executive at OE Construction, agrees to do any work as a subcontractor, she conducts a credit check on the contractor to see how promptly the contractor pays its bills. She also gathers information about the company's owner, financial manager, and the volume of work it does to gauge the credit risk it poses to OE Construction.[21]

The next step involves establishing a firm written credit policy and letting every customer know in advance the company's credit terms. "Our cash flow won't allow us to carry customers with a tendency to slow-pay," says Anita McKinney, controller of Luttrell Belting & Supply Co. "With a couple of potential customers, we said, 'We can't give you credit. Pay cash or give us a credit card.' They're not necessarily people who are out to do us wrong. It's just they're struggling like many people are to keep their businesses going."[22] The credit agreement must be in writing and should specify a customer's credit limit (which usually varies from one customer to another, depending on their credit ratings) and any deposits required (often stated as a percentage of the purchase price). It should state clearly all of the terms the business will enforce if the account goes bad, including interest, late charges, attorney's fees, and others. Failure to specify these terms in the contract means that they *cannot* be added later after problems arise. When will you send invoices? How soon is payment due: immediately, 20 days, or 30 days? Will you offer early-payment discounts? Will you add a late charge? If so, how much? The credit policies should be as tight as possible but remain within federal and state credit laws. According to the American Collectors Association, if a business is writing off more than 5 percent of sales as bad debts, the owner should tighten its credit and collection policy.[23]

The third step in an effective credit policy is to send invoices promptly because customers rarely pay before they receive their bills. Unfortunately, a recent study reports that 20 percent of small business owners forget to send invoices or to follow up on past-due invoices.[24] The sooner a company sends invoices, the sooner its customers will pay them. Manufacturers and wholesalers should make sure invoices are en route to customers as soon as the shipments go out the door (if not before). Service companies should keep track of billable hours daily or weekly and bill as often as the contract or agreement with the client permits. Online or computerized billing software makes managing accounts receivable much easier, is less expensive, and produces faster payments than paper invoices, but only 34 percent of small businesses use these programs.[25] Some businesses also use **cycle billing**, in which a company bills a portion of its credit customers each day of the month to smooth out uneven cash receipts.

**ENTREPRENEURIAL PROFILE: Bob Dempster: American Imaging Inc.** Bob Dempster, cofounder of American Imaging Inc., a distributor of X-ray tubes, once handled receivables the same way most entrepreneurs do: When customers ignored the "net 30" terms on invoices, he would call them around the forty-fifth day to ask what the problem was. Payments usually would trickle in within the next two weeks, but by then 60 days had elapsed, and American Imaging's cash flow was always strained. Then Dempster decided to try a different approach. Now he makes a "customer relations call" on the twentieth day of the billing period to determine whether the customer is satisfied with the company's performance on the order. Before closing, he reminds the customer of the invoice due date and asks if there will be any problems meeting it. Dempster's proactive approach to collecting receivables has cut his company's average collection period by at least 15 days, improved cash flow, and increased customer satisfaction![26]

When an account becomes overdue, entrepreneurs must take *immediate* action. The longer an account is past due, the lower is the probability of collecting it. As soon as an account becomes overdue, many business owners send a "second notice" letter requesting immediate payment. If that fails to produce results, the next step is a telephone call. A better system is to call the customer the day after the payment is due to request payment. If the customer cannot pay the entire amount, get him or her to commit to a schedule of smaller payments. If that fails, collection experts recommend the following:

- Send a letter from the company's attorney.
- Turn the account over to a collection attorney.
- As a last resort, hire a collection attorney.

Collection agencies collect nearly $55 billion annually in past due accounts for businesses.[27] Although collection agencies and attorneys take a portion of any accounts they collect (typically around 30 percent), they are often worth the price. According to the American Collector's Association, only 5 percent of accounts more than 90 days delinquent will be paid voluntarily.[28]

Business owners must be sure to abide by the provisions of the federal Fair Debt Collection Practices Act, which prohibits any kind of harassment when collecting debts (e.g., telephoning repeatedly, issuing threats of violence, telling third parties about the debt, or using abusive language). When collecting past-due accounts, the primary rule in dealing with past-due accounts is, "Never lose your cool." Even if the debtor launches into an X-rated tirade when questioned about an overdue bill, the *worst* thing a collector can do is respond out of anger. Keep the call strictly business and begin by identifying yourself, your company, and the amount of the debt. Ask the creditor what he or she intends to do about the past-due bill.

**TECHNIQUES FOR ACCELERATING ACCOUNTS RECEIVABLE** Although "net 30" credit terms are common, 64 percent of small business owners say that they have accounts receivable that have gone unpaid for more than 60 days.[29] Entrepreneurs can rely on a variety of techniques to speed cash inflow from accounts receivable:

- Speed up orders by having customers e-mail or fax them to you.
- Send invoices when goods are shipped rather than a day or a week later; consider e-mailing or faxing invoices to reduce "in transit" time to a minimum. For small monthly and per-transaction fees, Pat Jackson, an executive at Jackson Comfort Heating and Cooling Systems in Northfield, Ohio, equips her 22 fieldworkers with Bluetooth-enabled devices that can accept credit card payments on the job site. "It's one of the best things we've done by far," says Jackson. "It's speeded up our cash inflow."[30]
- Indicate in conspicuous print or color the invoice due date and any late-payment penalties imposed. (Check with an attorney to be sure all finance charges comply with state laws.) One study by Xerox Corporation found that highlighting the "balance due" section of invoices increased the speed of collection by 30 percent.[31]
- Include a telephone number and a contact person in your organization in case the customer has a question or a dispute about an invoice.
- Respond quickly and accurately to customers' questions about their bills.
- Allow customers to use multiple payment methods, including checks, credit cards, PayPal, money orders, and cash.
- Restrict the customer's credit until past-due bills are paid. Salespeople should know which of their customers are behind in their payments. If not, they will continue to sell (most likely on credit) to those delinquent customers!
- Deposit customer checks and credit card receipts daily.
- Identify the top 20 percent of your customers (by sales volume), create a separate file system for them, and monitor them closely. Twenty percent of the typical company's customers generate 80 percent of all accounts receivable.
- Ask customers to pay a portion of the purchase price up front. Tired of chasing late payers after completing their public relations projects, Mike Clifford, founder of Clifford Public Relations, began checking potential clients' credit ratings and requiring an up-front payment of one-third of the cost of a job. Clifford also instituted a monthly billing system that

tracks billable hours and related expenses. Since implementing the new system, Clifford has not experienced a single past-due account.[32]

- Watch for signs that a customer may be about to declare bankruptcy. Late payments from previously prompt payers and unreturned phone calls concerning late payments usually are the first clues that a customer may be heading for bankruptcy. If that happens, creditors typically collect only a small fraction, on average just 10 percent, of the debt owed.[33] Cynthia McKay, owner of a Le Gourmet Gift Basket franchise, lost thousands of dollars when five of her corporate clients filed for bankruptcy within a 10-month period. "That money is a weekly payroll for several employees," says McKay.[34]

- If a customer does file for bankruptcy, the bankruptcy court notifies all creditors with a "Notice of Filing" document. If an entrepreneur receives one of these notices, he or she should create a file to track the events surrounding the bankruptcy and takes action immediately. To have a valid claim against the debtor's assets, a creditor must file a proof-of-claim form with the bankruptcy court within a specified time, often 90 days. (The actual time depends on which form of bankruptcy the debtor declares.) If, after paying the debtor's secured creditors, any assets remain, the court will distribute the proceeds to unsecured creditors who have legitimate proof of claim.

- Consider using a bank's lockbox collection service (located near customers) to reduce mail time on collections. In a **lockbox** arrangement, customers send payments to a Post Office box that the bank maintains. The bank collects the payments several times each day and deposits them immediately into the company account. The procedure sharply reduces processing and clearing times from the usual two to three days to just hours, especially if the lockboxes are located close to the company's biggest customers' business addresses. The system can be expensive to operate and is most economical for companies with a high volume of large checks (at least 200 checks each month).

- Track the results of the company's collection efforts. Managers and key employees (including the sales force) should receive a weekly report on the status of the company's outstanding accounts receivable.

Another strategy that small companies, particularly those selling high-priced items, can use to protect the cash they have tied up in receivables is to couple a security agreement with a financing statement. This strategy falls under Article 9 of the Uniform Commercial Code (UCC), which governs a wide variety of business transactions, including the sale of goods and security interests. A **security agreement** is a contract in which a business selling an asset on credit gets a security interest in that asset (the collateral), protecting the company's legal rights in case the buyer fails to pay. To get the protection it seeks in the security agreement, the seller must file a financing statement called a UCC-1 form with the proper state or county office (a process that the UCC calls "perfection"). The UCC-1 form gives notice to other creditors and to the general public that the seller holds a secured interest in the collateral named in the security agreement. The UCC-1 form must include the name, address, and signature of the buyer; a description of the collateral; and the name and address of the seller. If the buyer declares bankruptcy, the small business that sells the asset is not *guaranteed* payment, but the filing puts its claim to the asset ahead of those of unsecured creditors. A small company's degree of safety on a large credit sale is much higher with a security agreement and a properly filed financing statement than it would be if it did not file the security agreement.

## Accounts Payable

The second element of the "big three" of cash management is accounts payable. Although it may be tempting to stretch out the payment of accounts payable as long as possible, there are a few cautions with this practice. First, developing good relationships with your suppliers ensures that they will provide good service. Second, when cash flow gets tight, having the goodwill of suppliers can make the phone call to let them know that you may be a bit late with your payment this month a lot easier on both ends. Third, many suppliers offer or are willing to negotiate discounts for quick payment. Fourth, when an entrepreneur strives to stretch out payables too long, there is a serious risk of *damaging the company's credit rating*. Paying late could cause suppliers to begin demanding prepayment or cash-on-delivery (C.O.D.) terms, which severely impair a company's cash flow. Finally, there is the ethical dimension; you expect prompt payment from your customers, so isn't it right to pay your suppliers promptly as well?

Unfortunately, many large companies use their economic power to delay payments to their small business suppliers and vendors. A survey of 5,000 small businesses by the Kauffman Foundation reports that 14 percent cite late payments as their biggest business challenge.[35]

**ENTREPRENEURIAL PROFILE: James Callahan: Callahan Aircraft Service, LLC** James Callahan was forced to lay off 16 of the 17 employees at his aircraft engineering company, Callahan Aircraft Service, LLC, which designs repairs for major airlines, because of customers' unpaid bills. One customer owed Callahan Aircraft Service, which is based in Albertville, Alabama, $50,000. Callahan believes that the airlines are trying to keep their maintenance costs down by delaying payments to their vendors.[36]

Small business owners should regulate their payments to vendors and suppliers to synchronize with their collection of accounts receivable. Ideally, a company will purchase an item on credit, sell it, and collect payment for it in time for the company to pay the supplier's invoice. In that case, the vendor's credit terms amount to an interest-free loan. Apple Inc. is an example of a company that turns the cash conversion cycle to its advantage. Its high inventory turnover ratio of 71 times a year, coupled with its ability to negotiate favorable credit terms with its suppliers and to collect customers' payments quickly, means that the company enjoys a cash conversion cycle of *negative* 61 days. On average, Apple collects payments from its customers and gets to use that cash before having to pay its suppliers 61 days later (see Figure 15.6).[37] Unfortunately, the typical small business experiences the opposite situation, paying its accounts payable in 40 days and collecting its accounts receivable in 59 days, which makes managing cash flow all the more important.[38]

Even when the timing of a company's cash flow isn't ideal, efficient cash managers benefit by setting up a payment calendar each month that allows them to pay their bills on time and to take advantage of cash discounts for early payment.

**ENTREPRENEURIAL PROFILE: Nancy Dunis: Dunis & Associates** Nancy Dunis, CEO of Dunis & Associates, a Portland, Oregon, marketing firm, recognizes the importance of controlling accounts payable. "Our payables must be functioning just right to keep our cash flow running smoothly," says Dunis. She has set up a simple five-point accounts payable system:

1. **Set scheduling goals.** Dunis strives to pay her company's bills 45 days after receiving them and to collect all her receivables within 30 days. Even though "it doesn't always work that way," her goal is to make the most of her cash flow.

2. **Keep paperwork organized.** Dunis dates every invoice she receives and carefully files it according to her payment plan. "This helps us remember when to cut the check," she says, and "it helps us stagger our payments over days or weeks," significantly improving the company's cash flow.

3. **Prioritize.** Dunis cannot stretch out all of her company's creditors for 45 days; some demand payment sooner. Those suppliers are at the top of the accounts payable list.

4. **Be consistent.** "Companies want consistent customers," says Dunis. "With a few exceptions," she explains, "most businesses will be happy to accept 45-day payments, so long as they know you'll always pay your full obligation at that point."

5. **Look for warning signs.** Dunis sees her accounts payable as an early warning system for cash flow problems. "The first indication I get that cash flow is in trouble is when I see I'm getting low on cash and could have trouble paying my bills according to my staggered filing system," she says.[39]

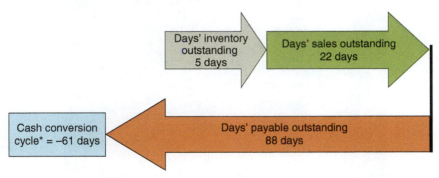

**FIGURE 15.6**

**Apple Inc.'s Cash Conversion Cycle**

*Cash conversion cycle = Days' inventory + Days' sales outstanding − Days' payable
= 5 + 22 − 88 = −61 days

Business owners should verify all invoices before paying them. Some unscrupulous vendors will send out invoices for goods they never shipped, knowing that many business owners will simply pay the bill without checking its authenticity. Someone in the company—for instance, the accounts payable clerk—should have the responsibility of verifying every invoice received.

Generally, taking advantage of cash discounts vendors offer benefits a small company. A cash discount (e.g., "2/10, net 30"—take a 2 percent discount if you pay the invoice within 10 days; otherwise, total payment is due in 30 days) offers a price reduction if the owner pays an invoice early. The savings that the discount provides usually exceeds the cost of giving up the use of a company's cash by paying early. Chris Zane of Zane's Cycles always pays his bills early and consistently captures discounts for doing so. "I make my salary on the discounts we get from paying our vendors early," Zane says.[40]

Clever cash managers also negotiate the best possible credit terms with their suppliers. Almost all vendors grant their customers trade credit, and entrepreneurs should take advantage of it. However, because trade credit can be relatively easy to get, entrepreneurs must be careful not to abuse it, putting their businesses in a precarious financial position. Favorable credit terms can make a tremendous difference in a firm's cash flow. Table 15.5 shows the same most likely cash budget (from Table 15.2) with one exception: Instead of purchasing on C.O.D. terms (Table 15.2), the owner has negotiated "net 30" payment terms (Table 15.5). Notice the drastic improvement in this small company's cash flow that results from the improved credit terms.

If owners do find themselves financially strapped when payment to a vendor is due, they should avoid making empty promises that "the check is in the mail." Instead, they should discuss openly the situation with the vendor. Most suppliers are willing to work out payment terms for extended credit, particularly if you have treated them fairly and paid them in a timely manner in the past. One small business owner who was experiencing a cash crisis claims,

> One day things got so bad I just called up a supplier and said, "I need your stuff, but I'm going through a tough period and simply can't pay you right now." They said they wanted to keep me as a customer, and they asked if it was okay to bill me in three months. I was dumbfounded: They didn't even charge me interest.[41]

Entrepreneurs also can improve their firms' cash flow by scheduling controllable cash disbursements so that they do not come due at the same time. For example, paying employees every two weeks (or every month) rather than every week reduces administrative costs and gives the business more time to use its cash. Owners of fledgling businesses may be able to conserve cash by hiring part-time employees or by using freelance workers rather than full-time, permanent workers. Scheduling insurance premiums monthly or quarterly rather than annually also improves cash flow.

## Inventory

Carrying too much inventory increases the chances that a business will run out of cash. Although inventory represents the largest investment for many businesses, many entrepreneurs manage it haphazardly. As a result, the typical small business has not only too much inventory but also too much of the wrong kind of inventory! Because inventory is illiquid, it can quickly siphon off a

Controlling inventory is an essential part of avoiding a cash crisis.
*Source:* © Blend Images/Alamy.

**TABLE 15.5  Cash Budget: Most Likely Sales Forecast After Negotiating "Net 30" Trade Credit Terms**

|  | Jan. | Feb. | Mar. | Apr. |
|---|---|---|---|---|
| *Cash Receipts:* | | | | |
| Sales | $150,000 | $200,000 | $200,000 | $300,000 |
| Credit Sales | 112,500 | 150,000 | 150,000 | 225,000 |
| *Collections:* | | | | |
| 60%—1st month after sale | $180,000 | $ 67,500 | $ 90,000 | $ 90,000 |
| 30%—2nd month after sale | 78,750 | 90,000 | 33,750 | 45,000 |
| 5%—3rd month after sale | 11,250 | 13,125 | 15,000 | 5,625 |
| Cash Sales | 37,500 | 50,000 | 50,000 | 75,000 |
| Interest | 0 | 200 | 0 | 0 |
| Total Cash Receipts | $307,500 | $220,825 | $188,750 | $215,625 |
| *Cash Disbursements:* | | | | |
| Purchases[a] | $105,000 | $140,000 | $140,000 | $210,000 |
| Rent | 2,000 | 2,000 | 2,000 | 2,000 |
| Utilities | 850 | 850 | 850 | 850 |
| Interest | 0 | 0 | 7,500, | 0 |
| Tax Prepayment | 0 | 0 | 50,000 | 0 |
| Capital Addition | 0 | 130,000 | 3 | 0 |
| Miscellaneous | 70 | 70 | 70 | 70 |
| Wage/Salaries | 30,000 | 40,000 | 45,000 | 50,000 |
| Total Cash Disbursements[a] | $137,920 | $312,920 | $245,420 | $262,920 |
| *End-of-Month Balance:* | | | | |
| Cash (beginning of month)[a] | $ 12,000 | $181,580 | $ 89,485 | $ 32,815 |
| +Cash Receipts | 307,500 | 220,825 | 188,750 | 215,625 |
| − Cash Disbursements[a] | 137,920 | 312,920 | 245,420 | 262,920 |
| Cash (end of month)[a] | 181,580 | 89,485 | 32,815 | (14,480) |
| Borrowing/Repayment | 0 | 0 | 0 | 24,480 |
| Cash (end of month [after borrowing/repayment])[a] | $181,580 | $ 89,485 | $32,815 | $ 10,000 |

[a]After negotiating "net 30" trade credit terms.

company's pool of available cash. Managing inventory requires entrepreneurs to play a balancing game. "In good times, you never want to lose a sale by running out of an item," says Jay Goltz, owner of several retail stores. "But if you're not vigilant when sales are slow, that mentality can fill your warehouse and empty your checking account."[42]

Small businesses need cash to grow and to survive, which is difficult to do if they have money tied up in excess inventory yielding a zero rate of return. "The cost of carrying inventory is expensive," says one small business consultant. "A typical manufacturing company pays 25 percent to 30 percent of the value of the inventory for the cost of borrowed money, warehouse space, materials handling, staff, lift-truck expenses, and fixed costs. This shocks a lot of people. Once they realize it, they look at inventory differently."[43] Tracking inventory consistently enables a business owner to avoid purchasing or manufacturing goods unnecessarily. Experienced entrepreneurs often maintain different levels of inventory for different items depending on how critical they are to the company's operation and how quickly they can be replenished. For instance, the owner of one small landscape company knew that hardwood mulch was one of his best-selling items in the spring, but he refused to purchase excessive amounts of it because his primary supplier was nearby and could deliver mulch within a few hours of receiving an order.

Marking down items that don't sell keeps inventory lean and allow it to turn over frequently. Even though volume discounts lower inventory costs, large purchases may tie up the company's valuable cash. Wise business owners avoid overbuying inventory, recognizing that excess inventory ties up valuable cash unproductively. In fact, only 20 percent of a typical business's inventory turns over quickly, meaning that owners must watch constantly for stale items.[44]

In addition to the cost of the inventory itself, the activities required to purchase, store, monitor, and control inventory are also costly. Efficient cash management calls for a business to commit just enough cash to inventory to meet demand. Paring down the number of suppliers enables a business to gain more bargaining power, minimize paperwork, and perhaps earn quantity discounts. Scheduling inventory deliveries at the latest possible date prevents premature payment of invoices. Finally, given goods of comparable quality and price, entrepreneurs should purchase goods from those suppliers who are best at making fast, frequent deliveries to keep inventory levels low.

Monitoring the "big three" of cash management—accounts receivable, accounts payable, and inventory—can help every business owner avoid a cash crisis while making the best use of available cash.

 **In the Entrepreneurial Spotlight**

# Be Ready for Inflation!

Mark and Nancy Roesner are owners of Copley Feed and Supply, and their business is highly susceptible to the effects of inflation. Operating expenses, including electricity to run their store and fuel used when delivering feed to customers, have been going up for several years. In addition, inventory costs, which are primarily seed, animal food, and fertilizer, have been hit particularly hard due to demand for corn for gasoline additives and demand in emerging markets overseas.

"In one year," Mrs. Roesner says, "the price of a 50-pound bag of fertilizer more than doubled to $19.99, from $7.89, a bale of hay rose to $6.29, from $4.29, and a 50-pound bag of horse feed to $10.49, from $6.99."

"We have always been very frugal," Mrs. Roesner says. They are careful to turn off lights in rooms that they are not using and have learned to spend more time planning their delivery routes. They are trying to do fewer routes and do them more efficiently whenever possible.

To deal with rising expenses, the Roesners have tried to keep pace with price increases. However, many of their customers are still feeling the pinch of the Great Recession, are not able to afford higher prices, and are beginning to cut back on their orders.

Although inflation has not raced out of control in the United States since the late 1970s, there has remained a consistent concern that inflation may heat up again sometime in the near future, particularly as the economy begins to grow. Many small business owners worry that the official measure of inflation does not reflect the inflation they experience in their businesses.

"Unfortunately, it's the steady and surging increase in fuel prices over the past few months that is the root of all this evil," says small business owner Jimmy Collins. "When fuel costs go up, so do manufacturing costs as well as transportation costs and so on. The end result is everything becoming more expensive, and when this type of inflation happens at an unexpected rate like it has been recently, my small business suffers."

Large businesses are better able to buffer themselves from the impacts of inflation. Small businesses are generally in a much weaker position to adjust prices when inflation heats up. Many small businesses are justifiably cautious about raising prices, especially in a weak economy.

Here are some steps that small businesses take to prepare for inflation:

- **Be aggressive with frequent small price increases.** This is generally a better strategy that waiting and trying to catch up at some point with one big jump in prices. For businesses that post prices, such as restaurant menus, this strategy creates a challenge. However, it is worth the effort, as customers are more willing to accept smaller increases in prices.

- **Build up cash reserves in the business.** This may sound counterintuitive because the value of cash decreases during inflation due to its diminishing buying power as prices go up. However, cash does become a critical asset for small businesses facing inflationary pressures. Cash reserves can serve as a buffer because costs can often increase faster than the entrepreneur can raise prices. "Cash is king" even during inflationary periods, so it is important to build cash reserves to buy time until you are able to pass along higher prices to your customers.

- **Stay vigilant in collecting accounts receivables.** Don't let your customers manage their own cash flow challenges at your expense.

- **Control your company's debt.** The Federal Reserve uses interest rate hikes to battle inflation. Pay down variable-interest loans as soon as possible when there is any hint of widespread inflation because interest rates are likely to increase and drive up the cost of using debt.

- **Stock up on inventory before prices from your suppliers go up.** However, be careful not to jeopardize your cash reserves when buying ahead with inventory.

- ***Focus on efficiency and productivity of your workforce.*** Workers demand higher wages to keep up with inflation. By increasing worker's productivity, you can offset some of the impact of higher wages on your company's profits.

- ***Watch your margins carefully.*** Focus on increasing your company's profits, not just its sales.

*Sources:* Based on Micky Meece, "Small Businesses (and Their Customers) Feel Sting of Inflation," *New York Times*, May 22, 2008, *www.nytimes.com/2008/05/22/ business/smallbusiness/22sbiz.html?_r=1&*; Jimmy Collins, "First Person: Inflation Is Hitting My Small Business Hard," *Yahoo! Finance*, April 23, 2012, *http://finance.yahoo.com/news/first-person-inflation-hitting-small-business-hard-160200537—finance.html*; Jeff Cornwall, "Inflation: How Small Businesses Can Deal with Soaring Prices," *Christian Science Monitor*, April 25, 2011, *www.csmonitor.com/Business/The-Entrepreneurial-Mind/2011/0425/ Inflation-how-small-businesses-can-deal-with-soaring-prices.*

## Bootstrapping to Avoid the Cash Crunch

Bootstrapping is defined as the "process of finding creative ways to exploit opportunities to launch and grow businesses with the limited resources available for most start-up ventures."[45] Bootstrapping is often associated with entrepreneurs who are able to launch businesses when they don't have access to significant start-up funding. They simply find ways to get done what has to get done despite their business's lack of funding, or, as the old saying goes, "They pull themselves up by their own bootstraps." Although bootstrapping is a common approach for many start-ups, it is also a key strategy for entrepreneurs managing growing businesses. By continuing to bootstrap, an entrepreneur can lower his or her breakeven point and better manage cash flow. Figure 15.7 displays the relationship between the various means of bootstrapping, its impact on breakeven, and the resulting benefits for a small business.

There are four basic rules for effective bootstrapping:

1. ***Overhead matters.*** The overhead used to run a business, also known as its fixed costs, is one of the two determinants of its break-even point (refer to Chapter 14). The lower a company's overhead, the lower the level of sales it must generate to break even and produce a profit. Lowering overhead expenses also makes a business more profitable as it grows.

2. ***Employee costs are the single biggest recurring cost.*** Because employee expenses are the biggest expense category for most small businesses, bootstrapping these expenses can have a significant impact on controlling costs and preserving cash.

3. ***Reduce operating costs.*** The contribution margin is the other determinant of a company's break-even point. By bootstrapping operating costs, an entrepreneur can increase the company's contribution margin and lower its break-even point. Thus, just like bootstrapping overhead, reducing operating costs can make a growing business more profitable and preserve its cash.

4. ***Marketing matters, but know your customers and where they go for information.*** The final aspect of bootstrapping involves marketing. Bootstrapping the marketing of a business is also known as *guerrilla marketing*, which was covered in detail in Chapter 9.

**5.** _____

Explain how bootstrapping can help a small business avoid a cash crunch.

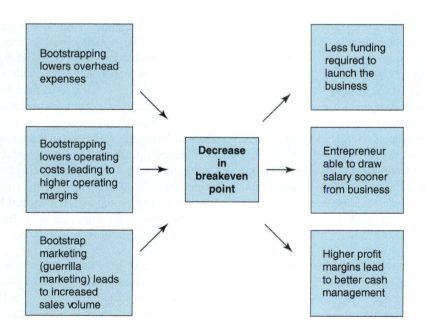

**FIGURE 15.7**

**Bootstrapping and the Breakeven Point**

Nearly every small business has the potential to improve its cash position. The key is to make an objective evaluation of a company's financial policies, searching for inefficiency in its cash flow and ways to squeeze more cash out of operations. Young firms cannot afford to waste resources, especially one as vital as cash. By utilizing the following bootstrapping tools, entrepreneurs can get maximum benefit from the company's pool of cash.

## Bootstrapping Overhead

**BUY USED OR RECONDITIONED EQUIPMENT, ESPECIALLY IF IT IS "BEHIND-THE-SCENES" MACHINERY** Many shrewd entrepreneurs purchase their office furniture at flea markets and garage sales! One restaurateur saved significant amounts of cash in the start-up phase of his business by purchasing used equipment from a restaurant equipment broker.

**ENTREPRENEURIAL PROFILE: John Paulsen: Lost Coffee** John Paulsen, cofounder of Lost Coffee, had been planning to make the transition from selling coffee out of a food truck to opening a coffee shop. However, the cost of equipment was a barrier. "Then a local Borders bookstore closed," said Paulsen, "and they liquidated everything, including the coffee shop. We went for everything we could get, spending about $15,000 for probably $250,000 worth of kitchen equipment." Paulsen and his partner were able to buy freezers, cabinets, and an espresso machine at a fraction of their value. The money they saved helped them to open two locations and cover staff costs. Within three months, Lost Coffee was operating at a profit.[46]

**WHEN PRACTICAL, LEASE INSTEAD OF BUY** U.S. businesses use leases to purchase 55 percent of the $1.3 trillion that they spend on equipment and software each year. Leasing is a common strategy among small businesses. Small companies (those with sales of less than $1 million) use leasing in 49 percent of their equipment acquisitions.[47] By leasing automobiles, computers, office equipment, machinery, and other assets rather than buying them, entrepreneurs can conserve valuable cash. The value of such assets is not in *owning* them but in *using* them. Leasing is popular among entrepreneurs because of its beneficial effects on a company's cash flow. Leasing also gives business owners maximum flexibility when acquiring equipment and protection against the risk of purchasing assets that become obsolete quickly.

**ENTREPRENEURIAL PROFILE: Andy Fleischer: Alabanza Corporation** Andy Fleischer, CFO of Web-hosting business Alabanza Corporation, recently switched from purchasing the company's servers to leasing them. Not only does leasing conserve the fast-growing company's precious cash, but it also enables it to keep its technology up to date, a vital factor given the nature of Alabanza's business. "In the past, we bought large blocks of servers up front," explains Fleischer. Leasing, however, allows Alabanza to spread the payment terms over 36 months, freeing up sizable amounts of cash the company can use elsewhere.[48]

Although total lease payments often are greater than those for a conventional loan, most leases offer 100 percent financing, meaning that the owner avoids the large capital outlays required as down payments on most loans. In addition, leasing is an "off-the-balance-sheet" method of financing; the lease is considered an operating expense on the income statement, not a liability on the balance sheet. Thus, leasing conserves not only a company's cash flow but also its borrowing capacity. Leasing companies typically allow businesses to stretch payments over a longer time period than those of a conventional loan. Lease agreements also are flexible; entrepreneurs can customize their lease payments to coincide with the seasonal fluctuations in their companies' cash balances.

Entrepreneurs can choose from two basic types of leases: operating leases and capital leases. At the end of an **operating lease**, a business turns the equipment back over to the leasing company with no further obligation. Businesses often lease computer and telecommunications equipment through operating leases because it becomes obsolete so quickly. At the end of a **capital lease**, a business may exercise an option to purchase the equipment, usually for a nominal sum. Table 15.6 compares the characteristics of leasing, borrowing, and paying cash for business assets.

**AVOID NONESSENTIAL OUTLAYS** Smart entrepreneurs spend cash only when it is necessary. By forgoing costly ego indulgences, such as ostentatious office equipment, first-class travel, and flashy company cars, business owners can make efficient use of their companies' cash. Even expenses that may at first seem unavoidable actually may not be necessary. Before putting scarce

**TABLE 15.6** Lease, Borrow, or Pay Cash?

When faced with the need to purchase equipment, many entrepreneurs wonder whether they should choose to lease the asset, borrow the money, or use the company's available cash to purchase it. The following table describes some of the characteristics of each option.

| Feature | Lease | Borrow | Cash |
|---|---|---|---|
| Time frame | Monthly payments made over life of lease | Monthly payments made over life of loan | No monthly payments; total payment made at time of purchase |
| Actual cost | Current value of all future lease payments | Cost of equipment plus interest on loan | Cost of equipment plus opportunity cost of investing cash up front |
| Initial cost | Small (sometimes no) down payment | Substantial down payment often required | Entire purchase price of equipment |
| Impact on company's borrowing capacity | None. Leasing is an "off-the-balance-sheet" method of financing | Reduced borrowing capacity | None. Company incurs no additional liabilities |
| Risk of obsolescence | Low. In an operating lease, company returns equipment to lessor at end of lease | High. Company owns the equipment after repaying the loan | High. Company owns the equipment up front |
| Tax implications | Lease payments are a deductible business expense | Interest payments on loan are a deductible business expense; company depreciates equipment over time | Company depreciates equipment over time |
| Impact on cash flow | Moderate. Company must make monthly lease payments | Moderate. Company must make monthly loan payments | Significant. Company pays entire purchase price up front. Cash is no longer available for other uses |

*Source:* Based on "Leasing Gives You More IT Bang for Your Buck," Small and Medium Businesses: Hewlett Packard, *HP.com,* http://h20330www3.hp.com/news_article.php?topiccode=20061212.

cash into an asset, every business owner should put the decision to the acid test by asking, "What will this purchase add to the company's ability to compete and to become more successful?"

**ENTREPRENEURIAL PROFILE: Evan Saks: Create-A-Mattress** Evan Saks, founder of Create-A-Mattress, kept his start-up costs low by launching a virtual mattress company. Create-A-Mattress employees work from home, and the company is able to use just-in-time manufacturing to keep inventory costs to a minimum. The company manages all administrative functions, including order processing, customer service, and payment processing, through a Web-based platform. This business model keeps overhead costs to a few hundred dollars a month. "A typical mattress retailer our size would have to raise $1.5 million to get started," says Saks. "My business started on one-tenth that amount."[49]

Evan Saks, founder of Create-A-Mattress.
*Source:* Rachel Aronis.

**NEGOTIATE FIXED LOAN PAYMENTS TO COINCIDE WITH YOUR COMPANY'S CASH FLOW CYCLE** Many banks allow businesses to structure loans so that they can skip specific payments when their cash flow ebbs to its lowest point. Negotiating such terms gives businesses the opportunity to customize their loan repayments to their cash flow cycles. For example, Ted Zoli, president of Torrington Industries, a construction-materials supplier and contracting business, consistently uses "skipped payment loans" in his highly seasonal business. "Every time we buy a piece of construction machinery," he says, "we set it up so that we're making payments for eight or nine months, and then skipping three or four months during the winter."[50]

**DO IT YOURSELF** Many creative entrepreneurs find ways to cut costs by doing work that they might normally hire someone else to do for them. For example, one coffee shop owner did all of his own renovation work on the old house he converted into his coffee shop, saving thousands of dollars. There are also ways to save on overhead costs by doing your own bookkeeping, maintenance, cleaning, and so forth.

**ENTREPRENEURIAL PROFILE: Brian Meert: *Handbago.com*** Brian Meert, CEO of *Handbago* .com, set up his own Web site when he first started his handbag Web site. He used an inexpensive template to create his initial Web site and registered his domain name through *GoDaddy* .com. Then he hired a freelance designer to customize the site to his specifications. In all, he spent about $1,000 on the site, which he used to test his business model and determine the features that customers really wanted. After a year, he was able to hire a professional designer to incorporate everything he had learned from his first year of business. "If I had spent all that money in the beginning," said Meert, "I would have had to spend it all over again in the redesign."[51]

### Bootstrapping Employee Costs

**HIRE PART-TIME EMPLOYEES AND FREELANCE SPECIALISTS WHENEVER POSSIBLE** Hiring part-timers and freelancers rather than full-time workers saves on both the cost of salaries and employee benefits. Robert Ross, president of Xante Corporation, a maker of laser printer products in Mobile, Alabama, hires local college students for telemarketing and customer support positions, keeping his recruiting, benefits, and insurance costs down.

**OUTSOURCE** One way that many entrepreneurs conserve valuable cash is to outsource certain activities to businesses that specialize in performing them rather than hiring someone to do them in-house (or doing the activities themselves). In addition to saving cash, outsourcing enables entrepreneurs to focus on the most important aspects of running their businesses.

**ENTREPRENEURIAL PROFILE: Sean Broihier: Fine Art America** Sean Broihier launched Fine Art America, an e-commerce marketplace for works of art, by outsourcing almost every function of his business. Artists upload digital images of their artwork to his Web site, where customers can purchase the images in a variety of formats ranging from framed prints to greeting cards. Fine Art America outsources the printing, framing, matting, stretching, packaging, shipping, and insuring. The company also outsources all administrative functions, including payroll, managing Web servers, and payments to businesses that specialize in performing these functions. All Broihier does is focus on creating a high-quality online storefront for artists.[52]

### Bootstrapping Operating Costs

**USE E-MAIL OR FAXES RATHER THAN MAIL** Whenever appropriate, entrepreneurs should use e-mails or faxes rather than mail to communicate with customers, suppliers, and others to reduce costs.

**LOOK FOR SIMPLE WAYS TO CUT COSTS** Allowing expenses to creep up over time is a common tendency in any business, but smart entrepreneurs are always on the lookout for ways to cut costs and to operate more efficiently. One useful technique is to sit down with employees periodically with a list of company expenses and brainstorm ways the company can conserve cash without endangering product quality or customer service. Ideas might range from installing more energy-efficient equipment to adding more fuel-efficient cars to the company fleet.

Entrepreneurs must be careful to avoid making across-the-board spending cuts to conserve cash, however. Doing so is a risky strategy because the owner runs the risk of cutting expenditures that literally drive the business. One common mistake during business slowdowns is cutting marketing and advertising expenditures. "As competitors pull back," says one adviser, "smart marketers will keep their ad budgets on an even keel, which is sufficient to bring increased attention to their products."[53] The secret to success is cutting nonessential expenditures. "If the lifeblood of your company is marketing, cut it less," advises one advertising executive. "If it is customer service, that is the last thing you want to cut back on. Cut from areas that are not essential to business growth."[54]

### Other Tools for Bootstrapping and Preserving Cash

**BARTER** Bartering, the exchange of goods and services for other goods and services, is an effective way to conserve cash. An ancient concept, bartering has remained an important cash preservation tool, especially during recessions. More than 500 barter exchanges (up from just 40 in 1980) operate across the United States, catering primarily to small- and medium-size businesses and many of them operating on the Internet. The dollar value of bartering transactions among companies in North America totals than $12 billion each year, with businesses trading everything from accounting services and computers to carpet and meals.[55] Nearly one-fourth of small companies in the United States use bartering as a cash management strategy, but more business owners turn to bartering during economic recessions.[56] These entrepreneurs use bartering to buy much-needed materials, equipment, and supplies—*without using cash*. The president of one barter exchange estimates that business owners can save "between $5,000 and

$150,000 in yearly business costs."[57] In addition to conserving cash, companies using bartering can transform slow-moving and excess inventory into much-needed goods and services. Often, business owners who join barter exchanges find new customers for the products and services they sell.

Of course, there is a cost associated with bartering, but the real benefit is that entrepreneurs "pay" for products and services at their wholesale cost and get credit in the barter exchange for the retail price. In a typical arrangement in a formal barter exchange program, businesses accumulate trade credits when they offer goods or services through the exchange. Then they can use accumulated trade credits to purchase other goods and services from other members of the exchange.

The typical formal barter exchange charges a one-time membership fee that ranges from $250 to $800 and a 5 to 10 percent transaction fee (usually split evenly between the buyer and the seller) on every deal. Some exchanges also charge a monthly fee of $10 to $30. The exchange acts as a barter "bank," tracking the balance in each member's account and sending monthly statements summarizing account activity. Rather than join a barter exchange, many enterprising entrepreneurs choose to barter on an individual basis. The natural place to start is with the vendors, suppliers, and customers with whom a company normally does business.

**ENTREPRENEURIAL PROFILE: Barbara Taylor: Synergy Business Services** Like many business brokers, Barbara Taylor, co-owner of Synergy Business Services, was hit hard by the Great Recession, but she discovered that bartering was an effective tool to keep her costs down. She has bartered her expertise in small business operations for various services. She traded consulting on social media for legal fees associated with a deposition, exit planning in exchange for search engine optimization services, and developing a marketing plan in exchange for general business coaching services. "While my husband and I feel lucky to still be in business," said Taylor, "we have had to regroup and find new ways to bolster our bottom line."[58]

**USE CREDIT CARDS TO MAKE SMALL PURCHASES** Using a credit card to make small purchases from vendors who do not offer credit terms allows entrepreneurs to defer payment for up to 30 days. Entrepreneurs who use this strategy must be disciplined, however, and pay off the entire credit card balance each month. Carrying a credit card balance from month to month exposes an entrepreneur to annual interest rates of 15 to 25 percent—*not* a cash conserving technique!

Many credit card companies now offer cash back when customers make certain types of purchases with their cards. The percentage of cash back can range from 1 to 5 percent of the amount purchased. Because business owners make many purchases with credit cards, they can earn large rebates by using these cards.

**ENTREPRENEURIAL PROFILE: Chris Zane: Zane's Cycles** Chris Zane, founder of Zane's Cycles, uses various business credit cards with cash-back programs to make almost all of the purchases for his company. Zane's Cycles buys most of its inventory with credit card that gives it 1.5 percent back. He and his employees use a different card that offers 2 percent back on travel. Its American Express card gives Zane's Cycles 5 percent back on supplies and on its cell phone bill. Zane estimates that he saves $40,000 a year with all of his various cash-back rebates. "The key is to use [the cards] like cash and pay them off immediately," says Zane.[59]

**ESTABLISH AN INTERNAL SECURITY AND CONTROL SYSTEM** Too many owners encourage employee theft by failing to establish a system of controls. Reconciling the bank statement monthly and requiring special approval for checks more than a specific amount, say, $1,000, helps minimize losses. Separating record-keeping and check-writing responsibilities rather than assigning them to a single employee offers more protection.

**DEVELOP A SYSTEM TO BATTLE CHECK FRAUD** Although the use of checks in the United States continues to decline, Americans still write more than 67 million checks per day. Unfortunately, nearly 336,000 of them are bad checks that "bounce," costing businesses nearly $123 billion annually.[60] Bad checks and check fraud can wreak havoc on a small company's cash flow. The most effective way to battle bad or fraudulent checks is to subscribe to an electronic check approval service. The service works at the cash register, and approval takes less than a minute. The fee a small business pays to use the service depends on the volume of checks. For most small companies, charges amount to 1 to 2 percent of the cleared checks' value.

**CHANGE YOUR SHIPPING TERMS** Changing a company's shipping terms from "F.O.B. (free on board) buyer," in which the seller pays the cost of freight, to "F.O.B. seller," in which the buyer absorbs all shipping costs, will improve cash flow.

**SWITCH TO ZERO-BASED BUDGETING** **Zero-based budgeting** primarily is a shift in the philosophy of budgeting. Rather than build the current year's budget on increases from the previous year's budget, zero-based budgeting starts from a budget of zero and evaluates the necessity of every item. The idea is to start the budget at zero and review all expenses, asking whether each one is necessary.

**START SELLING GIFT CARDS** Prepaid gift cards can be a real boost to a small company's cash flow. Customers pay for the cards up front, but the typical recipient does not redeem the gift card until later (sometimes much later), giving the company the use of the cash during that time. In addition, gift card recipients usually spend more than the value of the gift cards when they redeem them. Gift cards are appropriate for many businesses, especially those in the retail or service sector.

**ENTREPRENEURIAL PROFILE: Eva Sztupka-Kerschbaumer: ESSpa Kozmetika Organic SkinCare** Eva Sztupka-Kerschbaumer, owner of a day spa in Pittsburgh, Pennsylvania, found her company in a cash bind but needed $14,000 to replace two facial steamers and a microdermabrasion machine. To get the cash she needed, Sztupka-Kerschbaumer sent e-mails to her 8,000 customers, offering them discounted gift cards in return for payment up front. "This way, I lock in my customer base, purchase equipment, and get the cash flow," she says.[61]

**INVEST SURPLUS CASH** Because of the uneven flow of receipts and disbursements, a company will often temporarily have more cash than it needs—for a week, month, quarter, or even longer. When this happens, most small business owners simply ignore the surplus because they are not sure how soon they will need it. They believe that relatively small amounts of cash sitting around for just a few days or weeks are not worth investing. However, this is not the case. Small business owners who put surplus cash to work *immediately* rather than allowing it to sit idle soon discover that the yield adds up to a significant amount over time. This money can help ease the daily cash crunch during business troughs. "Your goal . . . should be to identify every dollar you don't need to pay today's bills and to keep that money invested to improve your cash flow," explains a consultant.[62]

However, when investing surplus cash, an entrepreneur's primary objective should *not* be to earn the highest yield (which usually carries with it high levels of risk); instead, the focus should be on the safety and the liquidity of the investments. Making high-risk investments with a company's cash cushion makes no sense and could jeopardize its future. The need to minimize risk and to have ready access to the cash restricts an entrepreneur's investment options to just a few such as money market accounts, zero-balance accounts, and sweep accounts. A **money market account** is an interest-bearing account offered by a variety of financial institutions ranging from banks to mutual funds. Money market accounts pay interest while allowing depositors to write checks (most have minimum check amounts) without tying their money up for a specific period of time. After surviving a cash crisis shortly after launching their branding and communications company, Jaye Donaldson and her partner Chester Makoski now keep enough cash invested in a money market account to cover at least three to six months' worth of expenses.[63] Some entrepreneurs try to store up as much as one year's worth of expenses as a cash surplus—just in case.

A **zero-balance account (ZBA)** is a checking account that technically never has any funds in it but is tied to a master account. The company keeps its money in the master account where it earns interest, but it writes checks on the ZBA. At the end of the day, the bank pays all of the checks drawn on the ZBA, then it withdraws enough money from the master account to cover them ZBAs allow a company to keep more cash working during the float period, the time between a check's being issued and its being cashed. A **sweep account** automatically "sweeps" all funds in a company's checking account above a predetermined minimum into an interest-bearing account, enabling it to keep otherwise idle cash invested until it is needed to cover checks.

**BE ON THE LOOKOUT FOR EMPLOYEE THEFT** Because small business owners often rely on informal procedures for managing cash (or no procedures at all) and often lack proper control procedures, they are most likely to become victims of employee theft, embezzlement, and fraud by their employees. The Association of Certified Fraud Examiners estimates that U.S. companies lose 5 percent of their annual revenue to fraud by employees. The median loss suffered by small businesses is $147,000, higher than the median loss of $140,000 experienced by all companies. The most common methods that employees use to steal from small businesses are fraudulent billing, corruption (for example, accepting bribes and kickbacks), and check tampering schemes. Alarmingly, the typical fraud lasts 18 months before the owner discovers it, usually as a result of a tip from another employee.[64] One source of the problem is the typical entrepreneur's attitude that "we're all family here; no one would steal from family."

## Conclusion

Successful owners run their businesses "lean and mean" by employing wise cash management and bootstrapping. Trimming wasteful expenditures, investing surplus funds, and carefully planning and managing the company's cash flow enable them to compete effectively in a hostile market. The simple but effective techniques covered in this chapter can improve every small company's cash position. One business writer says, "In the day-to-day course of running a company, other people's capital flows past an imaginative CEO as opportunity. By looking forward and keeping an analytical eye on your cash account as events unfold (remembering that if there's no real cash there when you need it, you're history), you can generate leverage as surely as if that capital were yours to keep."[65]

## Chapter Review

1. Explain the importance of cash management to the success of a small business.
   - Cash is the most important but least productive asset the small business has. Entrepreneurs must maintain enough cash to meet a company's normal operating requirements (plus a reserve for emergencies) without retaining excessively large, unproductive cash balances.
   - Without adequate cash, a small business will fail.
2. Differentiate between cash and profits.
   - Cash and profits are not the same. More businesses fail for lack of cash than for lack of profits.
   - Profits, the difference between total revenue and total expenses, are an accounting concept. Cash flow represents the flow of actual cash (the only thing businesses can use to pay bills) through a business in a continuous cycle. A business can be earning a profit and be forced out of business because it runs out of cash.
3. Understand the five steps in creating a cash budget and use them to build a cash budget.
   - The cash budgeting procedure outlined in this chapter tracks the flow of cash through the business and enables the owner to project cash surpluses and cash deficits at specific intervals.
   - The five steps in creating a cash budget are as follows: forecasting sales, forecasting cash receipts, forecasting cash disbursements, and determining the end-of-month cash balance.
4. Describe the fundamental principles involved in managing the "big three" of cash management: accounts receivable, accounts payable, and inventory.
   - Controlling accounts receivable requires business owners to establish clear, firm credit and collection policies and to screen customers before granting them credit. Sending invoices promptly and acting on past-due accounts quickly also improve cash flow. The goal is to collect cash from receivables as quickly as possible.
   - When managing accounts payable, an entrepreneur's goal is time payables to coincide with cash being collected from customers. Techniques to better manage payables include verifying invoices before paying them, taking advantage of cash discounts, and negotiating the best possible credit terms.
   - Inventory frequently causes cash headaches for small business managers. Excess inventory earns a zero rate of return and ties up a company's cash unnecessarily. Owners must watch for stale merchandise.
5. Explain how bootstrapping can help a small business avoid a cash crunch.
   - Minimizing a company's overhead expenses through bootstrapping lowers the break-even point for the business and makes it much more profitable over the long term.
   - Employee-related expenses are usually the highest single expense category for small businesses, so employing bootstrapping techniques to trim employee costs is critical for effective cash management.
   - Bootstrapping can also be used to trim operating expenses, which in turn increases the gross profit margin of the business and lowers breakeven.

## Discussion Questions

**15-1.** Why must small business owners concentrate on effective cash flow management?

**15-2.** Explain the difference between cash and profit.

**15-3.** Outline the steps involved in developing a cash budget.

**15-4.** How can an entrepreneur launching a new business forecast sales?

**15-5.** Outline the basic principles of managing a small firm's receivables, payables, and inventory.

**15-6.** How can bartering improve a company's cash position?

**15-7.** Alan Ferguson, owner of Nupremis, Inc., a Web-based application service provider, says, "We lease our equipment and technology because our core business is deploying it, not owning it." What does he mean? Is leasing a wise cash management strategy for small businesses? Explain.

**15-8.** What steps should business owners take to conserve cash in their companies?

**15-9.** What should be a small business owner's primary concern when investing surplus cash?

**15-10.** What are the four rules for effective bootstrapping? How could you apply these rules to a business that you have started or are hoping to start some day?

**15-11.** Fritz Maytag, owner of Anchor Steam, says, "Just because you are the best around doesn't mean that you have to expand. You can stay as you are and have a business that's profitable and rewarding and a great source of pride." Do you agree? Do you think that most entrepreneurs would agree? Explain.

# CHAPTER 16

# Sources of Equity Financing

*Don't confuse fundability with viability.*

—**Guy Kawasaki**

*There are two kinds of investors: [those] who try to create value by finding good people and helping them create something great, and others, who want a piece of someone else's things. The builders and the extractors. Avoid the extractors.*

—**Chris Dixon, cofounder/ CEO of Hunch**

## Learning Objectives

**On completion of this chapter, you will be able to:**

1. Explain the differences between the two types of capital small businesses require: fixed and working.

2. Describe the various sources of outside equity capital available to entrepreneurs, including friends and relatives, crowdsourcing, accelerators, angels, corporations, venture capital, and public stock offerings.

3. Describe the seven sources of funding that the founders can contribute to their new businesses.

4. Describe the types of businesses that attract venture capital financing and explain the criteria that venture capitalists use to decide on their investments.

5. Explain the process, the advantages, and challenges of making an initial public offering.

Raising the money to launch a new business venture has always been a challenge for entrepreneurs. Capital markets rise and fall with the stock market, overall economic conditions, and investors' fortunes. These swells and troughs in the availability of capital make the search for financing look like a wild roller-coaster ride. This ride has gotten even more challenging since the financial market crisis that began with the recession in 2008. Entrepreneurs, especially those in less glamorous industries or those just starting out, soon discover the difficulty of finding outside sources of financing. Many banks shy away from making loans to start-ups, venture capitalists are looking for ever-larger deals, private investors have grown cautious, and making a public stock offering remains a viable option for only a handful of promising companies with good track records and fast-growth futures. Family and friends, the most common source of outside funding for entrepreneurs, have not seen their personal investment portfolios recover to prerecession highs. Because of this, family and friends have become much more cautious about putting their money at risk in an uncertain entrepreneurial endeavor. The result has been a credit crunch for entrepreneurs looking for small to moderate amounts of start-up capital. Entrepreneurs and business owners who need between $100,000 and $3 million are especially hard hit because of the vacuum that exists at that level of financing.

In the face of this capital crunch, business's need for capital has never been greater. When searching for the capital to launch their companies, entrepreneurs must remember the following "secrets" to successful financing:

- *Choosing the right sources of capital for a business can be just as important as choosing the right form of ownership or the right location.* It is a decision that will influence a company for a lifetime; therefore, entrepreneurs must weigh their options carefully and understand the consequences of the deal before committing to a particular funding source. Avoid the tendency to jump at the first check that comes your way; instead, consider the long-term impact on your business of accepting that check.

- *The money is out there; the key is knowing where to look.* Entrepreneurs must do their homework *before* they set out to raise money for their ventures. Understanding which sources of funding are best suited for the various stages of a company's growth and then taking the time to learn how those sources work are essential to success.

- *Creativity counts.* To find the financing their businesses demand, entrepreneurs must use as much creativity in attracting financing as they did in generating the ideas for their products and services.

**ENTREPRENEURIAL PROFILE: Drue Kataoka and Svetlozar Kazanjiev: Aboomba** When Drue Kataoka and Svetlozar Kazanjiev began planning their wedding, they took a different approach to their wedding registry. Rather than list the typical household appliances that appear on most wedding registries, the couple created "The World's First Start-Up Registry," listing items to help them launch their e-commerce site called Aboomba. They took elements from their business plan, such as "feed an engineer for a day ($273.97)," "Red Bull for a week ($52.41)," and "Amazon EC2 Cloud Web hosting for a week ($134.40)," and incorporated them into their start-up registry. Guests and others responded to the creative approach to raising capital, providing the couple with every item on their start-up registry at least three times over.[1]

- *The Internet puts at entrepreneurs' fingertips vast resources of information that can lead to financing.* The Internet often offers entrepreneurs, especially those looking for relatively small amounts of money, the opportunity to discover sources of funds that they otherwise might miss. The growth of crowdsourcing further expands the power of the Internet as a fund-raising tool for small businesses. The Web site created for this book (*www.prenhall .com/scarborough*) provides links to many useful sites related to raising both start-up and growth capital. The Internet also provides a low-cost, convenient way for entrepreneurs to get their business plans into potential investors' hands anywhere in the world. When searching for sources of capital, entrepreneurs must not overlook this valuable tool!

- *Raise only as much money as you really need.* Entrepreneurs tend to fall into one of two traps when raising money for a new business. If the entrepreneur does not raise enough money, the business will most likely run out of cash before it reaches its break-even point. If the entrepreneur raises too much money, the temptation can be to spend the excess funding on unnecessary overhead and other expenses that become a burden if the business does not grow quickly enough. Careful business planning and financial forecasting determine the right balance between raising too much or too little cash for a start-up.

- *Be thoroughly prepared before approaching potential lenders and investors.* In the hunt for capital, tracking down leads is tough enough; don't blow a potential deal by failing to be ready to present your business idea to potential lenders and investors in a clear, concise, convincing way. That, of course, requires a solid business plan.

- *Looking for "smart" money is more important than looking for "easy" money.* Some entrepreneurs have little difficulty attracting investors' money. However, easy money is not always smart money. Even though it may be easy to acquire, money from the wrong investor can spell disaster for a small company. Entrepreneurs cannot overestimate the importance of making sure that the "chemistry" among themselves, their companies, and their funding sources is a good one. Too many entrepreneurs get into financial deals because they needed the money to keep their businesses growing only to discover that their plans do not match those of their financial partners.

**ENTREPRENEURIAL PROFILE: Brian Carlton: New Breed Wireless** When Brian Carlton launched CEIG, a company that sells content and applications for mobile phones under the brand name New Breed Wireless, he accepted an offer from a private investor who put up $400,000, payable in two installments, in exchange for 25 percent of the company. The relationship was rocky from the beginning, and the investor made clear his expectations of the company's performance. When CEIG missed one benchmark one year into the deal, the investor refused to invest the second installment, and Carlton was forced to scramble for money to keep the company afloat. "That investor didn't understand how technology businesses grow," says Carlton, whose company ultimately received the remaining $200,000 from the investor. Wiser for the experience, Carlton has revised his capital searching strategy, relying on smaller amounts of money and screening carefully every potential investor. With his new approach, Carlton has raised $1.1 million from 25 investors and has retained 75 percent of the equity in his business.[2]

- *Plan an exit strategy.* Although it may seem peculiar for entrepreneurs to plan an exit strategy for investors when they are seeking capital to *start* their businesses, doing so increases their chances of closing a deal. Investors do not put their money into a business with the intent of leaving it there indefinitely. Their goal is to get their money back—along with an attractive return on it. Entrepreneurs who fail to define potential exit strategies for their investors reduce the likelihood of getting the capital their companies need to grow.

Rather than rely primarily on a single source of funds as they have in the past, entrepreneurs must piece together capital from multiple sources tied to each stage of the growth of the business, a method known as **layered financing**. They have discovered that raising capital successfully requires them to cast a wide net to capture the financing they need to launch and grow their businesses. Much like assembling a patchwork quilt by using fabric from many different sources, financing a small business often requires entrepreneurs to find capital from many different sources. During the earliest stages of a business, financing most often comes from the entrepreneur, family, and friends. If the entrepreneur has partners, they also will be expected to help fund the business. Crowdfunding and accelerators are two emerging sources of funding for early stage businesses to help them move from an idea to launch. During a company's earliest growth stages, angel investors may provide growth capital. As increasing acceptance from the market proves the business model, venture capitalists provide additional financing for high-growth, high-potential ventures. All the while, most entrepreneurs add various forms of debt financing to the financing mix, which will be discussed in Chapter 17. Figure 16.1 shows how the various types of equity financing are layered over the stages of growth of an entrepreneurial firm.

**ENTREPRENEURIAL PROFILE: Matt Matros: The Protein Bar** Matt Matros lost 60 pounds by following a high-protein diet. He decided to turn his experience into a business and launched his Chicago-based restaurant, The Protein Bar, to offer urban professionals a quick, fast, healthy lunch alternative. Matros funded his start-up with a personal investment of $250,000. As the business began to take off, he was able to secure a loan guaranteed by the Small Business Administration (SBA). Matros successfully expanded his concept to four more locations in the Chicago area with a $1.3 million investment from angel investors. Based on the success of his initial expansion, he was then able to raise an additional $2 million angel investment from customers and local real estate investors who saw his business model's potential. Nine months later, he raised an additional $3.02 million in angel funding and expanded into Washington, D.C., where he opened two additional locations. Each new restaurant costs about $800,000 to open.[3]

Matt Matros, founder of The Protein Bar.

*Source:* Protein Bar.

**FIGURE 16.1**

**Possible Sources
of Equity Financing**

| Start-ups: | Early growth: | High growth and expansion: |
|---|---|---|
| Self-funding | Family and friends | Angels |
| Family and friends | Partners | Corporate venture capital |
| Partners | Crowdfunding | Venture capital |
| Crowdfunding | Angels | Public offering |
| Seed funding | | |

For most entrepreneurs, raising the money to start or expand their businesses is a challenge that demands time, energy, creativity, and a measure of luck. "Raising money is a marathon, not a sprint," says one entrepreneur who has raised $4 million for her four-year-old company.[4] This chapter and the next one will guide you through the myriad financing options available to entrepreneurs, focusing on both sources of equity (ownership) and debt (borrowed) financing.

## Planning for Capital Needs

**1.**

Explain the differences between the two types of capital small businesses require: fixed and working.

Becoming a successful entrepreneur requires one to become a skilled fund-raiser, a job that usually requires more time and energy than most business founders anticipate. The money required to launch a new business is known as **seed capital**. In start-up companies, raising seed capital can easily consume as much as one-half of the entrepreneur's time and can take many months to complete. Where to find this seed money depends, in part, on the nature of the proposed business and on the amount of money required. For example, the creator of a computer software firm would have different capital requirements than the founder of an ice cream shop. Although both entrepreneurs might approach some of the same types of lenders or investors, each would be more successful targeting specific sources of funds best suited to their particular financial needs and businesses.

The need for money is not limited to the start-up stage of a business. Once entrepreneurs prove the validity of their business models and attract a growing base of customers, they often must raise additional capital, called **growth capital**. For example, a small health care software business built its business pursuing a niche strategy selling software to small town hospitals. The business was profitable, but the entrepreneurs wanted to grow the business. To achieve this goal, they needed to acquire much larger customers. When they finally landed their first large, national hospital corporation as a customer, a new challenge emerged. The hospital corporation had multiple hospitals in cities across the country. To accommodate the demands of this new customer, the software company had to quickly add staff, buy more equipment and furniture, secure more computer servers, add satellite offices, and lease a much larger space for its headquarters. All of this required significant growth capital, which they secured from an investor. Investors providing growth capital expect the funds to improve a company's profitability and cash flow, thus ensuring a return on their investments.

**Capital** is any form of wealth employed to produce more wealth. It exists in many forms in a typical business, including cash, inventory, plant, and equipment. Entrepreneurs need two different types of capital: fixed and working.

### Fixed Capital

**Fixed capital** provides funding for the purchase of a business's permanent or fixed assets, such as buildings, land, computers, and equipment. Money invested in these fixed assets tends to be frozen because it cannot be used for any other purpose. Typically, large sums of money are involved in purchasing fixed assets. When using equity funding for fixed capital, investors expect their investment in the business to produce long-term growth that creates a return on the investment over time. If credit is used to purchase fixed assets, the terms of the loans usually are lengthy. The assumption is that the fixed assets create growth that leads to sufficient cash flow to ensure repayment.

## Working Capital

**Working capital** represents a business's temporary funds; it is the capital used to support a company's normal short-term operations. Accountants define working capital as current assets minus current liabilities. New businesses need working capital to help fund day-to-day expenses until the time that the business reaches its breakeven point and has positive cash flow. The need for working capital in an existing business arises because of the uneven flow of cash into and out of the business due to normal seasonal fluctuations or timing differences between when business sells a product or service and when the customer actually pays for it. Credit sales, seasonal sales swings, or unforeseeable changes in demand create fluctuations in *any* small company's cash flow. Working capital normally is used to buy inventory, pay bills, finance credit sales, pay wages and salaries, and take care of any unexpected emergencies. Equity financing is the most common source of working capital for a start-up business. Investors expect working capital to help launch the business so that it can achieve its high growth potential and generate a return on investment over time. Lenders are the most common source of working capital for seasonal or other short-term needs in established businesses. Lenders expect repayment as soon as the cash comes into the business from normal operations.

# Sources of Equity Financing

**Equity capital** represents the personal investment of the owner (or owners) and any investment from outside sources in a business. Equity capital is sometimes called *risk* capital because these investors assume the primary risk of losing their funds if the business fails.

> **2.**
>
> Describe the various sources of outside equity capital available to entrepreneurs, including friends and relatives, crowdsourcing, accelerators, angels, corporations, venture capital, and public stock offerings.

**ENTREPRENEURIAL PROFILE: Dan Hanlon: Excelsior-Henderson** Dan Hanlon's dream was to build a new motorcycle company that revived a classic brand called Excelsior-Henderson. At the age of 36, he launched his business and began raising money. During the 1990s, Hanlon raised more than $100 million in investments that helped build a state-of-the-art factory in Minneapolis-St. Paul, Minnesota, and fund the start-up expenses of the business. Early investments came from his family and friends. Eventually, the company raised money through a public offering of its stock. However, the business never was able to reach positive cash flow. Although Hanlon and his two cofounders were able to promote the concept of the business to investors and raise money, they were not as skilled at managing a growing business. Former employees said that they were micromanagers, unreceptive to suggestions from managers and employees, and unable to building a solid dealer network. In addition, they overbuilt what they needed for manufacturing, draining much of their capital. By the end of 1999, the company was down to its last million dollars, and the entrepreneurs were looking at various options to save it. In the end, however, the only option was to declare bankruptcy. "1999 was not a fun year. I started the year with a $20 million net worth and ended the year below zero," says Hanlon. "My brother Dave and his wife took a big hit. My mom and dad put in almost a third of their retirement savings." In addition, all of the shareholders in Excelsior-Henderson, many of whom were local citizens of the Twin Cities hoping to cash in on Hanlon's dream, lost all of the money they had invested in Excelsior-Henderson stock.[5]

If a venture succeeds, however, founders and investors share in the benefits, which can be quite substantial. The founders of and early investors in Yahoo!, Sun Microsystems, Federal Express, Intel, and Microsoft became multimillionaires when the companies went public and their equity investments finally paid off. To entrepreneurs, the primary advantage of equity capital is that it does not have to be repaid like a loan does. Equity investors are entitled to share in the company's earnings (if there are any) and usually to have a voice in the company's future direction.

The primary disadvantage of equity capital is that the entrepreneur must give up some—perhaps *most*—of the ownership in the business to outsiders. Although 50 percent of something is better than 100 percent of nothing, giving up control of your company can be disconcerting and dangerous. Many entrepreneurs who give up majority ownership in their companies or agree to the heavy-handed terms that professional investors insist on in exchange for equity capital find themselves forced out of the businesses they started! Entrepreneurs are most likely to give up more equity in their businesses in the start-up phase than in any other.

We now turn our attention to eight common sources of equity capital.

**3.**

Describe the seven sources of funding that the founders can contribute to their new businesses.

## Funding from Founders

The *first* place entrepreneurs should look for start-up money is in their own pockets. It's the least expensive source of funds available! For the majority of start-ups, self-funding is the only source of funding available. Limited funding does not stop entrepreneurs from pursing their vision, however. The amount of capital required to launch new businesses is surprisingly small. For new businesses with employees, more than half of start-ups launch with less than $50,000. For those entrepreneurs who start their businesses with no employees (about 80 percent of all start-ups), almost half start with less than $10,000.[6]

**ENTREPRENEURIAL PROFILE: Sharon Munroe: Little Green Beans** After spending 21 years working in large corporations, Sharon Munroe decided it was time to leave the long hours and stress that come with a corporate career and open her own business. Munroe volunteered at a nonprofit thrift store and observed the strong demand for used children's products, so she launched a consignment store, called Little Green Beans, which specializes in children's clothing, toys, and accessories such as strollers and high chairs. As a first-time entrepreneur, she knew that she would have to self-fund her business start-up. She had carefully saved her money for several years in anticipation of launching a business. "When it's your savings, it's a bit scary to take such a big risk," says Munroe. "But it was a calculated risk where I wasn't going to just throw money at things and hope they worked. I knew where I was going to get a return on my investment." Monroe developed a carefully planned start-up budget that fit within the savings she had accumulated for her new business. She was able to lease a space in a high-traffic area, build out that space, buy the latest technology available for a retail operation, and pay for rent and other operating costs—all for about $20,000. Unlike most other retailers, she had no inventory costs because everything was sold on consignment. She invested the remaining $10,000 of her budget in marketing and public relations to ensure that her store would get off to a strong start. Monroe had a successful launch and needed no additional financing.[7]

Lenders and investors *expect* entrepreneurs to put their own money into a business start-up. If an entrepreneur is not willing to risk his or her own money, potential investors are not likely to risk their money in the business either. Furthermore, failing to put up sufficient capital of their own means that entrepreneurs must either borrow excessive amounts of capital or give up significant shares of ownership to outsiders to fund their businesses properly. Excessive borrowing in the early days of a business puts intense pressure on its cash flow, and becoming a minority shareholder may dampen a founder's enthusiasm for making a business successful. Neither outcome presents a bright future for the company involved. Using their own money at start-up allows entrepreneurs to minimize the debt their companies take on and to retain control of their companies' future.

There are seven common approaches used by entrepreneurs to self-finance part or all of their new businesses.[8]

**PERSONAL SAVINGS** A common source of start-up funding is to use savings accounts, cash from the sale of investments such as publicly traded stocks, and funds withdrawn from retirement accounts. This cash provides seed capital for buying equipment and funding working capital. Entrepreneurs also rely on personal savings to cover their own living expenses until the business generates enough cash flow to provide them with a paycheck. Entrepreneurs forgoing their paychecks during the start-up phase is known as **sweat equity**. However, entrepreneurs' personal expenses don't stop during the start-up phase, which is why they should have enough money saved to cover the early financial needs of their businesses and to pay their own living expenses for up to six months.

As we saw in Chapter 5, entrepreneurs often do not launch a business alone. They may take on partners as cofounders to both expand the capital base for the business and provide complementary skills and experience.

**ENTREPRENEURIAL PROFILE: Lida Orzeck and Gale Epstein: Hanky Panky** Lida Orzeck and Gale Epstein cofounded Hanky Panky in New York in 1977. Hanky Panky manufactures and sells women's lingerie through department stores such as Nordstrom and Lord & Taylor as well as in upscale boutiques. Key to the success of their business partnership for more than 30 years is that Lida and Gale are quite different; they bring complementary skills to the business. "Gail designs, and I don't," explains Lida Orzeck. "Gale appreciates my style and my eye, but she thinks of me as the woman on the street, which is a very important role to play. I'm more in charge of the business." Orzeck is in charge of sales, marketing, and operations. The two also have very different personalities. Epstein is the creative spirit. She is a vegetarian who would rather be riding horses in the country. Orzeck prefers life in the big city, with its fast pace and excitement. They have found that their differences make working together easier, more effective, and enjoyable. With its founders' complementary skills, Hanky Panky has grown to 150 employees and sells more than $50 million a year in merchandise.[9]

Before entering into any partnership arrangement, entrepreneurs must consider the impact of giving up some personal control over operations and of sharing profits with others. Whenever entrepreneurs give up equity, they run the risk of losing control over the business.

**OTHER PERSONAL ASSETS** An entrepreneur may already own some of the equipment necessary to run a new business, such as a computer, a smart phone, or a vehicle. Rather than spending precious cash to buy duplicates of these items, their personal assets can become a part of the investment the entrepreneur makes in the business. It is not uncommon for a business to grow out of a hobby or out of an area studied in school. In this case, the entrepreneur may already have some of the specialized equipment needed for the business. For example, Kurt Nelson and Tyler Seymour started their video production company, Just Kidding Productions, as they were nearing graduation from college. They had already purchased much of the video equipment and computers that they needed to launch their business while they were students. The partners assigned a fair market value to the equipment that each contributed into the business, and this counted as a part of their investment in the corporation they formed.

**UNSECURED PERSONAL CREDIT** As you will learn in Chapter 17, banks rarely provide loans to start-up businesses. However, an entrepreneur may be able to secure a personal loan through credit cards or a personal line of credit. Although many entrepreneurs use multiple credit cards to fund their businesses, doing so is a risky strategy. By using credit cards to fund a new business, entrepreneurs put their personal credit rating at risk if their businesses fail. In addition, they may be violating the terms of use from the credit card company, which often prohibits the use of a personal credit cards for business purposes.

**ENTREPRENEURIAL PROFILE: Jane Poynter and Taber MacCallum: Paragon Space Development** Jane Poynter and Taber MacCallum started their business while living in the experimental Biosphere 2 outside of Tucson, Arizona. They had been experimenting with self-sustaining ecosystems—basically mini-biospheres—while part of the crew was sealed within the experimental Biosphere 2. Once their time in Biosphere 2 was over, Poynter and MacCallum relied on student loans and credit cards to finance their new company, Paragon Space Development, which was based on the prototypes they developed during their time in the Biosphere 2. Fortunately, Paragon Space was able to sell its miniature biospheres to NASA, JAXA (the Japan Aerospace Exploration Agency), and other governmental agencies for various experimental projects. The partners were able to pay back the personal credit they used to fund the launch of Paragon Space Development.[10]

**SECOND MORTGAGE ON PROPERTY** If an entrepreneur owns a house or a condominium—and has equity in the property above the amount he or she borrowed through a primary mortgage—he or she can use the equity in the home to secure a second mortgage on the property to help fund a business start-up. A second mortgage, just like unsecured personal credit discussed above, is a personal credit obligation. If the business fails, the entrepreneur must personally pay off the balance of the second mortgage.

**PLEDGING OTHER PERSONAL ASSETS** If an entrepreneur owns personal assets, such as publicly traded stock, rental property, or an interest in a family trust, he or she can use the property as collateral to secure a loan for the business. This approach is not without risk; if the business fails and the entrepreneur is unable to repay the loan, the lender can seize the personal assets pledged as collateral to repay the loan.

**WORKING A SECOND JOB** Because the entrepreneur's living expenses are an important part of the cash necessary to launch a business, many new business owners continue working other jobs as they launch their businesses. This is known as "extending the runway" for the launch of the new business because it gives the start-up more time to succeed before the owner takes money out of the business to cover personal living expenses. Because entrepreneurs can do much of what they have to do during the start-up at any time of day, they often work paying jobs by day and work on their new businesses at night and on weekends. Even after their business launches, some entrepreneurs continue to hold a second job at night, such as waiting tables or bartending, to make ends meet. At some point, the business will demand too much time to allow one to also work a second job. Ideally, this occurs when the new venture is able to pay you a regular salary!

 **ENTREPRENEURIAL PROFILE: Brian Morgan: Adventure Life** Brian Morgan traveled to Ecuador, Bolivia, and Peru to learn Spanish, trek in the shadow of volcanoes, and raft through the rain forest. After returning home to Montana, Morgan had an idea for a business that related to his experiences in South America. "I thought I could put a group of people together a few times a year and take them to Ecuador—show them the things that I found most spectacular," he says. He launched his business, Adventure Life, on a shoestring. He had only a couple of thousand dollars in savings, so he continued to work during the day at a software company. Morgan worked on Adventure Life evenings and weekends and used his limited start-up funding to print brochures and build a Web site. After a year of operations, the business was making enough to pay him a salary and cover all of its expenses. He was able to quit his job and focus on growing his business. Over the next 10 years, the company grew to more than $11 million in sales and sixteen employees.[11]

**BOOTSTRAPPING** As we saw in Chapter 8, because they are often unable to attract capital from outside sources, entrepreneurs bootstrap their companies. That is, the entrepreneur finds ways to accomplish all of the activities required to launch the business even though he or she has little or no money. It takes creativity, boldness, and a certain degree of brashness and moxie, but it works.

 **ENTREPRENEURIAL PROFILE: Johnny Earle: Johnny Cupcakes** Johnny Earle was a struggling rock musician. To pay for his living expenses, he worked at a music store. One of his co-workers gave him many nicknames that were variations on his name Johnny. One of them, Johnny Cupcakes, somehow stuck. When Earle was ordering T-shirts for his metal band, he decided on a whim to get some shirts printed with his nickname Johnny Cupcakes. The shirts were a hit, and he was soon selling dozens each week out of the trunk of his car. Earle soon began to come up with creative designs for his T-shirts combining cupcakes with cultural icons, such as the Statue of Liberty holding a cupcake and a skull and crossbones with a cupcake in place of the skull. His T-shirt designs developed a strong following of loyal customers. Earle signed up with an inexpensive Web store called Merchline.com to sell his shirts and stored his inventory at his parents' house. The popularity of his T-shirt designs continued to grow. After eight years of bootstrapped growth, Johnny Cupcakes had reached almost $4 million in sales and employed 30 people.[12]

## In the Entrepreneurial Spotlight

# Bootstrapping a Technology Start-Up

Debbie Gordon worked in a series of jobs in the technology industry. In a job she held in 2002, the entrepreneur for whom she worked was facing serious cash flow challenges. He came to Debbie to ask whether she would be willing to loan the company $15,000 to make payroll. Rather than put her money at risk for her employer, Debbie decided to leave and explore possible start-up opportunities for herself.

Debbie had become intrigued by the success of eBay as an online auction site and was curious about the opportunities it might hold. She began experimenting with eBay by selling items that she liked to buy—particularly shoes. Debbie would buy large quantities of designer shoes at a local outlet store of an upscale retailer. She bought the shoes at a significant discount and then marked them back up to retail price, offering them for sale on eBay. Because the store offered a 30-day return policy, her inventory risk was almost nonexistent. She found the process not only fun but also financially rewarding.

Many of her friends saw her success selling shoes using the auction site and began asking her to help them sell things they no longer wanted on eBay. Debbie realized that there must be many more people just like her friends who would be willing to pay her to sell items on eBay. Between the end of 2002 and the middle of 2003, Debbie developed a business plan for her new venture, Snappy Auction. Her plan was to set up retail locations where people who did not want to sell items on their own through eBay could drop these items off and they would be placed on eBay and sold by the staff at these retail outlets. She would take a significant percentage fee based on the sale price of each item.

While developing her business plan, Debbie recognized that she would need help establishing and growing the venture and began to recruit a number of veterans with experience in the areas of business development, software consulting, marketing, and legal representation to assist her in formulating a business model with a clear value proposition. She bootstrapped their compensation by offering them equity in the business and delayed bonuses to offset what their salaries would be in the open market.

Debbie soon found herself fielding calls from complete strangers wanting to franchise Snappy Auction. She decided that franchising was a cost-effective way to grow her business. She could bootstrap expansion by having her franchisees pay for each new Snappy Auction outlet. However, pursuing such an option would require her to develop a formal franchise agreement. The Federal Trade Commission (FTC) requires all franchisees to create a Uniform Franchise Disclosure Document (UFDD), a document designed to provide potential franchisees with the important information they need to make fully informed decisions about investing in a franchise. Debbie found that hiring consultants to develop the UFDD would cost at least $100,000, which was beyond the funding she had available to invest in the business. Rather than try to borrow money or find an investor, she decided to bootstrap this part of her company by writing her own UFDD agreement. With FTC regulations in one hand and a copy of *Franchising for Dummies* in the other, Debbie completed her franchise agreement just in time for an franchising expo. The expo resulted in significant interest from potential franchisees, confirming Debbie's belief. Based primarily on word-of-mouth and press coverage, the franchising of Snappy Auction had begun in earnest. Snappy Auction would go on to sign 40 franchise agreements in 10 states by early 2005. At of the beginning of 2006, the number of signed franchise agreements would reach more than 100, with 50 of those locations up and running.

Snappy Auction's software system helps the salesperson determine an item's value based on market demand and even determine the best day to kick off bidding. Once again, Debbie used bootstrapping to develop her software platform. She had a software background and was able to find a software engineer to work with her. The software allowed Snappy Auction to provide an easy eBay interface to franchisees, giving her company a significant competitive advantage over other retail auction businesses that were entering the market.

Snappy Auction was already at a crossroads because of its rapid growth. Debbie wanted to continue to grow the business as aggressively as possible. People had been coming to her eager to invest in her successful business. Up until this point, she had been the only shareholder and had no long-term debt. She had financed all of her company's growth from her initial investment, bootstrapping, and the cash flow that Snappy Auction generated from its operations.

1. Bootstrapping was an essential ingredient in Snappy Auction's successful and rapid growth. What advantages did bootstrapping offer Debbie as she grew her company? What limitations can bootstrapping create?

2. Evaluate possible sources of equity financing that Debbie could have used if she had not bootstrapped. What would equity investors expected from their investment in Snappy Auction? Is Snappy Auction an attractive business model for outside investors? Explain.

3. What would you recommend to Debbie in terms of future financing of Snappy Auction's growth? Should she continue to bootstrap? Should she seek outside investments? Justify your recommendations regarding future financing for Snappy Auction and give details on how you might implement them.

*Source:* Based on Mark Schenkel, Jeffrey Cornwall, and Jane Finley, "Snappy Auction," *Entrepreneurship Theory and Practice* 36, no. 3 (2012).

## Friends and Family Members

Although most entrepreneurs look to their own bank accounts first to finance a business, many do not have sufficient resources to launch their businesses alone. After emptying their own pockets, entrepreneurs should look to friends and family members who might be willing to invest in a business venture. Because of their relationships with the founder, these people are most likely to invest.

**ENTREPRENEURIAL PROFILE: Gauri Nanda: Nanda Home** Gauri Nanda had never really wanted to be an entrepreneur. Growing up, she had seen her parents struggle as small business owners. Nanda developed the first product for her business, Nanda Home, while attending graduate school at the Massachusetts Institute of Technology. The product was an alarm clock called Clocky that offered a unique way of waking up its owner. When the user presses the snooze bar, Clocky rolls off the table on its oversized wheels and finds a place to "hide" in the room. Clocky's mobile maneuvering forces the sleepy owner to get out of bed to turn off the alarm. Nanda had never intended her invention to become a business. It was simply a device she invented because of her own challenges with waking up for class on time. However, several tech bloggers discovered her product. The publicity, including being featured on national television news programs, convinced her that she should take advantage of the demand resulting from all the attention that Clocky had been getting. Nanda raised $80,000 from family members to launch her business. Because Nanda outsourced manufacturing, she was able to reach profitability without any additional outside investment beyond the funds from her family.[13]

The Global Entrepreneurship Monitor, a study of entrepreneurial trends across the globe, reports that family members and friends are the biggest source of external capital used to launch new businesses. Investments from family and friends are an important source of capital for entrepreneurs, but the amounts invested typically are small, often no more than just a few thousand dollars. In the United States, business founders and their family members investments in start-up businesses make up 36 percent of the typical start-up business's total capital.[14]

Investments (or loans) from family and friends are an excellent source of seed capital and can get a start-up far enough along to attract money from private investors or venture capital companies. Research by the Small Business Administration shows that 62 percent of start-up companies with employees and 59.6 percent of start-ups with no employees rely on personal and family savings to finance their businesses.[15] Inherent dangers lurk in family business investments and loans, however. Unrealistic expectations or misunderstood risks have destroyed many friendships and have ruined many family reunions. To avoid problems, an entrepreneur must honestly present the investment opportunity and the nature of the risks involved to avoid alienating friends and family members if the business fails. Smart entrepreneurs treat family members and friends who invest in their companies in the same way they would treat business partners. Some investments in start-up companies return more than friends and family members ever could have imagined. In 1995, Mike and Jackie Bezos invested $300,000 into their son Jeff's start-up business, Amazon .com. Today, Mike and Jackie own 6 percent of *Amazon.com*'s stock, and their shares are worth more than $8 billion![16]

Table 16.1 offers suggestions for structuring family and friendship financing deals.

## Crowdfunding

Historically, securities laws limited who can invest in small businesses. Investing in entrepreneurial businesses has been the realm of those with the knowledge and financial ability to assume the risks that come with such investments. These investors are called **accredited investors**. A few creative entrepreneurs have raised money from investors who do not meet the requirements of accredited investors using a funding technique called **crowdfunding**. Crowdfunding uses the Internet to generate many small contributions from a large number of people to fund a business. Crowdsourcing has been used primarily to help raise money to support social causes, help fund struggling artists, or support local small business start-ups. The money received from crowdfunding was considered a contribution or a donation rather than an investment. In most cases, something nominal is usually offered in return for financial support. For example, a musician might show appreciation to contributors by giving each of them a free download of a new song. Likewise, an owner of a new restaurant may offer contributors a special discount. The contributions are motivated by the desire to help out the struggling musician or restaurateur. The most commonly used Web sites that promote traditional crowdfunding are Kickstarter and IndieGoGo.

**ENTREPRENEURIAL PROFILE: Eric Migicovsky: Pebble** Eric Migicovsky had tried to raise money from traditional equity financing sources for his new wristwatch, called Pebble, that pairs with smart phones via Bluetooth. However, he was unable to attract the funding he needed, so he decided to take the unconventional approach of mounting a Kickstarter campaign. Although his initial goal was to raise $100,000, Migicovsky was able to raise more than $10 million to help launch Pebble. In exchange for their contributions, Migicovsky promised contributors that they would have preference to buy Pebbles when the watches were introduced to the market. "I think our campaign was successful because people can actually imagine themselves using Pebble," said Migicovsky. "If we're building something people want, why don't we ask the people?"[17]

The Jumpstart Our Business Startups (JOBS) Act of 2012 significantly expands the use of crowdfunding as a means for raising equity investment for small businesses. Crowdfunding for small business no longer must treated as a contribution. Under the provisions of this bill, those who provide funding can become equity investors with ownership in the business. The JOBS Act opens up funding of start-ups to a much broader group of investors who do not meet the legal criteria to be considered accredited investors. To be eligible for crowdfunding, the business must have annual revenues of less than $1 billion. An eligible business can raise up to $1 million from a crowdfunding offering each year. There are limitations on how much individuals can invest in a crowdfunding deal that is based on their income and net worth. Using crowdfunding under the JOBS Act, *anyone* can invest some amount in a business start-up. Entrepreneurs are no longer limited to seeking funding only from accredited investors.[18]

Attracting investors through crowdfunding requires a different approach than an entrepreneur uses when pursuing more sophisticated and experienced investors. Unlike experienced investors who invest more in people than in their ideas, crowdfunding investors are attracted to compelling stories and business ideas they can see themselves using. Crowdfunding works through social media, so the people in an entrepreneur's existing network must be advocates and

## TABLE 16.1 Suggestions for Structuring Family and Friendship Financing Deals

Tapping family members and friends for start-up capital, whether in the form of equity or debt financing, is a popular method of financing business ideas. In a typical year, some 6 million individuals in the United States invest in entrepreneurial ventures started by family members and friends. Unfortunately, these deals don't always work to the satisfaction of both parties. Chris Baggott, at the age of 31, quit his corporate job and bought a dry-cleaning store that he built into a chain with seven locations. He financed the business with a loan of $45,000 from his father-in-law, James Twiford Anderson, a physician. Anderson also cosigned a $600,000 bank loan for his son-in-law. However, the business soon fell on hard times, falling well short of Baggott's projections. Baggott was unable to meet his loan obligations. To try to find out what was going on, the bank went straight to Baggott's father-in-law, who would then call Baggott to get answers. "He'd call us and say, 'What the heck is going on here?'" says Baggott. "And then he'd have to write a check to cover it from his own funds." Eventually, Baggott had no choice but to sell his business. His father-in-law lost tens of thousands of dollars on the venture. "It was painful," says Baggott, who felt that the business failure strained the relationship with his father-in-law.

The following suggestions can help entrepreneurs avoid needlessly destroying family relationships and friendships:

- **Keep the arrangement strictly business.** The parties should treat all loans and investments in a business-like manner, no matter how close the friendship or family relationship, to avoid problems down the line. If the transaction is a loan exceeding $13,000, it must carry a rate of interest at least as high as the market rate; otherwise, the Internal Revenue Service may consider the loan a gift and penalize the lender.

- **Validate the business plan.** Seek business counseling from outside experts, such as a local SBDC (Small Business Development Center) or a SCORE (Service Corps of Retired Executives) chapter, to test the strength of the business plan before you present it to family members.

- **Educate "naive" investors.** Family members and friends usually invest in a business because of their relationships with the founder, not because they understand the business itself. Take the time to explain to potential investors the basics of the business idea, how it will make money, and the risks associated with investing in it.

- **Never accept more than investors can afford to lose.** No matter how much capital you may need, accepting more than family members or friends can afford to lose is a recipe for disaster—and perhaps financial hardship or even bankruptcy for the investors. Brian Scudamore, founder of 1-800-Got-Junk?, was unwilling to take money from family members even when his business was in danger of failing (it did not) because of a lack of cash. "My dad could have given me the money. However, I didn't want him to worry that things weren't going well . . . I wanted to show dad that I could do it myself, even if that meant stretching things a bit too far. Also, taking money from him would cause problems if things went sour."

- **Create a written contract.** Don't make the mistake of closing a financial deal with just a handshake. The probability of misunderstandings skyrockets! Settle all of the details of the deal up front in a formal agreement. Putting an agreement in writing demonstrates the parties' commitment to the deal and minimizes the chances of disputes from faulty memories and misunderstandings. If it is an equity agreement, create a formal shareholder agreement. If the money from family is a loan, use a formal promissory note.

- **Treat the money as "bridge financing."** Although family and friends can help you launch your business, it is unlikely that they can provide enough capital to sustain it over the long term. Sooner or later, you will need to establish a relationship with other sources of capital if your company is to grow. Consider money from family and friends as a bridge to take your company to the next level of financing. Have an exit plan for family members to show them how they will get their equity investment, plus a fair return, out of the business.

- **Develop a payment schedule that suits both the entrepreneur and the lender or investor.** Although lenders and investors may want to get their money back as quickly as possible, a rapid repayment or cash-out schedule can jeopardize a fledgling company's survival. Establish a realistic repayment plan that works for the parties without putting excessive strain on the young company's cash flow.

- **Keep everyone informed.** Entrepreneurs should keep investors informed about the company's progress, its successes and failures, and the challenges it faces. Investors will want to know both good news and bad news. Hold regular formal meetings with family investors.

*Sources:* Based on Alison Stein Wellner, "Blood Money," *Inc.*, December 1, 2003, *www.inc.com/magazine/20031201/gettingstarted.html*; Jenny McCune, "Tips for Feud-Free Financing from Friends and Family," *Bankrate*, July 24, 2000, *www.bankrate.com/brm/news/biz/Capital_borrowing/20000724.asp*; Paul Kvinta, "Frogskins, Shekels, Bucks, Moolah, Cash, Simoleans, Dough, Dinero: Everybody Wants It. Your Business Needs It. Here's How to Get It," *Smart Business*, August 2000, pp. 74–89; Alex Markels, "A Little Help from Their Friends," *Wall Street Journal*, May 22, 1995, p. R10; Heather Chaplin, "Friends and Family," *Your Company*, September 1999, p. 26; Nicole Carter, "How to Get Your Family to Invest Without Drama," *Inc.*, June 19, 2011, *www.inc.com/guides/201106/how-to-get-drama-free-funding-from-parents.html*; Noam Wasserman, *The Founder's Dilemmas* (Princeton, NJ: Princeton University Press, 2012), p. 259.

*Source:* CartoonStock.

*"I call my invention 'The Wheel', but so far I've been unable to attract any venture capital."*

lend credibility to a broader network of potential investors.[19] Although the JOBS Act significantly broadens the pool of people who can invest in small businesses, it also creates new challenges for entrepreneurs who use crowdfunding. The use of crowdfunding may complicate future fund-raising if an entrepreneur uses layered financing, so entrepreneurs should seek advice from financing experts to develop a long-term financing plan. Crowdfunding creates a large number of owners all of whom have a certain set of expectations and may require time and attention from the entrepreneur. If adding one additional partner increases the complexity of running a business, imagine what a crowd of partners can do to complicate an entrepreneur's life!

## Accelerators

Inexperienced entrepreneurs have difficulty finding early-stage seed funding. The first-time entrepreneur doesn't have the credibility to attract professional investors and typically doesn't have the personal wealth necessary to provide personal funding. To help bridge this gap in funding, many communities and universities have established **accelerator programs** that offer new entrepreneurs a small amount of seed capital and a wealth of additional support. Accelerator programs help move entrepreneurs from the idea stage to a point when the business has a proven story and a successful business model that they can pitch for more significant funding. "An accelerator takes single-digit chunks of equity in externally developed ideas in return for small amounts of capital and mentorship," says Paul Bricault, cofounder of Amplify, a Los Angeles–based accelerator.[20] Accelerators offer a structured program that lasts from three months to one year. A select group of entrepreneurs, typically 10 to 20, are invited to participate as a group in an accelerator program. The accelerator provides entrepreneurs with about \$15,000 to \$25,000 in seed capital, gives them temporary space to work on their businesses and their pitches, and connects them with a team of mentors, each of whom gets a small share of equity in the business in return for their guidance. All of this requires the entrepreneur to give up 6 to 10 percent of the ownership in the business. At the end of the program, the accelerator hosts a large pitch event. Local angel investors and venture capitalists are invited to hear accelerator participants pitch their business ideas. Investors who are interested can join the mentor team as investors in businesses that "graduate" from the accelerator program. There are private accelerators located in most major cities, and a growing number of universities, such as the Arizona State University program highlighted in the "Entrepreneurship in Action" section in this chapter, have accelerator programs to assist student and alumni entrepreneurs.

Two of the largest accelerator programs are Y Combinator and TechStars. Although accelerators do provide small investments, the most important contribution they offer is the coaching and mentoring from angel investors and experienced entrepreneurs. "Most angel investors have a couple of coffee-shop meetings, write a check, and then cross their fingers," explains David Cohen, founder of the global accelerator network called TechStars. "At TechStars, investors and mentors actually work with the companies for three months. At the end of that time, you've become part of the team—and you know whether or not you want to invest more."[21] The Techstars accelerator program reports that 70 percent of its participants receive subsequent funding after going through its program. An amazing 94 percent of businesses launched through the Y Combinator accelerator program receive additional funding.[22]

 **ENTREPRENEURIAL PROFILE: Ben Stucki: Dalo** Ben Stucki was an experienced software engineer and app developer and noticed that app developers had only one option for developing new apps—using their computers. He recognized that developers were not happy about having to lug their computers around when working with clients on new apps. He determined that there was a need in the market for software that would allow app developers to use their iPads or other tablets to develop new apps. "Many in our market want to work on mobile devices," said Stucki. "When you go to a client meeting, you don't really bring your laptop anymore. It's an iPad or a tablet." However, Stucki did not have the business experience necessary to secure funding for his new product, so he entered JumpStart Foundry, an accelerator that is part of the TechStars network. JumpStart Foundry provided Stucki with a space to work and seed capital. However, most important for Stucki, JumpStart Foundry provided mentors who had both investment and start-up experience. During the summer that he was in the accelerator program, Stucki worked on both developing his software and his business skills. After leaving the program at the end of the summer, he was able to raise $400,000 in capital from a venture capital firm and two angel investors, allowing him to hire his first employee, build his business, and begin to sell his product.[23]

## Entrepreneurship in Action

# Launching a Business in a University Accelerator

SkySong is a 43-acre technology park in Scottsdale, Arizona, developed by Arizona State University (ASU). SkySong will eventually include more than 1.2 million square feet of office, research and retail space; multifamily residential units; a hotel; and a conference center. One of the programs within SkySong is ASU's Edson Student Accelerator. Edson provides teams of student entrepreneurs from across the ASU campus with up to $20,000 in seed funding, office space for one year within SkySong, training and coaching, and an intensive mentoring program. The Edson accelerator program gives student entrepreneurs the opportunity to develop their innovative ideas and launch viable businesses. The program accepts student entrepreneurs pursuing any enterprise, large or small, for-profit or not-for-profit, domestic or global. Each year teams of aspiring student entrepreneurs submit written proposals to apply to become part of the accelerator program. It is a highly competitive process. The written proposals go through two rounds of judging. The finalists are invited to make presentations on their proposals to a panel of judges. Applications for a recent accelerator cohort included 340 start-up teams that included more than 1,000 ASU students from all university disciplines. Those 340 applicants were narrowed down to the top 30, who then pitched to an independent panel of judges comprised of local business leaders and successful entrepreneurs. The judges then chose the top 20 companies to receive funding and support from the Edson program. Brent Sebold, a venture manager at SkySong, says that helping entrepreneurs build the right team that can successfully transform the idea into a business that generates revenues and creates new jobs is the value of an accelerator program.

Three of the five finalists for *Entrepreneur* magazine's College Entrepreneur of 2011 participated in the Edson Student Accelerator program, including the winner of the award, Gabrielle Palermo. Palermo is COO and cofounder of a business called G3Box, which sells medical clinics made out of converted steel shipping containers to nonprofits and nongovernmental organizations. "I wasn't thinking I would be running a business while I was in college," said Palermo. The idea for the business came

*Source: ASU SkySong.*

Skysong, Arizona State University's Innovation Center

*Source: ASU SkySong.*

*(continued)*

## Entrepreneurship in Action *(continued)*

from a challenge posed by professors in one of her engineering classes. The challenge was to come up with a use for the numerous used shipping containers abandoned at ports around the world. The professor teamed Gabrielle Palermo with classmates Billy Walters, Susanna Young, and Clay Tyler. "The team's thinking immediately turned to ways to convert the containers into something that could help people," says Palermo. Their idea from the class project soon evolved into their start-up business.

G3Box solves two problems: It uses freight shipping containers that are left to rust in ports around the world, and it addresses the problem of inadequate medical facilities in rural areas. "For every seven containers we sell, we can donate a free maternity clinic," Palermo says. Shipping containers are ideal because they are durable, available all around the world, and can be made mobile, allowing access to remote locations. When converting the shipping container into clinics, G3Box must include an electrical power system, a ventilation/air-conditioning system, usable clinic space, and access to potable water.

G3Box is developing a prototype clinic to address maternal mortality in rural Africa, which has one of the highest maternal mortality rates in the world. In Malawi, Africa, for every 100,000 live babies born, 1,200 women will die. Most of these deaths, due to hemorrhage, sepsis, and hypertensive diseases, are preventable when there is access to quality medical facilities and educated health care administrators. "After the first clinic is set up, we will be able to tailor their designs for the future clinics based on the feedback from the villagers," says cofounder Susanna Young.

1. Work with a small team of your classmates to develop a plan to create an accelerator program on your campus. Make sure to develop a plan that fits within the mission and resource constraints of your school. If your school already has an accelerator program, what are the similarities and differences between your program and the program at ASU?

2. Evaluate possible equity funding options for G3Box as it prepares to leave its one-year stay in the accelerator program.

3. What tips can you offer the G3Box team before they approach the sources of financing you have listed?

4. Assuming that you have the financial means to invest in a small company, would you invest in G3Box? Explain. If so, what questions would you ask before investing?

*Sources:* http://skysong.asu.edu; Mary Shinn, "Engineering Classes Help Students Reach Out," Statepress.com, September 12, 2010, *www.statepress.com/2010/09/12/engineering-classes-help-students-reach-out*; Stacie Spring, "3 ASU Student Businesses Up for Entrepreneur Prize," *Ahwatukee Foothills News*, February 12, 2012, *www.ahwatukee.com/news/business/article_52964369-7515-550b-8af1-4057486e6bdf.html*; Carolyn Horwitz, "Meet the Entrepreneur of 2011 Award Winners," *Entrepreneur*, December 21, 2011, *http://www.entrepreneur.com/article/222469*; Maria Muto-Porter, "An Inside Look at Arizona State University's SkySong Incubator," *Young Entrepreneur*, May 17, 2012, *www.youngentrepreneur.com/blog/an-inside-look-at-arizona-state-universitys-skysong-incubator*.

### Angels

After they dip into their own pockets and convince friends and relatives to invest, some entrepreneurs still need even more money for seed and early growth capital. At this point, entrepreneurs often turn to private investors. These private investors, known as **angel investors**, are wealthy individuals, often entrepreneurs themselves, who invest in business start-ups in exchange for equity stakes in the companies. Angel investing has a long history of supporting successful start-ups. For example, Alexander Graham Bell, inventor of the telephone, used angel capital to start Bell Telephone in 1877. More recently, companies such as Google, Facebook, Apple, Starbucks, Amazon, and the Costco relied on angel financing in their early years to finance growth.

In many cases, angels invest in businesses for more than purely economic reasons (often because they have experience and a personal interest in the industry), and they are willing to put money into companies in the earliest stages (often before a company generates any revenue), long before venture capital firms jump in. Angel financing is ideal for companies that have outgrown the capacity of investments from friends and family but are still too small to attract the interest of venture capital companies.

**ENTREPRENEURIAL PROFILE: Elizabeth Thorpe: Posh Brood** Based on her experience as a mom trying to plan vacations for her own family, Elizabeth Thorpe decided that there was a need for a Web site that offered family-friendly choices on where to stay. Thorpe's business, Posh Brood, targets young, upscale families with incomes of $150,000 to $300,000. She started the business with a personal investment of $20,000, but her ability to build a sizable following of customers and the publicity from several very favorable reviews in the media attracted interest from investors. Posh Brood is a certified travel agency that generates revenues primarily through commissions paid by hotels. Thorpe built relationships with large hotel chains, such as Omni Hotels and Resorts, and established relationships with Expedia.com and Travelzoo. She chose to work with an angel investor to fund her business rather than seek a large investment from venture capital firms. The angel invests $12,000 each month to cover Posh Brood's payroll for five employees and other operating expenses. Thorpe believes that this approach to financing gives her time to fully develop her business model and determine the best growth path for Posh Brood over the long term.[24]

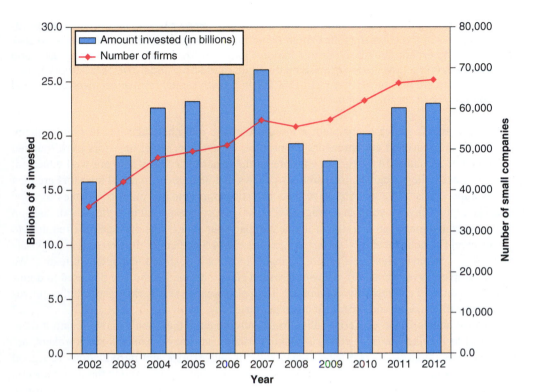

**FIGURE 16.2**
**Angel Financing**

Angels are a primary source of capital for companies that have the potential for significant growth in the start-up stage through the growth stage. The Center for Venture Research at the University of New Hampshire estimates that more than 268,000 angels invest $22.9 billion a year in more than 67,000 small companies, most of them in the start-up phase (see Figure 16.2).[25] Angels invest almost as much money in small companies as do venture capital firms, but they put it into nearly 18 times as many companies as do venture capital firms. Because the angel market is so fragmented and, in many cases, built on anonymity, we may never get a completely accurate estimate of its investment in business start-ups. However, experts concur on one fact: Angels are a vital source of equity capital for small businesses.

Angels fill a significant gap in the seed capital market. They are most likely to finance start-ups with capital requirements in the $10,000 to $2 million range, well below the $5 million to $25 million minimum investments most professional venture capitalists prefer. Because they invest in earlier stages of a business, angels also tolerate risk levels that would make venture capitalists shudder. In fact, 52 percent of angels' investments lose money, returning less than the angels' original investment. The potential for investing in big winners exists as well; 7 percent of angels' investments produce a return of more than 10 times their original investments.[26] In general, angel investors hope to realize a return of 10 times their original investment for seed stage funding, eight times their investment for a start-up business, and from three to five times their investment for funding in business seeking growth capital.[27]

Lewis Gersh, an experienced angel investor, says that out of 10 companies that an angel invests in, five will fail, two will break even, and two will return two to three times the original investment. Just one company out of 10 will produce a significant return, "which means that every one of them has to have the potential of being a home run," says Gersh. Most angels consider a "home run" investment to be one that results in a return of 10 to 30 times the original investment in five to seven years, somewhat lower than the returns that venture capital firms expect.[28] One angel investor, a retired entrepreneur, says that of the 31 companies he has invested in, "more than half have gone under, but four were home runs, returning 25 times my investment. The others gave me a small return or at least some of my money back."[29] Angel financing is important because angels often finance deals that venture capitalists will not consider.

**ENTREPRENEURIAL PROFILE: Angelo Nunez and Cary Williams-Nunez: Prime Time Boxing** Angelo Nunez and Cary Williams-Nunez combine the Baby Boomer Generation's interest in keeping in shape with nostalgia for boxing that can be traced back to the *Rocky* movies that were popular during their youth. Prime Time Boxing offers members boxing lessons as a path to fitness. The success of the company's  first three Prime Time Boxing locations led the owners to seek angel funding to expand their business to additional locations. They plan to buy existing gyms and convert them to Prime Time Boxing gyms using the funds raised from angel investors. Although their existing locations are profitable, they need $500,000 in growth capital from angel investors to fund their expansion goals for their company.[30]

Because angels prefer to maintain a low profile, the real challenge lies in *finding* them. Most angels are seasoned entrepreneurs themselves; on average, angel investors have founded 2.7 companies and have 14.5 years of entrepreneurial experience. They also are well educated; 99 percent have college degrees. Research also shows that 88 percent of angel investors are men (their average age is 57 years) who have been investing in promising small companies for nine years. The typical angel invests an average of $50,000 in a company that is at the seed or start-up growth stages and makes an investment in one company per year.[31] The average time required to close an angel financing deal is 67 days.[32] Angels accept 14.5 percent of the investment proposals they receive.[33] When evaluating a proposal, angels look for a qualified management team ("We invest in people," says one angel), a business with a clearly defined niche, the potential to dominate the market, and a competitive advantage. They also want to see market research that proves the existence of a sizable and profitable customer base.

Because angels frown on "cold calls" from entrepreneurs they don't know, locating them boils down to making the right contacts. Asking friends, attorneys, bankers, stockbrokers, accountants, other business owners, and consultants for suggestions and introductions is a good way to start. "Angels are more likely to invest in a company that was referred to them by someone they know and trust," says Marianne Hudson, director of the angel initiative at the Kauffman Foundation.[34] Networking is the key. Angels almost always invest their money locally, so entrepreneurs should look close to home for them—typically within a 50- to 100-mile radius. Angels also look for businesses they know something about, and most expect to invest their knowledge, experience, and energy as well as their money in a company. In fact, the advice and the network of contacts that angels bring to a deal can sometimes be as valuable as their money!

Angel investing has become more sophisticated, with investors pooling their resources to form angel networks and angel capital funds, dubbed "super-angels," that operate like miniature versions of professional venture capital firms and draw on their skills, experience, and contacts to help the start-ups in which they invest succeed. Angel networks are affiliations of independent angel investors. The network carefully screens potential deals before they are presented to the angel investors. Most networks have a team that works with entrepreneurs to improve their business plans and polish the pitches of those entrepreneurs who make it through the initial screening. Each angel investor makes an individual decision about whether to invest in each deal presented to the group. Membership fees from the angels and sponsorships paid by local professional organizations, such as law firms, accounting firms, and commercial banks, support the operating costs of the angel network. Angel super-funds go one step further and pool money from a group of angels to directly invest in deals. A committee of angels participating in the super-fund or staff hired to manage the pool of investment capital picks the companies in which the super-fund invests. Veteran angel investor Mike Maples operates Floodgate, a super-angel fund that manages $35 million in angel capital and invests between $250,000 and $1 million in promising start-ups, including Twitter and Digg.[35]

Today, more than 300 angel capital networks operate in cities of all sizes across the United States (up from just 10 in 1996) with as many operating in other countries.[36] Entrepreneurs can find angel networks in their areas with the help of the Angel Capital Association's directory (*www.angelcapitalassociation.org*). With the right approach, an entrepreneur can attract more money and a larger network of advisers from an angel capital group than from individual investors. The typical angel capital group has 44 members who invest $1.77 million each year in 6.3 companies on average.[37]

**ENTREPRENEURIAL PROFILE: Stephanie Hanbury-Brown: Golden Seeds** Golden Seeds's angel investor network of 250 members is the fourth-largest angel group in the United States. Its focus is on investing in women-led businesses. "It's very difficult for any entrepreneur to get capital, and it's even harder for women," says Stephanie Hanbury-Brown, founder of Golden Seeds. Members of the Golden Seeds angel network include both men and women, but the majority of members are women. So far, members of the network have invested approximately $34 million in 42 promising companies. "The top three things we look for are a great entrepreneur, a great entrepreneur, and a great entrepreneur," says Hanbury-Brown. "We back the jockey over the horse, unlike some venture capitalists who are OK backing the idea or the technology." Golden Seeds makes investments in multiple industries, including technology, consumer goods, life sciences, and media. The group has locations in New York, Boston, Philadelphia, and San Francisco. "I like investing in people who really know a particular industry and maybe worked at a corporation within a particular industry," says Hanbury-Brown. "And while they were there, they identified a real gap and need in the marketplace. Those people are in a really good position to know where the future of the industry is going and how they can disrupt that course."[38]

Angels are an excellent source of "patient money," often willing to wait five to seven years or longer to cash out their investments. They earn their returns through the increased value of the business, not through dividends and interest. For example, more than 1,000 early investors in Microsoft Inc. are now millionaires, and the original investors in Genentech Inc. (a genetic engineering company) have seen their investments increase more than 500 times.[39] Angels' return-on-investment targets tend to be lower than those of professional venture capitalists. Although venture capitalists shoot for 60 to 75 percent returns annually, angel investors usually settle for 20 to 50 percent (depending on the level of risk involved in the venture). A study by the Kauffman Foundation reports that the average return on angels' investments in small companies is 2.6 times the original investment in 3.5 years, which is the equivalent of an annual 27 percent internal rate of return.[40] Angel investors typically purchase 15 to 30 percent ownership in a small company, leaving the majority ownership to the company founder(s). They look for the same exit strategies that venture capital firms look for: either an initial public offering or a buyout by a larger company.

## Strategic Investments Through Corporate Venture Capital

Large corporations are in the business of financing small companies. Today, about 15 percent of all venture capital deals involve strategic investments by corporations. The average investment that large corporations make in small companies is $3.5 million, an amount that represents 8.4 percent of total venture capital investments.[41] Approximately 300 large corporations across the globe, including Intel, Motorola, Cisco Systems, Chevron, Comcast, Nokia, UPS, and General Electric, have venture capital divisions that invest on average $2.2 billion a year in young companies, most often those in the product development and sales growth stages. The large companies are looking not only for financial returns from the small companies in which they invest but also innovative products that can benefit them. Young companies get a boost from the capital injections that large companies give them, but they also stand to gain many other benefits from the relationship. The right corporate partner may share technical expertise, distribution channels, and marketing know-how and provide introductions to important customers and suppliers. Another intangible yet highly important advantage that an investment from a large corporate partner gives a start-up is credibility, often referred to as "market validation." Doors that otherwise would be closed to a small company magically open when the right corporation becomes a strategic partner.

Foreign corporations also are interested in investing in small U.S. businesses. Often, these corporations are seeking strategic partnerships to gain access to new technology, new products, or access to lucrative U.S. markets. In return, the small companies that they invest in benefit from the capital infusion as well as from their partners' international experience and extensive network of connections. Figure 16.3 shows recent trends in corporate venture capital.

**ENTREPRENEURIAL PROFILE: Cisco Systems** Since its inception, Cisco Systems's venture capital fund has invested more than 100 technology start-up companies. In addition, the Cisco venture capital fund leverages its funding by investing in regional venture capital funds that have a focus on technology investments around the globe. Cisco looks for more than just product fit in their investments. "The best way to think of our research and development organization is that, to some extent, it's a collection of tribes," says Guido Jouret, chief technology officer of Cisco's emerging technologies group. "We have business units focused on their own products, with their own competitors and their own partnership alliances. When it comes to acquiring new technologies, Cisco has a 'simple and rigorous checklist' for evaluating opportunities. In addition to proving its technology is beneficial to Cisco in both the short and long term, a company should have a corporate culture that blends seamlessly with Cisco." For example, Cisco's venture fund invested $100 million in Insieme, which develops software for cloud computing and networking. With its investment, Cisco also has the rights to acquire Insieme outright for an additional $750 million in the future. Cisco executives recognize that not all research and development can come from inside their company and that strategic investments broaden Cisco's development of new and innovative products.[42]

**FIGURE 16.3**

**Corporate Venture
Capital**

*Source:* Based on PriceWaterhouse-
Coopers MoneyTree Report.

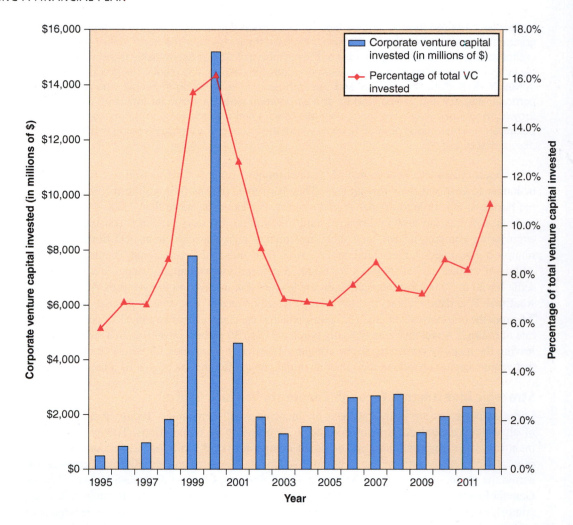

## In the Entrepreneurial Spotlight

# Funding Does Not Ensure Success

Christopher Cashman founded Protez Pharmaceuticals in 2003 using a creative financing plan. In exchange for 25 percent of the stock of Protez, Influx Pharmaceuticals agreed to give Protez some promising new drugs that it was not able to bring to market because of its commitment to several other new drugs. To develop these drugs, Protez received $3.3 million in government grants that Influx had been awarded. Protez also received an $800,000 investment from a small corporate venture capital division of a London-based drug company. Protez Pharmaceuticals's mission was to engage in the discovery and development of new antibiotics for difficult-to-treat infections, particularly those tied to infections in hospitals, using the technology they received from Influx.

In 2005, Cashman raised $800,000 in seed funding from an angel capital network, Robin Hood Ventures, and another $250,000 from Innovation Philadelphia, a nonprofit economic development organization that serves the Philadelphia

metropolitan region. His pitch to investors was that Protez was working on four different drug technologies, each of which could represent an annual market of $250 million to $500 million. The most promising of the four was known as Compound Y, a broad-spectrum antibiotic first developed in Japan.

Based on the progress Protez was making, Cashman quickly began pursuing a substantial B round of funding that he hoped would raise another $15 million. Cashman pitched to investors that $10 million would be enough to get Compound Y through Phase I clinical trials and that the full $15 million would take the drug all the way through Phase II. To be approved by the U.S. Food and Drug Administration, drugs must go through three phases of human trials: Phase I establishes safety and dosage, Phase II measures efficacy in a limited population, and Phase III measures efficacy in a broader population. Protez's monthly burn rate (the amount of negative cash flow each month) was $190,000. Cashman expected Protez's burn rate to double over the next six months, so a capital infusion was critical for Protez to move ahead. When fund-raising for the B round of financing was completed, Cashman had exceeded his goal, raising $21 million from a group of eight venture capital firms.

Only two years later, just as Compound Y was entering Phase II clinical trials, Protez announced that there was an agreement for Novartis to acquire the company. As optimistic as Cashman was about Protez, even he was surprised that the company was purchased so early in its development. Under the terms of the agreement, Novartis agreed to acquire Protez for up to $400 million in cash. The first $100 million was paid at closing. Novartis tied the remaining $300 million investment in Protez to meeting certain clinical milestones, regulatory approvals, and commercial targets. Protez became a stand-alone subsidiary of Novartis, maintaining its operations in Pennsylvania. The sale of Protez was Robin Hood Venture's biggest exit to date. Robin Hood investors could have ultimately reaped as much as 15 times their investment if the entire $400 million was paid out. Cashman's optimism soared.

Just two years later, however, Novartis made a stunning announcement about Protez. Officials at Novartis said that the company discontinued the development of Compound Y (now known as PZ-601) after observing a "high rate of adverse events" in testing the drug for patients with skin infections. Novartis closed Protez's headquarters and laid off its 16 employees. The former owners of Protez Pharmaceuticals never saw the $400 million payday they hoped for when Novartis bought the company. "There has not been, and there will be, no milestone payments made from the previously announced $300 million in potential milestones," says Sarah Kestenbaum of Novartis. Even without the additional $300 million, the company's former owners received a fourfold return on their investment from the $100 million in cash paid at the time of the acquisition.

"The [PZ-601] program termination is a reminder of how difficult the drug-development business is," says Barbara S. Schilberg, CEO of BioAdvance. "We look forward to seeing the members of the team find new opportunities in the region where they can use their entrepreneurial talent." They did find new opportunities as well. Three former Protez executives quickly moved on to launch a life sciences company called VenatoRx Pharmaceuticals, which began work on new antibacterial compounds to treat infections funded by a three-year, multi-million-dollar grant from the National Institutes of Health. Christopher Cashman was named to the board of directors of JDP Therapeutics, Inc., a specialty pharmaceutical company.

1. How typical is Protez's success in raising capital? How typical is the eventual demise of Protez even after it had been successful raising funds and negotiated an exit through its sale to Novartis? Explain.

2. Venture capitalists often view failure in previous deals to be at least as valuable as success when looking to invest in the teams that are leading entrepreneurial start-ups. Do you agree with this perspective? Explain. Discuss why the former Protez executives were able to move on so quickly to new endeavors after Protez was shut down.

3. Do you consider the demise of Protez to be a failure? Explain.

*Sources:* Jim Melloan, "Mr. Cashman, You're On," *Inc.*, July 1, 2005, *www.inc.com/magazine/20050701/cashman.html*; "Protez Pharmaceuticals to Be Acquired by Novartis," *Drugs.com*, June 4, 2008, *www.drugs.com/news/protez-pharmaceuticals-acquired-novartis-8264.html*; John George, "Novartis shutters Protez," *Philadelphia Business*, September 20, 2010, *www.bizjournals.com/philadelphia/stories/2010/09/20/story2.html?page=all*; "JDP Therapeutics, Inc. Appoints Christopher M. Cashman to Board of Directors," *Prweb.com*, June 18, 2010, *www.prweb.com/releases/JDP_Therapeutics/Pharmaceuticals/prweb4159384.htm*.

## Venture Capital Companies

**Venture capital companies** (VCs) are private, for-profit organizations that raise money from investors to purchase equity positions in young businesses that they believe have high growth and high profit potential, producing annual returns of 500 to 1,000 percent over five to seven years. More than 400 active venture capital firms operate across the United States today, investing in promising small companies in a variety of industries (see Figure 16.4). Companies in California's Silicon Valley and Boston's high-tech corridor attract 38 percent of all venture capital investments.[43] Some colleges and universities across the nation have created venture funds designated to invest in promising businesses started by their students, alumni, faculty, and others. Business schools at the University of Michigan, the University of Maryland, the University of North Dakota, Cornell University, and, in a joint venture called the University Venture Fund, the University of Pennsylvania, Brigham Young University, the University of Utah, and Westminster College operate venture capital funds that are comanaged by students, faculty, and sometimes professional venture capitalists.[44]

Venture capital firms, which provide funding for only 38 out of 100,000 of all start-up companies in the United States, have invested billions of dollars in high-potential small companies over the years, including notable businesses such as Apple Computer, Microsoft Inc., Intel, and Outback Steakhouse.[45] Although companies in high-tech industries such as communications, computer software, energy, medical care, and biotechnology are the most popular targets of venture capital, a company with extraordinary growth prospects has the potential to attract venture capital, whatever its industry.

**4.**

Describe the types of businesses that attract venture capital financing and explain the criteria that venture capitalists use to decide on their investments.

**FIGURE 16.4**

**Venture Capital Funding**

*Source:* Based on PriceWaterhouse-Coopers Money Tree Report.

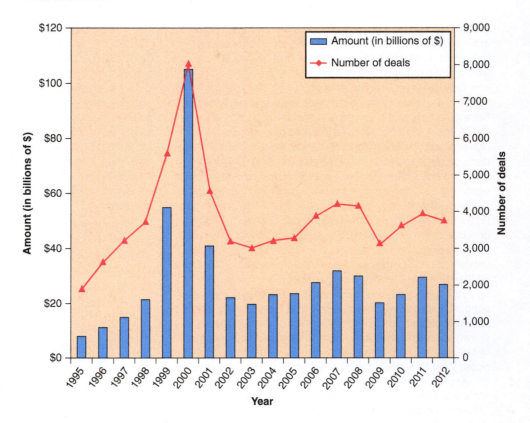

The opinions of entrepreneurs and venture capitalists often differ when it comes to the growth potential for their start-up businesses. The typical venture capital firm receives about 1,100 business plans each year. "It's rare that an unsolicited business plan shows up on the doorstep and becomes funded," says Bryan Stolle with Mohr Davidow Ventures. "We have large networks of trusted colleagues and advisors, and we have more brought to us through those networks than we can handle or deal with."[46] For every 100 business plans that the average venture capital firm receives, 90 of them are rejected immediately because they do not match the firm's investment criteria or requirements. The firm conducts a thorough due diligence investigation of the remaining 10 companies and typically invests in only one of them. That is only 1 percent of the deals they consider! Undoubtedly, every entrepreneur who submits a business plan to venture capitalists is convinced that their business was worthy of funding, but very few ever see any investment. Table 16.2 offers a humorous look at how venture capitalists decipher the language of sometimes overly optimistic entrepreneurs.

A traditional venture capital firm seeks funding for several separate funds managed within the firm. Investment in the venture funds comes from wealthy individuals, corporations, pension funds, endowments, foundations, and insurance companies. Each fund has a cap for the amount of investment and a defined period of time that the fund will invest in high-potential businesses. As each fund nears the end of its defined time of operation, the venture capital management team seeks to liquidate all investments made from that fund so that the investors in the fund can be paid and realize a return on their initial investment. A few venture capital firms, known as evergreen funds, do not put a defined life on their funds and simply pay out returns to their investors over time as companies they invest in reach an exit event, such as an acquisition or public offering.

## Policies and Investment Strategies

Venture capital firms usually establish stringent policies to govern their overall investment strategies.

**INVESTMENT SIZE AND SCREENING** The average venture capital firm's investment in a small company is $7.2 million. Depending on the size of the venture capital company and its cost structure, minimum investments range from $100,000 to $5 million. Investment ceilings, in effect, do not exist. Most firms seek investments in the $5 million to $25 million range to justify the cost of screening the large number of proposals they receive.

**TABLE 16.2 Deciphering the Language of the Venture Capital Industry**

By nature, entrepreneurs tend to be optimistic. When screening business plans, venture capitalists must make an allowance for entrepreneurial enthusiasm. Here's a dictionary of phrases commonly found in business plans and their accompanying venture capital translations.

*Exploring an acquisition strategy*—Our current products have no market.

*We're on a clear P2P (pathway to profitability)*—We're still years away from earning a profit.

*Basically on plan*—We're expecting a revenue shortfall of 25 percent.

*A challenging year*—Competitors are eating our lunch.

*Considerably ahead of plan*—Hit our plan in one of the last three months.

*Company's underlying strength and resilience*—We still lost money, but look how we cut our losses.

*Core business*—Our product line is obsolete.

*Currently revising budget*—The financial plan is in total chaos.

*Cyclical industry*—We posted a huge loss last year.

*Entrepreneurial CEO*—He is totally uncontrollable, bordering on maniacal.

*Facing challenges*—Our sales continue to slide, and we have no idea why.

*Facing unprecedented economic, political, and structural shifts*—It's a tough world out there, but we're coping the best we can.

*Going to market with a freemium model*—We don't know how we are going to make money, but we are going to start by giving our products away.

*Highly leverageable network*—No longer works but has friends who do.

*Ingredients are there*—Given two years, we might find a workable strategy.

*Investing heavily in research and development*—We're trying desperately to catch the competition.

*Limited downside*—Things can't get much worse.

*Long sales cycle*—Yet to find a customer who likes the product enough to buy it.

*Major opportunity*—It's our last chance.

*Niche strategy*—A small-time player.

*On a manufacturing learning curve*—We can't make the product with positive margins.

*Passive investor*—Someone who phones once a year to see if we're still in business.

*Positive results*—Our losses were less than last year.

*Refocus our efforts*—We've blown our chance, and now we have to fire most of our employees.

*Repositioning the business*—We've recently written off a multi-million-dollar investment.

*Selective investment strategy*—The board is spending more time on yachts than on planes.

*Solid operating performance in a difficult year*—Yes, we lost money and market share, but look how hard we tried.

*Somewhat below plan*—We expect a revenue shortfall of 75 percent.

*Expenses were unexpectedly high*—We grossly overestimated our profit margins.

*Strategic investor*—One who will pay a preposterous price for an equity share in the business.

*Strongest fourth quarter ever*—Don't quibble over the losses in the first three quarters.

*Sufficient opportunity to market this product no longer exists*—Nobody will buy the thing.

*Too early to tell*—Results to date have been grim.

*A team of skilled, motivated, and dedicated people*—We've laid off most of our staff, and those who are left should be glad they still have jobs.

*Turnaround opportunity*—It's a lost cause.

*Unique*—We have no more than six strong competitors.

*Volume sensitive*—Our company has massive fixed costs.

*We don't measure our success by financial results*—We are not sure whether this business model will ever result in profits.

*We're iterating like crazy right now*—We are no closer to a real product now than we were six months ago.

*Window of opportunity*—Without more money fast, this company is dead.

*Work closely with the management*—We talk to them on the phone once a month.

*A year in which we confronted challenges*—At least we know the questions even if we haven't got the answers.

*Sources:* Based on Scott Herhold, "When CEOs Blow Smoke," *e-company*, May 2001, pp. 125–127; Suzanne McGee, "A Devil's Dictionary of Financing," *Wall Street Journal*, June 12, 2000, p. C13; John F. Budd Jr., "Cracking the CEO's Code," *Wall Street Journal*, March 27, 1995, p. A20; "Venture-Speak Defined," *Teleconnect*, October 1990, p. 42; Cynthia E. Griffin, "Figuratively Speaking," *Entrepreneur*, August 1999, p. 26; Tom Ruhe, "The Most Pervasive, Pernicious Offense," *Wall Street Journal*, July 10, 2013, http://blogs.wsj.com/accelerators/2013/07/10/thom-ruhe-the-most-pervasisve-pernicious-offense/; Kevin Rouse, "Actual Things That Came Out of Humans Mouths at Day One of TechCrunch's Disrupt SF Conference," *New York*, September 9, 2012, http://nymag.com/daily/intelligencer/2012/09/techcrunch-jargon.html.

In a normal year, VCs invest in only 3,700 of the nearly 28 million small businesses in the United States! The venture capital screening process is *extremely* rigorous. The typical venture capital company invests in less than 1 percent of the business plans it receives. According to the Global Entrepreneurship Monitor, only about one in 1,000 businesses in the United States attract venture capital during its existence.[47] The average time required to close a venture capital deal is 80 days, slightly longer than the time required to complete angel financing.[48]

**OWNERSHIP** Most venture capitalists prefer to purchase ownership in a small business through common stock or convertible preferred stock. Although some venture capital firms purchase less than 50 percent of a company's stock, it is not uncommon for others to buy a controlling share of a company, leaving its founders with a minority share of ownership. Entrepreneurs must weigh the positive aspects of receiving needed financing against the disadvantages of owning a smaller share of the business. "Would you rather have 80 percent of a company worth zero or 50 percent of a company worth $500 million?" asks a partner at one venture capital firm.[49]

**STAGE OF INVESTMENT** Most venture capital firms invest in companies that are either in the early stages of development (called early-stage investing) or in the rapid-growth phase (called expansion-stage investing); few invest in businesses that are only in the start-up phase (see Figure 16.5). According to the Global Entrepreneurship Monitor, only one in 10,000 entrepreneurs worldwide receive venture capital funding at start-up.[50] About 97 percent of all venture capital goes to businesses in the early, expansion, and later stages.[51] Most venture capital firms do not make just a single investment in a company. Instead, they invest in a company over time across several stages, where their investments often total $10 to $25 million or more.

**ENTREPRENEURIAL PROFILE: Bismarck Lepe, Belsasar Lepe, and Sean Knapp: Ooyala** Ooyala allows creators of video content to deliver their content across all types of formats and devices. Founded by a group of former Google employees, Bismarck Lepe, Belsasar Lepe, and Sean Knapp, Ooyala received $77 million in funding from venture capitalists over five major rounds of

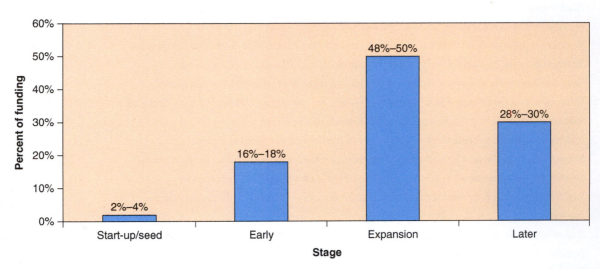

**Start-up/seed** – This is the initial stage in which companies are just beginning to develop their ideas into products or services. Typically, these businesses have been in existence less than 18 months and are not yet fully operational.

**Early stage** – These companies are refining their initial products or services in pilot tests or in the market. Even though the product or service is available commercially, it typically generates little or no revenue. These companies have been in business less than three years.

**Expansion stage** – These companies' products or services are commercially available and are producing strong revenue growth. Businesses at this stage may not be generating a profit yet, however.

**Later stage** – These companies' products or services are widely available and are producing ongoing revenue and, in most cases, positive cash flow. Businesses at this stage are more likely to be generating a profit. Sometimes these businesses are spin-offs of already established successful private companies.

**FIGURE 16.5**

**Venture Capital Funding by Stage**

financing. Sierra Ventures, a California venture capital firm, was the first venture capital firm to invest in Ooyala and was the only investor in Ooyala's Series B investment round of financing. Sierra Ventures also participated with other venture capital firms in all three subsequent rounds of fund-raising that followed its initial investment. Mark Fernandes, managing director of Sierra Ventures, serves on the board of Ooyala as a representative of Sierra's sizable investment in the company.

**ADVICE AND CONTACTS** In addition to the money they invest, venture capital companies provide the small companies in their portfolios with management advice and access to valuable networks of contacts of suppliers, employees, customers, and other sources of capital. One of their goals in doing so is to strengthen the companies in which they have invested, thereby increasing their value. Former National Basketball Association star David Robinson's company, Admiral Capital Group, recently invested in Centerplate, an event catering business that focuses on sports venues, and plans to use his network of contacts to help the company expand, particularly into professional basketball events.[52]

**CONTROL** In exchange for the financing they receive from venture capitalists, entrepreneurs must give up a portion of their businesses, sometimes surrendering a majority interest and control of its operations. Most venture capitalists prefer to let the founding team of managers employ its skills to operate a business *if* they are capable of managing its growth. However, most venture capitalists join the boards of directors of the companies they invest in or send in new managers or a new management team to protect their investments. The term sheets they negotiate often include the right to determine the CEO. In other words, venture capitalists are *not* passive investors! A study of new business ventures by Harvard professor Noam Wasserman reports that only half of the companies' founders were in the CEO position after three years and that the likelihood of a founder being replaced increases significantly after a company receives capital from outside investors, especially venture capitalists.[53]

Some venture capitalists serve only as financial and managerial advisers, whereas others take an active role managing the company—recruiting employees, providing sales leads, choosing attorneys and advertising agencies, and making daily decisions—which can cause friction with the founding entrepreneur(s). The majority of these active venture capitalists say they are forced to step in because the existing management team lacked the talent and experience to achieve growth targets.

**ENTREPRENEURIAL PROFILE: Jason Brown: Cotton Comfort** Jason Brown was just 26 years old when a group of venture capitalists offered to invest $5 million in Cotton Comfort, a small chain of clothing stores he had launched at age 20. He gave up 46 percent of his company in exchange for the capital investment and the investors' experience. Brown says that the venture capitalists pushed him to grow the company too fast, and when the economy slowed, Cotton Comfort ran out of cash and folded. "I was too young to know that my job was to listen to what the VCs had to say but to know that they had only a chapter out of the novel of understanding about my business," says Brown, who went on to launch two more successful businesses.[54]

As Jason Brown learned, a common complaint among entrepreneurs who accept venture capital is that their investors push too hard for too much growth too soon.

**INVESTMENT PREFERENCES** Venture capital funds are larger, more professional, and more specialized than they were 20 years ago. As the industry grows, more venture capital funds are focusing their investments in niches—everything from information technology services to biotechnology. Most venture capital firms also focus their investments within a specific geographic region. Some will invest in almost any industry but prefer companies in particular stages, including the start-up phase. Traditionally, however, only about 2 to 4 percent of the companies receiving venture capital financing are in the start-up (seed) stage, when entrepreneurs are forming a company or developing a product or service. Most of the start-up businesses that attract venture capital today are in the biotechnology, software, energy, and medical device industries.

**COMPETENT MANAGEMENT** Attracting venture capital takes more than just a good idea; it requires a management team that can transform an idea into a viable business. Venture capitalists believe in the adage "Money follows management." To them, the most important ingredient in the success of any business is the ability of the management team. They are looking for a team of managers who share the same vision for the company and have the experience and the ability to make that vision a reality. "The team is more important than the idea," says Jason Mendelson of the venture capital firm The Foundry Group. "Always has been, always will be. So you can have the cure for cancer but a crummy team, and it will fail. If you have a great team and kind of a medium idea, you can usually do OK."[55] From a venture capitalist's perspective, the ideal management team has experience, managerial skills, commitment, and the ability to build effective teams.

**COMPETITIVE EDGE** Investors are searching for some factor that will enable a small business to set itself apart from its competitors. This distinctive competence may range from an innovative product or service that satisfies unmet customer needs to a unique marketing or research-and-development approach. It must be something with the potential to make the business a leader in its field.

**GROWTH INDUSTRY** Hot industries attract profits—and venture capital. Most venture capital funds focus their searches for prospects in rapidly expanding fields because they believe the profit potential is greater in these areas. Venture capital firms are most interested in young companies in industries that have enough growth potential to become at least $100 million businesses within three to five years. Venture capitalists know that most of the businesses they invest in will flop, so their winners have to be *big* winners.

**VIABLE EXIT STRATEGY** Venture capitalists not only look for promising companies with the ability to dominate a market, but they also want to see a plan for a feasible exit strategy, ideally to be executed within three to five years. A recent study by the National Venture Capital Association reports that the number one factor that venture capitalists say creates a nonfavorable environment for venture capital is difficulty achieving successful exits.[56] Venture capital firms realize the return on their investments when the companies they invest in either make an initial public offering or sell out to a larger business. For instance, Dell recently purchased Equallogic, a company that developed highly efficient network data storage solutions for businesses, for $1.4 billion, creating a handsome payout for Equallogic's three founders and the venture capital companies that had invested in it. Paula Long, Peter Haden, and Paul Koning started Equallogic in the Haden's attic in 2003, and within three years, its sales had increased from $492,000 to more than $100 million.[57] "If your vision is to run a company and hand it over to your kids, VC funding is out of the question," says Mike Simon, CEO of LogMeIn, Inc., a remote software company that has raised $20 million in capital, half of it from venture capital firms.[58]

**INTANGIBLE FACTORS** Some other important factors considered in the screening process are not easily measured; they are the intuitive, intangible factors the venture capitalist detects by gut feeling. This feeling might be the result of the small firm's solid sense of direction, its strategic planning process, the experience and chemistry of its management team, or a number of other factors.

**ENTREPRENEURIAL PROFILE: Ofer Raz and Hod Fleishman: GreenRoad** In 2003, Ofer Raz and Hod Fleishman launched GreenRoad, a company whose software helps companies and individuals improve driving habits, reduce collisions, improve fuel economy, and reduce vehicle operating costs, and quickly realized that their company would require a significant investment to capitalize on the market opportunity that lay before it. The duo estimates that the cost of vehicle crashes in the United States alone is $235 billion and that 90 percent of all crashes are the result of driver behavior. Their subscription-based service provides real-time feedback and driver coaching and is designed to reduce those costs and save lives by improving drivers' behavior. Customers who use the company's technology (including Ryder, Ericsson, TMobile, LeFleur Transportation, and others) typically reduce the number of crashes by 50 percent and fuel consumption and emissions by up to 10 percent. After pitching their idea to many venture capital firms, Raz and Fleishman have received $42.5 million in financing across three rounds. Venture capitalists were impressed with the experience of the management team that Raz and Fleishman had assembled, the company's fast growth, and the size of the potential market. Representatives from the venture capital firms hold five of GreenRoad's board seats, but the company has the capital it needs to support continued research and development, product innovation, and a more concentrated sales and marketing effort.[59]

Despite its many benefits, venture capital is not suitable for every entrepreneur. "VC money comes at a price," warns one entrepreneur. "Before boarding a one-way money train, ask yourself if this is the best route for your business and personal desires, because investors are like department stores the day after Christmas—they expect a lot of returns in a short period of time."[60]

# CHAPTER 17
# Sources of Debt Financing

## Learning Objectives

**On completion of this chapter, you will be able to:**

1. Describe the various sources of debt capital and the advantages and disadvantages of each.

2. Explain the types of financing available from nonbank sources of credit.

3. Identify the sources of government financial assistance and the loan programs these agencies offer.

4. Describe the various loan programs available from the Small Business Administration.

5. Discuss state and local economic development programs.

6. Discuss other possible methods of financing growth.

7. Explain how to avoid becoming a victim of a loan scam.

*One of the greatest disservices you can do a man is to lend him money that he can't pay back.*

—Jesse Holman Jones

*Live within your means, never be in debt, and by husbanding your money you can always lay it out well.*

—Andrew Jackson

Rather than adding another owner to a business, as happens with an equity investment, **debt financing** is a temporary supply of funding with a contractual obligation to repay with interest. Debt financing, particularly from institutional lenders, is not a source of funding that is available to most start-ups. Most new entrepreneurs must rely on their own funding sources and on the business itself to generate capital internally. As a business begins to grow, its retained earnings, the portion of its profits that the owner keeps in the company, is the least expensive source of capital. Funding a growing business by its own cash flow is known as **organic funding**.

Small companies in the United States that are beyond the start-up phase rely heavily on debt capital to feed their growing businesses when internally generated cash flow is insufficient. The Small Business Administration estimates that lenders make $600 billion worth of loans of less than $1 million to small companies each year. Add to that amount loans from family members and friends and credit card borrowing, and total small business borrowing approaches $1 trillion a year. Lenders of capital are more numerous than investors, but small business loans can be just as difficult (if not more difficult) to obtain, especially given the recent turbulence in the financial markets. The amount that banks lend to small businesses has decreased by more than $100 billion since the credit crunch began in 2008.[1] A recent survey by the National Federation of Independent Businesses (NFIB) reports that small business owners have adjusted to the tighter lending conditions that began in 2008. Only 7 percent of small business owners say that their credit needs are not being met. However, the survey also found that 64 percent of small business owners did not apply for a loan of any kind. The NFIB also reports that small business owners continue to be cautious about capital spending, building up inventory, and hiring.[2] A survey by the New York Federal Reserve reports that entrepreneurs seeking small loans have had the hardest time finding banks willing to lend to them since 2008.[3] When entrepreneurs are not making capital investments, building inventory, and hiring, their companies do not grow, and the entire economy suffers. Table 17.1 displays the increase in small business debt leading up to the fiscal crisis that began in 2008 and decrease in small business debt during the subsequent years.

**ENTREPRENEURIAL PROFILE: Summit Kumar: Summit Telecom** Summit Kumar, president of Summit Telecom, a telecommunications company in Hicksville, New York, had success in the past getting credit for his business, but that changed when the economy entered a prolonged recession in 2008. "The banks are not lending. They claim they are, but they're not," says Kumar. "I got a line of credit from a bank five years ago, and I paid it back. Now the same bank says I'm 'high-risk business' and turns me away." Because of the weak economy and the resulting tightening of

### TABLE 17.1 Value of Small Business Loans

| Commercial real estate | 2006 | 2007 | 2008 | 2009 | 2010 | 2011 | 2012 |
|---|---|---|---|---|---|---|---|
| $100,000 or less | $28.7 | $28.4 | $28.5 | $26.4 | $22.1 | $19.8 | $18.0 |
| $100,000 to $250,000 | $65.0 | $68.8 | $68.6 | $67.1 | $59.6 | $56.4 | $53.1 |
| $250,000 to $1 million | $244.2 | $262.8 | $277.9 | $278.4 | $260.5 | $247.8 | $236.7 |
| Total commercial real estate | $337.9 | $360.1 | $375.0 | $372.0 | $342.3 | $323.9 | $307.8 |
| **Commercial and industrial** | | | | | | | |
| $100,000 or less | $117.0 | $131.2 | $141.7 | $134.5 | $137.2 | $119.8 | $120.2 |
| $100,000 to $250,000 | $54.7 | $57.5 | $57.3 | $55.1 | $51.2 | $47.3 | $46.3 |
| $250,000 to $1 million | $124.6 | $138.0 | $137.4 | $133.6 | $121.6 | $116.0 | $113.5 |
| Total commercial and industrial | $296.3 | $326.7 | $336.4 | $323.2 | $309.9 | $283.0 | $280.1 |
| **Total small** | | | | | | | |
| **Business loans ($1 million or less)** | $634.2 | $686.8 | $711.5 | $695.2 | $652.2 | $606.9 | $587.8 |

*Source:* Federal Deposit Insurance Corporation, Statistics on Depository Institutions.

credit by the banking industry, Kumar's business has suffered. Because he was unable to secure bank financing, Kumar had to turn to a cash advance company that would give him $50,000 but expected him to pay back $75,000 six months later.[4]

Although entrepreneurs who borrow capital maintain complete ownership of their businesses, they must carry the debt as a liability on the balance sheet and repay it with interest at some point in the future. In addition, because lenders consider small businesses to be greater risks than bigger corporate customers, small companies must pay higher interest rates because of the risk-return trade-off—the higher the risk, the greater the return demanded. Most small firms pay the **prime rate**, the interest rate banks charge their most creditworthy customers, *plus* two or more percentage points. Still, the cost of debt financing often is lower than that of equity financing because debt financing does not require entrepreneurs to dilute their ownership interest in the company.

The need for debt capital can arise from a number of sources, but financial experts identify the following reasons business owners should consider borrowing money:[5]

- *Increasing the company's workforce and/or inventory to boost sales.* Sufficient working capital is the fuel that feeds a company's growth.
- *Gaining market share.* Businesses often need extra capital as their customer bases expand and they incur the added expense of extending credit to customers.
- *Purchasing new equipment.* Financing new equipment that can improve productivity, increase quality, and lower operating expenses often takes more capital than a growing company can generate internally.
- *Refinancing existing debt.* As companies become more established, they can negotiate more favorable borrowing terms compared to their start-up days, when entrepreneurs take whatever money they can get at whatever rate they can get. Replacing high-interest loans with loans carrying lower interest rates can improve cash flow significantly.
- *Taking advantage of cash discounts.* Suppliers sometimes offer discounts to customers who pay their invoices early. As you will learn in Chapter 19, business owners should take advantage of cash discounts in most cases.
- *Buying the building in which the business is located.* Many entrepreneurs start out renting the buildings that house their businesses; however, if location is crucial to their success, it may be wise to purchase the location.
- *Establishing a relationship with a lender.* If a business has never borrowed money, taking out a loan and developing a good repayment and credit history can pave the way for future financing. Smart business owners know that bankers who understand their businesses play an integral role in their companies' ultimate success.
- *Retiring debt held by a "nonrelationship" creditor.* Entrepreneurs find that lenders who have no real interest in their companies' long-term success or do not understand their businesses can be extremely difficult to work with. They prefer to borrow money from lenders who are willing to help them achieve their business mission and goals.
- *Foreseeing a downturn in business.* Establishing access to financing before a business slowdown hits insulates a company from a serious cash crisis and protects it from failure.

Entrepreneurs seeking debt capital face an astounding range of credit options varying greatly in complexity, availability, and flexibility. Not all of these sources of debt capital are equally favorable, however. By understanding the various sources of capital—both commercial and government lenders—and their characteristics, entrepreneurs can greatly increase the chances of obtaining a loan.

Figure 17.1 shows the financing strategies that small business owners use for their companies. We now turn to the various sources of debt capital.

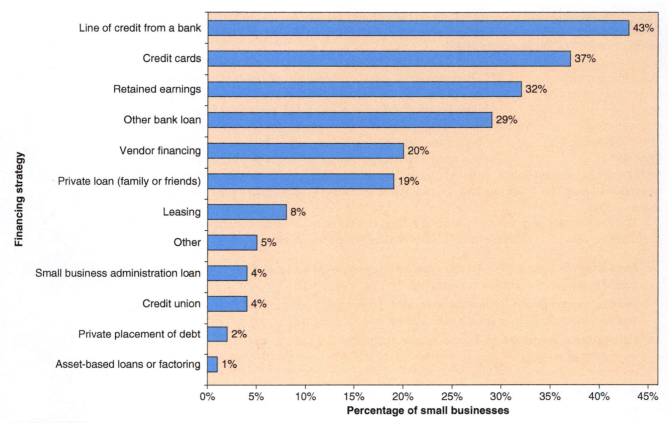

## FIGURE 17.1

### Small Business Financing Strategies

*Source:* Based on National Small Business Association, 2012 Small Business Access to Capital Survey, p. 4.

## In the Entrepreneurial Spotlight

# A Tale of Two Borrowers

### Busboys and Poets

Andy Shallal has been able to succeed in a market where most competitors are failing. Shallal owns several popular Busboys and Poets bookstore cafés in the Washington metropolitan area.

Shallal emigrated from Iraq at the age of 11 when Saddam Hussein assumed power. His experiences early in life led him to be a social activist and to bring his values into his business. Shallal was inspired to keep neighborhood development true to the history of an area. His vision was to make Busboys and Poets a neighborhood gathering place where people of different incomes, races, and identities could come together to exchange ideas. His first restaurant proved to be highly successful and allowed him to open two additional locations, each with its own identity tied to the local neighborhood.

Busboys and Poets cafés generate revenue of more than $14 million a year, but when Shallal wanted to borrow money to expand two of his highly successful stores, he could not find a bank that would lend him the money. One bank said that it would lend him the money personally if he used his house as

collateral. Shallal wanted a true business loan that uses the assets of the business as collateral. All of the banks he talked to turned him down, saying that they are not giving these types of business loans due to weak economic conditions.

Unless he secures some form of financing, he will be unable to expand his business to accommodate the growing demand for his concept.

### All American Real Estate

James and Sonia Conlin opened All American Real Estate NNY LLC after James had retired from the army after 21 years of service. James had been working in real estate on nights and weekends for a few years leading up to his retirement. The Conlins needed funding to help renovate the office space for the new real estate firm they founded. The building, which had been built in 1850, had not been updated since the 1950s. They decided to try to take out a loan to update the decor, straighten a few of the walls, and put up new drywall. The Conlins had estimated start-up cost to be about $120,000. The Conlins' loan request fit within the limits of the Small Business Administration's (SBA's) Patriot Express program, which they qualified for because of James's service in the army. The couple developed a business plan with the help of their local Small Business Development Center and submitted it to Community Bank.

"It's the fastest turnaround time for SBA approval because the loans are given preference," says Jennifer L. Huttemann-Kall, vice president at Community Bank, who was the loan officer for the loan. "SBA's pipeline has been so full that it is a huge help."

Patriot Express loans generally offer the lowest interest rates available for business loans and are guaranteed by the SBA for 85 percent for a loan the size that the Conlins were seeking for their new business.

"The fact that he is a retired military officer said a lot to me," says Huttemann-Kall. "And when I asked them for things, they were on it instantly—that says a lot about their business ethic. They have immediate access to soldiers and contacts at other bases."

The bank approved the loan, and the Conlins now operate their successful firm, along with two agents they have added to the company's staff, out of the renovated space made possible by the Patriot Express loan.

1. One of these businesses received a bank loan, and the other did not. Describe the differences between the two companies that led to one entrepreneur's receiving the financing he needed and the other one's failing to qualify for a loan.

2. What steps would you have recommended to Andy Shallal to increase the probability of qualifying for a loan?

3. Suppose that Shallal had approached you for help after being turned down by three banks. What other sources of capital would you have suggested he use?

*Sources:* Based on "Thriving Small Businesses Still Struggling to Get Loans," *CNN.com*, December 12, 2009, *www.cnn.com/2009/POLITICS/12/12/obama.bank.lenders/index.html*; "Andy Shallal: Restaurateur, Busboys and Poets," *Washington Business Journal*, April 6, 2009, *www.bizjournals.com/washington/stories/2009/04/06/tidbits21.html*; Nancy Madsen, "Two Catch 'Patriot Express'," *Watertown Daily Times*, December 19, 2010, *www.watertowndailytimes.com/article/20101219/NEWS03/312199981*.

## Sources of Debt Capital

### Commercial Banks

Commercial banks are the very heart of the financial market, providing the greatest number and variety of loans to small businesses. Commercial banks provide 50 percent of the dollar value of all loans to small businesses.[6] For small business owners, banks are lenders of *first* resort, especially as their companies grow. The typical loan amount is small; more than 88 percent of all small business bank loans are for less than $100,000. The average micro-business loan (those less than $100,000) is $6,820, and the average small business loan (those between $100,000 and $1 million) is $245,775.[7]

**1.**

Describe the various sources of debt capital and the advantages and disadvantages of each.

**ENTREPRENEURIAL PROFILE: Allison O'Neill: Bundle**  Allison O'Neill, founder of an infant and toddler clothing and accessory store in Soho, New York, called Bundle, launched her business just as the banking crisis and resulting recession began in 2008. Bundle is the type of business that tends to do well in any economy, which was one of the reasons she started the business. "One of the things I found was that, of all of retail, children's clothing is the most recession proof," says O'Neill. In addition to having cash on hand, O'Neill made sure to bootstrap her business start-up. "Everyone who works here wears many hats . . . everyone who's here is a sales associate, and a social media manager, and a marketing manager, and an inventory specialist." However, even with her frugal management and healthy personal finances, O'Neill had trouble securing a business loan. "I had great credit," she says. "I had basically four times the amount of a loan I was looking for, in my brokerage account, and they didn't care. They were just like, we're not taking any risks on start-ups."[8]

Allison O'Neill, founder of Bundle, a children's clothing store in Soho, New York.
*Source:* Allison O'Neill.

As Allison O'Neill learned, banks tend to be conservative in their lending practices and prefer to make loans to established small businesses rather than to high-risk start-ups. Small companies that are less than three years old are as much as 50 percent less likely to receive loans or lines of credit than older, more established businesses.[9] Because start-ups are so risky, bankers prefer to make loans to companies that have successful track records. Banks are concerned with a small company's operating past and scrutinize its records to project its position in the immediate future. They also want proof of a company's stability and its ability to generate adequate cash flow that ensures repayment of the loan. If they do make loans to a start-up venture, banks like to see significant investment from the owner, sufficient cash flow to repay the loan, personal guarantees by the entrepreneurs to repay the loan if the business cannot, and the ample collateral (such as compensating balances) to secure it. Bankers also prefer to see more than one source of repayment on loans to small businesses. An SBA guarantee to insure the business loan is another avenue to make a small business "bankable." Entrepreneurs should not overlook small community banks (those with less than $10 billion in assets) for loans. These small banks, which make up 98.7 percent of U.S. banking institutions, account for almost 52 percent of the dollar volume of all small business loans.[10] They also tend to be "small business friendly" and are more likely than their larger counterparts to customize the terms of their loans to the particular needs of small businesses, offering, for example, flexible payment terms to match the seasonal pattern of a company's cash flow or interest-only payments until a piece of equipment begins generating revenue. Small community banks approve 49.5 percent of small business loan requests, far higher than the small business loan approval rate of 17.3 percent at large banks.[11]

When evaluating a loan application, banks focus on a company's capacity to create positive cash flow because they know that's where the money to repay their loans will come from. The first question in most bankers' minds when reviewing an entrepreneur's business plan is "Can this business generate sufficient cash to repay the loan?" Even though they rely on personal guarantees and collateral to secure their loans, the last thing banks want is for a borrower to default, forcing them to sell the collateral (often at "fire sale" prices) and use the proceeds to pay off the loan or seek repayment from the owners individually. That's why bankers stress cash flow when analyzing a loan request, and that's why it is so difficult for a business start-up to find bank financing. "Cash is more important than your mother," jokes one experienced borrower.[12]

Banks, as well as many other lenders, also require that entrepreneurs sign personal guarantees for any loans they make to the small businesses. By making a personal loan guarantee, an entrepreneur pledges that he or she will be personally liable for repaying the loan in the event that the business itself cannot repay the loan. Recall from Chapter 5 that in the eyes of the law, a sole proprietor or a general partner and the business are one and the same; therefore, for them, personal loan guarantees are redundant. However, because the owners of S corporations, corporations, and limited liability companies are separate from their businesses, they are not automatically responsible for the company's debts. Once the owners of these businesses sign personal loan guarantees, however, they become liable for their companies' loans. (It is as if these individuals have "cosigned" the loan with the business.) Working with a partner, Rosalind Resnick launched NetCreations, an Internet marketing company, using money from various sources, including bank loans. The bank required the partners to provide personal guarantees of $2 million for NetCreation's line of credit and equipment leases. The personal guarantees remained in effect until the company went public.[13]

## Short-Term Loans

Short-term loans, extended for less than one year, are the most common type of commercial loan banks make to small companies. These funds typically are used to replenish the working capital account to finance the purchase of inventory, finance credit sales to customers, take advantage of cash discounts, or handle other short-term needs. As a result, an owner repays the loan after converting inventory and receivables into cash. There are several types of short-term loans.

**COMMERCIAL LOANS (OR TRADITIONAL BANK LOANS)** The basic short-term loan is the commercial bank's specialty. Business owners typically repay the loan, which often is unsecured because secured loans are much more expensive to administer and maintain, as a lump sum within three to six months. In other words, the bank grants a loan to the small business owner without requiring him or her to pledge any specific collateral to support the loan in case of default. The owner repays the total amount of the loan at maturity. Sometimes the interest due on the loan is prepaid—deducted from the total amount borrowed. Until a small business is able to prove its financial strength and liquidity (cash flow) to the bank's satisfaction, it will probably not qualify for this kind of commercial loan.

**LINES OF CREDIT** One of the most common requests entrepreneurs make of banks is to establish a **line of credit**, a short-term loan with a preset limit that provides much-needed cash flow for day-to-day operations. With a commercial (or revolving) line of credit, business owners can borrow up to the predetermined ceiling at any time during the year quickly and conveniently by writing themselves a loan. Banks set up lines of credit that are renewable for anywhere from 90 days to several years, and they usually limit the open line of credit to 40 to 50 percent of a firm's present working capital, although they may lend more for highly seasonal businesses. Bankers may require a company to rest its line of credit during the year, maintaining a zero balance, as proof that the line of credit is not a perpetual crutch. Like commercial loans, lines of credit can be secured or unsecured. Small lines of credit often are unsecured, and large ones usually are secured by accounts receivable, inventory, equipment, or other business assets.

## TABLE 17.2 How Large Should Your Line of Credit Be?

Determining how large a small company's line of credit should be is an important step for a growing business. As a company's sales grow, so will its inventory and accounts receivable balances, both of which tie up valuable cash. To avoid experiencing a cash crisis, many growing companies rely on a line of credit. How large should that line of credit be? The following formulas will help you answer that question:

$$\frac{\text{Average collection}}{\text{period ratio}} + \frac{\text{Average inventory}}{\text{turnover ratio}} - \frac{\text{Average payable}}{\text{period ratio}} = \frac{\text{Cash}}{\text{flow cycle}}$$

Cash flow cycle $\times$ Average daily sales $-$ Forecasted annual profit $=$ Line of credit requirement

**Example:** Suppose that Laramie Corporation has an average collection period ratio of 49 days and an average inventory turnover ratio of 53 days. The company's average payable period is 39 days, its annual sales are $5,800,000, and its net profit margin is 6.5 percent. What size line of credit should Laramie seek?

| | |
|---|---:|
| Average collection period ratio | 49 days |
| Average inventory turnover ratio | 53 days |
| Total | 102 days |
| Minus average payable period ratio | 39 days |
| Cash flow cycle | 63 days |
| Annual sales | $5,800,000 |
| Average daily sales (annual sales ÷ 365 days) | $15,890 |
| Cash flow cycle | 63 days |
| Times average daily sales | $15,890 |
| Equals | $1,001,096 |
| Minus forecasted profit (annual sales × net profit margin) | 377,000 |
| Equals line of credit requirement | $624,096 |

Laramie Corporation should seek a line of credit of $624,000.

*Source:* Based on George M. Dawson, "It Figures," *Entrepreneur Start-Ups*, December 2000, p. 27.

A business typically pays a small handling fee (1 to 2 percent of the maximum amount of credit) plus interest on the amount borrowed—usually at least prime plus one or more point. Because banks prefer the security of established businesses, securing a line of credit can be difficult for some small companies, especially new ones. A study by the National Federation of Independent Businesses reports that the most difficult type of loan for small business owners to obtain is a line of credit; only 37.6 percent of the small companies that applied received one.[14] Table 17.2 shows one method for determining how large a line of credit a small company should seek.

**ENTREPRENEURIAL PROFILE: David Meinert: Onto Entertainment, Big Mario's New York Style Pizza, and The 5 Point Cafe** David Meinert has been a successful restaurateur in Seattle for many years. He owns Onto Entertainment, Big Mario's New York Style Pizza, and The 5 Point Cafe. Meinert has strong credit and profitable businesses that generate $2 million in annual revenue. Meinert recently switched to Chase Bank after 12 years banking with Bank of America. He chose large banks because of the convenience of their many locations. Meinert applied for a $50,000 line of credit from Chase. However, the bank denied his loan application within 12 hours. "It was insulting and made no sense, even to the banker. And there was no one to even talk to about it," Meinert says. After Chase Bank denied his request for the line of credit, Meinert decided to switch all of his business accounts to Seattle Bank, a small community bank. Meinert has been happy with his choice. "For one, I had a conversation with the executive vice president. That's a huge difference in itself," he said. "The higher-ups of the bank are able to come to my restaurant and have a meal. They are customers of my business, and I'm a customer of theirs. It's also just the whole vibe of knowing people and knowing they're decision makers of the bank. I've been able to meet board members of the bank. They're local people who live here, work here—they're going to be at this bank for a long time."[15]

**FLOOR PLANNING** Floor planning is a form of financing frequently employed by retailers of "big-ticket items" that are easily distinguishable from one another (usually by serial number), such as automobiles, recreational vehicles, boats, and major appliances. For example, Thrifty Car Sales makes a floor plan financing program available to the network of franchised dealers who sell the used cars that are taken out of service from its Thrifty Car Rental system. Bombadier Capital, the provider of the floor plan, finances Thrifty Car Sales dealers' purchases of automobiles from Thrifty Car Rental and maintains a security interest in each car in the order by holding its title as collateral.[16] Dealers pay interest on the loan monthly and repay the principal as the cars are sold. The longer a floor-planned item sits in inventory, the more it costs a business owner in interest expense. Banks and other floor planners often discourage retailers from using their money without authorization by performing spot checks to verify prompt repayment of the principal as items are sold.

### Intermediate- and Long-Term Loans

Banks primarily are lenders of short-term capital to small businesses, although they will make certain intermediate- and long-term loans. Intermediate- and long-term loans are extended for one year or longer and are normally used to increase fixed- and growth-capital balances. Commercial banks grant these loans for starting a business, constructing a plant, purchasing real estate and equipment, and other long-term investments. Loan repayments are normally made monthly or quarterly.

**TERM LOANS** Another common type of loan banks make to small businesses is a **term loan**. Typically unsecured, banks grant these loans to businesses whose past operating history suggests a high probability of repayment. Some banks make only secured term loans, however. Term loans impose restrictions (called **covenants**) on the business decisions an entrepreneur makes concerning the company's operations. For instance, a term loan may set limits on owners' salaries, prohibit further borrowing without the bank's approval, or maintain certain financial ratios. Term loans often have a balloon feature, which means that after three to five years, the full amount of principal is due before the amortized payments fully repay the loan. If the business is in good financial shape, the bank will renew the loan with the business, charging new loan fees and possibly changing the interest rate. An entrepreneur must understand all of the terms attached to a loan before accepting it.

**INSTALLMENT LOANS** These loans are made to small firms for purchasing equipment, facilities, real estate, and other fixed assets. When financing equipment, a bank usually lends the small business from 60 to 80 percent of the equipment's value in return for a security interest in the equipment. The loan's amortization schedule typically coincides with the length of the equipment's usable life. When financing real estate (commercial mortgages), banks typically lend up to 75 to 80 percent of the property's value and allow a lengthier repayment schedule of 10 to 30 years.

The accompanying "Lessons from the Street-Smart Entrepreneur" feature describes how small business owners can maintain positive relationships with their bankers.

 **Lessons from the Street-Smart Entrepreneur**

# How to Maintain a Positive Relationship with Your Banker

Too often, entrepreneurs communicate with their bankers only when they find themselves in a tight spot and needing money. Unfortunately, that's not the best way to manage a working relationship with a bank. "Businesspeople have a responsibility to train their bankers in their businesses," says one lending adviser. "A good banker will stay close to the business, and a good business will stay close to the banker." A good banking relationship has the power to influence in a significant way the success of a small business.

How can business owners develop and maintain a positive relationship with their bankers? The first step is picking the right bank and the right banker. Some banks are not enthusiastic about making small business loans, and others target small businesses as their primary customers. It's a good idea to visit several banks—both small community banks and large national banks—and talk with a commercial loan officer about your banking needs and the bank's products and services. After finding the right banker, an entrepreneur must focus on maintaining effective *communication*. The best strategy is to keep bankers informed—*of both good news and bad*.

Jamey Bennett is CEO of LightWedge, which manufactures specialty reading lights. Bennett has always made it a practice to keep his banker informed. For example, when Bennett decided to replace his CFO, he immediately let his banker know. A change in key personnel, especially one that deals with the finances of the business, is important to a banker. "I don't think anybody likes surprises, especially your banker," says Bennett. "If something material to the business changes significantly, I keep [my banker] abreast of it." Sometimes the news a business owner has to share with a banker is not good news. "Right now, we're feeling pretty good about where we are in respect to managing our cash, but some of our customers are not in such good shape," says Bennett. "We've got one of our biggest customers looking very, very sick right now." In this case, Bennett's banker was able to offer some advice that helped fend off a possible major problem later. His banker recommended that he purchase credit insurance to help protect against a loss resulting from a large accounts receivable becoming uncollectable. "I need him as a partner in what we're doing today and what I expect to be doing tomorrow," says Bennett.

What else can entrepreneurs do to manage their banking relationships?

***Understand the factors that influence a banker's decision to lend money.*** Bankers *want* to lend money to businesses; that's how they generate a profit. However, they want to lend money to businesses they believe offer a very high probability of repaying their loans on time. Bankers look for companies that are good credit risks and that have clear plans for success.

***Invite the banker to visit your company.*** An on-site visit gives the banker the chance to see exactly what a company does and how it does it. It's also a great opportunity to show the bank where and how the business puts the bank's money to use.

***Make a good impression.*** A company's physical appearance can go a long way toward making either a positive or a negative impression on a banker. Lenders appreciate clean, safe, orderly work environments and view sloppily maintained facilities (such as spills, leaks, and unnecessary clutter) as negatives.

***Send customer mailings to the banker as well.*** "Besides the numbers, we try to give our bankers a sense of our vision for the business," says Mitchell Goldstone, president of Thirty-Minute Photos Etc. Goldstone sends customer mailings to his bankers "so they know we're thinking about opportunities to generate money."

***Send the banker samples of new products.*** "I try to make my banker feel as if he's a partner," says Drew Santin, president of a product development company. "Whenever we get a new machine, I go out of my way to show the banker what it does."

***Show off your employees.*** Bankers know that one of the most important components of building a successful company is a dedicated team of capable employees. Giving bankers the opportunity to visit with employees and ask them questions while touring a company can help alleviate fears that they are pumping their money into a high-risk "one-person show."

***Know your company's assets.*** Almost always interested in collateral, bankers want to judge the quality of your company's assets—property, equipment, inventory, accounts receivable, and others. Be sure to point them out. "As you walk the lender through your business," says one experienced banker, "it's always a good idea to identify assets the banker might not think of."

***Be prepared to personally guarantee any loans the bank makes to your business.*** Even though many business owners choose the corporate or limited liability company forms of ownership for their limited liability benefits, some are surprised when a banker asks them to make personal guarantees on business loans. It's a common practice, especially on small business loans.

***Keep your business plan up to date and make sure your banker gets a copy of it.*** Bankers lend money to companies that can demonstrate that they will use the money wisely and productively. They also want to make sure that the company offers a high probability of repayment. The best way to provide bankers with that assurance is with a solid business plan.

***Know how much money you need and how you will repay it.*** When a banker asks, "How much money do you need?" the correct answer is not "How much can I get?"

1. What advantages do entrepreneurs gain by communicating openly with their bankers?

2. What are the consequences of an entrepreneur's failing to communicate effectively with a banker?

*Sources:* Based on Kasey Wehrum, "How to Get Chummy with Your Banker," *Inc.*, April 1, 2009, *www.inc.com/magazine/20090401/finance-buddy-can-you-spare-a-loan.html*; Emily Maltby, "Uptick Catches Entrepreneurs by Surprise," *Wall Street Journal*, December 8, 2009, p. B7; Keith Lowe, "Keep Your Banker Informed," *Entrepreneur*, April 1, 2002, *www.entrepreneur.com/article/0,4621,298380,00.html*; David Worrell, "Attacking a Loan," *Entrepreneur*, July 2002, *www.entrepreneur.com/article/52678*; Maggie Overfelt, "How to Raise Cash During Crunch Time," *FSB*, March 2001, pp. 35–36; Joan Pryde, "Lending a Hand with Financing," *Nation's Business*, January 1998, pp. 53–59; Joseph W. May, "Be Frank with Your Bank," *Profit*, November/December 1996, pp. 54–55; "They'll Up Your Credit If . . .," *Inc.*, April 1994, p. 99; Jane Easter Bahls, "Borrower Beware," *Entrepreneur*, April 1994, p. 97; Jacquelyn Lynn, "You Can Bank on It," *Business Start-Ups*, August 1996, pp. 56–61; Stephanie Barlow, "Buddy System," *Entrepreneur*, March 1997, pp. 121–125; Carlye Adler, "Secrets from the Vault," *FSB*, June 2001, p. 33.

# Nonbank Sources of Debt Capital

Although they are usually the first stop for entrepreneurs in search of debt capital, banks are not the only lending game in town. We now turn our attention to other sources of debt capital that entrepreneurs can tap to feed their cash-hungry companies.

**2.**
Explain the types of financing available from nonbank sources of credit.

## Asset-Based Lenders

**Asset-based lenders**, which are usually smaller commercial banks, commercial finance companies, or specialty lenders, allow small businesses to borrow money by pledging otherwise idle assets, such as accounts receivable, inventory, or purchase orders, as collateral. This form

"It's a mistake to borrow money from a friend."

of financing works especially well for manufacturers, wholesalers, distributors, and other companies with significant stocks of inventory, accounts receivable, equipment, real estate, or other assets. Even unprofitable companies whose income statements could not convince loan officers to make traditional loans can get asset-based loans. Because asset-based lenders focus more on collateral than on a company's credit rating, these cash-poor but asset-rich companies can use normally unproductive assets—accounts receivable, inventory, equipment, and purchase orders—to finance rapid growth and the cash crises that often accompany it.

Like banks, asset-based lenders consider a company's cash flow, but they are much more interested in the quality of the assets pledged as collateral. The amount a small business can borrow through asset-based lending depends on the **advance rate**, the percentage of an asset's value that a lender will lend. For example, a company pledging $100,000 of accounts receivable might negotiate a 70 percent advance rate and qualify for a $70,000 asset-based loan. Advance rates can vary dramatically depending on the quality of the assets pledged and the lender. Because inventory is an illiquid asset (i.e., hard to sell), the advance rate on inventory-based loans is quite low, usually 10 to 50 percent. Steven Melick, CEO of the Sycamore Group, an e-business software developer, gets an 85 percent advance rate on his company's loans from GE Capital by pledging high-quality accounts receivable as collateral.[17] The most common types of asset-based financing are discounting accounts receivable and inventory financing.

**DISCOUNTING ACCOUNTS RECEIVABLE** The most common form of secured credit is accounts receivable financing. Under this arrangement, a small business pledges its accounts receivable as collateral; in return, the lender advances a loan against the value of approved accounts receivable. The amount of the loan tendered is not equal to the face value of the accounts receivable, however. Even though the lender screens the firm's accounts and accepts only qualified receivables, it makes an allowance for the risk involved because some receivables will be uncollectible. A small business usually can borrow an amount equal to 55 to 85 percent of its receivables, depending on their quality. Generally, lenders accept only accounts receivable that are current.

**ENTREPRENEURIAL PROFILE: Robison Oil** Robison Oil, of Elmsford, New York, sells and services heating, ventilating, and air-conditioning equipment and is a supplier of heating oil, natural gas, electricity, biofuel, and green energy alternatives to both residential and commercial customers. Robison Oil is a highly seasonal business, sometimes showing a loss at the end of the year. As a result, its bank was unable to provide the company with financing. Instead, Robison Oil turned to an asset-based lender, which was willing to extend an $11 million term loan and $18 million line of credit based on the strength of its long-term customer accounts. "We thought about going back to a bank, but we have found this segment of lenders much more flexible," said Dan Singer, copresident of Robison. The total financing costs of the asset-based lender were about one percentage point more than the company would have gotten with a traditional bank loan.[18]

**INVENTORY FINANCING** A small business can use its inventory of raw materials, work in process, and finished goods to secure loan. If the business defaults on the loan, the lender claims the firm's inventory, sells it, and uses the proceeds to satisfy the loan (assuming that the bank's claim is superior to the claims of other creditors). Because inventory usually is not a highly liquid asset and its value can be difficult to determine, lenders are willing to lend only a portion of its worth, usually no more than 50 percent of the inventory's value. Most asset-based lenders avoid inventory-only deals; they prefer to make loans backed by inventory *and* more secure accounts receivable.

**PURCHASE ORDER LOANS** Small companies that receive orders from large customers can use those purchase orders as collateral for loans. The customer places an order with a small business that needs financing to fill the order. The small business pledges the future payment from the order as security for the loan, and the lender verifies the credit rating of the customer (not the small business) before granting the short-term loan, which often carries annual rates of 40 percent or more. Borrowers usually repay the loan within 60 days.

**ENTREPRENEURIAL PROFILE: George Tarrab: Slider the UNscooter** George Tarrab is the founder of Slider the UNscooter, which sells ride-on scooters out of its operation located in Simi Valley, California. When the economic downturn came in 2008, Tarrab was unable to convince banks to extend credit to his business. The Slider's sales were strong and growing faster than the company's cash flow could handle. Tarrab had several orders from major customers. To fulfill the orders, Tarrab turned to purchase order financing and was able to secure more than $200,000 in funding to get the scooters made. Although the purchase order lender charged substantial fees, Tarrab was able to get his orders filled and keep his growing business moving ahead.[19]

Asset-based financing is a powerful tool. A small business that could obtain a $1 million line of credit with a bank would be able to borrow as much as $3 million by using accounts receivable as collateral. It is also an efficient method of borrowing because entrepreneurs borrow only the money they need when they need it. Asset-based borrowing is an excellent just-in-time method of borrowing, one that often is available within just hours. As bank credit has tightened in the aftermath of the financial crisis of 2008, the popularity of asset-based lending has increased.

Asset-based loans are more expensive than traditional bank loans because of the cost of originating and maintaining them and the higher risk involved. To ensure the quality of the assets supporting the loans they make, lenders often monitor borrowers' assets, perhaps as often as weekly, making paperwork requirements on these loans intimidating, especially to first-time borrowers. Rates usually run from two to eight percentage points (or more) above the prime rate. Because of this rate differential, small business owners should not use asset-based loans over the long term; their goal should be to establish their credit through asset-based financing and then to move up to a line of credit.

## Trade Credit

Because of its ready availability, trade credit is an extremely important source of financing to most entrepreneurs. In fact, 60 percent of small businesses use trade credit as a source of financing.[20] Trade credit involves convincing vendors and suppliers to sell goods and services without requiring payment up front. When banks refuse to lend money to a small business because they see it as a poor credit risk, an entrepreneur may be able to turn to trade credit for capital. Getting vendors to extend credit in the form of delayed payments (e.g., "net 30" credit terms) usually is much easier for small businesses than obtaining bank financing. Essentially, a company receiving trade credit from a supplier gets a short-term, interest-free loan for the amount of the goods purchased.

Vendors and suppliers usually are willing to finance a small business owner's purchase of goods from 20 to 90 days, interest free. The key to maintaining trade credit as a source of funds is establishing a consistent and reliable payment history with every vendor.

**ENTREPRENEURIAL PROFILE: Ed and Jennifer Foy: eFashion Solutions** In 2000, Ed and Jennifer Foy started eFashion Solutions, a company that provides e-commerce solutions for well-known companies in the apparel, entertainment, and specialty retail industries, in Secaucus, New Jersey. The company provides a full range of services, including purchasing, merchandising,

Web site design, marketing, business intelligence, customer service, order management, and order fulfillment for its clients. As their company grew, the Foys raised $24 million in equity capital and used a variety of traditional bank financing to support its operations. When the company's regular lender shut off access to credit because of the financial crisis, eFashion Solutions began using trade credit from its vendors. eFashions Solutions has been able to negotiate "net 60" credit terms with some vendors but takes advantage of cash discounts (more on these in Chapter 19) from other vendors that range from 1 to 10 percent for early payment.[21]

## Equipment Suppliers

Most equipment suppliers encourage business owners to purchase their equipment by offering to finance the purchase over time. This method of financing is similar to trade credit but with slightly different terms. Usually, equipment vendors offer reasonable credit terms with only a modest down payment and the balance financed over the life of the equipment (often several years). In some cases, the vendor repurchases equipment for salvage value at the end of its useful life and offers the business owner another credit agreement on new equipment. Start-up companies often use trade credit from equipment suppliers to purchase equipment and fixtures such as counters, display cases, refrigeration units, machinery, and the like. It pays to scrutinize vendors' credit terms, however; they may be less attractive than those of other lenders.

## Commercial Finance Companies

When denied bank loans, small business owners often look to commercial finance companies for the same types of loan. Commercial finance companies are second only to banks in making loans to small businesses and, unlike their conservative counterparts, are willing to tolerate more risk in their loan portfolios.[22] For instance, Chris Lehnes, a top manager at CIT Small Business Lending, says that his company regularly makes loans to small businesses with debt to equity ratios of 10:1 (10 times as much debt as equity), a situation that would send most bankers scurrying back to their vaults.[23] Of course, like banks, finance companies' primary consideration is collecting their loans, but finance companies tend to rely more on obtaining a security interest in some type of collateral, given the higher risk loans that make up their portfolios. Because commercial finance companies depend on collateral to recover most of their losses, they do not always require a complete set of financial projections of future operations as most banks do. However, this does *not* mean that they neglect to evaluate carefully a company's financial position, especially its cash balance, before making a loan. "We're looking at the projected cash flow—the ability of the business to repay us," says CIT's Lehnes. "We put a lot of weight on what the business has done in the past couple of years."[24]

Approximately 150 large commercial finance companies, such as UPS Capital, GE Capital Solutions, CIT Small Business Lending, and others, make a variety of loans to small companies, ranging from asset-based loans and business leases to construction and Small Business Administration-guaranteed loans. Dubbed "the Wal-Marts of finance," commercial finance companies usually offer many of the same credit options as commercial banks do, including intermediate- and long-term loans for real estate and fixed assets as well as short-term loans and lines of credit. P.C. Richard & Son, one of the oldest private, family-owned appliance and consumer electronics retailers in the United States, uses GE Capital to provide inventory financing to offer a large selection of products to its customers. Based on inventory turnover and cash flow, GE Capital terms are often more flexible than those that a manufacturer can provide, allowing P.C. Richard to account for seasonal variation and to act quickly on new opportunities, such as the introduction of the new Apple iPad. In an era when many regional and national competitors have suffered, P.C. Richard has not just survived but thrived, generating robust Internet sales and expanding the number of its stores by 15 percent. Since 2009, P.C. Richard has opened 10 new showrooms.[25]

Finance companies offer small business borrowers faster turnaround times, longer repayment schedules, and more flexible payment plans than traditional lenders, all valuable benefits to cash-hungry small companies. However, because their loans are subject to more risks, finance companies charge higher interest rates than commercial banks (usually at least prime plus 2 percent). Their most common methods of providing credit to small businesses are asset based—accounts receivable financing and inventory loans. Rates on loans from commercial finance companies are higher than those at banks—as high as 15 to 30 percent (including fees), depending on the risk a particular business presents and the quality of the assets involved. Because many of the loans they make are secured by collateral (usually the business equipment, vehicle, real estate, or inventory purchased with the loan), finance companies often impose more onerous reporting requirements, sometimes requiring weekly (or even daily) information on a small company's inventory levels or accounts receivable balances. However, entrepreneurs who cannot secure financing from traditional lenders because of their short track records, less-than-perfect credit ratings, or fluctuating earnings often find the loans they need at commercial finance companies.

## Stock Brokerage Houses

Stockbrokers also make loans, and many of them offer loans to their customers at lower interest rates than banks. These **margin loans** carry lower rates because the collateral supporting them—the stocks and bonds in the customer's portfolio—is of high quality and is highly liquid. Moreover, brokerage firms make it easy to borrow. Usually, brokers set up a line of credit for their customers when they open a brokerage account. To tap that line of credit, a customer simply writes a check or uses a debit card. Typically, there is no fixed repayment schedule for a margin loan; the debt can remain outstanding indefinitely as long as the market value of the borrower's portfolio of collateral meets minimum requirements. Aspiring entrepreneurs can borrow up to 50 percent of the value of their stock portfolios, up to 70 percent of their bond portfolios, and up to 90 percent of the value of their government securities.

There is risk involved in using stocks and bonds as collateral on a loan. Brokers typically require a 30 percent cushion on margin loans. If the value of the borrower's portfolio declines, the broker can make a **margin call**—that is, the broker can call the loan in and require the borrower to provide more cash and securities as collateral. Swings in the stock market may translate into margin calls for many entrepreneurs, requiring them to repay a significant portion of their loan balances within a matter of days—or hours. If an account lacks adequate collateral, the broker can sell off the customer's portfolio to pay off the loan.

## Insurance Companies

For many small businesses, life insurance companies can be an important source of business capital. Insurance companies offer two basic types of loans: policy loans and mortgage loans. **Policy loans** are extended on the basis of the amount of money paid through premiums into the insurance policy; with a policy loan, a business owner serves as his or her own bank, borrowing against the money accumulated in the investment portion of an insurance policy. It usually takes about two years for an insurance policy to accumulate enough cash surrender value to justify a loan against it. Once he or she accumulates cash value in a policy, an entrepreneur may borrow up to 95 percent of that value for any length of time. Interest is levied annually, but the entrepreneur determines the repayment rate, or repayment may be deferred indefinitely. However, the amount of insurance coverage is reduced by the amount of the loan. Policy loans typically offer very favorable interest rates, sometimes below the prime rate. Only insurance policies that build cash value—that is, combine a savings plan with insurance coverage—offer the option of borrowing. These include whole life (permanent insurance), variable life, universal life, and many corporate-owned life insurance policies. Term life insurance, which offers only pure insurance coverage, provides no borrowing capacity.

Insurance companies make **mortgage loans** on a long-term basis on real property worth a minimum of $500,000. They are based primarily on the value of the real property being purchased. The insurance company extends loans of up to 75 or 80 percent of the real estate's value and allows a lengthy repayment schedule over 25 or 30 years so that payments do not strain the firm's cash flows excessively. Many large real estate developments, such as shopping malls, office buildings, and theme parks, rely on mortgage loans from insurance companies.

## Credit Unions

**Credit unions**, nonprofit financial cooperatives that promote saving and provide loans to their members, are best known for making consumer and car loans. However, many are also willing to lend money to their members to launch businesses, especially since many banks have restricted loans to higher-risk start-ups. The first credit union in the United States was chartered in New Hampshire in 1909.[26] Today, more than 7,500 federally and state-chartered credit unions operate in the United States, and many of them make business loans, usually in smaller amounts than commercial banks typically make. In fact, the average credit union business loan is $217,000, but some credit unions have made business loans in the millions of dollars.[27] Because credit unions are exempt from federal income tax, they often charge lower interest rates than banks.

Credit unions make $12 billion in small business loans to their members each year.[28] However, the small business loan approval rate at credit unions has slipped from 57.6 percent in 2012 to 45 percent today, which is slightly below the 49.5 percent small business loan approval rate at small banks.[29] Lending practices at credit unions are very much like those at banks, but they are subject to constraints that banks are not. For instance, credit unions are prohibited from making business loans that total more than 12.25 percent of their assets (a cap that Congress is considering increasing to 27.5 percent). Recent changes in legislation, however, exempt certain business loans from that limitation. In another move that favors entrepreneurs, the SBA recently opened its 7(a) loan programs to credit unions, providing even more avenues for entrepreneurs seeking financing.

Increasingly, entrepreneurs are turning to credit unions to finance their businesses' capital needs.

**ENTREPRENEURIAL PROFILE: Muhammad Abdullah: Legacy Business Group** Muhammad Abdullah, who owns Legacy Business Group in Des Moines, Iowa, needed a line of credit to fill large orders from customers of his safety and medical-supplies business. Abdullah's company took a $60,000 order for fire extinguishers, fire extinguisher cabinets, whiteboards, bike racks, and other items needed for an Armed Forces Readiness Center in Middletown, Iowa. However, Abdullah was unable to get financing from a bank to fill the order, so he turned to a credit union where he was able to get a $25,000 line of credit. "It's not the normal way, but I guess I've been doing business with credit unions personally for a good while," says Abdullah. "They said they want to work with small business, and so we called them."[30]

Entrepreneurs searching for a credit union near them can use the online database at the Credit Union National Association's Web site at *www.cuna.org*.

### Bonds

Bonds, which are corporate IOUs, have always been a popular source of debt financing for large companies, but few small business owners realize that they can also tap this valuable source of capital. Although the smallest businesses are not viable candidates for issuing bonds, a growing number of small companies are finding the funding they need through bonds when banks and other lenders say no. Because of the costs involved, issuing bonds usually is best suited for companies generating annual sales between $5 million and $30 million and having capital requirements between $1.5 million and $10 million. Although they can help small companies raise much needed capital, bonds have certain disadvantages. The issuing company must follow the same regulations that govern businesses selling stock to public investors. Even if the bond issue is private, the company must register the offering and file periodic reports with the Securities and Exchange Commission.

**Convertible bonds**, bonds that give the buyer the option of converting the debt to equity by purchasing the company's stock at a fixed price in the future, have become more popular for small companies. In exchange for offering the option to convert the bond into stock, the small company issuing the convertible bonds gets the benefit of paying a lower interest rate on the bond than on a traditional bond. The conversion feature is valuable only if the company is successful and the value of its stock increases over time.

Small manufacturers needing money for fixed assets with long repayment schedules have access to an attractive, relatively inexpensive source of funds in **industrial development revenue bonds** (IDRBs). To issue IDRBs, a company must work with a local or state government agency that issues the bonds on the company's behalf. The company, not the government entity, is responsible for repaying both the principal and the interest on the bond issue. Typically, the amount of money companies that issue IDRBs seek to raise is at least $2 million, but some small manufacturers have raised as little as $500,000 using a mini-bond program that offers a simple application process and short closing times. Each government entity has its own criteria, such as job creation, expansion of the tax base, and others, that companies must meet to be eligible to issue mini-bonds. NGK Spark Plugs, a company founded in 1936 that produces spark plugs for automotive, marine, motorcycle, and small engines, issued $15 million in industrial revenue bonds with the help of the West Virginia Economic Development Agency to build an 85,000-square-foot factory in Sissonville, West Virginia, that created 80 new jobs.[31]

To open IDRBs up to even smaller companies, some states pool the industrial bonds of several small companies too small to make an issue alone. By joining together to issue composite industrial bonds, companies can reduce their issuing fees and attract a greater number of investors. The issuing companies typically pay lower interest rates than they would on conventional bank loans.

### Private Placements

A private placement involves selling debt to one or a small number of investors, usually insurance companies or pension funds. Private placement debt is a hybrid between a conventional loan and a bond. At its heart, it is a bond, but its terms are tailored to the borrower's individual needs, as a loan would be.

Privately placed securities offer several advantages over standard bank loans. First, they usually carry fixed interest rates rather than the variable rates banks often charge. Second, the maturity of private placements is longer than most bank loans: 15 years rather than five. Private placements do not require hiring expensive investment bankers. Finally, because private investors can afford to take greater risks than banks, they are willing to finance deals for fledgling small companies.

## Small Business Investment Companies

The Small Business Investment Company program was started after Russia's successful launch of the first space satellite, *Sputnik*, in 1958. Its goal was to accelerate the American position in the space race by funding high technology start-ups. Created by the 1958 Small Business Investment Act, **small business investment companies** (SBICs) are privately owned financial institutions that are licensed and regulated by the Small Business Administration. In a unique public–private partnership, the more than 300 SBICs operating across the United States use a combination of private capital and federally guaranteed debt to provide long-term venture capital to small businesses. In other words, SBICs operate like any other venture capital firm, but, unlike traditional venture capital firms, they use private capital and borrowed government funds to provide both debt and equity financing to small businesses.

In 2012, SBICs provided $3.1 billion in financing to more than 1,000 small businesses, which was a 17 percent increase from 2011 and an 83 percent increase from 2010.[32] Most SBICs prefer later-round financing to funding raw start-ups. Because of changes in their financial structure made a few years ago, however, SBICs now are better equipped to invest in start-up companies. On average, about 30 percent of SBIC investments go to companies that are less than two years old.[33] Funding from SBICs helped launch companies such as Apple, Costco, Intel, Federal Express, Whole Foods Market, Outback Steakhouse, and Build-a-Bear Workshop.

SBICs must be capitalized privately with a minimum of $5 million, at which point they qualify for up to $3 in long-term SBA loans for every dollar of private capital invested in small businesses up to the ceiling of $150 million. As a general rule, SBICs may provide financial assistance only to small businesses with a net worth of less than $18 million and average after-tax earnings of $6 million during their past two years. However, employment and total annual sales standards vary from industry to industry. SBICs are limited to a maximum investment or loan amount of 30 percent of their private capital to a single client.

Operating as government-backed venture capitalists, SBICs provide both debt and equity financing to small businesses. Because of SBA regulations affecting the financing arrangements an SBIC can offer, many SBICs extend their investments as loans with an option to convert the debt instrument into an equity interest later. Most SBIC loans are between $100,000 and $5 million, and although interest rates can be higher than traditional bank loans, the loan term is longer than most banks allow. Borrowers typically do not make installment payments; instead, the loan is due at an agreed-on date. When they make equity investments, SBICs are prohibited from obtaining a controlling interest in the companies in which they invest (no more than 49 percent ownership). SBICs must invest at least 25 percent of their capital in smaller businesses, which are defined by the SBA as those with tangible net worth of less than $6 million and an average of $2 million in net income over the previous two years at the time of investment. The most common methods of SBIC financing are straight debt instruments (49 percent), debt instruments combined with equity features (35 percent), and equity-only investments (16 percent).[34]

**ENTREPRENEURIAL PROFILE: Terry, Barry and Mark Awalt: JSI Store Fixtures** In 1991, brothers Terry and Barry Awalt started JSI Store Fixtures, a company that provides a wide range of attractive and functional fixtures to retail stores, in the family basement in Milo, Maine, with a single table saw. Brother Mark joined the family business in 1997. JSI grew quickly, and the Awalts moved the business into a nearby former shoe factory. In 2006, the Awalts had the opportunity to acquire a regional competitor and needed capital to invest in more efficient, more productive equipment. Champlain Capital Partners, an SBIC with offices in Boston and San Francisco, provided the necessary capital to fuel the company's growth. Since receiving equity financing from the SBIC, JSI Store Fixtures has doubled its customer base, more than doubled its workforce, and now generates nearly $40 million in annual sales.[35]

## Federally Sponsored Programs

**3.**

Identify the sources of government financial assistance and the loan programs these agencies offer.

Federally sponsored lending programs have suffered from budget reductions in the past several years. Current trends suggest that the federal government is reducing its involvement in the lending business, but many programs are still active, and some are actually growing.

### Economic Development Administration

The Economic Development Administration (EDA), a branch of the Commerce Department, offers a variety of grants, loan guarantees, and loans to create new businesses and to expand existing businesses in areas with below-average income and high unemployment. Focusing on economically distressed communities, the EDA finances long-term investment projects needed to stimulate economic growth and to create jobs by making loan guarantees. The EDA guarantees up to 80 percent of business loans between $750,000 and $10 million. Entrepreneurs apply for loans through private lenders for whom an EDA loan guarantee significantly reduces the risk of lending. Start-up companies must supply 15 percent of the guaranteed amount in the form of equity, and established businesses must make equity investments of at least 15 percent of the guaranteed amount. Small businesses can use the loan proceeds in a variety of ways, including supplementing working capital and purchasing equipment and buying land and renovating buildings.

EDA business loans are designed to help replenish economically distressed areas by creating or expanding small businesses that provide employment opportunities in local communities. To qualify for a loan, a business must be located in a disadvantaged area, and its presence must directly benefit local residents. Some communities experiencing high unemployment or suffering from the effects of devastating natural disasters have received EDA Revolving Loan Fund grants to create loan pools for local small businesses. The EDA provides grants to a state or local agency that makes loans at or below market rates to small companies that otherwise have difficulty borrowing money. Loan amounts range from as little as $1,000 to more than $1 million, but most fall between $25,000 and $175,000.

**ENTREPRENEURIAL PROFILE: Ralph Cole: West Wind Farm** Ralph Cole wants to make his West Wind Farm located in Morgan County, Tennessee, 100 percent sustainable. Cole secured a rural development grant from the U.S. Department of Agriculture and a loan from Pathway Lending to install a new dairy barn with 120 solar panels housed on the south-facing roof. "Sunlight is free, effortless to harvest, and does not harm the environment," says Cole, "So you have to ask, 'why not?'" The solar energy collected at West Wind is sent back to the Tennessee Valley Authority's electricity grid. Cole estimates that the solar panels will pay for West Wind Farm's current electricity consumption and eventually will pay for themselves.[36]

The EDA's Trade Adjustment Assistance for Firms (TAAF) program provides financial assistance to manufacturers and service companies that have been affected adversely by imports. Small companies work with one of 11 Trade Adjustment Assistance Centers to receive grants that cover 50 to 75 percent of the cost of projects (from market research and product development to e-commerce and inventory control) that are aimed at improving the company's competitive position. For instance, after Wayne and Mechelle Williams bought a struggling custom door manufacturing company, they used a variety of funding, including a TAAF grant, to bring the company out of bankruptcy and to achieve 700 percent growth in just four years by taking market share back from Chinese competitors.[37]

### Department of Housing and Urban Development

The Department of Housing and Urban Development (HUD) sponsors several loan programs to assist qualified entrepreneurs in raising needed capital. Community Development Block Grants (CDBGs) are extended to cities and towns that, in turn, lend or grant money to entrepreneurs to start small businesses that will strengthen the local economy. Grants are aimed at cities and towns in need of revitalization and economic stimulation. Some grants are used to construct buildings and plants to be leased to entrepreneurs, sometimes with an option to buy. Others are earmarked for revitalizing a crime-ridden area or making start-up loans to entrepreneurs or expansion loans to existing business owners. No ceilings or geographic limitations are placed on CDBG loans and grants, but projects must benefit low- and moderate-income families.

HUD also makes loan guarantees through its Section 108 provision of the Community Block Development Grant program. The agency has funded more than 1,200 projects since its inception in 1978. These loan guarantees allow a community to transform a portion of CDBG funds into federally guaranteed loans large enough to pursue economic revitalization projects that can lead to the renewal of entire town. For instance, the city of Greenville, South Carolina, used Section 108 funds to renovate a public market designed to serve as an anchor in its West End section that was targeted for revitalization. Since its construction, 16 small businesses have located in the market, creating new jobs and stimulating economic growth in the area, and a new stadium modeled after Boston's Fenway Park is home to the local minor league baseball team.[38]

## U.S. Department of Agriculture's Rural Business and Cooperative Program and Business Program

The U.S. Department of Agriculture (USDA) provides financial assistance to certain small businesses through its Rural Business-Cooperative Service (RBS). The RBS program is open to all types of businesses (not just farms) and is designed to create nonfarm employment opportunities in rural areas—those with populations below 50,000 and not adjacent to a city where densities exceed 100 people per square mile. Entrepreneurs in many small towns, especially those with populations below 25,000, are eligible to apply for loans through the RBS program, which makes almost $900 million in loan guarantees each year.

The RBS does make a limited number of direct loans to small businesses, but the majority of its activity is in loan guarantees. Through its Business and Industry Guaranteed Loan Program, the RBS will guarantee as much as 80 percent of a commercial lender's loan up to $25 million (although actual guarantee amounts are almost always far less, usually between $200,000 and $1 million) for qualified applicants. Entrepreneurs apply for loans through private lenders, who view applicants with loan guarantees favorably than because the agency's guarantee reduces the lender's risk dramatically.

To make a loan guarantee, the RBS requires much of the same documentation as most banks and most other loan guarantee programs. Because of its emphasis on developing employment in rural areas, the RBS requires an environmental impact statement describing the jobs created and the effect the business has on the area. The RBS also makes grants available to businesses and communities for the purpose of encouraging small business development and growth.

## Small Business Innovation Research Program

Started as a pilot program by the National Science Foundation in the 1970s, the Small Business Innovation Research (SBIR) program has expanded to 11 federal agencies, ranging from NASA to the Department of Defense. The total SBIR budget across all 11 agencies is more than $2.1 billion annually. These agencies award cash grants or long-term contracts to small companies wanting to initiate or to expand their research-and-development (R&D) efforts. SBIR grants give innovative small companies the opportunity to attract early-stage capital investments *without* having to give up significant equity stakes or taking on burdensome levels of debt.

The SBIR process includes three phases. Phase I (project feasibility) grants, which determine the feasibility and commercial potential of a technology or product (called "proof of concept"), last for up to six months and have a ceiling of $150,000. Phase II (prototype development) grants, designed to develop the concept into a specific technology or product, run for up to 24 months with a ceiling of $1 million. Approximately 40 percent of all Phase II applicants receive funding. Phase III is the commercialization phase, in which the company pursues commercial applications of the R&D conducted in Phases I and II and must use private or non-SBIR federal funding to bring a product to market.

Competition for SBIR funding is intense; only 17 percent of the small companies that apply receive funding. So far, 112,500 SBIR awards totaling more than $26.9 billion (26 percent in Phase I and 74 percent in Phase II) have gone to more than 15,000 small companies, which traditionally have had difficulty competing with big corporations for federal R&D dollars. The government's dollars have been well invested. Nearly 45 percent of small businesses receiving second-phase SBIR awards have achieved commercial success with their products.[39]

**ENTREPRENEURIAL PROFILE: Dr. Jim Stefansic: Pathfinder Therapeutics, Inc.** Pathfinder Therapeutics, Inc., is a medical device company that developed an image-guided surgery system for abdominal surgery that works like a GPS for surgeons. Jim Stefansic, cofounder of Pathfinder Therapeutics, secured four SBIR grants totaling almost $3.4 million from the U.S. Department of Health and Human Services to help support the development of the company's products and supporting software.[40]

## Entrepreneurship in Action

# Where Do We Turn Now?

Tim Erven founded Custom Gaming in 2008 when he was 18 years old. Over the next five years, the company grew to become the leader in rapid-fire controllers for serious gamers. Custom Gaming was not Erven's first entrepreneurial endeavor, however. At the age of 10, Erven started an e-commerce company that sold strategy guides for video games, Pokemon cards, and custom-made skateboards. He was able to use the money from his various ventures to pay his way through college at Drew University in New Jersey.

After five years of operation, Custom Gaming had grown to about 250 orders a week through its Amazon storefront, which generated about $300,000 in revenues. Although the business is profitable, like any small companies Erven has had to struggle with cash flow issues as the company grew. Erven tried to secure a $10,000 loan to help pay for improvements to the Web site and to rent a warehouse to store products. He supplied the banks with tax returns that demonstrated the profitability of his business. However, each of the six banks that he approached for a loan rejected his application. His parents offered to put their home up as collateral for the loan, but banks still rejected his loan application. The bankers expressed concerns about Erven's age and the fact that his business had no credit record. Because he has not been able to get a bank loan, Erven has relied on several personal credits cards to fund cash flow in his business and support its growth.

Erven's loan requests were within the amount that banks typically approve for business loans. However, even though Erven was willing to reduce the amount of the loan below conventional standards, he was unable to secure approval from the banks.

Desperate for funding, Erven has explored nontraditional financing. However, he is concerned about the costs of this type of funding when compared to a bank loan. He has even explored getting equity financing from Chinese investors who are interested in having him move his production to China.

"I'm either going to have to give up a portion of the company or pay a high [interest rate]," says Erven. "I'd be able to get a much lower rate [from a bank], but that's the reality of what I have to do to get the funding."

1. What other sources of financing do you recommend that Erven consider for the financing he needs for his business?

2. Erven had never borrowed money for his business before the opportunity to expand his business and rent warehouse space. What steps can entrepreneurs take to make sure that they have financing arrangements in place when opportunities such as this one arise?

*Sources:* Based on Nick Leiber, "Why Banks Won't Lend to This Guy's Profitable Business," *Bloomberg Businessweek*, February 27, 2012, *www.businessweek.com/articles/2012-02-27/why-banks-wont-lend-to-this-guys-profitable-business*; "Lack of Small Business Loans Driving US Entrepreneurs to China," *Personal Money Network*, May 1, 2012, *personalmoneynetwork.com/moneyblog/2012/03/01/finding-small-business-loans*; Tim Erven, "Tim Erven," *Huffington Post*, July 9, 2012, *www.huffingtonpost.com/tim-erven*.

### The Small Business Technology Transfer Program

The Small Business Technology Transfer (STTR) program complements the SBIR program. Whereas the SBIR focuses on commercially promising ideas that originate in small businesses, the STTR allows small companies to exploit the Small Business Innovation Research (SBIR) program. While SBIR focuses on developing vast reservoir of commercially promising ideas that originate in universities, federally funded R&D centers, and nonprofit research institutions. Researchers at these institutions can join forces with small businesses and can spin off commercially promising ideas while remaining employed at their research institutions. Five federal agencies award grants in two of three phases (up to $100,000 in Phase I and up to $750,000 in Phase II) to these research partnerships. The STTR's annual award budget is approximately $1 billion.

### Small Business Administration

**4.**

Describe the various loan programs available from the Small Business Administration.

The Small Business Administration (SBA) has several programs designed to help finance both start-up and existing small companies that cannot qualify for traditional loans because of their thin asset bases and their high risk of failure. The SBA has come under recent criticism because of the diversion of funding to large corporations that was intended for small businesses. There also have been concerns about mismanagement and waste within the SBA. However, strong political support remains for the agency.

In 2012, the SBA guaranteed more than $30 billion in lending to more than 47,000 small businesses. In the wake of the upheaval in the financial markets in 2008, banks maintain much tighter lending standards, and many small businesses cannot qualify for loans. Although SBA loan programs account for less than 10 percent of all small business lending, tight credit conditions make them all the more important for small companies in search of capital.[41] "SBA programs help newer businesses and businesses that don't have a lot of collateral," says an executive at a bank that makes SBA-guaranteed loans.[42]

The SBA's $102.6 billion loan portfolio makes it the largest single financial backer of small businesses in the nation.[43] The SBA does *not* actually lend money to entrepreneurs directly; instead, entrepreneurs borrow money from a traditional lender (about 4,500 lenders in the United States make SBA loans), and the SBA guarantees a percentage of the loan to the lender in case the borrower defaults. To be eligible for SBA backing, a business must be within the agency's criteria that define a small business. In addition, some types of businesses, such as those engaged in gambling, pyramid sales schemes, or real estate investment, among others, are ineligible for SBA loans. The loan application process can take from between three days to many months, depending on how well prepared the entrepreneur is and which bank is involved. To speed up processing times, the SBA created three "express" programs that give entrepreneurs responses to their loan applications within 36 hours. Table 17.3 summarizes the various SBA lending programs.

## SBA*Express* Loan Programs

**THE SBA*EXPRESS* PROGRAM**  The **SBA*Express* Program**, in which participating lenders use their own loan procedures and applications to make loans of up to $350,000 to small businesses, streamlines the application process for SBA loan guarantees. Because the SBA guarantees up to 50 percent of the loan, banks are often more willing to make small loans to entrepreneurs who might otherwise have difficulty meeting lenders' standards. Lenders can charge up to 6.5 percent above the prime interest rate on SBA*Express* loans below $50,000 and up to 4.5 percent above prime on loans above $50,000. Loan maturities on these loans typically are seven years. Mike Robillard, president of San Antonio Clippers in San Antonio, Texas, used an SBA*Express* loan to add two locations to his Sports Clips hair salon franchise operation. Robillard needed growth capital quickly to secure the best locations, a key to success in his industry. "We had to start laying out money quickly to lock down those locations," he says.[44]

**PATRIOT EXPRESS PROGRAM**  The **Patriot Express loan program** is designed to assist some of the nation's 25 million veterans and their spouses who want to become entrepreneurs. The loan ceiling is $500,000, and the SBA guarantees up to 90 percent (more than the normal 85 percent) of the loan amount in case the borrower defaults. The business must be at least 51 percent owned by an eligible veteran. Like SBA*Express* loans, the turnaround time on loan applications is just 36 hours. Patriot Express loans carry interest rates that range from 2.25 to 4.75 percent above the prime interest rate.

**ENTREPRENEURIAL PROFILE: Jason Kuhn and Evan Kranzley: J&E Technical Services**  Jason Kuhn and Evan Kranzley are partners in J&E Technical Services located in Martinsburg, West Virginia. They needed a business loan to purchase a portable X-ray device for their business to perform nondestructive testing on aircraft. If they could not get financing to purchase the device, they would lose a huge opportunity to obtain a contract with Northrop Grumman Corporation. The business was able to secure an SBA Patriot Express Loan Program through its local BB&T branch bank. "Knowing Jason was a U.S. Navy veteran, and the SBA's Patriot Express program was designed for entrepreneurs with military experience, this was a good fit for J&E," says Matt Coffey, assistant vice president and business services officer for BB&T. "We could see the contract opportunities they had were real, they just needed funding to get started." Since receiving the loan, J&E Technical has expanded into other markets, including testing power-generating wind turbines, petrochemical plants, and pipelines.[45]

## SBA Loan Programs

**SMALL LOAN ADVANTAGE PROGRAM**  The SBA Small Loan Advantage program was launched in 2011. This program expands access to capital for small businesses and entrepreneurs in specifically designated underserved communities. The Small Loan Advantage program allows for loans up to $350,000 with SBA guarantees 85 percent for loans up to $150,000 and 75 percent for those greater than $150,000. Most Small Loan Advantage loans are approved in a matter of minutes through electronic submission.

**COMMUNITY ADVANTAGE**  Community Advantage is a pilot program of the SBA that also is aimed at increasing the number loans in specifically designated underserved communities. This program partners with community-based, mission-focused financial institutions rather than banks and other traditional SBA lenders. Potential new SBA lending partners include Community Development Financial Institutions, SBA's Certified Development Companies, and SBA's nonprofit microlending intermediaries. The maximum loan size for this program is $250,000,

**TABLE 17.3 SBA Loan Program Overview**

| Program | Maximum Loan Amount | Guaranty Percentage | Use of Proceeds | Loan Maturity | Maximum Interest Rates |
|---|---|---|---|---|---|
| Standard 7(a) | $5 million | 85% on loans up to $150,000; 75% on loans between $151,000 and $5 million | Term loan. Purchase land or buildings; expand or renovate existing buildings; acquire equipment and fixtures; make leasehold improvements; working capital; refinance existing debt (in special cases); purchase inventory; establish seasonal line of credit | Working capital, equipment—5 to 10 years; real estate—up to 25 years | Loans of 7 years or less: prime + 2.25%; loans longer than 7 years: prime + 2.75%; for loans of less than $50,000, rates can be up to prime + 4.25% |
| SBA*Express* | $350,000 | 50% | Same as 7(a) loan purposes and revolving line of credit | Same as 7(a) | Loans of $50,000 or less: prime + 6.5%; loans of greater than $50,000: prime + 4.5% |
| Patriot *Express* | $500,000 | Same as 7(a) | Same as SBA*Express* | Same as 7(a) | Same as 7(a) |
| Export *Express* | $500,000 | 90% on loans of $350,000 or less; 75% on loans greater than $350,000 | Proceeds for entering new export market or to expand and existing export market | Same as SBA*Express* | Same as 7(a) |
| CAPLines | $5 million | Same as 7(a) | Working capital needs that are associated with specific contracts | Up to 5 years | Same as 7(a) |
| International Trade | $5 million | 90% up to $4.5 million maximum guarantee | Acquire long-term fixed assets | Up to 25 years | Same as 7(a) |
| Small Loan Advantage Program | $250,000 | Same as 7(a) | Same as 7(a) | Same as 7(a) | Same as 7(a) |
| Community Advantage Program | $250,000 | Same as 7(a) | Same as 7(a) | Same as 7(a) | Prime + 4% |
| Export Working Capital | $5 million (may be combined with International Trade loan) | 90% up to $4.5 million maximum guarantee | Short-term working capital for exporting | Generally 1 year or a single transaction cycle (3-year maximum) | No cap |
| 504 Loans | $5 to $5.5 million, depending on type of business | 40% up to $2.2 million maximum | Long-term, fixed-asset projects, such as constructing new buildings, purchasing and renovating existing buildings, and purchasing equipment and machinery | Equipment—up to 10 years; real estate—up to 20 years | Fixed rate depends on when SBA's debenture-backed loan is sold |
| Microloan | $50,000 | N/A | Purchase machinery and equipment, fixtures, leasehold improvements, financing receivables, or working capital; cannot be used to repay existing debt. | Up to 6 years | Variable; generally between 8% and 13% |

*Source:* "Quick Reference to SBA Loan Guaranty Programs," U.S. Small Business Administration, Washington, DC, *www.sba.gov/sites/default/files/Quick%20Reference%20Guide%20to%20SBA%20Loan%20Guaranty%20Programs.pdf*.

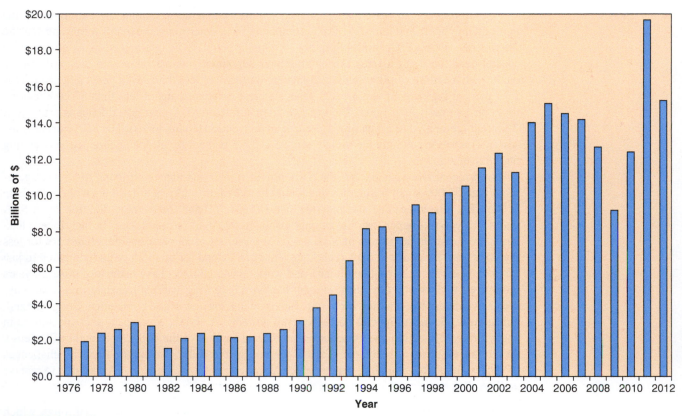

**FIGURE 17.2**

## SBA 7(A) Guaranteed Loans

*Source:* Based on SBA, Quarterly Indicators and Summary of Performance and Financial Information.

with guarantees of 85 percent for loans up to $150,000 and 75 percent for those greater than $150,000. Approval times for most Community Advantage loans are within 5 to 10 days.

**7(A) LOAN GUARANTY PROGRAM** The SBA works with local lenders (both bank and nonbank) to offer a variety of loan programs designed to help entrepreneurs who cannot get capital from traditional sources to gain access to the financing they need to launch and grow their businesses. By far the most popular SBA loan program is the **7(A) loan guaranty program** (see Figure 17.2), which makes partial guarantees on loans up to $5 million to small businesses. Private lenders actually extend these loans to companies, but the SBA guarantees them in case the borrower defaults. Normally, the SBA guarantees 85 percent of loans up to $150,000 and 75 percent of loans above $150,000 up to the loan guarantee ceiling of $3,750,000. Sheila Tucker worked in chain pharmacies for more than twenty years before she secured a 7(a) loan guaranty to open her first pharmacy. Based on that store's success, she obtained a second 7(a) loan guaranty to open a second location.[46]

The SBA does not actually lend any money to small businesses; it merely acts as an insurer, guaranteeing the lender a certain level of repayment in case the borrower defaults on the loan. Because the SBA assumes most of the credit risk, lenders are more willing to consider riskier deals that they normally would refuse.

**ENTREPRENEURIAL PROFILE: Susan Nolte and Marissa Hanley: May Cookie Co.** Susan Nolte founded May Cookie Co. based on her vision to start a business that would create a world of healthy people who eat well, live well, and smile a lot. While attending her first national trade show in 2009, she landed her first big retail account, a national home furnishings store. This account helped Nolte build steady cash flow for her business while pursuing regional distribution through Whole Foods and several other distribution outlets. However, May Cookie Co. needed access to capital to expand and to fulfill its growing orders. Nolte met with an SBA lending specialist at Connecticut Bank & Trust, who helped her secure a $75,000 loan guaranteed by the SBA's 7(a) program to help get her company's natural cookie mixes produced, marketed, and distributed. May Cookie Co. built sales through independent and small-chain specialty stores, Whole Foods, and online. In 2010, Nolte decided to bring her daughter, Marissa Hanley, into the company to handle new business development in California. "I'm really trying to get the word out to the public at large," says Nolte, "But I don't want to grow too fast!"[47]

Marissa Hanley and Susan Nolte of May Cookie Co.
*Source:* May Cookie Co.

Qualifying for an SBA loan guarantee requires cooperation among the entrepreneur, the participating bank, and the SBA. The participating bank determines the loan's terms and sets the interest rate within SBA limits. Contrary to popular belief, SBA guaranteed loans do *not* carry special deals on interest rates. An entrepreneur negotiates interest rates with the participating bank, with a ceiling of prime plus 2.25 percent on loans of less than seven years and prime plus 2.75 percent on loans of seven to 25 years. Interest rates on loans of less than $25,000 can go up to prime plus 4.75 percent. The average interest rate on SBA-guaranteed loans is prime plus 2 percent (compared to prime plus 1 percent on conventional bank loans). The SBA normally assesses a one-time guaranty fee of between 2.5 and 3.5 percent for all loan guarantees, depending on the loan amount.

In a recent five-year period, the SBA provided 7(a) guarantees on loans to an average of more than 51,000 small businesses that would have had difficulty getting loans without the help of the SBA guarantee. The average 7(a) loan is $337,730 and the average duration of an SBA loan is 12 years—longer than the average commercial small business loan. In fact, longer loan terms are a distinct advantage of SBA loans. At least half of all bank business loans are for less than one year. By contrast, SBA real estate loans can extend for up to 25 years (compared to just 10 to 15 years for a conventional loan), and working capital loans have maturities of seven years (compared with two to five years at most banks). These longer terms translate into lower payments, which are better suited for young, fast-growing, cash-strapped companies. Craig Hartzell, a disabled U.S. Army Special Forces veteran, founded Azimuth, a company that specializes in engineering, fabrication and engineering services in support of the U.S. Department of Defense. At its start-up, Hartzell's company lacked the necessary capital to meet the financial challenges of successful contract bidding against much larger competitors, but Hartzell was able to receive an SBA 7(a) guaranteed loan secured through a local lender.[48]

**THE CAPLINE PROGRAM** In addition to its basic 7(a) loan guarantee program (through which the SBA makes about 70 percent of its loans), the SBA provides guarantees on small business loans for start-up, real estate, machinery and equipment, fixtures, working capital, exporting, and restructuring debt through several other methods. About two-thirds of all of the SBA's loan guarantees are for machinery and equipment or working capital. The **CAPLine Program** offers short-term capital to growing companies needing to finance seasonal buildups in inventory or accounts receivable under five separate programs, each with maturities up to five years: seasonal line of credit (provides advances against inventory and accounts receivable to help businesses weather seasonal sales fluctuations), contract line of credit (finances the cost of direct labor and materials costs associated with performing contracts), builder's line of credit (helps small contractors and builders finance labor and materials costs), standard asset-based line of credit (an asset-based revolving line of credit for financing short-term needs), and small asset-based line of credit (an asset-based revolving line of credit up to $200,000). CAPLine is aimed at helping cash-hungry small businesses by giving them a credit line to draw on when they need it. These loans built around lines of credit are what small companies need most because they are so flexible, efficient, and, unfortunately, so hard for small businesses to get from traditional lenders.

**SECTION 504 CERTIFIED DEVELOPMENT COMPANY PROGRAM** Established in 1980, the SBA's Section 504 program is designed to encourage small businesses to purchase fixed assets, expand their facilities, and create jobs (see Figure 17.3). Section 504 loans provide long-term financing at fixed rates to small companies to purchase land, buildings, or equipment. Because they are designated for fixed-asset purchases that provide basic business infrastructure to small companies that otherwise might not qualify, 504 loans are intended to serve as a catalyst for economic development. Three lenders play a role in every 504 loan: a bank, the SBA, and a **certified development company** (CDC). A CDC is a nonprofit organization licensed by the SBA and designed to promote economic growth in local communities. Some 270 CDCs now operate across the United States and make more than 9,000 504 loans in an average year. An entrepreneur generally is required to make a down payment of just 10 percent of the total project cost. The CDC puts up 40 percent at a low, long-term, fixed rate, supported by an SBA loan guarantee in case the entrepreneur defaults. The bank provides at market rates long-term financing for the remaining 50 percent, which also is supported by an SBA guarantee. The major advantages of Section 504 loans are their fixed rates and terms, their 10- to 20-year maturities, and the low down payment required.

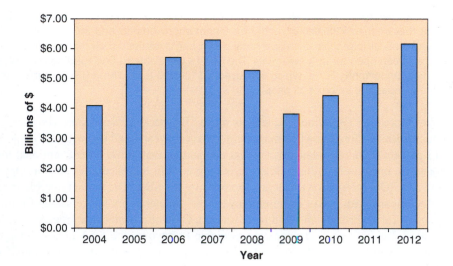

**FIGURE 17.3**

**SBA 504 Loan Volume**

*Source:* Based on SBA, Quarterly Indicators and SBA's Summary of Performance and Financial Information.

**ENTREPRENEURIAL PROFILE: Jim Tankersley: Laser-Tronics** Jim Tankersley owns and operates Laser-Tronics, a company in San Marcos, California that uses computer-guided machines to cut computer frames, auto parts, and other products out of raw-metal plates and bars. Tankersley needed an 18,000-square-foot building to house his business and was able to purchase a building for $2.2 million with financing from Union Bank of California and CDC Small Business Finance, a local certified development company. "Union Bank suggested SBA 504 financing because of the low down payment, which allowed me to save my cash for the business," says Tankersley.[49]

As attractive as they are, 504 loans are not for every business owner. The SBA imposes several restrictions on 504 loans:

- For every $65,000 ($100,000 for small manufacturers) that the SBA provides, the project must create or preserve at least one new job or achieve a public policy goal, such as rural development, expansion of exports, minority business development, and others.

- Machinery and equipment financed must have a useful life of at least 10 years.

- The borrower must occupy at least two-thirds of a building constructed with the loan, or the borrower must occupy at least half of a building purchased or remodeled with the loan.

- The borrower must qualify as a small business under the SBA's definition and must have neither a tangible net worth in excess of $15 million nor an average net income in excess of $5 million after taxes for the preceding two years.

Because of strict equity requirements, existing small businesses usually find it easier to qualify for 504 loans than do start-ups. The average 504 loan has ranged from $500,000 to $600,000 in recent years.

**MICROLOAN PROGRAM** Recall from the previous chapter that the majority of entrepreneurs require less than $100,000 to launch their businesses. Indeed, research suggests that most entrepreneurs require less than $50,000 to start their companies. Unfortunately, loans of that amount can be the most difficult to get, especially since the financial crisis of 2008. Lending these relatively small amounts to entrepreneurs starting businesses is the purpose of the SBA's microloan program. Called **microloans** because they range from just a hundred dollars to as much as $50,000, these loans have helped thousands of people take their first steps toward entrepreneurship. Banks typically have shunned loans in such small amounts because they considered them to be unprofitable. In 1992, the SBA began funding microloan programs at 96 private nonprofit lenders in 44 states in an attempt to "fill the void" in small loans to start-up companies, and the program has expanded from there. In 2012, microloan lenders provided 3,973 microloans amounting to $44.7 million. The average microloan was about $11,250 and carried an 8.18 percent interest rate.[50]

**ENTREPRENEURIAL PROFILE: Mitesh and Chetna Parikh: Threads** Mitesh and Chetna Parikh started a salon, called Threads, in a tiny start-up space in a Holiday Inn in Dublin, California. The Parikhs were able to support their business's initial growth with cash flow that the business generated. However as word-of-mouth grew, they could not handle any new customers within such a small space. The Parikhs found a larger space across the street that had great freeway access, but they needed $100,000 in capital for tenant improvements and for purchasing additional salon equipment. Despite their strong personal credit, banks declined their loan request because the business had been open for only two years. The Parikhs were able to find funding through a micro-lender called Opportunity Fund, which approved a $100,000 loan. Threads now generates several million in revenues and employs 26 people.[51]

Today, more than 170 authorized lenders make SBA-backed microloans. The average maturity of microloans is three years (the maximum term is six years) and interest rates range between 8 and 13 percent. Lenders' standards are less demanding than those on conventional loans. All microloans are made as installment loans through nonprofit intermediaries such as Opportunity Fund and ACCION International that are approved by the SBA. The typical microloan recipient is a small company with five or fewer employees and collateral that bankers shun for traditional loans, such as earthworms from a fish bait farmer in Ohio or a Minnesota grocery store's frozen fish inventory.[52] Although microloans are available to anyone, the SBA hopes to target those entrepreneurs who have the greatest difficulty getting start-up and expansion capital: women, minorities, and people with low incomes.

**ENTREPRENEURIAL PROFILE: Michael Golata: UPS** Retailer Sam's Club, a division of Wal-Mart, works with a nonbank SBA lender, Superior Financial Group, to offer its small business members microloans up to $25,000 through the SBA. "Access to capital is a major pain point for our [small business] members," says Catherine Corley, vice president of membership. Michael Golata, a contractor for UPS who delivers emergency medical equipment to hospitals, had the opportunity to expand his business by bringing other delivery drivers into his business. Golata found a used Sprinter van for $12,500 and applied to two local banks for a loan, but both rejected his loan application. A commercial finance company offered to lend him the money, but Golata balked at the 21 percent interest rate and $450 monthly payments. He learned about the microloans that Sam's Club offered with Superior Financial Group and applied online for a $10,000 loan. The next day, Superior approved his loan with a 7.25 percent loan over 10 years. "I thought I was dreaming," says Golata, whose business with UPS immediately increased from $3,000 a week to $8,000.[53]

**LOANS INVOLVING INTERNATIONAL TRADE** For small businesses going global, the SBA has the **Export Express Program**, which, like other express programs, offers quick turnaround times on applications for guarantees of 75 to 85 percent on loans up to $500,000 to help small companies develop or expand their export initiatives. Loan maturities range from 5 to 25 years, depending on the purpose of the loan.

The SBA also offers the **Export Working Capital Program**, which is designed to provide working capital to small exporters by providing loan guarantees of 90 percent of the loan amount up to $5 million. The SBA works in conjunction with the Export-Import Bank (Ex-Im Bank) to administer this loan guarantee program. Applicants file a one-page loan application, and the response time normally is 10 days or less. Small businesses must use loan proceeds to finance small business exports.

**ENTREPRENEURIAL PROFILE: Mike Brown: American Aluminum International** Mike Brown is the owner of American Aluminum International, a small Missouri company that wholesales aluminum sheet, coil, bar, and other metals that are used to make large trailers, gas tanks, and electrical transformers. The company exports all of its production output to companies in Mexico. Its customers typically take a long time to pay, causing a cash flow problem. To offset his company's high accounts receivables due to slow payments, Brown was able to secure a $1.5 million credit line with Bank of America, guaranteed by the Export-Import Bank of the United States. "The funds were used to stock inventory and pay our vendors despite our customers often taking 90 to 120 days to pay," says Brown.[54]

The **International Trade Loan Program** is for small businesses that are engaging in international trade or are adversely affected by competition from imports. The loan ceiling is $5 million, and maturities run up to 25 years.

**DISASTER ASSISTANCE LOANS** As their name implies, **disaster assistance loans** are made to small businesses devastated by financial or physical losses from hurricanes, earthquakes, floods, tornadoes, and other disasters. Business physical disaster loans are designed to help companies repair or replace damage to physical property (buildings, equipment, inventory, and so on) caused by the disaster, and economic injury loans provide working capital for businesses throughout the disaster period. For businesses, the maximum disaster loan usually is $2 million, but Congress often raises that ceiling when circumstances warrant. Disaster loans carry low interest rates of 4 percent and long payback periods up to 30 years. After Hurricane Sandy slammed into the coastal region of the Northeast United States, shutting down thousands of businesses, the SBA granted $260 million in disaster assistance loans to more than 2,500 small businesses that suffered financial losses.[55]

## State and Local Loan Development Programs

Just when many federally funded programs are facing cutbacks, state and local loan and development programs are becoming more active in providing funds for business start-ups and expansions. Many states have decided that their funds are better spent encouraging small business growth rather than "chasing smokestacks"—trying to entice large businesses to locate in their boundaries. These programs come in many forms, but they all tend to focus on developing small businesses that create the greatest number of jobs and economic benefits. Entrepreneurs who apply for state and local funding must have patience and must be willing to slog through some paperwork, however.

Although each state's approach to economic development and job growth is unique, one common element is some kind of small business financing program: loans, loan guarantees, development grants, venture capital pools, and others. One approach many states have had success with is **Capital Access Programs** (CAPs). First introduced in 1986 in Michigan, 22 states now offer CAPs that are designed to encourage lending institutions to make loans to businesses that do not qualify for traditional financing. Under a CAP, a bank and a borrower each pay an up-front fee (a portion of the loan amount) into a loan-loss reserve fund at the participating bank, and the state matches this amount. The reserve fund, which normally ranges from 6 to 14 percent of the loan amount, acts as an insurance policy against the potential loss a bank might experience on a loan and frees the bank to make loans that it otherwise might refuse. One study of CAPs found that 55 percent of the entrepreneurs who received loans under a CAP would not have been granted loans without the backing of the program.[56]

Even cities and small towns have joined in the effort to develop small businesses and help them grow. More than 7,500 communities across the United States operate **revolving loan funds** (RLFs) that combine private and public funds to make loans to small businesses, often at below-market interest rates. As money is repaid into the funds, it is loaned back out to other entrepreneurs.

In addition to RLFs, more than 1,000 communities across the United States have created **community development financial institutions** (CDFIs) that designate at least some of their loan portfolios for entrepreneurs and small businesses. CDFIs operate through a variety of mechanisms, including microenterprise loan funds, community development loan funds, and others, and provide loans to people who do not meet traditional lenders' criteria. Because the loans that they make are higher risk, the interest rates that CDFIs charge are higher than those charged by traditional lenders.

**5.** _____
Discuss state and local economic development programs.

## In the Entrepreneurial Spotlight

# Alternative Sources of Financing

Although banks tend to be lenders of first resort for small businesses, accounting for the greatest volume of loans to small businesses, they are not the only lending game in town, as the following profiles illustrate.

### Take2Chic

Mari Alstin needed $25,000 to open her women's clothing boutique, Take2Chic, in Philadelphia. Although she had $10,000 in savings and credit, she had to find another source for the remaining

$15,000. She had used the peer-to-peer lending site Prosper for personal loans in the past, so she decided to return to it to raise the money she needed for her new store. "I needed something that was quick, easy, and guaranteed," says Alstin. "It was all about timing because I didn't want the place that I wanted to lease to be given away." Alstin posted a description of her entrepreneurial project at the Prosper Web site. She was able to quickly raise the full $15,000. The loan came from a large number of people who each of whom loaned Alstin between $25 and $2,000.

*(continued)*

# In the Entrepreneurial Spotlight *(continued)*

## Material Culture

George Jevremovic began importing and selling Turkish rugs in 1982. Because of the growth in his business, he eventually moved into a 60,000-square-foot storefront called Material Culture, where he sells imported rugs and furnishings imported from around the world to designers, homeowners, and collectors. Jevremovic wanted to refinance Material Culture's debt to accommodate a restructuring of the business. He knew that he could use the company's primary asset, its inventory, to secure a loan, but that asset-based loans typically carry high interest rates and fees. Instead, Jevremovic turned to MultiFunding, a Philadelphia-based loan broker. Loan brokers help entrepreneurs find a wide range of funding options, including merchant cash advances, accounts receivable and inventory financing, lease buybacks, purchase order financing, and conventional SBA loans. MultiFunding introduced Material Culture to a regional bank that provided two conventional loans—a line of credit and a term loan. Through this arrangement, Material Culture refinanced its debts at low rates and secured some working capital. MultiFunding's fee is typically between 1 and 2.5 percent of the total loan amount.

## Able Planet

Kevin Semcken had been working with his current bank for almost three years. He had a $2.5 million line of credit for his business, Able Planet, which manufactures audio headphones that it sells to big box retailers. Semcken had never missed a payment, but one day he got an unexpected call from his banker. The bank would no longer allow Able Planet to use the line of credit for financing the cost of raw materials and manufacturing. Without that line of credit, Semcken would have no way to pay for inventory that he sold to retailers such as Wal-Mart and Costco. "They waited until the last minute and dropped it on us," says Semcken. The timing of the bank's decision came at the worst time. His business was approaching the busiest season. The time from back-to-school through Christmas was when his company sold 60 percent of its products each year. Semcken had invested a good deal of his own money into Able Planet and had gotten investments from family members. He was concerned about protecting all of the money his family had invested, but without funding, he would not be able to fill the orders for his retail customers.

1. What steps can business owners take when banks refuse their loan applications?

2. Assume the role of consultant to Kevin Semcken, owner of Able Planet. What advice can you offer him about getting the financing he needs to support his company?

*Sources:* Based on Michelle Goodman, "Anonymous Investors Offer a Lending Alternative," *Entrepreneur*, January 7, 2013, *www.entrepreneur.com/article/225022*; Jeremy Quittner, "How to Get a Loan? Let Us Count the Ways," *Inc.*, February 4, 2013, *www.inc.com/jeremy-quittner/alternatives-to-banking.html*; "Multifunding Success Stories: George Jervemovic," *Multifunding*, April 16, 2012, *www.multifunding.com/success_stories/george-jevremovic*; Nitasha Tiku, "When Your Bank Stops Lending," *Inc.*, July 1, 2009, *www.inc.com/magazine/20090701/case-study-when-your-bank-stops-lending.html*.

# Other Methods of Financing

**6.**

Discuss other possible methods of financing growth.

Small business owners do not have to rely solely on financial institutions and government agencies for capital.

## Factoring Accounts Receivable

Rather than carry credit sales on its own books (some of which may never be collected), a small business can sell outright its accounts receivable to a factor. A **factor** buys a company's accounts receivable and pays for them in two parts. The first payment, which the factor makes immediately, is for 50 to 80 percent of the accounts' agreed-on value, which is typically discounted at a rate of 3 to 5 percent of the value of the invoice. The factor makes the second payment of 15 to 18 percent, which makes up the balance less the factor's service fees, when the original customer pays the invoice. Because factoring is a more expensive type of financing than loans from either banks or commercial finance companies, many entrepreneurs view factors as lenders of last resort. However, for businesses that cannot qualify for those loans, factoring may be the only choice!

Begun by American colonists to finance their cotton trade with England, factoring has become an important source of capital for many small businesses that depend on fast billing turnaround across a multitude of industries ranging from hardware stores and pharmacies to pest control firms and hiring agencies. Factoring deals are either with recourse or without recourse. Under deals arranged with recourse, a small business owner retains the responsibility for customers who fail to pay their accounts. The business owner must take back these uncollectible invoices. Under deals arranged without recourse, however, the owner is relieved of the responsibility of collecting them. If customers fail to pay their accounts, the factor bears the loss. Because the factoring company assumes the risk of collecting the accounts, it normally screens the firm's credit customers, accepts those judged to be creditworthy, and advances the small business owner a portion of the value of the accounts receivable. Factors will discount anywhere from 2 to 40 percent of the face value of a company's accounts receivable, depending on the following characteristics of a small company:

- Its customers' financial strength, credit ratings, and ability to pay invoices on time
- Its industry and its customers' industries because some industries have a reputation for slow payments
- Its history and financial strength, especially in deals arranged with recourse
- Its credit policies

The discount rate on deals without recourse usually is higher than on those with recourse because of the higher level of risk they carry for the factor.

Although factoring is more expensive than traditional bank loans (a 2 percent discount from the face value of an invoice due in 30 days amounts to an annual interest rate of 24.5 percent), it is a source of quick cash and is ideally suited for fast-growing companies, especially start-ups that cannot qualify for bank loans. "Factoring provides a business with immediate cash for accounts receivable because a business can sell receivables as soon as they are generated," explains the head of one factoring operation.[57] Small companies that sell to government agencies and large corporations, both famous for stretching out their payments for 60 to 90 days or more, also find factoring attractive because they collect the money from the sale (less the factor's discount) much faster.

Susan Brown, founder of Boppy Company.
*Source:* Boppy Company.

**ENTREPRENEURIAL PROFILE: Susan Brown: Boppy Co.** Susan Brown created a pillow, called Boppy, that is used to help breast-feeding moms give their infants added support. She grew her company to about $2 million in revenues, selling her product to 100 specialty children's stores, but as the business grew, cash was running low because of the company's growing accounts receivable. Brown couldn't secure a loan from a traditional bank, so she turned instead to a factoring agency. The factor gave her 80 percent of the value of her invoices so that she wouldn't have to wait the typical 30 days for payment. The business inched along until acquiring its first major retail account. Boppy Co. now generates $40 million in retail sales annually.[58]

## Leasing

Leasing is another common alternative financing technique. Today, small businesses can lease virtually any kind of asset—from office space and telephones to computers and heavy equipment. By leasing expensive assets, a small business owner is able to use them without tying up valuable capital for an extended period of time. In other words, entrepreneurs can reduce the long-term capital requirements of their businesses by leasing equipment and facilities, and they are not investing capital in depreciating assets. In addition, because no down payment is required and because the cost of the asset is spread over a longer time (lowering monthly payments), the company's cash flow improves.

## Cash Advances

Restaurants and other retailers often have difficulty finding financing because they do not have accounts receivable or invoices to borrow against. Lending companies such as AdvanceMe and RapidAdvance will provide businesses cash advances in the form of a lump sum. The lender then takes a percentage of the business's daily credit card receipts until the borrower repays the loan and a predetermined fee. Cash advances are a last resort source of debt financing because its cost is so high.

**ENTREPRENEURIAL PROFILE: Dennis Sick: Mohegan Manor** Dennis Sick, owner of the Mohegan Manor restaurant in Baldwinsville, New York, needed money to cover utilities and taxes during the slow winter months, so Sick took out an advance on credit card receipts. Using cash advance financing, his business received a lump sum of $45,000 from the lender. In return, the lender took a percentage of the business's daily credit card receipts until Sick repaid the loan, plus a fixed fee. The lender took 13 to 18 percent of Mohegan Manor's daily credit card sales until Sick was able to repay the loan. Seven months later Sick had paid a total of $64,000, giving the lender an annual return of about 70 percent![59]

### Peer-to-Peer Loans

New online funding options are emerging to help small businesses with credit. **Peer-to-peer loans** are Web-based vetting platforms that create an online lending community of investors who provide funding to creditworthy small-business owners. Two of the most popular online vetting platforms are Lending Club and Prosper. Lending Club reports that it makes more than $120 million in loans to small businesses *each month*! Interest rates can range from less than 7 percent to more than 25 percent. Lending Club has a maximum loan limit of $35,000. Hannah Attwood wanted to raise money to open a cloth diaper supply and cleaning service called Adore Diaper Service. She first tried to secure bank financing. "They just laughed at me," she says. Attwood then applied to Lending Club, and within a week, more than 60 investors had jointly given her a three-year, $6,000 loan at 11.36 percent. She combined the loan with an equal amount of savings to buy industrial washers and dryers and cloth diapers for her business.[60]

### Credit Cards

Unable to find financing elsewhere, some entrepreneurs have launched their companies using the fastest and most convenient source of debt capital available: credit cards. It is a common financing technique for start-ups. However, credit cards are expensive, and if the business fails, the entrepreneur is left with a mountain of unpaid credit card bills to pay personally. Although it is sometimes part of the mythology of entrepreneurship, experts do not recommend using credit cards to finance a new business. Putting business start-up costs on credit cards charging 20 percent or more in annual interest is expensive and risky and can lead to severe financial woes, however. A study by Robert Scott of Monmouth University and the Kauffman Foundation reports that taking on credit card debt reduces the likelihood that a start-up company will survive its first three years of operation. Every $1,000 increase in credit card debt results in a 2.2 percent increase in the probability that a company will fail.[61]

## Where *Not* to Seek Funds

**7.**

Explain how to avoid becoming a victim of a loan scam.

Entrepreneurs searching for capital must be wary of con artists whose targets frequently include financially strapped small businesses. The swindle usually begins when the con artist scours an area for "DEs"—desperate entrepreneurs in search of quick cash injections to keep their businesses going. Usually, the scam involves advance fees and follows one of two patterns (although a number of variations exist). Under one scheme, scammers guarantee a small business owner a loan from a nonexistent bank with false credentials. The con artist tells the owner that loan processing will take time and that in the meantime the owner must pay a percentage of the loan amount as an advance fee. Of course, the loan never materializes, and the small business owner loses the deposit, sometimes several thousands of dollars.

Another common scam begins with a loan broker who promises a capital-hungry small business owner an SBA loan if the owner pays a small processing fee. Again, the loan never appears, and the small business owner loses his or her deposit. Other scammers charge entrepreneurs excessive fees to help them apply for SBA loan guarantees.

Unfortunately, schemes by con artists preying on unsuspecting business owners who are in need of capital are more common when credit tightens. Scams most commonly involve the SBA's smallest loan programs, such as the SBA*Express* and Microloan programs. The Internet has made crooks' jobs easier. On the Web, they can establish a legitimate-looking presence, approach their targets anonymously, and vanish instantly—all while avoiding mail fraud charges if they happen to get caught. These con artists move fast, cover their trails well, and are extremely smooth. The best protection against such scams is common sense and remembering the adage "If it sounds too good to be true, it probably is." Experts offer the following advice to business owners:

- Be suspicious of anyone who approaches you—unsolicited—with an offer for "guaranteed financing."
- Watch out for red flags that indicate a scam: "guaranteed" loans, up-front fees, and unsolicited pitches over the Web.
- Conduct a thorough background check on any lenders, brokers, or financiers with whom you intend to do business. Is the lender registered to do business in your state? Does the Better Business Bureau have a record of complaints against the company?

- Make sure you have an attorney review all loan agreements before you sign them.
- *Never* pay advance fees for financing, especially on the Web, unless you have verified the lender's credibility.

## Chapter Review

1. Describe the various sources of debt capital and the advantages and disadvantages of each.
   - Commercial banks offer the greatest variety of loans, although they are conservative lenders. Typical short-term bank loans include commercial loans, lines of credit, discounting accounts receivable, inventory financing, floor planning, and character loans.
2. Explain the types of financing available from nonbank sources of credit.
   - Asset-based lenders allow small businesses to borrow money by pledging otherwise idle assets, such as accounts receivable, inventory, or purchase orders, as collateral.
   - Trade credit is used extensively by small businesses as a source of financing. Vendors and suppliers commonly finance sales to businesses for 30, 60, or even 90 days.
   - Equipment suppliers offer small businesses financing similar to trade credit but with slightly different terms.
   - Commercial finance companies offer many of the same types of loans that banks do, but they are more risk oriented in their lending practices. They emphasize accounts receivable financing and inventory loans.
   - Stock-brokerage houses offer loans to prospective entrepreneurs at lower interest rates than banks because they have high-quality, liquid collateral—stocks and bonds in the borrower's portfolio.
   - Insurance companies provide financing through policy loans and mortgage loans. Policy loans are extended to the owner against the cash surrender value of insurance policies. Mortgage loans are made for large amounts and are based on the value of the land being purchased.
   - SBICs are privately owned companies licensed and regulated by the SBA that qualify for SBA loans to be invested in or loaned to small businesses.
3. Identify the various federal loan programs aimed at small businesses.
   - The EDA, a branch of the Commerce Department, makes loan guarantees to create and expand small businesses in economically depressed areas.
   - HUD extends grants (such as CDBGs) to cities that, in turn, lend and grant money to small businesses in an attempt to strengthen the local economy.

- The USDA's RBS loan program is designed to create nonfarm employment opportunities in rural areas through loans and loan guarantees.
- The SBIR program involves 11 federal agencies that award cash grants or long-term contracts to small companies wanting to initiate or to expand their R&D efforts.
- The STTR program allows researchers at universities, federally funded R&D centers, and nonprofit research institutions to join forces with small businesses and develop commercially promising ideas.

4. Describe the various loan programs available from the SBA.
   - SBA loan activity is in the form of loan guarantees rather than direct loans. Popular SBA programs include the SBA*Express* Program, Patriot Express Program, Small Loan Advantage program, Community Advantage program, the 7(a) loan guaranty program, the CAPLine Program, the Microloan program, the 504 Certified Development Company Program, several export loan programs, and the disaster loan program.
5. Discuss state and local economic development programs.
   - In an attempt to develop businesses that create jobs and economic growth, most states offer small business financing programs, usually in the form of loans, loan guarantees, and venture capital pools.
   - Many state and local loan and development programs, such as CAPs and RLFs, complement those sponsored by federal agencies.
6. Discuss other possible methods of financing growth.
   - By factoring accounts receivable, leasing equipment instead of buying it, cash advances on credit card receipts, peer-to-peer lending, and using credit cards, owners can stretch their supplies of capital.
7. Explain how to avoid becoming a victim of a loan scam.
   - Entrepreneurs hungry for capital for their growing businesses can be easy targets for con artists running loan scams. Entrepreneurs should watch out for promises of "guaranteed" loans, up-front fees, and offers that seem too good to be true.

# Discussion Questions

**17-1.** What role do commercial banks play in providing debt financing to small businesses? Outline and briefly describe the major types of short-, intermediate-, and long-term loans commercial banks offer.

**17-2.** What is trade credit? How important is it as a source of debt financing to small firms?

**17-3.** Explain how asset-based financing works. What is the most common method of asset-based financing? What are the advantages and disadvantages of using this method of financing?

**17-4.** What function do SBICs serve? How does an SBIC operate? What methods of financing do SBICs rely on most heavily?

**17-5.** Briefly describe the loan programs offered by the following:
  a. EDA
  b. HUD
  c. USDA
  d. Local development companies.

**17-6.** Explain the purpose and the methods of operation of the SBIR program and the STTR program.

**17-7.** Which of the SBA's loan programs accounts for the majority of its loan activity? How does the program work?

**17-8.** Explain the purpose and the operation of the SBA's microloan program.

**17-9.** What is a factor? How does the typical factor operate? Explain the advantages and the disadvantages of factoring. What kinds of businesses typically use factors?

# CHAPTER 18

# Location, Layout, and Physical Facilities

## Learning Objectives

**On completion of this chapter, you will be able to:**

1. Explain the stages in the location decision.

2. Describe the location criteria for retail and service businesses.

3. Outline the basic location options for retail and service businesses.

4. Explain the site selection process for manufacturers.

5. Discuss the benefits of locating a start-up company in a business incubator.

6. Describe the criteria used to analyze the layout and design considerations of a building, including the Americans with Disabilities Act.

7. Explain the principles of effective layouts for retailers, service businesses, and manufacturers.

*It is not the strongest of the species that survive, nor the most intelligent, but the ones most responsive to change.*

—Charles Darwin

*It is choice—not chance— that determines your destiny.*

—Jean Nidetch

## Stages in the Location Decision

Few decisions that entrepreneurs make have as lasting and as dramatic an impact on their businesses as the choice of a location. Entrepreneurs who choose their locations wisely—with their customers' preferences and their companies' needs in mind—can establish an important competitive advantage over rivals who choose their locations haphazardly. Because the availability of qualified workers, tax rates, quality of infrastructure, traffic patterns, quality of life, and many other factors vary from one site to another, the location decision is an important one that can influence the growth rate and the ultimate success of a company. Thanks to widespread digital connectivity, mobile computing, extensive cellular coverage, and affordable air travel, entrepreneurs have more flexibility when choosing a business location than ever before.

The characteristics that make for an ideal location often vary dramatically from one company to another because of the nature of the business. In the early twentieth century, companies looked for ready supplies of water, raw materials, or access to railroads. For instance, West Virginia once was home to a thriving glass-making industry because it provided entrepreneurs with ample supplies of quality sand (a key raw material), natural gas for heating glass furnaces, and inexpensive river transportation to get finished products to market.[1] Today, businesses are more likely to look for sites that are close to universities and offer high-speed Internet access and accessible interstate highways and airports. In fact, one study concluded that the factors that make an area most suitable for starting and growing small companies include access to dynamic universities, an ample supply of skilled workers, a nearby airport, a temperate climate, and a high quality of life.[2]

The key to finding a suitable location is identifying the characteristics that can give a company a competitive edge and then searching out potential sites that meet those criteria. For example, businesses that depend on face-to-face contact with customers must identify locations that attract high volumes of well-qualified walk-in customers. Although online sales continue to increase steadily, brick-and-mortar businesses stores still dominate consumer sales, accounting for 92 percent of all retail sales.[3] One reason for the staying power of physical locations is the appeal of their real-world presence. An inviting physical location enables people to touch, feel, and experience the products and services a business offers. Potential buyers can pick up merchandise, try it on, and compare it side by side with other items. An optimal location also provides a gathering place where people can share experiences and one-on-one interactions. The ability to look someone in the eye and ask questions or watch a demonstration appeals to human nature and provides a powerful sales tool for the business. Investing time collecting and analyzing the data relevant to choosing a location pays off in customer traffic, higher sales, and greater efficiencies.

**ENTREPRENEURIAL PROFILE: Steve Kuhnau: Smoothie King** Smoothie King, a company started in 1973 when founder Steve Kuhnau began blending fresh fruit, nutrients, and proteins to combat his allergies, is one of the leading retailers of nutritional smoothies, diet supplements, and healthy snacks. Headquartered in New Orleans, Louisiana, the company has grown to 639 franchised locations (103 of them outside the United States) and is one of the top-performing and fastest-growing companies in the industry. With 21 years of experience, Richard Leveille, a senior vice president whose main responsibility is location analysis for new outlets, knows that choosing the right location is a key element to Smoothie King's success. The company has three primary criteria for selecting a site for a new outlet: high visibility, maximum customer convenience, and successful businesses in the surrounding area that complement Smoothie King's products. Managers and franchisees know from experience that the most important factor in selecting a site is its visibility, a location with high traffic counts that customers can easily see. Convenient locations translate into more frequent visits from customers, which is why the chain looks for locations that allow the installation of drive-through windows. The final criterion is a location that supports other successful businesses whose products complement Smoothie King's or that attract the same customer base. Smoothie King works with Buxton, a company that specializes in site selection for restaurants and retailers, to find its locations. Buxton's analytical tools allow Smoothie King to identify those locations that provide the best match for its target customers and to make projections about which areas offer the greatest potential to support large numbers of outlets.[4]

The location decision process resembles an inverted pyramid. The first level of the decision is the broadest, requiring an entrepreneur to select a particular region of the country. Then an entrepreneur must choose the right state, then the right city, and, finally, the right site within the city (see Figure 18.1). The "secret" to selecting the ideal location lies in knowing the factors that are

**FIGURE 18.1**

**The Location Decision**

*Source:* From Dale M. Lewison and M. Wayne DeLozier, Retailing (Columbus, OH: Merrill/Macmillan Publishing, 1984), p. 341.

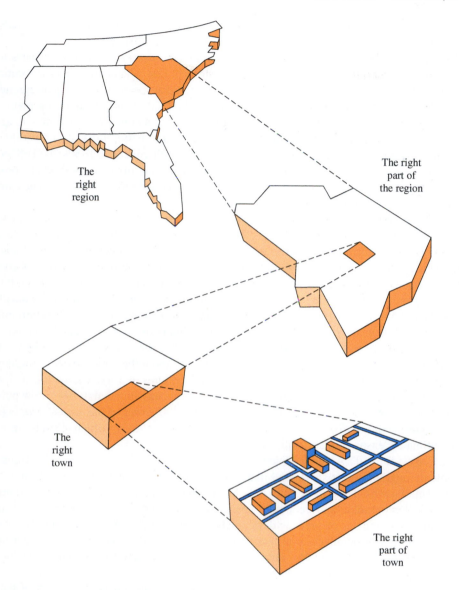

The right region

The right part of the region

The right town

The right part of town

most important to a company's success and then finding a location that satisfies as many of them as possible, particularly those that are most critical. For instance, one of the most important location factors for high-tech companies is the availability of a skilled labor force, and their choice of location reflects this.

**ENTREPRENEURIAL PROFILE: Terry Golding: Amethyst Research, Inc.** Terry Golding, president of Amethyst Research, Inc., a small company that has developed an advanced semiconductor technology used to manufacture infrared night-vision imagers, chose a location in the Technology Transfer Center in Ardmore, Oklahoma, that provides both office and lab space for the company's 10 employees, five of whom have PhDs. Although Ardmore is a small town (just 25,000 residents), it has attracted numerous small high-tech companies, such as Amethyst Research, with its specialized technology parks and a technology incubator that will soon be in operation. Ardmore also offers start-up companies the advantage of low costs and easy access to major markets, such as nearby Dallas and Oklahoma City. The support of local government officials and a pro-business climate clinched the deal for Golding. "We wouldn't be nearly as far along with our business had we not located here," he says.[5]

## Selecting the Region

The first step in selecting the best location is to focus on selecting the right region. This requires entrepreneurs to look at the location decision from the "30,000-foot level," as if he or she were in an airplane looking down. In fact, in the early days of their companies, Sam Walton, founder of retail giant Wal-Mart, and Ray Kroc, who built McDonald's into a fast-food giant, actually used private planes to survey the countryside for prime locations for their stores.

Which region of the country has the characteristics necessary for a new business to succeed? Above all, entrepreneurs must place their customers first when considering a location. As Smoothie King's experience suggests, facts and statistics, not speculation, lead entrepreneurs to the best locations for their businesses. Common criteria include rapid population growth, rising disposable incomes, the existence of necessary infrastructure, a nonunion environment, and low operating costs. At the broadest level of the location decision, entrepreneurs prefer to locate in regions of the country that are experiencing substantial growth. Since the 1950s, the U.S. population has shifted to the South and the West and from rural areas to urban and suburban communities.[6] Studying these shifts in population and the resulting economic growth gives entrepreneurs an idea of where the action is—and isn't.

One of the first stops entrepreneurs should make when conducting a regional evaluation is the U.S. Census Bureau (*www.census.gov*). There entrepreneurs can access for specific locations vital demographic information, such as age, income, educational level, employment level, occupation, ancestry, commuting times, housing data (house value, number of rooms, mortgage or rent status, number of vehicles owned, and so on), and many other characteristics. With a little practice, entrepreneurs can prepare customized reports on the potential sites they are considering. These Web-based resources give entrepreneurs instant access to important site-location information that only a few years ago would have taken many hours of intense research to compile! In 2012, the Census Bureau ceased publication of the *U.S. Statistical Abstract* (published annually since 1878), which contained about 1,400 useful data sets about the United States, ranging from basic population characteristics and leisure activity expenditures to poverty rates and energy consumption. However, ProQuest, an information gateway company founded in 1943, now publishes in both print and online formats the *ProQuest Statistical Abstract of the United States* (*http://cisupa.proquest.com/ws_display.asp?filter=Statistical%20Abstract*), which closely resembles the discontinued Census Bureau publication.

The Census Bureau's American FactFinder site (*http://factfinder.census.gov*) provides easily accessible demographic fact sheets and maps on nearly every community in the United States, including small towns. The Census Bureau's American Community Survey provides annual updates on the demographic and economic characteristics of areas with populations of at least 65,000, three-year updates on areas with populations between 20,000 and 65,000, and five-year updates on areas with populations of less than 20,000. Both the American FactFinder and the American Community Survey allow entrepreneurs to produce easy-to-read, customizable maps of the information they generate in their searches.

ZoomProspector is a useful Web site that gives entrepreneurs access to much of the same information that large companies use when selecting locations and allows them to search for the ideal location using a multitude of factors, including population size, job growth rate, number of patents issued, venture capital invested, education level, household incomes, and proximity to interstate highways, railroads, and airports. Once entrepreneurs locate a city that matches their customer profiles, they find other cities across the United States that have similar profiles with a single mouse click! Entrepreneurs who are considering a particular region can display "heat maps" that visually display the areas that have the highest concentrations of people who have a particular characteristic, such as a bachelor's degree or the highest household incomes.

**ENTREPRENEURIAL PROFILE: Steve Sarowitz: Paylocity** Steve Sarowitz, CEO of Paylocity, a provider of human resources and payroll services to small and medium-size businesses, uses ZoomProspector to find the best locations across the United States for the rapidly expanding company's new offices. Sarowitz says that ZoomProspector helps his company answer the important question: Would this be a good market for us? "What's great about ZoomProspector is that we can get so much information about each individual market we are considering—market demographics, which industries are strongest, education levels, and more," says Sarowitz. Founded in 1997, Paylocity, which is based in Arlington Heights, Illinois, and has appeared on *Inc.'s* list of the 5,000 fastest-growing companies seven times, now has 14 locations and, with ZoomProspector's help, is looking to add more.[7]

ePodunk, a Web site that provides in-depth Census-based information about more than 46,000 towns and cities of all sizes around the United States, is another useful tool for entrepreneurs. Zipskinny is a Web site that provides Census profiles and comparisons with other communities using ZIP codes.

The Population Reference Bureau (*www.prb.org*) provides a detailed breakdown of the most relevant data collected from the most recent census reports. Its DataFinder is a database that includes 244 variables for the United States and 132 variables for 210 other nations. The site also includes helpful articles that discuss the implications of the changing demographic and economic profile of the nation's (and the world's) population, such as the impact of aging Baby Boomers on business and the composition of the U.S. workforce.

Other helpful resources merit mention as well. *Lifestyle Market Analyst*, a four-part annual publication, matches population demographics with lifestyle interests. Section 1 provides demographics and lifestyle information for 210 "Designated Market Areas" across the United States. Section 2 gives demographic and geographic profiles of 77 lifestyle interests that range from avid readers and dieters to wine aficionados and pet owners. Section 3 describes the dominant lifestyle interests for each of the 210 market areas. Section 4 provides comparisons of other activities that correspond with each lifestyle interests. Entrepreneurs can use *Lifestyle Market Analyst* to determine, for example, how likely members of a particular market segment are to own a dog, collect antiques, play golf, own a vacation home, engage in extreme sports, invest in stocks or bonds, or participate in a host of other activities.

Other sources of demographic data include Nielsen Marketplace, *Editor and Publisher Market Guide*, *The American Marketplace: Demographics and Spending Patterns*, and *Zip Code Atlas and Market Planner*. Nielsen Marketplace provides a comprehensive tool for market analysis, allowing customers to generate customized reports and maps that show basic demographics, lifestyle patterns, and purchasing behavior for almost any market in the United States. The site also includes several unique statistics. Effective buying income (EBI) is a measure of disposable income, and the buying power index (BPI) is a unique measure of spending power that takes population, EBI, and retail sales into account to determine a market's ability to buy goods and services.

The *Editor and Publisher Market Guide* includes detailed economic and demographic information, ranging from population and income statistics to information on climate and transportation networks for all 3,096 counties in the United States and more than 1,600 key cities in both the United States and Canada.

*The American Marketplace: Demographics and Spending Patterns* provides useful demographic information in eight areas: education, health, income, labor force, living arrangements, population, race and ethnicity, and spending and wealth. Most of the tables in the book are derived from government statistics, but *The American Marketplace* also includes a discussion of the data in each table as well as a forecast of future trends. Many users say the primary advantage of *The American Marketplace* is its ease of use.

The U.S. Census Bureau also offers the ZIP Code Tabulation Areas (ZCTA) Web site (*www.census.gov/geo/ZCTA/zcta.html*) that organizes the wealth of census data by zip code. The database of 33,120 ZCTAs across the United States allows users to create tables and plot maps of census data by ZIP code.

*Site Selection* magazine (*www.siteselection.com*) is another useful resource that helps entrepreneurs determine the ideal location for their companies. Issues contain articles that summarize the incentive programs that states offer, profiles of each region of the country, and the benefits of locating in different states.

The task of analyzing various potential locations—gathering and synthesizing data on a wide variety of demographic and geographic variables—has become much easier and less expensive because much of the data required to determine the ideal location are available online. Many states and counties across the United States now provide geographic information systems (GIS) files online that allow entrepreneurs to identify sites that meet certain location criteria for their businesses. GIS packages allow users to search through virtually any database containing a wealth of information and plot the results on a map of the country, an individual state, a specific city, or even a single city block. The visual display highlights what otherwise would be indiscernible business trends. For instance, using GIS programs, entrepreneurs can plot their existing customer base on a map with various colors representing the different population densities. Then they can zoom in on those areas with the greatest concentration of customers, mapping a detailed view of ZIP code borders or even city streets. GIS street files originate in the U.S. Census Department's TIGER (Topographically Integrated Geographic Encoding Referencing) file, which contains map information broken down for every square foot of Metropolitan Statistical Areas (MSAs). TIGER files contain the name and location of every street in the country and detailed block statistics for the 345 largest urban areas. In essence, TIGER is a massive database of geographic features such as roads, railways, and political boundaries across the entire United States that, when linked with mapping programs and demographic databases, gives entrepreneurs incredible power to pinpoint existing and potential customers on easy-to-read digital maps.

The Small Business Administration's (SBA's) Small Business Development Center (SBDC) program also offers location analysis assistance to entrepreneurs. These centers, numbering more than 900 nationwide, provide training, counseling, research and other specialized assistance to entrepreneurs and existing business owners on a wide variety of subjects—all at no charge! They are an important resource, especially for those entrepreneurs who may not have access to a computer. (To locate the SBDC nearest you, contact the SBA office in your state or go to the SBA's SBDC locator page at *www.sba.gov/local-assistance*.)

For entrepreneurs interested in demographic and statistical profiles of international cities, Euromonitor International (*www.euromonitor.com*) and the Organization for Economic Development and Cooperation (*www.oecd.org*) are excellent resources.

Once an entrepreneur has identified the best region of the country, the next step is to evaluate the individual states in that region.

## Selecting the State

Every state has a business development office working to recruit new businesses. Although the publications produced by these offices will be biased in favor of locating in that state, they still are excellent sources of information and can help entrepreneurs assess the business climate in each state. Some of the key issues to explore include the laws, regulations, and taxes that govern businesses and incentives or investment credits the state may offer to businesses locating there. Other factors to consider include proximity to markets, proximity to raw materials, wage rates, quantity and quality of the labor supply, general business climate, and tax rates. Table 18.1 shows the most friendly and least friendly states for small businesses, a ranking based on a survey conducted by the Kauffman Foundation and Thumbtack that asked more than 6,000 small business owners to evaluate the states in which they operated on multiple factors, including the ease of starting a business, hiring costs, the regulatory burden that states impose, worker training programs that are available, and others.

**PROXIMITY TO MARKETS**  Locating close to the markets they plan to serve is critical to manufacturers, especially when the cost of transporting finished goods is high relative to their value. Locations near customers offer a competitive advantage. Service firms often find that

**TABLE 18.1 Most and Least Small Business Friendly States**

| Ranking (A+ [Most Friendly] to F [Least Friendly] | States |
|---|---|
| A+ | Arkansas, Idaho, Oklahoma, Utah |
| A | Georgia, Louisiana, New Hampshire, Texas |
| A− | Kansas, Oregon, South Carolina, Virginia |
| B+ | Alabama, Colorado, Indiana, Nebraska |
| B | Missouri, Nevada, Tennessee |
| B− | Arizona, Minnesota, Washington |
| C+ | Maryland, Pennsylvania, Kentucky, Wisconsin |
| C | Connecticut, Florida, Illinois, North Carolina |
| C− | Iowa, Louisiana, Montana, New Jersey |
| D+ | Delaware, Massachusetts, Michigan, Ohio |
| D | Alaska, California, Maine, New Mexico, New York |
| F | Hawaii, Vermont, Rhode Island |
| Not rated | North Dakota, South Dakota, West Virginia, Wyoming |

*Source:* Based on "Which State Is Best for Small Business?" *Entrepreneur*, November 12, 2012, *http://www.entrepreneur.com/article/224704*; "United States Small Business Friendliness," Thumbtack and Kauffman Foundation, 2012, *http://www.thumbtack.com/survey*.

proximity to their clients is essential. If a business is involved in repairing equipment used in a specific industry, it should be located where that industry is concentrated. The more specialized a business or the greater the relative cost of transporting the product to the customer, the more likely it is that proximity to the market will be of importance in the location decision. Many quick-service restaurants prefer locations near college and university campuses because of the high concentration of their target customers. One disadvantage of a college town location is that sales decline when college students leave for Christmas and summer breaks; however, many chains report that, despite the predictable decrease in sales when students are away, their college town locations are among their highest-performing units.

**ENTREPRENEURIAL PROFILE:  Scott Gittrich: Toppers Pizza** Toppers Pizza, founded in 1991 by Scott Gittrich and based in Whitewater, Wisconsin, has expanded to 50 locations by focusing primarily on cities that are home to at least one college or university. Toppers Pizza's outlets feature an unusual menu—the Potato Topper pizza (potato chunks, bacon, and onions), the Hangover Helper (Canadian bacon, onions, bell peppers, and potatoes), and the Mac' N Cheese—and stay open until 3 A.M., features that are popular with its college-age target market. Gittrich says that stores that are located near college campuses generate 50 percent of their sales after 9 P.M. "It's not easy to do," he admits, "but our stores are buzzing with activity after our competitors have closed." Annual sales at Toppers Pizza outlets average $930,000, well above the industry average.[8]

**PROXIMITY TO NEEDED RAW MATERIALS**  A business that requires raw materials that are difficult or expensive to transport may need a location near the source of those raw materials. For example, fish-processing plants benefit from locating close to ports. Some companies locate close to the source of raw materials because of the cost of transporting heavy low-value materials over long distances. Bel Brands USA, maker of Mini Babybel cheese, selected Brookings, South Dakota, as the location for its newest manufacturing plant in the United States. Managers included 40 criteria in the selection process, including labor supply and costs, utilities cost, land price and availability, and operating costs, but the most important factor was the availability of an essential raw material, milk, in the area to support the company's annual production of 40 million pounds of cheese. Other factors that made Brookings an ideal choice include South Dakota State University, which has a renowned dairy science program, a friendly business climate, and a low cost of living.[9] For products in which bulk or weight is not a factor, locating close to suppliers can facilitate quick deliveries and reduce inventory holding costs. The value of products and materials, their cost of transportation, and their unique functions all interact to determine how close a business should be to its suppliers.

**WAGE RATES** Existing and anticipated wage rates provide another measure for comparing states. Wages vary from one state or region to another, significantly affecting a company's cost of doing business. For instance, according to the Bureau of Labor Statistics, the average hourly compensation for workers (including wages and benefits) ranges from a low of $26.32 in the South to a high of $33.18 in the Northeast. (The average hourly compensation for the nation is $28.95.[10]) Wage rate differentials within geographic regions can be even more drastic. When reviewing wage rates, entrepreneurs must be sure to measure the wage rates for jobs that relate to their particular industries or companies. In addition to surveys by the Bureau of Labor Statistics (*www.bls.gov*), local newspaper ads can give entrepreneurs an idea of the pay scale in an area. In addition, entrepreneurs can obtain the latest wage and salary surveys with an e-mail or telephone call to the local chambers of commerce for cities in the region under consideration. Entrepreneurs should study not only prevailing wage rates but also *trends* in rates. How does the rate of increase in wage rates compare to those in other states? Another factor influencing wage rates is the level of union activity in a state. How much union organizing activity has the state seen within the last two years? Is it increasing or decreasing? Which industries have unions targeted in the recent past?

**LABOR SUPPLY** For many businesses, especially technology-driven companies, one of the most important characteristics of a potential location is the composition of the local workforce. The number of workers available in an area and their levels of education, training, and experience determine a company's ability to fill jobs with qualified workers at reasonable wages. According to a recent survey by *Site Selection* magazine, site selection consultants ranked workforce availability and quality as the most important location factor.[11]

**ENTREPRENEURIAL PROFILE: Andy Lim: Lavu Inc.** Andy Lim, who spoke no English when he emigrated to the United States in 2000, started Lavu Inc., a company that makes a simple iPad- and iPhone-based tableside ordering and restaurant management software system, from his kitchen table in Albuquerque, New Mexico, in 2010. The groundbreaking system has proved to be so effective that restaurants all across the nation have adopted it, and celebrity chef Gordon Ramsay has featured it on his television show, *Kitchen Nightmares.* For Lavu, Albuquerque is the ideal location, mainly because of an ample supply of highly educated, talented workers. "We are going head-to-head against Silicon Valley," says Lim, "but we are staying in Albuquerque. We are very efficient here. The living costs are cheaper, and we have been able to hire the best and brightest employees, many of whom are graduates of the nearby University of New Mexico."[12]

Entrepreneurs should know how many qualified people are available in the area to do the work required in the business. Some states attempt to attract industry with the promise of cheap labor. Unfortunately, businesses locating in those states may find unskilled, low-wage labor and unskilled laborers who can be difficult to train. The size of an area's labor pool and the education, skills, and ability of its members determine a company's ability to fill jobs with qualified workers at reasonable wages. "The single biggest reason why anyone is moving companies is access to talent," says Tim Nitti, co-owner of location strategy company KLG.[13]

Knowing the exact nature of the labor force needed and preparing job descriptions and job specifications in advance help business owners determine whether there is a good match between their companies and the available labor pool. Checking educational statistics in the state to determine the number of graduates in relevant fields of study provides an idea of the local supply of qualified workers. Drawn by the strength of a technology cluster and the presence of 17 colleges and universities near Boston with 221,000 students, a thriving video game industry that is comprised mainly of small companies such as Harmonix ("Guitar Hero" and "Rock Band"), Turbine ("Lord of the Rings"), Tilted Mill Entertainment ("SimCity"), and others has made Massachusetts home. Becker College in Worcester, Massachusetts, houses the Digital Game Institute, which provides a reservoir of young talent for these fast-growing high-tech companies.[14]

**BUSINESS CLIMATE** According to a recent survey by *Site Selection* magazine, 87 percent of site consultants say that a state's business climate is very or somewhat important in companies' location decisions.[15] A state's business climate is its overall attitude toward businesses; some states have created environments that are more "entrepreneur friendly" than others. Has the state passed laws that place restrictions on the way a company can operate? Does the state impose a corporate income tax? (Four states do not.) Does it support education at all levels so that a supply of qualified employees is available? Does the state offer small business support programs or financial assistance to entrepreneurs?

**ENTREPRENEURIAL PROFILE: John and Tullaya Akins: Bangkok Cuisine Thai Restaurant** John and Tullaya Akins, owners of the Bangkok Cuisine Thai Restaurant in Sandpoint, Idaho, wanted to open a second Mediterranean-themed restaurant. The copreneurs had selected a brick building in Sandpoint's downtown district that had housed a bicycle shop but changed their minds when they learned that the city would impose an impact fee (to tap into the city's water and sewer systems and to cover fire and police protection) of $26,000 to convert the building into a 45-seat restaurant. "That's make or break for us," says John. "We are shopping for a location in Ponderay (a nearby town with minimal impact fees) and the surrounding area that is more business friendly. It's too bad. We love this community."[16]

**TAX RATES** Another important factor entrepreneurs must consider is the tax burden that states impose on businesses and individuals. Income taxes may be the most obvious tax states impose on both business and individual residents, but entrepreneurs also must evaluate the impact of payroll taxes, sales taxes, property taxes, and specialized taxes on their cost of operations. Currently, seven states impose no income tax on their residents, but state governments always impose taxes of some sort on businesses and individuals.[17] In some cases, states offer special tax rates or are willing to negotiate fees in lieu of taxes (FILOT) for companies that create jobs and stimulate the local economy.

**ENTREPRENEURIAL PROFILE: Peter Farrell: ResMed Inc.** When California passed Proposition 30, a proposal that raised taxes on its wealthiest citizens, many entrepreneurs began making plans to relocate their businesses to states where the tax burden is significantly lower. "There are states with no personal income tax," says David Kline, vice president of a taxpayers advocacy

The IRS of site 2 is as follows:

$$IRS = \frac{27,750 \times 43.50}{8,400}$$

$$= \$143.71 \text{ sales potential per square foot}$$

Although site 2 appears to be more favorable on the surface, site 1 is supported by the index; site 2 fails to meet the minimum standard of $175 per square foot.

### Reilly's Law of Retail Gravitation

Reilly's Law of Retail Gravitation, a classic work in market analysis published in 1931 by William J. Reilly, uses the analogy of gravity to estimate the attractiveness of a particular business to potential customers. The ability to draw customers is directly related to the extent to which customers see it as a "destination" and is inversely related to the distance that customers must travel to reach the business. Reilly's model also provides a way to estimate the trade boundary between two market areas by calculating the "break point" between them. The break point between two primary market areas is the boundary between the two where customers become indifferent about shopping at one or the other. The key factor in determining this point of indifference is the size of the communities. If two nearby cities have the same population sizes, then the break point lies halfway between them. The following is the equation for Reilly's Law:[44]

$$BP = \frac{d}{1 + \sqrt{P_b/P_a}}$$

where

$BP$ = distance in miles from location A to the break point

$d$ = distance in miles between locations A and B

$P_a$ = population surrounding location A

$P_b$ = population surrounding location B

For example, if city A and city B are 22 miles apart and city A has a population of 22,500 and city B has a population of 42,900, the break point according to Reilly's law is as follows:

$$BP = \frac{22}{1 + \sqrt{42,900/22,500}} = 9.2 \text{ miles}$$

The outer edge of city A's trading area lies about nine miles between city A and city B. Although only a rough estimate, this simple calculation using readily available data can be useful for screening potential locations.

 **In the Entrepreneurial Spotlight**

## Transformed Locations

Entrepreneurs, by their nature, are risk takers, but the most successful entrepreneurs take the necessary steps to minimize the risks they face in their businesses. Rob Stumm, who operates three Pinkberry Frozen Yogurt franchises with his daughters Courtney and Celie, and John Jeter, founder of The Handlebar, a pub/café/concert venue in Greenville, South Carolina, personify the dogged persistence and willingness to step out and take a chance when they are confident that they have made the right decisions. Stumm opened his first Pinkberry franchise in an ideal location in the center of New Orleans, an area he had researched thoroughly and, as a New Orleans native, knew quite well. "With

a Whole Foods and other similar stores across the street, we knew our customers would be there," he says. "We knew our second location had to yield the same results."

With his first franchise outlet operating successfully, Stumm began to focus on finding the location for his second franchise. The location that Stumm selected, however, caused some observers to doubt. "Before we came in, the site of our second store was not what you would consider ideal," he admits. Located on an odd-shaped lot in what was then a rough section of the French Quarter, the site was home to an old gazebo where employees of a neighboring hotel took their smoke breaks, yet Stumm, a

*(continued)*

# In the Entrepreneurial Spotlight (continued)

Pinkberry Frozen yogurt.
*Source:* Jonathan Alcorn/Newscom.

miscellaneous businesses and envisioned a city gem—a "cultural anchor," a place with a bohemian attitude that would house a village of creative ventures. "People thought we were nuts," recalls Jeter. "Everybody said we should move to the West End (the thriving sector of the city that was the first to benefit from its revitalization efforts), but the real estate was exorbitant."

Jeter's risk paid off. By booking up-and-coming musicians such as John Mayer, Jennifer Nettles, Corey Smith, Indigo Girl Amy Ray, Zac Brown, and others, The Handlebar began attracting a loyal following of customers. "That's what an entertainment venue does," he says. "It brings people into a part of town after hours. There's life on the street. Everybody feels safer, and things take off from there." Soon, entrepreneur Gene Burger transformed a nearby former Amoco gas station into Horizon Records, and Mike Goe opened the Wood and Wire Guitar Shop. Other businesses, including a florist, an antique store, and a bevy of artists, quickly followed, and the North End began to look like the thriving cultural anchor that Jeter had envisioned all along. "[It was] a ghost town around there in the evenings, but now a whole cluster of entertainment activities and businesses have come in and more are coming," says a city economic development official. "Something like The Handlebar makes all the difference in revitalizing a neighborhood."

The Handlebar is an integral part of Greenville's cultural infrastructure and was the key component in the revitalization of the city's North End. A new master plan for the area calls for a $200,000 streetscape project that includes pocket parks, bike paths, flower beds, and wider sidewalks that are designed to draw more shoppers. Many merchants say it is the tipping point that will allow their unique cultural village to become the gem that Jeter envisioned many years ago. "We're marching out of the mainstream," he jokes, "but we've been doing that since we started."

licensed architect, saw the site as a diamond in the rough. Retail shops thrived less than a block away, and the historic French Quarter drew millions of tourists and potential customers annually. Undeterred, Stumm convinced Pinkberry officials that the location would be successful and purchased it. "Franchisees should never compromise on real estate," advises Stumm. "We knew our target market going into our second location and didn't want to settle on a location that might be easier to set up but would be farther away from our customers." Stumm says that the second outlet was the most expensive to build, in part because of the need to customize the building to fit onto the odd-shaped lot. The location also has proved to be the most successful of the three (soon to be four) outlets that Stumm owns. In fact, the French Quarter location is one of the most successful units in the entire Pinkberry chain.

John Jeter faced a similar issue when he decided to open The Handlebar, which he bills as a "listening room, pub, and café," in a former Oldsmobile dealership in Greenville's North End. The city has won numerous awards and has become a model of downtown revitalization, but none of the revitalization efforts had reached the North End when Jeter opened for business in 2001. However, Jeter looked around at the crumbled buildings, weed-choked sidewalks, and tattered strip of gas stations and

1. What risks did Rob Stumm and John Jeter take by choosing what many people considered less-than-ideal locations for their businesses?

2. Work with several of your classmates to select an area of your community that suffers from some of the maladies that Stumm and Jeter faced and develop a plan for revitalizing it. What steps would you have to take first to make the area attractive to potential entrepreneurs? What could local government do to encourage entrepreneurs to locate there?

*Sources:* Based on Robert Thomas, "Finding the Real Estate Diamond in the Rough," *QSR Magazine*, May 2012, www.qsrmagazine.com/growth/finding-real-estate-diamond-rough; Anna Lee, "The Handlebar's Song," *Greenville News*, May 19, 2012, pp. 1A, 3A.

## Location Options for Retail and Service Businesses

**3.**

Outline the basic location options for retail and service businesses.

Retail and service business owners can locate in nine basic areas: the central business district, neighborhoods, shopping centers and malls, near competitors, shared spaces, inside large retail stores, nontraditional locations, at home, and on the road. According to Reis Inc., the average cost to lease space in a shopping center is about $19 per square foot, and at malls, lease rates average $39 per square foot. In central business locations, the average cost is between $22 and $45 per square foot (rental rates vary significantly, depending on the city).[45] Of course, cost is just one factor a business owner must consider when choosing a location.

## Central Business District

The central business district (CBD) is the traditional center of town—the downtown concentration of businesses established early in the development of most towns and cities. Entrepreneurs derive several advantages from a downtown location. Because businesses are centrally located, they attract customers from the entire trading area of the city. In addition, small businesses benefit from the traffic generated by other stores clustered in the downtown district. However, locating in a CBD does have certain disadvantages. Intense competition, high rental rates, traffic congestion, and inadequate parking facilities characterize some CBDs. In addition, many cities have experienced difficulty in preventing the decay of their older downtown business districts. Downtown districts withered as residents moved to the suburbs and began shopping at newer, more convenient shopping centers and malls.

Today, however, many of these CBDs are experiencing rebirth as cities restore them to their former splendor and shoppers return. Many customers find irresistible the charming atmosphere that traditional downtown districts offer with their rich mix of stores, their unique architecture and streetscapes, and their historic character. Cities have begun to reverse the urban decay of their downtown business districts through proactive revitalization programs designed to attract visitors and residents alike to cultural events by locating theaters and museums, hosting festivals, and sponsoring special events such as ice skating in the downtown area. In addition, many cities are providing economic incentives to real estate developers to build apartment and condominium complexes in the heart of their downtown districts. Vitality is returning as residents live and shop in the once nearly abandoned downtown areas. The "ghost-town" image is being replaced by both younger and older residents who love the convenience and excitement of life at the center of the city.

**ENTREPRENEURIAL PROFILE: Casey Karnes: B1 Bicycles** Columbus, Ohio's, CBD suffered from many of the same maladies as other cities, but city officials have focused their efforts on refurbishing it. A study that the city conducted concludes that a $375 million retail gap exists in downtown Columbus. "There is a huge unmet demand for goods and services downtown," says one city official. "It's one of the largest untapped retail markets in central Ohio." The 100,000 employees who work downtown make up the largest potential customer base, but more than 39,000 students who attend classes at four locations in the CBD are also a significant market. More than 6,200 people live downtown, and neighborhoods that are within two miles of the CBD are home to 65,000 residents. Casey Karnes, who opened B1 Bicycles, a full-service bicycle shop in the CBD in 2007, in the early stages of the downtown revitalization effort, is pleased with his downtown location and says that his company's sales are growing fast. "There's still a lot of room for expansion, a lot of room for people to be part of downtown retail, but having more restaurants and more people moving downtown is helping."[46]

## Neighborhood Locations

Small businesses that locate near residential areas rely heavily on the local trading areas for business. For example, many grocers and convenience stores located just outside residential subdivisions count on local customers for successful operation. One study of food stores reports that the majority of the typical grocers' customers live within a five-mile radius. The primary advantages of a neighborhood location include relatively low operating costs and rents and close contact with customers.

**ENTREPRENEURIAL PROFILE: Danny Meyer: Shake Shack** Danny Meyer, founder of Union Square Hospitality Group, owns three of the *Zagat Guide's* top five fine-dining restaurants in Manhattan. Meyer also operates Shake Shack, an upscale hamburger restaurant (plus wine, beer, and ShackMeister Ale) with nine locations in major urban areas or in sports venues. Meyer recently opened the first Shake Shack outlet in suburbia, choosing a location in affluent West Port, Connecticut, as the site for his experiment to determine whether the business model will succeed outside of densely populated urban areas. Unlike the typical fast-food chains, Shake Shack uses soft, muted colors that fit into the upscale neighborhood. "Our customer is the person who says, 'I don't eat at fast-food restaurants, but when I choose to eat a burger and fries or a shake, I want a good one, and that's why I'm coming to Shake Shack,'" says Randy Garutti, Shake Shack's CEO.[47]

## Shopping Centers and Malls

Until the early twentieth century, CBDs were the primary shopping venues in the United States. As cars and transportation networks became more popular in the 1920s, shopping centers began popping up outside cities' CBDs. Then in October 1956, the nation's first shopping mall, Southdale, opened in the Minneapolis, Minnesota, suburb of Edina. Designed by Victor Gruen, the fully enclosed mall featured 72 shops anchored by two competing department stores (a radical concept at the time), a garden courtyard with a goldfish pond, an aviary, hanging plants, and artificial trees. With its multilevel layout and parking garage, Southdale was a huge success and forever changed the way Americans would shop.[48] Today, the nation's nearly 113,000 shopping centers and malls, which encompass more than 8.8 billion square feet of retail space, have become a mainstay of the American landscape. Because many different types of stores operate under one roof, shopping malls give meaning to the term "one-stop shopping." In a typical month, nearly 187 million adults visit malls or shopping centers, generating $2.4 trillion in annual sales, representing 55 percent of all retail sales.[49] There are eight types of shopping centers (see Table 18.6):

- *Neighborhood shopping centers.* The typical neighborhood shopping center is relatively small, containing from 3 to 12 stores and serving a population of up to 40,000 people who live within a 10-minute drive. The anchor store in these centers is usually a supermarket or a drugstore. Neighborhood shopping centers typically are straight-line strip malls with parking available in front and primarily serve the daily shopping needs of customers in the surrounding area.

- *Community shopping centers.* A community shopping center contains from 12 to 50 stores and serves a population ranging from 40,000 to 150,000 people. The leading tenant often is a large department or variety store, a super drugstore, or a supermarket. Community shopping centers sell more clothing and other soft goods than do neighborhood shopping centers. Of the eight types of shopping centers, community shopping centers take on the greatest variety of shapes, designs, and tenants.

- *Power centers.* A power center combines the drawing strength of a large regional mall with the convenience of a neighborhood shopping center. Anchored by several large specialty retailers, such as warehouse clubs, discount department stores, or large specialty stores, these centers target older, wealthier Baby Boomers, who want selection and convenience. Anchor stores usually account for 80 percent of power center space, compared with 50 percent in the typical community shopping center. Just as in a shopping mall, small businesses can benefit from the traffic generated by anchor stores, but they must choose their locations carefully so that they are not overshadowed by their larger neighbors.

- *Theme or festival centers.* Festival shopping centers employ a unifying theme that individual stores display in their decor and sometimes in the merchandise they sell. Entertainment is a common theme for these shopping centers, which often target tourists. Many festival shopping centers are located in urban areas and are housed in older, sometimes historic buildings that have been renovated to serve as shopping centers.

- *Outlet centers.* As their name suggests, outlet centers feature manufacturers' and retailers' outlet stores selling name-brand goods at a discount. Unlike most other types of shopping centers, outlet centers typically have no anchor stores; the discounted merchandise they offer draws sufficient traffic. Most outlet centers are open-air and are laid out in strips or in clusters, creating small "villages" of shops.

- *Lifestyle (or town) centers.* Typically located near affluent residential neighborhoods where their target customers live, lifestyle centers are designed to look less like shopping centers and malls and more like the busy streets in the CBDs that existed in towns and cities in their heyday. Occupied by many upscale national chain specialty stores, such as Williams Sonoma, Talbot's, Pottery Barn, Pier 1 Imports, Jos. A. Bank Clothiers, and others, these centers combine shopping convenience, dining, and entertainment, ranging from movie theaters and open-air concerts to art galleries and people watching. Some centers also include residential space, often located above the ground-level retail shops. "Lifestyle centers create a shopping-leisure destination that's an extension of customers' personal lifestyles," says one industry expert. The typical lifestyle center generates between $400 and $500 in sales per square foot compared to $350 to $375 in sales per square foot in traditional malls.[50] Lifestyle centers are among the most popular types of shopping centers being built today. The first lifestyle center, The Shops of Saddle Creek, opened in Germantown, Tennessee, in 1987. Today, more than 400 lifestyle centers operate across the United States.[51]

- *Regional shopping malls.* The regional shopping mall serves a large trading area, usually from 5 to 15 miles or more in all directions. These enclosed malls contain from 50 to

**TABLE 18.6 Types of Shopping Centers**

| Type of Shopping Center | Concept | Square Footage (including anchors) | Acreage | Typical Anchor | | Anchor Ratio (%)[a] | Primary Trade Area (miles)[b] |
|---|---|---|---|---|---|---|---|
| | | | | **Number** | **Type** | | |
| **Malls** | | | | | | | |
| Regional center | General and fashion merchandise; mall (typically enclosed) | 480,000–800,000 | 40–100 | 2 or more | Full-line department store; junior department store; mass merchant; discount department store; fashion apparel | 50–70 | 5–15 |
| Super-regional center | Similar to regional center but offers more variety | >800,000 | 60–120 | 3 or more | Full-line department store; junior department store; mass merchant; fashion apparel | 50–70 | 5–25 |
| **Open-air centers** | | | | | | | |
| Neighborhood center | Convenience | 30,000–150,000 | 3–15 | 1 or more | Supermarket | 30–50 | 3 |
| Community center | General merchandise; convenience | 100,000–350,000 | 10–40 | 2 or more | Discount department store; supermarket; drug; home improvement; large specialty or discount apparel | 40–60 | 3–6 |
| Lifestyle center | Upscale national chain specialty stores, dining, and entertainment in an outdoor setting | 150,000–500,000 but can be larger or smaller | 10–40 | 0–2 | Not usually anchored in the traditional sense but may include bookstore; large specialty retailers; multiplex cinema; small department store | 0–50 | 8–12 |
| Power center | Category-dominant anchors; few small business tenants | 250,000–600,000 | 25–80 | 3 or more | Category killer; home improvement; discount; department store; warehouse club; off-price | 75–90 | 5–10 |
| Theme/festival center | Leisure; tourist oriented; retail and service | 80,000–250,000 | 5–20 | Unspecified | Restaurants; entertainment | N/A | 25–75 |
| Outlet center | Manufacturers' outlet stores | 50,000–400,000 | 10–50 | N/A | Manufacturers' outlet stores | N/A | 25–75 |

[a]The share of a center's total square footage that is occupied by its anchors.
[b]The area from which 60% to 80% of the center's sales originate.
*Source:* International Council of Shopping Centers, New York.

100 stores and serve a population of 150,000 or more living within a 20- to 40-minute drive. The anchor is typically one or more major department stores with smaller specialty stores occupying the spaces between the anchors. Clothing is the most popular item sold in regional shopping malls.

- *Super-regional shopping malls.* A super-regional mall is similar to a regional mall but is bigger, containing more anchor stores and a greater variety of shops selling deeper lines of merchandise. Its trade area stretches up to 25 or more miles. Canada's West Edmonton Mall, the largest mall in North America, with more than 800 stores and 100 restaurants in 5.3 million square feet, is one of the most famous super-regional malls in the world. In addition to its abundance of retail shops, the mall contains an ice skating rink, a water park, two hotels, an amusement park, a bungee tower, miniature golf courses, and a 21-screen movie complex. Currently, more than 1,500 regional and super-regional shopping malls operate in the United States.

When evaluating a mall or shopping center location, an entrepreneur should consider the following questions:

- Is there a good fit with other products and brands sold in the mall or center?

- Who are the other tenants? Which stores are the anchors that will bring people into the mall or center?

- Demographically, is the center a good fit for your products or services? What are its customer demographics?

- How much foot traffic does the mall or center generate? How much traffic passes the specific site you are considering?

- How much vehicle traffic does the mall or center generate? Check its proximity to major population centers, the volume of tourists it draws, and the volume of drive-by freeway traffic. A mall or center that scores well on all three is more likely to be a winner.

- What is the mall's vacancy rate? What is the turnover rate of its tenants?

- How much is the rent, and how is it calculated? Most mall tenants pay a base amount of rent plus a small percentage of their sales above a specified level.

- Is the mall or center successful? How much does it generate in sales per square foot? (Experts say that if a mall's sales per square foot slips below $300, it is doomed.[52]) The International Council of Shopping Centers in New York (*www.icsc.org*) is a good source of industry information.

A mall location is no guarantee of business success, however. Malls have been under pressure lately. About one-third of the malls in the United States are thriving, and many weaker ones (known as "greyfields") have been demolished or redeveloped. The basic problem is an oversupply of mall space; there is 22.5 square feet of mall retail space for every person in the United States! The last new enclosed mall in the United States opened in 2006.[53] In addition, the demographic makeup of an area's shoppers often changes over time, creating a new socioeconomic customer base that may or may not be compatible with a small company's target customer profile. As a result, many malls have undergone extensive renovations to emphasize "entertailing," adding entertainment features to their existing retail space in an attempt to generate more traffic. For instance, in addition to its 520 retail shops and 60 restaurants, Minneapolis's Mall of America, the largest mall in the United States (located only a few miles from Southdale, the nation's first mall), includes a Nickelodeon Universe amusement park at its center, a 1.2-million-gallon aquarium, a flight simulator, and a 14-screen movie complex in its 4.2 million square feet of space. The Mall of America, which attracts 40 million visitors per year, could hold seven Yankee Stadiums but does not make the top 10 list of largest malls in the world.[54]

### Near Competitors

One of the most important factors in choosing a retail or service location is the compatibility of nearby stores with the retail or service customer. For example, stores selling high-priced goods such as cars or merchandise that requires comparisons, such as antiques, find it advantageous to locate near competitors to facilitate comparison shopping. Locating near competitors might be a key factor for success in businesses that sell goods that customers compare on the basis of price, quality, color, and other factors.

Although some business owners avoid locations near direct competitors, others see locating near rivals as an advantage. For instance, restaurateurs know that successful restaurants attract other restaurants, which, in turn, attract more customers. Many cities have at least one "restaurant row," where restaurants cluster together; each restaurant feeds customers to the others. In Worcester, Massachusetts, more than 40 restaurants coexist on Shrewsbury Street's Restaurant Row. Entrepreneur Greg Califano, who studied in Naples, Italy, to become certified to make authentic Neapolitan pizzas, chose Restaurant Row for the location of his pizza wood-fired pizza restaurant, Volturno. Califano found a historic building that fits the "Old World" ambiance of the restaurant, which includes two special pizza ovens flown in from Naples.[55]

Locating near competitors has its limits, however. Clustering too many businesses of a single type into a small area ultimately erodes their sales once the market reaches the saturation point. As the number of gourmet coffee shops has exploded in recent years, many have struggled to remain profitable, often competing with three or four similar shops, all within easy walking distance of one another. When an area becomes saturated with competitors, the stores cannibalize sales from one another, making it difficult for them to survive.

## Shared Spaces

Because outstanding locations can be expensive or hard to find, some small companies are sharing spaces with other small businesses. Entrepreneurs can reduce their rent and maintenance costs (and, therefore, their financial risk) by operating in a joint space. Entrepreneurs often find that sharing space with other businesses sparks creativity because their employees have the opportunity to interact with people outside of their industries. Others who share space with businesses that sell complementary products often see their sales increase.

**ENTREPRENEURIAL PROFILE: Jessica Swiggum Goldman, Emmy Rigali, and Trisha Reynolds: All About Dance, Go Cycle, and Free to Be** When Jessica Swiggum Goldman, owner of a dance studio, All About Dance, decided to expand her business, she moved into a 15,000-square-foot building in Chicago's Old Town section and struck a deal with Emmy Rigali, owner of a fitness studio, to rent a portion of the building. The location gave Rigali the opportunity to offer a spin class that her customers had been requesting. She invested in 26 stationary bikes and a sound system and opened Go Cycle. Goldman also rented a portion of her building to a third complementary business, Free to Be, which sells dance and fitness apparel. "I have a built-in customer base," says owner Trisha Reynolds. "They're here every day." The three entrepreneurs not only share the building's rent expense but also benefit from sharing a common front desk and receptionist, studio space, and locker rooms. They also have discovered intangible benefits of their shared space. "There's an energy here, a buzz," says Rigali. "In shared space, I was successful more quickly and with less stress."[56]

## Inside Large Retail Stores

Rather than compete against giant retailers, some small business owners are cooperating with them, locating their businesses inside the larger company's stores. These small companies offer products that the large retailers do not and benefit from the large volume of customer traffic that the large stores attract. Large retailers, including Wal-Mart, Target, and others, are hosts to small businesses, including franchisees of fast-food chains Subway, McDonald's, and Checkers and medical clinics and banks. Checkers, a quick-service hamburger chain that operates 770 drive-through outlets in the United States, recently opened restaurants inside Wal-Mart stores. "It has to be the right type of partnership," says Jennifer Durham, who is in charge of franchise development. "We wouldn't go into a Neiman-Marcus because that's not where our customers are."[57] These stores within a store reap the benefits of the large volume of traffic from the more than 100 million people who shop at Wal-Mart each week.

## Nontraditional Locations

Rather than select a location and try to draw customers to it, many small businesses are setting up locations where their customers already are. Many of these are nontraditional locations, such as airports, museums, office buildings, churches, casinos, college and university campuses, athletic arenas, and others, that offer high concentrations of potential customers. In many cases, these locations are smaller and less expensive to build but generate more sales per square foot than traditional, full-size stores. Dunkin' Donuts has more than 500 nontraditional locations out of 6,800 outlets in the United States, including locations in theme parks, military bases, universities, travel centers on interstate highways, and others. More than 8,000 of Subway's 35,000 restaurants worldwide are in nontraditional locations, including a high school in Detroit in which students operate the outlet, and account for 20 percent of the chain's total sales. Subway also has an outlet in a Jeep assembly plant and in a church in Buffalo, New York, where the pastor is a franchisee.[58]

## Home-Based Businesses

For more than 15 million entrepreneurs, home is where the business is, and their numbers are swelling. One recent study from the SBA reports that 52 percent of all small companies are home based and that more than 21 percent of home-based businesses generate more than $100,000 in annual revenue.[59] Many service businesses operate from entrepreneurs' homes. Because many service companies do not rely on customers to come to their places of business, incurring the expense of an office location is unnecessary. For instance, customers typically contact plumbers or exterminators by telephone, and the work is performed in customers' homes. Internet-based and catalog retailers also operate from their homes.

 **ENTREPRENEURIAL PROFILE: Wendy Navarro: Saige Nicole** In 2006, Wendy Navarro, a stay-at-home mother, started Saige Nicole, an online boutique that specializes in clothing and accessories for babies and toddlers, from her home in Costa Mesa, California. Ninety percent of Navarro's upscale product line features unique items created by other "mompreneurs," including brands such as Right Bank Babies, Lilliputians-NYC, Wendy Anne Moses Baskets, Cape Clogs, and others. Navarro's entire family is involved in running the business, which has become so successful that she recently opened a retail store in Costa Mesa. The SBA recently presented Navarro with the Home-Based Champion of the Year Award.

Choosing a home location has disadvantages. It may affect family life, interruptions are more frequent, the refrigerator is all too handy, work is always just a few steps away, and isolation can be a problem. Another difficulty that some home-based entrepreneurs face involves zoning laws. As their businesses grow and become more successful, entrepreneurs' neighbors often begin to complain about the increased traffic, noise, and disruptions from deliveries, employees, and customers who drive through their residential neighborhoods to conduct business.

## On the Road

Some entrepreneurs are finding that the best location is not a permanent location but a mobile business that takes products and services to its customers. Veterinarians, dentists, restaurants, and others are outfitting mobile units and taking their businesses on the road. Although mobile entrepreneurs avoid the costs of building or renovating permanent locations, they must incur the expense of setting up their mobile businesses. They also face other obstacles, such as finding suitable parking spaces in high-traffic areas, complaints from owners of nearby businesses, and securing the necessary permits to operate. In some cities, ordinances prohibit food truck entrepreneurs from operating within a set distance (often 200 to 300 feet, but some cities have established a minimum of 1,500 feet) of an existing restaurant.

## Lessons from the Street-Smart Entrepreneur

# How to Launch a Successful Pop-Up Shop

One of the hottest trends in the retail and restaurant industries is pop-up shops, temporary locations that are open for only a few hours, days, or weeks before shutting down. Many pop-up stores operate in the busy shopping period leading up to Christmas. Entrepreneurs are using pop-up stores to test ideas for new businesses, move excess inventory, explore the viability of new markets, and capitalize on a market opportunity. Sisters Christina Bartkus and Lisa Trifone, cofounders of Purefections, a chocolate shop in Quincy, Massachusetts, that makes delectable concoctions from fine Belgian chocolate, spotted an opportunity to reach customers in nearby Boston and in November opened a pop-up shop in an unused section of their brother's interior design business on Boston's busy Tremont Street. They posted an adhesive version of their business name and logo in large cocoa-colored letters on the space's white walls, put a sign outside announcing their shop, and began selling their chocolate goodies. "We have many customers who come to our Quincy store and beg us to open up more locations," says Bartkus. "Pop-ups allow us to be more convenient for our existing customers and to reach a whole new customer base."

The Street-Smart Entrepreneur offers business owners the following lessons learned by studying the factors behind successful pop-up stores:

***Decide what you want your pop-up shop to accomplish.*** Entrepreneurs create pop-up shops for many reasons; be sure to identify the goals and objectives your shop should achieve. On a visit to New York City, Jason Revilla and Jim Grumbine, cofounders of Faith & Fortune, an online company that sells "socially conscious" T-shirts, sweatshirts, hoodies, and other apparel, noticed several successful pop-up shops and decided to open their own in their hometown of in Beverly, Massachusetts. Their goal was to raise awareness of their company among potential customers. "Because we're a Web-based business, we were looking to get more people to interact with our brand," says Grumbine. "[We want] people to come in and see our clothing because the materials we use are unique, soft, comfortable, and vintage-like."

***Develop a unified plan for your concept.*** By definition, pop-up shops have only a limited time to accomplish their purposes, and entrepreneurs must make the most of the brief opportunity they have. The best way to achieve that is to develop a plan to create a unique, one-of-a-kind shopping experience, an event that will attract customers and keep them talking for weeks about it. Every pop-up shop should have a unified theme that resonates with the company's target audience. Women's handbag retailer Kate Spade had success with an igloo-shaped pop-up shop set up next to a skating rink in New York City's Bryant Park for three weeks before Christmas that offered shoppers a selection of signature handbags, accessories, jewelry, and stocking stuffers in addition to free hot chocolate.

*Select the right location for your pop-up store.* Because a pop-up store is temporary, an entrepreneur must find the ideal location for it. Jason Revilla and Jim Grumbine worked with a friend who is a real estate agent to find an empty storefront on a street with a high volume of foot traffic for their Faith & Fortune pop-up store. Alfredo Sandoval, a restaurateur and managing partner of the Mercadito Hospitality Group in Chicago, opened a pop-up restaurant, PT, that operated during the Windy City's summer months on the spacious sidewalk patio at the Talbott Hotel, which is located in a prime spot in Chicago's upscale Gold Coast Historic District. The temporary restaurant set up 100 seats on the patio and 50 in a converted space inside the boutique hotel. PT was able to field test its drink and menu items on customers and generate a significant "buzz" for its brand, enabling the company to open a full-time, permanent restaurant in the Talbott Hotel several months later.

*Manage your costs.* Some entrepreneurs use pop-up stores to test their business ideas on a small scale before committing significant resources to them. Others see pop-up shops as a way to generate additional profits. Whatever purpose entrepreneurs have for their pop-up shops, they must manage their costs carefully. Entrepreneurs often can negotiate reasonable rental rates with landlords on properties that otherwise would remain vacant. At Faith & Fortune, the landlord allowed Revilla and Grumbine to use the storefront in exchange for a few T-shirts. They also spent $150 to purchase business signs (which they can reuse), office supplies, and food and, as they promised, donated 20 percent of their sales to charitable causes.

*Get the word out.* One key to a successful pop-up event is promotion, and social media marketing tools are ideal for reaching potential customers. Cheri Caso, owner of Merchant No. 4, an online shop that sells modern housewares, opened a pop-up shop in an unused loft in her friend's architecture firm in New York City. Because of the fourth-floor location, Caso knew that promoting her pop-up store would be essential. To generate traffic, she announced the event on Facebook and Twitter and sent press releases to local publications and design blogs that were popular with her target customers. She also placed a sidewalk sign outside the building. In just four days, she covered her costs (just $1,000), sold a lot of slow-moving merchandise, generated a small profit, and promoted her company to the nearly 300 people who went through the shop. Other entrepreneurs have been successful by hosting a wine and cheese grand opening, inviting shoppers to a VIP blogger night, or offering discounts to customers who sign in on Foursquare.

*Use mobile technology to make the checkout process seamless for customers.* One practical issue that pop-up entrepreneurs must deal with is making sure that the checkout process works smoothly and efficiently. Greg Turner, owner of Fringe Outfitters, an online retailer of men's and women's clothing, uses Square, a mobile credit card reader that allows merchants to accept credit cards on any smart phone or tablet device that operates on either iOS or Android operating systems, when he launches a pop-up store. Entrepreneurs can set up an account at *Squareup.com* and receive a free Square card reader that plugs into the headphone jack of their phones or tablets. Square charges a processing fee of 2.75 percent for credit card swipe transactions and 3.5 percent plus 15 cents for keyed-in transactions.

Pop-up shops are useful tools for entrepreneurs who want to create a lean start-up. Rather than build a business model or full-featured product in secrecy and then launch it with great fanfare, a lean start-up launches a "minimum viable product," one that includes just enough features to get meaningful feedback from customers. In a customer-focused, iterative process, entrepreneurs observe customers' purchasing behavior and use the feedback they get from the minimum viable product to revise and improve the original product or business model before going back to the market to get more feedback from customers. The idea is to get to market much faster with a product or business model whose features reflect just what customers want and to reduce the probability of wasting time incorporating features that customers don't want. One business writer who has watched pop-up shops lead to successful permanent small businesses says,

> Why does this pop-up storefront option work so well? It lowers the barriers to entry for a person interested in starting a business, creates a temporary timeline to test out the businesses potential, and mitigates the risk associated with a traditional start-up. It also does away with the tedium, and minutia associated with filing endless permits, developing long-range accounting forecasts, reviewing costly insurance packages, multi-year leases, navigating bureaucracy, and more. In the end, it's the Lemonade Stand philosophy: All it takes to start one is a stand and lemonade. The other pieces are necessary but can be added and enhanced as the business grows.

*Sources:* Based on Kathleen Pierce, "The Anatomy of a Pop-Up Store," *Boston Globe*, December 5, 2012, *www.bostonglobe.com/lifestyle/style/2012/12/05/the-anatomy-pop-store/cy2daeKoRS1gy5jmus0GVL/story.html*; Matt Robinson, "Purefections Brings the Sweet to the Street Starting November 17," *Exhale*, November 2, 2012, *http://exhalelifestyle.com/main/index.php/purefections-brings-the-sweet-to-the-street-starting-november-17*; Jason Del Rey, "How to Open a Pop-Up Store," *Inc.*, July 1, 2010, *www.inc.com/magazine/20100701/how-to-open-a-pop-up-store.html*; "Tips for Starting a Pop-Up Shop," *Fox Small Business Center*, April 18, 2012, *http://smallbusiness.foxbusiness.com/sbc/2012/04/02/how-to-start-pop-up-shop*; Bob Krummert, "How Pop-Up Restaurants Can Help You Expand," *Restaurant Hospitality*, May 31, 2012, *http://restaurant-hospitality.com/new-restaurant-concepts/how-pop-restaurants-can-help-you-expand*; Charlie Duerr, "Summer Pop-Up Restaurant Craze Hits Chicago," *Nation's Restaurant News*, June 27, 2012, *http://nrn.com/latest-headlines/summer-pop-restaurant-craze-hits-chicago*; Melanie McIntyre, "How to Open a Pop-Up Retail Shop," *Metropreneur Columbus*, April 1, 2011, *www.themetropreneur.com/columbus/open-pop-up-shop*; Alyson Shontell, "18 Amazing Pop-Up Stores That Stopped Shoppers in Their Tracks," *Business Insider*, May 3, 2011, *www.businessinsider.com/17-most-creative-pop-up-stores?op=1*; Robert Wilonsky, "The Power of the Pop-up Shop," *Dallas Observer*, June 10, 2011, *http://blogs.dallasobserver.com/unfairpark/2011/06/the_power_of_the_pop-up_shop.php*.

# The Location Decision for Manufacturers

**4.**

Explain the site selection
process for manufacturers.

The criteria for the location decision for manufacturers are very different from those of retailers and service businesses; however, the decision can have just as much impact on the company's success. In some cases, a manufacturer has special needs that influence the choice of a location. When one manufacturer of photographic plates and film was searching for a location for a new plant, it had to limit its search to those sites with a large supply of available freshwater, a necessary part of its process. In other cases, zoning ordinances dictate a company's location decision. If a manufacturer's process creates offensive odors or excessive noise, it may be even further restricted in its choices.

The type of transportation facilities required dictates the location of a factory in some cases. Some manufacturers may require a location on a railroad siding, whereas others may need only access to interstate highways. Some companies ship bulk materials by ship or barge and consequently require a facility near a navigable body of water. Developers are building the 6,700-acre Americas Gateway Logistics Center, a mixed-use industrial park in Florida's heartland that will minimize the transportation costs of its tenants by providing ready access to interstate highways, railways, seaports, and international air cargo airports. "International access is tremendous through the ports, and we are criss-crossed with highways and Class 1 railroads," says one official.[60]

As fuel costs escalate, the cost of shipping finished products to customers also influences the location decision for many manufacturers, forcing them to open factories or warehouses in locations that are close to their primary markets to reduce transportation costs.

**ENTREPRENEURIAL PROFILE: Mickey Walker: Viking Air Movers** Mickey Walker, founder of Viking Air Movers, a small, family-owned business that makes pressurized drying systems, recently opened a factory in Hesperia in southern California's San Bernardino County. Walker cites the area's inexpensive land, reasonable wage rates, and sizable, qualified workforce as benefits of locating there, but low transportation costs were the primary driver of the company's decision. "We ship our products worldwide from our plant," says Walker. "The transportation assets of this area are outstanding. The major railroad hubs and Interstate 15 give us access to our [West Coast and Asian] customers." Viking Air Movers also operates a distribution center in Fairfield, Ohio. "We ship products east of the Mississippi out of Fairfield," he says.[61]

## Foreign Trade Zones

Created in 1934, foreign trade zones can be an attractive location for small manufacturers that engage in global trade and are looking to reduce or eliminate the tariffs, duties, and excise taxes they pay on the materials and parts they import and the goods they export. A **foreign trade zone** (see Figure 18.5) is a specially designated area in or near a U.S. customs port of entry that allows resident companies to import materials and components from foreign countries; assemble, process, manufacture, or package them and then ship the finished product back out while either deferring, reducing, or eliminating completely tariffs and duties. As far as tariffs and duties are concerned,

**FIGURE 18.5**

**How a Foreign Trade Zone (FTZ) Works**

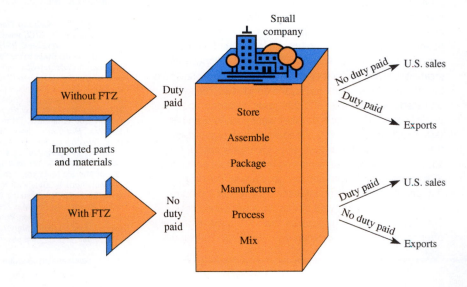

a company located in a foreign trade zone is treated as if it is located outside the United States. For instance, a maker of speakers can import components from around the world and assemble them at its plant located in a foreign trade zone. The company pays no duties on the components it imports or on the speakers it exports to other foreign markets. The only duties the manufacturer pays are on the speakers it sells in the United States. There are 257 foreign trade zones and 514 subzones, which are special foreign trade zones that are established for limited purposes, operating in the United States. (The International Trade Administration provides a list of foreign trade zones by state at *http://ia.ita.doc.gov/ftzpage/letters/ftzlist-map.html*.) More than 12 percent of foreign goods enter the United States through foreign trade zones.[62] The value of shipments into foreign trade zones has increased from $147 billion in 1998 to nearly $534 billion today; foreign trade zone tenants export nearly $35 billion worth of goods annually.[63]

## Business Incubators

For many start-up companies, a business incubator may make the ideal initial location. A **business incubator or accelerator** is an organization that combines low-cost, flexible rental space with a multitude of support services for its small business residents. The primary reason that communities establish incubators is to enhance economic development, create jobs, and diversify the local economy. The strategy works; 84 percent of the companies that graduate from incubators stay in the local community.[64]

> **ENTREPRENEURIAL PROFILE: Andrew Torba and Charles Szymanski: Kuhcoon**  Andrew Torba and Charles Szymanski recently moved their start-up, Kuhcoon, a company that builds, maintains, and manages social networking accounts for businesses into the Scranton Enterprise Center, a business incubator created in 2003 in downtown Scranton, Pennsylvania. "The incubator really gave us the legitimacy and credibility we needed as young entrepreneurs," says Torba, who is just 21 years old. "Before this, we were operating out of a shed in my parents' backyard." Kuhcoon moved into the incubator after Torba and Szymanski won the annual Great Valley Technology Alliance business plan competition. Since entering the incubator, Kuhcoon has grown from four employees to 10 and now has clients around the world for its social media services platform.[65]

An incubator's goal is to nurture young companies during the volatile start-up period and to help them survive until they are strong enough to go out on their own (see Figure 18.6). Three types of incubators exist: mixed-use incubators host start-up companies from a variety of industries, technology incubators target companies that are creating or commercializing new technologies, and empowerment incubators are mixed-use facilities that focus on businesses whose founders are underserved, such as minority or women entrepreneurs.[66] Deborah Jackson, Kelly Hoey, and Veronika Sonsev founded New York City based startup accelerator Women Innovative Mobile (WIM) Accelerator. WIM Accelerator targets and invests in mobile technology ventures with gender diverse founding

**5.** _____
Discuss the benefits of locating a start-up company in a business incubator.

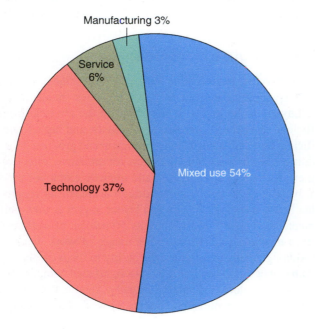

**FIGURE 18.6**

**Business Incubators by Industry Focus**

*Source:* Based on National Business Incubation Association, Athens, OH, 2012.

Veronika Sonsev, Deborah Jackson, and Kelly Hoey, cofounders of Women Innovative Mobile, a business accelerator.

*Source:* Lisa Tanner Photography.

teams. Companies accepted into the WIM Accelerator receive access to expert mentors and advisors, services and perks such as free office space plus a seed-capital investment from WIM Accelerator, in exchange for which WIM Accelerator takes an 8% equity stake in the ventures.[67]

The shared resources that accelerators and incubators typically provide their tenants include secretarial services, a telephone system, computers and software, high-speed Internet connections, audiovisual equipment, meeting space, and, sometimes, access to mentors, management consulting services, and financing. Not only do these services save young companies money (reducing a small company's start-up costs in some cases by 40 to 50 percent), but they also save them valuable time. Entrepreneurs can focus on getting their products and services to market rather than searching for the resources they need to build their companies. Many business incubators help their tenants gain access to capital by providing access to angel investors and venture capital firms; a survey by the National Business Incubation Association reports that 83 percent of incubators provide some kind of access to seed capital, ranging from help with obtaining federal grants to making connections with angel investors.[68]

The typical incubator has entry requirements that prospective residents must meet. Incubators also have criteria that establish the conditions a business must maintain to remain in the facility as well as the expectations for "graduation" into the business community. The typical start-up that lives in an incubator stays for an average of three years. More than 1,250 incubators operate across the United States, up from just 12 in 1980. Perhaps the greatest advantage of choosing to locate a start-up company in an incubator is a greater chance for success. The National Business Incubation Association reports that graduates from business incubators have an 87 percent survival rate. Each year, business incubators help an estimated 49,000 start-up companies that provide full-time employment for more than 200,000 workers and generate annual revenue of almost $15 billion.[69]

## Layout and Design Considerations

**6.**

Describe the criteria used to analyze the layout and design considerations of a building, including the Americans with Disabilities Act.

Once an entrepreneur chooses the best location for his or her business, the next issue to address is designing the proper layout for the space to maximize sales (retail) or productivity (manufacturing or service). **Layout** is the logical arrangement of the physical facilities in a business that contributes to efficient operations, increased productivity, and higher sales. Planning for the most effective and efficient layout in a business environment can produce dramatic improvements in a company's operating effectiveness and efficiency. An attractive, effective layout can help a company's recruiting efforts, reduce absenteeism, and improve employee productivity and satisfaction. A recent *U.S. Workplace Survey* by global design firm Gensler reports that 90 percent of employees believe that better workplace design and layout improves their performance and productivity and the company's competitiveness. Yet only 50 percent of workers say that their work environment encourages innovation.[70] The changing nature of work demands that work space design also changes. Although many jobs require the ability to focus on "heads down," individual tasks, collaboration with coworkers is becoming a more significant component of work even when workers are scattered across the globe and "meet" virtually. An effective work space must be flexible enough to accommodate and encourage both types of work. Increasingly, work is becoming more complex, team based, technology dependent, and mobile, and work spaces must change to accommodate these characteristics. The study by Gensler concludes that top-performing companies have work spaces that are more effective than those of average companies, particularly for collaboration. Gensler also reports that employees at top-performing companies spend 23 percent more time collaborating with their coworkers than do employees at average companies.[71]

When creating a layout, managers must consider its impact on space itself (comfort, flexibility, size, and ergonomics), the people who occupy it (type of work, special requirements, need for interaction, and tasks performed), and the technology they use (communication, Internet access, and equipment).[72] The following factors have a significant impact on a space's layout and design.

## Size and Adaptability

A building must offer adequate space and be adaptable to accommodate a business's daily operations. If space is restrictive at the outset of operations, efficiency will suffer. There must be room enough for customers' movement, inventory, displays, storage, work areas, offices, and restrooms. Haphazard layouts undermine employee productivity and create organizational chaos. Businesses that launch in locations that are too small at the outset must make premature and costly moves to larger spaces, interfering with their ability to maintain a loyal customer base. Although entrepreneurs want locations capable of accommodating their companies' growth, they should avoid spaces that are too big because they waste valuable resources in the form of higher rent and unused space. "Don't take on more space than you need," advises Bill Armstrong, an experienced commercial real estate broker.[73] In fact, many businesses are reducing the space they allocate for their office workers because technology allows some people to work from almost anywhere rather than from a traditional office. In 1985, the average amount office space per employee was 400 square feet; today, it is 250 square feet, and experts predict that by 2021, the average office employee will work in just 150 square feet.[74] Companies are moving away from private offices and even cubicles to unassigned work spaces, communal tables or desks that workers share and that can be rearranged easily, depending on the task at hand. The result is a fluid layout that changes during the day. Studies show that employees utilize just 50 percent of a traditional office space because of meetings, travel, vacation, and sick days.

**ENTREPRENEURIAL PROFILE: Rob Watts: Traction Systems, LLC** Rob Watts, founder of Traction Systems, LLC, a Web site development company in West Sacramento, California, created an office that includes L-shaped desks for each of the company's four employees in a single 30-square-foot room. Web designer Vitaly Zavortny says that the open space makes interaction and collaboration on projects easy; when he has to concentrate on "heads-down" work, he uses noise-canceling headphones. "We constantly collaborate on different projects and discuss different solutions for various problems so we love this environment," he says.[75]

A start-up often requires the founder to customize a location to fit the company's specific layout needs. These upgrades to a rental space are known as **tenant improvements**, and sometimes landlords will contribute toward the cost of the improvements if an entrepreneur signs a long-term lease (typically at least three years). Entrepreneurs who lease buildings must consider other costs associated with the property in addition to the lease rate, which usually is expressed as a dollar amount per square foot. Additional costs include a fee for common area maintenance (CAM) (which covers the expense of maintaining the property), for property taxes, and for insurance; a lease agreement in which the tenant pays all three of these expenses is called a **triple net lease**.

## External Appearance

The physical appearance of a building determines the first impression that customers have of a business and contributes significantly to establishing its identity in customers' minds. Therefore, a building's appearance must be consistent with the entrepreneur's desired image for the business. Retailers, in particular, must recognize the importance of creating the proper image for their stores and how their shop's layout and physical facility influence this image. In many ways, the building's appearance sets the tone for the customer's quality and service expectations. The appearance should reflect the "personality" of the business. Should the building project an exclusive image or an economical one? Is the atmosphere informal and relaxed, or it is formal and businesslike? Externally, the storefront—its architectural style and color, signs, entrances, and general appearance—gives important clues to customers about a business's image.

Communicating the right signals through layout and physical facilities is an important step in attracting a steady stream of customers. Retail consultant Paco Underhill advises merchants to "seduce" passersby with their storefronts. "The seduction process should start a minimum of 10 paces away," he says.[76] A building's exterior should have "curb appeal" to entice shoppers, and one of the best ways to create curb appeal is to emphasize cleanliness. Trash in the parking area, fingerprints on glass doors and windows, peeling exterior paint, and stained, sticky floors send a negative message to potential customers and discourage them from shopping. Bojangles, the chicken and biscuits restaurant, emphasizes cleanliness in its restaurants, requiring managers to patrol their units at least once an hour to make sure that they measure up to the chain's standards.[77]

**ENTREPRENEURIAL PROFILE: Huddle House** Huddle House, an Atlanta, Georgia-based chain of family restaurants with 400 locations in 20 states, recently redesigned its restaurants to include a contemporary look with a unique tower entrance, subdued earth-tone color palette, and plush seating. Outlets sporting the new look have seen sales increase of at least 30 percent. "Our plans call for 90 percent of our system to be reimaged by 2017," says Michael Abt, the company's CEO.[78]

A store's window display can be a powerful selling tool if used properly. Often, a store's display window is an afterthought, and many business owners neglect to change their displays often enough. The following tips help entrepreneurs create displays that sell:

- *Keep displays simple.* Simple, uncluttered arrangements of merchandise draw the most attention and have the greatest impact on potential customers.

- *Keep displays clean and up to date.* Dusty, dingy displays or designs that are outdated send the wrong message to customers.

- *Promote local events.* Small companies can show their support of the community by devoting part of the display window to promote local events.

- *Change displays frequently.* Customers don't want to see the same merchandise every time they visit a store. Experts recommend changing window displays at least quarterly. Businesses that sell fashionable items, however, should change their displays at least twice a month, if not weekly.

- *Get expert help, if necessary.* Some business owners have no aptitude for design! In that case, their best bet is to hire a professional to design window and in-store displays. If a company cannot afford a professional designer's fees, the entrepreneur should check with the design departments at local colleges and universities. There might be a faculty member or a talented student willing to work on a freelance basis.

- *Appeal to all of a customer's senses.* Effective displays engage more than one of a customer's senses. Who can pass up a bakery case of freshly baked, gooey cinnamon buns with their mouth-watering aroma wafting up to greet passersby?

- *Contact the companies whose products you sell to see whether they offer design props and assistance.* These vendors may offer additional insight and are aware of industry trends and competitor tactics.

## Entrances

All entrances to a business should *invite* customers in. Wide entryways and attractive merchandise displays that are set back from the doorway can draw customers into a business. A store's entrance should catch passing customers attention and draw them inside. "That's where you want somebody to slam on the brakes and realize they're going someplace new," says retail consultant Paco Underhill.[79] Retailers with heavy traffic flows, such as supermarkets or drugstores, often install automatic doors to ensure a smooth traffic flow into and out of their stores. Retailers should remove any barriers that interfere with customers' easy access to the storefront. Broken sidewalks, sagging steps, mud puddles, and sticking or heavy doors not only create obstacles that might discourage potential customers but also create legal hazards for a business if they cause customers to be injured.

## The Americans with Disabilities Act

Approximately 18.7 percent of people in the United States are disabled.[80] The Americans with Disabilities Act (ADA), passed in July 1990, requires most businesses to make their facilities available to physically challenged customers and employees. In addition, the law requires businesses with 25 or more employees to accommodate physically challenged candidates in their hiring practices. Most states have similar laws, many of them more stringent than the ADA, that apply to smaller companies as well. The rules of the these state laws and the ADA's Title III are designed to ensure that mentally and physically challenged customers have equal access to a firm's goods or services. For instance, the act requires business owners to remove architectural and communication barriers when "readily achievable" (accomplished without much difficulty or expense). The ADA allows flexibility in how a business achieves this equal access, however. For example, a restaurant could either provide menus in Braille or offer to have a staff member read the menu to blind customers. A small dry cleaner might not be able to add a wheelchair ramp to its storefront without incurring significant expense, but the owner could comply with the ADA by offering curbside pickup and delivery services for disabled customers at no extra charge.

The Department of Justice revised the ADA in 2010, and all newly constructed or renovated buildings that are open to the public and were occupied after March 15, 2012, must comply with the 2010 requirements. For example, in retail stores, checkout aisles must be wide enough—at least 36 inches—to accommodate wheelchairs. Restaurants must have at least 5 percent of their tables accessible to wheelchair-bound patrons. Miniature golf courses must make at least 50 percent of the holes on the course accessible to disabled customers.

Complying with the ADA does not necessarily require businesses to spend large amounts of money. The Department of Justice estimates that more than 20 percent of the cases that customers have filed under Title III involved changes that the business owners could have made at no cost, and another 60 percent would have cost less than $1,000![81] In addition, companies with $1 million or less in annual sales or with 30 or fewer full-time employees that invest in making their locations more accessible to everyone qualify for a tax credit. The credit is 50 percent of their expenses between $250 and $10,250. Businesses that remove physical, structural, and transportation barriers for disabled employees and customers also qualify for a tax deduction of up to $15,000.

The ADA also prohibits any kind of employment discrimination against anyone with a physical or mental disability. A physically challenged person is considered to be "qualified" if he or she can perform the essential functions of the job. The employer must make "reasonable accommodation" for a physically challenged candidate or employee without causing "undue hardship" to the business. Most businesses have found that making these reasonable accommodations for customers and employees has created a more pleasant environment and offers additional conveniences for all.

## Signs

One of the lowest-cost and most effective methods of communicating with customers is a business sign. Signs communicate what a business does, where it is, and what it is selling. The United States is a highly mobile society, and a well-designed, well-placed sign can be a powerful vehicle for reaching potential customers.

A sign should be large enough for passersby to read from a distance, taking into consideration the location and speed of surrounding traffic arteries. To be most effective, the message should be short, simple, and clear. A sign should be legible both in daylight and at night; proper illumination is a must. Contrasting colors and simple typefaces are best. Signs that customers can read or understand at a glance are most effective. The most common problems with business signs are that they are illegible, poorly designed, improperly located, and poorly maintained and have color schemes that are unattractive or hard to read.

Before investing in a sign, an entrepreneur should investigate the local community's sign ordinance. In some cities and towns, local regulations impose restrictions on the size, location, height, and construction materials used in business signs.

## Interiors

Designing a functional, efficient interior layout demands research, planning, and attention to detail. Successful retailers recognize that their stores' interior layouts influence their customers' buying behavior. "A store's interior architecture is fundamental to the customer's experience—the stage upon which a retail company functions," says retail consultant Paco Underhill.[82] Retailers such as Cabela's, Barnes & Noble, and Starbucks use layouts that encourage customers to linger and spend time (and money). Others, such as Lowe's, Aldi, and Wal-Mart, reinforce their discount images with layouts that communicate a warehouse environment, often complete with pallets, to shoppers. Luxury retailers such as Tiffany & Company, Coach, and Nordstrom create opulent layouts in which their upscale customers feel comfortable.

Technology has changed drastically the way employees, customers, and the environment interact with one another, but smart entrepreneurs realize that they can influence the effectiveness of those interactions with well-designed layouts. The result can be a boost to a company's sales and profits. For instance, as their customers' needs and expectations have changed, retailers have modified the layouts of their stores to meet those needs. Because shoppers are busier than ever and want an efficient shopping experience (particularly men), many retail stores have moved away from the traditional departments (e.g., shoes, cosmetics, and men's suits) and are organizing their merchandise by "lifestyle categories," such as sports, women's contemporary, men's business casual, and others. These displays expose customers to merchandise that they otherwise might have missed and make it easier for them to, say, put together an entire outfit without having to roam from one department to another.

Designing an effective layout is an art and a science. **Ergonomics**, the science of adapting work and the work environment to complement employees' strengths and to suit customers' needs, is an integral part of a successful design. For example, chairs, desks, and table heights that allow people to work comfortably can help employees perform their jobs faster and more easily. Design experts claim that improved lighting, better acoustics, and proper climate control benefit the company as well as employees. An ergonomically designed workplace can improve a company's ability to recruit new workers, increase workers' productivity significantly, and lower days lost due to injuries and accidents. A study for the Commission of Architecture and the Built Environment and the British Council for Offices reports that simple ergonomic features, such as proper lighting and seating, reduce absenteeism by 15 percent and increase productivity between 2.8 and 20 percent.[83]

Unfortunately, many businesses fail to incorporate ergonomic design principles into their layouts, and the result is costly. The most frequent and most expensive workplace injuries are repetitive strain injuries (RSIs), which cost U.S. businesses $20 billion in workers' compensation claims and $600 million in lost productivity each year. According to the Bureau of Labor Statistics, RSIs are responsible for 33 percent of all workplace injuries and cause an injured worker to miss an average of 11 days of work per year, 38 percent more than the time missed for the average injury. RSIs also are a major driver of workers' compensation claims.[84] Workers who spend their days staring at computer monitors (a significant and growing proportion of the workforce) often are victims of RSIs.

The most common RSI is carpal tunnel syndrome, which occurs when repetitive motion causes swelling in the wrist that pinches the nerves in the arm and hand. The good news for employers, however, is that preventing injuries, accidents, and lost days does *not* require spending thousands of dollars on ergonomically correct solutions. Most of the solutions to RSIs are actually quite simple and inexpensive, ranging from installing equipment that eliminates workers' repetitive motions to introducing breaks during which workers engage in exercises designed by occupational therapists to combat RSIs.

### Drive-Through Windows

For many businesses, a drive-through window adds another dimension to the concept of customer convenience and is a relatively inexpensive way to increase sales. In the quick-service restaurant business, drive-through windows are an essential design component, accounting for 70 percent of sales, an increase from 60 percent in 2002.[85] Although drive-through windows are staples at fast-food restaurants and banks, they can add value for customers in other businesses as well, including drugstores, convenience stores, hardware stores, and even wedding chapels. Archaeologists have found evidence of a "drive-through" window in an ancient building in Godin Tepe, a 5,000-year-old village in the mountains of Iran, through which residents distributed food and weapons to soldiers.[86]

Seattle's Best Coffee recently opened 15 drive-through-only locations in the Dallas–Fort Worth market. With a footprint of only 600 square feet, the outlets can fit in almost any high-volume location and sell coffee, other beverages, and "dashboard friendly" food to busy customers who are too pressed for time to get out of their cars. The company selected Dallas–Fort Worth as the location for the first outlets because people there dine out 70 percent more than the national average.[87]

## Sight, Sound, Scent, and Lighting

Retailers can increase sales by sending important subconscious signals to customers using what design experts call "symbolics." For instance, when shoppers enter a Whole Foods supermarket, the first items they see are displays of fresh flowers. Not only are the flowers' colors and the smells pleasing, but they also send a clear message to customers: "You are embarking on an adventure in freshness in our store—flowers, produce, meats, seafood, *everything*."[88] Layouts that engage all of customers' senses also increase sales. Retail behavioral expert Paco Underhill, founder of Envirosell, a market research company, says that most of customers' unplanned purchases come after they touch, taste, smell, or hear something in a store. For example, stores that sell fresh food see sales increase if they offer free samples to customers. One study reports that offering shoppers free samples increases not only the sales of the item offered but the sales of other products as well.[89] Research also shows that customers are willing to pay more for products they can see, touch, taste, or try.[90] "If somebody doesn't try 'em, they're not going to buy 'em," quips Underhill.[91] Sight, sound, scent, and lighting are particularly important aspects of retail layout.

**SIGHT** A business can use colors and visual cues in its interior designs to support its brand and image in subtle yet effective ways. For instance, many high-tech companies use bright, bold colors in their designs because they appeal to their young employees. On the other hand, more conservative companies, such as accounting firms and law offices, decorate with more subtle, subdued tones because they convey an image of trustworthiness and honesty. Upscale restaurants that want their patrons to linger over dinner use deep, luxurious tones and soft lighting to create the proper ambiance. Fast-food restaurants, on the other hand, use strong, vibrant colors and bright lighting to encourage customers to get in and out quickly, ensuring the fast table turnover they require to be successful. Table 18.7 shows how businesses can use colors to target specific groups of customers or elicit particular emotions among customers.

At the Vermont Country Deli in Brattleboro, Vermont, wooden bookshelves and odd tables filled with colorful displays of jams, jellies, and desserts greet customers as they enter the store. The mismatched tables and shelves give the store an authentic, down-home look, and signs such as "Life is short. Eat cookies" entice customers to make purchases. At Whole Foods, prices for fresh fruits and vegetables appear to be hand scrawled on fragments of black slate, a tradition in outdoor markets in Europe—as if a farmer had pulled up that morning, unloaded the produce, and posted the price before heading back to the farm. Some of the produce also is sprinkled with water droplets. When customers at the restaurant Tallulah on the Thames in Newport, Rhode Island, are seated, waiters hand them a rustic clipboard with a handwritten list of the daily "farm-to-table menu."[92] The subtle message these symbolics send to customers is *freshness*.[93]

### TABLE 18.7 The Power of Color

Colors can be used to target different demographics or create certain emotions in consumers

| Pinks/Reds | Oranges | Yellows | Greens | Blues | Purples |
|---|---|---|---|---|---|
| Activating, exciting, powerful | A balanced color, vibrant, energetic, friendly | Brightest and most energizing, warm, happy, stimulating | Calming, balancing, cool | Dependability, trust, stability, security | Abundance, dignity, creativity, imagination |
| Used minimally as an accent to draw attention or create sense of urgency | Used to give an inviting impression or to show movement and energy | Used in design focused on kids and to express happiness | Used to bring harmony and stability, often used in residential application to denote verdant or modern sustainable environment | Conservative dark hues used for business and lighter hues used for more social environments | Used to show wealth and luxury |

*Source:* Based on Yellow Duck Marketing, cited in Regina Wood, "85 Percent of Consumers Buy Products Based on Color," *Ragan,* June 13, 2012, *www.ragan.com/Main/Articles/85_percent_of_consumers_buy_products_based_on_colo_45039.aspx#.*

**SCENT** Research shows that scents can have a powerful effect in retail stores. The Sense of Smell Institute reports that the average human being can recognize 10,000 different aromas and can recall scents with 65 percent accuracy after one year, a much higher recall rate than visual and aural stimuli produce. Studies show that introducing the proper scent into a retail environment can increase sales from 20 to 90 percent. In one experiment, when Eric Spangenberg of Washington State University diffused a subtle scent of vanilla into the women's department of a store and rose maroc into the men's department, he discovered that sales nearly doubled. He also discovered that if he switched the scents, sales in both departments fell well below their normal average. Scents also enhance customers' perceptions of product quality and value.[94] Spangenberg's research suggests that simple scents, such as orange and vanilla, are more effective than complex scents that combine multiple fragrances.[95]

Many companies—from casinos to retail stores—are beginning to understand the power of using scent as a marketing tool to evoke customers' emotions. Almost every bakery uses a fan to push the smell of fresh-baked breads and sweets into pedestrian traffic lanes, tempting them to sample some of their delectable goodies. Stores selling swimsuits see sales increase when they introduce a coconut scent, and in intimate apparel shops, a soft lilac scent increases sales.[96] "Smell has a greater impact on purchasing than everything else combined," says Alan Hirsch of the Smell & Taste Treatment & Research Foundation. "If something smells good, the product is perceived as good."[97] Lavender, vanilla, and chamomile scents encourage shoppers to relax and slow down; floral and citrus scents encourage them to browse longer and spend more.[98] Sony infuses its Style Stores with a blend of vanilla, orange, and cedar that is designed to make women shoppers feel more at ease.[99]

**SOUND** Retailers that use the right sounds to "decorate the silence" can increase sales as well.[100] Background music can be an effective marketing tool if the type of music playing in a store matches the demographics of its target customers. "[Music] sets the tone for the whole place," says Jonathan Schoen, manager of Basso, an Italian restaurant in St. Louis, Missouri. "People walk in and can immediately hear what you're about."[101] Abercrombie and Fitch plays loud, upbeat music with a rhythmic beat that creates a nightclub-like atmosphere for its youthful customers, but Victoria's Secret uses classical music in its stores to reinforce an upscale image for its brand.[102] Many restaurants invest considerable time selecting just the right play lists for different day parts that reflect the image they want to create, increase food and bar sales, and encourage customers to "eat to the beat." Studies show that playing slow-tempo music during dinner increases bar sales by more than 40 percent and that playing music with a fast beat increases lunch sales. "We are a rock 'n' roll pizza joint, and we want music that reflects that," says Frank Uible, owner of Pi, a four-unit pizza chain in St. Louis, Missouri. "The music may be a little softer when we are not as busy and more up-tempo at peak hours."[103]

Research shows that music is a stimulant to sales because it reduces resistance; warps the sense of time, allowing shoppers to stay longer in the store; and helps to produce a positive mental association between the music and the intended image of the store.[104] One audible rule seems clear for retail soundscapes: Slow is good. Because people's biorhythms often mirror the sounds around them, a gently meandering mix of classical music or soothing ambient noise encourages shoppers to slow down and relax. Classical music, in particular, makes shoppers feel affluent and boosts sales more than other types of music.[105] "If customers are moving less quickly," says shopping psychologist Tim Dennison, "they're more likely to engage with a product and make a purchase." The growing competition for the attention of time-pressed shoppers forces businesses to focus more on the total sensory experience they provide. "Retailers will have to make their stores more stimulating" says Dennison.[106]

**LIGHTING** Good lighting allows employees to work at maximum efficiency. Proper lighting is measured by the amount of light required to do a job properly with the greatest lighting efficiency. In a retail environment, proper lighting should highlight featured products and encourage customers to stop and look at them. "The lighting and the atmosphere created with the lighting really makes your store more spectacular," says the president of a design firm that specializes in restaurants and retail stores.[107] Efficiency also is essential because lighting consumes 25 percent of the total energy used in the typical commercial building.[108] Traditional incandescent lighting is least efficient. Only 10 percent of the energy it generates is light; the remaining 90 percent is heat. Although incandescent bulbs are the cheapest to purchase, they have the shortest life span, averaging between 750 and 1,200 hours. Compact fluorescent lights (CFLs) generate far less heat, use 75 percent less energy, and last 8 to 10 times longer than traditional incandescent lights. Technology advances are increasing the popularity of light-emitting diode (LED) lighting. Although still more expensive to purchase, LEDs use just 20 percent of the electricity of incandescent lights and 50 percent of CFLs. They also last five times longer than CFLs and 45 times longer than incandescent lights. LEDs generate the least amount of heat, reducing business's cooling costs. The estimated total costs of operating each type of bulb over 50,000 hours are $352.50 (incandescent), $89.75 (CFL), and $85.75 (LED).[109] Mike Hardin, owner of Hodad's, a hamburger restaurant in San Diego, California, worked with a local utility to convert all of the outlet's incandescent lights to LEDs. Hardin saw immediate results; Hodad's energy bill decreased by more than 50 percent. Now an LED convert, Hardin says, "It doesn't make sense to me anymore to screw in a light bulb that is going to cost me and our world a lot more energy."[110]

Lighting provides a good return on investment given its overall impact on a business. Few people seek out businesses that are dimly lit because they convey an image of untrustworthiness. The use of natural gives a business an open and cheerful look and actually can boost sales. A series of studies by energy research firm Heschong Mahone Group reports that stores using natural light experience sales that are 40 percent higher than those of similar stores using fluorescent lighting.[111] Similarly, a study by office furniture maker Haworth reports that employees who work in more natural environments (with natural light and external views) exhibit less job stress, more job satisfaction, and fewer ailments.[112]

### Sustainability and Environmentally Friendly Design

Businesses are designing their buildings in more environmentally friendly ways not only because it is the right thing to do but also because it saves money. In addition to saving energy (and the planet), companies that create well-planned, environmentally friendly designs see employee productivity increase by 3.5 to 10 percent.[113] Companies are using recycled materials; installing high-efficiency lighting, fixtures, and appliances; and using LEED (Leadership in Energy and Environmental Design) principles in construction and renovation.

**ENTREPRENEURIAL PROFILE: Chipotle Mexican Grill** Chipotle Mexican Grill, a chain of Mexican restaurants that Steve Ells started in 1993 in Denver, Colorado, recently built three LEED-certified restaurants. The outlet in Gurnee Mills, Illinois, uses 43 percent less water than the typical restaurant by including in its design a 2,500-gallon underground cistern that captures rainwater that is used for landscape irrigation, high-efficiency water fixtures, tankless water heaters, and waterless urinals. The restaurant, which was built mainly with recycled materials, features plenty of windows that let in natural light, and low-E glazing on the windows repels heat during the summer and cold during the winter. It also uses highly efficient LED lighting and Energy Star–rated kitchen equipment. An on-site wind turbine produces 10 percent of the restaurant's energy, and a computerized energy management system monitors all of the building's systems. Chipotle says that the restaurant's energy usage is 33 percent below that of a typical outlet and plans to build more LEED-certified outlets.[114]

Businesses that have not yet implemented LEED principles into the design of their buildings can lower the cost of and increase the efficiency of their operations by conducting energy audits, reducing the impact of "energy hogs" on their business expenses. Many local utilities conduct energy audits for free, and implementing their suggestions can produce significant savings. The U.S. Department of Energy offers simple checklists (*www1.eere.energy.gov/femp/services/energy_aware.html*) that serve as good starting points for defining an energy-savings plan.

## Layout: Maximizing Revenues, Increasing Efficiency, and Reducing Costs

The ideal layout depends on the type of business and on the entrepreneur's strategy for gaining a competitive edge. Retailers design their layouts with the goal of maximizing sales revenue; manufacturers design their layouts to increase efficiency and productivity and to lower costs.

**7.** _____

Explain the principles of effective layouts for retailers, service businesses, and manufacturers.

### Layout for Retailers

Retail layout is the arrangement of merchandise in a store. A retailer's success depends, in part, on well-designed floor displays. The displays should pull customers into the store and make it easy for them to locate merchandise; compare price, quality, and features; and ultimately make a purchase.

Paco Underhill, retail consultant and author of *Why We Buy: The Science of Shopping*, calls a store's interior design "the stage on which a retail company functions."[115] Unfortunately, according to Underhill, most retail shopping spaces do not include what customers want to experience.[116]

Research shows that 66 percent of all buying decisions are made once a customer enters a store, meaning that the right layout can boost sales significantly.[117] A retail layout should pull customers into the store and make it easy for them to locate merchandise; compare price, quality, and features; and ultimately make a purchase. An effective layout also should take customers past displays of other items that they may buy on impulse. One of the most comprehensive studies of impulse purchases found that one-third of shoppers made impulse purchases. The median impulse purchase amount was $30 but varied by product category, ranging from $6 for food items to $60 for jewelry and sporting goods. Although the urge to take advantage of discounts was the most common driver of unplanned buying decisions, the location and attractiveness of the display also were important factors.[118] Research shows that shoppers are influenced by in-store displays, especially end-cap displays—those at the ends of aisles.[119]

Retailers have always recognized that some locations within a store are superior to others. Customer traffic patterns give the owner a clue to the best location for the highest gross margin items. Merchandise purchased on impulse and convenience goods should be located near the front of the store. Items that people shop around for before buying and specialty goods attract their own customers and should not be placed in prime space. Prime selling space should be restricted to products that carry the highest markups.

Retail store layout evolves from a clear understanding of customers' buying habits. If customers come into the store for specific products and have a tendency to walk directly to those items, placing complementary products in their path increases sales. Observing customer behavior helps business owners identify "hot spots," where merchandise sells briskly, and "cold spots," where it may sit indefinitely. By experimenting with factors such as traffic flow, lighting, aisle size, music type and audio levels, signs, and colors, an owner can discover the most productive store layout. For instance, one of the hot spots in a Barnes & Noble bookstore during the busy holiday season is the "Christmas table" at the front of the children's department. The table, which holds between 75 and 125 titles, draws consistent traffic and is the most desired spot for a book aimed at children.[120]

Business owners should display merchandise as attractively as their budgets will allow. Customers' eyes focus on displays, which tell them the type of merchandise the business sells. It is easier for customers to relate to one display than to a rack or shelf of merchandise. Open displays of merchandise can surround the focal display, creating an attractive selling area. Retailers can boost sales by displaying together items that complement each other. For example, displaying ties near dress shirts or handbags next to shoes often leads to multiple sales.

When planning in-store displays, retailers should remember the following:

- *Make products easy to reach.* The average man is 69.3 inches tall, and the average woman is 63.8 inches tall. The average person's normal reach is 16 inches, and the extended reach is 24 inches. The average person's standing eye level is 63.1 inches from the floor.[121] Placing merchandise on very low or very high shelves discourages customers from making purchases. For example, putting hearing aid batteries on bottom shelves where the elderly have trouble getting to them or placing popular children's toys on top shelves where little ones cannot reach them hurts sales of these items.

- *Shoppers prefer wide aisles.* One study found that shoppers, especially women, are reluctant to enter narrow aisles in a store. Narrow aisles force customers to jostle past one another, creating what experts call the "butt-brush factor." Open aisles allow customers to shop comfortably and encourage them to spend more time in a store.

- *Placing shopping baskets in several areas around a store increases sales.* Seventy-five percent of shoppers who pick up a basket buy something, compared to just 34 percent of customers who do not pick up a basket.[122] Smart retailers make shopping baskets available to customers throughout the store, not just at the entrance.

- *A store's layout should enable customers to easily locate the items they want.* Easy-to-read signs, clearly marked aisles, and displays of popular items located near the entrance make it easy for shoppers to find their way around a store.

- *Whenever possible, allow customers to touch the merchandise.* Customers are much more likely to buy items if they can pick them up. The probability that customers who are shopping for clothing will make purchases increases if they try on the garments. Shoppers who use fitting rooms to try on garments make purchases 67 percent of the time, compared to a 10 percent purchase rate for shoppers who do not use a fitting room.[123]

Retailers should separate the selling and nonselling areas of a store and should never waste prime selling space with nonselling functions, such as storage, receiving, office, and fitting areas. Although nonselling activities are necessary for a successful retail operation, they should not take precedence and occupy valuable selling and merchandising space. Many retailers place their nonselling departments in the rear of the building, recognizing the value of each foot of space in a retail store and locating their most profitable items in the best-selling areas. Entrepreneurs should use at least 80 percent of available retail space for selling and merchandising.

One nonselling activity, the checkout process, is a particularly important ingredient in customer satisfaction and often ranks as a sore spot with shoppers. Research shows that shoppers tend to be impatient, willing to wait only about four minutes in a checkout line before becoming exasperated. One study reports that 43 percent of customers say that long checkout lines make them less likely to shop at a store.[124] Retailers are discovering that simplifying and speeding up the checkout process increases customer convenience, lowers shoppers' stress levels, and makes them more likely to come back. Some retailers use roving clerks equipped with handheld credit card swiping devices, especially during peak hours, to hasten the checkout process.

The various areas within a small store's interior space are not equal in generating sales revenue. Certain areas contribute more to revenue than others. The value of store space depends on floor location in a multistory building, location with respect to aisles and walkways, and proximity to entrances. Space values decrease as distance from the main entry-level floor increases. Selling areas on the main level contribute a greater portion to sales than do those on other floors because they offer greater exposure to customers than either basement or higher-level locations. Therefore, main-level locations carry a greater share of rent than other levels.

## In the Entrepreneurial Spotlight

# The Secrets of Successful Retail Layouts

Fraser Ross, owner of Kitson, a 10-store retail chain in southern California that sells pop culture fashions, accessories, books, and gift items and novelties, plans the layout for his stores strategically, using his many years of retail experience and keen observation of shoppers and their buying habits. Ross frequently changes the displays and the layout of his stores, but he relies on one underlying principle: lure shoppers into the store with attractive displays of lower-priced gifts, entice them with a flashy jewelry counter in the center, and guide them toward the back, where eye-catching shelves of colorful, expensive handbags and shoes and orderly racks of the latest fashions await. Ross starts seducing customers before they enter his store with unusual, attention-grabbing window displays that might use a popular movie or book as its theme. In Ross's eclectic stores, which are well-known destinations for celebrity shoppers, including the Kardashians, Alicia Keys, Channing Tatum, Heidi Klum, Jessica Alba, Lenny Kravitz, Taylor Swift, and others, round tables in the gift area along one wall steer customers back into the heart of the store, where they continue to fill their shopping baskets.

During the all-important holiday season, which accounts for half of Kitson's $30 million in annual sales, layout takes on even more importance. Ross plots a very intentional path for shoppers to follow through the store. He places unusual gift items at the front of the store and uses displays of jewelry and accessories to draw shoppers to the rear of the store, which is home to the most expensive items. He puts carefully selected impulse items from inexpensive bracelets to pricier colognes and perfumes near cash registers. Ross also carefully selects his stores' play lists of background music. Beginning on the first Saturday before Thanksgiving, every fourth song on the track is a Christmas song. As Christmas draws closer, he increases the frequency of holiday music until every song is a Christmas song, but the choices, like the stores' merchandise, is eclectic, including classics such as Bing Crosby's "White Christmas" and modern songs such as "Christmas Tree" by Lady Gaga and Space Cowboy. Ross also changes in-store displays more frequently during the holidays. "You've got to feed customers today," he explains. The men's shop and a selection of about 400 books priced between $10 and $30 are located upstairs.

Like Fraser Ross, David DeMattei, CEO of Lucky Brand, a retailer of casual apparel, shoes, jewelry, and accessories with 209 stores in the United States, understands the importance of an effective layout to his company's sales and profits. "Retail is in the details," quips DeMattei. Lucky Brand, a division of Fifth & Pacific, recently engaged in a methodical revamp of its stores, doing away with a cluttered look that often displayed merchandise out of customers' reach and appeared outdated. Replacing it is an orderly layout with a clean look, lighter colors, and displays positioned to allow shoppers to create complete outfits easily. Although a great deal of research went into the design, DeMattei says that

*(continued)*

# In the Entrepreneurial Spotlight *(continued)*

"we don't want it to look like a science. We just want it to look relaxed." The goal of the newly designed stores, whose signature item is Lucky Brand jeans (which contain the message "Lucky You" stitched inside the fly), is to "romance" shoppers. "It starts with the [display] windows," says Patrick Wade, the company's creative director, gazing at a window mannequin wearing a carefully coordinated casual outfit. Just behind the mannequin inside the store are tables displaying the items in the same outfit and in other color variations of the outfit. "The idea is to get shoppers thinking, 'I could buy it just the way it is in the window—or make the look my own with the red blouse,'" he says.

Lucky Brand has been conducting experiments to determine whether putting menswear or womenswear at the front of its stores increases sales. A yearlong study has proved inconclusive, so DeMattei decided to leave women's clothing up front and to put men's clothing at the back of the store.

Inspired by the success of cosmetics retailer Sephora, makeup and skin care retailers have switched from "don't touch" layouts to "open layouts" that allow customers to browse through open shelves and experiment without interference from a salesperson. Launched in 1993 as a French perfume chain, Sephora stormed the makeup market in the United States and forced other makeup retailers to change their tactics. For years, women shopping for makeup had two choices: drugstores that offered products in tightly sealed packages or department stores that required a hovering salesperson whose sales commission was tied to particular brands. Spotting an opportunity, managers at Sephora decided to break out of the traditional mold for

marketing makeup and offer more than 13,000 products in one store and give customers the freedom to explore and sample various types of makeup. In the company's open sell environment, women can try lipsticks, eyeliners, blushes, and other products from more than 250 brands on their own, or they can ask for assistance from one of Sephora's highly trained sales associates.

An open sell strategy with minimal involvement from trained beauty consultants means that proper layout is more important than ever before. Despite stocking more than 13,000 products, Sephora stores are always neat and orderly. The unspoken message they send to customers is clear: We offer a large selection of products, but they are always easy to find. Displays organize fragrances in alphabetical order and cosmetics by brand. Large storefront windows allow passersby to have a bird's-eye view of the store instantly and to see the breadth and depth of its product line, both of which have proved to be effective at drawing in shoppers.

1. Identify at least two layout principles that the three retailers described here utilize.

2. Work with a team of your classmates to identify a local business and use the layout principles that you have learned in this chapter to develop a more effective layout. How would you test your layout to determine whether it actually is more effective?

*Sources:* Based on Christina Binkley, "How Stores Lead You to Spend," *Wall Street Journal*, December 2, 2010, pp. D1, D8; Christina Binkley, "The Shopping Science Behind Lucky's Revamp," *Wall Street Journal*, January 19, 2012, p. D8; Elizabeth Holmes, "Leave Me Alone, I'm Shopping," *Wall Street Journal*, June 28, 2012, pp. D1, D4.

---

The layout of aisles in the store has a major impact on the customer exposure that merchandise receives. Items located on primary walkways should be assigned a higher share of rental costs and should contribute a greater portion to sales revenue than those displayed along secondary aisles. Space values also depend on the spaces' relative position to the store entrance, which serves as the "landing strip" for shoppers. A critical moment occurs when shoppers walk into a store as they slow down, try to orient themselves, and expand their peripheral vision to get a panoramic view of the retail spaces. An effective layout allows them to familiarize themselves with the retail landscape as quickly as possible.

**ENTREPRENEURIAL PROFILE: Old Navy** Clothing retailer Old Navy recently created a new look for its stores using a "racetrack" layout in which the primary aisle starts at the store's entrance and loops through the entire store in a circular, square, or rectangular pattern. The goal of a racetrack layout is to expose customers to as much merchandise as possible and to encourage them to browse through other merchandise displayed on smaller "rabbit trails" that branch off of the main aisle. The new Old Navy layout also includes dressing rooms, a children's play area, and cash registers located in the center of the store and a "fundamentals" wall that displays low-priced items.[125]

Most American shoppers turn to the right when entering a store and will move around it counterclockwise.[126] That makes the front right-hand section of a retail store the "retail sweet spot." Retailers should put their best-selling and highest-profit-margin items in this prime area. Only about one-fourth of a store's customers will go more than halfway into the store. Therefore, the farther away an area is from the entrance, the lower its value. Using these characteristics, Figure 18.7 illustrates space values for a typical small-store layout.

## Layout for Manufacturers

Manufacturing layout decisions take into consideration the arrangement of departments, work stations, machines, and stock-holding points within a production facility. The objective is to

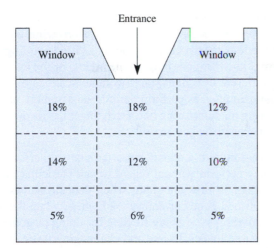

**FIGURE 18.7**

**The Space Value for a Small Store**

arrange these elements to ensure a smooth work flow (in a production area) or a particular traffic pattern (in a service area). Manufacturing facilities have come under increased scrutiny as firms attempt to improve quality, reduce inventories, and increase productivity through facilities that are integrated, flexible, and controlled. Facility layout has a dramatic effect on product mix, product processing, materials handling, storage, control, and production volume and quality.

**FACTORS IN MANUFACTURING LAYOUT** The ideal layout for a manufacturing operation depends on several factors, including the following:

- *Type of product.* Product design and quality standards, whether the product is produced for inventory or for order, and physical properties, such as the size of materials and products special handling requirements, susceptibility to damage, and perishability
- *Type of production process.* Technology used types of materials handled, means of providing a service, and processing requirements in terms of number of operations involved and amount of interaction between departments and work centers
- *Ergonomic considerations.* To ensure worker safety, to avoid unnecessary injuries and accidents, and to increase productivity
- *Economic considerations.* Volume of production; costs of materials, machines, work stations, and labor; pattern and variability of demand; and length of permissible delays
- *Space availability within facility itself.* Ensure that the space will adequately meet current and future manufacturing needs

**TYPES OF MANUFACTURING LAYOUTS** Manufacturing layouts are categorized either by the work flow in a plant or by the production system's function. There are three basic types of layouts that manufacturers can use separately or in combination—product, process, and fixed position—and they differ in their applicability of different levels of manufacturing volume.

*Product Layouts* In a **product (or line) layout**, a manufacturer arranges workers and equipment according to the sequence of operations performed on the product. Conceptually, the flow is an unbroken line from raw materials input to finished goods. This type of layout is applicable to rigid-flow, high-volume, continuous or mass-production operations or when the product is highly standardized. Automobile assembly plants, paper mills, and oil refineries are examples of product layouts. Product layouts offer the advantages of lower materials handling costs; simplified tasks that can be done with low cost, lower-skilled labor; reduced amounts of work-in-process inventory; and relatively simplified production control activities. All units are routed along the same fixed path, and scheduling consists primarily of setting a production rate.

Disadvantages of product layouts include their inflexibility, monotony of job tasks, high fixed investment in specialized equipment, and heavy interdependence of all operations. A breakdown in one machine or at one work station can idle the entire line. Such a layout also requires the owner to duplicate many pieces of equipment in the manufacturing facility; duplication can be cost prohibitive for a small business. German automaker BMW, in which the heirs of Herbert

Quandt (who acquired majority ownership of the company in 1960) own a controlling interest, recently expanded its factory in Greer, South Carolina. Borrowing the layout of a factory in Leipzig, Germany, BMW redesigned the Greer factory in a "hand-and-finger" concept. "The plant has a main [manufacturing] line that goes through the middle of the building, and there are 'fingers' that branch off in different directions," says communications director Max Metcalf. The fingers are corridors where employees perform various subassembly and installation activities that are then fed into the main manufacturing line. Each finger has its own receiving docks so that components from suppliers can arrive just in time.[127]

*Process Layouts*  In a **process layout**, a manufacturer groups workers and equipment according to the general function they perform without regard to any particular product. Process layouts are appropriate when production runs are short, when demand shows considerable variation and the costs of holding finished goods inventory are high, or when the product is customized. Process layouts have the advantages of being flexible for doing customer work and promoting job satisfaction by offering employees diverse and challenging tasks. Its disadvantages are the higher costs of materials handling, more skilled labor, lower productivity, and more complex production control. Because the work flow is intermittent, each job must be individually routed through the system and scheduled at the various work centers, and its status must be monitored individually.

*Fixed-Position Layouts*  In a **fixed position layout**, materials do not move down a line as in a product layout. Because of the bulk or weight of the final product, workers go to the materials and assemble them into finished products in one spot. Aircraft assembly shops and shipyards typify this kind of layout.

**DESIGNING LAYOUTS**  The starting point in layout design is determining how and in what sequence product parts or service tasks flow together. One of the most effective techniques is to create an overall picture of the manufacturing process using assembly charts and process flowcharts. Given the tasks and their sequence, in addition to a knowledge of the volume or products that can be produced, an entrepreneur can analyze space and equipment needs. Two important criteria for selecting and designing a layout are worker productivity and materials handling costs.

*Worker Productivity*  Designing layouts ergonomically so that they maximize workers' strengths is especially important for manufacturers. Creating an environment that is comfortable and pleasant for workers pays big benefits over time in the form of higher productivity, lower absenteeism and tardiness, and fewer injuries. Designers must be sure that they match the environment they create to workers' needs rather than trying to force workers to adapt to the environment.

*Materials Handling Costs*  Manufacturers can lower materials handling costs by using layouts designed to automate product flow whenever possible and to minimize flow distances and times. The extent of automation depends on the level of technology and amount of capital available as well as behavioral considerations of employees. Flow distances and times are usually minimized by locating sequential processing activities or interrelated departments in adjacent areas. The following features are important to a good manufacturing layout:

- Smooth materials flow pattern
- Straight-line layout where possible
- Straight, clearly marked aisles
- Backtracking kept to a minimum
- Related operations close together
- Minimum of in-process inventory
- Easy adjustment to changing conditions
- Minimum materials handling distances
- Minimum of manual handling
- No unnecessary rehandling of material

- Minimum handling between operations
- Materials delivered to production employees quickly
- Use of gravity to move materials whenever possible
- Materials efficiently removed from the work area
- Materials handling done by indirect labor
- Orderly materials handling and storage
- Good housekeeping

## Chapter Review

1. Explain the stages in the location decision.
   - The location decision is one of the most important decisions an entrepreneur will make, given its long-term effects on the company. An entrepreneur should look at the choice as a series of increasingly narrow decisions: Which region of the country? Which state? Which city? Which site?
   - Demographic statistics are available from a wide variety of sources, but government agencies such as the Census Bureau have a wealth of detailed data that can guide an entrepreneur in her location decision.
2. Describe the location criteria for retail and service businesses.
   - For retailers and many service businesses, the location decision is especially crucial. They must consider the size of the trade area, the volume of customer traffic, the number of parking spots, the availability of room for expansion, and the visibility of a site.
3. Outline the basic location options for retail and service businesses.
   - Retail and service businesses have six basic location options: CBDs, neighborhoods, shopping centers and malls, near competitors, outlying areas, and at home.
4. Explain the site selection process for manufacturers.
   - A manufacturer's location decision is strongly influenced by local zoning ordinances. Some areas offer industrial parks designed specifically to attract manufacturers. Two crucial factors for most manufacturers are the accessibility to (and the cost of transporting) raw materials and the quality and quantity of available labor.
5. Discuss the benefits of locating a start-up company in a business incubator.
   - Business incubators are locations that offer flexible, low-cost rental space to their tenants as well as business and consulting services. Their goal is to nurture small companies until they are ready to "graduate" into the larger business community. Many government agencies and universities offer incubator locations.

6. Describe the criteria used to analyze the layout and design considerations of a building, including the Americans with Disabilities Act.
   - When evaluating the suitability of a particular building, an entrepreneur should consider several factors:
     - *Size.* Is the structure large enough to accommodate the business with some room for growth?
     - *Construction and external appearance.* Is the building structurally sound, and does it create the right impression for the business?
     - *Entrances.* Are they inviting?
     - *Legal issues.* Does the building comply with the ADA, and, if not, how much will it cost to bring it up to standard?
     - *Signs.* Are they legible, well located, and easy to see?
     - *Interior.* Does the interior design contribute to your ability to make sales, and is it ergonomically designed?
     - *Lights and fixtures.* Is the lighting adequate to the tasks workers will be performing, and what is the estimated cost of lighting?
7. Explain the principles of effective layout for retailers, service businesses, and manufacturers.
   - Layout for retail store and service businesses depends on the owner's understanding of customers' buying habits. Retailers have three basic layout options from which to choose: grid, free-form, and boutique layouts. Some areas of a retail store generate more sales per square foot and are, therefore, more valuable than others.
   - The goal of a manufacturer's layout is to create a smooth, efficient work flow. Three basic options exist: product layout, process layout, and fixed-position layout. Two key considerations are worker productivity and materials handling costs.

# Discussion Questions

**18-1.** How do most small business owners choose a location? Is this wise?

**18-2.** What factors should a manager consider when evaluating a region in which to locate a business? Where are such data available?

**18-3.** Outline the factors entrepreneurs should consider when selecting a state in which to locate a business.

**18-4.** What factors should a seafood-processing plant, a beauty shop, and an exclusive jewelry store consider in choosing a location? List factors for each type of business.

**18-5.** What intangible factors might enter into the entrepreneur's location decision?

**18-6.** What are zoning laws? How do they affect the location decision?

**18-7.** What is the trade area? What determines a small retailer's trade area?

**18-8.** Why is it important to discover more than just the number of passersby in a traffic count?

**18-9.** What types of information can an entrepreneur collect from census data?

**18-10.** Why may a cheap location not be the best location?

**18-11.** What function does a small firm's sign serve? What are the characteristics of an effective business sign?

**18-12.** Explain the following statement: "The portions of a small store's interior space are not of equal value in generating sales revenue." What are some of the major features that are important to a good manufacturing layout?

# CHAPTER 19
# Supply Chain Management

## Learning Objectives

**On completion of this chapter, you will be able to:**

1. Understand the components of a purchasing plan.

2. Explain the principles of total quality management, including Lean, 5S, and Six Sigma, and their impact on quality.

3. Conduct economic order quantity analysis to determine the proper level of inventory.

4. Differentiate among the three types of purchase discounts that vendors offer.

5. Calculate a company's reorder point.

6. Develop a vendor rating scale.

7. Describe the legal implications of the purchasing function.

*We are too busy mopping the floor to turn off the faucet.*

*—Anonymous*

*Continuous improvement is not about the things you do well—that's work. Continuous improvement is about removing the things that get in the way of your work. The headaches, the things that slow you down, that's what continuous improvement is all about.*

*—Bruce Hamilton*

This chapter discusses the activities involved in managing a small company's supply chain—purchasing, quality management, and vendor analysis. Although none of these is the most glamorous or exciting job that an entrepreneur undertakes, they form an important part of the foundation that supports every small business. When entrepreneurs begin producing products or providing services, they quickly learn how much their products or services depend on the quality of the components and services they purchase from their suppliers. Success today depends on higher levels of collaboration among the businesses that make up a company's supply chain. "Many businesses still regard the supply chain as the back end of their businesses, but the modern supply chain has a much bigger contribution to make," concludes a study of supply chain management. "It can help companies differentiate themselves from the competition and achieve greater sustainable growth."[1] Today, thriving companies operate as part of seamless network of alliances and partnerships with customers, suppliers, and distributors. For many businesses, the quality of the supply chain determines their ability to satisfy their customers and to compete effectively. "Competition is not really company vs. company," says one expert, "but supply chain vs. supply chain."[2] In other words, supply chain management has become an important strategic issue rather than merely a tactical matter for companies. Several studies have found that companies that utilize best-practice supply chain management tools outperform those with average supply chains. They not only have faster delivery times, lower costs, and higher levels of customer service but also achieve superior financial performance, producing 30 percent higher profit margins than companies with average supply chains. Top-performing companies also have on-time delivery rates of 96 percent (compared to 89 percent for average performing companies) and generate 15.3 inventory turns per year (compared to just 8.2 turns for average performing companies)—all while carrying less inventory.[3]

**Supply chain management** (SCM) is the process by which a company forecasts, plans for, and acquires the materials and goods it purchases from vendors and suppliers to maximize the value it provides to its customers at minimum cost. Proper SCM requires transparency, a smooth flow of information up and down the chain, and collaboration among a company and its supply chain partners. Managing the supply chain has become more challenging, however, because the globalization of business makes supply chains longer and adds layers of complexity to supply chain activities. The Outsourcing World Summit reports that 58 percent of medium-size companies and 43 percent of small companies engage in global sourcing for at least some of their purchases. Nearly 75 percent of these companies also say that they plan to expand their global purchases over the next three years.[4] According to a recent study by PriceWaterhouseCoopers, 85 percent of managers say that their companies' global purchasing patterns have increased the level of complexity in their supply chains.[5] Figure 19.1 shows the greatest pressures that companies face in managing their supply chains. Purchasing goods and services from companies scattered across the globe means that entrepreneurs must manage the elements of their supply chains more closely to avoid disruptions, inventory shortages, and quality problems.

Selecting the right vendors and designing a fast and efficient supply chain influences a small company's ability to produce and sell quality products and services at competitive prices. These decisions have far-reaching effects for a business as well as a significant impact on its bottom line.

Most shoppers give little thought to the path that the goods they buy in stores took to get there. However, entrepreneurs know that a flexible, reliable supply chain is essential to business success.

*Source:* © Patti McConville/Alamy.

## The Final Decision

Once business owners identify potential vendors and suppliers, they must decide which one (or ones) to do business with. Entrepreneurs should consider the following factors before making the final decision about the right supplier.

**NUMBER OF SUPPLIERS** One important question entrepreneurs face is "Should I buy from a single supplier or from several different sources?" Concentrating purchases at a single supplier (or sole sourcing) results in special attention from the supplier, especially if orders are substantial. Second, a business may be able to negotiate quantity discounts if its orders are large enough. Finally, a small company can cultivate a closer, more cooperative relationship with the supplier. Suppliers are more willing to work with companies that prove to be loyal customers. The result of this type of partnership can be better-quality goods and services. Stratsys, a company that makes plastic prototypes for the aerospace, automotive, and medical industries, purchases some of its most important raw materials from a single source. Company managers admit that doing so involves risk, but they believe that their company produces better-quality products by eliminating the variability that multiple sources of supply would introduce into their production process.[34]

However, using a single vendor also has disadvantages. A company can experience shortages of critical materials if its only supplier suffers a catastrophe, such as bankruptcy, a fire, a strike, or a natural disaster. To offset the risks of sole sourcing, many companies rely on the 80/20 rule. They purchase 80 percent of their supplies from their premier supplier and the remaining 20 percent from several "backup" vendors. If a catastrophe shuts down the company's principal supplier, the business can shift its orders to its "minor" suppliers with whom it has established relationships. Although this strategy may require a compromise on getting the lowest prices, it removes the risk of sole sourcing and lets a company's primary suppliers know that they have competition.

**RELIABILITY** Business owners must evaluate a potential vendor's ability to deliver adequate quantities of quality merchandise on time. One common complaint that small businesses have against their suppliers is late delivery. Late deliveries and the resulting shortages they often cause result in lost sales and customer ill will. Large customers often take precedence over small ones when it comes to service.

**PROXIMITY** A supplier's physical proximity is an important factor when choosing a vendor. The cost of transporting merchandise can increase significantly the total cost of merchandise to a buyer. Foreign manufacturers require longer delivery times, and because of the distance that shipments must travel, a hiccup anywhere in the distribution channel often results in late deliveries. In addition, entrepreneurs can solve quality problems more easily with nearby suppliers than with distant vendors. Some companies that once outsourced production of products or components to factories in foreign countries because they offered lower costs than domestic factories are bringing their orders back to companies in the United States, a trend called **reshoring**. Rapidly rising labor costs in countries such as China and India, the high cost of oil that makes shipping goods around the world more expensive, and the complexity of dealing with suppliers located 7,000 miles away have made domestic suppliers much more attractive to U.S. businesses.

**ENTREPRENEURIAL PROFILE: Sonja Zozula and Jerry Anderson: LightSaver Technologies** When Sonja Zozula and Jerry Anderson started LightSaver Technologies in 2009, they outsourced production of the company's emergency lights for home owners to a factory in China. Two years later, Zozula and Anderson decided to shift production back to a company in Carlsbad, California, located just 30 miles from their headquarters in San Clemente, California. "It's 30 percent cheaper to manufacture in China," says Anderson. "But [you must] factor in shipping and all the other [problems] you have to endure." Neither Zozula nor Anderson has ever been to China, which made communicating with their suppliers there more difficult, and shipments of the company's emergency lights often were stuck in customs for some reason, sometimes for several weeks. Sometimes, product quality was an issue, and Anderson would spend hours on the phone with managers at the Chinese factory trying to explain necessary changes to their products. "[Now] if we have an issue in manufacturing, we can walk down to the plant floor," he says. "We can't do that in China." Anderson estimates that the total cost of producing LightSaver Technologies' products in the United States is 2 to 5 percent cheaper than producing them in China.[35]

Some companies also consider the proximity of their suppliers to one another when selecting vendors. Suppliers often locate in clusters (refer to Chapter 16), which can create operating efficiencies; however, locating near one another increases the risk of every supplier being shut down by a natural disaster, such as a flood, a hurricane, or an earthquake, or a man-made disaster, such as an explosion at a power plant.

## In the Entrepreneurial Spotlight

# Back in the USA

Like many manufacturers in the United States, managers at K'Nex Brands LP, a family-owned company that makes plastic building toys that children can assemble into a multitude of designs, decided a few years ago to move most of the production operation from its factory in Hatfield, Pennsylvania, to subcontractors with factories in China. Two of K'Nex Brands's rivals, Hasbro Inc. and Mattel Inc., the giants in the toy industry, had made the same move years earlier. Recently, however, Joel Glickman, K'Nex Brands's founder and chairman, began "reshoring" its manufacturing operations, returning production of the company's toys to the factory in Hatfield. "In the long term, it's much better for us to manufacture here," says Glickman, pointing out that the company can respond much faster to changes in the toy market, which tend to occur quickly, creating high demand for the latest must-have toy before dropping it in favor of the next hot toy. Not only does local production enable K'Nex Brands, which generates annual sales of $100 million, to deliver high-demand toys to retail stores much faster, but it also gives the company greater control over the materials used in and the quality of its toys, both of which are vital to ensuring safety for the children who play with its toys. Other toy makers have suffered damaged reputations and lost sales when they recalled toys manufactured in China because they posed safety or health hazards to children. One company recalled nearly 1 million toys that it sold in the United States after its lab tests showed that a subcontractor in China had coated them in lead paint.

Like K'Nex, companies that outsourced production to "low-cost" countries have discovered many hidden costs associated with moving production to factories thousands of miles away and are reconsidering their decisions. Less control over materials and quality, longer delivery times, higher shipping costs, greater risk of supply chain interruption, and more difficulty communicating with factories thousands of miles away make the manufacturing process more difficult to coordinate. In addition, rapidly rising wages in China and higher productivity of domestic workers have made bringing manufacturing back home more attractive. "We expect net labor costs for manufacturing in China and the U.S. to converge around 2015," says the author of a report from the Boston Consulting Group. "Companies should undertake a rigorous, product-by-product analysis of their global supply networks that fully accounts for total costs rather than just factory wages. For many products sold in North America, the U.S. will become a more attractive manufacturing option."

Companies that "reshore" their manufacturing operations face challenges, however. Some companies have difficulty hiring skilled employees with manufacturing experience, and

sophisticated networks of companies linked in an efficient supply chain can be hard to find domestically. K'Nex has struggled to find domestic suppliers because toy-making skills have faded over time as more companies shifted toy production to other countries. The company still imports small battery-powered motors for its toys from suppliers in China because it has not been able to locate a domestic supplier that can provide motors at competitive prices. It also imports the head of an "Angry Birds" toy that requires a rubberized coating that would be expensive to replicate in the United States.

Although most companies will continue to make labor-intensive products in foreign factories, many of those that manufacture goods that require less manual labor and allow for more automation are returning production to factories in the United States. Because toy making involves a great deal of manual labor (which still costs more in the United States than in many other countries), K'Nex redesigned some of its toys to make them less labor intensive to produce. For instance, the company's old roller-coaster tracks were held together by metal pins that employees in China inserted by hand; its new tracks simply snap together. A roller-coaster car that once had a shiny metallic finish now comes with decals that children apply. K'Nex eliminated the metallic coating because the process used to apply it was "expensive and dirty, and we can't do it here [in the United States], so we designed it out of the product," says Joseph Smith, the company's chief development officer. Hubcaps that Chinese employees once attached to car wheels are now included as separate parts in the kit so that children can snap them into place. K'Nex also has invested in technology to make its manufacturing operation more efficient. A $30,000 robot from Rethink Robotics Inc. currently performs simple packaging tasks, but K'Nex managers are planning to install more sophisticated robots that will enable the company to move more production and assembly tasks back to its Hatfield factory.

1. What advantages have companies gained by outsourcing their manufacturing operations to factories in foreign countries?

2. What forces are driving companies such as K'Nex to "reshore" their manufacturing operations to the United States? What benefits and challenges do they face as they pursue their reshoring strategies?

*Sources:* Based on James R. Hagerty, "A Toy Maker Comes Home to U.S.A.," *Wall Street Journal,* March 11, 2013, pp. B1–B2; "Coming Home," *The Economist,* January 19, 2013, *www.economist.com/news/special-report/21569570-growing-number-american-companies-are-moving-their-manufacturing-back-united*; *Made in America, Again: Why Manufacturing Will Return to the U.S.,* Boston Consulting Group, August 2011.

**SPEED** How fast can a supplier deliver products to your business? A speedy supply chain can be a competitive advantage for a company. Zara, a popular clothing chain owned by Spanish company Inditex, is known for its tightly controlled supply chain that zips the latest fashions at very affordable prices (the average item sells for $27) to its stores in 73 countries. The company's high-tech logistics system gets the latest designer styles from the drawing board to store shelves in less than two weeks, compared to an industry average of nine months![36]

**SERVICES** Entrepreneurs must evaluate the range of services that vendors offer. Do salespeople make regular calls on the firm, and are they knowledgeable about their product line? Will the sales representatives assist in planning store layout and in creating attractive displays? Will the vendor make convenient deliveries on time? Is the supplier reasonable in making repairs on equipment after installation and in handling returned merchandise? Are sales representatives able to offer useful advice on purchasing and other managerial functions? Is the supplier willing to take the time to help you solve problems that inevitably will crop up?

**ENTREPRENEURIAL PROFILE: PayCycle** CPA Charles Ross uses payroll services company PayCycle to handle the payroll function for his own business and for many of his small business clients. PayCycle won Ross as a loyal customer after he discovered that he had entered a client's payroll information incorrectly, creating a problem that PayCycle remedied quickly. It was Friday afternoon, and the client's W-2 forms had to go out the following Monday, meaning that PayCycle had to recalculate an entire year's payroll. Even though it required almost a full day's work for someone at PayCycle over a weekend, the payroll service fixed the problem, and the forms went out on schedule on Monday. That level of service explains why Ross is a lifelong customer and why 90 percent of PayCycle's customers refer new customers to the company.[37]

**COLLABORATION** The goal is to find a supplier that is eager to join forces with the intent of building a long-term partnership with your company. Other small companies make ideal candidates.

**ENTREPRENEURIAL PROFILE: Scott Fischer and Harriet Donnelly: Center for Systems Management and Technovative Marketing** When NASA approached Scott Fischer, president of the Center for Systems Management (CSM), a Vienna, Virginia, company that provides training and consulting services for corporations and government agencies, about creating a video for an internal marketing campaign, Fischer knew that the job was beyond his company's ability. Wanting the chance to expand his work with the space agency, Fischer began looking for a company with which he could partner to create the video. He had to work quickly because NASA needed the video in just 45 days. Fischer and a team of employees selected Technovative Marketing, a seven-person marketing firm headed by Harriet Donnelly. Donnelly worked on the video herself and attended every meeting that Fischer had with NASA officials. (On every project, Donnelly assigns both a staff person and a senior manager to every Technovative project to make sure that clients always have two points of contact.) Because of the partnership that CSM and Technovative Marketing forged, the project turned out to be a huge success. NASA has enlisted CSM for similar projects, and, in turn, CSM is partnering with Technovative Marketing.[38]

**ENVIRONMENTALLY FRIENDLY AND SOCIALLY RESPONSIBLE BUSINESS PRACTICES** A trend that has emerged recently is customers holding companies responsible for the actions of their suppliers. Therefore, when selecting vendors, businesses must consider whether potential suppliers, especially those in foreign countries, obey child labor laws, provide workers with safe working conditions and fair wages, and comply with environmental laws. Failure to do so can tarnish a company's reputation, causing it to lose luster among customers. Apple Inc., a company whose supply chain extends throughout Asia, has struggled to ensure that its suppliers operate according to environmentally friendly and socially responsible business practices. The company conducted a thorough audit of its suppliers after combustible dust created an explosion in a Chinese factory that produced its popular iPad, killing two workers and injuring more than a dozen others. The audit revealed that 62 percent of Apple's suppliers were not complying with work-hour limits, 35 percent failed to meet the company's standards for preventing worker injuries, and 32 percent failed to comply with rules for handling hazardous substances. Other companies have faced similar problems, uncovering violations of child labor laws in the production of cocoa in Ivory Coast, deforestation in Indonesia in the production of palm oil, and forced labor in mining operations in the Democratic Republic of the Congo.[39]

**PRICE**  Small firms usually must pay list price for items that they purchase infrequently or in small quantities. However, this is not the case for goods that they purchase regularly in large quantities. Entrepreneurs should always attempt to negotiate the best prices and terms of sale with their vendors, especially on the products that they purchase in volume.

## Legal Issues Affecting Purchasing

**7.**

Describe the legal implications of the purchasing function.

When a small business purchases goods from a supplier, ownership passes from seller to buyer, but when do title to and the risk associated with the goods pass from one party to the other? The answer is important because any number of things can happen to the merchandise after a customer orders it but before a company delivers it. When entrepreneurs order merchandise and supplies from their vendors, they should know when the ownership of the merchandise—and the risk associated with it—shifts from supplier to buyer.

### Title

Before the Uniform Commercial Code (UCC) was enacted, the concept of title—the right to ownership of goods—determined where responsibility for merchandise fell. Today, however, three other concepts, identification, risk of loss, and insurable interest, play a more important role when disputes arise over lost, damaged, or destroyed shipments of goods.

**IDENTIFICATION**  Identification is important because it gives the buyer an insurable interest in the goods. Before title can pass to the buyer, the goods must already be in existence and must be identifiable from all other similar goods. Specific goods already in existence are identified at the time the sales contract is made. For example, if Graphtech, Inc., orders a laser printer, the goods are identified at the time the contract is made. Fungible goods, those that cannot be separated from a larger mass (e.g., wheat in a silo), are identified when they are marked, shipped, or otherwise designated as the goods in the contract. For example, an order of oil may not be identified until it is loaded into a transfer truck for shipment.

### Risk of Loss

**Risk of loss** determines which party incurs the financial risk if the goods are damaged, destroyed, or lost while in transit. Risk of loss does *not* always pass with title. Three particular rules govern the passage of title and the transfer of risk or loss:

> *Rule 1: Agreement.*  A supplier and a small business owner can agree (preferably in writing) to shift the risk of loss at any time during the transaction. In other words, any explicit agreement between buyer and seller determines when risk of loss passes to the buyer. For example, if an entrepreneur whose business is located in Freeport, Maine, orders goods from a vendor in St. Louis, Missouri, the contract may specify that risk of loss transfers from seller to buyer as soon as the truck carrying the goods crosses the Missouri border.

> *Rule 2: F.O.B. Seller.*  Under a sales contract designated F.O.B. ("free on board") seller, title and risk of loss pass to the buyer as soon as the seller delivers the goods into the care of a carrier or shipper. In addition, an **F.O.B. seller contract** (also known as a **shipment contract**) requires that the buyer pay all shipping and transportation costs. For example, a North Carolina manufacturer sells 100,000 capacitors to a buyer in Ohio with terms "F.O.B. North Carolina." Under this contract, the Ohio firm (buyer) pays all shipping costs, and title and risk of loss pass from the manufacturer as soon as the carrier takes possession of the shipment. If the goods are lost or damaged in transit, the *buyer* suffers the loss. Of course, the buyer can purchase insurance (see insurable interest below) and has legal recourse against the carrier if the carrier is at fault. If a contract is silent on shipping terms, the courts assume that the contract is a shipment contract (F.O.B. seller), and the buyer bears the risk of loss while the goods are in transit.

> *Rule 3: F.O.B. Buyer.*  A sales contract designated F.O.B. buyer requires that the seller deliver the goods to the buyer's place of business (or to a place that the buyer designates,

frequent feedback and rewards. At the end of every quarter, all 80 of the company's employees meet with their supervisors, who assign up to 25 points in each of four areas: initiative, aptitude, flexibility, and aptitude. Employees who score at least 70 points earn incentive pay—the higher their scores, the greater the bonus amount. More than 90 percent of TruFast's employees receive some bonus. Roth says that the program has reduced employee turnover and produces a return on investment of between 15 and 18 percent. "My employees keep asking me when the next review is and what they need to know to score well on it," says Roth. "That tells me all I need to know."[88]

Some companies allow employees to evaluate each other's performance in **peer reviews** or evaluate their boss's performance in **upward feedback**. These are aspects of a technique called **360-degree feedback**. Peer appraisals can be especially useful because an employee's coworkers see his or her on-the-job performance every day. As a result, peer evaluations tend to be more accurate and more valid than those of some managers. In addition, they may capture behavior that managers miss. Disadvantages of peer appraisals include potential retaliation against coworkers who criticize, the possibility that appraisals will be reduced to "popularity contests," and the refusal of some workers to offer any criticism because they feel uncomfortable evaluating others. Some bosses using upward feedback report similar problems, including personal attacks and extreme evaluations by vengeful subordinates.

Regardless of the technique, employee feedback should be honest, clear, and respectful. Entrepreneurs will benefit from developing effective feedback skills as they grow the business and delegate additional responsibilities to employees.

## Chapter Review

1. **Explain the challenges involved in the entrepreneur's role as leader and what it takes to be a successful leader.**
   - Leadership is the process of influencing and inspiring others to achieve a common goal and then giving them the power and the freedom to achieve it.
   - Management and leadership are not the same, yet both are essential to a small company's success. Leadership without management is unbridled; management without leadership is uninspired. Leadership gets a small business going; management keeps it going.

2. **Describe the importance of hiring the right employees and how to avoid making hiring mistakes.**
   - The decision to hire a new employee is an important one for every business, but its impact is magnified many times in a small company. Every "new hire" an entrepreneur makes determines the heights to which the company can climb or the depths to which it will plunge.
   - To avoid making hiring mistakes, entrepreneurs should develop meaningful job descriptions and job specifications, plan and conduct an effective interview, and check references before hiring any employee.

3. **Explain how to build the kind of company culture and structure to support the entrepreneur's mission and goals and to motivate employees to achieve them.**
   - Company culture is the distinctive, unwritten code of conduct that governs the behavior, attitudes, relationships, and style of an organization. Culture arises from an entrepreneur's consistent and relentless pursuit of a set of core values that everyone in the company can believe in. Small companies' flexible structures can be a major competitive weapon.

4. **Understand the potential barriers to effective communication and describe how to overcome them.**
   - Research shows that entrepreneurs spend about 80 percent of their time in some form of communication, yet their attempts at communicating sometimes go wrong.
   - Barriers to effective communication include that managers and employees don't always feel free to say what they really mean, ambiguity blocks real communication, information overload causes the message to get lost, selective listening interferes with the communication process, defense mechanisms block a message, and conflicting verbal and nonverbal messages confuse listeners.
   - To become more effective communicators, entrepreneurs should clarify their messages before attempting to communicate them, use face-to-face communication whenever possible, be empathetic, match their messages to their audiences, be organized, encourage feedback, tell the truth, and not be afraid to tell employees about the business, its performance, and the forces that affect it.

5. **Discuss the ways in which entrepreneurs can motivate their workers to higher levels of performance.**
   - Motivation is the degree of effort an employee exerts to accomplish a task; it shows up as excitement about work. Four important tools of motivation are empowerment, job design, rewards and compensation, and feedback.
   - Empowerment involves giving workers at every level of the organization the power, the freedom, and the responsibility to control their own work, to make decisions, and to take action to meet the company's objectives.

- Job design techniques for enhancing employee motivation include job enlargement, job rotation, job enrichment, flextime, job sharing, and flexplace.
- Money is an important motivator for many workers but not the only one. The key to using rewards such as

recognition and praise to motivate involves tailoring them to the needs and characteristics of the workers.
- Giving employees timely, relevant feedback about their job performance through a performance appraisal system can also be a powerful motivator.

## Discussion Questions

**21-1.** What is leadership? What is the difference between leadership and management?

**21-2.** What behaviors do effective leaders exhibit?

**21-3.** Why is it so important for small companies to hire the right employees? What can entrepreneurs do to avoid making hiring mistakes?

**21-4.** What is a job description? A job specification? What functions do they serve in the hiring process?

**21-5.** Outline the procedure for conducting an effective interview.

**21-6.** What are some alternative techniques to traditional interviews?

**21-7.** What is company culture? What role does it play in a small company's success? What threats does rapid growth pose for a company's culture?

**21-8.** What mistakes do companies make when switching to team-based management? What might companies do to avoid these mistakes? Explain the four phases teams typically experience.

**21-9.** What is empowerment? What benefits does it offer workers? The company? What must a small business manager do to make empowerment work in a company?

**21-10.** Explain the differences among job simplification, job enlargement, job rotation, and job enrichment. What impact do these different job designs have on workers?

**21-11.** Is money the "best" motivator? How do pay-for-performance compensation systems work? What other rewards are available to small business managers to use as motivators? How effective are they? What motivates workers of Generation Y?

**21-12.** Suppose that a café and coffee shop that sells organic, mostly locally grown foods and fair trade coffee identifies its performance as a socially responsible company as a "critical number" in its success. Suggest some ways for the owner to measure this company's "social responsibility index."

**21-13.** What is a performance appraisal? What are the most common mistakes managers make in performance appraisals? What should small business managers do to avoid making those mistakes?

## CHAPTER 22

# Management Succession and Risk Management Strategies in the Family Business

### Learning Objectives

**On completion of this chapter, you will be able to:**

1. Explain the factors necessary for a strong family business.
2. Understand the exit strategy options available to an entrepreneur.
3. Discuss the stages of management succession.
4. Explain how to develop an effective management succession plan.
5. Understand the four risk management strategies.
6. Discuss the basics of insurance for small businesses.

*When it works right, nothing succeeds like a family firm. The roots run deep, embedded in family values. The flash of the fast buck is replaced with long-term plans. Tradition counts.*
—Eric Calonius

*Soul is what drives all of what happens in family businesses, and it is the indefinable essence of a family's spirit and being. Soul is not something that can be measured or quantified, but it is easily recognizable by both its presence and its absence.*
—Tom Hubler

## Family Businesses

1.
Explain the factors necessary for a strong family business.

Nearly 90 percent of all companies in the United States, about 24.5 million businesses, are family owned. Yet family-owned businesses, those in which family members control owner-ship and/or decision making, are often overlooked by the media that focus most of their atten-tion on the largest companies in our economy. In reality, family businesses generate 64 percent of the U.S. gross domestic product, account for 63 percent of all employment and 78 percent of job creation, and pay 65 percent of all wages.[1] Despite common perceptions, not all fam-ily businesses are small: 33 percent of *Fortune* 500 companies are family businesses.[2] Glob-ally, family-owned businesses account for 70 to 90 percent of world gross domestic product (GDP).[3] Some of the best-known companies in the world are family owned, including Ford Motor Company, Samsung, Hyundai, Mars, Sainsbury, Marriott, and Wal-Mart. In fact, Sam Walton's heirs own 49 percent of the stock in the world's largest company, Wal-Mart, and those shares are worth an estimated $128 billion, an amount that exceeds the GDP of 124 countries in the world.[4]

When a family business works right, it is a thing of beauty. Family members share deeply rooted values that guide the company and give it a sense of harmony. Family members understand and support one another as they work together to achieve the company's mission. That harmony can produce a significant financial payoff. A study by Jim Lee of Texas A&M University–Corpus Christi shows that family-owned businesses are more profitable and experience faster employ-ment and revenue growth over time than nonfamily businesses.[5] Another study of companies in the Standard & Poor's 500 Index by Ronald Anderson, David Reeb, and Sattar Mansi found that family firms outperformed their nonfamily counterparts on a variety of financial measures.[6] Other research comparing the financial performances of similar sets of family and nonfamily businesses shows that family businesses produce a return on assets that averages 6.65 percent higher than that of nonfamily firms.[7]

### Benefits of Family Businesses

Family businesses have many advantages over their nonfamily rivals, including the following.

**LONG-TERM FOCUS** Because owners of family businesses usually see themselves as stewards of their companies for the next generation, they make decisions for the long term rather than for the next quarter. Their focus is on building an enduring legacy rather than on producing quick returns, a tendency that plagues most publicly held companies. "I would have been fired a couple of times in a publicly-traded company, where you are judged according to quarterly earnings," says Count Anton-Wolfgang von Faber-Castell, eighth generation CEO of the family-owned Faber-Castell Company that started making pencils in Stein, Germany, in 1761.[8]

**ENTREPRENEURIAL PROFILE: Chris McCormick: L.L. Bean** Chris McCormick, the first non-family CEO of venerable outdoor gear and apparel retailer L.L. Bean, which Leon Leonwood Bean started in 1912, recently went to the board of the family-owned company in Freeport, Maine, and recommended that the company "have an 'investment year,' and allow profits to fall because we needed to make a big investment in marketing and attracting younger customers." The decision was an easy one. "They agreed," says McCormick. "Family members understand that we want to be around another 100 years and investments in growth are critical to the long-term financial health of the business."[9]

**FASTER DECISION MAKING** Family business owners say that they are more agile than their nonfamily competitors because they can make decisions faster. Their companies can identify emerging market niches and enter them quickly because decision makers share similar values and vision for the company, which streamlines the decision-making process. Anthony Halas, second-generation CEO of Seafolly, a highly successful swim- and casual-wear company based in Australia, says that "the ability to make good decisions and react quickly and not being bound by outside investors who are looking solely at the bottom line are definite advantages to operating a family firm. A family business can really invest in the future."

**AN ENTREPRENEURIAL MIND-SET** Family business owners pride themselves on retaining their entrepreneurial spirit, which means that they sometimes must reinvent their companies to survive and thrive.

**ENTREPRENEURIAL PROFILE: Andrew Cornell: Cornell Iron Works,** now in its fifth generation of ownership, began in 1828 in New York City as a blacksmith shop before morphing into an ironworks company. (It created the iron base and the spiral stairs for the Statue of Liberty and ironwork for the Brooklyn Bridge.) In its more than 185-year history, the company has reinvented itself several times. During the Great Depression, the company made sidings for sanitation trucks and security doors for buildings, including the Metropolitan Museum of Art in New York City. Today, under the leadership of CEO Andrew Cornell, the company, now located in Mountaintop, Pennsylvania, focuses on a profitable niche, making specialty overhead doors for industrial, institutional, and retail customers.[10]

**STRONG COMMITMENT TO THEIR EMPLOYEES** Family businesses' long-term focus carries over to a long-term commitment to their employees. Many family-owned companies see their employees as an extension of the family and do everything they can to avoid layoffs, even in difficult economic times. The result is intense loyalty and dedication from employees. During the Great Depression, Crane and Company, a family-owned papermaking business founded in Dalton, Massachusetts, in 1770, saw demand for its paper plummet. Rather than institute layoffs, however, Crane paid workers to paint the nearly 160 houses that the company owned and rented to its workers.[11]

**LOCAL PHILANTHROPY** Like most small businesses, family-owned companies give back to the communities in which they operate, particularly to causes that align with the family's shared values. A study by Family Enterprise USA reports that 94 percent of family businesses donate money to charitable organizations, 81 percent of owners volunteer in community organizations, and 53 percent encourage their employees to volunteer their time in the local community.[12] Family-owned businesses "are using philanthropy as part of their business strategies," says the head of Strategic Philanthropy. "It makes sense and can be extremely beneficial to achieving business objectives such as retaining great employees and improving the company's reputation as a good corporate citizen."

**ENTREPRENEURIAL PROFILE: Eliot Orton: Vermont Country Stores** Vrest and Ellen Orton, who cofounded the Vermont Country Stores in tiny Weston, Vermont, in 1945, donated time and money to local charitable causes, choosing specific projects by talking with customers while sitting around the small store's potbellied stove. Today, their grandson, Eliot Orton, is the CEO of Vermont Country Stores, which has grown into a 15,000-square-foot tourist destination and an online and catalog retail company with more than $100 million in annual sales. Eliot continues his grandparents' generosity, donating an estimated 10 percent of its annual profits and his own time as well as that of most of the company's 500 employees to charitable causes, ranging from local volunteer fire departments and food pantries to nonprofits with an international focus.[13]

### The Dark Side of Family Businesses

Family businesses also have a dark side, and it stems from their lack of continuity. Sibling rivalries, quarrels about management succession, fights over control of the business, and personality conflicts often lead to nasty battles that can tear families apart and threaten or destroy once thriving businesses. Long-standing family feuds can make family relationships difficult, and when mixed with business decisions and the wealth family businesses can create, the result can be explosive.

**ENTREPRENEURIAL PROFILE: Luray Caverns** Luray Caverns, one of the most visited show caves in the United States, is in its fourth generation of family ownership, but since 2003, the six siblings who are the current owners of the popular tourist attraction in Luray, Virginia, have been engaged in legal battles that threaten the family's ownership. In 1905, Theodore Clay Northcott, known as The Colonel, purchased Luray Caverns, and his descendants have owned the attraction, which is now worth an estimated $20 million, since then. In the latest legal volley, the three youngest siblings, John Graves, Rod Graves, and Cornelia Graves Spain, filed a lawsuit against their older sisters, Rebecca Graves Hudson, Katherine Graves Fichter, and Elizabeth Graves Vitu, claiming that the oldest sisters had violated provisions of the trusts that governed their inheritance and, therefore, had disqualified themselves from receiving any shares in Luray Caverns Corporation. A district court judge recently dismissed the case, stating that "this case is simply one skirmish in the complicated and contentious battle that has been waged among the descendants of Colonel Northcott over the distribution of stock and control of Luray Caverns." One observer describes the family skirmishes as "'Dallas' meets the National Geographic Channel."[14]

**TABLE 22.1 The World's Oldest Family Businesses**

William O'Hara, director of the Institute for Family Enterprise at Bryant College, and Peter Mandel have compiled a list of some of the world's oldest family businesses.

| Company | Country | Nature of Business | Year Established |
|---|---|---|---|
| Hoshi Ryokan | Japan | Hotel | 718 |
| Château de Goulaine | France | Vineyard, museum, butterfly collection | 1000 |
| Fonderia Pontificia Marinelli | Italy | Bell Foundry | 1000 |
| Barone Ricasoli | Italy | Wine and olive oil | 1141 |
| Barovier & Toso | Italy | Artistic glassmaking | 1295 |
| Hotel Pilgram Haus | Germany | Innkeeping | 1304 |
| Richard de Bas | France | High-quality papermaker | 1326 |
| Torrini Firenze | Italy | Goldsmiths | 1369 |
| Antinori | Italy | Wine | 1385 |
| Camuffo | Italy | Shipbuilding | 1438 |
| Baronnie de Coussergues | France | Wine | 1495 |
| Grazia Deruta | Italy | Ceramics | 1500 |
| Fabbrice D'Armi Beretta | Italy | Firearms production | 1526 |
| William Prym GmbH & Company | Germany | Copper, brass, haberdashery | 1530 |
| R.J. Balson & Son | Great Britain | Butcher | 1535 |
| Codorniu | Spain | Wine | 1551 |
| Fonjallaz | Switzerland | Wine | 1552 |
| Von Poschinger Manufaktur | Germany | Glassmaking | 1568 |
| Wachsendustrie Fulda Adam Gies | Germany | Candles and wax figures | 1589 |
| Berenberg Bank | Germany | Banking | 1590 |

Source: Based on William T. O'Hara and Peter Mandel, "The World's Oldest Family Companies," Family Business, www.familybusinessmagazine.com/oldworld.html.

The stumbling block for most family businesses is management succession: 70 percent of first-generation businesses fail to survive into the second generation, and of those that do, only 13 percent make it to the third generation. Just 3 percent of family businesses survive to the fourth generation and beyond.[15] The leading causes of family business failures are inadequate estate planning, failure to create a management succession plan, and lack of funds to pay estate taxes.[16] Just when they are ready to make the transition from one generation of leaders to the next, family businesses are most vulnerable. As a result, the average life expectancy of a family business is 24 years, although some last much longer (see Table 22.1).[17]

**ENTREPRENEURIAL PROFILE: Zenas Crane: Crane & Company** Crane & Company, based in Dalton, Massachusetts, is one of the oldest family businesses in the United States. Founded in 1801 by Zenas Crane, the company generated most of its revenue from sales of high-quality stationery (including stationery that the White House uses), but as technology and social media began to dampen the demand for fine stationery, Crane & Company shifted its focus to providing paper to the U.S. government for making currency. Today, the company generates most of its revenue from sales of currency-grade paper (which it is constantly updating to thwart counterfeiters) to foreign governments. Crane & Company, which has about 100 shareholders, most of whom are sixth-, seventh-, and eighth-generation descendants of Zenas Crane, recently sold an equity stake to private equity firm Lindsay Goldberg. Only five members of the Crane family currently work for the company, and its CEO, Max Mitchell, is not a Crane family member.[18]

According to a study of family businesses across the globe by PriceWaterhouseCoopers, 32 percent of family business owners are apprehensive about transferring their businesses to the next generation, and 9 percent say that management succession is likely to cause family conflict.[19] The best way to ensure the legacy of a family business and a successful transition from one generation of family owners to the next is to develop a succession plan for the company. Although business founders inevitably want their businesses to survive them and most intend to pass them on to their children, they do not always support their intentions with a plan to accomplish that goal. The study by PriceWaterhouseCoopers reports that 47 percent of family businesses have no succession plans in place.[20] Another survey of family business owners by MassMutual Financial Group and Arthur Andersen reports that 19 percent had not engaged in any kind of estate planning other than creating a will.[21] For most family businesses, the greatest threat to survival comes from *within* the company rather than from outside it. Many entrepreneurs dream of their businesses continuing in the family but take no significant steps to make their dreams a reality.

## Characteristics of Successful Family Businesses

Successful family businesses that have survived across multiple generations of family ownership share several important qualities: shared values, shared power, tradition, a sense of stewardship, a willingness to learn, family behavior, and strong family ties.[22]

**SHARED VALUES** The first and probably most overlooked quality is a set of shared values. What family members value and believe about people, work, and money shapes their behavior toward the business. Families that share similar values instill those values into the family business, where they become a vital and enduring part of the company's legacy. According to the global family business survey by PriceWaterhouseCoopers, 78 percent of family business owners say that their families' shared values and culture are an important strength of their companies.[23] Without shared values, creating a sense of vision and direction for a business is difficult. "We have an edge," explains Chris McCormick, CEO of L.L. Bean. "We stick to our beliefs—customer service, quality, outdoor recreation, and our family ownership. We work as a team with shared values. These shared values have allowed the business to maintain a consistent point of view, a consistent experience, a consistent message. This is what differentiates our brand in the marketplace and keeps us relevant. If we do these basics well, profitability will follow, as it has now for more than 100 years."[24]

To avoid the problems associated with conflicting values and goals, family business owners should consider taking the following actions:

- Make it clear to all family members that they are not required to join the business. Family members' goals, ambitions, and talents should be foremost in their career decisions. W.S. Darley and Company, a company in Itasca, Illinois, that makes firefighting equipment, including fire trucks, and is in its fourth generation of family ownership has a family participation plan that states that the business has no obligation to hire any family member, nor does any family member have an obligation to work in the family business. Andrew Cornell, fifth-generation CEO of Cornell Iron Works, has a similar philosophy. "A family business can't be a home for wayward family members," he says. "We're building a business for the good of employees and shareholders."[25]

- Do not assume that a successor must come from within the family. Simply being born into a family does not guarantee that a person will make a good business leader. In fact, nonfamily executives manage between 10 and 15 percent of all family-owned businesses.[26] "For a family business to appoint a nonfamily chief executive is an extraordinarily big decision," says Paul Drechsler, the first nonfamily CEO to manage Wates Group, a family-owned construction firm founded in 1897 in Surrey, United Kingdom. "It's a great privilege to lead a family business, but it's also a huge responsibility."[27]

- Give family members the opportunity to work outside the business initially to learn firsthand how others conduct business. Working for others allows family members to develop knowledge, confidence, and credibility before stepping back into the family business. Family members who work outside the family business also bring with them new ideas when they return.

**ENTREPRENEURIAL PROFILE: Ed and Norma Mitchell: Mitchell's Family of Stores**
Mitchell's Family of Stores, founded by Ed and Norma Mitchell in 1958 in Westport, Connecticut, is now in its third generation of family ownership and, with annual sales of more than $100 million, has grown into the largest family-owned upscale clothing store in the United States. Jack and Bill Mitchell, the second generation of owners, instituted "the five-year rule," which says that family

members must work outside the family business for at least five years before joining the company. "The five-year rule not only gives the next generation work experience, but it also gives them wisdom they can bring to the family business," explains Jack.[28]

**SHARED POWER** Shared power does not necessarily mean equality of power. Rather, shared power is based on the idea that family members allow those people with the greatest expertise, ability, and knowledge in particular areas to handle decisions in those areas. Dividing responsibilities along the lines of expertise is an important way of acknowledging respect for each family member's talents and abilities. When the third generation of family members (all sons) began working for Mitchell's Family of Stores, each one chose a different functional area depending on his skills, talent, and ability. "One picked finance and administration, another sales and merchandising, another marketing, and several managing newly acquired stores," says Jack Mitchell.[29]

**TRADITION** Tradition is necessary for a family business because it serves to bond family members and to link one generation of business leaders to the next. However, founders must hold tradition in check when it becomes a barrier to change. The key is to select those traditions that provide a solid foundation for positive behavior while taking care not to restrict the future growth of the business. "The companies that are successful change their strategy after each generation," says Joachim Schwass, a professor of family business at Switzerland's IMD business school. "Bringing in the new generation and saying, 'Son, do as I did,' will not work."[30]

**ENTREPRENEURIAL PROFILE: Peter and Anthony Halas: Seafolly** In 1996, after a short stint as an actor, Anthony Halas began working for Seafolly, the Australian swimwear company that his father, Peter, had started with a partner in 1975. Two years later, Halas bought out his father's partner, took on a leadership role, and began transforming from a company that once provided private-label swimwear for the discount sector into a company marketing fashionable swimwear under its own label. Within 14 years under Halas's leadership, Seafolly became the leading swimwear company in Australia with about 40 percent market share and the operator of Sunburn, the country's largest chain of multibrand swimwear stores. Every business decision that Halas makes is steeped in 50 years of family business history, but he continues to show that he is willing to take bold steps to innovate and keep the family business in tune with the ever-changing demands of a highly competitive industry, including expanding the product line to include casual wear and a push into international markets. Twenty-five percent of the company's sales now come from its clothing line. Seafolly sells its products in 44 countries, but Halas is focusing on five key markets—the United States, France, Germany, Canada, and the United Kingdom.[31]

**A SENSE OF STEWARDSHIP** Family business owners whose businesses thrive for generations see themselves as more than just entrepreneurs; they view their roles as stewards of a family tradition, caretakers of the family business for future generations. "The core value of stewardship that family businesses embrace—leaving the company in a better place than when you took it over—drives their internal attitudes and behavior," says the owner of one family business.[32] Creating an ongoing legacy in the form of a family business requires a family to focus on five interrelated components (see Figure 22.1):

1. Heritage—maintaining the company's and the family's values, vision, and traditions.
2. Family and self—sustaining the family and supporting its members, enabling them to realize their goals both inside and outside the family business.
3. Business legacy—creating a sound management succession plan.
4. Community—giving back to the local community by being a good corporate citizen, volunteering, and engaging in philanthropy.
5. Wealthcare—preserving the family's and the company's wealth with proper estate planning strategies.[33]

**ENTREPRENEURIAL PROFILE: Avedis Zildjian: Zildjian**, the oldest family-owned business in the United States, traces its roots to Constantinople, Turkey, where, in 1623, Avedis Zildjian developed an alloy of copper, tin, and silver and began making cymbals with spectacular power and sound clarity. The company moved to the United States in 1929 and remains the world leader in the cymbal industry. Each generation of the Zildjian family has guided the company with a focus on future generations. Now in its fifteenth generation of family leadership, the company recently introduced a new line of electronic cymbals named "the 16th" after the next generation of Zildjians who are expected to take over the family business.[34]

**A WILLINGNESS TO LEARN AND ADAPT** A willingness to learn and grow is the hallmark of any successful firm, and it is essential to a family business. A family business that actively seeks new ideas and innovative techniques reduces its risk of obsolescence.

**ENTREPRENEURIAL PROFILE: Tom Flottman: Flottman Company** "If you do the same thing for more than five years in a row, you're going to fall behind," says Tom Flottman, CEO of Flottman Company, a third-generation printing company founded in 1921 by Flottman's grandfather. The company, based in Crestview Hills, Kentucky, started as a commercial job shop but by the 1960s had become a full-color lithographer. In the 1970s, Flottman's entered a lucrative niche, printing drug labels and leaflets for the pharmaceutical industry. Although that business still makes up more than half of the company's $6 million in annual sales, Tom has taken Flottman's into new markets, including multichannel communications and marketing. "To survive, we must be more than a company that puts ink on paper," he explains.[35]

The current generation of leadership must set the stage for new ideas by involving the next generation in today's decisions. In many cases, a formal family council serves as a mechanism through which family members can propose new ideas. Perhaps more important than a family council is fostering an environment in which family members trust one another enough to express their ideas, thoughts, and suggestions. Open discussion of the merits of new ideas is a characteristic that has proved valuable for many family businesses' ability to sustain their competitive advantages.

**BEHAVING LIKE FAMILIES** Families that play together operate family businesses that are more likely to stay together. Time spent together outside the business creates the foundation for the relationships family members have at work. Too often, life in a family business can degenerate into nothing but day after day of work and discussions of work at home. When a family adds activities outside the scope of the business, however, new relationships develop in a different arena. A family should not force members to "play together" but instead should create an

**FIGURE 22.1**
**The Legacy Model for Sustaining a Successful Family Business**

*Source: "Fine Tuning Your Legacy,"
Hubler For Business Families, http://
www.hublerfamilybusiness.com/
OwnershipPlanning/FineTuning
YourLegacy.aspx.*

environment that welcomes every member into fun family activities. Planned activities should be broad enough in scope to involve all family members. Over time, trust, respect, openness, and togetherness lead to behavior that communicates genuine caring and concern for the well-being of each family member, and that spills over into the working relationship as well.

**A STRONG FAMILY SUPPORT NETWORK**  According to a global survey of family business owners, the most important advantage family businesses have is the strong support network from family members.[36] Strong family ties grow from one-on-one relationships. Shared time conveys the message that the family business is *more* than just a business; it is a group of people who care for one another working together for a common goal. (Think "Duck Dynasty.") The bond that a family business creates among relatives can be strong and enduring. "There's a love and a trust and a respect that can be very powerful when they are brought into a business environment," says Ross Nager, director of a center for family business.[37]

The same emotions that hold family businesses together can also rip them apart if they run counter to the company's and the family's best interest. Emotions run deep in family businesses, and the press is full of examples of once successful companies that have been ruined by family feuds over who controls the company and how to run it. Conflict is a natural part of any business but can be especially powerful in family businesses because family relationships magnify the passions binding family members to the company. Without a succession plan, those passions can explode into destructive behavior that can endanger the family business.

## Exit Strategies

2.

Understand the exit strategy options available to an entrepreneur.

Most family business founders want their companies to stay within their families, although in some cases maintaining family control is not practical (see Figure 22.2). Sometimes no one in the next generation of family members has an interest in managing the company or has the necessary skills and experience to handle the job. Under these circumstances, the founder must look outside the family for leadership if the company is to survive. Whatever the case, entrepreneurs must confront their mortality and plan for the future of their companies. Having a solid management succession plan in place well before retirement is near is critical to success. Entrepreneurs should examine their options once they decide it is time to step down from the businesses they have founded. Three options are available to entrepreneurs planning to retire: sell to outsiders, sell to (nonfamily) insiders, or pass the business on to family members with the help of a management succession plan. We turn now to these three exit strategies.

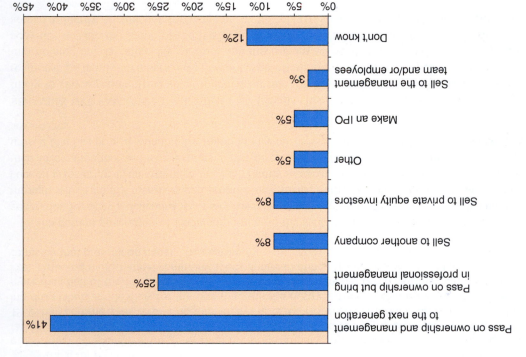

**FIGURE 22.2**

**Plans for Passing on the Family Business**

*Source:* Based on Family Firm: A Resilient Model for the 21st Century, PriceWaterhouseCoopers Family Business Survey, 2012, p. 14.

Chart "Plans for Passing on the Family Business":

- Pass on ownership and management to the next generation — 41%
- Pass on ownership but bring in professional management — 25%
- Sell to another company — 8%
- Sell to private equity investors — 8%
- Other — 5%
- Make an IPO — 5%
- Sell to the management team and/or employees — 3%
- Don't know — 12%

(X-axis: 0%, 5%, 10%, 15%, 20%, 25%, 30%, 35%, 40%, 45%)